TOURISM MANAGEMENT
Towards the New Millennium

ADVANCES IN TOURISM RESEARCH SERIES

Series Editor: Professor Stephen Page
Centre for Tourism Research, Massey University, New Zealand

Advances in Tourism Research is a new series of monographs and edited volumes which comprise state of the art research findings, written and edited by leading researchers working in the wider field of tourism studies. Each book has been designed to provide a cutting edge focus for researchers interested in tourism, particularly the management issues now facing decision-makers, policy analysts and the public sector. The audience is much wider than just academics and each book seeks to make a significant contribution to the literature in the field of study by not only reviewing the state of knowledge relating to each topic but by questioning some of the prevailing assumptions and research paradigms which currently exist in tourism research. The series also aims to provide a platform for further studies in each area by highlighting key research agendas which will stimulate further debate and interest in the expanding area of tourism research. The series is always willing to consider new ideas for innovative and scholarly books and inquiries can be made to the Series Editor.

Forthcoming titles include:

ASHWORTH & TUNBRIDGE
The Tourist-Historic City: Prospect and Retrospect of Managing the Heritage City

BAUM & LUNDTORP
Seasonality in Tourism: An Exploration of Issues

SONG & WITT
Tourism Demand Modelling and Forecasting: Modern Econometric Approaches

TEO, CHANG & HO
Interconnected Worlds: Tourism in Southeast Asia

Related Elsevier journals – sample copies available on request

Annals of Tourism Research
Cornell Hotel and Restaurant Administration Quarterly
International Journal of Hospitality Management
International Journal of Intercultural Relations
Tourism Management
World Development

TOURISM MANAGEMENT
Towards the New Millennium

Edited by

Chris Ryan

and

Stephen Page

2000

PERGAMON

An Imprint of Elsevier Science

Amsterdam – Lausanne – New York – Oxford – Shannon – Singapore - Tokyo

ELSEVIER SCIENCE Ltd
The Boulevard, Langford Lane
Kidlington, Oxford OX5 1GB, UK

First edition 2000

Library of Congress Cataloging in Publication Data
Tourism management: towards the new millennium/edited by Chris Ryan and Stephen Page.
    p.cm.—(Advances in tourism research series)
    Includes bibliographical references and index.
    ISBN 0-08-043589-0
    1. Tourism. I. Ryan, Chris, 1945- II. Page, Stephen, 1963- III. Series.

G155.A1 T59237 2000
338.4'791—dc21   99-047662

British Library Cataloguing in Publication Data
A catalogue record from the British Library has been applied for.

ISBN 0-08-043589-0

♾ The paper used in this publication meets the requirements of ANSI/NISO Z39.48-1992 (Permanence of Paper).
Printed in the Netherlands.

Contents

Preface

The journal *Tourism Management* was first launched in March 1980 and at the start of the new millennium it has now been in existence for two decades. This is an opportune time to reflect on the second of these decades, thereby continuing a process initiated in 1990 with the first compilation of articles from the journal edited by Rik Medlik (1991) in the volume *Managing Tourism*. It is evident that a great deal of change has occurred in tourism research since the journal was first published. In 1980, tourism journals were limited in scope and range; in 1999, there are over 50 academic and professional tourism and leisure journals developed for an international readership with the needs of the academic and practitioner research audience in mind. Yet it is with confidence that we feel the journal has continued to grow in strength and authority as a leading forum for the dissemination of research findings from a broad range of researchers with a common interest in the management implications of tourism. Yet the journal does not always publish material exclusively with that focus in mind. It is also a forum for critical debate of issues of current concern and seeks to sustain an information dissemination role through the publication of shorter research notes of work completed but not fully developed, case studies, book reviews of new literature in the field, and reports of conferences. Although this book does not include any of these latter aspects, it does highlight the wider research focus of the journal with reference to one of its principal aims – to publish articles based on new research.

Although it is not the place of this book to question the quality, quantity and range of journal articles now being published under the heading of tourism studies, one cannot fail to acknowledge that within the last decade – perhaps even the last five years – significant changes have occurred in the range of methodologies and research paradigms being adopted by researchers. In consequence, many of the current articles are more sophisticated and analytical than their predecessors, and while description retains its role as a primary research source, most papers being published today seek to go beyond that initial research function. Whether greater sophistication at the level of the specific translates into more conceptual development of wider theories unique to tourism is, however, a moot point. In a special issue of *Tourism Management* related to 'research methods' in tourism, it is perhaps indicative of the current debate that the editors (Faulkner and Ryan, 1999) simply expressed their lack of agreement as to this issue. It could be argued that until recently qualitative research methods (other than simple description) had not been part of the prevailing research paradigm in tourism studies other than in specific anthropologically or ethnographically based work. Although this assessment may be overly critical of the past state of the discipline, the real difficulty now facing tourism researchers is the incredible information overload and volume of articles, book chapters and texts now being published. For researchers it is an enormous amount of material to peruse in order to assess what is relevant and notable. Perhaps this is the sign of a maturing discipline or perhaps it is the sign of increased pressures on academics for research outputs: 'never mind the quality – feel the width' is a persuasive description of the policy now being pursued in many quarters.

It is against this background that the present volume of selected articles published in *Tourism Management* since 1989–90 seeks to take stock of some of the key developments in the literature and to examine the role and effect of some of the notable articles. This in itself is a far from easy task.

First, it is a highly subjective process, and by no means uses many of the prevailing scientific measures such as citation indices. Yet the articles have been carefully selected as representing the journal's contribution to scholarship, the evolution of thinking and the development of the subject area, particularly in the emergence of research sub-areas. Second, we have tried to provide a series of sections within the book which reflect the development of established and new research areas together with comments that try to relate the articles to the wider literature and current progress of knowledge in each area. Unlike Medlik's (1991) *Managing Tourism*, the articles have not been amended in any form or shape: they are reprinted in their entirety.

Selecting the articles was a very challenging task, simply because of the volume of material published in the last decade. It would have been very easy to begin with the special issue of the journal on research methods (*Tourism Management*, 20(1), 1999), but the selection of articles was taken from the period 1989 through to the end of 1998 (thereby excluding the special issue on research methods of February 1999). It also needs to be stated that as editors we were seeking to identify themes by which the articles related to each other and to the wider literature. We also sought to identify some of the major themes of research of the past decade, and to highlight some of the growing areas of concern and changing research methodologies. Because of this, we would be the first to admit that several excellent articles published in the last decade have not been reproduced in this collection. This may have been because they were single items, or perhaps because, within the wider context of time and with the benefit of hindsight, the issues being described have not established themselves, or seem to be establishing themselves, as concerns of international significance. Clearly articles of a parochial, localised or extremely descriptive nature have been omitted, and we have sought to emphasise articles of analytical merit or those that have made a significant impact on research methodology or future research.

It will be noted that, in terms of simple quantity, the largest number of articles relate to the issue of ecotourism, or sustainable tourism. Sustainability of tourism has been an issue for a period much longer than the last decade, but it continues not only to elicit concern and research, but arguably has become an ever increasingly important topic for management decisions and planning. With emergent middle classes in the Indian sub-continent and, more widely, in Asia, showing every sign of wishing to engage in travel like their counterparts in North America and Europe, pressures on 'natural' spaces will continue to escalate. New concerns, albeit with antecedents in a wider social science literature, that are coming more to the fore in tourism research include those relating to gender issues and the role of indigenous peoples in tourism. Thus far there have been comparatively few research-based articles published on these topics in the last decade in *Tourism Management*, but there has been a significant increase in books being devoted to these topics. In the early literature relating to ecotourism, there was a tendency to view all the impacts of tourism on the natural environment as being detrimental. Subsequent research began to advance a series of scenarios wherein this was not necessarily true. Thus too, in these fields of gender and indigenous peoples, it might be expected that the broad, sweeping contentions contained in books will increasingly be questioned in research articles which examine the particular, and in doing so researchers will evolve new conceptual frameworks.

In some topics, the advances have generally been in terms of new means of analysis. Thus, for example in economics, past research into tourism forecasting has now meant that those forecasts have become data for subsequent researchers who have sought to develop and improve their means of predicting future trends. On the other hand, in some sub-areas, like that of urban tourism, geographers seem to be engaged in processes of recycling theoretical approaches, and in this collection Page (2000) comments that urban tourism, for all of its importance, has not perhaps made the theoretical advances that might have been expected.

Underlying this book is a view that only through a continuing dialogue between specific tourism journal articles and a wider social science literature can one consider the 'cutting edge' nature of tourism research and the manner in which it is then developed and disseminated into a more general synthesis such as in student texts. This book is one way of allowing readers to assess the merits of each article and its wider contribution to the tourism literature. Whilst many may not totally agree with the selection, the overall thrust of the book is to provide readers with a broad overview of the journal's past publications of the decade commencing in 1989–90 and, through the commentaries, to locate those papers in a wider discussion of the way the literature has developed. Through the commentaries we also hope to provide some indicators as to the way tourism research might develop in the next decade. Finally, we would want to thank all of those who have contributed to *Tourism Management* by submitting their research papers, and to those who have acted as referees. In one sense a journal is a collective effort of a wider academic community who express their concerns, make public their thoughts and expertise, and in doing so hope to influence other researchers, students and the wider community. While at times change is sometimes slow, the editors are convinced that over time academics do influence agendas of debate outside of academia. Journals like *Tourism Management* are part of that process, and as such can only fulfil that role because of support from the academic community. We would like therefore to thank all the authors, referees and the publication team for their efforts.

Chris Ryan
Stephen Page

References

Faulkner, B. and Ryan, C. (1999). Innovations in tourism management research and conceptualisation, *Tourism Management*, February, 20(1): 3–6.

Medlik, R. (1991). *Managing Tourism*, Oxford: Butterworth Heinemann.

Page, S. (2000). Urban tourism, in C. Ryan and S. Page (eds), *Tourism Management: Towards the New Millennium*, Oxford: Elsevier Science. pp. 197–202.

Part I

Selecting holidays: the purchase decision and its antecedents

Introduction by Chris Ryan

Within marketing theory the actual purchase decision has long formed an important focus for research and comment. While books and articles on the marketing of tourism are far from new, what is apparent is that recent publications have taken cognisance of both modelling procedures and research that has informed the wider marketing literature and has gone beyond some of the previously simplistic approaches that characterised some of the earlier publications in tourism. Recent books that incorporate these new approaches and contribute new research have included Teare et al. (1994), Crotts and van Raaij (1994), Swarbrooke and Horner (1999) and Pizam and Mansfeld (1999). As discussed elsewhere in this volume, a significant advance in the conceptualisation of tourism and subsequent research can be discerned in the last decade and this is as true of tourism marketing as in other aspects of the subject.

It can be said that a number of theories seek to explain why people travel and why they go on holiday. Some travel arises from patterns of work as the need to meet people, exchange ideas, sign contracts and be exposed to new work practices are important reasons for travel. As an aside, it is interesting to note just how little research has been reported in the academic journals on work-related travel. From time to time it has been noted that during periods of recession business-related travel tends to fall, whereas in times of plenty it tends to increase. From one perspective this is to be expected, but we know little about why corporate travel budgets may fall more than say, percentage increases in unemployment. Some corporate travel may be deemed to contain a 'reward' component. Fellow academics may be familiar with the terminology adopted by some universities in times of tight budgets that conference travel is a 'privilege' and not a right. In short, corporate business has not been explored much in the academic literature, although from time to time research undertaken by credit and cash card companies, or studies related to business travel loyalty schemes might be reported in the trade press. Partly because it is easier to access holiday takers, the vacation market has been subject to much more research. Some of this has been motivated by market research reasons, such as a desire to map perceptions of alternative destinations or to devise ways of making attractions, destinations and/or activities more popular with designated market segments.

In assessing recreational products and their purchase, researchers have often sought to develop models based upon the following considerations.

The nature of the attraction

What are the physical components of the destination in terms of aesthetics, the nature of resources, and the activities that might be undertaken there? In simple terms these may be described as pull factors.

The characteristics of the holidaymaker

What are the personality variables that are attracted by the above-mentioned activities and places? Should there not be a congruence between place and personality? In one of the most enduring conceptualisations of this approach, Plog (1977, 1990) devised the much cited categorisation of allocentric, mid-centric and psychocentric holidaymakers and, within an American context, allocated these types to destinations as varied as Coney Island and Kenya. However, beyond this broad generalisation, the research provides an image of a much more complex set of arrangements. Pearce (1988) has argued that tourists have a travel career whereby their tastes change over time, learning from their experiences and thereby becoming more adventuresome. On the other hand Laing (1987) has a different perception of holiday careers. For him the holidaymaker seeks to maximise utility within constraints of budget and time, and having once identified those things that create satisfaction, the holidaymaker's choice of destinations and activities will be comparatively stable over time as they seek to repeat their experiences. This is particularly true of package holiday takes, yet he observes:

(package holiday taking) is less easily explained than is first thought . . . for many people package holiday taking is an habitual action – they rarely consider the reasons behind the preference . . . (the) preference for packaged travel may be more an outcome of personal and highly individual factors which demand particular detailed analysis. (Laing, 1987: 179)

The roles tourists play

Here the work of social psychologists like Argyle et al. (1981) is of importance. They categorised eight features of social situations. These are:

Goals:	purposes or ends of social behaviour.
Rules:	shared beliefs that regulate behaviour.
Roles:	duties and obligations attending social positions people occupy.
Repertoire of elements:	sum of behaviours appropriate to a situation.

Sequences:	ordering of the repertoire of behaviours.
Concepts and structure:	shared definitions and understandings needed to operate in social cognitive situations.
Environmental setting:	props, spaces, barriers, modifiers which influence the setting situation.
Language and speech:	the codes of speech inherent in language.

For Yiannakis and Gibson (1992) tourist roles arise from a mixture of motivation, selected place and the product structure associated with that place. While they simply denote structure in terms of degrees of organisation, it can be easily seen that the social structures of place help determine the roles that tourists play as social entities. Perhaps the importance of work such as that of Yiannakis and Gibson (1992) is that it delineates the ways in which the same person can engage in different roles at different times and places. Additionally, and to confuse matters even more, some observers have commented that tourist places are multi-product locations, able to appeal to a mix of tourists who interact with a place in different ways to suit their own ends. Ashworth and Voogd (1994: 7) carefully locate place as both 'an assemblage of products and the product in itself' and also define it as being within a series of nesting hierarchies of places. They thus note that 'each individual holiday is unique to the extent that the use and experience derived from each element in the place is unique to a particular customer' (Ashworth and Voogd, 1994: 7).

The motivation of tourists

Many studies exist as to the motivation of tourists and much of the earlier literature has been encapsulated in Pearce's (1982) book *The Social Psychology of Tourist Behaviour* while his colleague, Ross (1994), has sought to update some of the material by reference to what may be called well-established psychological schools of thought in his text *The Psychology of Tourism*. From the viewpoint of consumer marketing theory it is comparatively easy to adapt the theories of Howard and Sheth (1969), Nicosia (1966) and Engel et al. (1968) and other market theorists to tourist products. Some writers like Ryan and Glendon (1998) and Swarbrooke and Horner (1999) have sought to use the Leisure Motivation Scale of Beard and Ragheb (1983) within a touristic setting. In a number of cases commentators have sought a more integrative approach. It can be said that different people possessing the same motivations can exhibit varying behaviours in the same location, and the relationship between motivation, exhibited behaviour and role adaptation and adoption are not simple matters. Thus Jamal and Hollinshead (2000) observe that truths in touristic settings are negotiated truths.

The role of intruding variables

In identifying linkages between place, motivation and behaviour it can be observed that no experience of place is necessarily the same even if place, motive and even outward behaviour is the same. Repetition of action is not a replication of experience because the tourist brings to the place and time the accumulation of past experiences which shape expectations and perceptions. Past experience is thus a moderating or intruding variable of greater or less importance depending on the circumstance. In addition, other factors may be present which induce change within the place and potential experience. As social creatures, the presence or absence of significant others can certainly impact upon displayed behaviour. Notable as a factor determining behaviour is whether other family members or members of valued social groups are present. Social settings within groups of people with whom there are varying degrees of familiarity are determinants of roles that tourists play.

Another factor is that the purchase decision in tourism is often a delayable decision. This is not always the case. For example a decision to attend the Olympic Games in Sydney in the year 2000 is time- and place-specific, but, on the other hand, a decision to simply visit Sydney could be actualised either tomorrow, next month, next year or whenever. The timing of the visit may be dependent upon a list of variables that affect a purchase decision, such as current prices, available holiday time, disposable income, school holidays, age of children, whether sufficient holiday time is possessed by both partners and significant others and work patterns. The actual visit is also associated with a potential series of substitutable actions – these include not only switching time of arrival, but also length of stay, accommodation used, mode of travel and types of activities undertaken at the resort. In consequence the relationships implied by simple AIDA marketing models – that is, Attention, Intention, Decision, Action are – to the mind of this author, woefully inadequate in coming to any understanding of tourist purchase decisions and subsequent behaviours.

Attempts to place tourist purchase decisions within more inclusive and coherent models do exist. One of the more complete is offered by Woodside and MacDonald (1993) and Figure 1 illustrates both its approach and its grounding in the work of Howard and Sheth (1969), Nicosia (1966) and Engel et al. (1968). It seeks to locate purchase decisions within the social milieu of the tourist, the internal psychological processes and thence the subsequent experience and its evaluation into subsequent purchase decisions. Teare (1994) reviews a number of similar approaches, including that of Moutinho (1986) and ends with a number of research statements, including the view that satisfaction, and by implication future purchases, arise from a series of cumulative experiences.

Within the wider market research literature, as is observed by Dellaert et al. (1998), an increasingly used research process is that of logit-type models. Since theirs is one of the papers selected, it might be of value to briefly explain what this form of modelling requires. Essentially, in probit and logit forms of models, the researcher is concerned with how much of a determining variable is required to bring about a change in a dichotomous variable. In our case, how low does a price need to be to bring about a holiday purchase? The purchase is the dichotomous variable in that only two stages exist – purchase or non-purchase. In the modelling process one notes the number of people who are aware of price changes and become purchasers as the price of the holiday changes over a period of time. In logit analysis, unlike regression analysis, the determined variable is not regressed on the basis of a list of determining variables, but rather the proportion responding to a change in stimuli is transformed. In a logit

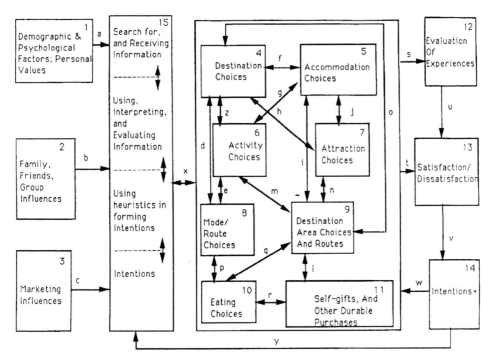

Figure 1. General systems of customer choice decisions of tourism services.
(*Source*: Woodside and MacDonald, 1993)

transformation, the observed proportion *P* is replaced by

$$\frac{\ln\left(p/(1-P)\right)}{2} + 5$$

and the quantity $\ln\left(p/(1-P)\right)$ is the *logit*, while the division by 2 and addition of the constant, 5, maintains positive values. Using a statistical package like SPSS^{TM}, it thus becomes possible, as in chi-squared tests, to compare observed with expected frequencies and to measure the significance thereof. An associated technique is linear logistic regression analysis, which is similar to regular multiple regression but where again the determined variable is binary (0 or 1) instead of continuous. In short, with the advent of cheaper desktop computers and more sophisticated statistical packages, it becomes possible to test for more subtle nuances in consumer behaviours if the researcher wishes to use such positivistic approaches.

Traditionally, within the consumer behaviour literature, especially that based on a North American tradition, this positivistic paradigm has been the conventional approach. However, given that from one perspective, tourism is essentially about experiences of place, there is a growing role being attributed to alternative research processes.

For this section, the following texts were selected:

Dellaert, B.G.C., Ettema, D.F. and Lindh, C. (1998). Multi-faceted tourist travel decisions: a constraint-based conceptual framework to describe tourists' sequential choices of
travel components, *Tourism Management*, August, 19(4): 313–20.

Thornton, P.R., Shaw, G. and Williams, A.M. (1997). Tourist group holiday decision-
making and behaviour: the influence of children, *Tourism Management*, August, 18(5):
287–98.

The first of these studies is based on a Swedish sample, and is interesting because not
only does it postulate a concept of the purchase decision, but subsequently tries to
support it with empirical evidence. The paper therefore produces detailed information
as to factors such as the length of period between decisions about destination choice,
accommodation, travel companions, mode of travel, departure date and trip duration
and the actual departure date. While Dellaert and his co-authors show that the choice
of destination is generally the first decision made, it is very noticeable that the standard
deviation is very high for this variable, implying that the importance of destination
in the travel decision varies significantly. This is partly explained by the constraints
that they identify, which include some of the items listed above as moderating or
intervening variables in the decision-making process. In short, these are items like the
incidence of school holidays and presence of young children. What does emerge from
their study is that econometric models of demand really need to involve socio-
economic and social structure data in that economic variables like price and income
alone do not explain the decisions made by holidaymakers. As noted above, they also
consider the implications of their findings for methods of modelling.

Thornton, Shaw and Williams consider a very important theme in holiday choice in
a study based on visitors to Cornwall. Within conventional marketing theory it can be
argued that holiday-taking decisions are, within families, carefully researched and
considered, because of the need to satisfy the preferences of significant others, and the
large sums of money that are involved. The purchases of holidays are not frequently
made in the sense that, for example, a purchase of breakfast cereals is, and thus holiday
purchase decisions are not programmable as discussed by, for example, Howard and
Sheth (1969). While it might be objected that the sample used in this paper is
comparatively small, i.e. 85 tourist parties, as any researcher knows who has used a
diary approach, the quality of such data can indeed be very rich. This proved to be the
case here, as the data covered holiday periods within which records were made at 2-
hourly intervals. Thus a diverse pattern of activities were recorded: from trips to the
beach, engaging in sports, visiting pubs, walking, sleeping and just relaxing.
In addition, all of these activities were mapped to provide not only a diary of activity,
but also a flow of spatial use. The main issue of the paper is, however, just how
important were children in determining the actual holiday activity in which the visitors
engaged? As might be expected, the age of the child is an important factor. Nonetheless, some significant findings emerge from this paper. One such, for example, is the
strong destination loyalty factor shown by children between the ages of 6 and 10.
Obviously this leads to high levels of repeat visitation. What provides additional
credibility for this research project is the use of interviews for a subset of the total
sample, thereby providing additional interpretive material for the diary records

obtained. The paper also thereby illustrates the trend towards using both quantitative and qualitative research techniques within research design.

When one considers these papers in the wider context of research relating to the role of the family in holiday decision making (for example the work of Lawson (1991), Bojanic (1992), Seaton and Tagg (1995)) it becomes very clear that Crompton's (1979) suggestion that holidays perform a very important family bonding function is indeed sustained.

In a sense, therefore, the research reviewed here forms a closed system. Initially, this discussion commenced with a view that holiday purchases were based on an interaction between, on the one hand, the characteristics of the holidaymaker and their background, and on the other hand, the attributes of place and the activities made possible therein. This may be described as a simple push–pull relationship. However, it is also evident that the timing of purchase decisions is significantly affected by intervening variables, among which are the immediate social conditions of the domestic life of the purchaser. In that sense, studies which (a) seek to devise general models like that of Dellaert et al. (1998) and (b) attend to more specific factors like family roles (e.g. Thornton et al. 1997) form important complementary processes.

References

Argyle, M., Furnham, A. and Graham, J.A. (1981). *Social Situation*. Cambridge: Cambridge University Press.

Ashworth, G.J. and Voogd, H. (1994). Marketing of tourism places: What are we doing? *Journal of International Consumer Marketing*, 6(3/4): 5–19.

Beard, J.G. and Ragheb, M.G. (1983). Measuring leisure motivation, *Journal of Leisure Research*, 1983, 15(3): 219–28.

Bojanic, D. (1992). A look at a modernised family life cycle and overseas travel, *Journal of Travel and Tourism Marketing*, 1(1): 61–80.

Crompton, J.L. (1979). Motivations for pleasure vacation, *Annals of Tourism Research*, 6(4): 408–24.

Crotts, J.C. and van Raaij, W.F. (eds) (1994). *Economic Psychology of Travel and Tourism*. New York: The Haworth Press, Inc.

Dellaert, B.G.C., Ettema, D.F. and Lindh, C. (1998). Multi-faceted tourist travel decisions: a constraint-based conceptual framework to describe tourists' sequential choices of travel components, *Tourism Management*, 19(4): 313–20.

Engel, J.F., Kollat, D.J. and Blackwell, R.D. (1968). *Consumer Behavior*. New York: Holt, Rinehart and Winston.

Howard, J.A. and Sheth, J.N. (1969). *The Theory of Buyer Behaviour*. New York: Wiley and Sons.

Jamal, T. and Hollinshead, K. (2000). Tourism and the forbidden zone: the underserved power of qualitative inquiry, *Tourism Management*, in press.

Laing, A. (1987). The package holiday participant: choice and behaviour. Unpublished PhD thesis, University of Hull.

Lawson, R. (1991). Patterns of tourist expenditure and types of vacation across the family life cycle, *Journal of Travel Research*, 29(4): Spring, 12–18.

Moutinho, L. (1986). Consumer behaviour in tourism, *Management Bibliographies and Reviews*, 12(3): Bradford: MCB University Press.

Nicosia, F.M. (1966). *Consumer Decision Processes*. Englewood Cliffs, NJ, Prentice-Hall.

Pearce, P.L. (1982). *The Social Psychology of Tourist Behaviour*, Oxford: Pergamon Press.

Pearce, P.L. (1988). *The Ulysses Factor: Evaluating Visitors in Tourist Settings*. New York: Springer Verlag.

Pizam, A. and Mansfeld, Y. (eds) (1999). *Consumer Behavior in Travel and Tourism*. New York: The Haworth Press, Inc.

Plog, S.C. (1977). Why destinations rise and fall in popularity, in E.M. Kelly (ed.), *Domestic and International Tourism*. Wellesley, MA: Institute of Travel Agents. pp. 26–8.

Plog, S.C. (1990). A carpenter's tools: an answer to Stephen L.J. Smith's review of psychocentric/allocentrism, *Journal of Travel Research*, 28(4) Spring: 43–4.

Ross, G.F. (1994). *The Psychology of Tourism*, Elsternwick, Vic: Hospitality Press.

Ryan, C. and Glendon, I. (1998). Application of leisure motivation scale to tourism, *Annals of Tourism Research*, 25(1):169–84.

Seaton, A.V. and Tagg, S. (1995). The European family vacation: paedonomic aspects of choices and satisfactions, *Journal of Travel and Tourism Research*, 4(1): 1–21.

Swarbrooke, J. and Horner, S. (1999). *Consumer Behaviour in Tourism*. Oxford: Butterworth Heinemann.

Teare, R. (1994). The consumer decision process: a paradigm in transition, in R. Teare, J.A. Mazanec, S. Crawford-Welch and S. Calver (eds), *Marketing in Hospitality and Tourism: A Consumer Focus*. London: Cassell.

Teare, R., Mazanec, J.A., Crawford-Welch, S. and Calver, S. (eds) (1994). *Marketing in Hospitality and Tourism: A Consumer Focus*, London: Cassell.

Thornton, P.R., Shaw, G. and Williams, A.M. (1997). Tourist group holiday decision-making and behaviour: the influence of children, *Tourism Management*, 18(5): 287–98.

Woodside, A.G. and MacDonald, R. (1993). General systems framework of customer choice and behaviour processes for tourism services. Paper presented at the International Conference, 'Decision Making Processes and Preference Changes of Tourists: Intertemporal and Intercountry Perspectives' of the Institute of Tourism and Service Economics, University of Innsbruck, 25–27 November 1993.

Yiannakis, A. and Gibson, H. (1992). Roles tourists play, *Annals of Tourism Research*, (19)2: 287–304.

1

Multi-faceted tourist travel decisions: a constraint-based conceptual framework to describe tourists' sequential choices of travel components

Benedict G C Dellaert

Center for Economic Research and Economics Institute Tilburg (EIT), Tilburg University, PO Box 90153, 5000 LE Tilburg, The Netherlands

Dick F Ettema

Hague Consulting, The Hague, The Netherlands

Christer Lindh

Transport and Traffic Planning Group, Royal Institute of Technology, Stockholm, Sweden

Introduction

Imagine the following scenario:

It is February 1998 and the Jones family are considering their holiday plans for the year. They roughly know where they want to go – a mountain area where they've been several times before – and in which period they would like to travel. After a few weeks of contemplation and some further orientation they decide on a 3-week camping trip in the middle of August. One of the children will not come along because she prefers to go somewhere else with some friends. The family decides to book one of five campgrounds in the region, depending on availability, and will decide on the route to take later.

Many decisions tourists make are not single independent choices of separate elements (such as destination, accomodation or travel companions), but rather, are complex multi-faceted decisions in which the choices for different elements are interrelated and evolve in a decision process over time. Although travelers may also book pre-packaged travel tours, many of the decisions that travelers face are not between fully packaged alternatives, and the above anecdote illustrates how a travel decision process for a holiday might take place if it involved multiple components. The anecdote illustrates that different facets of a trip are decided upon (such as destination, accommodation, travel timing) and in some temporal sequence (for example, trip type was selected before specific destination). It also illustrates that decision-makers may face some constraints that may restrict their options (such as working hours and accommodation availability).

Assume that tourists' travel choices can be regarded as the outcome of a sequential scheduling process in which a number of decisions are scheduled over a longer period (e.g. varying from a few days to several months) and that those decisions take into account restrictions because of time and money budgets and coupling constraints caused by work, family and friendship-based relationships. Then, the specific contribution of this paper is to introduce a conceptual framework that allows one to analyze tourists' travel behavior that incorporates this type of temporal sequencing of multi-faceted travel decisions as well as relevant decision-making constraints. In line with most research on travel choice, our discussion will be restricted to holiday travel only. It should also be noted that though our analysis allows us to look at multiple facets within the trip choice, we focus on tourists' choices of single trips. Thus, we leave the extension of the proposed framework to include choices of multiple trips over longer periods of time for future research.

Tourist travel choice: a brief review

Most studies of tourists' travel choice address tourists' *destination* choices as the key element in the travel decision-making process. In some studies, this element is combined with accommodation or activity choices.[1,2] The duration of overnight stays has also been investigated.[3]

Generally, the factors investigated when studying these aspects of travel decision-making are fairly similar and two main categories of destination characteristics are distinguished in the literature.

(1) The possibility to undertake certain *activities* at the destination. Examples of activities that may influence tourists' choices are: sports (e.g. golf or tennis), dining, cultural activities (e.g. visiting museums, galleries, opera, theatre, dance, festivals), gambling, night life, visiting historical attractions, shopping and outdoor recreation (e.g. mountains and beaches).
(2) The *attributes of the destination itself* such as general price level, accessibility, climate, health, safety, residents' attitude toward tourists, existence of language barriers,[4] scenery, availability and quality of accommodation, and air quality.

Traveler characteristics can also influence tourists' travel choices. They include elements such as the number of people traveling as a group, traveler income, age and possible relationships to people in certain destinations.[5]

Other research has emphasized the *structure of tourists' travel decision-making* processes rather than the outcome of the choice. For example, Crompton[6] proposed that travelers first create a cognitive set of possible destinations, which is narrowed down in the course of the decision process into smaller consideration sets, until the final travel alternative is selected. His findings suggest that people consider five to six alternatives up to 5–6 months before their trip. Two months before departure, the number of alternatives considered is decreased to two to three. This process was observed in high involvement travel decisions, for example, for trips to a new destination, and may not apply to low involvement routine decisions.

Similarly, Woodside and MacDonald[7] introduced the 'trip frame' concept, which describes a set of interrelated travel choices. These include destination choice, route/mode choice, accommodation choice, choice of activities, choices of areas to visit, choice of attractions and choice of visiting shops. For each choice element, different consideration sets, motives and information search procedures can exist. Furthermore, the choices for each element can be made at different points in time. For instance, the destination may be chosen a considerable time before the trip, while the choice to visit attractions may be made during the trip. The trip frame concept also includes an evaluation of outcomes of choices, which in turn may influence future choices. Thus, the decision process is viewed as a complex multi-dimensional process consisting of a number of separate but possibly interdependent choices that are made at different points in time.

Other studies have focused on understanding the evolution of tourist travel choices over longer periods of time. For example, Oppermann[8] distinguishes three time horizons in describing changes tourism patterns over time: average changes in travel behavior across all tourists, that may occur over the years; changes in travel behavior within each tourist, as his or her travel experience and family situation evolve; and changes between generations of travelers, as shifts occur between the common backgrounds of each generation.

Similarly, Lawson[9] studied the relationships between the family life-cycle and tourist choice behavior and observed that differences in travel choices occurred depending on family structure. Recently, Dellaert, Prodigalidad and Louviere[10] further explored the role of family member interactions in travel decision-making and analyzed the influence of different family members. Although these latter three studies did not particularly focus on the structure of the travel choice process *per se*, they do stress the possibility of social limitations on travel choice, and the relevance of measuring, tourist preferences over time.

Taken together, the total set of research findings show that many aspects that influence tourists' travel decisions have been identified, as well as many different stages that may occur in tourists' travel choices. However, some elements of the travel choice process still deserve more attention.

Specifically, Woodside and McDonald[7] show that even decisions concerning the choice of a single trip need not be taken at one moment in time, but may be spread out over a longer period. In fact, the decision process consists of a number of different stages, which are marked by specific actions such as a first discussion of the idea to make a trip, the start of the information search, the final decision to make the trip, etc.

Given that it is the case that tourists do not always decide on all facets simultaneously, it is particularly worthwhile to understand how tourists' choices of different aspects of their travel decisions are distributed over time. Different timing of these choices would influence the decision when strategic policy and management actions and/or marketing and communications strategies could be implemented most effectively. For example, if tourists decide on their geographical destination before they decide on their accommodation, information or pricing strategies regarding hotel facilities could be implemented more effectively once market communications on countries and regions were implemented already.

Furthermore, although travel constraints have been recognized implicitly in the discussion of the travel life-cycle (for example, by taking into account possible differences in travel behavior between travelers with and without children), most research on tourist decisions to date is still somewhat limited in how it deals with the general concept of so called *space–time constraints*. This concept was introduced by Hägerstrand in 1970[11] and describes the total range of physical and social limitations that may exist to the timing, length and speed of travel. Most travelers face several types of limits to the set of destinations that they can visit for a holiday. For instance, time and duration of a trip may depend on holiday schedules of schools and work of the individual, and individuals may be limited by the time schedules of their travel companions.

Specifically, the following three types of constraints can be distinguished.[11]

(1) Authority constraints, these are constraints imposed by law (e.g. opening hours of shops) or institutions (e.g. work or school hours).
(2) Coupling constraints, these are constraints that stem from restrictions faced by household members, friends and colleagues.
(3) Capacity constraints, these are constraints caused by the availability of travel options (modes with their specific speeds) and money resources.

Together these constraints provide a comprehensive overview of how tourists' travel choices may be limited by factors beyond their direct control.

The proposed framework

In the proposed framework, we focus on the choices that travelers make in booking and planning their travel facilities, i.e. the choices that they make *before* they undertake their actual traveling, as these choices are most relevant to tourism planners and marketers who want to understand the demand for long-distance travel. The framework describes tourists' choices of a single trip given their current stage in the travel life-cycle and their current knowledge level of travel options. Based on the previous review, we identify the following decisions that tourists need to make for each trip.

First, the decision whether or not to make a trip has to be made. This decision will depend upon goals that individuals wish to attain and will determine the activities to perform during the trip.

Second, if a trip is made, decisions have to be taken about: (i) trip destination, (ii) type of accommodation, (iii) travel companions, (iv) travel mode for the trip, (v) when to make the trip, and (vi) duration of the trip. Fesenmaier's[12] findings indicate that those are the decisions that are generally taken prior to the trip.

Third, other factors such as choices of special attractions to visit, travel routes to follow, day-to-day expenditure, and rest and food stop locations and timing, are more often made during the trip.

Generally, the decisions that tourists make are strongly interrelated. For instance, the choice of accommodation will depend on the available accommodation at the destination. At the same time, the destination choice will also depend on requirements that individuals have about the accommodation. Similar dependencies exist for most of the decisions that have to be taken. Furthermore, it should be noted that decisions are made subject to the constraints defined by Hägerstrand. These constraints determine restrictions to the set of possible alternatives from which tourists can choose their travel options. In more formal terms, they set the boundaries for the space in which the consumer utility maximization process can take place. The proposed framework is graphically summarized in Figure 1. It shows the various components in multi-faceted tourist travel decisions, the possible timing and sequencing of the components, and the fact that choices occur subject to a set of constraints.

In summary, this conceptualization and the combined findings in research on tourist choice processes suggest that the following elements should be addressed in models of multi-faceted tourist travel choice.

(1) Analysis of destination choice, accommodation choice, choice of travel companions, mode choice, choice of travel date and duration of the trip for each separate trip.
(2) Analysis of the planning horizon of decisions on different aspects of trips, such as initiation of the first idea, start of information search, and the final decision taken.

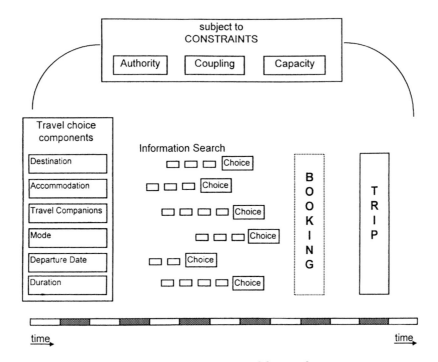

Figure 1. Proposed conceptual framework.

(3) Analysis of how overnight long-distance trip decisions are affected by different types of constraints such as temporal and budgetary limitations.

We illustrate the role of these components in the study described below.

Exploratory study

Data for an exploratory study of the proposed framework were collected in March, April and May 1995 from 300 respondents in Sweden. Respondents were randomly approached by telephone and were screened on the basis of the question if they had made in the past year at least one overnight long-distance trip. They were asked to indicate their holiday traveling plans for the period June 1995 to December 1995, day trips and business trips were not included.

For each of their intended trips, respondents were asked to indicate, if applicable, the timing and selection of the different travel choice components included in the proposed framework: thus, their intended destination, accommodation, travel companions, departure date, duration of the their trip and date of booking. Because of a miscommunication in the data collection process, no data were collected on respondents intended transportation modes. Respondents were specifically asked at what time they had made choices for each of the above aspects of their trip in order to be able to study possible sequencing of their choice of different travel components.

To illustrate the impact of constraints on respondents' travel choices, questions about some possible limiting factors were also included in the survey. Household composition was included as a possible coupling constraint, assuming that families with children would be more limited in their choice of travel period and trip length. As possible capacity constraints, respondents' income and car-ownership were also measured. The latter is a common explanatory variable in daily transportation research.[13] In our study it was included because we expected that non-car owners would be more limited in terms of the number of trips that they could make as compared with tourists that did own a car.

Timing of choices

Table 1 summarizes the main results of the data collection. In the first column, it shows for each of the months in the period from April 1995 to December 1995 how many trips were planned across all respondents. The table shows a clear preference of the respondents for the months June, July and August. In the other columns, the table shows how many respondents planned each of the aspects of their trips in each of the months for the period May 1994 to May 1995.

The results show that most trips planned between June and December 1995 took place between January and April 1995, with a small secondary peak in July to September 1994. In general, most trip elements were planned a few months before the actual trip, with approximately 1 or 2 months' variation between planning for different elements, such as accommodation, destination and duration.

This is further underlined in the data presented in Table 2, which offers a more detailed picture of the average period between the different choices that tourists made

Table 1. Timing of the various factors in tourists' travel choice processes.

Month	Planned trip date	Date of destination choice	Date of accommodation choice	Date of travel companions choice	Date of travel mode choice	Date of departure date choice	Date of trip duration choice	Date of booking
Before May 1994	—	43	6	31	N/A	6	3	1
June 1994	—	6	2	6	—	2	1	—
July 1994	—	4	3	9	—	—	5	—
August 1994	—	9	6	7	—	2	5	—
September 1994	—	12	4	9	—	3	3	—
October 1994	—	15	1	10	—	3	2	—
November 1994	—	15	3	8	—	3	2	—
December 1994	—	14	5	17	—	6	5	2
January 1995	—	16	11	35	—	13	11	15
February 1995	—	32	19	33	—	18	16	16
March 1995	—	28	19	37	—	27	18	20
April 1995	23	23	18	40	—	24	20	11
May 1995	54	—	7	12	—	5	11	4
June 1995	102	—	—	—	—	—	—	—
July 1995	113	—	—	—	—	—	—	—
August 1995	63	—	—	—	—	—	—	—
September 1995	13	—	—	—	—	—	—	—
October 1995	9	—	—	—	—	—	—	—
November 1995	4	—	—	—	—	—	—	—
December 1995	8	—	—	—	—	—	—	—
Total	389	200	104	254	N/A	114	102	65

Table 2. Periods between planning factors and actual trip.

Planning activity	Average period planned before trip (in months)	Standard deviation*
Destination choice	7.17	8.16
Accommodation choice	5.58	4.42
Travel companions choice	6.20	4.77
Travel mode choice	N/A	—
Departure date choice	4.92	3.65
Trip duration choice	5.57	4.29
Booking	3.81	2.35

*Differences between categories are not significant at 95% confidence level.

in the planning process and the actual travel date. In line with Fesenmaier's findings, destination choices and travel companion choices were typically made early on in the planning process, on average 6 to 7 months before the actual travel date. The timing of the choices for destination and travel companions follows that of the choices of accommodation and trip duration. These are made at approximately 5.5 months before the travel date. The choice of the exact departure date was made on average about 5 months before departure and bookings were not made until 3 to 4 months before departing. Standard deviations on all of these average periods were found to be quite high, which indicates a considerable difference in timing of the planning process across respondents and perhaps also trips. This also explains the fact that no significant differences were found between the average planning periods for each travel facet.

A note of caution is needed when interpreting this data. The method of data collection did not allow us to distinguish between respondents that had not (yet) made a decision on a specific element of the trip and respondents that chose not to answer the question. This may have reduced the number of observations of choices for factors that are generally decided upon closer to the actual travel date. As a consequence, the estimated averages for the planning periods may be somewhat higher than those in reality.

Constraints

Examples of constraints that were relevant in this study are given in Tables 3–5. They illustrate the effect of possible constraints on trip timing, trip length and number of trips. Table 3 illustrates coupling constraints and, to a certain extent, authority constraints. It confirms that households with children are more limited in their choice of travel date and travel duration because of legal and social requirements that exist with regard to children's attendance in school. The tables show a general tendency for households with children to make most important long-distance overnight trips in June, July and August and to focus on medium-length holidays of about 1 week. Although both trends also apply to households without children, the latter category shows more variation in their travel timing and duration choices. The main trips of households without children are more evenly spread across the year, and households

Table 3. Household composition as a coupling constraint.

	Percentage of trips made	
Factor	With children	No children
Travel date		
April	5.0	5.4
May	3.3	16.1
June	25.0	29.0
July	45.0	33.4
August	15.0	8.1
September	1.7	4.3
October	1.7	2.1
November	1.7	0.5
December	1.6	1.1
Total	100%	100%
	($n = 60$)	($n = 186$)
Trip length		
1 night	6.5	4.2
2–3 nights	10.9	12.7
4–6 nights	6.5	6.0
1 week	43.5	38.5
2 weeks	19.6	19.9
More than 2 weeks	13.0	18.7
Total	100%	100%
	($n = 46$)	($n = 166$)

Table 4. Income as a capacity constraint: Destinations visited on longest trip and number of trips for low and high-income groups.

Income group	Destinations visited (no. of respondents)	Average no. of trips (s.d.)*
Low income (< 150 000 SKR) ($n = 36$)	Sweden (1), Denmark (2), Finland (2), Norway (5), UK (2), France (4), Germany (2), Holland (1), Austria (2), Spain (3), Italy (1), Greece (7), Eastern-Africa (1), USA (3)	1.28 (0.80)
High income (> 310 000 SKR) ($n = 32$)	Denmark (3), Finland (1), Norway (3), Great-Britain (4), Ireland (3), France (4), Germany (1), Belgium (1), Switzerland (1), Spain (1), Italy (1), Greece (7), USA (1), Malaysia (1)	1.88 (1.14)

*Differences between categories are not significant at 95% confidence level.

without children make relatively more short (2 to 3 nights) and very long trips (more than 2 weeks). It should be noted that although these trends could be observed in the data, the differences were not significant at the 95% confidence level.

Tables 4 and 5 illustrate the role of capacity constraints on tourists' choices. Table 4 shows that the destinations that low-income respondents chose for their longest trip

Table 5. Car ownership as a capacity constraint: Average number of trips for car owners and non-car owners.

Car ownership	Average no. of trips	(s.d.)*
Car owners ($n = 104$)	1.72	1.06
Non-car owners ($n = 24$)	1.67	0.90

*Differences between categories are not significant at 95% confidence level.

were very similar to those selected by high-income respondents. However, it can also be seen that low-income respondents on average made considerably fewer trips per year than did high-income respondents. Table 5 shows that a similar but smaller difference exists between car owners and non-car owners. This indicates that not having a car did not restrict respondents very much in terms of their travel behavior.

In summary, the data collected in this study illustrates the use and relevance of the various components in the proposed analytical framework. Various aspects of tourists' long-distance overnight travel choices were measured and illustrated. It shows how the timing of the choices for these components can differ across components that depend on the constraints that people face. The potential impact of various constraints on tourists' travel choice behavior was also illustrated on the basis of household coupling constraints and income and car-ownership constraints.

Conclusion and discussion

The main contribution of this paper was to propose a conceptual framework that can be used to model and understand multi-faceted tourist travel decisions that involve subsequent choices for different facets of a single trip as well as the constraints that may limit the number of feasible travel alternatives.

The framework was illustrated with an empirical application. The main findings of this study are the following.

(1) The choice of the different facets of travel (e.g. destination, accommodation, or travel duration choices) do indeed represent subsequent, yet interrelated, decisions that jointly make up the total travel decision process.
(2) The timing of the choices for these facets differed in terms of the average period between decision-making and the travel moment.
(3) There is a relatively large variance between the timing of different tourists' choices for each of the travel decision facets.
(4) Constraints that tourists face when making their travel decisions determine, at least in part, their travel decisions.

The main implications for future travel decision research are that more attention might be paid to interrelate tourists' choices of various components of travel decision making, which jointly affect tourists' ultimate travel choices. Factors such as the timing of choice-making and the constraints that tourists face when making their choices, have so far received relatively little attention in tourism research, but we have shown that they can be significant factors in tourists' travel decision-making processes. This implies that formal econometric models of tourists' decision-making may need to be extended to include relevant socioeconomic constraints and social structures (such as working hours and travel timing regimes), which may affect tourists' opportunities to travel. Also, the proposed framework can be used to better understand the potential impact of changes in social and legal structures over time, as it can incorporate the structure of constraints that is included in these social and legal structures. For example, family life-cycle theory can be incorporated in terms of changing coupling constraints over time.

To some extent, analytical tools that address the issues raised in the proposed conceptual framework are already available. For instance, logit type choice models can be used to separately model the choices involved in trip scheduling, such as destination choice, accommodation choice and mode choice.[13] In this approach, characteristics of the destination, accommodation, mode, or company can be used as explanatory variables. To account for interdependencies between these choices, multidimensional choice models of the nested logit or probit type can be applied. These more complex models allow one to account for, e.g. the dependency of mode choice on the destination choice. For example, Dellaert, Borgers and Timmermans[14] presented such a model in the context of city trips.

However, logit type models do not allow one to incorporate timing decisions directly in the modeling framework. Therefore, another useful way of analyzing trip scheduling could be to make use of duration models.[15] These models are especially suitable in capturing changes in choice probabilities over time, as well as expected time intervals between choice moments. Specifically, the models describe the probability that an event will occur conditionally on the fact that it has not yet occurred. A difficulty in applying these models is that there is no clear theoretical framework to determine why one planning period should be more optimal than another.

For businesses and government organizations that operate in the travel industry, the conceptual framework and our empirical findings offer insight in the question of when to target different facets in tourists' choices most effectively. For example, differences in timing of destination choices and accommodation choices have become apparent in this study, which implies that sequential communication and/or sales strategies may be more effective in interacting with potential travelers than simultaneous approaches. On the other hand, our findings also indicate that potential benefits may exist in bundling several aspects of travel choices, which may open up opportunities for early sales if later travel decision elements can be tied in with earlier decision elements. For example, destination choices, which are the earliest choices in the travel choice sequence, might be tied in with accommodation choices. Also, our findings offer insights into the limits that exist when attempting to change tourists travel choices and travel considerations, because our results include the constraints that different tourists face. For example, it will be quite difficult to move a tourist's travel time if he or she is traveling in a group in which timing was mutually agreed upon. These insights can be used to better predict and manage demand for travel services in different periods of the year and potentially, in the long run, to develop more effective time and environmental resource-use strategies at the community level.

References

1. Hu, Y. and Brent Ritchie, J. R., Measuring destination attractiveness: a contextual approach. *Journal of Travel Research* 1993, **32**, 25–34.
2. Shoemaker, S., Segmenting the US travel market according to benefits realized. *Journal of Travel Research* 1994, **32**, 8–21.
3. Dadgostar, B. and Isotalo, R.M., Factors affecting time spent by near-home tourists in city destinations. *Journal of Travel Research* 1992, **31**, 34–39.
4. Um, S. and Crompton, J.L., The roles of perceived inhibitors and facilitators in pleasure travel destination decisions. *Journal of Travel Research* 1992, **30**, 18–25.
5. Woodside, A. G. and Lysonski, S., A general model of traveller destination choice. *Journal of Travel Research* 1989, **27**, 8–14.
6. Crompton, J., Structure of vacation destination choice sets. *Annals of Tourism Research* 1992, **19**, 420–434.
7. Woodside, A. G. and MacDonald, R., General system framework of customer choice processes of tourism services. In R. Gasser and K. Weiermair (eds.), *Spoilt for Choice*. Kultur Verlag, Austria, 1994.
8. Oppermann, M., Travel life cycle. *Annals of Tourism Research* 1995, **22**, 535–552.
9. Lawson, R., Patterns of tourist expenditure and types of vacation across the family life cycle. *Journal of Travel Research* 1991, **29**, 12–18.
10. Dellaert, B., Prodigalidad, M. and Louviere, J., Using conjoint analysis to study family travel preference structures: a comparison of day trips and one-week holidays. *Tourism Analysis* 1998, **2**, 67–75.
11. Hägerstrand, T., What about people in regional science? *Papers of the Regional Science Association* 1970, **23**, 7–21.
12. Fesenmaier, D., A preliminary examination of the complex tourism decision making process. Working paper, Urbana-Champaign IL: Department of Leisure Studies, University of Illinois, 1995.
13. Ben-Akiva, M. and Lerman, S. R., *Discrete Choice Analysis: Theory and Application to Travel Demand*. MIT Press, Cambridge, MA, 1985.
14. Dellaert, B. G. C., Borgers, A. W. J. and Timmermans, H. J. P., Conjoint models of tourist portfolio choice: theory and illustration. *Leisure Sciences* 1997, **19**, 31–58.
15. Hensher, D. A. and Mannering, F.L., Hazard-based duration models and their application to transport analysis. *Transport Reviews* 1994, **14**, 63–82.

2

Tourist group holiday decision-making and behaviour: the influence of children

Paul R Thornton

Institute of Cornish Studies, University of Exeter, Hayne Corfe Centre, Sunningdale, Truro, TR1 3ND, UK

Gareth Shaw and Allan M Williams

Department of Geography, University of Exeter, Amory Building, Rennes Drive, Exeter, EX4 4RJ, UK

Introduction

Olmsted and Hane defined a group as 'a plurality of individuals who are in contact with one another, who take each other into account, and who are aware of some significant commonality'.[1] With this definition in mind, tourism can be seen as a form of leisure behaviour where activities are or, at least, able to be intensively group-based to an extent unlikely to be matched in most other non-holiday situations, including weekend leisure activities. Despite this the tourist group has often been ignored in favour of collecting data on the perceptions and motivations of the individual.

The significance of group-based behaviour lies in its modification of individual behaviour. Individual behaviour becomes the outcome of personal motivations after they have been filtered and redirected by the social circle of the group. Since the group exerts a powerful influence on the individual to conform to particular values and norms, the result, in terms of behaviour, is often a negotiated (or imposed) compromise rather than the enactment of any one individual's desires.[2] Furthermore, the more significant the differences between individuals in a group, the greater will be the required compromise. Therefore, an individual tourist's experiences are often based on group defined goals, expectations and standards. The eventual holiday activities of each member of the group will be affected by the preferences of the other members of the group, unless the individual leaves the group for a significant period of time.

In many cases the 'significant commonality' behind groups are family relationships. While mature adults will vary in their motivations and desires, larger differences are likely to exist between generations, particularly adults and children. The dynamics of family-based group decision-making processes have been the subject of considerable research. However, most research has concentrated on the purchase of general leisure products rather than tourist products. Nevertheless the literature provides some pointers for the analysis of tourist group behaviour. The following section presents a brief review of the research of relevance to this article, and is not intended to be an exhaustive discussion of the extensive literature on family decision-making. A more complete review of the literature may be found in Seaton and Tagg.[3] The review will be followed by an examination of the major components of differentiation between different types of tourist group and some initial explanations for these variations.

Research on family decision-making

Research on family decision-making has generated several theories concerning the role of individuals within family groups. Initially the decision-making process was perceived as unilateral, with later theories becoming more complex and hybrid as choices were perceived as involving both individual and joint decisions.[4] The early literature, mostly pre-1950, assumed the husband, as head of the household, made all of the family's decisions unilaterally.[5] From the 1950s this approach was supplanted by the notion of the wife acting as a 'purchasing agent'.[6] Fodness notes that while there is superficial support for this theory, it incorrectly equates the action of purchasing with the responsibility and authority for making family decisions. In addition, both the husband's and wife's responsibility theories operated on the basis that one member of the family held complete responsibility for decisions.

In contrast to these theories Sharp and Mott argued that decision-making was shared, with differing levels of responsibility depending on the specific nature of particular projects.[7] Empirical evidence provided some support for their hypotheses, and largely discredited the view that only one member of the family makes consistent and unilateral decisions. Indeed Sharp and Mott concluded that vacation decision-making, in particular, was an area where husband and wife actively co-operated as a marital dyad. Later research developed these theories further. Davis, for example, broke down family decision-making into more detailed sub-decisions.[8] These sub-decisions included choices of when to purchase, where to purchase and how much to spend. Davis found that decision-making varied not only by product category but by sub-decision as well. Thus, it is misleading to refer to husbands and wives controlling decision-making, since this ignores a whole level of complexity, namely the sub-decisions.

Jenkins extended Davis' research by analysing which member of the family exerted most influence in each sub-decision. Results suggested that while husbands dominated sub-decisions on length of trip, timing of vacations and expenditure, sub-decisions over whether to take children, the mode of transport, activities, lodging and destination were all joint husband/wife choices. However, Jenkins found that wives appeared to have no primary influences compared to husbands.[9]

Filiatrault and Ritchie's work on joint decision-making between husband and wives also analysed sub-decisions within vacation travel.[10] They concluded that husband/wife influence varied according to different sub-decisions and different decision-making units (that is married couples and family groups of varying compositions). More specifically they found that: firstly, husbands dominate decisions in families where there are children, with more joint decision-making where there are no children;

secondly, the relative influence of husbands and wives across sub-decisions varied more in families than in couples; thirdly, children had little influence on the overall decision-making process, and their best chance to do so was to 'ally' themselves with either the husband or wife (to produce a 'majority' position).[11]

Overall, the results appear to be confusing. For example, Sharp and Mott found in their study that joint decisions between husband and wife were more likely in high income families than low income families.[12] In contrast, Wolgast's work indicated the situation was the reverse, with individual, husband-dominated, decision-making more prevalent in wealthier families.[13]

Fodness, in studying family vacation decision-making, found evidence to support the conclusion that holiday choice was usually a joint decision.[14] However, contrary to previous studies they indicated that wives, rather than husbands, were more likely to be responsible for individual decisions in families with children. Furthermore, unlike previous research, it was the wife who dominated information–search processes (such as writing-off for brochures), rather than the husband. Other findings suggested an association between observable changes in family dynamics and the progression of the family life cycle, particularly with respect to who has primary responsibility for the care of children. Fodness concludes that such results might provide a differential advantage in product decisions and promotional strategies for those involved in tourism marketing.[15]

More recently, the role of children in family decision-making has continued to be reassessed. Originally ignored, and later dismissed as having little or no influence, they have gradually attracted more attention.[16] Usually the role assigned to children as either tourists or visitors has been a passive one. For example, Ryan identified children as important from the viewpoint of their actual numbers and their role as a determining factor that accounts for the satisfaction of adults.[17] He notes satisfying the child generates a satisfactory experience for the adult.

This 'passive role' is further seen in the effect children have on the influence of the husband and wife according to the stage of the family life cycle. Filiatrault and Ritchie's research indicates that in a situation where a mother halts her career to care for children, the father assumes a position of greater economic dominance, with the potential for exerting more decision-making power over infrequent, expensive choices.[18] However, in such circumstances an additional relationship may develop, (between mother and child) which will modify future decision-making, with the mother operating as an arbiter upon a child's purchasing decision, either allowing a purchase to go ahead or halting it.

In tourism research, few researchers have identified children as having an active role in decision-making. Children have often been viewed as expressing demands that parents have to plan for, or plan around, but:

Children are not the target audience for the tourist industry as a whole, especially when it comes to travel abroad for a major holiday. It is generally assumed that they submit to whatever choices their parents make, and that they have little secondary influence on their parents' particular choice of holiday destination.[19]

This possibility of children being active participants, or negotiators, in family decisions has mostly been ignored, but there are some exceptions. For example,

Ryan found that children were a catalyst in generating a family visit to an attraction. However, it is not clear whether this 'catalyst' effect derived from the parents deciding a trip to a site would be beneficial, or a result of the child's expressed desire to visit. Intuitively, two factors may indicate the latter. Firstly the satisfaction of children is highly rated by parents, and if the child does not wish to visit a site then satisfaction may be difficult to achieve (in effect a form of veto). Secondly, children are among the most discerning customers and the least prepared to accept mediocre experiences.[20] Children, therefore, may play a significant role in some decision-making and have the ability to exert influence.

This was later confirmed in a multinational study conducted by Seaton and Tagg.[21] The work of the greatest relevance here created a sample of 970 interviews with United Kingdom families on how they formed their vacation decisions.[22] In line with their desire to explore 'paedonomic' decisions (those most affected by children) the survey was initially addressed, in the form of a self-completed questionnaire, towards collecting children's opinions. The respondents were required to recall data from their last holiday, which could have been up to two years before. Subsequently questionnaire forms were distributed to parents.

It is difficult to make effective comparisons between the Seaton and Tagg survey and the Cornwall study described here. Principally, there are fundamental differences in methodological approach. The Cornwall study made use of a self-completed space–time budget survey (described below) rather than a recall questionnaire. This was as a result of the Cornwall survey's aim to investigate the behaviour of tourist parties over an extended period of time during their holidays, rather than examining the behaviour that led up to the decisions to travel and where to go. In addition Seaton and Tagg chose to survey children aged between 12 and 18 and their mothers and fathers or custodial parent/cohabiting parents. The Cornwall survey, for reasons described below, looked at tourist groups as a whole. These could include children aged between 0 and 16 (17- and 18-year olds were considered adults), and all adults including other relatives such as grandparents. However since Seaton and Tagg's work produced interesting, and in some cases contradictory, results reference will be made to it.

In contrast to this tendency to ignore children, the tourist industry does seem to have recognised their importance. Boyer and Viallon suggest that much of the promotional material for holidays is designed so as to construct codes which are familiar to children.[23] Similarly, Mayo and Jarvis argue that the tourist industry targets the child's interest by appealing to desires to play and through stimulating curiosity.[24]

More general research on leisure-related family decision-making suggests children only possess a role in making small-scale choices and none in major resource-binding (expensive) and infrequent purchases, such as holidays.[25] These pre-travel decisions remained firmly within the parent's influence.[26] Therefore, children seem to have little influence in the decision to travel, since it is a major, infrequent and expensive choice, their only effect being to modify the relationship between husband and wife. In contrast, little research is available on decision-making whilst actually on vacation. In this situation tourist groups face a larger number of individually less important choices, yet the outcomes of these choices are significant in shaping behaviour while on holiday. For example, Cullingford notes:

This view [of the tourist industry] of children's lack of influence contrasts with that of industry, which is exemplified in advertising, especially when related to toys. As is clearly demonstrated by advertisements for toys on television, children are assumed to wield great power over their parents' spending habits, power fostered by peer-group pressure and fashion. There is also a sense of relief for parents in having choices made for them, wanting to win approval and avoid disappointment, in succumbing to easy gratification.[27]

This suggests children do have some direct influence on holiday behaviour, particularly relating to higher frequency/limited resource-binding decisions. However, there is a need for detailed empirical research on whether differences can be identified between the holiday activities of tourist groups with children present, and those without. One method of doing so is to quantify variations in the activities of holiday-makers. Pearce suggests one of the most effective means of collecting data on behaviour is through the space–time budget diary survey.[28] This facilitates an examination of fluctuating patterns of activities through time that is not possible with a single moment-in-time questionnaire survey.

Space–time budgets and tourist behaviour

The value of a space–time budget survey lies in its ability to record data on patterns of behaviour spatially and temporally too complex and detailed for behavioural observation or questionnaire surveys to be practical options.[29] Unfortunately, diary surveys are difficult to operationalize and have seen limited use in tourism research. Two significant examples of space–time budget surveys are D Pearce[28] and Dietvorst,[30] both of which faced difficulties in operationalization and in the analysis of the completed diaries.[30]

A space–time budget diary may vary in exact format, but must record the starting time of an activity, the duration of that activity, the frequency with which the activity occurred, the sequential order of activities in the period of study concerned and the location of these activities.[31]

The data on the activities of the tourist parties in this paper were collected through a space–time budget diary survey of a random sample of tourists staying in two different locations in Cornwall (Newquay and the Bodmin area), stratified to take account of differences between serviced and self-catering accommodation. The diaries were completed by the self-administered method during the period June–September 1993. Only respondents staying at least one week were included in the survey. Each of the first six days of their holiday was represented by a grid based on two hour time blocks, for the period 9 am to 9 pm. This time limitation was introduced both to control the amount of information collected, and to minimise the intrusiveness of the survey (a major cause of low response rates with space–time diary research). The respondents were asked to record their activities and locations in each of these time blocks. If the members of the holiday group were involved in different activities, these were recorded separately. A total of 143 diaries were completed and returned in usable condition by tourist parties, producing more than 10 300 hours of activities to be analysed. Appendix one suggests some possible sources of bias in the diaries. Finally, a smaller follow-up diary/interview survey was undertaken with thirteen respondents from different types of tourist groups. The diary/interview survey used the same basic survey form, but also included an interview session with the tourist party at the end of the first week of their holiday.

The diary sample consisted of 85 tourist parties with one or more children aged 0–16 and 58 parties with no children. A Mann–Whitney test of the average hours tourist parties spent on each activity demonstrated the behaviour of those parties with children was significantly different to those without ($p < 0.05$). These differences are summarised in terms of main activity types in Figure 1. There were some striking similarities such as the percentage of time spent on eating and refreshments and in the amount of time budgeted to visiting fee paying attractions and shopping. However, there were variations between the time budgets of tourist parties containing children and those consisting solely of adults. Parties without children spent more time travelling by car or coach and walking. In contrast tourist parties with children spent more time using swimming pools and taking part in activities based on the beach. Adult-only tourist parties used their extra time principally for relaxing (over 17% of their time budgets on average).

A more detailed disaggregation of the data reveals additional differences (Table 1). For example, Figure 1 implies similar amounts of time are spent visiting fee paying attractions by both types of tourist party. However, nearly two-thirds of this component of the adult-only groups' time budgets was spent visiting historic sites and heritage attractions, compared to approximately one third for groups with children. Furthermore, adult-only parties spent twice as much time sightseeing by car or coach than parties with children; this variation is also reflected in the tourist parties' contrasting activity spaces (Figure 2), with adult-only parties spending more time and reaching greater distances from their accommodation than groups with children.

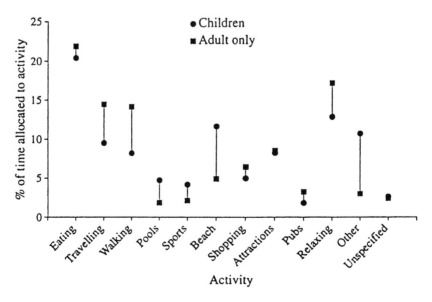

Figure 1. Tourist group time budgets.

Table 1. Activities of groups with and without children.

Activity	Time (% of available budget)	
	With children	Adult only
Eating and Refreshments		
At accommodation	15.4	15.3
Away from accommodation (purchased)	3.2	5.1
Away from accommodation (picnic)	0.9	0.2
Refreshments	0.9	1.1
Total	20.4	21.6
Travelling by Car or Coach		
Sightseeing by car or coach	3.0	6.9
Moving between locations	6.5	7.4
Total	9.6	14.3
Walking		
Walking in the country	4.5	6.9
Walking around town	3.7	6.9
Total	8.2	13.9
Use of Swimming Pools		
Accommodation's own pool	4.2	1.7
Other pools	0.5	0.1
Total	4.7	1.8
Taking Part in Sporting Activities		
High effort sports	2.2	1.0
Low effort sports	2.1	1.0
Total	4.3	1.9
Beach Activities	8.1	1.6
Beach leisure	2.0	0.3
Swimming	0.0	0.0
Surfing	0.7	2.1
Walking on beach	0.9	0.7
Total	11.7	4.7
Going Shopping	3.9	5.3
Pleasure shopping	0.5	0.5
Essential shopping	0.6	0.4
Total	5.0	6.3
Visiting Fee Paying Attractions		
Amusement arcades	0.5	0.1
Theme parks	2.2	1.5
'Educational' sites	2.4	1.0
NT/EH type sites	3.1	5.6
Total	8.2	8.3
Visiting Pubs, Clubs and Bars	0.3	0.0
Within accommodation base	0.8	1.4
Outside of accommodation base	0.7	1.7
Total	1.8	3.1

Continued

Table 1. (Continued)

	Time (% of available budget)	
Activity	With children	Adult only
Relaxing		
Sleeping	0.7	0.8
Relaxing outdoors	1.4	3.2
Relaxing indoors	10.8	13.0
Total	12.9	17.0
Other Activities	2.5	2.1
Using accommodation facilities	1.8	0.4
Farm activities	2.3	0.3
Care of children	4.0	0.0
Total	10.7	2.7
Unspecified Activities	2.6	2.2

Note: Sub-totals subject to 'rounding'.

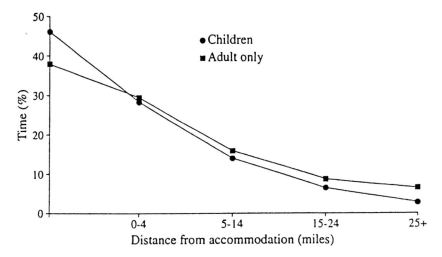

Figure 2. **Tourist group activity spaces.**

A further dimension of such variations is highlighted in Figure 3, which compares the activity locations of 'adult-only' parties and tourist parties including children aged six to ten. This demonstrates the substantially greater amount of time adult-only parties spend in a wider variety of locations, including more time spent inland (Appendix 2). In contrast, tourist parties containing children spent 46% of their time budgets within the immediate vicinity of their accommodation. While some of these differences may be expected, this research has helped to chart some of the major components of differentiation.

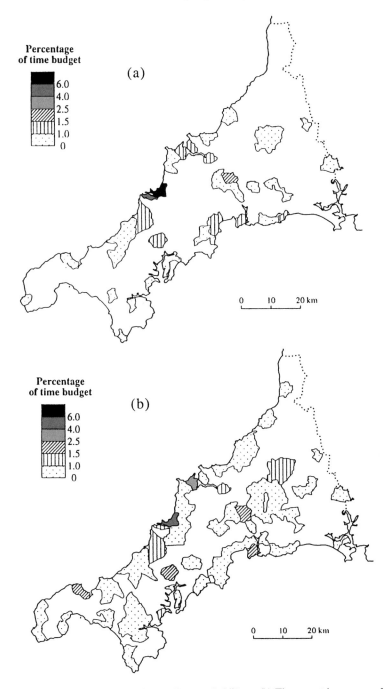

Figure 3. (a) **Time spent in accommodation-medium aged children.** (b) **Time spent in accommodation-adult only parties.**

The influence of children on holiday behaviour

While the presence of children does have a clearly identifiable influence on the behaviour of tourists while on holiday, it is important to consider the extent to which this is contingent on the age of the children. Previous research has suggested that the influence of children on behaviour declines with increasing age. For example, Kelly found that, in non-holiday leisure activities, pre-school children had the greatest influence on activity participation.[32] In other words the presence of a young child outweighed other influences, including the presence of older children.

In order to test the influence of children's ages on holiday activities, tourist parties with children were further subdivided according to the age of their youngest child into three types of party: those with children aged up to 5, those with children aged 6–10, and those with children aged 11–16. The ages of the rest of the party were not considered, even if the party included other children or even, in a number of cases, when grandparents accompanied the party. All parties that contained no children were classified as 'adult-only', and these included adults of all ages, both young and retired. Therefore, the only difference between tourist parties was the presence or absence of children, and the age of the youngest child. Table 2 provides more detailed confirmation of the results of Figure 1, showing there are relatively high correlations between all types of tourist parties, i.e. all tourists take part in some basic 'tourist activities'. However, the weakest correlation is between adult-only tourist parties and tourist parties with pre-school aged children. The strength of the correlations, in general, increases with the age of children, with tourist parties containing children aged up to 16 showing the strongest similarities to adult-only parties. In addition, groups with a child of up to 5 have the strongest correlation with parties with children aged between 6 and 10. Therefore, children can be said to have an observable influence on the behaviour of tourist parties, and this influence generally declines with increasing age. This appears to contradict the findings of Seaton and Tagg, who suggested that the level of decision consultation increased with the age of children.[33] It is important to note that the results of the Cornwall survey suggest that it is incorrect to equate increased direct decision consultation with an ability to influence behaviour. Younger children can influence behaviour to a greater extent simply through their presence, and not through their ability to negotiate. While increasing age may bring an ability to

Table 2. Correlation matrix of tourist parties.

	Pearson's product moment			
	Adult only	0–5	6–10	11–16
Adult only	—	0.6800	0.8195*	0.8258**
0–5	0.6800	—	0.9454**	0.8494**
6–10	0.8195*	0.9454**	—	0.9473**
11–16	0.8258**	0.8494**	0.9473**	—

No of cases: 12. 2-tailed significance: $*P = 0.01$, $**P = 0.001$. Correlations of the similarity in the behaviour of different types or tourist parties using 12 types of main activities.

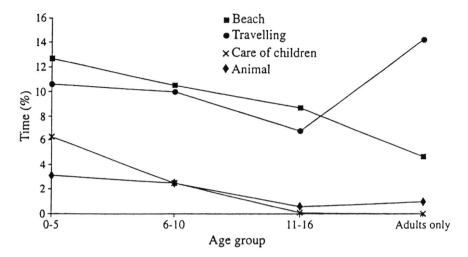

Figure 4. Activities influenced by children's age.

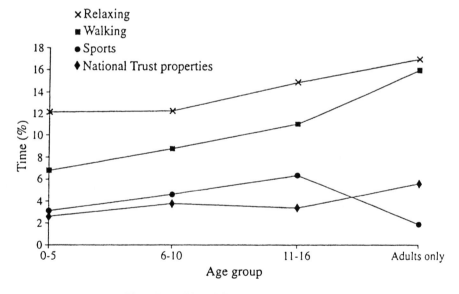

Figure 5. Activities influenced by children's age.

make suggestions, it also creates an expectation of flexibility or willingness to accept compromises not expected from younger children.

While there are similarities in the time budgets of all tourist parties, the amount of time spent on individual activities relates to the presence and age of children (Figures 4 and 5). As would be expected, walking is directly affected by the age of children – increasing from about 6% of the time budget of parties with a youngest child aged under 5, to 11% for groups with older children (11–16). Walking is a very important activity for adult-only parties, accounting for 16% of their time budgets. Similarly, the visiting of historic sites and heritage attractions is much more popular with groups that do not contain children. In contrast, the popularity of visiting attractions such as animal sanctuaries declines with the age of children. The amount of time spent on caring for children, including bathing them is obviously highly dependent on the age of the child concerned. In the 0–5 age group this accounts for over 6% of the groups' total time budgets, although this declines to only 2.5% with 6–10 year olds and to effectively zero with the oldest children.

The question of how children influence the behaviour of a tourist party was investigated through a diary–interview survey. This included similar space–time diaries but added in-depth interview sessions at the end of the survey period. The tourist parties interviewed were not involved in the main diary survey. The basis of the interview was provided by the diary. Since all members of the tourist party were present in the interview the aim was to create a discussion within the group about the behaviour recorded by the diary instrument. The parties in the interview sample were selected on the basis of their representing different types of tourist group: parties without children; parties with young children; parties with children aged 6–10; and parties with children aged 11–16. In total 936 hours of activities were discussed. This sample was then analysed on the basis of a transcript of its contents. The diary/interview survey was only used to make qualitative statements that were indicative of general quantitative findings.

The first point to note is the high degree of group cohesion amongst tourist parties observed in the main space–time budget survey: tourists spent 90% of the surveyed period in each other's company. The results of the diary/interview survey indicated that children were active in influencing the nature and frequency of holiday activities. Part of this influence derived from the way in which the initial objectives of the holiday had been formulated: several parties reported in the interviews that they only took a summer holiday in Cornwall because of their children. In addition, repeat visits to the same resort, the same accommodation unit and even the same week of the year, were explained by reference to their children's demands. Product loyalty proved strongest amongst groups containing 6- to 11-year olds, who also most desired the company of other children.

In terms of decision-making, all parties with children reported the importance of negotiation in deciding holiday activities. For example, a family group with two children in the 0–5 and 6–10 age groups described their situation:

There's certainly a kind of negotiation going on fairly continuously about what people want. I mean [C] wants to go bike riding. I just know eventually we'll end up hiring bikes and going along the Camel Trail. That's the bee in her bonnet at the moment. Everybody's representing themselves. (Father)

Apart from the youngest, [D]. She's too young to read up on things, but she makes her views known in other ways. She remembered the pony rides from last year, and that's all she's been eager to do, isn't it? I mean we're surprised. We thought she'd want to got to the seaside, but she wasn't overly bothered. She was the one who was fed up first. (Mother)

The youngest children, in general, are unable to take part in negotiations – their influence derives from a need to have set meal times and be kept content. One parent suggested 'I think you keep the children happy before you keep yourself happy'. However, all parents stressed that they retained the right to veto children's choices:

The kids know what they want to do and make regular suggestions. They don't have things thought up for them. Never short of suggestions. (Mother)

No, quite often they do what we decide, don't they? (Father)

Oh yes. What I mean is they're always wanting to do their things. They've always got a list of things they'd like to do. We try and get a balance for the children with what we like. (Mother)

Decision-making on holiday, then, is a complex process of negotiation between individuals with unequal powers of influence. In many ways the necessary compromises are greatest within parties containing the youngest children. In all cases, decisions are not simply taken at one point in time but are almost constantly negotiated over the course of the holiday. This implies those questionnaire surveys taken at one point in time are failing to record data on some complex issues.

Conclusion

Overall, the findings of the space–time budget and the diary–interview surveys suggest holiday activities are heavily group based. Even those parties with teenage children proved to be very cohesive over tourist space. This contradicts the results of the Seaton and Tagg, who found that 20% of children claimed to have spent little or no time with their parents. There are several explanations for this contradiction. Firstly the Cornwall survey covered domestic holidays only, whereas the Strathclyde survey contained a significant proportion of foreign holidays. It is possible that there are different trends according to holiday location. Secondly, the children surveyed by Seaton and Tagg were between the ages of 12 and 18, the Cornwall survey children between 0 and 16 (with 17- and 18-year olds classified as adults). Thirdly, Seaton and Tagg used a questionnaire to record the perceptions and opinions of children on their holiday experiences recalled from up to two years before. The Cornwall survey, which also examined other aspects of the activities of tourists and the way they used space, required a space–time budget survey, which should – theoretically – produce a more objective recording of elapsed time. Finally, the Cornwall survey may be using a different definition of cohesiveness to that perceived by the child respondents in the Seaton and Tagg survey. The Cornwall survey equated continued spatial proximity as representing cohesiveness, and not joint activities involving both adults and children. Therefore the apparent contradiction may derive from methodological and evidential differences.

The cohesiveness discovered by the Cornwall survey has important implications for the ability of children to influence the activities of parents. In particular, the influence of children can be seen in two forms. The first is an obvious outcome of the caring requirements of children who are both dependent on their parents and inflexible in their time-tabling needs (i.e. meals, etc.). To simplify, these are principally children under the age of 5. The alternative means of influence is through negotiation with parents. While children possess the ability to make suggestions, the ultimate decision appears to remain with the parents. However, the satisfaction of children is rated more highly by parents than their own. Of interest to the tourist industry should be the fairly high level of product loyalty of 6- to 10-year olds. However, they remain notoriously discerning customers. Even more damaging is the likelihood that an experience that fails to satisfy a child will have a strong knock on effect on their parents.

Further implications for planning lie in the differences in the spatial use which various tourist parties make of tourist destination areas. Firstly, the domination of the accommodation base in the activity spaces of parties with children, and the high degree of product loyalty among the latter has important design implications for the owners/managers of these establishments. Secondly, the beach activities of a traditional holiday are less important to many adult-only groups. The holiday activities that form a large part of their space–time budgets indicate the importance of interesting and rewarding walks, areas to sightsee by car and the presence of heritage features. There is, therefore, a need for further research on the detailed activities (space–time budgets) of groups in the different market segments, and the need to inform the development of tourist policies in these areas. The study of tourist holiday activities, and the use tourists make of time and space is resource-binding, and therefore unlikely to replace more traditional questionnaire approaches, but it does make a rewarding and important supplement to the usual type of data collected.

References

1. Olmsted, M. and Hane, A., *The Small Group.* Random House, New York, 1978.
2. Crompton, J., Dimensions of the social group role in pleasure vacations. *Annals of Tourism Research* 1981, **VIII**, 550–568.
3. Seaton, A. V. and Tagg, S., The European family vacation: paedonomic aspects of choices and satisfactions. *Journal of Travel and Tourism Research* 1995, **4**(1), 1–21.
4. Fodness, D., The impact of family life cycle on the vacation decision making process. *Journal of Travel Research* 1992, **2**(2), 8–13.
5. Sharp, H. and Mott, P., Consumer decisions in the metropolitan family. *Journal of Marketing* 1956, **21**, 149–156.
6. Davis, H., Decision-making within the household. *Journal of Consumer Research* 1976, **2**, 241–260.
7. Sharp and Mott, 1956.
8. Davis, 1976.
9. Jenkins, R., Family vacation decision making. *Journal of Travel Research* 1978, **16**(4), 2–7.
10. Filiatrault, P. and Ritchie, J., Joint purchasing decisions: a comparison of influence structure in family and couple decisions making units. *Journal of Consumer Research* 1980, **7**, 131–140.
11. Filiatrault and Ritchie, 1980, p. 139.
12. Sharp and Mott, 1956.
13. Wolgast, E., Do husbands or wives make the purchasing decisions? *Journal of Marketing* 1958, **23** (October), 151–158.
14. Fodness, 1992, p. 12.
15. Fodness, 1992, p. 13.
16. Howard, D. and Madrigal, R., Who makes the decision: the parent or the child? the perceived influence of parents and children on the purchase of recreation services. *Journal of Leisure Research* 1990, **22**(3), 244–258.
17. Ryan, C., The child as a visitor. *World Travel and Tourism Review*, 1992, 135–139.
18. Filiautrault and Ritchie, 1980, p. 137.
19. Cullingford, C., Children's attitudes to holidays overseas. *Tourism Management* 1994, **16**(2), 121–127.

20. Ryan, 1992, p. 138.
21. Seaton and Tagg, 1995.
22. Seaton, A. V. and Tagg, S., How different are Scottish family holidays from English? In *Tourism: the state of the art*, ed. A. V. Seaton. Wiley, Chichester, 1994, pp. 540–548.
23. Boyer, M. and Viallon, P., La Communication Touristique. In *The Language of Tourism*, ed. G. Dann. CAB International, Wallingford, 1996.
24. Mayo, E. and Jarvis, L., *The Psychology of Leisure Travel: Effective Marketing and Selling of Travel Services*, CBI, Boston, 1981.
25. Ekstrom, K., Tansuhaj, P. and Foxman, E., Children's influence in family decisions and consumer socialization: a reciprocal view. In *Advances in Consumer Research*, Vol. 14, eds M. Wallendorf and P. Anderson. Association for Consumer Research, Provo, Utah, 1986, pp. 283–288.
26. Darley, W. and Lim, J., Family decision making in leisure-time activities: an exploratory investigation of the impact of locus of control, child age influence factor and parental type on perceived child influence. In *Advances in Consumer Research*, Vol. 13, ed. R. Lutz. Association for Consumer Research, Provo, UT, 1986, pp. 370–374.
27. Cullingford, 1994, p. 121.
28. Pearce, D., The spatial structure of coastal tourism: a behavioural approach. *Tourism Recreation Research* 1988, **13**(2), 11–14.
29. Anderson, J., Space–time budgets and activity studies in urban geography and planning. *Environment and Planning* 1971, **3**, 353–368.
30. Dietvorst, A., Cultural tourism and time–space behaviour. In *Building a New Heritage: Tourism, Culture and Identity in the New Europe*, eds G. Ashworth and P. Larkham. Routledge, London, 1994, pp. 69–89.
31. Anderson, 1981.
32. Kelly, J., *Leisure Identities and interactions*. George, Allen and Unwin, London, 1983.
33. Seaton and Tagg, 1994.
34. Tourism Research Group, *The Cornwall Holiday Survey 1993*. University of Exeter, Exeter, 1994.

Appendix A

A total of 280 diaries were distributed with the offer of a gift voucher as reward for completing and returning them. 143 were returned in a usable condition. However the quality of data in these was quite variable, a common failing of space–time diaries. This was not a problem since only the minimum data of activity and location were required for the survey.

Response rates were not consistent over location and type of accommodation. Overall there was a bias towards the Newquay sites (61% of responses) owing to the diligence of hotel operators in encouraging their guests to complete the diaries.

There may also be an age bias. To ensure that the instructions associated with the diaries were understood the diary form requested that respondents were over the age of 16. It is not possible to tell to what extent this was complied with. However, this should be irrelevant since the diary recorded the activities of all members of the tourist parties, even if they spent time apart. The instructions did ask the respondents to indicate which member of the tourist party completed the diary. Assuming the respondents were truthful, more females completed the diary than males (44.8% compared with 30.8%). A further 24.5% of diaries either did not indicate who completed them or were the result of a combined effort.

A further cause of bias often associated with diaries involves the occupational or socio-economic backgrounds of respondents. There has been the suggestion that the complexity of diaries may put respondents from lower socio-economic groups off completing them. There is some evidence of bias: 47% of tourist parties were from professional or managerial backgrounds. However, a separate visitor survey in Cornwall around the same time found 42% of respondents were from occupational groups A or B, demonstrating that if this technique is biased so too are others.[34]

Appendix B

See Figure 3.

The maps are based on the location of activities according to parishes. Tourist parties with children show a less exploratory nature – staying mainly around the Newquay area. Their activities are mainly located along the coast. In contrast, adult-only parties are more exploratory, and more likely to travel inland. In particular, the National Trust properties in the Bodmin and Truro areas encourage visits to these sites. Newquay remains attractive, but time is also spent in the smaller resorts with a stronger 'heritage' theme, such as St Ives, Padstow and Fowey.

Part II

Economic forecasting in tourism

Introduction by Chris Ryan

The forecasting of tourist demand would appear to be a pre-requisite for successful strategic planning and management at national and regional level. Certainly there is evidence that national tourism organisations think so. As indicated by Smith (1999) and Ryan and Simmons (1999), Canada, New Zealand and Australia have all considered ways of improving research in this area. Australia has established a specific Tourism Forecasting Council to undertake such research and disseminate its findings to the Australian tourism industry. The importance of understanding economic forces is illustrated by the British Tourism Authority's response in September 1998 when its then chairman, David Quarmby (1998) commented that, 'The 16 percent rise in the value of the pound against European currencies will have cost Britain over £850 million of revenue from European visitors in 1997 and 30 000 tourism jobs in this country'. Most general textbooks on tourism spend considerable time describing the basic economic demand functions for tourism, and how movements in such variables as income, exchange rates and travel costs determine the numbers of incoming, outgoing and domestic tourists. The importance of economic factors as a determinant of tourism movement was significantly demonstrated by the slow down in the Asian economies at the end of the 1990s. Thus, while tourism in the East Pacific Region had been growing at 7.5 percent per annum in the period 1988 to 1997, in 1997 it was but 1.1 percent (Office of National Tourism, 1998). Yet, while such experience indicates the potential value of economic forecasting, it also indicates some of the limitations in the sense that few forecasters actually saw the forthcoming downturn in the Asian economies, although the problems relating to the Japanese banking sector had been recognised for some time. Nonetheless, the apparent rate of recovery in PATA regional tourism would appear to support the contention that as the rate of increase in income falls, or as the absolute level of incomes fall, the downward pressure on tourism demand can exhibit income inelasticity, while 'for any given increase in the growth of income, there may be a faster percentage growth in tourism demand' (Ryan, 1991: 13), although such arguments are made more complex by behaviour that substitutes between destinations and duration of stay.

The most commonly used methods of forecasting tourism flows can be divided into two categories: econometric approaches and the use of univariate time series. These are not, of course the sole methods and Frechtling (1996) also describes what he terms 'qualitative methods', which include subjective probability assessments and the use of the Delphi method.

Econometric forecasting

The parameters and problems of econometric forecasting are comparatively well known. The basis of the neo-classical approach is generally well understood and is explained in many introductory books on both economics and tourism. Following Smeral (1994: 497) it may be said that tourism demand can be represented as

$$D_{ij} = f\left(p_{ij} \ldots p_{nj}, Y_j\right)$$

$$\vdots$$

$$D_{nj} = f\left(p_{ij} \ldots p_{nj}, Y_j\right)$$

where the demand components can be subdivided as

$D_{ij} \ldots D_{(n-2)j}$ = demand for non-tourism consumer goods in country j
$D_{(n-1)j}$ = domestic consumption of tourism services by country j
D = tourism consumption abroad by country j

Similarly, price functions can be subdivided as

$p_{ij} \ldots p_{(n-2)j}$ = prices of non-tourism consumer goods in country j
(expressed as units of a homogeneous currency)
$p_{(n-1)}$ = prices of domestic tourism goods and services in country j
(expressed as units of a homogeneous currency)
p_{nj} = prices of foreign tourism goods and services in units of a homogenous currency for country j

with

$$p_{nj} = \sum_{k=1}^{l} g_k p_{(n-1)k}$$

where

$$g_k = D_{njk}/D_{nj}$$

and

$$\sum_{k=1}^{l} g_k = 1, \qquad j \neq k$$

Y_j = disposable income in country j in units of a homogenous international currency

$$\sum_{I=1}^{n} p_{ij} D_{ij} = Y_j$$

n = number of consumer goods, $i = 1 \ldots n$

m = number of countries of origin, $j = 1 \ldots m$

l = number of destinations countries, $k = 1 \ldots l$

Thus, in this simple model, the demand for each consumer good, including tourism, is solely a function of prices and disposable income. It represents a single-stage model in that it looks only at the demand from the origin country j for the destination country k. In practice, the tourist may consider a number of alternative countries and competing flows between countries occur, and thus the model has to be extended to take into account the possible flows of travel to all possible destinations. The extension of the model into this stage is demonstrated by a number of writers, while Crouch (1994) and Athiyaman (1997) have reviewed the various modes such modelling has taken and the variables considered. From a simple macro-economic perspective it is easy to identify additional factors that need to be taken into account. The cost of travel is one immediate factor, especially when considering long haul destinations and their attractiveness relative to destinations nearer to the point of origin. Prices are affected by exchange rate movements as indicated by Quarmby's statement above. Relative differences in inflation between competing countries can also affect perceptions of 'expensiveness', while such differences may offset any gains made by one destination in terms of exchange rate movements.

The technical difficulties of econometric forecasting may be categorised as being at least three-fold – these being concerns about the data, statistical techniques and how the model is defined.

Issues of data quality and volume

The first problem relates to the quality of data, and associated with this, the volume of data required for such exercises. For example, actual airfares paid by passengers on any one flight may vary from nothing for employees using travel passes to maximum full rate for first class passengers. Hence forecasters use various indices. Within Europe the geographical proximity and range of alternative airports and the resultant complex flight patterns and air fare structures mean that considerable volumes of data are required, some of which may be of uncertain quality (Witt, 1978). Another difficulty identified by Witt is the derivation of data about promotional effort by national tourism offices. Witt (1994: 517) argued that:

... promotional expenditure is expected to play a role in determining the level of international tourism demand and thus should feature as an explanatory variable in the demand function.

but noted that it was often difficult to obtain data which specified levels of promotional spending in different countries. There is some evidence to suggest that this may be a factor, for example in the increase of tourism arrivals in South Africa following the dismantling of apartheid. In this case overseas arrivals increased from 2 703 191 in 1992 to 4 944 430 in 1996 (WTO, 1998). This was considerably in excess of the 18 percent growth rate in world tourism (as measured by arrivals) that took place in the same period. No doubt much of this was due to special factors, but equally it is true that the South African tourism authorities took every opportunity to promote themselves, particularly in the markets of Northern Europe and North America. However, in 1998, at the New Zealand National Tourism and Hospitality Research Conference, Witt stated in response to a question, that he felt that the evidence on the whole did not support, at least for New Zealand, any reason for including promotional expenditure of this nature as it had not been shown to be an important determinant when compared with others like prices and income, which usually accounted for most of the variance.

Statistical problems

The second group of difficulties are related to statistical issues, and these too are generally well described in the literature. First, regression techniques assume independence of variables. In practice, particularly perhaps in inflationary periods characterised by high cost-push inflation which is associated with increasing labour costs, the relationship between incomes and prices is obviously one of action and reaction. Equally, if considering travel costs in areas of major land masses, then substitutability between air and surface transport may exist. Accordingly, under these conditions *multicollinearity* – the existence of high degrees of correlation between variables – will exist, and may invalidate the forecasting model. Witt and Witt (1992) and Witt (1994) are among those who provide examples of such issues. A second common issue is that of *heteroscedasticity*: namely, the violation of the assumption that all residuals maintain a constant variance over time. This violation is common if the data cover long periods of time, particularly in the case of tourism, which in many instances has experienced fast rates of growth. Patterns of variance are easily identified by charting the residuals. Frechtling (1996) suggests the use of data transformation to overcome this problem, for example the use of logarithmic scales or the use of squared roots. The former is often related to the use of the Cobb–Douglas production function (Wynn and Holden, 1974). A third problem that may be encountered is that of *autocorrelation*. This is where a variable correlates strongly with its own past values. One reason for its existence may be the continuing effects of specific events. Thus, for example, the Asian crisis might have created a high correlation between tourist expenditure in periods t and $t + 1$ even though income in period $t + 1$ has increased. This might be because a change has taken place between the income/tourist activity relationship. This change could theoretically occur because behaviour is being affected more by recent past experience than expectation about future increases in income, with the result that tourism expenditure remains a constant between periods t and $t+1$, thereby generating the observed correlation between expenditure in both periods. Kane (1968) observes that because regression models will often evidence some degree of stochastic dependence between successive values of the error term it is thus important to test patterns of residuals to determine if the relationship is too large to attribute to chance, or whether an omitted variable is accounting for the observed autocorrelation.

The modelling process

The above theoretical example highlights another problem, and that is how the relationships are modelled. It could be argued that the introduction of lagged variables relating to expenditure variables would overcome the potential problem and that really the problem is one of defining relationships and not autocorrelation. Therefore, the nature of the regression is based upon the modelling process. This requires, first, a selection of the variables thought to determine tourist demand, and then, secondly, a determination of the relationship between them. As just noted, one common question is whether a lagged relationship might apply where demand in period t is partially dependent upon the existence of a variable in the period $t-1$. It might also be thought that the relationships are not linear ($Y=a+bT$), but, say, quadratic ($Y=a+bT+cT^2$).

Time series

A second common method of forecasting is the use of time series. This, essentially, is the extrapolation of past trends into the future, and thus to a large degree their validity rests upon the assumption that the underlying relationships between determining variables remain constant over the period being tested. 'Raw' time series data may, however, consist of four constituent parts: trend, cycle, seasonal and irregular component parts. In tourism applications seasonality of data is, of course, common, and economists and statisticians have developed widely known techniques of smoothing to cope with these problems. The simplest of these is the single moving average (SMA), while other techniques include single exponential smoothing, double exponential smoothing, autoregression, Box–Jenkins, ARMA (autoregression/moving average combined) and ARIMA (autoregression/integrated/moving average). One of the comments often made about these approaches is that they are essentially atheoretical in that they extrapolate from a known set of data, like visitor numbers, without examining the underlying determinants of those numbers. However, on the other hand, they work from easily accessible data while, as described above, that is not always the case for regression-based methods.

Do these methods work?

One of the issues that has exercised the minds of econometricians is the accuracy of the resultant forecasts. One of the main researchers who has led attempts to examine this issue, and to devise means of improving forecasts has been Stephen Witt. The papers reproduced here include one from 1989 when Witt began to compare the accuracy of various forms of forecasting, using as a basic comparison, two simple modes of forecasting. Naive method one was simply to say that tourism flows in period $t + 1$ would be the same as in period t, while the second would state that flows in period $t + 1$ would simply be those of period t plus the average rate of growth prevailing at period t. He has shown that in some circumstances, these naive forecast methods produced lower error rates than more sophisticated methods. However, to conclude that forecasting is simply a statistical process of little value is to miss one of the points of forecasting. If forecasting has, as its strategic aim, the development of desired outcomes and the avoidance of undesirable ones, then acting on the results of the forecast may change the relationship of the variables upon which the forecast was based. For example, if a downturn in tourist arrivals is expected, and a government then increases the promotional budget and provides tax incentives to companies, a subsequent increase in tourism arrivals is not the proof of poor forecasting.

Nonetheless, statisticians continue to seek new ways of improving forecasts. One comparatively recent introduction is the use of *cointegration analysis* in tourism forecasting. This arises in part from the observation of the relationship of variables, for it has been found that, although many economic time series may trend up or down together in a non-stationary way, *groups* of variables may drift together. Underlying this is the assumption that, theoretically, there may be good reasons for believing that such groups may adhere over time in a linear fashion. The article by Seddighi and Shearing (1997) in *Tourism Management* illustrates the use of this method.

A second recent innovation in tourism forecasting is the use of *neural network modelling*. Unlike techniques such as nonlinear regression, neural networks do not require the *a priori* assumption of the functional form of the model (linear, first-order polynomial and logarithmic). And, unlike expert systems and fuzzy logic, neither do they require an elicitation of expert knowledge, which is particularly useful when a large number of variables are being considered (Petri et al., 1998). Neural networks, which may be described as a subset of the science of artificial intelligence, have been used in a range of applications, including forecasting tourist flows and behaviours (Pattie and Snyder, 1996; Law and Au, 1999).

Caudill and Butler (1990: 7–8) and Ryan (2000) list the characteristics of neural networks thus:

- Simple processing elements (neurodes) communicate with each other through a rich set of inter-connections.
- Memories are represented by variable patterns of weighted neurodes in changing patterns of communication.
- Neural networks are not programmed – they learn.
- Operations are the functions of structures of connections, transfer functions of neurodes and learning laws.
- Neural networks act as an associative memory; they can retrieve information from partially incorrect, noisy or incomplete cues.
- A neural network can generalise.

- A neural network is fault tolerant; it can continue as neurodes and connections become defective. It exhibits 'graceful degradation'.
- A neural network acts as a processor for time-dependent spatial patterns.
- A neural network can be self-organising.

This technique represents potentially an exciting forecasting approach for the new millennium. The articles reproduced here are

Faulkner, B. and Valerio, P. (1995). An integrative approach to tourism demand forecasting, *Tourism Management*, February, 16(1): 29–38.

Witt, C.A. and Witt, S.F. (1989). Measures of forecasting accuracy – turning point error *v* size of error, *Tourism Management*, September, 10(3): 255–60.

Witt, S.F. (1992). Tourism forecasting. How well do private and public sector organisations perform? *Tourism Management*, March, 13(1): 79–84.

The first of these articles has been included because it reinforces the notion that forecasting is not an exercise complete in itself, but is undertaken for purposes of strategic management. In addition, it was one of the first articles published in which Faulkner began to discuss his belief that one of the better ways of understanding changes within tourism was to treat it as a system subject to non-linear, chaotic and spontaneous change – that is, it could be analysed through the use of chaos theory. He has subsequently published more work on this subject in *Tourism Management* (Russell and Faulkner, 1999), albeit in the period outside of that which is reviewed in this book. Should a collection of articles from the third decade of *Tourism Management* be collected, it will be of interest to see to what extent chaos theory has been adopted by fellow researchers.

For tourism scholars with an interest in economics, the work of Stephen Witt needs little introduction. In the 1989 article Witt and Witt revisited past forecasts for the period 1965–1983 and assessed to what degree forecasts had been accurate and reached two main conclusions – first, that econometric forecasts are better than naive approaches, and secondly, that measures of accuracy need themselves to be closely examined before any firm conclusion can be reached about which is the better method of forecasting. In the final article Witt examines forecasting for flows of visitors to New Zealand, and argues that one way of improving forecasts is to not only disseminate results but incorporate feedback into those results. The article has been selected for this insight and not so much for the data contained. Indeed, it might be argued that the apparent strength of the naive method for New Zealand at the time of the study was simply due to there being more consistent flows of tourists in the 1980s, and as New Zealand has become more closely incorporated into Asian-Pacific trade patterns, these flow patterns have become more complex.

In short, the articles cover some of the important issues relating to forecasting – the techniques, their purposes, their adequacies and their development.

References

Athiyaman, A. (1997). Knowledge development in tourism: tourism demand research, *Tourism Management*, 18(4): 221–28.

Caudill, M. and Butler, C. (1990). *Naturally Intelligent Systems*. Boston, Mass: Massachusetts Institute of Technology.

Crouch, G. (1994). The study of international tourism demand: a survey of practice, *Journal of Travel Research*, 32: 41–5.

Faulkner, B. and Valerio, P. (1995). An integrative approach to tourism demand forecasting, *Tourism Management*, February, 16(1): 29–38.

Frechtling, D. (1996). *Practical Tourism Forecasting*. Oxford: Butterworth-Heinemann.

Kane, E.J. (1968). *Economic Statistics and Econometrics – An Introduction to Quantitative Economics*. New York: Harper and Row.

Law, R and Au, N. (1999). A neural network model to forecast Japanese demand for travel to Hong Kong, *Tourism Management*, 21(1): 89–98.

Office of National Tourism. (1998). *Tourism Industry Trends*. October. Canberra: Ministry of Industry, Science, Tourism.

Pattie, D.C. and Snyder, J. (1996). Using a neural network to forecast visitor behaviour, *Annals of Tourism Research*, 23(1): 151–64.

Petri, K.L., Billo, R.E. and Bidanda, B. (1998). A neural network process model for abrasive flow machining operations, *Journal of Manufacturing Systems*, 17(1): 52–64.

Quarmby, D. (1998). *Inbound Tourism Hit by Strong Pound*. British Tourist Authority published annual report – press release. Hammersmith: British Tourist Authority, 17 September 1998.

Ryan, C. (1991). *Recreational Tourism – A Social Science Perspective*. London: Routledge.

Ryan, C. and Simmons, D. (1999). Towards a tourism research strategy for New Zealand, *Tourism Management*, 20(3): 305–12.

Ryan, C. (2000). Tourist behaviour research – subjectivity and neural networks, in E. Laws, B. Faulkner and G. Moscardo (eds), *Tourism in the Twenty-First Century: Reflections on Experience*. London: Academic Press.

Russell, R. and Faulkner, B. (1999). Movers and shakers: chaos makers in tourism development, *Tourism Management*, 20(4): 411–23.

Seddighi, H.R. and Shearing, D.F. (1997). The demand for tourism in North East England with special reference to Northumbria: an empirical analysis, *Tourism Management*, 18(8): 499–512.

Smeral, E. (1994). Economic models, in S.F. Witt and L. Moutinho (eds), *Tourism Marketing and Management Handbook*, 2nd edn. Hemel Hempstead: Prentice Hall. pp. 497–503.

Smith, S.L.J. (1999). Toward a national tourism research agenda for Canada, *Tourism Management*, 20(3): 297–304.

Witt, S.F. *The Demand for Foreign Holidays*, unpublished Ph.D thesis, Bradford University 1978.

Witt, S.F. (1992). Tourism forecasting. How well do private and public sector organisations perform? *Tourism Management*, March, 13(1): 79–84.

Witt, S.F. (1994). Econometric demand forecasting, in S.F. Witt and L. Moutinho (eds), *Tourism Marketing and Management Handbook*, 2nd edn. Hemel Hempstead, Prentice Hall. pp. 516–20.

Witt, C.A. and Witt, S.F. (1989). Measures of forecasting accuracy – turning point error *v* size of error, *Tourism Management*, 10(3): 255–60.

Witt, S.F. and Witt, C.A. (1992). *Modeling and Forecasting Demand in Tourism*. London: Academic Press.

WTO (1998). *Yearbook of Statistics*, vol 2, 50th edn. Madrid: World Tourism Organisation.

Wynn, R.F. and Holden, K. (1974). *An Introduction to Applied Econometric Analysis*. London: Macmillan.

3

An integrative approach to tourism demand forecasting

Bill Faulkner

Griffith University (Gold Coast), PMB 50, Gold Coast Mail Centre, QLD 4217, Australia

Peter Valerio

Australian Tourist Commission, GPO Box 2721, Sydney, NSW 2001, Australia

Progress has been made in the development of tourism forecasting techniques in Australia over the last few years to the extent that we have moved beyond a reliance on guesswork and gut feelings to more rigorous approaches involving, for instance, the use of econometric models. Yet, by viewing forecasting as simply an attempt to anticipate the future, we have tended to lose sight of the fact that the forecasting process itself is an integral part of strategic management. An appreciation of this aspect of forecasting, and the limitations of the methodologies currently being applied, highlights the need for a reorientation towards an integrative approach.

However, in addition to employing a combination of existing approaches, we need to explore also innovations that may help us cope with what appears to be an increasingly volatile and unpredictable environment. This point is pursued below in three stages. First, the background to the problem is outlined by referring briefly to the role of forecasting and some of the observations that have been made about the limitations of existing approaches. Second, some insights are drawn from the emerging field of chaos theory to provide a different perspective on forecasting, which is in turn used as a basis for elaborating on elements of the integrative approach being advocated. Finally, a methodology being developed by the Australian Tourist Commission (ATC) is described to illustrate how an integrative approach might be applied. The recency of this technique's introduction in the ATC context precludes any meaningful comparison between forecast and actual trends at this stage. However, its potential has been demonstrated by immediate beneficial effects on the involvement of management and stakeholders in the organization's goal-setting process.

On the need for an integrative approach

In any context, forecasting is an essential step in the minimization of disparities between the demand for, and supply of, services and facilities. Given the lead times usually involved in the development of the infrastructure required to service markets, future demand must often be anticipated up to several years in advance if we are to avoid missed opportunities through insufficient and inappropriate capacity on the one hand, or wasteful and counter-productive under-utilized capacity on the other. This applies equally to situations where elaborate physical structures have to be put in place or where skills have to be developed in the workforce through training programmes.

As considerable lead times are involved in both these aspects of tourism product development, the above observation regarding the central role of forecasting in the management process is certainly no less applicable to this industry. Indeed, there are two distinctive (but not necessarily unique) features of tourism which accentuate this point. First, the necessity of matching supply and demand is heightened by the perishability of the tourism product.[1,2] Unused capacity at a particular point in time cannot be stored or stockpiled for later use and, as a consequence, represents a loss of revenue which cannot be recovered. Second, the inherent volatility of tourism demand, stemming from its predominantly discretionary nature, underscores both the need for, and difficulty of, forecasting in this field. If, as Poon suggests, we are witnessing a transformation to a predominance of so-called 'new tourists' whose behaviour is increasingly unpredictable, then this volatility is likely to become even more pronounced in the future.[3]

Forecasting has therefore become an important element of tourism management in both the private and public sectors. However, its potential contribution to this process has not always been realized because of the general failure to adopt an integrative approach. In this context, the term 'integrative' has a double meaning. First, it refers to the application of a combination of methodologies to a particular forecasting problem. Second, it is concerned with the relationship between these methodologies and the decision-making process itself.

Integration by the combination of methodologies

Descriptions of the various techniques employed in the forecasting of tourism demand have been documented in some detail by several authors.[4-9] The main general conclusion one can draw from these contributions is that each approach has specific strengths and weaknesses and, accordingly, it would be prudent to apply a combination of such approaches to a given situation. Specifically, approaches that complement each other in terms of their respective strengths and weaknesses might be considered.

However, there are several specific observations that can be drawn from this literature, which have a particular bearing on the following discussion:

- Over the past 30 years there has been a considerable emphasis on econometric approaches concentrating on income and price factors as determinants of demand.[10]
- The emphasis placed on modelling is a matter of concern if, as some authors have noted,[5,6] data limitations result in an over-reliance on a limited range of variables.
- As Witt and Witt observe, complex econometric modelling approaches do not necessarily produce more accurate forecasts than simpler time-series approaches and, as a consequence, the benefits derived from such approaches may not be commensurate with the additional time and cost involved.[11]

- These approaches nevertheless provide a systematic basis for understanding relationships among variables and exploring the effects of alternative scenarios for the future.[12]
- Approaches such as the Delphi technique offer the dual advantage of enabling a broader range of quantifiable and non-quantifiable variables to be taken into account, while at the same time providing a framework for consultation. More specifically, these techniques provide a vehicle for integrating a range of approaches.

Integration with the decision-making process

As emphasized at the outset of this paper, the ultimate purpose of tourism demand forecasting is to assist in management decision-making. Yet, forecasting has, to a large extent, become an end in itself, resulting in its alienation from the planning process and, in association with this, naïve perceptions of the nature and role of forecasting prevail among users.

This point is highlighted in a more general commentary on forecasting by Schaffer:[13]

Experts need their own private world where ignorant outsiders cannot penetrate. The very obscurity of the sums in which cost benefit analysts or astrologers engage helps give them impressive authority. But the expert predictors also need outsiders' trust: They need to show that the terms they use are, in some way, connected to what matters to the customers. (p. 54)

Forecasting often becomes an end in itself, rather than an integral part of the strategic management process, because of the complexity of the methodologies used and the consequent need for specialist analysts to be involved. The analysts, however, have become isolated and detached, and forecasting has become a black box as far as most users are concerned. With the decision-makers becoming mesmerized by the 'science' of forecasting, much of the debate about the outcome has focused on the bottom-line numbers, rather than the methodologies and assumptions on which they are based.

Under these circumstances, the role of the forecasting process in strategic planning has become very limited. The technicians need to make forecasting a transparent and iterative process through the installation of consultative mechanisms that give users an opportunity to challenge the assumptions made and explore the implications of their own scenarios.

As a consequence of the alienation process described above, there is a general naïvety in attitudes towards forecasting which is reflected in, for instance, the frequent acceptance of forecasts at face value without questioning underlying assumptions. Another symptom of naïvety is the tendency to regard those forecasts that turn out to be accurate as necessarily superior.[4,14]

There are several reasons that can be put forward to suggest that this may not necessarily be the case:

- The accurate forecast might be right for the wrong reasons. While this situation may not have negative planning implications in the short term, it will in the longer term if it results in too much faith being placed in an ostensibly 'proven' but potentially flawed approach.

- Under certain circumstances a good forecast may be one which does not eventuate. That is, if a forecast foreshadows the prospect of negative developments, and thereby triggers remedial action to prevent these from occurring, it will have served its purposes without being accurate in the long run. It is easy in retrospect, for instance, to condemn the Club of Rome's[15] predictions about the resource implications of global population growth as being unrealistically alarmist. However, these predictions were instrumental in the initiation of programmes which alleviated some of the problems in advance.
- There are occasions when forecasts have such an influence on planning targets that they become self-fulfilling prophecies. This has a positive effect if it results in the infrastructure required to take up growth opportunities being put in place. On the other hand, unduly conservative forecasts can also become self-fulfilling prophecies if they discourage the development of capacity and, as a consequence, restrict growth in demand. The fear of the latter has resulted in the promotion of unrealistically high growth scenarios by some tourism industry commentators in the Australian context.

Effective integration of tourism demand forecasting with management decision-making implies the establishment of a meaningful dialogue between technicians and users. Such a dialogue would arrest the alienation process referred to above and lead to a more informed view of the nature and role of forecasting across the board. Furthermore, through the use of Delphi and similar techniques, there will be more scope for bringing a range of alternative approaches to bear on the problem and the overreliance on modelling techniques will be reduced. There are, however, more fundamental reasons for diversifying the range of approaches we rely on. These are explored in the following section.

Chaos and uncertainty

The development of methodologies for understanding the underlying causal relation-ships affecting changes in tourism demand is fundamental to the development of better forecasting systems. While the modelling approaches referred to in the previous section have provided valuable frameworks for assembling available data, exploring relation-ships between variables and (on the basis of this) considering the implications of possible future developments, insights from the physical sciences in particular highlight limitations in the ability of such approaches to further our understanding of causal relationships. On the one hand, such limitations might be construed as signalling the need for a 'paradigm shift' in accord with Thomas Kuhn's interpretation of scientific revolutions.[16] However, on the other hand, the utility of existing appro-aches and the lack of fully operational alternatives suggests that it would be more appropriate to supplement, rather than actually displace, existing methodologies.

In the physical sciences, the probing of sub-atomic phenomena at one extreme and of the outer reaches of the cosmos at the other has highlighted the limitations of the mechanistic Newtonian–Cartesian paradigm as a basis for understanding the mysteries of the universe. It is being increasingly recognized that our physical environment does not operate like a gigantic clockwork machine, with its various parts fitting neatly together and acting in unison in a manner which can be both measured and predicted with mathematical precision. A new wave of thought has grown out of Einstein's theory of relativity, quantum mechanics, Heisenberg's uncertainty principle and, more recently, chaos theory to challenge the mechanistic worldview.[17] The linear, machine vocabulary of classical physics is thus being displaced by concepts which depict a confusing world of non-linearity, spontaneity and surprise juxtaposed with attributes normally associated with living organisms, such as adaptation, coherence and organization.[18]

In their analysis of the implications of these developments, Davies and Gribbin offer the following interpretation:[18]

Physicist Joseph Ford has described the materialistic, mechanistic paradigm as one of the 'Founding myths' of classical science. Myths of course are not literal expressions of truth. Are we to suppose, then, that the immense progress made in science during the past three hundred years is rooted in a complete misconception about the nature of nature? No, this would be to misunderstand the role of scientific paradigms. A particular paradigm is neither right nor wrong, but merely reflects a perspective, an aspect of reality that may prove more or less fruitful depending on circumstance – just as a myth, although not literally true, may contain allegorical insights that prove more or less fruitful depending on circumstances. In the event, the mechanistic paradigm proved so successful that there has been an almost universal tendency to identify it with reality, to see it not as a facet of truth but as the whole truth. Now, increasing numbers of scientists are coming to recognise the limitations of the materialistic view of nature, and to appreciate that there is more to the world than cogs in a gigantic machine. (p. 3)

If the reservations are being expressed about the ability of the mechanistic framework to explain the behaviour of inanimate objects, then its applicability to the explanation of human behaviour, as reflected in tourism demand, must also be questioned.

The neo-classical economic theory, on which the modelling approach referred to in the previous section is largely based, is analogous to Newtonian physics in several respects. First, it is based on the application of the 'materialistic, mechanistic' paradigm to socio-economic phenomena. Second, it has so dominated the field of tourism demand analysis and forecasting that, despite its limited success in explaining this aspect of human behaviour, there has also been a tendency to 'see it not as a facet of truth but as the whole truth'. Finally, in a broader context, there is a growing body of opinion which sees conventional economic theory as being demonstrably incapable of understanding modern economic events and, as a consequence, increasingly irrelevant as a framework for guiding policy development towards the solution of current economic problems. Indeed, some commentators have suggested that it is the moribund status of economic theory which is responsible for modern economic problems and that this is symptomatic of the need for a paradigm shift.[19]

One of the basic assumptions of the prevailing methodologies, and the reason they are generally only suitable for relatively short-term forecasts, is that relationships between variables remain constant. The possibility, indeed likelihood, of these relationships changing over time tends to be over-looked. Meanwhile, social commentators such as Toffler[20] have emphasized the accelerating pace of change in modern society and the associated destabilization of social relations, which have resulted in increasing levels of uncertainty and greater pressure on adaptive capabilities at both the institutional and individual level. This process is undoubtedly reflected in factors which have a bearing on tourism demand and will have a compounding effect on forecasting efforts in this field.

The limitations of the mechanistic orientation of orthodox economics and the simpler mathematical time-series approach to forecasting stand out in the context of this dynamic setting. Both these approaches are analogous to Newtonian physics in that they assume constancy and linearity (or quasi-linearity) in relationships and, implicitly, a tendency towards an equilibrium state owing to the dominance of negative feedback mechanisms. Drawing on insights from the new wave in physics, Waldrop argues that socio-economic systems are: open rather than closed; organic as opposed to mechanistic; dynamic rather than static; and driven by positive feedback rather than negative feedback.[19] It is ironic that, whereas the imitation of the physical sciences by the social sciences has resulted in mechanistic qualities being attributed to socio-economic systems, we could perhaps be witnessing over the next few years a situation where lessons from the physical sciences may result in the recognition of lifelike characteristics in such systems.

The notion of socio-economic systems driven by positive feedback mechanisms points to the possible relevance of chaos theory to the forecasting process. Positive feedback refers to the progressive accentuation of small changes or deviations and contrasts with negative feedback, where the effects of such shifts are ameliorated with the system being restored to equilibrium. Chaos theory focuses on the non-linearity of phenomena and the tendency for initially small changes eventually to produce large cumulative effects which precipitate fundamental changes in the system.

Obvious examples of non-linearity in tourism include the slow-down in the growth of a maturing market as demand approaches saturation,[21] and the passage of a destination through the product life cycle as described by Butler.[22] The opposite process, whereby an initial small perturbation cascades upwards through a system to produce eventually an event or shift of considerable magnitude, has been referred to by chaos theorists as the 'butterfly effect'.[23] Examples of the butterfly effect in tourism would include instances where an exponential growth in visitor numbers arises from the compounding effect of a single event, such as the extension of jet airline services to a previously isolated destination or the development of an innovative holiday package which taps a particularly significant emerging market.

It is not yet clear how a realignment in the theoretical foundations of our analysis might be translated into new forecasting methodologies. If we take Davies and Gribbin's reference to different paradigms reflecting different facets of the truth literally, then we should accept that conventional econometric techniques may have a continuing role to the extent that they may be useful in broadly defining constraints on tourism demand. It is obvious, however, that this approach needs to be used in conjunction with other methodologies which are less limited in terms of assumptions made about the underlying dynamics of change. Accordingly, an approach which permits the integration of conventional methodologies with others that incorporate the new perspective described in this section may lead to more innovative and effective forecasting in the future.

The certainty of the unexpected

While, at this stage, it may not be clear where chaos theory might lead us, this perspective at least helps to highlight our general naïvety regarding the capabilities of existing methodology to actually predict the future. Chaos theory and numerous instances of recent events have demonstrated that, if anything, the only certainty about the future is that the unexpected will happen. Who in 1974 predicted the 1975 oil crisis? Yet this single event precipitated a global recession and an associated slump in world travel. Nobody could predict the Chernobyl and Lockerbie disasters, which impacted dramatically on travel patterns owing to heightened concerns over the safety of travel in Europe. Did anyone predict the dismemberment of the Soviet bloc more than a few months or even weeks in advance? Closer to home in Australia, no one predicted the 1989 domestic pilots' dispute and its devastating impact on tourism more than a few days before it actually happened.

If forecasting tourism demand is so difficult, and if it is virtually impossible to predict the future with any certainty in any case, why bother?

There are two rejoinders to the question. First, whatever the limitations of our forecasting capabilities, management outcomes based on partially correct visions of the future will be superior to those based on no vision at all. Second, and more importantly, if it is done properly, forecasting involves a structured analysis of recent and possible future developments. As noted above, such analyses should be an integral part of the management routine of all enterprises and organizations. Yet this has not generally been the case among decision-makers in both industry and government, where there has been a tendency to accept or reject forecasts produced by the 'experts' at face value without any serious attempt being made to become involved in the forecasting process itself. As argued previously, a dialogue between the technicians who produce the forecasts and the decision makers who use them is essential if underlying assumptions are to be questioned and debated, and if insights generated by the analysis of trends are to be utilized in the management process.

A step towards the development of a more open consultative approach to tourism forecasting has been taken in Australia with the establishment of the Federal Government's Tourism Forecasting Council. The Council will provide a consultative framework which will have the potential not only to facilitate an industry input to the forecasting process, but also it will enable the development of a broader understanding of the assumptions on which the forecasts are based and the insights produced by associated analyses. A similar approach needs to be developed at the enterprise level, with forecasting exercises becoming an integral part of the ongoing management process.

No matter how far we go in this direction, we still cannot alter the fact that the future is intrinsically unpredictable and, accordingly, we will inevitably be surprised by events no matter how sophisticated our forecasting technology becomes. An important adjunct to the integration of the forecasting and management processes should therefore be the development of contingency planning capabilities. This involves the development of a relatively free-wheeling approach to the generation of alternative scenarios, the assignment of notional probabilities to these scenarios and the planning of specific strategies for coping with each one. The value of this approach is that, by considering potential developments and responses in advance, the organization will not be forced to make quick, ill-considered decisions when the unexpected occurs.

Given the unavoidable uncertainties of the future, the tourism management process should involve not only a sceptical consideration of various forecasts, but also an examination of alternative extreme scenarios. For example:

- What if the OPEC countries suddenly doubled the price of oil?
- What if there is a global financial crisis of the same magnitude as the 1930s Wall Street crash?
- What if domestic air services are again disrupted by another pilots' dispute?
- What if the ozone layer precipitously disintegrates, resulting in severe constraints on outdoor activities?
- What if a major military conflict erupts in Asia or Europe?

Some of these scenarios may appear to be outlandish. But are they any more improbable than some of the actual events referred to earlier? To become overly concerned by such possibilities is a recipe for personal and corporate neuroses. In our personal lives we should not fuel anxieties by worrying about future developments that may never eventuate. However, it is sensible for organizations periodically to assess the potential impacts of extreme events, and consider alternative coping strategies so that these can be mobilized quickly in response to events if and when they occur.

The Australian Tourist Commission approach

The Australian Tourist Commission (ATC) promotes Australia internationally as a tourist destination. As part of its ongoing management process, the Commission sets targets which are expressed in terms of the expected number of visitors from respective overseas markets in future years. These targets provide a basis for planning the organization's marketing strategies and allocating resources within its marketing programme. They also serve as benchmarks for evaluating the ATC's overall performance. The targets are published to provide the industry with an indication of the market potential of various international markets and, in this respect, they are instrumental in the development of a coordinated approach to the international marketing of the Australian tourism product.

Targets are distinct from forecasts in that, in effect, they define a set of aspirations for the ATC and the Australian tourism industry to aim at, and in this sense provide a focus for action. On the other hand, forecasts provide an assessment of what is likely to happen, given certain assumptions about the conditions affecting demand. However, the ATC's process of setting targets is intrinsically a forecasting exercise to the extent that the determination of targets must ultimately take into account background conditions affecting demand and an assessment of what is likely to happen in the absence of the ATC's intervention. While targets must therefore inevitably exceed forecasts, they need to be considered in the context of existing forecasts in order to ensure that they remain in touch with reality.

The approach to target setting which has evolved within the ATC reflects an appreciation of several observations that can be drawn from previous discussion.

First, as all techniques currently employed for tourism forecasting have limitations, a combination of these techniques needs to be applied so that their respective strengths and weaknesses complement each other. In particular, it has been noted that, by limiting analyses to the impact of quantifiable economic factors, conventional methodologies overlook the numerous other factors involved in a potential tourist's decision-making process. Second, a systematic approach to forecasting should be an integral part of the planning process, as this provides the basis for assessing emerging opportunities and threats. Third, as a consequence of the previous point, forecasting (and target setting) should be a consultative process and the approaches adopted should be 'transparent' from the point of view of all parties involved. Furthermore, participants should be encouraged not to accept forecasts produced by the technicians at face value. The assumptions on which forecasts are based should be scrutinized and challenged, while the implications of methodological limitations should be understood and taken into account. While this approach demands that managers and decision-makers become more sophisticated, it also demands that the technicians involved become more effective in communicating with, and educating, users.

Key features of the ATC's forecasting and target-setting methodology applied in the recent past include:

- structured and unstructured consultation with the tourism industry and ATC staff, both in Australia and overseas;
- consideration of a wide range of demand factors, in addition to quantifiable economic variables;
- an assessment of the competitive environment through the conduct of market share analysis; and
- travel propensity and outbound trend analysis.

The integration of these components into the overall approach is depicted in Figure 1.

The Australian Bureau of Tourism Research's (BTR) forecasts, which are based on econometric models, provide a benchmark for the analysis of individual markets. This is supplemented by an analysis of such factors as GDP growth projections, existing and projected future travel propensities, aviation market trends and political/trade considerations such as agreements on the establishment of closer economic relations.

A key feature of the ATC approach is market share analysis. Market share analysis is rarely incorporated in tourism demand estimation, possibly because of the difficulties associated with the collation of meaningful outbound data. For example, certain countries may only record outbound travel *en masse*, capturing short and long haul together. In a market such as the UK, this could mean including all trips to Continental Europe. Some countries do not produce any outbound data at all, in which case it is necessary to capture arrivals from that country as reported at several destinations and combine these figures.

Despite these limitations, ATC considers that market share estimates provide useful input to the target-setting process, particularly as they have not previously been used in demand estimation work in Australia and are rarely used (if at all) by other countries. Using market share trend analysis gives us a snap-shot of how Australia is performing in relation to its competitors. Relying on trends in gross visitor arrivals obscures the gains to be made from exploiting competitive advantage in a market. By looking at

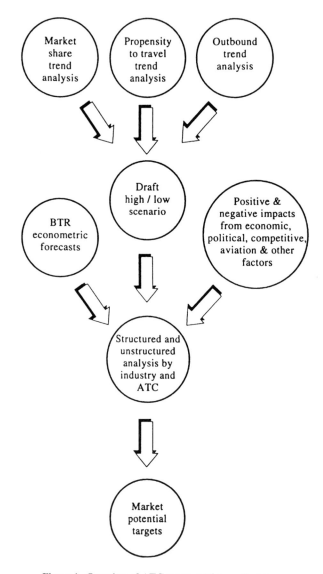

Figure 1. Overview of ATC target-setting methodology.

market share trends, the overall prospect for the origin market can be related to Australia's likely performance. In some cases, where market share has been increasing, this may override a downfall in general travel prospects from a market. In this scenario, relying on income projections for a market will indicate a decline in travel whereas the opposite may occur.

Predictably, some measures of market share are better than others but using the same method to measure market share over time is relevant from a trend analysis perspective. For example, only total outbound figures are available for Malaysia with no distinction made between short-haul travel to neighbouring countries and more relevant long-haul travel. Despite this limitation, a useful measure of Australia's relative performance in this market can be derived.

Market share trends are calculated over a period of approximately 10 years. This analysis is then used, in combination with outbound projections, to produce two scenarios: a 'trend' scenario and a 'static' scenario. The trend scenario assumes that the market share trend which exists will apply in the future, whereas the 'static' scenario assumes that market share remains constant.

In combination with outbound projections, these scenarios form 'working' or draft targets. The outbound projections used are themselves given considerable considera-tion. A number of outbound estimates are reviewed including actual forecasts, simple outbound trend analysis and travel propensity trend analysis in conjunction with population projections. The final outbound figure used is opened to debate.

The consultative phase is largely based on the workshop format with participants drawn from airlines, hotels, attractions, inbound operators and the Bureau of Tourism Research. Representatives of the latter body provide technical input on forecasts based on econometric models. Some emphasis is placed on the presentation of data and analytical material in a format which can readily be interpreted by participants from a range of backgrounds and critical comment is invited on the proposed targets for each country. An example of the style of presentation is provided in Figure 2. In addition to the data provided by ATC, participants involved in the review process were requested to combine these data with their knowledge of each market when commenting on individual country targets. A more structured written feedback form is also provided to enable participants to record their assessment of the targets after further con-sideration. An extract from this pro forma is shown as Figure 3. Meanwhile, ATC overseas offices organize industry involvement in the target revision process within individual origin countries. Briefings on the output of ATC research (segmentation studies, satisfaction surveys, internal marketing evaluation research such as tracking studies and barriers to travel studies) are given as an integral part of this process.

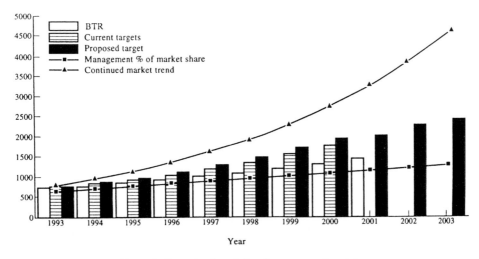

Figure 2. **Example of workshop data presentation style.**

NEW ZEALAND	1993	1994	1995	1996	1997
Draft target (000)	475	505	533	560	580
% Growth	6%	6%	6%	5%	4%
Growth assessment (H/L/OK)					
Suggested growth (optional)					

Comments

Figure 3. Example of industry feedback pro forma (actual form extended to year 2003).

When viewed in the light of the analysis contained in earlier sections of this paper, the approach to forecasting and target setting being developed by the ATC represents a significant step forward. In particular, the previous dependence upon econometric modelling has been reduced, with this approach being supplemented by others that take into account factors which are less amenable to quantitative analysis. In addition, more emphasis is being placed on a consultative approach which not only permits a more diverse range of factors to be taken into account, but also facilitates the integration of forecasting with the management decision process.

However, at this stage, the ATC's approach does not adequately take into account the implications of the chaos theory perspective. This requires the inclusion of a stage in the target-setting process where extreme scenarios are canvassed so that the need to consider contingency plans for coping with these potential eventualities can be signalled to the industry. It also requires background analysis to be carried out in an effort to identify positive feedback-driven phenomena that may precipitate dramatic shifts in the dynamics of tourism demand in the near or distant future.

Conclusion

Forecasting is a fundamental element of strategic planning. Without a systematic and rigorous assessment of emerging market trends, the tourism industry at individual destinations will have difficulty positioning itself in order to take advantage of opportunities as they arise, or to counteract potentially threatening developments. Where forecasting has been embraced as a tool for planning, however, there has been a tendency to rely on a limited range of methodologies, while the technical sophistication of popular approaches has hindered the establishment of an effective dialogue between specialist analysts and decision makers.

Reliance on a limited range of approaches denies planners access to the varied perspectives other approaches can bring to bear on the problem. More importantly, it means that the deficiencies of one approach are not compensated by the strengths of another. The emphasis placed on econometric methods, in particular, could contribute to significant blind spots in our vision of the future because of the mechanistic orientation of this approach. Specifically, the incidence of non-linear phenomena highlighted by chaos theory (such as the butterfly effect and saturation cycles) may have more significant tourism marketing implications than the linear relationships highlighted by conventional methodologies based on economic theory. Whatever approach is adopted, however, we have no option but to accept the fact that we cannot predict the future with any degree of certainty. The inclusion of a contingency planning phase within the planning cycle is therefore a useful adjunct to the planning process.

The establishment of a dialogue between specialist forecasters and decision-makers is essential for the effective integration of forecasting and the planning process. Forecasters therefore need to develop more user-friendly approaches to presenting information to, and educating, users. They also need to devise a format of presentation which facilitates more meaningful two-way discussion not only to ensure that the underlying assumptions and logic of their forecasts are scrutinized, questioned and debated, but also to make the forecasting process open to alternative perspectives.

The system being developed by the ATC has been presented as an example of the move towards a more open, consultative approach to forecasting which epitomizes the integrative approach advocated in this paper. Even in this instance, however, there is scope for further development to take into account limitations of the forecasting methodologies described above.

References

1. Greenley, G E and Matcham, A S 'Problems in marketing services: the case of incoming tourism' *European Journal of Marketing* 1971 **17** (6) 57–64
2. Middleton, V T C *Marketing in Travel and Tourism* 1st edn, Heinemann, Oxford (1990)
3. Poon, A *Tourism Technology and Competitive Strategies* CAB International, Wallingford (1993) 115
4. Archer, B 'Demand forecasting and estimation', in Brent Ritche, J R and Goeldner, C R (eds) *Travel Tourism and Hospitality Research: A Handbook for Managers and Researchers* Wiley, New York (1987) 77–85
5. Armstrong, J S *Long Range Forecasting*, 2nd edn, Wiley, New York (1985)
6. Calantone, R J, Benedito, A and Bojanic, D 'A comprehensive review of tourism forecasting literature' *J Travel Research* 1987 (Fall) 28–39
7. Bar On, R V 'Forecasting tourism and travel series' in Van Doorn, J W M (ed) *Problems of Tourism* **3** (1984) 24–39
8. Uysal, M and Crompton, J L 'An overview of approaches used to forecast tourism demand' *Journal of Travel Research* 1985 (Spring) 7–15
9. Van Doorn, J W M 'Tourism forecasting techniques: a brief overview' in Van Doorn, J W M (ed) *Problems of Tourism* **3** (1984) 7–15
10. Crouch, G I and Shaw, R H 'Determinants of international tourist flows: findings from 30 years of empirical research' *Monash University Graduate School of Management, Management Papers* No 29 (1990)
11. Witt, S F and Witt, C A *Modelling and Forecasting Demand in Tourism* Academic Press, London (1992)
12. Makridakis, S 'The art and science of forecasting: an assessment of future directions' *International Journal of Forecasting* **2** (1986) 15–39
13. Schaffer, S 'Comets and the world's end', in Howe, L and Wain, A *Predicting the Future* Cambridge University Press, Cambridge, 52–76
14. Carbone, R and Armstrong, J S Note. Evaluation of extrapolative forecasting methods: results of a survey of academicians and practitioners *J Forecasting* **1** (1982) 215–217
15. Meadows, D H, Meadows, D L, Randers, J and Behrens, W W III *The Limits of Growth* Universe Books, New York (1972)
16. Kuhn, T S *The Structure of Scientific Revolutions* 2nd edn, University of Chicago Press, Chicago (1962)
17. Capra, F *The Turning Point: Science, Society and the Rising Culture* Flamingo, London (1982)

18. Davies, P and Gribbin, J *The Matter Myth: Beyond Chaos and Complexity* Penguin, London (1992)
19. Waldrop, M *Complexity: The Emerging Science and the Edge of Order and Chaos* Simon and Schuster, London (1992)
20. Toffler, A *Future Shock* Bodley Head, London (1970)
21. Mazanie, J 'The tourism/leisure ratio: anticipating the limits of growth' *Tourist Review* 1981 **36** (4) 2–12
22. Butler, R W 'The concept of a tourist area cycle of evolution: implications for management of resources' *Canadian Geographer* 1980 **24** (1) 5–12
23. Gleick, J *Chaos: Making a New Science* Heinemann, London (1987)

4

Measures of forecasting accuracy – turning point error vs size of error

Christine A Witt

Lecturer in Operations Management, University of Bradford Management Centre, Emm Lane, Bradford, West Yorkshire

Stephen F Witt

Lewis Professor of Tourism Studies, Department of Management Science and Statistics, University College of Swansea, Singleton Park, Swansea

A comparison of the forecast accuracy of several quantitative methods applied to international tourism demand data has shown that the simple naive 'no change' extrapolation model (termed 'naive 1') is relatively accurate when forecasting accuracy is measured in terms of the magnitude of forecasting error.[1] Specifically, the 'no change' forecasts resulted in lower average percentage errors over a one-year time horizon than forecasts generated by any of the following six models – constant rate of growth ('naive 2'), exponential smoothing, trend curve, Gompertz, stepwise auto-regressive and econometric.

   Given the above result, together with the fact that fairly large percentage errors were present using naive 1 (the overall mean absolute percentage error associated with the forecasts generated by naive 1 over a one-year-ahead time horizon was in excess of 10%), it may be the case that it is more important to be able to forecast the *direction of change* of tourism demand (i.e. whether there will be *more or fewer* tourist visits next year than this year) rather than the absolute level. In this situation accuracy is measured by turning point error.[2] The superiority of naive 1 when accuracy is measured by the size of the forecasting error implies that firms in the international tourism industry should plan for no change in demand compared with the previous year, and yet it is well known that tourism markets are volatile, with some destinations increasing in popularity – often quite rapidly – while others are decreasing in popularity. The assumption of no change is, therefore, rather unsatisfactory. Hence, if a forecasting method can be found which generates reasonably accurate forecasts of turning points, then airlines, ferry operators, coach operators, hoteliers, tour operators, etc will at least receive an indication as to whether to plan for an *increase or decrease* in demand, even if the magnitude of the expected increase or decrease is somewhat uncertain. For example, if a relatively accurate method can be found for generating turning point forecasts, and these forecasts suggest that there is likely to be an increase in demand, then, e.g. coach operators can plan to increase their fleet of coaches. If, on the other hand, 'no change' were assumed, it would be unlikely that they could satisfy the probable increase in demand.

This article examines the relative accuracy of forecasts of international tourism demand, where accuracy is defined in terms of turning point error. The results are then compared with those obtained when accuracy is defined in terms of the magnitude of forecasting error. The relative ranking of the various forecasting techniques may well change when the measure of forecasting performance changes – as Makridakis notes, 'the relative accuracy of forecasting methods depends upon the loss function employed'.[3]

Data requirements and sources

Models are developed to forecast the following tourist flows:

- France to Italy, Morocco, Portugal, Spain, Switzerland and the UK;
- West Germany to Austria, France, Italy, Spain, Switzerland and Yugoslavia;
- the UK to Austria, France, West Germany, Greece, Italy and Spain; and
- the USA to Canada, France, West Germany, Italy, Mexico and the UK.

The data used in the study are annual and for outward tourism from France and West Germany they cover the period 1965 to 1983, from the USA the period 1965 to 1984, and from the UK the period 1965 to 1985 (the most recent data available at the time the analysis was carried out). The various forecasting models are estimated over the periods 1965–80, 1965–81 and 1965–82 for all origins, 1965–83 for the UK and USA, and 1965–84 for the UK. These models are used to generate forecasts of tourist flows for one year ahead – sets of one-year-ahead out-of-sample forecasts are thus generated for each origin.

Forecasts are made of 24 one-year-ahead tourist flows (four origins each to six destinations) over several time periods (three for France and West Germany, four for the USA and five for the UK) using seven different estimation techniques. This gives a total of about 600 errors for analysis.

In the case of France, the data relate to holidays plus visits to friends and relatives (minimum four days) and were obtained from *L'Economie du Tourisme* and *Annuaire Statistique de la France*. West German data refer to holidays plus visits to friends and relatives (minimum five days) and are published in *Fachserie F, Reihe 8, Sonderbeitrag Urlaubs- und Erholungsreisen*. For the UK, the data refer to holidays only (minimum one night) and were supplied by the Department of Trade and Industry. In the case of the USA, the figures relate to holidays plus visits to friends and relatives plus business visits (minimum one night) and were obtained from several sources – Statistics Canada provided the data on travel to Canada, the Banco de Mexico and Ministry of Tourism in Mexico supplied the data on travel to Mexico, and the remaining data are published in the Survey of Current Business. For certain origin–destination pairs, there were missing observations in some years and it was necessary to use supplementary data obtained from destination national tourist offices.

Forecasting methods

The forecasting methods included in the analysis are now described:

Naive 1

The forecast for period $t + 1$ is equal to the actual number of visits in period t:

$$\hat{V}_{t+1} = V_t \tag{1}$$

where V_t denotes the number of tourist visits in period t and '$\hat{}$' denotes a forecast value.

Naive 2

The forecast for period $t + 1$ is equal to the actual number of visits in period t multiplied by the growth rate over the previous period:

$$\hat{V}_{t+1} = V_t \left(1 + \frac{V_t - V_{t-1}}{V_{t-1}} \right) \tag{2}$$

Exponential smoothing

Some of the origin–destination pair data series contain trends, and hence an appropriate form of exponential smoothing is Brown's one parameter double exponential smoothing model.[4] Where no trend is present this technique reduces to single exponential smoothing.

Trend curve analysis

Ten linear equation trend curves are fitted to each data series and the curve exhibiting the best fit is selected to generate the forecasts. The trend curves comprise linear, constrained hyperbola, exponential, geometric, semilog, modified exponential, hyperbola, modified hyperbolic, quadratic and log quadratic:

linear

$$\hat{V}_t = \alpha + \beta_1 t \tag{3}$$

constrained hyperbola

$$\frac{1}{\hat{V}_t} = \alpha + \beta_1 \frac{1}{t} \tag{4}$$

exponential

$$\ln \hat{V}_t = \alpha + \beta_1 t \tag{5}$$

geometric

$$\ln \hat{V}_t = \alpha + \beta_1 \ln t \tag{6}$$

semilog

$$\hat{V}_t = \alpha + \beta_1 \ln t \tag{7}$$

modified exponential

$$\ln \hat{V}_t = \alpha + \beta_1 \frac{1}{t} \tag{8}$$

hyperbola

$$\hat{V}_t = \alpha + \beta_1 \frac{1}{t} \tag{9}$$

modified hyperbolic

$$\frac{1}{\hat{V}_t} = \alpha + \beta_1 t \tag{10}$$

quadratic

$$\hat{V}_t = \alpha + \beta_1 t + \beta_2 t^2 \tag{11}$$

log quadratic

$$\ln \hat{V}_t = \alpha + \beta_1 t + \beta_2 t^2 \tag{12}$$

where α, β_1, β_2 are parameters to be estimated, and t represents the time period.

Gompertz

This S-shaped curve is often used to represent the pattern of a product life cycle, and is estimated using non-linear estimation techniques. Given the popularity of, and theoretical justification for, the product life cycle concept, it was decided specifically always to include this particular form of trend curve in the forecasting comparisons.

Stepwise autoregression

The autoregressive model takes the form:

$$\hat{V}_{t+1} = \alpha + \beta_0 V_t + \beta_1 V_{t-1} + \beta_2 V_{t-2} \tag{13}$$

where $\alpha, \beta_0, \beta_1, \beta_2$ are parameters to be estimated.

A stepwise process based on incremental F-statistics is used to determine whether a variable is added to or removed from Equation 13 until the coefficients of each variable in the equation are statistically significant at the 5% level. Note that in some instances, no acceptable autoregressive model was estimated – a statistically significant coefficient could not be obtained for any of the potential explanatory variables – and hence forecasts were not generated.

Econometrics

Separate models are constructed for each origin–destination pair and potential explanatory variables include:

- origin income;
- the cost of living for tourists in the destination;
- the cost of living for tourists in substitute destinations;
- the cost of travel between the origin and destination;
- the cost of travel between the origin and substitute destinations;
- the exchange rate between the currencies of the origin and destination;
- oil crisis dummy variables;
- a foreign currency restriction dummy variable;
- a lagged dependent variable; and
- a trend term.[5]

The basic model is specified in log-linear form as follows:

$$\ln \frac{V_{ijt}}{P_{it}} = \alpha_1 + \alpha_2 \ln \frac{Y_{it}}{P_{it}} + \alpha_3 \ln C_{jt} + \alpha_4 \ln CS_{it} + \alpha_5 \ln EX_{ijt}$$
$$+ \alpha_6 \ln TA_{ijt} + \alpha_7 \ln TAS_{it} + \alpha_8 \ln TS_{ijt} + \alpha_9 \ln TSS_{it}$$
$$+ \alpha_{10} DV1_t + \alpha_{11} DV2_t + \alpha_{12} DV3_{it} + U_{ijt} \qquad (14)$$

$t = 1, 2 \ldots 16 \ (1 = 1965, \ldots 16 = 1980)$

where

V_{ijt}	is the number of tourist visits from origin i to destination j in year t;
P_{it}	is the origin i population in year t;
Y_{it}	is personal disposable income in origin i in year t (1980 prices);
C_{jt}	is the cost of living for tourists in destination j in year t (1980 prices);
CS_{it}	is a weighted average of the cost of tourism in substitute destinations for residents of origin i in year t (1980 prices);
EX_{ijt}	is the rate of exchange between the currencies of origin i and destination j in year t;
TA_{ijt}	is the cost of travel by air from origin i to destination j in year t (1980 prices);
TAS_{it}	is a weighted average of the cost of travel by air to substitute destinations from origin i in year t (1980 prices);
TS_{ijt}	is the cost of travel by surface from origin i to destination j in year t (1980 prices);
TSS_{it}	is a weighted average of the cost of travel by surface to substitute destinations from origin i in year t;
$DV1$	is a dummy variable which picks up the effects of the 1974 oil crisis: $DV1_t = 1$ if $t = 10(1974)$ or $11(1975)$ otherwise $= 0$;
$DV2$	is a dummy variable which picks up the effects of the 1979 oil crisis: $DV2_t = 1$ if $t = 15(1979)$ otherwise $= 0$;

DV3	is a dummy variable which picks up the effects of the 1967–69 UK currency restrictions (applies to UK origin models only);

$DV3_{it} = 1$ if i refers to the UK and $t = 3(1967)$, $4(1968)$ or $5(1969)$, otherwise $= 0$;

U_{ijt}	is a random disturbance term; and
$\alpha_1, \alpha_2, \ldots, \alpha_{12}$	are unknown parameters.

In addition, a trend term $\alpha_{13}t$ and/or lagged dependent variable term $\alpha_{14} \ln (V_{ij(t-1)}/P_{i(t-1)})$ is incorporated in the model for those origin–destination pairs where the preliminary empirical results indicate that this may be necessary.

The procedure adopted for selecting a 'best' econometric forecasting model for each origin–destination pair is described in Martin and Witt.[6] In this study, when generating forecasts of tourism demand using econometric models, known values of the explanatory variables have been substituted into the model. Hence, the econometric forecasts are *ex post* (as opposed to *ex ante*) forecasts – information has been used which would not have been available to the forecaster at the point in time from which the forecasts are generated. This proved necessary on account of the difficulties involved in obtaining retrospective forecasts of the explanatory variables in particular forecasts of travel costs. The econometric method may, therefore, appear more accurate than would be the case in practice on account of the additional uncertainties involved in forecasting the explanatory variables, and this point should be borne in mind when accuracy comparisons are made.

Measures of forecast accuracy

Turning point error

A turning point error occurs when the forecast misses the actual direction of change, i.e. if the forecast change is positive and the actual change is negative, or if the forecast change is negative and the actual change is positive.[7] Equally, a turning point error occurs if the data series exhibits a turning point, but this is not picked up by the forecast, or if the data series does not exhibit a turning point, but one is forecast.

In order to compress the comparison over several observations of forecast direction of change with actual direction of change into a single measure of turning point error, the concept of the percentage of directions of movement forecast correctly may be used.[8]

As the naive 1 model forecasts no change, it will neither generate a correct nor an incorrect forecast of direction of change. In order to outperform the naive 1 model, a forecasting method must, therefore, forecast over 50% of directions of movement correctly. Clearly if a technique only yields 40% accuracy on this basis, it would be better to assume no change.

Measures based on size of error

As the forecasting tests are carried out on data series of origin–destination tourist flows of widely differing sizes, it is necessary to use criteria of forecast accuracy which are measured in unit-free terms. Two measures of accuracy, mean absolute percentage error (MAPE) and root mean square percentage error (RMSPE), are considered. Although the use of MAPE is widely supported,[9] many authors consider that an accuracy criterion specified in terms of squared errors is often more appropriate than one in terms of absolute errors,[10] and thus RMSPE is also examined.

The error (e) is defined as

$$e_t = \hat{V}_t - V_t \tag{15}$$

If there are n forecasts, then

$$\text{MAPE} = \frac{1}{n}\sum_{t=1}^{n}\frac{|e_t|}{V_t} \times 100 \tag{16}$$

where $|e_t|$ denotes the absolute value of the error.

$$\text{RMSPE} = \sqrt{\frac{1}{n}\sum_{t=1}^{n}\left(\frac{e_t}{V_t}\right)^2} \times 100 \tag{17}$$

Both MAPE and RMSPE are subject to distortion caused by outlying observations, in that one or two poor forecasts will affect the average error measures. However, given the number of forecast errors under consideration, this is unlikely to be a serious problem. Turning point error is, by contrast, not affected by outliers at all, in that the *size* of error is not considered, only whether the forecast direction of change is correct.

Empirical results

Turning point error

Table 1 summarizes the performance of the seven forecasting methods across the various origin countries in terms of the percentage of directions of movement forecast

Table 1. Forecasting performance: percentage of directions of movement forecast correctly.

	Origin country			
Forecasting method	France	West Germany	UK	USA
Naive 1	150 (3=)	50 (4=)	50 (3=)	50 (2=)
Naive 2	39 (7)	39 (7)	67 (2)	50 (2=)
Exponential smoothing	67 (1)	50 (4=)	70 (1)	43 (5)
Trend curve analysis	50 (3=)	50 (4=)	47 (6)	33 (7)
Gompertz	50 (3=)	61 (3)	33 (7)	42 (6)
Autoregression	60 (2)	67 (2)	49 (5)	44 (4)
Econometrics	50 (3=)	72 (1)	50 (3=)	75 (1)

Note: Figures in brackets denote rankings.

correctly over a one-year time horizon. The relative forecasting accuracy of a par-ticular method varies considerably according to origin country. For example, expo-nential smoothing yields the most accurate forecasts of turning points for France and the UK, whereas econometrics yields the most accurate forecasts for West Germany and the USA. By contrast exponential smoothing comes in fourth equal position for West Germany (together with naive 1) and fifth for the USA (where it is outperformed by naive 1). Econometrics is ranked third equal for both France and the UK (together with naive 1 in each case). Other forecasting methods also display considerable variation in the ranking, e.g., naive 2 ranges from second position in the case of the UK to seventh (i.e. worst) position for France and West Germany and Gompertz ranges from third position for West Germany to seventh position for the UK.

The forecasting methods which outperform naive 1 are given below according to origin country:

- France – exponential smoothing and autoregression;
- West Germany – econometrics, autoregression, and Gompertz;
- UK – exponential smoothing and naive 2; and
- USA – econometrics.

Three methods outperform naive 1 for two origins (econometrics, exponential smoothing and autoregression), and Gompertz and naive 2 are just better than naive 1 for one origin.

Trend curve analysis does not outperform naive 1 for any origin, and therefore does not appear to be of any help in forecasting one-year-ahead tourism flows. By contrast, econometrics does not underperform naive 1 for any origin, and forecasts the direction of movement of tourism demand correctly in over 70% of cases for two origins, and so should prove useful in tourism forecasting. Exponential smoothing outperforms naive 1 for two origins and underperforms for one origin. Autoregression beats naive 1 twice and is beaten by naive 1 twice, but a problem with autoregression is that in some cases no acceptable model was estimated and hence no forecasts generated. For the remaining forecasting methods – naive 2 and Gompertz – naive 1 outperforms for more origins than it underperforms.

It appears that for forecasting direction of change in tourism flows over a one-year time horizon, econometric forecasting models provide valuable information when the origin country is West Germany or the USA, and exponential smoothing models provide valuable information when the origin country is France or the UK. The percentage of turning points forecast accurately using these methods for these origins varies between 67% and 75%.

Comparison of turning point error with MAPE and RMSPE

Table 2 shows the rankings of the seven forecasting methods across the various origin countries over a one-year time horizon when the accuracy criteria are MAPE and RMSPE. As already discussed, naive 1 outperforms all other forecasting methods for all origin countries. Some of the rankings correspond to some extent across the turning point error/size of error criteria. For example, econometrics is ranked first for the USA on the turning point error criterion and second on the MAPE criterion. Exponential

Table 2. Forecasting performance: MAPE and RMSPE.

Accuracy criterion	Forecasting method	Origin country			
		France	West Germany	UK	USA
MAPE	Naive 1	9.06 (1)	5.80 (1)	12.73 (1)	11.94 (1)
	Naive 2	12.76 (5)	10.55 (6)	15.73 (2)	14.10 (4)
	Exponential smoothing	9.38 (2)	7.29 (3)	16.72 (4)	12.95 (3)
	Gompertz	13.41 (6)	9.07 (5)	24.12 (7)	16.48 (6)
	Trend curve analysis	12.54 (4)	8.33 (4)	22.12 (6)	20.93 (7)
	Autoregression	13.45 (7)	5.96 (2)	15.81 (3)	15.03 (5)
	Econometrics	10.98 (3)	11.28 (7)	20.91 (5)	12.35 (2)
RMSPE	Naive 1	11.91 (1)	7.57 (1)	14.45 (1)	15.14 (1)
	Naive 2	17.85 (7)	13.07 (6)	20.21 (3)	16.75 (4)
	Exponential smoothing	12.68 (2)	9.56 (3)	21.41 (4)	15.99 (2)
	Gompertz	17.45 (6)	10.84 (4)	28.10 (7)	20.37 (6)
	Trend curve analysis	17.15 (5)	11.02 (5)	27.83 (6)	23.74 (7)
	Autoregression	16.86 (4)	8.30 (2)	18.05 (2)	18.16 (5)
	Econometrics	13.61 (3)	13.87 (7)	27.42 (5)	16.03 (3)

Note: Figures in brackets denote rankings.
Source: C.A. Witt and S.F. Witt, 'Accuracy of econometric forecasts of tourism', *Annals of Tourism Research*, Vol 16, No 3, 1989, forthcoming.

smoothing is ranked first for France on the turning point error criterion and second on the size of error criteria. However, in general the rankings do not correspond, e.g. econometrics has the lowest turning point error for West Germany but the highest MAPE and RMSPE. These results are in contrast to those obtained by Wright and co-workers, who when using monthly data to forecast interest rate changes found that 'the ranking of methods based upon . . . MAPE and MSPE is the same as that based on number of correct decisions', where a correct decision is equivalent to a correct forecast of the direction of change.[11]

Overall, the greatest improvement in performance on moving from size of error to turning point error as a measure of forecasting accuracy occurs for econometrics – it appears that although econometric models do not generate particularly accurate forecasts of the size of the change in tourism demand, they do generate relatively accurate forecasts of the direction of change in tourism demand.

Conclusions

The performance of several quantitative forecasting methods has been assessed in the context of flows of international tourist visits. Previous results obtained when forecasting accuracy was defined in terms of error magnitude yielded the conclusion that the naive 'no change' extrapolation model outperformed the six other techniques under consideration for one-year-ahead forecasts. But the present study shows that it is possible to outperform the 'no change' model when forecasting accuracy is defined in terms of turning point error, i.e. it is possible to forecast the direction of change of tourism demand with some degree of accuracy. This could benefit firms in the tourism industry who would know whether to plan for an increase or decrease in demand.

Econometric models do not underperform the 'no change' model for any of the four origin countries considered, and yield the most accurate forecasts of turning points for West Germany and the USA. Overall, therefore, econometrics appears to be the best technique for forecasting turning points. Exponential smoothing forecasts of turning points are the most accurate for France and the UK, but the 'no change' model outperforms exponential smoothing for one origin. The forecasts generated by the econometric and exponential smoothing models should be of practical value to those involved in planning in the international tourism industry. In reality it will be necessary to generate forecasts of the explanatory variables in order to use the econometric models to yield forecasts of tourism demand, which may reduce the accuracy of the forecasts, but this is not necessarily the case. As Fildes discovered when examining studies which compared econometric and extrapolative forecasts:

In the short term, of 39 studies where *ex post* comparisons are made, the score is 22 to 11 in favour of econometric models. But . . . of 15 *ex ante* comparisons, a higher proportion, 11, favour causal models, despite the additional handicap they have of uncertainty in the explanatory variables.[12]

The results regarding the relative forecasting accuracy of the various techniques differ considerably according to whether the measure of forecasting accuracy is based on turning point error or size of error. Although the rankings for MAPE and RMSPE are similar for each origin, when the ranking according to percentage of directions of movement forecast correctly is compared with the MAPE/RMSPE rankings there is little similarity. The relative accuracy of the forecasting methods examined is, therefore, critically dependent upon the accuracy measure chosen.

Acknowledgement

The authors wish to thank COMSHARE for allowing access to their ORION forecasting package which was used to generate the time series forecasts discussed in this paper.

Notes and references

1. See C.A. Martin and S.F. Witt, 'An empirical analysis of the accuracy of forecasting techniques', *Proceedings of Travel and Tourism Research Association 19th Annual Conference*, University of Utah, Salt Lake City, 1988, pp 285–298; C.A. Martin and S.F. Witt, 'Forecasting tourism demand: a comparison of the accuracy of several quantitative methods', *International Journal of Forecasting*, Vol 5, No 1, 1989, pp 7–19; and C.A. Witt and S.F. Witt, 'Accuracy of econometric forecasts of tourism', *Annals of Tourism Research*, Vol 16, No 3, 1989, forthcoming.

2. Other studies which utilize accuracy measures based on forecasting the direction of change include J. Cicarelli, 'A new method of evaluating the accuracy of economic forecasts', *Journal of Macroeconomics*, Vol 4, 1982, pp 469–475; and G. Thury, 'Macroeconomic forecasting in Austria: an analysis of accuracy', *International Journal of Forecasting*, Vol 1, 1985, pp 111–121.

3. See p 22 of S. Makridakis, 'The art and science of forecasting; an assessment and future directions', *International Journal of Forecasting*, Vol 2, No 1, 1986, pp 15–39.
4. R.G. Brown, *Smoothing, Forecasting and Prediction*, Prentice Hall, NJ, USA, 1963.
5. For a full discussion of the justification and data sources for the explanatory variables see: C.A. Martin and S.F. Witt, 'Tourism demand forecasting models: choice of appropriate variable to represent tourists' cost of living', *Tourism Management*, Vol 8, No 3, September 1987, pp 233–246; and C.A. Martin and S.F. Witt, 'Substitute prices in models of tourism demand', *Annals of Tourism Research*, Vol 15, No 2, 1988, pp 255–268.
6. Martin and Witt, 1988, *op cit*, Ref 5.
7. See R.K. Chisholm and G.R. Whitaker, Jr, *Forecasting Methods*, Irwin, Homewood, IL, USA, 1971, pp 4–5; and R.F. Wynn and K. Holden, *An Introduction to Applied Econometric Analysis*, Macmillan, London, 1974, pp 190–191.
8. See D.J. Wright, G. Capon, R. Pagé, J. Quiroga, A.A. Taseen and F. Tomasini, 'Evaluation of forecasting methods for decision support', *International Journal of Forecasting*, Vol 2, No 2, 1986, pp 139–152; and A. Zellner, C. Hong and G.M. Gulati, 'Turning points in economic time series, loss structures and Bayesian forecasting', *8th International Symposium on Forecasting*, Amsterdam, Netherlands, June 1988.
9. See, for example, M.J. Lawrence, R.H. Edmundson and M.J. O'Connor, 'An examination of the accuracy of judgemental extrapolation of time series', *International Journal of Forecasting*, Vol 1, No 1, 1985, pp 25–35.
10. See, e.g., N. Meade and I.M.D. Smith, 'ARAMA vs ARIMA – a study of the benefits of a new approach to forecasting', *Omega*, Vol 13, No 6, 1985, pp 519–534.
11. Wright, Capon, Pagé, Quiroga, Taseen and Tomasini, *op cit*, Ref 8, p 148.
12. See pp 571–572 of R. Fildes, 'Quantitative forecasting – the state of the art: econometric models', *Journal of the Operational Research Society*, Vol 36, No 7, 1985, pp 549–580.

5

Tourism forecasting: how well do private and public sector organizations perform?

Stephen F Witt

Lewis Professor of Tourism Studies, European Business Management School, University of Wales, Singleton Park, Swansea

In this article the forecasts of international tourist flows produced by three commercial organizations and one national tourist office are examined. The commercially produced forecasts comprise the following:

- US outbound travel split by destination country;
- UK outbound travel split by destination country, transport mode and holiday type (independent or inclusive tour); and
- New Zealand inbound travel split by origin country.

The public sector produced forecasts also relate to New Zealand inbound travel split by origin country.

Tourism forecasting organizations

Forecasts of US outbound travel split by destination country have been produced by Coopers and Lybrand and published by the American Express Publishing Corporation in the *World Travel Overview* annually since 1986.[1] Forecasts of UK outbound travel split by destination country were produced by Brooke, Buckley and Witt and published by Industry Forecasts in *The International Travel and Tourism Forecast* as a one off in 1985.[2] Forecasts of New Zealand inbound travel split according to origin country have been produced by the McDermott Miller group and published by the New Zealand Tourist and Publicity Department in 1985 in *Economic Determinants of Tourist Arrivals Model 1985*, and annually since then in *The Economic Outlook for New Zealand's Major Tourism Markets*.[3] In addition the joint New Zealand Tourist and Publicity Department and Tourism Council Forecasting Group have produced a set of official international tourist arrivals forecasts (of which the McDermott Miller group forecasts form one of the inputs) annually since 1986 and these are published by the New Zealand Tourist and Publicity Department in *New Zealand International Visitor Arrival Forecasts.*[4]

Coopers and Lybrand and the McDermott Miller Group use econometric models to generate forecasts of international tourist flows. In *The International Travel and Tourism Forecast* a combination of forecasting techniques is employed – econometrics and state-space forecasting. The New Zealand Tourist and Publicity Department and Tourism Council Forecasting Group uses the Delphi technique to generate forecasts; a range of key experts in the tourism industry is brought together to consider three sets of quantitative forecasts (weighted moving average, linear trend, econometric (McDermott Miller)) and industry surveys, and subsequently arrive at final consensus forecasts.

Assessment of forecasting performance

In order to measure forecasting performance, it is necessary to select particular measures of accuracy. As the forecasting tests are carried out on data series of origin–destination tourist flows of widely differing sizes, it is essential to use an error magnitude criterion of forecast accuracy which is measured in unit-free terms. Thus absolute percentage error figures are calculated for each forecast value considered in this study; where average error values are required, the mean absolute percentage error (MAPE) is calculated. (The use of MAPE as a measure of forecast accuracy is widely supported in the forecasting literature.)[5]

In addition to measuring forecasting performance in terms of error magnitude, forecasting accuracy can be measured in terms of 'direction of change error'. Here the ability of models to forecast the direction of movement of tourism demand (i.e. whether there will be *more* or *fewer* tourist visits next year than this year) is examined. A direction of change error occurs when the forecast misses the actual direction of change, i.e. if the forecast change is positive and the actual change is negative, or vice versa. Equivalently, a direction of change error occurs if the data series exhibits a change in direction, but this is not picked up by the forecast, or if the data series does not exhibit a change in direction, but one is forecast. Directional accuracy measures are employed by numerous authors.[6] In order to compress the comparison over several observations of forecast direction of change with actual direction of change into a single measure of direction of change error, the concept of the percentage of directions of movement forecast correctly may be used.[7]

The accuracy of the forecasts produced by the four organizations may be examined in relative terms, by comparing the forecasting performances with that of the simple 'no change' naive model (denoted N1), where the forecast number of visits in a given year is taken to be equal to the actual number in the previous year:

$$\hat{V}_{t+1} = V_t \tag{1}$$

where V_t denotes the number of tourist visits in year t and '$\hat{}$' denotes a forecast value. Given the considerable time, effort and expense necessarily incurred in the development of the sophisticated forecasting procedures used by these organizations, it is to be expected that there would be a corresponding improvement in the accuracy of the forecasts generated as compared with the forecasts produced by using the naive model. If indeed the published forecasts do not outperform the no change model, then the usefulness of the forecasting techniques employed by the organizations in the context of international tourism demand must be brought into question.

The no change naive model will neither generate a correct nor an incorrect forecast of direction of change. In order to outperform this model in terms of direction of change error, a forecasting organization must, therefore, forecast over 50% of directions of movement correctly; clearly if a technique yields only 40% accuracy on this basis, it would be better to assume no change.

An alternative naive model which can be used for assessing forecasting performance is the no change growth rate model (denoted N2), where the forecast number of visits in a given year is taken to be equal to the actual number in the previous year multiplied by the growth rate over the year prior to that:

$$\hat{V}_{t+1} = V_t \left[1 + \frac{V_t - V_{t-1}}{V_{t-1}} \right] \tag{2}$$

Each of the forecasting organizations being considered makes annual forecasts for several years ahead, but this article concentrates on assessing the accuracy of the published one-year ahead forecasts. As Means and Avila point out when discussing the performance of the TRAM model, 'it is inescapable that many analysts will want to use TRAM for short-term, one-year forecasts as part of their planning processes'.[8]

Empirical results

New Zealand inbound tourism

Error magnitude results. Table 1 presents the percentage error figures for overseas visitor arrivals in New Zealand for the year to March 1989 from its most important source countries – Australia, USA, Japan, UK, Canada and Germany[9] – split according to tourist segment. Thus, where possible, arrivals are divided into holiday visits, visits to friends and relatives (VFR) and business visits, but in certain cases holiday visits and VFR are combined to give leisure visits. The percentage errors are given for the econometric forecasts produced by the McDermott Miller group (MM forecasts) and the Delphi forecasts produced by the New Zealand Tourist and Publicity Department and Tourism Council Forecasting Group (NZTP/NZTC forecasts), together with the two sets of naive forecasts.

Examination of the first part of Table 1 does not immediately show that one of the four forecasting methods is clearly more accurate than the others. For example, when considering the various categories of Australian tourists visiting New Zealand, N2 has the lowest absolute percentage error for the holiday and business segments, and MM for the VFR segment. By contrast, for inbound tourism from the USA, the most accurate forecasts of holiday visits are generated by MM, whereas the most accurate VFR and business visit forecasts are produced by NZTP/NZTC. By calculating

Table 1. New Zealand inbound tourism forecasting accuracy – error magnitude, 1988–89.

Origin country	Segment	MM[a]	NZTP/NZTC[b]	N1	N2
Absolute percentage error					
Australia	Holiday	30.8	24.9	34.2	22.5
	VFR	0.8	3.9	2.0	18.6
	Business	10.6	6.4	12.7	0.4
USA	Holiday	9.4	14.7	12.4	18.3
	VFR	2.9	1.5	5.9	3.0
	Business	8.7	2.4	11.0	11.7
Japan	Leisure[c]	7.4	0.5	17.0	0.9
	Business	8.6	5.2	10.3	2.9
UK	Holiday	5.5	2.7	11.8	2.3
	VFR	10.6	0.3	7.2	27.6
	Business	3.0	4.5	0.0	19.6
Canada	Holiday	5.7	8.6	6.6	12.3
Germany	Leisure[c]	13.1	0.5	12.6	29.5
Total arrivals	Holiday	1.7	9.6	3.8	7.2
	VRF	7.2	3.7	6.0	16.3
	Business	9.9	9.8	12.0	2.0
Mean absolute percentage error					
	Holiday	12.9	12.7	16.3	13.9
	VFR	4.8	1.9	5.0	16.4
	Leisure	10.3	0.5	14.8	15.2
	Business	7.7	4.6	8.5	8.7

Notes: [a]Econometric forecast; [b]Delphi forecast; [c]leisure = holiday + VFR.
Sources: Derived from New Zealand Tourist and Publicity Department, *New Zealand International Visitor Arrival Forecasts*, Wellington, NZ, various issues; and New Zealand Tourist and Publicity Department, *New Zealand Visitor Statistics, 1988–1989*, Wellington, NZ, 1989.

MAPEs for the various visit segments over the most important source countries, however, a clearer pattern begins to emerge, and these are presented in the second part of the table. For each visit category, the Delphi technique is the most accurate – marginally so for holiday visits, but substantially more accurate than the other forecasting methods for all other visit categories.

Table 2 examines forecasts of total arrivals for each of the main source countries over a three-year period in terms of error magnitude. Here again, as for Table 1, no clear pattern emerges on studying the first part of the table. For example, the most accurate forecasts of Australian tourist visits to New Zealand are generated by MM in 1988–89, NZTP/NZTC and N1 in 1987–88 and NZTP/NZTC in 1986–87. The most accurate forecasts of US visits are produced by N1 in 1988–89 and 1987–88 and N2 in 1986–87. By averaging the absolute percentage errors over the three-year period for each origin, however, a much clearer picture of relative forecasting performance becomes apparent, and these values are presented in the second part of the table. The Delphi technique is the most accurate forecasting method for five of the six most important source countries and for total arrivals; only in the case of Canada is a different method (econometrics) ranked first.

Table 2. New Zealand inbound tourism forecasting accuracy – error magnitude, 1988–89, 1987–88, 1986–87.

	Origin country	MM[a]	NZTP/NZTC[b]	N1	N2
Absolute percentage error					
1988–89	Australia	8.6	9.6	8.9	17.5
	USA	9.7	12.5	9.5	17.7
	Japan	7.1	0.3	16.3	0.7
	UK	6.4	0.7	7.6	16.0
	Canada	4.7	6.8	5.5	5.8
	Germany	9.0	0.5	11.8	25.0
	Total arrivals	4.7	4.0	1.4	10.5
1987–88	Australia	9.0	7.3	7.3	13.3
	USA	11.8	7.0	6.9	13.6
	Japan	7.1	3.0	16.9	5.7
	UK	17.1	11.5	20.4	7.1
	Canada	2.9	6.1	0.3	7.8
	Germany	10.2	11.8	29.4	15.3
	Total arrivals	11.7	2.2	10.8	1.2
1986–87	Australia	2.1	1.0	6.9	17.1
	USA	23.1	8.2	18.1	6.8
	Japan	14.0	9.6	21.4	12.9
	UK	10.5	5.8	14.3	5.6
	Canada	3.8	6.9	6.9	25.9
	Germany	0.0	1.5	16.7	9.2
	Total arrivals	11.5	5.7	9.7	4.2
Mean absolute percentage error					
	Australia	6.6	6.0	7.7	16.0
	USA	14.9	9.2	11.5	12.7
	Japan	9.4	4.3	13.0	6.4
	UK	11.3	6.0	14.1	9.6
	Canada	3.8	6.6	4.2	13.2
	Germany	6.4	4.6	19.3	16.5
	Total arrivals	9.3	4.0	7.3	5.3

Notes: [a]Econometric forecast; [b]Delphi forecast.
Sources: Derived from New Zealand Tourist and Publicity Department, *New Zealand International Visitor Arrival Forecasts*, Wellington, NZ, various issues; and New Zealand Tourist and Publicity Department, *New Zealand Visitor Statistics, 1981–1989*, Wellington, NZ, 1989.

Of the four forecasting methods considered, the Delphi technique is clearly the most complex, requiring various inputs including econometric forecasts. It appears, therefore, that when accuracy is measured in terms of error magnitude, the method which involves the greatest effort generally generates the most accurate forecasts.

The second part of Table 1 also demonstrates that econometrics – the second most complex forecasting technique – is ranked second in terms of accuracy for each visit segment. On moving to the second part of Table 2, however, the results are less clear cut; econometrics outperforms the naive methods for just three of the seven origin countries/country groups.

Direction of change error results. Table 3 presents the forecast direction of change (positive or negative) of tourist flows between 1987–88 and 1988–89 for the various source countries split according to tourist segment. The forecast directions of movement are given for the MM, NZTP/NZTC and N2 methods, together with the actual direction of change. Each of the three techniques forecasts directions of movement correctly in 78% of cases, and hence outperforms N1. However, the two complex forecasting procedures are no more accurate than the naive no change growth rate model in terms of predicting direction of change.

Table 4 examines forecasts of total arrivals from the main source countries over a three-year period in terms of direction of change error. Each technique outperforms N1 for each year considered. The Delphi method generates the most accurate forecasts for two of the years and overall. Econometrics is the most accurate technique in the third year, but is ranked behind N2 for the years when the Delphi method is ranked first.

The econometric, Delphi and N2 forecasting methods clearly outperform N1 in terms of direction of change error. The evidence regarding the relative forecasting performance of the three former methods is not as strong, but the Delphi technique is somewhat more accurate than the other two.

Table 3. New Zealand inbound tourism forecasting accuracy – direction of change error 1988–89.

Origin country	Segment	Actual	MM[a]	NZTP/NZTC[b]	N2
			Direction of movement		
Australia	Holiday	−	−	−	−
	VFR	+	+	+	+
	Business	+	+	+	+
USA	Holiday	−	−	+	+
	VFR	+	+	+	+
	Business	+	+	+	+
Japan	Leisure[c]	+	+	+	+
	Business	+	+	+	+
UK	Holiday	+	+	+	+
	VFR	+	−	+	+
	Business	nc	+	+	+
Canada	Holiday	+	+	−	−
Germany	Leisure[c]	+	−	+	+
Total arrivals	Holiday	−	−	+	+
	VFR	+	−	+	+
	Business	+	+	+	+
Percentage of wrong forecast directions			22	22	22

Notes: [a]Econometric forecast; [b]Delphi forecast; [c]leisure = holiday + VFR.
Sources: Derived from New Zealand Tourist and Publicity Department, *New Zealand International Visitor Arrival Forecasts*, Wellington, NZ, various issues; and New Zealand Tourist and Publicity Department, *New Zealand Visitor Statistics, 1988–1989*, Wellington, NZ, 1989.

Table 4. New Zealand inbound tourism forecasting accuracy – direction of change error 1988–89, 1987–88, 1986–87.

		Direction of movement			
	Origin country	Actual	MM[a]	NZTP/NZTC[b]	N2
1988–89	Australia	–	–	+	+
	USA	–	–	+	+
	Japan	+	+	+	+
	UK	+	+	+	+
	Canada	+	+	–	–
	Germany	+	+	+	+
	Total arrivals	+	–	+	+
	Percentage of wrong forecast directions		14	43	43
1987–88	Australia	+	–	nc	–
	USA	+	–	+	+
	Japan	+	+	+	+
	UK	+	+	+	+
	Canada	–	–	+	+
	Germany	+	+	+	+
	Total arrivals	+	–	+	+
	Percentage of wrong forecast directions		43	21	29
1986–87	Australia	–	–	–	+
	USA	+	–	+	+
	Japan	+	+	+	+
	UK	+	+	+	+
	Canada	+	+	+	+
	Germany	+	+	+	+
	Total arrivals	+	–	+	+
	Percentage of wrong forecast directions		29	0	14
	Overall percentage of wrong forecast directions		29	21	29

Notes: [a]Econometric forecast; [b]Delphi forecast.
Sources: Derived from New Zealand Tourist and Publicity Department, *New Zealand International Visitor Arrival Forecasts*, Wellington, NZ, various issues; and New Zealand Tourist and Publicity Department, *New Zealand Visitor Statistics, 1988–1989*, Wellington, NZ, 1989.

US outbound tourism

The author has examined the accuracy of the TRAM econometric model compared with the N1 and N2 models in terms of error magnitude.[10] For the 42 US tourist destinations considered in 1986, TRAM has a lower absolute percentage error than the naive no change model in only 31% of cases. When the destinations are grouped into geographical regions (Western Europe, Middle East, South America, Asia/Pacific, Caribbean and Central America), TRAM has a lower regional MAPE than N1 in only one of the five cases. However, the TRAM model is more accurate than N2 for 67% of destinations, and when the regional areas are considered the TRAM MAPE is lower than the N2 MAPE in four out of five cases and equal in one. The ranking of forecasting methods in terms of error magnitude for US outbound tourism is very clear: N1 is the most accurate method, followed by econometrics and then N2.

The author has also compared the forecasting ability of the TRAM and N1 models in terms of direction of change error.[11] Examination of the forecast direction of change of tourist flows between 1985 and 1986 shows that the TRAM model forecasts directions of movement correctly for 39% of destinations. Once again, N1 is the more accurate method, followed by econometrics.

The very poor forecasting performance of the TRAM model in 1986 may have been caused by significant unforeseen events, such as the Chernobyl nuclear accident together with the USA–Libya conflict and terrorist-related activities which substantially reduced US travel to Europe during that year. The possibility that the relative forecasting performance of the TRAM model was influenced by the special events which occurred in 1986 may be investigated by examining the two-year ahead forecasts for 1987. As Means and Avila point out, 'the events of 1986 were not perceived by the public as part of a persistent, on going pattern; thus a bounce-back should be expected in 1987.'[12]

In terms of error magnitude the TRAM model yields more accurate forecasts than the random walk model in 44% of cases in 1987. Furthermore, as for the 1986 forecasts, the TRAM model only outperforms the random walk model in terms of regional MAPEs for the Caribbean and Central America. When direction of change is considered, however, the situation alters. For the 1987 forecasts, the TRAM model forecasts directions of movement correctly in 59% of cases, compared with 39% of cases when forecasting 1986 tourist flows. The volume of tourism from the USA was forecast to increase for virtually all destinations in 1986 compared with 1985; but as a result of the unforeseen events of 1986, a decrease was recorded for many destinations. The 1986 forecasting performance in terms of direction of change error was thus markedly affected by the events of this year. It appears, therefore, that for normal years the TRAM econometric model outperforms the no change model in terms of percentage of directions of movement forecast correctly. In fact, the TRAM model also outperforms N2: the latter model correctly forecasts direction of change in 55% of cases compared with 59% for the TRAM model.

For US outbound tourism the relatively complex econometric model is outperformed by the simple no change naive model in terms of error magnitude, but it outperforms the no change model in terms of directional accuracy. The TRAM model is more accurate than the no change growth rate model both in terms of error magnitude and direction of change error.

UK outbound tourism

The author has examined the accuracy of the *International Travel and Tourism Forecast* (ITTF) compared with the N1 and N2 models in terms of error magnitude.[13] For the 48 alternative holidays (12 destinations split into independent/inclusive tour and air/surface transport) considered in 1985, the ITTF outperforms N1 in 56% of cases. However, examination of the MAPEs for each of the four holiday categories shows that the ITTF only outperforms N1 for one category – independent air holidays. N1 is more accurate than the ITTF for inclusive tour air holidays, independent surface holidays and inclusive tour surface holidays. Comparison of the ITTF with the no change growth rate model shows that the forecasting performance of the former model is relatively good – it has a lower MAPE than N2 for each of the four categories of holiday.

The relative forecasting ability of the ITTF and N1 models has also been assessed in terms of direction of change error.[14] The ITTF model correctly forecasts the direction of change of tourist flows between 1984 and 1985 in 61% of cases, thus outperforming N1. In fact, the ITTF also outperforms N2 – the latter model correctly forecasts directions of change in only 44% of cases.

For UK outbound tourism the forecasting ability of the ITTF and N1 models appears to be similar in terms of error magnitude, whereas the ITTF is more accurate than N1 in terms of the ability to forecast directions of movement correctly. The ITTF is more accurate thitn N2 both in terms of error magnitude and direction of change error.

Conclusions

This study has examined the accuracy of forecasts of international tourism demand produced by four organizations, and compared this with the forecasting ability of two naive models. Attention has been restricted to those forecasting services that publish tourism demand forecasts on an origin country–destination country basis (e.g. the UK to Spain) rather than just on a more aggregated basis (e.g. total UK outbound tourism).

It appears that the (econometric) forecasts of international tourism demand generated by the three private sector organizations considered are not particularly accurate compared with naive forecasts, although limited success has been achieved with the forecasts of New Zealand inbound and UK outbound tourism. Given the considerable expense and effort incurred in generating econometric forecasts compared with naive forecasts, it must be demonstrated that the former are *clearly* more accurate than the latter in order to justify their use. This has not been shown to be the general case in international tourism demand forecasting.

The Delphi forecasts of New Zealand inbound tourism are generated by combining quantitative forecasts with expert judgement. Two sets of univariate time series forecasts are examined as well as econometric forecasts. In addition, the findings of industry surveys are considered. Finally, qualitative inputs are provided by tourism experts. The resulting forecasts are generally more accurate than the econometric and naive no change and no change growth rate forecasts, both in terms of error magnitude and direction of change error. Hence, it appears that the accuracy of forecasts of international tourism demand can be substantially improved if forecasts generated by several methods are considered and qualitative inputs are incorporated in the forecast generation process. Furthermore, although econometric models alone do not provide particularly accurate forecasts of tourism demand, they can be a valuable input in a Delphi forecasting exercise.

Notes and references

1. G. Means and R. Avila, 'Econometric analysis and forecasts of US international travel: using the new TRAM model', *World Travel Overview 1986/87*. American Express Publishing, New York, 1986, pp 90–107; G. Means and R. Avila, 'An econometric analysis and forecast of US travel and the 1987 TRAM model update', *World Travel Overview 1987/88*, American Express Publishing, New York, 1987, pp 102–123; G. Means and R. Avila, 'Globalization redirects the travel industry: the 1988 TRAM analysis', *World Travel Overview 1988/89*, American Express Publishing, New York, 1988, pp 86–100.
2. M.Z. Brooke, P.J. Buckley and S.F. Witt, *The International Travel and Tourism Forecast*, Industry Forecasts, London, 1985.
3. McDermott Miller Group, *Economic Determinants of Tourist Arrivals Model 1985*, New Zealand Tourist and Publicity Department, Wellington, NZ, 1985; McDermott Miller Group, *The Economic Outlook for New Zealand's Major Tourism Markets*, New Zealand Tourist and Publicity Department, Wellington, NZ, various issues.
4. New Zealand Tourist and Publicity Department, *New Zealand International Visitor Arrival Forecasts*, Wellington, NZ, various issues.
5. See, for example, J.L. Kling and D.A. Bessler, 'A comparison of multivariate forecasting procedures for economic time series', *International Journal of Forecasting*, Vol 1, 1985, pp 5–25; M.J. Lawrence, R.H. Edmundson and M.J. O'Connor, 'An examination of the accuracy of judgemental extrapolation of time series', *International Journal of Forecasting*, Vol 1, 1985, pp 25–35; C.D. Lewis, *Industrial and Business Forecasting Methods*, Butterworths, London, 1982.
6. See, for example, R.J. Brodie and C.A. de Kluyver, 'A comparison of the short term forecasting accuracy of econometric and naive extrapolation models of market share', *International Journal of Forecasting*, Vol 3, 1987, pp 423–437; J. Cicarelli, 'A new method of evaluating the accuracy of economic forecasts', *Journal of Macroeconomics*, Vol 4, 1982, pp 469–475; G. Thury, 'Macroeconomic forecasting in Austria: an analysis of accuracy', *International Journal of Forecasting*, Vol 1, 1985, pp 111–121; D.J. Wright, G. Capon, R. Page, J. Quiroga, A.A. Taseen and F. Tomasini, 'Evaluation of forecasting methods for decision support', *International Journal of Forecasting*, Vol 2, 1986, pp 139–152.
7. *Ibid*, D.J. Wright *et al.*
8. *Op cit*, Ref 1, Means and Avila, 1987.
9. As the data refer to the period before reunification, all references to Germany are in fact to West Germany.
10. S.F. Witt, 'The track records of tourism forecasting services', in P. Johnson and B. Thomas, eds, *Choice and Demand in Tourism*, Mansell, London, 1992.
11. S.F. Witt, 'Assessing the accuracy of published econometric forecasts of international tourism demand', *Proceedings of Travel and Tourism Research Association (TTRA) 22nd Annual Conference*, University of Utah, Salt Lake City, 1991.
12. *Op cit*, Ref 1, Means and Avila, 1987, p 116.
13. *Op cit*, Ref 10.
14. *Op cit*, Ref 11.

Part III

Gender and sex in tourism

Introduction by Chris Ryan

'Gender issues' have a long tradition of being a subject of academic concern. One only needs to recall turn of the century writers and works like Vera Brittain's *Testament of Youth: An Autobiographical Study of the Years 1900–1925,* or the radical works of Emma Goldman, who, as early as 1917, explored some of the wider social reasons for prostitution in her essays, *The Traffic in Women and Other Essays on Feminism.* It can be said that tourism research lagged behind in this respect. Indeed, it might be further argued that tourism researchers, with a few exceptions (see Mathieson and Wall, 1982), were behind their counterparts working in the area of 'recreation and leisure' as they, with a stream of works identified with writers like Winter (1982) and Melamed (1986), began writing almost two decades ago about constraints upon females' participation in leisure pursuits, women's perceptions of leisure and their female roles and other similar concerns. It is perhaps notable that in his work drawing on past articles of *Tourism Management,* Medlik (1991) makes no specific reference to gender issues. The irony thus existed of many studies into tourist behaviours, attitudes and perceptions being developed from what may be described as market research orientated studies wherein gender was being used as a discriminant variable, yet where the nature of women's experiences were not really discussed.

Among the studies that reflected a recent change in attitudes was the special issue of *Annals of Tourism Research,* edited by Margaret Swain, that appeared in 1995. In addition, a key book was that of Kinnaird and Hall (1994) followed by the work of Sinclair in 1997. Indeed Swain (1995: 248) described the former book as 'one of the first published collections on the topic of gender in tourism'. This is not to say, however, that tourism scholars had been blind to the basic issues of gender, if only because of the vexed question of sex tourism. In one of the first widely used textbooks about tourism, Mathieson and Wall (1982: 149) noted a sequence of contentions about tourism and prostitution and commented that 'detailed studies do not exist'. It is also to their credit that they recognised the impacts that tourism had on the role of women, and were able to cite various studies from the late 1970s (see Mathieson and Wall, 1982: 146). A significant work based on ethnography was that of Lever, who in 1987, reported on the changes in lifestyles experienced by young women from the Spanish hinterland who went to work at the tourist resort of Lloret de Mar.

Articles published in *Tourism Management* also reflected these concerns. Among those published in the last decade in *Tourism Management* have been work by Frew and Shaw (1999), Carr (1999), Small (1999), Jordan (1997), Kinnaird and Hall (1996), Ryan and Kinder (1996) and Lutz and Ryan (1993). These articles have examined a number of issues – from the experience of women working in the industry (Jordan, 1997), to the expectations of businesswomen as guests in hotels (Lutz and Ryan, 1993) to issues of how gender relates to personality and tourist experience (Frew and Shaw, 1999) among other topics.

However, just as the 1990s have seen an increased recognition of female experiences as being distinct and important, so too the traditional male hegemony has been challenged from other directions. If the 1990s have consolidated the subject of female studies within tourism research, it has also introduced the topic of gay and lesbian studies. Articles in *Tourism Management* have again been part of a wider trend. For example, Hughes (1997), Pritchard et al. (1998) and Clift and Forrest (1999) are recent contributors on this subject. As yet though, and this would be true of other tourism journals besides *Tourism Management*, there has thus far been little published research on the lesbian market or their tourist demands and experiences.

That these issues have come to the fore may be explained by a number of factors, but a specific one must surely be the economic implications of gender, especially with reference to the demand for travel experiences. As Lutz and Ryan (1993) pointed out, the emergence of service industries and the growing female managerial class within those industries, has meant that females now account for about 50 percent of all business travel in the USA, and a growing and significant proportion in other western countries. Similarly, as Ryan (1999) points out, the growing economic importance of the gay sectors of society, as evidenced by the success of Sydney's Mardi Gras and San Francisco's Gay Games, has led to more visible consumption by both 'gays' (and 'straights') of gay locations. But the studies listed above have also indicated that gender is an issue of not only the demand for tourism but also of the nature of its impacts. Tourism has both created new economic opportunities for some women in some locations, while in others it has confirmed the status quo where males continue to enjoy most of the economic benefits of tourism. While tourism has been thought to generate new opportunities for female workers in the developing world, as Smith (1994) has shown, the truth is far more complex. In some instances tourism has negatively impacted upon family care, created new responsibilities for women and yet not brought the desired economic benefits. And if any topic brings together gender, sex, social and economic impacts, it is the vexed question of sex tourism, as is explored by Bishop and Robinson (1998), Manderson and Jolly (1997), Oppermann (1998) and Ryan and Hall (2000).

What, in outline, has been learnt from these studies? First, the distinction between sex and gender, whereby the former refers to biology and the latter to social conditioning has become well established. In creating this distinction the issue of what established a 'gay' or 'lesbian' identity has become that much easier in perhaps two ways. First, there is a wider acceptance of the genetic basis of homosexuality, even if the 'gay' or 'lesbian' gene has not been conclusively identified. Secondly, a wider social tolerance of more diverse social gender roles has slowly gained ground, although such gains may still be fragile. In that sense tourism has a significant social role to play. As the industry accedes to demand for gay locations and legitimises those demands by absorbing them into the mainstream of touristic activity, partly by a process of commodification by which 'straight' people come to view gay bars as another 'authentic experience', so tourism enables the gay community to play a larger role in society through acceptance of them being but another social group. Such processes are not without tensions. Thus, for example, Baptist churches in the southern United States of America have sought to ban their members from visiting Disney World because of the resort's willingness to develop 'gay products'. Thirdly, it poses issues for the gay community as it implies the danger of de-gaying those places and activities which helped generate a sense of identity among gay people.

Fourthly, the studies show that in spite of gains made by women in the years since the commencement of 'modern feminism' in the 1960s, there remain differences in employment opportunities between men and women. This is part of a wider social issue, but tourism has its own problems in part due to the use of glamour in its marketing images. Adkins (1992) has pointed out that such images, based on females, can contribute to stereotyping, while Richter (1994: 155) has argued that the very globalisation of the tourism industry 'may deprive further those with the least influence and political access', among which number she includes women in many parts of the world. Such issues cut across not only the divide of the First and Developing Worlds, but across social divides in advanced societies and within industries as women seek parity with males in management roles. Gender issues are thus not simply about distinctive patterns of demand for tourism, recreation and leisure but they are also about the social and political frameworks within which we all live our lives.

Fifthly, the studies on gender continue to show that sex retains a special function and sensitivity within touristic lives. While sex tourism remains 'big business' the illegal status of many who work within the sex industry and the ambiguity of laws which often render the generally male client immune from prosecution continue to exemplify the social and political tensions which writers like Richter (1994) and others describe. To these issues of sociology and political studies can be added the psychological and medical dimensions. There are the issues of how women rationalise and come to terms with their participation in an industry that at best is often merely tolerated by wider society. Such tolerance is often physically marked by geographically defined 'red light zones' that occupy ambiguous locations. They may be, as in Amsterdam, specific tourist attractions in their own right. They may be associated with criminal activities, although neither client nor working woman wishes for any intrusion from other criminal activities which may attract the police – indeed, the criminality associated with prostitution may be solely one of legal definition because the acts of commercial sex do not often intrude upon other members of society. Where such intrusion is felt due to lower property values, or the harassment of non-prostitute women by males, it may be argued such problems arise because of inability of the interested parties to properly regulate their business in their own way.

Added to these legal, political, psychological and social factors is the spectre of sexually transmitted diseases. Although few such studies have been reported in the main tourism journals, such work is published in either journals like the *Journal of Travel Medicine* or books like those edited by Clift and Page (1996), Clift and Grabowski (1997) and Carter and Clift (Ryan, 1999). Although AIDS and HIV have dominated headlines, especially with reference to the incidence of such diseases in countries like Thailand, other diseases like syphilis, genital herpes, and chlamidyia continue to adversely affect the quality of peoples' lives.

Sex tourism also presents a problem for a simplistic feminist analysis, whereby it is presented primarily as a further example of male hegemonies that reinforce the subordinate position of women in our society. As a number of tourism studies show, women may be equally predatory in the sense of seeking out sexual adventure. Wickens (1994, 1997), Yamba (1988) and Ryan and Hall (2000) are among those who provide examples of such behaviours in the settings of Greece, the Gambia and the Caribbean. Truly the beaches are liminal areas sociologically as well as geographically. This presents difficulties for some commentators, as evidenced by O'Connell-Davidson (1998: 181) who noted that 'heterosexual female sex tourism is, in numerical terms, a far, far smaller phenomenon than male sex tourism' and therefore, she argued, it is not really worth considering. Yet there exists evidence that it is a growing phenomenon (e.g. Wickens, 1994, 1997; Albuquerque, 1998, 1999). The issue of sex tourism is not simply one of which gender exploits or is exploited in terms of the sexual act, but of much wider socio-economic factors which generate inequalities in wealth, power and employment opportunities. For some commentators like Richter (1994) and Bishop and Robinson (1998) the inequalities are embedded and condoned by a global economic system which seeks to protect the interests of 'haves' against 'have nots'. Certainly that system and its expression at a local level inhibits the expression of sexual freedom and identity that some feminist writers like Bell (1994) and Kruhse Mount-Burton (1996) would advocate. Yet of course, tourism permits opportunities for significant amounts of non-commercial sexual activity with other than a usual partner, which somehow has generally escaped the same sort of socio-political analysis that has accompanied commercial sexual arrangements (Clift and Grabowski, 1997; Ryan, 1999; Ryan and Hall, 2000). Yet such activities cannot also but help speak volumes about sexual needs and social *mores*.

Gender and sexual issues have thus increasingly played an important role in the debate about tourism and its wider social significance. Sex and tourism, or even gender and tourism, as terms, no longer simply mean descriptive work about the brothels of Patpong or even the role of farmers' wives who earn a little extra 'pin money'. Rather, in the research that is currently taking place, the voices of women, gay men, male and female patrons of the sex industry, and the whispers of lesbians, are being added to the Babel that constitutes tourism research. It is but a further example of the maturation of the subject of tourism that increasingly this topic and its various facets of women's roles in the developing world, their employment in the First World, the ability of women to participate in leisure and the thorny issues of commercial sex are attracting researchers who tend to specialise in these areas, or at least, are prepared to allocate some part of their research effort to these issues.

Among the contributions to *Tourism Management* over the last decade, three such examples have been selected. These are

Jordan, F. (1997). An occupational hazard? Sex segregation in tourism employment, *Tourism Management*, December, 18(8): 525–34.

Hughes, H. (1997). Holidays and homosexual identity, *Tourism Management*, February, 18(1): 3–7.

Ryan, C. and Kinder, R. (1996). Sex, tourism and sex tourism: fulfilling similar needs? *Tourism Management*, November, 17(7): 507–18.

These papers have been selected as generally discussing a number of the issues previously described. Jordan's work is derived from a study of the opinions of managers and female employees within the travel agency industry in the United Kingdom. In this article she describes how female employees, in spite of their superior number within the industry, still view the industry as being dominated by males. Stereotyping of the nurturance role associated with being female was institutionalised by comments like '...women are natural carers' (Jordan, 1997: 530). However, Jordan's analysis goes beyond this confirmation of what is already known. She begins to consider the strategies of resistance by women and how open to them such avenues of change are. She notes how opportunities are closed by the low level of importance attached to training. Thus, she takes these issues beyond the normal debate about skill levels and client satisfaction into a wider issue of the roles of women in employment in what is one of the main 'gatekeeper' functions in the chain of distribution.

The second article, by Hughes, while relatively short, addresses some very specific issues about the nature of the relationship between tourism and gay identity. Among the points made are first, the comparative lack of gay venues means that gays often have to travel to find a supportive milieu within which to express their identity. Secondly, such locations represent, yet again, the 'pull/push' dichotomy that has underlain much of tourism analysis for the last 40 or more years. Thirdly, like other aspects of sex tourism, anonymity is important to many gays – a reflection of the marginality occupied by the expression of overt sexuality that exists in our society. Fourthly, the short duration of the gay man's encounters at the location to which he has travelled is also reflective of much that characterises tourism. Fifthly, Hughes considers the contribution that consuming a gay holiday implies to self-conceptualisation.

Finally, the longer article by Ryan and Kinder draws upon a series of telephone interviews with clients of New Zealand prostitutes. The questions ranged over a number of topics, including the reasons why they patronised sex workers while travelling. The research was also informed by a number of interviews with sex workers, and this article represents one in a series of research reports (the others being Ryan and Kinder, 1995; Ryan et al., 1998; Ryan, 1999; and Ryan and Hall, 2000). In the article reproduced here, Ryan and Kinder examine the concept of deviance as it applies to sex tourism, and conclude that it is found wanting. Rather, they argue, many of the motives for visiting sex workers are closely paralleled by the motivations for holiday taking itself. Both activities are motivated by a desire for relaxation, by fantasy and enactment of those fantasies, by a desire for change, by social needs, by a sense of adventure and similar reasons. They also argue that both the act of patronage of a sex worker and of going on holiday are actually examples of liminal activities – the latter socially condoned, while the former is at best merely tolerated and is often condemned. As such, the article represents an attempt to place sex tourism within a wider social context and, by reference, to a wider set of theoretical concepts than have generally been true of the tourism literature prior to that date.

Taken as a whole these three examples cover many of the issues associated with gender, sex and tourism. It may be noted that all three have adopted a qualitative research approach – a fact which reflects a need to construct a series of different and sometimes conflicting truths or texts. Finally, it must be admitted that these three articles, general as they are, do not cover the whole gamut of research in this expanding field. As initially mentioned, there is a rich quantitative literature on the importance of gender as a determinant in purchasing holidays, and in actual tourist behaviours. Some of this is related to life-stage (e.g. Lawson, 1991; Bojanic, 1992). The above discussion and the selected articles have not located the subject within specific ontologies, although it is implied that they exist primarily within critical reality and constructionist approaches. This perhaps is in contrast to much of the literature that emanates from, specifically, North American researchers as is illustrated by Bolla et al. (1991), Shaw (1991) or Brown et al. (1991) who, in a special issue of the *Journal of Applied Recreation Research* on female issues, use quantitative measures of women's leisure experiences, body images and well-being.

Consequently it can be concluded that gender, sex and tourism represents a further example of the complexities of tourism in a social setting. Yes, tourism research is about people on holiday, or travelling for business purposes. But we are all members of social groups, absorbing norms and value systems, and hence our holiday behaviours continue to confirm, challenge or cloud in ambiguity not only our own identities but the identities of others with whom we come in contact, and the power relationships that are exercised in those interactions. The literature on gender, sex and tourism reflects this process, as do the three selected articles presented here.

References

Adkins, L. (1992). Sexual work and the employment of women in the service industries, in M. Savage and A. Witz (eds), *Gender and Bureaucracy*. Oxford: Blackwell Publishers and The Sociological Review.

Albuquerque, de, K. (1998). Sex, beach boys and female tourists in the Caribbean, *Sexuality and Culture*, 2: 87–11.

Albuquerque, de, K. (1999). In search of the big bamboo: Female sex tourists in the Caribbean, *Transitions*, 77: 48–57.

Bell, S. (1994). *Reading, Writing and Rewriting the Prostitute Body*. Bloomington and Indianapolis: Indiana University Press.

Bishop, R. and Robinson, L.S. (1998). *Night Market: Sexual Cultures and the Thai Economic Miracle*. London: Routledge.

Bojanic, D. (1992). A look at a modernised family life cycle and overseas travel, *Journal of Travel and Tourism Marketing*, 1(1): 61–80.

Bolla, P., Dawson, D. and Harrington, M. (1991). The leisure experience of women in Ontario, *Journal of Applied Recreation Research*, 16(4): 322–48.

Brittain, V. (1994). *Testament of Youth: An Autobiographical Study of the Years 1900–1925*. Harmondsworth: Penguin Twentieth-Century Classics (reprint).

Brown, B.A., Frankel, B.G. and Fennell, M. (1991). Happiness through leisure: The impact of type of leisure activity, age, gender and leisure satisfaction on psychological well-being, *Journal of Applied Recreation Research*, 16(4): 368–92.

Carr, N. (1999). A study of gender differences: young tourist behaviour in a UK coastal resort, *Tourism Management* 20(2): 223–8.

Clift, S. and Forrest, S. (1999). Gay men and tourism: destinations and holiday motivations, *Tourism Management*, 20(5): 615–27.

Clift, S. and Grabowski, P. (eds) (1997). *Tourism and Health: Risks, Research and Responses*. London: Pinter.

Clift, S. and Page, S. (eds) (1996). *Health and the International Tourist*. London: Routledge.

Frew, E. and Shaw, R. (1999). The relationship between personality, gender, and tourism behaviour, *Tourism Management*, 20(2): 193–202.

Goldman, E. (1970). *The Traffic in Women and Other Essays on Feminism*. Ojai, California: Times Change Press. p. 1917.

Hughes, H. (1997). Holidays and homosexual identity, *Tourism Management*, 18(1): 3–7.

Jordan, F. (1997). An occupational hazard? Sex segregation in tourism employment, *Tourism Management*, 18(8): 524–34.

Kinnaird V. and Hall, D. (1994). *Tourism: A Gender Analysis*. Chichester: Wiley.

Kinnaird V. and Hall, D. (1996). Understanding tourism processes: a gender-aware framework, *Tourism Management*, 17(2): 95–102.

Kruhse Mount-Burton, S. (1996). The contemporary client of prostitution in Darwin, Australia. Unpublished PhD thesis, Griffith University, Nathan, Queensland.

Lawson, R. (1991). Patterns of tourist expenditure and types of vacation across the family life cycle, *Journal of Travel Research*, Spring, 29(4): 12–18.

Lever, A. (1987). Spanish tourism migrants: The case of Lloret de Mar, *Annals of Tourism Research*, 14(4): 449–70.

Lutz, J. and Ryan, C. (1993). Hotels and the businesswoman: an analysis of businesswomen's perceptions of hotel services, *Tourism Management*, 14(5): 349–56.

Manderson, L. and Jolly, M. (1997). *Sites of Desire Economies of Pleasure: Sexualities in Asia and the Pacific*. Chicago: University of Chicago Press.

Mathieson, A. and Wall, G. (1982). *Tourism: Economic, Physical and Social Impacts*. Harlow: Longmans.

Medlik, S. (ed.) (1991). *Managing Tourism*. Oxford: Butterworth-Heinemann.

Melamed, L. (1986). The experience of play in women's development, *Recreation Research Review*, 13(1): 7–13.

O'Connell-Davidson, J. (1998). *Prostitution, Power and Freedom*. London: Polity Press.

Oppermann, M. (ed.) (1999). *Sex Tourism and Prostitution: Aspects of Leisure, Recreation and Work*. New York: Cognizant Communication Corporation.

Pritchard, A., Morgan, N.J., Sedgeley, D. and Jenkins, A. (1998). Reaching out to the gay tourist: opportunities and threats in an emerging market, *Tourism Management*, 19(3): 273–82.

Richter, L. (1994). Exploring the political role of gender in tourism research, in W.F. Theobald (ed.), *Global Tourism: The Next Decade*. Oxford: Butterworth-Heinemann. pp. 146–58.

Ryan, C. (1999). Sex tourism: paradigms of confusion, in S. Clift and S. Carter (eds), *Tourism and Sex: Culture, Commerce and Coercion*. London: Pinter. pp. 15–26.

Ryan, C. and Hall, C.M. (2000). *Sex Tourism: Margins and Liminalities*. London: Routledge.

Ryan, C. and Kinder, R. (1995). The deviant tourist and the crimogenic place in A. Pizam and Y. Mansfeld (eds), *Tourism Crime and International Security Issues*. Chichester: Wiley. pp. 23–36.

Ryan, C. and Kinder, R. (1996). Sex, tourism and sex tourism: fulfilling similar needs? *Tourism Management*, 17(7): 507–18.

Ryan, C., Murphy, H. and Kinder, R. (1998). The New Zealand sex industry and tourist demand: illuminating liminalities, *Pacific Tourism Review*, 1(4): 313–28.

Shaw, S.M. (1991). Body image among adolescent women: the role of sports and physically active leisure, *Journal of Applied Recreation Research*, 16(4): 349–67.

Sinclair, M.T. (ed.) (1997). *Gender, Work and Tourism*. London: Routledge.

Small, J. (1999). Memory-work: a method for researching women's tourist experiences, *Tourism Management*, 20(1): 25–36.

Smith, V. (1994). Privatization in the Third World: small-scale tourism enterprises, in W.F. Theobald (ed.), *Global Tourism: The Next Decade*. Oxford: Butterworth-Heinemann. pp. 163–73.

Swain, M.B. (ed.) (1995). Gender in tourism – special issue, *Annals of Tourism Research*, 22(2): 247–489.

Wickens, E. (1994). Consumption of the authentic: the hedonistic tourist in Greece, in A.V. Seaton, C.L. Jenkins, R.C. Wood, P.U.C. Dieke, M.M. Bennett, L.R. MacLellan and R. Smith (eds), *Tourism: The State of the Art*. Chichester: Wiley. pp. 818–25.

Wickens, E. (1997). Licensed for thrill: risk taking and tourism, in S. Clift and P. Grabowski (eds), *Tourism and Health: Risks, Research and Responses*. London: Pinter. pp. 151–64.

Winter, W. (1982). The double whammy: physical activity and the older woman, *Recreation Research Review*, 9(4): 40–7.

Yamba, B. (1988). Swedish women and the Gambia, Conference on the Anthropology of Tourism, edited by Tom Selwyn, Froebel College, London.

6

An occupational hazard? Sex segregation in tourism employment

Fiona Jordan

Cheltenham and Gloucester College of Higher Education, Department of Leisure Management, Francis Close Hall, Swindon Road, Cheltenham GL50 4AZ, UK

The poor image of tourism employment, especially with reference to the position of women, is often justified in relation to the nature of the industry itself. Tourism is claimed to function through the supply of often intangible benefits such as hospitality and by catering to human feeling.[1] It has been argued by some in the tourism industry, that its dependence upon human resources[1-3] necessitates the creation of jobs which are part-time, low-paid and generally unskilled.[4,5] That these jobs are primarily carried out by women[6,7] is often viewed as a coincidence, or as supplying supplementary work to enhance the family income. This culture of gendered employment is promoted by tourism organizations through the manipulation of the image of women and their appropriate work roles. Thus, as Castelberg-Koulma[8] suggests, female labour provides an 'essential prop' for the tourism industry.

Policy-making within tourism organizations has significant implications for the role of women, and for the interaction of the tourism industry with its customers. As Richter[3] states:

The power of tourism to capture our imagination and shape our sense of our own identity and that of others means that the control of tourism is important.

In addition to existing legal requirements,[9,10] labour market changes, associated with demographic shifts, are providing increased impetus for tourism companies in the UK to develop equal opportunities strategies.[11] Enhancing equality of opportunity in the workplace can also play a part in reducing recruitment costs and the low morale often associated with high labour turnover.[12-14]

This article presents data from an exploratory, qualitative study of the opinions and perceptions of policy-makers and female employees within a small sample of tourism organizations. It examines factors which contribute to the segregation of tourism employment by sex, and the role of equal opportunities policies in resisting segregationary practices. The characteristics of tourism work cannot be considered in isolation from external influences, such as the role of women in the workforce, and the nature of the industry itself. Thus these issues are also addressed within the article.

Whilst research examining the role of female managers has been carried out in the related fields of leisure services,[15–17] and hospitality management,[13,18,19] tourism employment has not yet been the subject of widespread academic analysis.[20] More specifically, previous research has largely neglected issues of sex discrimination,[14] and of the effectiveness of equal opportunities policies in redressing the imbalance of employment conditions.[11] As some estimates suggest that the travel and tourism industry accounts for about 7% of global employment, making it the world's largest employer,[21] this is a worrying omission.[3] Over the past three decades the range of tourism products and services has steadily increased,[22,23] with expenditure on tourism by UK residents rising by almost 50% between 1990 and 1994.[24] Given this expansion it is felt that the role of women's employment in tourism constitutes a significant issue for future research. It is hoped that the findings of this initial project will provide the basis for further study.

The problems of definition

It is necessary, initially to construct appropriate definitions for both 'tourism' and 'tourism employment'. Discussion of the characteristics of tourism employment is problematic, given the complexity of what may be defined as 'tourism' and the organizations which support it. Kinnaird et al.[6] differentiate between those definitions arising from attempts to quantify tourism-related activities and the movement of people,[25] and those which define tourism as a social phenomenon.[26] The latter definitions, arising from sociological and anthropological studies, focus upon the social relations involved in the provision of, and participation in, tourism. As the characteristics of female employment in tourism are largely determined by social and cultural factors[8,10,27] these definitions have more direct relevance to this study. Lanfont[28] provides a useful definition of tourism which takes account of these issues:

... it is a combination of services (accommodation, catering, transport), culture, particular geographical features, which provide different activity spaces, and other intangibles such as hospitality.

This view of tourism emphasizes the breadth and complexity of tourism, and allows for the inclusion of social characteristics, such as gender and race.

The problems inherent in identifying 'tourism' as a concept are reflected in attempts to define 'tourism employment'. If the measurement of tourism as a tangible product is difficult, then identification of exactly what constitutes tourism employment is bound to be problematic.[22] Employment within tourism varies considerably, encompassing everything from direct employment in travel agencies, tour operators, food service and accommodation, to indirect employment in souvenir production and retail. There is concern that some previous studies have attempted to cover too many diverse issues, thereby suffering from an 'homogenizing tendency',[29] or that they have focused on employment within the hotel and catering sectors, and suffered from 'hospitality-bias'.[30] For the purposes of this study, the empirical research primarily concerns employment in organizations directly related to tourism, such as tour operators and travel agencies.

The position of women in the workforce

Prior to consideration of the specific characteristics of women's employment in tourism, it is useful to examine general working conditions for women. Studies[31,32] suggest that employment across a wide spectrum of industries is segregated by sex. Stockdale,[33] defines such segregation as:

> The jobs that women do are different from those done by men (horizontal segregation) and women work at lower levels than men in the occupational hierarchy (vertical segregation).

Thus women workers predominate in 'female' occupations, such as secretarial, administrative and catering work, and the 'caring' professions, such as teaching and nursing, but are still under-represented in the management structures of these sectors.[10,32,34] Previous research,[9,35] has shown that sex segregation has tended to locate women in areas regarded as less skilled and therefore less valuable to the economy. This has created a corresponding imbalance of financial reward. Reskin and Padavic,[9] suggest that occupational segregation does not have to be actively encouraged, but can be reproduced simply through 'organizational inertia'. Collinson et al.[14] state that such job segregation is 'reproduced, rationalized and resisted' within organizations, forming what they describe as the 'vicious circles of job segregation' (see Figure 1). This model identifies various means by which sex segregation is perpetuated within organizations.

Collinson et al.[14] claim that, where necessary, firms justify retention of current management profiles and recruitment practices in a variety of ways. This rationalization of existing employment structures, and the corresponding division of labour, generally takes the form of blaming individuals, society and/or the nature of the business. One example of this type of justification is the generalization by some employers that the disproportionately high concentration of women in low-paid, part-time jobs, is primarily attributable to women's preference for these patterns of employment. Women, it is argued, seek these jobs in order to accommodate their domestic/family commitments. Previous research,[5,13] has questioned the validity of such assertions but nevertheless such rationalization of work patterns still exists.

Collinson et al.[14] also argue that the way in which recruitment procedures (internal and external) are managed, has significant implications for the reproduction of existing organizational structures. They consider that managerial and patriarchal control strategies, along with informal recruitment practices, are key factors in this process. Their conclusion is that an open, objective and documented system of internal recruitment is necessary to prevent the passive reproduction of current management structures. The 'vicious circles of sex segregation' also incorporates the notion of resistance of segregationary practices, both inside and outside organizations. Research findings[14] suggest that the most successful forms of resistance are those operated by collectives, such as trade unions. It is argued that resistance by individuals is seldom effective

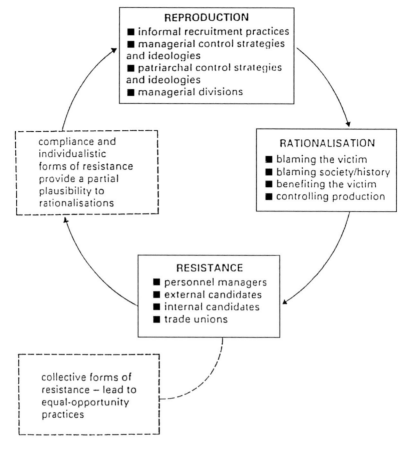

Figure 1. The vicious circles of job segregation.

and can, in fact, provide a 'partial plausibility' to the rationalizations put forward by employers.

One area of contention in academic circles is the extent to which progress has been made in equalizing conditions of employment. Rosen[36] and Bacon and Lewis[37] put forward a very positive view of women's achievements in the workplace and advancement in the field of management. This view is not commonly held amongst those who have studied working conditions for women. On the contrary, a survey of women on the boards of the top 200 companies in Britain[38] revealed that women represent only 4% of all directorship appointments. Kay[39] points to the fact that the major increase in women's participation in the workforce has been their enhanced contribution in the sphere of part-time employment. This, she says, has implications for the status of women's work, which is often lower than that of their male counterparts.

There is evidence[34] that, although more women are participating in paid employment, they are concentrated in lower-paid, less skilled and repetitive jobs with fewer employment-related benefits. These characteristics of female employment are not confined to Britain, but have been identified as an international problem.[10] A 1995 survey by the Central Statistical Office[40] shows that whilst the proportion of women who are economically active has risen by 9% over the past 25 years, they are still under-represented in policy and decision-making positions. The response of many ambitious women has been to establish their own businesses rather than pursuing management careers within companies.[13,41]

Characteristics of employment for women in tourism

Whilst the complexity and heterogeneity of tourism employment makes generalization problematic, previous studies[27,42,43] suggest that women have only limited access to well-paid, skilled and managerial positions. Despite the fact that women form the majority of the workforce in most sectors of tourism, their employment is gendered in nature.[2,6] Richter[44] likens tourism employment to a pyramid, with many women located in seasonal and part-time jobs at the lower end, but few reaching the management positions at the top. Research focusing on the hospitality sector has highlighted the specific problems experienced by women in this area, where only 4% of middle/senior managers, and only 1% of top management, are female.[45] It has been suggested that relatively low levels of union membership[1,2,13] and a 'lack of organization amongst women workers'[46] has inhibited progress towards equality of opportunity.

The poor position of women in tourism employment has been exacerbated by international focus on tourism development as 'a panacea for many different types of local economies'.[25] This 'quick fix' view of tourism development has been criticized for concentrating on the creation o f a large quantity of jobs, whilst overlooking the nature and conditions of the employment generated.[6,29] Leontidou[47] suggests that traditional gender distinctions have promoted the image of men as travellers and women as hostesses. This social construction has enabled national governments and tourist organizations to portray women in a service role. Richter[3] and Enloe[2] state that the overall control of power and decision-making by men has a direct bearing on the exploitation of women in the tourism workplace.

There is evidence to suggest that women's employment in tourism is both horizontally and vertically segregated, with the majority of female workers located in subordinate posts, receiving lower levels of remuneration.[3] The tourism industry also segregates women into areas of employment which commercialize their perceived domestic skills and 'feminine' characteristics.[2,6,42] As Kinnaird and Hall[46] comment:

... the greatest degree of segregation is found amongst the semi-skilled, domestic and servicing-type occupations, many mirroring functions carried out in the home. Women thus tend to remain segregated in occupations which are predominantly female.

They cite Walby in suggesting that an understanding of the origins and maintenance of occupational segregation by sex is an important factor in explaining women's subordinate position in the workforce.

The study

The findings discussed are the result of a small-scale, exploratory project carried out in 1996, during the last full year of the UK's new right Conservative government. This research project undertook a provisional investigation of the underlying issues of women's employment in tourism organizations. The objective was to provide descriptive and experiential data, rather than quantitative analysis of the current situation. The intention of the study was to examine factors contributing to sex segregation of employment in participating tourism organizations, and to determine what role, if any, equal opportunities policies might have in providing resistance to segregationary practices. It is hoped that the results will provide the basis for further work in this area.

A series of in-depth interviews were conducted with policy-makers from nine tourism organizations. These respondents held senior management posts such as Chief Executive, Managing Director, Head of Training and Development and Group Personnel Manager. The participating companies included travel agencies, tour operators, an airline and a national hotel chain. Small samples of women working in various roles, such as Travel Consultant, Section Supervisor and Operations Manager, within three of these companies were also interviewed. The three organizations from which both policy-makers and employees were interviewed included two tour operators and one travel agency. Two of these companies were based in the South East and one in the North West of England. All three companies had a predominantly female workforce, with the number of employees varying from 35 to 180. The management structure of two of the organizations was male-dominated, whilst the third had an even split of male and female managers. All information provided for the study is being treated as confidential, and thus the participating companies are not named here.

Given the sensitivity of the subject matter being explored, it was felt that face-to-face discussions would yield more valid information than questionnaires or telephone conversations. The interviews provided data to explore the conditions of work for women, and test the effectiveness of policies adopted by the organizations studied. Whilst the women involved in the study all volunteered to participate, respondents were, in some cases, selected by managers, thus potentially affecting the representativeness of the sample. Of those interviewed, the majority were female, white, middle class and aged between 20 and 40 years old. This may appear to be an unrepresentative sample. However, observation of the workforce in the organizations studied leads the researcher to believe that this mirrors the general characteristics of female employees. The focus of this particular study is the gendered nature of tourism employment. Thus, whilst the age bias of the workforce is discussed as a contributory factor in job segregation, matters of race and class have not been addressed here. It is suggested that further studies could usefully examine these important issues.

The qualitative data were interrogated do determine which particular features of tourism employment were most significant in influencing the horizontal and vertical segregation of female employees in participating companies. The role of equal opportunities policies in resisting the continuance of segregation in the workplace was then investigated. The model of the 'vicious circles of job segregation'[14] was adapted to provide a theoretical framework for the analysis of the data collected. The intention was to test the application of the concepts put forward by Collinson et al.[14] within the specific context of these tourism organizations.

Discussion of results

The findings of the study will be discussed in three main sections. Firstly, the degree to which the culture of tourism organizations internalizes, institutionalizes, and, in doing so, rationalizes, sex segregated employment is examined. This is followed by consideration of the internal recruitment and promotion systems in the tourism companies, and their potential contribution to the reproduction of existing, segregated, workplace structures. Finally, the role of formalized equal opportunities policies, as a method of resisting further segregation, will be analysed.

The culture of tourism

The culture of individual organizations can legitimate sexism informally, providing barriers to female progression, and preventing change. Thus, it has significant influence over the extent to which organizations remain horizontally and vertically segregated. The management profiles of the majority of the tourism organizations studied in this research were male-dominated. Women tended to be located in 'traditional' female areas such as personnel, retail and marketing, whilst being under-represented in departments such as financial services, and in planning and development roles. The participating companies displayed some similarities in their approach to rationalizing current management structures. These justifications tended to relate to the nature of the tourism industry and to the specific needs of individual businesses, legitimizing a culture of recruitment oriented primarily to attracting young, female employees.

A number of respondents suggested that the predominance of young, female employees in tourism employment was inextricably linked to image creation and promotion of tourism services. Tourism is an industry dependent on the creation of fantasy through imagery, its advertisers being described as 'dream packagers'[48] and 'purveyors of escape'.[49] This is reflected in the commodification of perceived female characteristics in areas of tourism literature and advertising. Adkins[42] and Richter[44] warn that this can contribute to stereotyping and the formation of potentially damaging power relations. Respondents commented that age and sex were important factors governing work in tourism. As one female manager stated:

The travel industry is very age conscious. You only have to look at stewardesses to see it. It's purely the image that attracts young girls.

The tourism industry was considered to be oriented towards recruiting young, female workers in order to perpetuate is glamorous image. Likewise, the perceived glamour of tourism work was thought to be a key factor in attracting women into the workforce.

As one travel consultant put it:

Women are attracted to this industry because of all the different things to do, and the glamour of travel. They want the fringe benefits like cheap flights.

Another commented:

Maybe men just don't think of being a travel agent.

Generally, tourism was seen as being a 'female-friendly' industry which was more attractive to women than to men because of the nature of the work involved. This view of tourism employment as positively alluring provides employers with a useful explanation for the number of women working in poorly paid jobs within the industry. Their justification is that women are happy to accept the poor conditions because the work is glamorous. This questionable rationalization of the position of women, therefore relates to the unique nature of tourism work. Previous studies undertaken in the hospitality industry have, however, been critical of this 'myth of uniqueness' being used as an excuse for poor conditions of employment.[13,18]

A number of respondents suggested that the high level of female employment was indicative of an industry in which there is equality of opportunity. This view does not, however, take account of the nature of much of the work undertaken by women, or their status in the workforce. Many of the female employees interviewed perceived tourism to be an industry which is still male-dominated at senior management levels, despite the number of women employed. They did not generally agree that a climate of equal opportunities already existed.

The constantly busy environment of tourism firms was put forward as an excuse for a lack of formal training programmes in most of the organizations studied. Given the administrative nature of much of the work required, most training was 'on-the-job' and skills-oriented. When employees were undergoing training, they were not carrying out their usual tasks, and business was interrupted. Often, therefore, training was viewed as a distraction or an inconvenience. Thus, in many cases, only practical, task-related, skills development was considered, by employers, to be worthwhile. Just one of the companies studied operated a professional staff development programme targeting individual training needs. In partnership with local educational institutions, this company offers all staff the opportunity to gain nationally recognized qualifications, such as National Vocational Qualifications. The company views investment in staff training as ultimately beneficial in terms of both staff and customer retention. The development of individual employee skills profiles is thus justified in commercial terms. Unfortunately, this attitude was not representative of most of the organizations studied.

The horizontal segregation of women into areas of employment which reflect their 'feminine' characteristics was primarily explained by reference to the specific requirements of tourism businesses. A typical comment from one travel agency employer was:

Women are better in service industry jobs because they have more patience. Because women are natural carers, people on the other end of the 'phone react better to them than they would to a man.

Another manager stated:

Customers prefer to deal with females, because they find it easier to talk to them. Women are more relaxed – they don't get as stressed as men.

There was evidence that women tended to be recruited into jobs which commercially utilized their perceived inherent domestic skills and/or femininity. Employers felt that this was justifiable on the basis of enhanced income generation. Some tourism organizations appear to use the nature of tourism as an industry as an excuse to locate women in certain prescribed work roles. With reference to the 'vicious circles of job segregation',[14] the most common rationalizations for the maintenance of current organization structures relate to the specific features of tourism and the needs of individual businesses within that industry.

Promotion systems within tourism organizations

This section discusses the promotions systems of the organizations studied to assess the contribution of these structural factors in reproducing the current management profile. The internal promotions procedures of participating tourism organizations were examined to determine the extent to which they influence the position of female employees. The majority of the companies studied operated informal internal recruitment systems, which they claimed embodied the principles of meritocracy. There was seldom open advertisement of internal vacancies for supervisor or line management positions. Promotion decisions were generally made by middle and senior managers, based on recommendations by line managers.

Only one of the companies had any written criteria governing procedures for upgrading staff. In most cases, those selected for promotion were approached directly by line managers and asked to perform the job, rather than being interviewed. Criteria for advancement tended to relate to a person's character and ability to perform their current role effectively. One Managing Director stated that decisions were based on '*a proven track record*' and another General Manager claimed that staff needed to demonstrate a good '*all round performance*'. This type of informal, unregulated system has been identified as potentially contributing to the perpetuation of job segregation.[14] Whilst policy-makers generally felt that the present system was adequate, a number of difficulties were identified.

Some female respondents claimed that the assessment of an individual's abilities, by those in more senior positions, could be adversely influenced by factors such as personality conflicts and preconceived notions of female characteristics. The implication was that the procedure contained elements of subjectivity which tended to result in bias. As one female manager put it:

It (tourism) is still a male-dominated industry. It isn't women who stop; it is still men who assess potential, and that's why women don't get as far as they could.

Some female employees doubted the effectiveness of the internal recruitment process. As one female supervisor said:

Promotion can be more a matter of luck and tenacity – i.e. long service.

The lack of formalized policies governing promotion decisions, combined with very limited company investment in individual training, appeared to undermine the confidence of some female employees. They considered that their opportunities to progress into management roles were limited by this system. A number of women were reluctant to apply for managerial positions for which they believed themselves to be underqualified. As one female supervisor put it:

Some of the others don't have the confidence to apply for supervisor's posts because they haven't had the training and all the managers are men.

These findings echo those of previous studies carried out in other industries.[50,51] The erosion of female confidence can lead to dearth of applications from women, forcing tourism firms to recruit experienced managers externally. This, then, provides a further rationalization on the part of organizations to justify the continuing male dominance of tourism management. As one company director stated:

All appointments are made by the Board of Directors based on merit and experience. Men generally have more experience and are better placed to get promotion.

This type of system serves to perpetuate the 'vicious circles of job segregation'.[14] Without formal selection procedures, there is little company control over the extent to which gendered organizational structures are being reinforced. The lack of specific targets and monitoring arrangements allows the existing management profile to be reproduced through 'organizational inertia'.[9]

Equal opportunities policies as a means of resistance

This section explores the role of formalized equal opportunities policies in resisting the continuance of such employment segregation. Collinson et al.[14] have identified various forms of resistance to discriminatory and segregationary practices. They discovered that resistance by individuals, both internal and external to the organization, tends to be limited in its effectiveness. Thus, in relatively non-unionized working environments, such as tourism,[1,2,13,46] there is unlikely to be significant active opposition on the part of workers. This researcher was interested in exploring the role of the equal opportunities policy in providing support to individual employees seeking to resist segregationary practices.

Whilst it is acknowledged that creation of policy is not in itself sufficient to generate a climate of equality of opportunity, it can be regarded as a useful tool. Whether or not an organization adopts an equal opportunities policy has implications for organizational culture. The Employment Department's '*Ten Point Plan for Employers*'[12] describes an equal opportunities policy as:

... the first essential step in implementing an equal opportunities programme. A policy is not an end in itself, but provides a framework for action and initiatives. (EDG PL922)

Such policies can be used to raise awareness within organizations, helping to stimulate cultural change. There is, however, the potential danger that policy documents which do not deliver their message effectively will undermine the efforts of well-intentioned employers. In addition, companies may falsely raise the expectations of employees by introducing policies, but then failing to implement them.[52]

Four of the participating tourism companies had not devised equal opportunities policies. Policy-makers in these firms believed that their companies already embodied the principles of equality and therefore no further measures were required. As one female Managing Director stated:

We have a very female organization culture, so we don't need a written equal opportunities policy.

Generally, these companies displayed what might be described as a 'typically' male-dominated management structure. One organization did contain an even number of male and female managers. However, whereas the male managers headed up departments with a number of staff reporting in to them, female managers ran less prestigious departments. In addition, female managers tended to be horizontally segregated into 'traditional' female areas such as marketing, reservations and sales. This indicates that company cultures may not be as supportive of women's progression as the policy-makers believe them to be.

Some female employees disputed the assertion by policy-makers that written policies were unnecessary. As one female manager said:

The informal, no policy, system only works if you are a valued member of staff.

Where women working within organizations perceived there to be a male-dominated management profile (offering little chance of female career development) this was reflected in a corresponding lack of employee commitment. These women commented that they viewed their companies merely as a stepping stone or a short-term career move as they offered no visible route for progression. Such attitudes are, understandably, damaging to the morale of women within the organizations. In addition, when such discontent is expressed in high staff turnover, extra expense is incurred by the firms concerned.

Equal opportunities policy documents were collected from the remaining tourism organizations. The size, scale and scope of these varied widely. The policies considered most useful were those concisely stated on one or two pages. These were circulated to all staff members using a variety of communication media, such as external recruitment information, induction material and staff handbooks. Such policies made specific reference to the extent of management commitment to equal opportunities. They detailed forms of behaviour and practice which would be considered inappropriate in the workplace. In addition, the related grievance and disciplinary procedures were outlined. These policies indicate to potential and existing employees that the company is endeavoring to create an internal culture of equality of opportunity.

The attitudes of women working in companies which had implemented equal opportunities programmes were (not surprisingly) more positive than those discussed previously. A manager in one company described how the policy impacted on female employees:

This is an excellent company to work for. Your sex doesn't matter at all. The equal opportunities policy is a good way of determining whether or not people have any prejudices; because if they do this organization is not for them.

Another female worker referred to the '*climate of trust*' created within the company. This particular organization demonstrates its dedication to equality of opportunity by undertaking individual staff development plans linked to training programmes. Female employees praised this system, and expressed their loyalty to the company, which, they felt, provided a highly supportive working environment. The organization appears to have successfully combined formalized policy with its existing culture, to embed equal opportunities for both sexes in its structures and processes. This strategy is likely to be mutually beneficial to both the business and the workforce in the longer term. Women within the company generally have enhanced confidence in their abilities to perform a variety of work roles, for which they are fully trained. They are thus better equipped to make the transition into management positions in different areas of the company.

One national tour operator underpins its formal equal opportunities policy by targeting crêche facilities towards its more senior female managers. This controversial policy has been criticized internally for providing extra support to those who are in the best position to afford private childcare. However, the company believes that by organizing its childcare in this way, it is sending a positive message to women wishing to progress into management roles. The organization is also targeting external recruitment campaigns at mature women wishing to return to the workforce. The company considers that this not only increases equality of opportunity but makes sound business sense. Demographic statistics indicate that more holidays are likely to be purchased by those in the older age groups. This company believes that by hiring mature staff, it will be able to develop a workforce which has increased empathy with its future customers.

The results of this study suggest that formalized policy has a role to play in ensuring that women are provided with both practical and cultural support within tourism organizations. This can contribute to the creation of a climate of confidence in which women are more likely to seek managerial posts. The equal opportunities policy, backed up by use of targets and monitoring, is one tool which can be used by individuals and companies to resist the perpetuation of job segregation. There is evidence that formalization of policy, underpinned by a commitment to training, can exert a positive influence over organizational culture. The perceived supportiveness of this culture is a significant factor in determining the level of female employees' commitment to the organization.

Conclusions

The results of this exploratory study suggest that the majority of the tourism organizations studied do reproduce and rationalize job segregation, and that there is only limited resistance to the perpetuation of the 'vicious circles of job segregation'.[14] The horizontal segregation of women in these tourism organizations is rationalized in relation to the unique nature of the industry and its specific work requirements. Employers believe that the exploitation of perceived feminine characteristics and domestic skills is justified by commercial needs. The glamorous image of tourism work is considered to be particularly attractive to women, possibly compensating for relatively poor remuneration and limited opportunities. One Head of Personnel provided a further, realistic, explanation of the segregation of female employees into lower level tourism jobs:

Tourism is a very low margin business and the major cost is payroll. Women are more likely to accept the low pay and conditions than men.

The equity of this situation remains generally unquestioned by employers, whose main concern is income generation. Such attitudes assist in maintaining the existing male-dominated management structure of tourism organizations studied. Whilst such rationalizations are accepted, rather than challenged, there is little incentive for the tourism organizations to alter their existing practices.

Few of the companies studied have devised any formal procedures or criteria governing promotion. The lack of structured processes allows elements of subjectivity to influence promotion decisions. When combined with the cultural factors used by tourism businesses to rationalize preservation of the status quo, this tends to disadvantage female employees. Most of the organizations claimed to be operating a promotion system based on the principles of meritocracy. These assertions can surely only be validated if selection criteria are specified and then adhered to. Where decisions rely on subjective opinion, the dangers of furthering sex segregation of employment are significantly enhanced. In order to overcome these problems, decisions concerning advancement within companies should be made on the basis of objective criteria rather than on false notions of meritocracy. The tourism companies could consider the use of standardized procedures to regulate recruitment and progression. Such measures would enable promotion decisions to be made on a more impartial, gender-neutral basis. This would enhance equality of opportunity, thereby resisting, rather than reproducing, existing management structures.

In some tourism organizations, the lack of coherent and effective policies on equal opportunities, combined with informality of internal recruitment processes, has created a culture of promotion based on patronage. Given the male bias which already exists, opportunities for female seeking promotion are significantly reduced. This results in continued horizontal and vertical segregation – a perpetuation of the 'vicious circles of job segregation'.[14] In the majority of the companies studied there was little evidence of resistance to the continuance of occupational segregation.

Female employees within firms which had implemented equal opportunities policies did, however, comment on the positive influence exerted on organizational culture. The expression of company commitment to equality of opportunity, underpinned by appropriate training initiatives, engenders greater confidence in women wishing to progress into management roles. Whilst it is naive to suggest that such documents are themselves evidence that a supportive climate definitely exists, policy statements can provide written reassurance for female employees. Given the extent to which employment for women in many tourism organizations is horizontally and vertically segregated, policy itself is unlikely to be sufficient to accomplish the level of change required. However, it can be viewed as one valuable weapon with which to combat continuing occupational segregation.

Recent studies have stressed the importance of developing our understanding of gender relations in the context of tourism.[43,44,46] The findings of this research indicate that the culture of tourism itself is considered to be a contributory factor in maintaining existing gendered patterns of employment. Ramsay and Parker[53] point out that wholesale cultural change is unlikely to occur in any industry. This is especially true of an industry as heterogenous as tourism. They suggest that what is required is publicity concerning successful initiatives within one or two companies being utilized as a means of stimulating others to follow suit. A number of the tourism organizations studied have implemented policies aimed at enhancing equality of opportunity.

Unfortunately the dissemination of information on such successful schemes is hampered by the 'fractionated' nature of the UK tourism industry.[54] The fragmented structure of the industry also limits the possibility of organizations adopting a coherent approach to improving the working environment for women. Baum[20] states that, for this reason, human resources need to be regarded as a central issue of national tourism policies. Whilst this may be the case, individual organizations should also take responsibility for generating internal cultural changes.

For tourism organizations, enhancing equality of opportunity may assist in reducing recruitment and training costs associated with high labour turnover[13,14] and can boost the confidence and morale of employees.[12] In an industry where around 80% of purchasing decisions are made by women[24] the extent of female input into strategic policy decisions also has significant implications for the interaction of organizations with their customers. By designing and implementing equal opportunities policies, organizations can provide their workers with a useful means of resisting job segregation. Whilst policies may not be a total solution to the problem of occupational segregation in tourism, their importance should not be overlooked. Without some form of active resistance, organizations can passively continue to segregate women, denying them the opportunity to participate fully in tourism management.

Acknowledgements

I would like to thank Cara Aitchison and Celia Brackenridge for their help and support throughout the research project. Thanks also to Derek Hall, Frances Brown, Vivian Kinnaird and two anonymous referees for their valuable comments on earlier versions of this article.

References

1. Burns, P. M., Sustaining tourism employment. *Journal of Sustainable Tourism* 1993, **1**, (2), 81–96.
2. Enloe, C., *Bananas, Beaches, and Bases: Making Feminist Sense of International Politics*, Pandora, London, 1989.
3. Richter, L. K., Gender and race: neglected variables in tourism research. In *Change in Tourism: People, Places, Processes*, ed. R. Butler and D. Pearce. Routledge, London, 1995.
4. Hudson, R. and Townsend, A., Tourism employment and policy choices for local government. In *Perspectives on Tourism Policy*, ed. P. Johnson and B. Thomas, Mansell, London, 1992.
5. Bagguley, P., Gender and labour flexibility in hotel and catering, *Service Industries Journal* 1990, **10**, (4), 737–747.
6. Kinnaird, V., Kothari, U. and Hall, D., Tourism: gender perspectives. In *Tourism: A Gender Analysis*, ed. V. Kinnaird and D. Hall, Wiley, New York, 1994.
7. Murphy, P. E., *Tourism: A Community Approach*, Routledge, London, 1985.
8. Castelberg-Koulma, M., Greek women and tourism: women's co-operatives as an alternative form of organization. In *Working Women: International Perspectives on Labour and Gender Ideology*, ed. N. Redclift and M. T. Sinclair. Routledge, London, 1991.
9. Reskin, B. F. and Padavic, I., *Women and Men at Work*. Pine Forge Press, Oxford, 1994.
10. Coyle, A., Continuity and change: women in paid work. In *Women and Work: Positive Action for Change*, ed. A. Coyle and J. Skinner. MacMillan Education, Basingstoke, 1988.

11. Aitkenhead, M. and Liff, S., The effectiveness of equal opportunity policies. In *Women at Work: Psychological and Organizational Perspectives*, ed. J. Firth-Cozens and M. A. West. Open University Press, Miltion Keynes, 1991.

12. Anon, *Equal Opportunities: Ten Point Plan for Employers*. Employment Department Group, PL 922. HMSO, London.

13. Wood, R. C., *Working in Hotels and Catering*. Routledge, London, 1992.

14. Collinson, D. L., Knights, D. and Collinson, M., *Managing to Discriminate*. Routledge, London, 1990.

15. White, J., Women in leisure service management. In *Relative Freedoms: Women and Leisure*, ed. E. Wimbush and M. Talbot. Open University Press, Milton Keynes, 1988.

16. Henderson, K. and Bialeschki, M. D., The feminization of the leisure services profession: possible explanations and implications. *Journal of Parks and Recreation Administration* 1990, **8**, (3), 1–11.

17. Frisby, W., Women in leisure service management: alternative definitions of career success. *Society and Leisure* 1992, **15**, (1), 155–173.

18. Hicks, L., Excluded women: how can this happen in the hotel world? *The Service Industries Journal* 1990, **10**, (2), 348–363.

19. Diaz, P. E. and Umbreit, W. T., Women leaders – a new beginning. *Hospitality Research Journal* 1995, 18(3) and 19(1), (double issue), 49–60.

20. Baum, T., National tourism policies: implementing the human resources dimension. *Tourism Management* 1994, **15**, (4), 259–266.

21. Theobold, W. F., The context, meaning and scope of tourism. In *Global Tourism: The Next Decade*, ed. W. Theobold. Butterworth Heinemann, Oxford, 1994.

22. Johnson, P. and Thomas, B., Tourism research and policy: an overview. In *Perspectives on Tourism Policy*, ed. P. Johnson and B. Thomas. Mansell, London, 1992.

23. Hawkins, D. E., Global assessment of tourism policy. In *Tourism Research: Critiques and Challenges*, ed. D. Pearce and R. Butler. Routledge, London, 1993.

24. Anon, *UK Travel and Tourism: 1996 Market Review*. Key Note Report, 5th ed. 1996. Key note, Middlesex, UK.

25. Williams, A. M. and Shaw, G., Tourism: candyfloss industry or job generator? *Town Planning Review* 1988, **59**, (1), 81–101.

26. Urry, J., The sociology of tourism. In *Progress in Tourism, Recreation and Hospitality Management*, Vol. 3, ed. C. Cooper. Belhaven Press, London, 1991.

27. Ireland, M., Gender and class relations in tourism employment. *Annals of Tourism Research* 1993, **20**, 666–684.

28. Lanfont, M. F., Tourism in the process of internationalisation. *International Social Science Journal* 1980, **32**, 14–43.

29. Bull, P. and Church, A., The hotel and catering industry of Great Britain during the 1980s: sub regional employment change, specialisation and dominance. In *Progress In Tourism, Recreation and Hospitality Management*, Vol. 5, ed. C. P. Cooper and A. Lockwood. Belhaven Press, London, 1994.

30. Baum, T., Human resource issues in tourism: an introduction. In *Human Resource Issues in International Tourism*, ed. T. Baum. Butterworth Heinemann, Oxford, 1993.

31. Sinclair, M. T., Women, work and skill: economic theories and feminist perspectives. In *Working Women: International Perspectives on Labour and Gender Ideology*, ed. N. Redclift and M. T. Sinclair. Routledge, London, 1991.

32. Witz, A. and Savage, M., The gender of organizations. In *Gender and Bureaucracy*, ed. M. Savage and A. Witz. Blackwell Publishers/The Sociological Review, Oxford, 1992.

33. Stockdale, J. E., Sexual harassment at work. In *Women at Work: Psychological and Organizational Perspectives*, ed. J. Firth-Cozens and M. A. West. Open University Press, Milton Keynes, 1991.

34. Little, J., *Gender, Planning and the Policy Process*. Pergamon, Oxford, 1994.

35. Imray, L. and Middleton, A., Public and private: marking the boundaries. In *The Public and the Private*, ed. E. Gamarnikov, D. H. J. Morgan, J. Purvis and D. Taylorson. Heinemann, London, 1983.

36. Rosen, B. C., *Women, Work and Achievement: The Endless Revolution*. MacMillan Press, Basingstoke, 1989.

37. Bacon, W. and Lewis, R., Strategies for professional development and training in leisure management: an analysis of the views of the female members of ILAM. In *Ideology, Leisure Policy and Practice*, ed.

A. Tomlinson and D. Botterill. Leisure Studies Association Conference Papers, LSA Publications, University of Brighton, Eastbourne 1991, pp. 85–94.

38. Holton, V., Women on the boards of Britain's top 200 companies. *Women in Management Review* 1995, **10**, (3), 16–21.

39. Kay, T., Women, work and leisure futures: the leisure implications of changing female employment patterns. Conference paper given at the *World Leisure and Recreation Association 4th International Congress*, Cardiff, July 1996.

40. Church, J. and Summerfield, C., *Social Focus on Women*. Central Statistical Office report, 1995. HMSO, London, 1995.

41. Moody, A., Women on Top. *Supermarketing*, 22nd March 1996, 18–20.

42. Adkins, L., Sexual work and the employment of women in the service industries. In *Gender and Bureaucracy*, ed. M. Savage and A. Witz. Blackwell Publishers/The Sociological Review, Oxford, 1992.

43. Aitchison, C., Gendered Tourist Spaces and Places: The Masculinisation and Militarisation of Scotland's Heritage. Conference paper given at the *LSA/VVS International Conference*, Wageningen September, 1996.

44. Richter, L. K., Exploring the political role of gender in tourism research. *Global Tourism: The Next Decade*, ed. W. Theobold. Butterworth Heinemann, Oxford, 1994.

45. Jones, M., Failure to promote women: a serious loss. In *Caterer and Hotelkeeper*, 1992, 9 January, 12.

46. Kinnaird, V. and Hall, D., Understanding tourism processes: a gender-aware framework. *Tourism Management* 1996, **17**, (2), 95–102.

47. Leontidou, L., Gender dimensions of tourism sub-cultures and restructuring. In *Tourism: A Gender Analysis*, ed. V. Kinnaird and D. Hall. Wiley, New York, 1994.

48. Reimer, G. D., Packaging dreams: Canadian tour operators at work. *Annals of Tourism Research*, 1990, **17**, 501–512.

49. Uzzell, D., An alternative structuralist approach to the psychology of tourism marketing. *Annals of Tourism Research* 1984, **11**, 79–99.

50. Skinner, J., Who's changing whom? Women, management and work organisation. In *Women and Work: Positive Action for Change*, ed. A. Coyle and J. Skinner. MacMillan Education, Basingstoke, 1988.

51. Alban-Metcalfe, B. and West, M. A., Women Managers. In *Women at Work: Psychological and Organizational Perspectives*, ed. J. Firth-Cozens and M. A. West. Open University Press, Milton Keynes, 1991.

52. Gilling, J., Room at the top. *Leisure Opportunities*,1995, March, 40.

53. Ramsay, K. and Parker, M., Gender, bureaucracy and organizational culture. In *Gender and Bureaucracy*, ed. M. Savage and A. Witz. Blackwell Publishers/The Sociological Review, Oxford, 1992.

54. Plog, S. C., Leisure travel: an extraordinary industry facing superordinary problems. In *Global Tourism: The Next Decade*, ed. W. Theobold. Butterworth Heinemann, Oxford, 1994.

7

Holidays and homosexual identity

Howard Hughes

Department of Hotel Catering and Tourism Management, The Manchester Metropolitan University, Old Hall Lane, Manchester M14 5HR, UK

There has been a recent interest in gender perspectives on tourism[1] but the perspective of 'sexuality' remains unexplored. A similar development is evident in the study of geography where 'the recognition of the importance of gender in informing the use and experience of urban space' has not been matched by 'adding sexuality to the equation'.[2] Sexuality – hetero, homo and bi – is considered, however, to be an important focus for future research in geography;[3] sexuality is deemed to influence the 'social character of space'[2] and that space may itself influence sexual identities. Given the evident spatial dimension of tourism, a sexuality perspective to its analysis may be of particular significance. It has, however, been recognized by geographers who have initiated sexuality-focused studies that there are particular difficulties in researching sexuality, especially homo and bi. These are areas of human behaviour about which there is a certain 'sensitivity'.[4] There are also practical difficulties in obtaining data about activities which are often marginalized; there is, therefore, a necessary reliance on anecdotal evidence, informal 'interviews' and participant observation.

It is intended that this paper should contribute to sexuality studies of tourism. The discussion is confined to homosexual men, also referred to as 'gay' men.

Given that there are holidays aimed at the senior citizen market, at families, young singles, culture-seekers of all ages and life-stages, the physically adventurous, etc., then it is hardly surprising that there are holidays aimed specifically at the gay men's market. There are a number of UK tour operators offering overseas holidays exclusively to gay men, e.g. Uranian, In Touch, Sensations, Man Around. There are hotels in the UK that advertize themselves as 'gay' venues and there are destinations, both in the UK and overseas, that are identified as (though not necessarily exclusively) gay resorts. There is a concentration on a number of particular destinations such as Amsterdam, Sitges, Ibiza (Town), Mykonos and Gran Canaria. Further afield, popular destinations include San Francisco, New York, Miami (South Beach),

Australia (especially Sydney) and Thailand. In the UK the most favoured gay centres include London, Manchester, Brighton and Blackpool.

Gay travel guides are published: Spartacus, Best, Gai Pied, Ferrari for Men. In such guides, the gay press and in tour operators' brochures there are overtones of opportunity for casual sexual encounter on holiday. The sex–holiday association is more direct than in equivalent heterosexual publications. This association is, however, inconsequential for this paper, because it is argued here that the significance of holidays for gay men lies in their contribution to the process of establishing 'identity'.

Sexual identity

The homosexual

Identity is a very fluid concept and is subject to continual change. There is a view that identity, for many, is created and affirmed by the act of consumption.[5] Leisure activity, in particular, is considered to play an important role in the construction of individual identity.[6] It is the symbolic meanings and signs of the product, rather than the product or service itself, that are consumed. According to the meanings attached to products, a consumer constructs and demonstrates a particular identity. This assumes a shared sense of the symbolism; for it to convey meaning, symbolism must be recognized by others.

The identity that an individual might seek to establish will have a sexual/gender dimension though there are many additional strands to identity such as race, class and nationality. For gays, in particular, sexuality may be a paramount dimension of identity-formation.[7] Sexual identity itself may not be a biological issue but more a social construction located in particular historical contexts. It has been argued that 'before the nineteenth century homosexuality existed but "the homosexual" did not'.[8] The categorisation of 'the homosexual' is associated with the process of industrialisation and strengthening of the capitalist system. One interpretation is that the capitalist system fostered both 'the family' and its stability as a means of ensuring a supply of labour and an ordered workforce.[9] Any other lifestyle such as homosexuality was seen as threatening and labelled 'aberrant'. It was important to have criteria for identifying the aberrant individual and this encouraged interest in 'scientific' bases for classification. There was an undoubted move to identify and condemn 'the homosexual' in the nineteenth century.

The process of industrialisation transformed family life and the division of labour within the family. Male and female roles became more sharply distinguished. Prior to this, certain forms of sexual activity may have been proscribed but the nineteenth century saw medico-scientific attempts to give credence to a definite heterosexual–homosexual distinction and the identification of 'the homosexual' as a distinctive sort of person. Homosexuality became a source of identity rather than a sexual act and the homosexual 'identity' was created. A homosexual identity is a choice though it may have some other, perhaps, biological basis.

The choice of a homosexual identity may be a particularly painful one given society's reaction to the homosexual. The certain and inexorable knowledge of sexuality is set against the equally certain knowledge of social (and often legal) censure. Unable to express their sexuality openly, gay men often have had to meet furtively. They have also generally experienced a legal and social climate which is not supportive of long-term same-sex relationships.

Nonetheless the choice or acceptance of a homosexual identity is seen by many as quite fundamental[10] though for others, other (non-sexual) criteria will be more important in identity. Acceptance of that identity may well imply a particular way of life including wearing distinguishing clothes and following certain leisure activities and patronising gay bars, clubs and similar facilities. Being gay may now be increasingly regarded as following a particular lifestyle rather than solely having a particular sexuality.[11] This is probably no more than the wider societal preoccupation with constructing identity through consumption and leisure noted earlier. The growing power of the 'pink pound' may be a liberating force in its own right that will ensure recognition from 'straight' society; for the gay consumer, however, spending may be an expression of freedom which is illusory[12] and which distracts from more fundamental restrictions.

A sexual identity is partly an individual construct but it has to be 'validated' by others, both homosexual and heterosexual. The individual may recognize his difference from the 'norm' but there may be several stages involving contact with others before full acceptance of the identity of 'homosexual'.[8] The existence of a 'gay space' – a 'physical manifestation of gay community'[13] usually as a spatially discrete concentration of pubs and clubs but also cafés, shops, residences and public space – permits gay identity to be validated by relationships with others; it offers havens for gay self-expression[12] (though it may have the effect of reinforcing difference[14]). (Some gay spaces, e.g., Manchester, may have become so 'open' that the identity-giving role may be threatened.[15]) Many 'openly' gay men may choose not to frequent gay space and may confirm their identity in other ways. Not all homosexuals will choose a 'gay life style' and some will opt for a 'hetero life style'.

The gay space (essentially a leisure arena) has, however, become representative of the gay community and may offer the most significant opportunity for confirming gay identity (and possibly contributing to its increased 'masculinisation'[16]). This gay identity is a lifestyle that a gay buys into and only gays with the appropriate purchasing power can buy into it. Arguably, it reflects a particular middle class (and young) lifestyle.[14]

Gay space and tourism

The potential support to individual gays that exists within the gay space is more likely in larger urban areas. Gay pubs, clubs and other facilities in any one town exist in rough proportion to the total population but 'it is clear that there are remarkably few gay venues in total . . . ; most gays have to travel a long way to reach a gay venue'.[13] The lack of gay venues in non-urban areas may be compounded by rather less liberal attitudes towards homosexuality.[17]

There is therefore a degree of congruence between homosexual identity and 'tourism'. The acceptance of a homosexual identity is often dependent upon the act of being 'a tourist', at least in the limited sense of travel, if not stay. Even in large urban areas such as London and Manchester it is often necessary to seek out and travel some distance to gay venues. This is the 'pull' factor. The 'Gay Village' of Manchester acts as a magnet for gay men (and, to a lesser extent, women) not only from Greater Manchester but also from all over the UK.

Regardless of the 'pull' factor of limited concentrations of gay facilities, there are associated 'push' factors. There is the push of the exclusion from 'normal' society and the consequent need for the reassurance of the open and secure company of other gay men; opportunities for this are limited (the 'pull'). The gay man is, in large part, able to be himself only in the gay space,[7] which may be primarily a leisure environment. This is an environment that is limited and 'artificial' but is often the only one where the gay man can be himself. (In a related way, it is argued that the 'occupation' of space, though in the form of residences, may be a necessary condition for the expression of sexual identity.[18]) The heterosexual man has more opportunity to be himself in work, at home and in leisure. A similar point has been made in respect of lesbians living in the parental home: 'many women . . . use time/space strategies to separate the performance of their lesbian identity from the performance of their identity as a daughter'.[19]

In addition many gays will choose to travel in search of an anonymous or safe environment in which to be gay. Gays from Manchester may forego frequenting local gay space because of the fear of discovery and choose to 'be gay' elsewhere; some who do frequent local gay space may choose to travel for encounters they wish to conceal from others.

Given that the fulfillment or achievement of gay identity often involves travel and is thus, in practice, a variation of tourism, it may also be argued that the search for gay identity is itself conceptually a form of tourism. A man may live and work in what is basically a heterosexual society and visit 'the resort' of gay society in his leisure time. (A similar point has been made with respect to bisexuals.[20]) Holidays are to do with change of location and behaviour and escape, and identity is affirmed by the act of consumption, by behaviour before, during and after the holiday. It is often the occasion for 'abnormal' behaviour; guest/host encounters and guest/guest relationships are short-term and different from personal interactions at home and activities are unlike at home. The experience of the gay man entering the gay space is analogous to this. Paradoxically the gay man needs to be a tourist in order to be at home! He needs to be in the 'resort' in order to be himself.

Sexual identity and holidays

Holidays

Gay men may go on gay holidays as well as seeking gay space at home. Holidays are associated with 'change' if only of location. A holiday is a form of non-work activity with particular temporal and spatial dimensions; it takes place away from home and over a prolonged period of time. What occurs during that time could well be similar to non-work activity when not on holiday. In some cases tourists may see the holiday as an opportunity to extend their 'home' activities such as visiting pubs and clubs, playing sports, visiting the theatre, etc. Others will seek the opportunity to do something completely different, if only beach activity and acquiring a tan. A holiday is a 'non-instrumental' trip associated with pleasure.[21] The absence from home would seem to give opportunities for satisfactions to be achieved which are *additional* to those achieved from leisure time spent at or close to home.

There is a growing interest generally in determining why people go on holiday at all.[22] A holiday is more than an opportunity for physical recuperation, though that may be the case for some. The needs satisfied by going on holiday are many and varied and any one tourist is likely to be motivated by a complex set of needs. Tourists themselves are not always aware of or are unable to articulate what motivates them. 'Most attempts to explain tourist motivation take a content theory approach to the problem and, despite its limitations, many show marked similarities to Maslow's need hierarchy'.[23] Studies have interpreted tourist motivation in terms such as social interaction, regeneration, self-realisation, freedom, ego-enhancement, evaluation of self, prestige and escape. The holiday gives a considerable opportunity to 'escape into a world of fantasy . . . and indulge in kinds of behaviour generally frowned on at home'.[30] There is every reason to believe that these factors can be applied with equal validity to gays going on holiday but 'motivations behind travel are constructed out of the social realities of the lives of those who participate . . . . This implies that these motives are gendered'.[24] Equally, motives are sexualized. These aspects of holiday motivation are unexplored and there may well be motives that are specific to gay men.

Gay men and gay holidays

Some of the reasons why gay men seek gay holidays are fairly obvious; given that a holiday has become part of the 'good life' it is a form of consumption that most of the population at large aspires to. The consumption of a holiday is one aspect of the process of forming and consolidating identity which applies to all, regardless of sexuality. Holiday products as seen in tour operators' brochures for instance, are, however, very much a reflection of heterosexual society (especially couples and families) and as such will be alienating to many gay men.

On a more positive note the very process of consuming a gay holiday is a statement about 'self' and a confirmation of identity. Further it provides extra opportunity to validate identity by living and playing, over a continuous period of time, in a gay milieu. Such environs are, by definition, more sympathetic to gay lifestyles and the more liberal atmosphere is one wherein the holidaymaker is able to be gay without fear of stigmatisation, harassment or arrest. For the gay man the holiday provides an extended temporal opportunity to be gay. Gay men, on holiday, may feel more comfortable in the company of other gay men and the holiday may be the only opportunity to express sexuality openly. This may be an extension of 'domestic' behaviour or, more significantly for some, may be behaviour which does not occur at home. For some the holiday may provide the only possibility of openly being gay and acting differently from when at home. Holidays provide opportunities for all to behave 'out of character' and to do this away from those who may disapprove.

Given that much gay activity is forced to be covert the holiday is an ideal way of ensuring that covertness.

It does also include the prospect of casual and anonymous sex which is an extra opportunity for some gay men and a new opportunity for others.

Gays are not, though, welcome in all places. There are some countries where any form of homosexual activity remains a criminal offence and, even where legal, gays may be subject to harassment. It has been reported, for instance, that police in Bavaria had been stamping the word 'homosexual' on the passports of foreigners found in gay bars.[25]

Gay holidays do not appeal to all gay men, anymore than does frequenting gay space. It can be very claustrophobic and insular. The inherent attraction of a holiday – 'change' – may lead some gays to deliberately seek non-gay holidays. Also the range of gay holidays is limited; those who seek more than sea and sun may need to look to the 'mainstream' holiday market. In addition, as identity has validity only if recognized by 'outsiders' who share the same code of signifiers, restriction to gay space may be considered by some to be counter-productive.

Not all gays are necessarily able to take a holiday any more than all can occupy gay space when not on holiday. The single most important reason, amongst the population as a whole, for not having a holiday is limited income.[26] It is conventional wisdom that gay purchasing power is strong[27] and it is undoubtedly true that the financial burden of family life is not borne by most gays but gays are not homogeneous in terms of employment and income.[28]

Conclusions

Tourism and being gay are inextricably linked. Because of social disapproval of homosexuality many gay men are forced to find gay space (the 'push'); the ability to establish and confirm identity usually necessitates relationships with other gay men. Gay space is limited (the 'pull') and gays find it necessary to travel in order to enter that space. Others choose to travel away from local to other gay space because of a need to preserve anonymity (the 'push'). This travel may not be 'a holiday' but it is analogous to tourism in as much as it involves movement from usual surroundings over distances that are often greater than heterosexual men travel for their leisure purposes.

The holiday itself can provide for the gay man an opportunity to confirm his identity. For some gay men it may be the only opportunity and for others it may augment the opportunities at home. There is probably a large number of gay men for whom it is important to confirm that gay identity. Not all gay men are able to do this in their 'normal' lives, whether in work or at leisure. Given that society has discouraged openness about being gay the holiday provides the perfect chance to come out, if only temporarily. The gay identity can be adopted and confirmed 'in secret'.

Those who frequent the gay space at home may be expected to feel less need to have a gay holiday. Nonetheless many do have such holidays. For them it is a further statement about identity. Much of their leisure may occur in gay space and the holiday provides an extended chance to confirm identity. During the holiday the gay man can be gay all day and every day, a prospect which is unlikely at home. The gay man can be himself.

It is arguable, however, to what extent the gay identity itself risks becoming distorted under these circumstances. The gay man finds himself in the situation of being 'authentic' only in an 'artificial' situation. Authentic relationships with friends, partners and holiday acquaintances occur in a leisure, non-work, 'non-domestic' context; roles are assumed, holiday encounters are often short-term and relationships may be contrived. The gay man returns to a reality where his opportunities to be authentic are restricted. It may well be difficult for an identity to develop fully when it is deemed by society to be an aberration and when it can only be authenticated at limited times and in limited circumstances.

The holiday, nonetheless, is likely to make a very significant contribution to the creation and validation of identity for many gay men. The nature and dimension of this contribution remain to be examined further.

References

1. Richter, L., Exploring the political role of gender in tourism research. In *Global Tourism: The Next Decade*, ed. W. Theobald. Butterworth-Heinemann, Oxford, 1995; Kinnaird, V. and Hall, D. (eds), *Tourism: A Gender Analysis*. Wiley, Chichester, 1994; Gender in tourism. *Annals of Tourism Research*, 1995, **22**.
2. Bell, D., Insignificant others: lesbian and gay geographies. *Area*, 1991, **23**, 327.
3. Bell, D. and Valentine, G., Introduction: orientations. In *Mapping Desire: Geographies of Sexualities*, eds D. Bell and G. Valentine. Routledge, London, 1995, pp. 1–27.
4. Binnie, J., The twilight world of the sadomasochist. In *The Margins of the City: Gay Men's Urban Lives*, ed. S. Whittle. Arena, Aldershot, 1994, pp. 157–169.
5. Featherstone, M., Lifestyle and consumer culture. *Theory, Culture and Society*, 1987, **4**, 55–70.
6. Wearing, B. and Wearing, S., Identity and the commodification of leisure. *Leisure Studies*, 1992, **11**, 3–18.
7. Bell, D., Insignificant others: lesbian and gay geographies. *Area*, 1991, **23**, 323–329.
8. Weeks, J., The body and sexuality. In *Social and Cultural Forms of Modernity*, eds R. Bocock and K. Thompson. Polity Press in association with the Open University, Cambridge, 1992, pp. 219–266.
9. Halifax, N., *Gay Liberation and the Struggle for Socialism*. Socialist Workers Party, London, 1988.
10. Weeks, J., *Sexuality and its Discontents: Meaning, Myths and Modern Sexualities*. Routledge and Kegan Paul, London, 1985.
11. Edge, S., The Nineties so far. *Gay Times*, February 1996, 18–20, 22, 24.
12. Binnie, J., Trading places: consumption, sexuality and the production of queer space. In *Mapping Desire: Geographies of Sexualities*, eds D. Bell and G. Valentine. Routledge, London, 1995, pp. 182–199.
13. Hindle, P., Gay communities and gay space in the city. In *The Margins of the City: Gay Men's Urban Lives*, ed. S. Whittle. Arena, Aldershot, 1994, pp. 7–25.
14. Field, N., *Over the Rainbow: Money, Class and Homophobia*. Pluto Press, London, 1995.
15. Whittle, S., Consuming differences: the collaboration of the gay body with the cultural state. In *The Margins of the City: Gay Men's Urban Lives*, ed. S. Whittle. Arena, Aldershot, 1994, pp. 27–41.
16. Forrest, D., We're here, we're queer and we're not going shopping: changing gay male identities in contemporary Britain. In *Dislocating Masculinity*, eds A. Cornwall and N. Lindisfarne. Routledge, London, 1994, pp. 97–110.
17. Kramer, J., Bachelor farmers and spinsters: gay and lesbian identities and communities in rural North Dakota. In *Mapping Desire: Geographies of Sexualities*, eds D. Bell and G. Valentine. Routledge, London, 1995, pp. 200–213.

18. Castells, M. and Murphy, K., Cultural identity and urban structure: the spatial organisation of San Francisco's gay community. In *Urban Policy Under Capitalism*, eds N. Fainstein and S. Fainstein. Sage, London, 1982, pp. 237–259.

19. Johnston, L. and Valentine, G., Wherever I lay my girlfriend, that's my home. In *Mapping Desire: Geographies of Sexualities*, eds D. Bell and G. Valentine. Routledge, London, 1995, pp. 99–113.

20. Bell, D., Bisexuality: a place on the margins. In *The Margins of the City: Gay Men's Urban Lives*, ed. S. Whittle. Arena, Aldershot, 1994, pp. 129–141.

21. Cohen, E., Who is a tourist? A conceptual clarification. *Sociological Review*, 1974, **22**, 527–555.

22. Burns, P. and Holden, A. *Tourism: A New Perspective*. Prentice Hall, London, 1995.

23. Witt, C. and Wright, P., Tourist motivation: life after Maslow. In *Choice and Demand in Tourism*, eds P. Johnson and B. Thomas. Mansell, London, 1992, pp. 33–55.

24. Kinnaird, V., Kothari, U. and Hall, D. Tourism: gender perspectives. In *Tourism: A Gender Analysis*, eds V. Kinnaird and D. Hall. Wiley, Chichester, 1994, pp. 1–34.

25. *The Guardian*, 23 August 1995.

26. Hughes, H., Holidays and the economically disadvantaged. *Tourism Management*, 1991, **12**, 193–196.

27. Anonymous, The gaying of America. *Restaurant Business*, 1995, **20**, 42, 46, 51.

28. Northmore, D., Stretching it to the limit. *The Pink Paper*, 26 July 1996, p. 10.

8

Sex, tourism and sex tourism: fulfilling similar needs?

Chris Ryan and Rachel Kinder

Department of Management Systems, Massey University, Private Bag 11-222, Palmerston North, New Zealand

This paper briefly reviews two areas of literature. First, prostitution and tourist behaviour as found in the mainstream publications of tourism research. Second, the conceptual themes of marginality, deviance and liminality, which are then extended to a consideration of tourism and prostitution. After outlining some of the research upon which the paper is based, it examines the motivations of the clients of sex workers, and the motivations for tourism, and finds a commonality between these two sets of motives. From this perspective, it is argued that tourists who go to sex workers are not simply just tacking on an activity to their tour, but are engaging in a fulfilment of types of motivations which are consistent with needs met by other forms of tourism. To explain visits to sex workers simply in terms of a want for sex is contended to be too simple a view. The paper then considers the view of the prostitute, before trying to show that both tourism and prostitution are margins that express much about the nature of our society. The paper draws upon both a literature review and research undertaken in New Zealand based on telephone interviews with clients who visited sex workers while away from home, and face-to-face interviews with female sex workers.

The paper is thus about liminality, and in the subject of commercial sexual activity as a tourist behaviour many margins are involved. These are the margins between the world of being a tourist away from home, and the usual space of home and work; between the encounter of tourist and prostitute; between the prostitute and her non-work world and the way she is regarded; between the sexual encounter and other tourist activities; and between commercial and non-commercial sex. The encounter between sex worker and tourist is a nexus between such margins, possessing some commonalities but having its own functions too.

Sex tourism

Within the tourism literature there is a considerable amount of data relating to sex tourism. However, much relates to the countries of Southeast Asia, is often descriptive in nature and does not relate to other studies of deviancy or models of social interaction. For example, Hall,[1] in his book on Pacific Rim tourism, describes current changes of attitude towards sex tourism in Thailand but does not introduce any theoretical concepts. Where additional concepts have been introduced they have sometimes been of a controversial nature based on interpretation of evidence. For example, Thitsa[2] and Truong[3] both argue that Buddhism embodies strong misogynistic strands which degrade women, while Truong also maintains that prostitution was encouraged by small hotels as a means of competing with larger, new hotels. Indeed, within the tourism literature there are some interesting omissions when seeking data on the tourist as a client of prostitutes. For example, Law[4] and Page[5] in their respective books, both entitled *Urban Tourism*, are able to describe tourism within cities without a single reference to prostitution, even though, within the standard texts such as Mathieson and Wall[6] and Ryan[7], there are discussions about prostitution and its association with tourism, and in many cases prostitution is an urban phenomenon as evidenced by Amsterdam.[8,9]

   This is not to state that all work is descriptive in nature. Ryan and Kinder[10] apply models of 'intervening opportunity' to explain the circumstances that lead to tourist patronage of prostitutes, arguing that given the presence of a series of predispositions, both general and particular spatial patterns create opportunities for the visit to the prostitute to occur. Cohen[11-14] has published a number of studies which not only describe the relationships between *farangs* (foreigners) and Thai prostitutes, but which utilize an ethnomethodological perspective where the marginality of existence becomes illustrative of longings and needs. This marginality can be interpreted in a number of ways. The holiday is itself marginal in a temporal sense – it takes up but a small proportion of a working life. The relationship with a Thai woman is a feature of an entrapment by the perceived exotic – a formulation of something which, as revealed by the letters of the tourists, is missing from their daily lives. Urry comments, when writing of tourism, that:

... there are interesting parallels with the study of deviance. This involves the investigation of bizarre and idiosyncratic social practices which happened to be defined as deviant in some societies but not necessarily in others ... a similar analysis can be applied to tourism.[15]

Conceptualization of margins, liminality and deviance are well established in anthropology and sociology when applied to communities that exist on the margins of society. Although related concepts, and fuzzy in the boundaries of the concepts, they are simultaneously different and the same. Turner writes that:

The attributes of liminality or of liminal *personae* ('threshold people') are necessarily ambiguous, since the condition and these persons elude or slip through the network of classifications that normally locate states and positions in cultural space.[16]

Yet, within this space they offer a blend of 'lowliness and sacredness, of homogeneity and comradeship' ([16] p. 96), and by reason of their state of betwixt and between define states of culture and society. Thus, quite separately, Rojek[17] is able in his discussion of the development of late Victorian tourism to analyse the meaning of the vulgar seaside holiday in terms of carnivalization – a site of the profane which defined the norms of Victorian society.

Deviance, on the other hand, represents a structured rejection of those norms, albeit the structures may be defined by the norms of the dominant social classes. For example, Becker and Quinney[18,19] construct deviance as a revolt against current patterns of power. Marginality, on the other hand, as used by Ryan and Kinder[10] in their discussion of tourist–prostitute relationships, is a construct of the interaction, the interface between that which is the dominant set of norms, and that which is subordinate.

A common theme among such writers is the dialectic that exists between the norms, cultures and social processes at either end of the continuum. Turner ([16] p. 106) lists a series of binary oppositions or discriminations. Such dualities are also to be found in the literature of tourism and prostitution. In the debate about the motivation for recreational tourism dichotomies of 'push–pull', the search for the 'unfamiliar' and the security of the 'familiar', the risk-taker and the risk-averse are all concepts that have been discussed.[7] Feminists and other writers have noted the duality of women. Bell notes that:

Prostitutes were analyzed and categorized in relation to the bourgeois females ideals: the good wife and the virginal daughter. The prostitute might be the same, she might be different; often she was located on a continuum somewhere between sameness and difference, but she was always the disprivileged other in relation to the determinant site: wife, mother, daughter. The sameness/difference opposition provided the framework for derivative couples inside the category 'woman' good girl/bad girl, madonna/whore, normal/abnormal, licit/illicit, wife/prostitute, as well as the high and low images that have fragmented and categorised the female body.[23]

Hence, what exists in the literature is a common thread between apparently different spheres of concern. It is contended that this commonality of dialectics of the liminal people is what helps to explain the relationship between tourism and prostitution, and that the relationship is more complex than one of simply stating that some tourists 'use' the services of 'working girls'. Rather, it can be argued that both tourism as, at the very least, a behaviour that temporally is marginal, and prostitution as a social phenomenon pervading both tourist and non-tourist life, illustrate an unspoken consensus among what might be termed 'mainstream society'. Downes and Rock comment that:

It has been remarked that phenomenological sociology argues that society can be analysed only as a set of experiences, that experiences are experiences by consciousness, and that order is built on a vital framework of categorization . . . social order is a fragile human accomplishment achieved in the face of the meaningless.[24]

Holiday-taking is an important set of purchased experiences for people who construct their own meanings from situations that may offer the potential for catharsis. The 'Shirley Valentine' syndrome, where a holiday causes significant change in people's lives, is not born of fiction alone, but can be observed in the increased case load of marriage counselling services during and after main holiday periods. Combining the potential of holiday-taking for emotional experience with the action of patronizing sex workers generates an interesting case study of marginality or liminality. Its importance is illustrated by Downes and Rock's comments on deviancy when they note:

> Those who deny or defy important separations and definitions within society do more than merely break a rule. They may be thought to challenge the very legitimacy and structure of order, becoming agents or instances of chaos. ([24] p. 203)

By definition the structure of order is a determining site; the legitimate defines the illicit and illegitimate; it posits and produces the other. Hence the interest of postmodernist writers who seek to examine the absent and the excluded as part of the text that is to be deconstructed – the disprivileged or secondary concept carries traces of the legitimate. Both licit and illicit are conditional and dependent upon the other. Finally, it should be noted that in the following discussion, the terms 'marginal' and 'liminal' are used interchangeably unless otherwise stated, simply to avoid unnecessary repetition.

Holidaying as a marginal activity

It may seem strange to define holiday-taking as a marginal activity when, as is often noted, tourism is the world's largest industry. Hence care must be taken to understand the context with which the term 'marginality' is being used in the context of tourism. It may be noted that comments about the size of tourism are based on technical definitions which include many forms of non-leisure travel such as journeys for business purposes. Additionally, data often record numbers of visits rather than the number of visitors; this in part masks the numbers of repeat trips and multiple journeys being undertaken. Nonetheless, it cannot be seriously maintained that holiday-taking is a 'marginal' economic activity. The stance that it is a liminal activity can only be defended on the basis that, as noted, it represents a small proportion of an individual's total time, and possibly only a fraction of total leisure time if the position of a declining tourism–leisure ratio in advanced societies is maintained.[7]

There is, however, a second proposition to note, which is the phenomenological perspective. Within the patterns of daily working life individuals fit into roles that operate within scripted occasions. The conventions of the roles are widely understood, and it is this understanding which permits the easy fulfilment of functions. However, as Pearce[24] has noted, such occasions are difficult for individuals to recall clearly, and have little emotional impact. Indistinguishable days pass and the only subjective assessment of their importance might be a sense of loss in that no clear purpose to activities is discernible. Leisure is deemed to be important because it does indeed represent an opportunity for *recreation*, although even here commentators such as Podilchak[25] have noted the industrialization of leisure and the loss of fun, and others like Rojek[17] have contested the distinction between leisure and work. Therefore, holidays possess at least two paradoxical attributes in any claim to marginality. First, as noted, there is a temporal marginality, and second, the potential for a richness of experience makes them markedly different from non-holiday time. It is this potential for an enriching experience in short, limited and constrained time periods that makes holidays so different from other pursuits. A third component also exists, and that is the consumption of space. Holidays occur within specific geographical locations – some of which owe their rationale only to tourism. Cohen[11] refers to marginal paradises, and uses the imagery of the beach, a littoral strip, a geographical marginality, in an analysis of holiday lifestyles and their subsequent meaning. In short, a time–space compression occurs. Urry[15] identifies five effects of such a time–space compression: volatility and ephemeral nature of products, instantaneity and disposability, the encouragement of short-termism, the development of certain signs and images, and the production of simulacra.

Urry's proposition, however, denies that tourism is a special case of the liminal – rather it becomes simply one further case of the fragmentation of a previously modern, homogenous society. Urry's book, *The Tourist Gaze*, is devoted to the thesis that holiday-taking epitomizes a new analysis of contemporary life – an analysis often labelled as 'post-modernism'. Hence, tourism is but one more example of a process of commoditization occuring within a world of increased differentiation where consumers signal their game playing and matters of the moment through a purchase of items and symbols which evoke 'a particular set of relations between the signifier, the signified and the referent'([15] pp. 88–84). One possible implication of postmodernism is that the whole world consists of thresholds, and hence the thresholds between tourism and work, between tourist and prostitute, between prostitute and her non-working world are not unique by reason of being thresholds engaged in by the people who occupy space 'betwixt and between', because all occupy such spaces in a post-modern world.

Nonetheless, to argue that the world consists of thresholds does not deny that tourism is itself a revealing margin. Tourism is not simply a temporal constrained activity – it is a significant period when, as noted before, people feel able to do things they really want to do freed from the constraints of responsibilities to employers and social roles they normally occupy. This type of comment is itself revealing of how society is perceived; it is a social network of reciprocal responsibilities which while supportive of individuals also restrict life. The tourist becomes a temporary 'outsider', answerable to no one but him- or herself. The modern age accepted the need for this type of freedom, and then channelled it by permitting periods of leave from work, and in the postmodern age commercialized and packaged the holiday, and subjected it to industrial processes of air schedules and advanced booking. Yet, the reality of the holiday as an experience of difference continues, and it is this experience that is the liminal nature of tourism.

The nature and context of the research

In order to further explore the relationship between tourism and prostitution telephone interviews were undertaken with clients of female sex workers. This was done in New Zealand. The legal situation of prostitution in New Zealand is one that reflects the ambiguities and confusions that characterize the 'threshold people'. An appendix provides a fuller explanation of the law embodied in the 1978 Massage Parlours Act, but the effective position is one of licensing an illegal trade. Indeed, in some cities, sex workers have to register with the police before advertising in the press.

This apparent contradiction, which illustrates at the least a process of legal ambiguity, gives rise to a series of conventions within the industry. Managers and owners of massage parlours generally require payment from clients for a 'massage only', or for an opportunity to visit one of their hostesses. Anything else that happens is of no concern of theirs, but is simply a personal matter between the two other parties. Section 149 of the 1961 Crimes Act makes anyone who, 'for gain or reward, procures ... any women or girl to have sexual intercourse with any male who is not her husband' liable to imprisonment. Thus, sex workers do not directly ask for payment, but may engage in the use of well-known synonyms which are recognizable by both parties as to their meaning, but which are not explicit requests for money in return for sex. Practices thus skirt around the intent of the law – yet the law is ambiguous. On the one hand it threatens the prostitute and the provider of the venue, while on the other it provides for the recognition of the venue for purposes such as taking prostitution off the streets to avoid offence to others and possible harassment of local residents, as happens in other countries such as the United Kingdom.

The legislation is generally successful in this latter objective, with one or two exceptions. Certainly it aids access to prostitutes by clients. The 1993–94 New Zealand telephone directories, in their yellow pages, list 128 escort agencies and 125 massage parlours. Of these, 48 escort agencies are located in Auckland, as are 52 massage parlours. Additionally many newspapers carry advertisements in their classified advertising columns under the category of 'adult entertainment'.

As noted, there was no problem for the researchers in identifying the location of massage parlours. The research concentrated on those working in Auckland and Wellington, the two major cities in New Zealand. The population of the two city zones is approximately 1 000 000 and 500 000 respectively, and both are major tourist centres for recreational, VFR and business tourism. Access to information was also aided by discussions with the New Zealand Prostitutes Collective which has branches in both cities, and with the police in Auckland. There are significant differences between the two cities. Wellington has what has been called the 'smallest red light district in the world'. It consists of but a handful of establishments, and many massage parlours are located outside the business district in places such as Lower Hutt, near industrial areas. Indeed, from a survey of the advertisements in the press, Wellington has many more women working privately than is the case in Auckland. This might be because the main daily Wellington newspaper will carry these advertisements, whereas its Auckland counterpart does not. Auckland, however, has a well-known red-light district, Fort Street, which could be described as a tourist attraction, consisting as it does of not only massage parlours but also strip clubs, 'adult cinemas', 'adult bookshop', pubs and nearby restaurants. There is also a second 'red light' area; smaller, with a longer tradition, less 'glitzy' with fewer neon lights, and also servicing a wider range of requirements including homosexuals and transsexuals. As such it is thought it attracts far fewer tourists.

Ryan and Kinder[26] estimated the value of the Auckland sex industry as being at least NZ$25 million, of which about 25–30% was thought to come from out-of-town clients and others who could be described as 'tourists'. The figures were also consistent with what evidence existed from studies undertaken by researchers financed by health authorities.[27,28]

The problem was how to reach the clients. It was decided to use telephone interviewing because this permits direct questioning of sensitive matters as the respondent is neither talking directly to another person, nor picking up clues from facial movement or body language which might suggest disapproval, and creates a situation where people will respond more easily to a 'disembodied' voice which poses no threat when discussing delicate matters.[29] An advertisement was placed in the adult entertainment columns of the Wellington press which asked the question, 'do you visit massage parlours?' It continued, 'if you do, could you please telephone a university researcher' and a name and number was given. Such an approach poses the difficulty that the respondents are self-selecting. Detailed conversations with 42 clients were recorded during a period of two days. The transcripts and notes were shown to others and the consensus view of this informed opinion is that the material contained in the conversations is consistent with what is known of clients and their attitudes. It is also consistent with the literature.[30-32] In these interviews questions were asked about matters such as why they went to prostitutes, the frequency of visits, whether patronage increased during trips away from home, and details were sought as to the person's occupation, age and frequency of travel. Although the ordering of questions varied as conversations developed, a checklist of questions was maintained and adhered to as far as was possible. Respondents varied from the hesistant to others who were far more forthcoming, talked with ease about their activities, and indeed, in one case, even offered to send research material. It did not arrive! The details recorded covered the clients' motivations and behaviours when they visited prostitutes, the frequency of visits and journey patterns. This last form of questioning established whether visits occurred within the clients' residential areas, or when travelling away from home on a tourist trip (i.e. when requiring overnight accommodation away from home). Of the 42, 35 visited prostitutes when away from home, and the following discussion is based on their comments about motivations. Additionally the discussion draws upon unstructured individual discussions with nine sex workers in different parts of North Island, New Zealand.

The motivation for visiting prostitutes: comparisons with holidaying motivation

Many researchers have examined the motivation for tourist behaviour. Crompton[33] notes that travel consumers are not motivated by the specific qualities of the destination and its attractions, but rather by the broad suitability of the destination to fulfil their particular psychological needs. He proposes that 'instead of distance, culture and climate being used to classify destinations, one can envisage clusters of vacation centres which are predominantly self-exploration, or social interaction or indeed sexual arousal'. Mathieson and Wall[6] refer to the physical motivational category, which includes motivations such as refreshment of body and mind and pleasure – fun, excitement, romance and entertainment. It is not hard to extend these motivations to the client visiting a prostitute. For example, it has been noted that the geographical nature of many urban tourist destinations mean a reduction in the effectiveness of social guardians.[10,35,36,37]

Yiannakis and Gibson[38] develop a typology of holidaymaker clusters based on three different continuums. The first is the desire for a vacation that is either highly structured or has little structure. The second axis indicated whether tourists preferred their tourist destination to be a stimulating or tranquil environment. The final axis was a continuum to determine whether the tourist aspired to visiting a strange or familiar environment. Hence the tourist seeking contact with prostitutes might choose a vacation with a structure that permits flexibility, seeking a stimulating environment, but also one with familiarity. They describe the 'action seeker' as:

Mostly interested in Partying, going to night clubs and meeting the opposite sex for uncomplicated romantic experiences. ([38] p. 33)

Evidence of this type of client for a prostitute is given by Winter who comments:

Some clients thrive on the ability to engage an anonymous prostitute for sexual relations: to them the whole experience is a novel sexual adventure filled with surprises and fantasies.[39]

Crompton[33] identifies a series of motivations which help to explain the need for tourism, and which can be applied to commercial sex. Like holidays, a visit to a prostitute can meet relaxation, social and friendship needs. Evidence of this emerged from conversations with clients. 'Charlie' stated that he sees ladies to 'get a little bit of happiness'. 'Fred' commented that 'I just usually want a cuddle and some company. It gives me friendship and some social activity . . . ' 'Nick', a business traveller who often visits prostitutes, stated that he used 'high class' escorts who are usually well educated, that he had a need to interact with them on an intellectual level – that 'it is more important to be with the girl and have intelligent, cheerful conversation, than just to have sex'. Additionally tourists visit different places in order to see and do new things: they search for novelty. So too do those who visit prostitutes. 'Sam' met escorts 'because of a search for variety'. Michael 'feels the need to do something different'. Peter, who frequently uses prostitutes when on business trips, commented 'yes, my sexual [activity] is different than with my normal partner . . . [it] involves excitement at the unknown'. Again, 'Basil' stated 'Trying to get more of a cover of what different people are like – mainly for the variety'.

Some commentators on tourist movation have noted the role of a holiday as an outlet for fantasizing – as an escape from the 'ordinary'.[6,7,33] This, too, occurs in the statements of those who visited prostitutes. Thus 'Tony' notes that 'it is more exciting, more uninhibited and there is no holding back. I enjoy the whole experience, the sex, the fantasies, being able to 'talk dirty' and the fact that there are no demands on men. Holidays have also been noted by Crompton[33] as opportunities for regression into childhood. The tourist visiting a prostitute may also be engaged in another form of regression. Sheehy[40] has made the observation that, for a man, prostitution represents an opportunity of 'buying the nostalgic illusion that things are how they were when he was a boy'. Further, if holidays present opportunities for many to enjoy, however limited the time, the lifestyle of the wealthy, so too sex tourism, particularly in Asia, permits an exhilaration usually open only to the wealthy, that is of having access to many women of youth and beauty. It can also be regarded as an acting out of the fantasy of being powerful. Lindi St Clair is quoted by Thomson[41] as saying 'Let's look at half these politicians. Let's look at half the royals. Who would give them a second glance if they weren't rich and famous? Power makes an ugly man attractive'.

The 'holiday romance' that can be found in literature and fact (although not often researched) has several features. One is that it is understood by both parties to be temporary – that its boundaries are those of the holiday place and period. There were examples of respondents who simply wanted sex without emotional involvement. Indeed, parallels could be drawn between the actions of some younger respondents and the type of tourist featured in media portrayal of 18–30 holidaymakers.[42] 'Ted', aged 25, was one such example. He went to a prostitute the first time two years ago when 'out with the boys and we were drinking'. He had no time for emotional involvement with a girl; 'I don't want to have to go through all that bullshit'. On the other hand, there is a significant literature relating to sex tourists who want friendship with young women. Kruhse Mount-Burton cites one interviewee as stating:

It's true there is no chance of rejection. But now maybe I'm a bit idealistic in the sense that I think, wouldn't it be nice if during that day, and that encounter, that there developed a genuine friendliness . . . [43]

Cohen[13] reproduces letters sent by former clients to the Thai women with whom they have shared time. In this study similar motives were also stated by respondents. Thus one man said:

It's like meeting a girl friend for the first time . . . the affection may be purchased, but I am continually pleasantly surprised by just how nice the women are, and that I very much appreciate.

The difference in attitudes, between seeking or rejecting emotional support, is possibly demonstrated by the language used by respondents. Those who share the views of 'Ted' seemed to have a greater tendency to 'use a prostitute'; others would 'visit a prostitute'. Such language difference can be held to be significant. The transcripts were subjected to a frequency count of the motivational statements. This found that sex and concealment needs were mentioned by almost all respondents. The separate motivations of 'friendship' and 'variety' were equally important in that about 40% of respondents mentioned these needs, while 'relaxation' and 'sex with no emotional ties' were mentioned by about 15% of the respondents. 'Relaxation', however, was a more complex item, in that it was inferred in statements about 'friendship', and hence simple frequency counts of the number of mentions underestimates this motivation.

Another motivation that emerged (albeit associated with concealment needs) was the role of prostitutes in family bonding – a need recognized in the tourism literature as one met by holidaying.[33] For example, 'Roger' is happy in his marriage, but feels a need to visit prostitutes for a sexual relief. He would never want his wife to find out as it would ruin his marriage and the trust between him and his wife. For almost all of the men involved, concealment and discretion were of paramount importance, often because of a need to sustain a marriage.

In this listing of motivations, there are leitmotifs; namely, the desire for sex and concealment. The desire for sex is, as already noted, not unknown to observers of tourist behaviour. Nor, but from a different perspective, is the desire for concealment. Pizam and Mansfeld[44] illustrate the linkage between crime and tourism, and the fact that tourist locations can offer concealment for criminal action. In the context of the tourist and the prostitute, the tourist location offers the concealment of anonymity which reduces ties of responsibility. However, what emerges from the discussions with clients and prostitutes is a need to conceal actions from cared-for others. Clients wish to conceal their actions from their partners and, for many prostitutes, there is a wish to conceal their actions from parents and/or children.

The tourist–prostitute relationship shares many features with other forms of client – prostitute relationships. Concealment is one such feature, and is illustrative of the way both clients and prostitutes operate at the margin of many social activities. The margins can be identified as legal, the question of sexual roles and spatial marginality. In both the legal and social contexts a continuum might be identified which ranges from that which is accepted and legal to that which is not tolerated, not accepted and is illegal. The relationship between client and prostitute occupies not only the middle ground in this continuum, but does so in a 'fuzzy' manner that attracts ambivalence and hypocrisy.

The complexity of prostitute liminality

The legal ambivalence has already been noted in the case of New Zealand's legislation. Indeed, the position is more 'fuzzy' than previously discussed. New Zealand's Inland Revenue Department has a specific taxation officer whose role is to assess the earnings of sex workers for taxation purposes. Some sex workers wryly observe that this is an example of the state living off 'immoral' earnings as prohibited by the 1961 Crimes Act. Under the legislation police have various powers, but in practice rarely use them. In a number of towns the police have no desire to close down massage parlours or escort agencies for a number of reasons. One is the acceptance that such actions might be self-defeating in simply driving activities further underground in such a way that it reduces some channels of information on more serious crime. Other reasons also exist such as the fact that the legislation protects prostitutes to some extent. However, that extent is limited. Currently, under New Zealand legislation, women with a criminal record for prostitution are legally, and often practically, unable to work in massage parlours, and are thus working privately or on the streets. This means they are at greater risk from assault.

The margin is also illustrated in other ways. Massage parlour management tends to be prepared to sponsor 'straight' sex, but not homosexual or transsexual relationships. Hence, in Auckland, such prostitutes tend to work outside the main red-light district of Fort Street with its parlours, restaurants and strip clubs, and on an older 'sex centre' of streets around 'K-Road' – there again running higher personal risks.

The fuzzy nature of the legality of the sex trade is also illustrated by its association with crime. Prostitutes may be managed by pimps. In some cases prostitutes and pimps trade because of a need for illegal drugs. Historically, in some parts of the world, there has been an association between organized crime and prostitution; for example, where brothels are illegal they might be financed by criminal money. However, within the New Zealand context of licensed massage parlours, the linkage between pornography, crime, drugs and prostitution is not self-evident. Nonetheless, some linkage does exist at the margins of this already marginal activity. Thai women have been deported from New Zealand by the Immigration Department on arrival at Auckland Airport 'for their own safety' and after raids on massage parlours. It is of interest to note in this respect the draft statements of the Second World Whores' Conference which noted:

Women who choose to migrate as prostitutes should not be punished or assumed to be the victims of abuse. They should enjoy the same rights as other immigrants. For many women, female migration through prostitution is an escape from an economically and socially impossible situation in one country to hopes for a better situation in another. The fact that many women find themselves in another awful situation reflects the lack of opportunities for financial independence and employment satisfaction for women, especially for third world women, throughout the world.[45]

Hence, deportation without choice again illustrates the marginal position occupied by sex workers.

This social marginality of the sex industry covers many aspects of social functioning. Arguably, as indicated by 15% of the sample of 42 respondents, the notion of a demand for sex without emotional ties is a male one. Such a view is questionable, as already noted, but it also raises the question of what of the supply of sex? Two questions arise: do prostitutes possess power over clients, and do prostitutes necessarily feel degraded by their work? Clients do report being used and abused. Two respondents referred to the clinical nature of the encounter. Kruhse Mount-Burton also notes that:

...prostitution in the Australian context is often appraised by clients as deficient, in that prostitutes are criticised for being emotionally and sexually cold and for making little effort to please, or to disguise the commercial nature of the interaction. ([43] p. 193)

The creation of a commercial transaction out of a sexual act implies a commoditization, and the nature of the sexual act advertised is diverse. Yet, of the total of 42 respondents, only three referred to cross-dressing, bondage or similar practices. Indeed, more noted that they required company and the sexual act was either not a prime motivation or not always indulged in. However, one theme that did emerge was a sense of relief on the part of some that they did not have to play the role of initiating sexual action. There was no 'duty' to arouse a partner, and indeed the female would take the initiative.

The wider literature includes interviews with sex workers, and indicated some themes followed in this research project. On being asked why they had entered prostitution the sex workers all stated that it was because of the money. This is a conventional finding as indicated by Nina Lopez-Jones, spokeswoman for the English Collective of Prostitutes, who is quoted by Silver as saying:

Actually, in most cases it's simply a means of making ends meet. Because ours is a sexual activity, people forget we're on the game for money. At least seventy per cent are mothers. They see prostitution as a way not to descend into poverty. Men do all kinds of things for money; more ways are open to them than to women.[46]

In interviews with New Zealand sex workers the same motivation was also advanced, although in one case the woman involved was introduced to prostitution by her mother, who had also been a prostitute. This relates to another theme in the literature[47] – to what extent do women become prostitutes as a result of past abuse? Silver recognizes this argument when she states:

According to FCP's figures, approximately seventy per cent of all prostitutes are single mothers. One way they explain this relates to the high level of domestic violence in general. If you are going to be beaten up and/or raped anyway at home, it is not such a leap to risk it happening outside the home whilst at least making a good independent living. ([46] p. 105)

Hence, having money means independence, it means avoiding rape and violence in the woman's life. As Nina Lopez-Jones of the ECP notes:

It means you can afford to take a cab rather than waiting out on the street for a bus and running the risk of being attacked there. It means that you don't have to work necessarily in a job where either sex with your boss, or some kind of sexual work with your boss, is a requirement. It means you don't have to sleep with your landlord so that he doesn't evict you. ([49] p. 106)

But the work of the prostitute cannot simply be explained by financial need alone. The feminist literature and the writings of prostitutes themselves increasingly seek more complex explanations relating to the role of females in society, female independence and their concepts of their own sexuality. Thus Bell argues when she writes:

... from the view of the clitoris – that part of the body not associated with reproduction, but with pleasure ... Yet the sexual body is the underside, the shadow of the spirit, that had to be mastered: a subtext always present, insistent in the text's denial of the body. ([23] p. 20)

On both sides of the Atlantic, there is an awareness of a tradition of prostitution prior to that of the 19th century which dates back to the period of the *hetaira*, the priestess of ancient Greece, who held their own schools and who engaged in the 'mysteries'. Veronica Vera of Prostitutes of New York (PONY) maintains that:

Sex is a nourishing, life-giving force and as a consequence sex work is of benefit to humanity ... Sex workers are providing a very valuable service to be honoured. Sex work ... is a good service, it is the best service that one individual can do for another individual ... ([23] p. 108)

Similar sentiments can be found in work by Jordan,[32] McLeod[30] and Delacoste and Alexander.[40] At one level sex work is perceived as a continuation of the nurturance female role. But it is more, for it is also a recognition of the sexuality of at least some females, of their own pleasures, and, in part, of their own role playing. Women dress for the role, and the act of dressing gives them the thrill of being able to exercise power over men. Hence the danger of prostitution for sex workers – in its promise of financial independence and senses of sexuality and power, it becomes addictive. Kasl writes that the 'addiction part is the ritual of getting dressed, putting on makeup, fantasizing about the hunt, and the moment of capture. "To know that you go out there and they would come running. What power!" '[50]

The problem of addiction is also recognized, and some feminist organizations perceive such notions as not only dangerous in themselves, but as pandering to male fantasies. Wynter, spokesperson for WHISPER (Women Hurt in Systems of Prostitution Engaged in Revolt) writes of the rejection of the lies that women freely choose prostitution from an array of economic alternatives, that turning tricks is sexual pleasure, that women can and do become wealthy in systems of prostitution, and that 'we reject the lie that women control and are empowered in systems of prostitution'.[51] Other WHISPER advocates maintain that prostitution is a reflection of male domination within a capitalist system (e.g. Giobbe,[52,53]), while others[49,54] equate prostitution to the normal contract of employment enforced by capitalism. There is, therefore, no consistent view of prostitution and its meanings for wider society. For some writers it is a confirmation of the subordinate role of women and the reduced employment opportunities they face, for others it is a means of reclaiming past status of the role, and yet for other writers it is a means of acquiring new recognition of one's own sexuality and pride in being a 'working woman'.

These same mixtures of feelings were confirmed by different sex workers in New Zealand. 'Louise' stated that she was delaying entry into university to earn some money, but she enjoyed working in a massage parlour. She met nice men, they enjoyed her services, and she for the most part similarly enjoyed sex. However, when asked, she admitted her mother did not know what she did. For 'Chantelle', it was a way of life – her mother had introduced her to the work, she had two children and two broken marriages, it was a means of economically sustaining herself in a way she could not otherwise do, and as for the work 'it was alright!'.

What have these experiences to do with the tourist as client? The conversations with both clients and prostitutes raise many questions about sexuality in society, and a number of dialects arise. There is the search for the familiar and the new, a concept familiar in leisure and tourism literature. Some clients seek a familiar experience by regular patronage of a sex worker; others, a majority of our interviewees, wanted some variety; hence their patronage when away from home, even if they were also regulars for other sex workers. Many felt able to talk more openly about sex and their wants to a prostitute then they are to their own partners – prostitutes are professional sex workers. If, as argued above, there is merit in researching the fringe of society in order to better understand society as a whole, then this oneness and male appreciation of sex with prostitutes as a source of relaxation which is not found within their homes says much about the attitudes of males in their relationships with their partners. While husbands seemingly wish not to inflict their own sexual needs upon their wives, they at the same time might be denying the sexual needs of their wives. It can only be recorded that the 'Madonna' syndrome accorded to females by males seemed present in responses by those interviewed in this research. In short, the study of tourists and prostitutes reveals the period of travel away from home to be not simply a period of opportunity, fantasy, relaxation or renewal, but a reflection of dysfunctioning in a wider society. In a sense, there is a reversal of Krippendorf's[55] thesis that sick society produces 'sick tourists' as evidenced by 'irresponsible' behaviours. Rather, the tourist's very visit to a prostitute can be interpreted, once the motivations are examined, to mean attempts at self-cure, for the holiday visit to the sex worker has a potential to aid the search for self-identity and recognition of individual needs.

It has been noted that a number of clients sought concealment to preserve their marriage. In interpreting this wish, the authors would argue that this desire is not a question of simply sustaining a social picture; more underlying motivations are involved. Basically, to use the language of Theweleit,[56] it would seem males continue to perpetuate the notion of the 'White' and 'Red' Woman. He argued that the bourgeoisie fantasized about women as falling into two classifications. The 'White'

Woman supported men within the home, and served man's (and family's) needs. The 'Red' Woman threatened male composure and tormented male self-control. She was young, beautiful, intensely sexual, independent – a figure of continuous fascination; a flame to which the male is drawn. Such female figures are part of romantic literature – but the dangerous appeal of Mérimée's Carmen is countered by the tradition of the soft-hearted prostitute, a girl of big bosom and heart who understands male weakness. The 'White' woman, or Madonna myth, is persistent as is evidenced by writings of those who seek to counter feminism. Carroll argues that women are 'the true defenders of the humanist values that emanate from the household, the values of tenderness, nurture and compassion'.[57]

Such discussions about the meanings of femininity apply to any consideration of sexual roles in our society. Where tourism occupies an additional niche, this lies in some of the inherent attributes of tourism. Urry ([15] p. 100) notes in *The Tourist Gaze* that the 'post-tourist' knows that tourism is a game whereby the concept of travel as a voyage of discovery of other places is rejected in order to seek experience as an end in itself. From the perspective of the ludic (games playing) tourist, the travelling client of the prostitute is taking advantage of an opportunity to seek an experience that makes real a need, however fantastical. The sex act becomes part of the experience of travel – both become an abstraction that contrasts strongly with 'normal' life. On the other hand, however attractive this idea might be as a variant upon 'The Gaze', it is not entirely supported by this research. Frank commented 'All the sales reps, especially, do it, because it is socially acceptable in the business world'. Harry sought prostitutes away from home simply because 'it was safer'. In short, the paradox of the marginal act is that it becomes a conventional act, undertaken for conventional reasons. It exposes one weakness in the research: that the sample was too small to find whether significant differences existed between business travellers and recreational tourists. It is suggested, from admittedly flimsy evidence, that men who visit sex workers as business travellers will also visit prostitutes as recreational travellers – the constraint when undertaking holiday travel is the existence of opportunity, dependent upon place visited and whether family members are present.

Hence, what tourism opens up is a series of alternative opportunities and experiences. On the one hand patronage of prostitutes is one of variety, play, sexual need, fantasy, comfort and companionship, regardless of wherever it takes place, but travel reinforces both opportunity and each of these motivations. Alternatively, for some it has been reduced to being a 'business perk'; simply part of the business of travel. In short, going to a prostitute is akin to any leisure activity which might be done on holiday. Those who go to climb, sail or play golf obtain additional enjoyment from the opportunities produced by the new destination – so too is the case for prostitution. At one level, therefore, the paradox of the margin is that it is no different from many other acceptable pursuits in the way in which it affords leisure and recreation, while at another level, it is an act barely tolerated by many – a tolerance level conditioned by social mores of what is and what is not acceptable.

Marsh[58] noted that it was sometimes 'hard to understand why more girls did not take to the streets' when reviewing the freedom and support systems Victorian prostitutes could enjoy. The same factors can apply today, and the current debate about prostitution is, as noted, complex. From the perspective of social exchange theory, reciprocity, defined by Gouldner as 'a mutually gratifying pattern of exchanging goods and services' must be present for both client and prostitute. Exchange theory is concerned with transaction arising from the need to mutually satisfy wants. The theory[59,60] considers exchange formation, relationships, the exchange transaction evaluation and consequences of the exchange. Thus, as Ap notes, 'Outputs refer to the physical, social, or symbolic objects of events that are valued and accrue to the actors' ([60] p. 685). However, social exchange theory assumes rationality on the part of the actors, but the definition of rationality as defined by Ap[60] is one of simply a need being met. Thus sub-optimal decisions are simply outcomes of satisficing processes that exist when insufficient information occurs. Hence the propositions advanced by the theory become no more than statements of the obvious. For example, as Ap again notes, 'When the value of resources exchanged between the host and guest actors is greater for one than for the other, the exchange transaction is likely to be perceived as unfair by the disadvantaged actor' ([60] p. 677).

Such rationalizations do little to explain the tourist client–prostitute relationship and its status in society. Hall has argued that:

Most fundamentally, however, the motivations for sex tourism are an outcome of a desire on the part of the tourist for self-gratifying erotic power through the control of another's body.[61]

In the view of the present authors this too is a simplification. The provision alone of B&D (bondage and domination) services is sufficient to make one ask whose body is being controlled. The needs for leisure, social interaction and exploration make the process more complex than that being envisaged by Hall. What perhaps this paper does illustrate is a much wider truth: that much of the 'tourist gaze' (to use Urry's phrase), like that of wider society, is a male-orientated gaze.[62] It is this that is being challenged by the growth of feminist literature on recreation and prostitution.

Conclusions

This paper argues that tourism is a marginal, or liminal, experience; that while the industrial infrastructure behind the provision of the experiences has made it a significant contributor to economic activity, the essence of tourism remains the escape from the reality of daily life, the ability to fulfil fantasy. Prostitution is also a liminal behaviour from different but sometimes shared perspectives. It too has a significant economic impact, and for many women offers financial independence. Sex workers work at fulfilling needs for escape, relaxation, fantasy fulfilment and family bonding – just as workers in the tourist industry do. It can be argued that tourism has offered employment, career and political awareness to women.[62] Tourism is part of the entertainment business; pornography is too. Tourism is sometimes regarded as a 'sexy' business – it is glamorized, can be exploitative, and certainly has used sexual imagery to sell its products. Everywhere one looks the interconnecting and overlapping nature of tourism and prostitution can be found. Hence to regard sex tourism as some form of deviance, as something that is foreign to the intrinsic nature of tourism, is a mistake. Additionally, like all social thresholds, both say much about the nature of our society. Can it be concluded that society, for all the technical advances and social progress that have been made in overcoming problems of poor health, housing and education, nonetheless remains not only unsatisfying, but denying aspects of our humanity, and our sexual identities?

Finally, it should again be emphasized that this paper is written generally from a perspective of client–sex worker relationships within a western society, and more specifically from a New Zealand context of, as noted, legalized massage parlours. Indeed, the work is even more specific than that, in that the sex workers involved within the research were themselves New Zealanders. This specificity is important because it means that the research does not address issues relating to tourism to Asian countries (which as originally noted is well documented). Nor does it refer to another growing phenomenon, which is the presence of Asian female sex workers in New Zealand. This is important in that it appears to the authors that the New Zealand female workers have greater discretion, choice and control than might be the case for Asian women. Again, however, it must be noted that this conclusion is primarily anecdotal, although Cohen (E Cohen 1995, private correspondence) feels there is some journalistic evidence for an 'export' trade in Thai women. The authors are therefore reluctant to extend their analysis to other situations of sex tourism, but equally feel that studies relating to, in particular, Asian sex tourism are not totally pertinent to the situation within a country such as New Zealand. So too, the analysis cannot necessarily be extended into gay and transsexual prostitution. The reasons for these caveats are that in the case of Asian sex tourism the question of economic dominance and power is more to the fore according to some authors such as Hall,[1,61] while in the case of gay and transsexual prostitution the authors do not know enough to come to any conclusion, All that can be noted is that, at least in New Zealand, it appears to work through different venues from that of traditional prostitution.

Acknowledgements

The authors want to thank members of the Auckland and Wellington Offices of the New Zealand Prostitutes Collective for their time and interest, and a number of working women in the sex industry who were interviewed during this research, Additionally the authors want to thank the anonymous referees for their comments. The final interpretation is of course that of the authors.

References

1. Hall, C M (1994) *Introduction to Tourism in the Pacific Rim: Development Impacts and Markets* Longman, Cheshire, 101–102
2. Thitsa, K *Providence and Prostitution: Image and Reality for Women in Buddhist Thailand* Change International Reports, London (1980)
3. Truong, T *Sex, Money and Morality* Zed Books, London (1990)
4. Law, C M *Urban Tourism: Attracting Visitors to Large Cities* Mansell, New York (1993)
5. Page, S J *Urban Tourism* Routledge, London (1995)
6. Mathieson, A and Wall, G *Tourism, Its Economic, Social, and Environmental Impacts* Longman, Harlow (1982)

7. Ryan, C *Recreational Tourism – a Social Science Perspective* Routledge, London and New York (1991)
8. Ashworth G J White, P E and Winchester, H 'The redlight distrist of the West European city: a neglected aspect of the urban landscape' *Geoforum* 1998 **19** 201–212
9. Velten, D and Kleiber, D 'Characterisitcs and sexual behavior of clients of female prostitutes', poster presented at the VIII International Conference on Aids, Amsterdam, 19–24 July 1992
10. Ryan, C and Kinder, R 'The deviant tourist and the crimogenic place – the case of the tourist and the New Zealand prostitute', in Pizam, A and Mansfield, Y (eds) *Crime and International Security Issues* Wiley, Chichester (1996) 23–35
11. Cohen, E 'Marginal paradises; bungalow tourism on the islands of Southern Thailand' *Annals of Tourism Research* 1982 **9** (2) 189–228
12. Cohen, E 'The dropout expatriates: a study of Marginal *Farangs* in Bangkok' *Urban Anthropology* 1984 **13** (1) 91–114
13. Cohen, E 'Lovelorn *Farangs*: the correspondence between foreign men and Thai girls' *Anthropological Quarterly* 1986 **59**, vol, pp 115–127
14. Cohen E 'Open-ended prostitution as a skilful game of luck: opportunity, risk and security among the tourist oriented prostitutes in a Bangkok *soi*' Hitchcock, M, King, V T and Parnwell, M J C (eds) *Tourism in South East Asia* Routledge, London (1993)
15. Urry, J *The Tourist Gaze* Sage, London (1990) 2
16. Turner, V *Drama, Fields and Metaphors – Symbolic Action in Human Society* Cornell University Press, Ithaca (1969)
17. Rojek, C *Ways of Escape – Modern Transformations in Leisure and Travel* Macmillan, Basingstoke (1993)
18. Becker, H S *Outsiders: Studies in the Sociology of Deviance* Free Press, Glencoe (1963)
19. Quinney, R *Class, State and Crime: On the Theory and Practice of Criminal Justice* David MacKay, New York (1977)
20. Krippendorf, J *The Holidaymakers* Heinemann, Oxford (1987)
21. Pearce, P L *The Social Psychology of Tourist Behaviour* Pergamon Press, Oxford (1982)
22. Pearce, P L *The Ulysees Factors: Evaluating Visitors in Tourist Settings* Springer-Verlag, New York (1988)
23. Bell, S *Reading, Writing and Rewriting the Prostitute Body* Indiana University Press, Bloomington and Indianapolis (1994) 40–41
24. Downes, D and Rock, P *Understanding Deviance – a Guide to the Sociology of Crime and Rule-Breaking* 2nd edn, Clarendon Press, Oxford (1988) 202
25. Podilchak, W 'Distinctions of fun, enjoyment and leisure', *Leisure Studies* 1991 **10** (2) 133–148
26. Kinder, R and Ryan, C 'The deviant tourist and the crimogenic place – the case of the tourist and the New Zealand prostitue' in *Proceedings of Tourism Down Under* Massey University (1994) 55–71
27. Chetwynd, J *The New Zealand Prostitutes' Collective – a Process Evaluation of its Formation and Operation* Christchurch School of Medicine, Christchurch (1991)
28. Woods, K A 'You have sex with a condom. You're making love without. Condom use by parlour workers in and out of work' unpublished paper, component of PhD, University of Auckland, 1993
29. Ryan, C *Researching Tourist Satisfaction – Issues, Concepts, Problems* Routledge, London and New York (1994)
30. McLeod, E *Women Working: Prostitution Now* London, Croom Helm (1982)
31. Barnard, M A, McKeganey, N P and Leyland, A H 'Risk behaviours among male clients of female prostitutes' *British Medical Journal* 1993 **307** 361–362
32. Jordan, J *Women in the New Zealand Sex Industry talk to Jan Jordan* Penguin, Auckland (1991)
33. Crompton, J L 'Motivation for pleasure vacation' *Annals of Tourism Research* 1979 **6** (4) 408–424
34. Cohen, E 'Rethinking the sociology of tourism' *Annals of Tourism Research* 1979 **6** (1) 18–35
35. Cohen, L E and Felson, M 'Social change and crime rate trends: a routine activity approach' *American Sociological Review* 1979 **44** (August) 588–608
36. Felson, M 'Linking criminal choices, routine activities, informal control, and criminal outcomes' in Cornish, D B and Clarke, R V *The Reasoning Criminal – Rational Choice Perspectives on Offending* Springer-Verlag, New York (1986)
37. Schiebler, S A, Crotts, J and Hollinger, R C 'Florida tourists' vulnerability to crime' in Pizam, A and Mansfield, Y (eds) *Crime and International Security Issues* Wiley, Chichester (1996) 37–50

38. Yiannakis, A and Gibson, H 'Roles tourists play' *Annals of Tourism Research* 1992 **19** (2) 287–303
39. Winter, M *Prostitution in Australia* Purtaboi Publications, Balgowah, NSW (1976)
40. Sheehy, G *Hustling: Prostitution in Our Wide Open Society* Delacorte. New York (1971) 3
41. Thomson, A 'Political mistresses reveal state of affairs' *Dominion* 1996 (3 April) 7
42. Benny Dorm (pseudonym) *Beach Party – the Last Resort* New English Library, Hodder and Stoughton, London (1988)
43. Kruhse Mount-Burton, S 'Sex toursim and traditional Australian male identity' in Lanfant, M-F, Allcock, J B and Bruner, E M (eds) *International Tourism – Identity and Change* Sage, London (1995) 194
44. Pizam, A and Mansfeld, Y *Crime and International Security Issues*, Wiley, Chichester (1996)
45. '2nd World Whores' Congress, 1986', Draft Statements' cited in Delacoste, F D and Alexander, P *Sex Work, Writings by Women in the Sex Industry* Cleis Press, Pittsburgh (1987) 307
46. Silver, R *The Girl in Scarlet Heels* Century, London (1993)
47. Caplan, G M 'The facts of life about teenage prostitution' *Crime and Delinquency* 1984 **30** (1) 69–74
48. Gibson-Ainyette, I, Templer, D I, Brown, R and Veaco, L 'Adolescent female prostitutes' *Archives of Sexual Behaviour* 1988 **17** (5) 431–438
49. Delacoste, F D and Alexander, P *Sex Work, Writings by Women in the Sex Industry* Cleis Press, Pittsburgh (1987)
50. Kasl, C D *Women, Sex and Addiction* Ticknor & Fields, New York (1989) 154
51. Wynter, S 'WHISPER, Women Hurt in Systems of Prostitution Engaged in Revolt' in Delacosta, F and Alexander, P (eds) *Sex Work, Writings by Women in the Sex Industry* Cleiss Press, Pittsburgh (1987) 269
52. Giobbe, E 'When sexual assault is a job description' *WHISPER Newsletter* 1990 **4** (3) 4
53. Jenness, V 'From sex as sin to sex as work: COYOTE and the reorganization of prostitution as a social problem' *Social Problems* 1990 **37** (August) 403–420
54. Op cit Ref. 46, Silver, 1993, p. 97
55. Krippendorf, J *The Holidaymakers*, Oxford, Heinemann (1987)
56. Theweleit, K *Male Fantasies, Vol 1: Women, Floods Bodies and History*, Cambridge, Polity (1987)
57. Carroll, J *Guilt*, London and New York, Routledge (1985) 98
58. Marsh, J *Pre-Raphaelite Sisterhood* St Martin's Press, New York (1985)
59. Searle, M S 'Propositions for testing social exchange theory in the context of ceasing leisure participation' *Leisure Studies* 1991 **13** 279–294
60. Ap, J 'Residents' perceptions of tourism impacts' *Annals of Tourism Research* 1992 **19** (4) 665–690
61. Hall, C M 'Tourism prostitution: the control and health implications of sex tourism in south-east Asia and Australia' in Clift, S and Page, S J (eds) *Health and the International Tourist*, Routledge, London (1995) 182
62. Kinnaird, V, Kothari, U and Hall, D 'Tourism gender perspectives' in Kinnaird, V and Hall, D (eds) *Tourism, a Gender Analysis* Wiley, Chichester (1994)

Appendix

In New Zealand, massage parlours are legal under the 1978 Massage Parlours Act, which, in section 3, states that the Act does not apply to massage undertaken for sports purposes or by those pursuing massage under a licence or registration in pursuit of a profession – that is, the Act does not apply to what might be termed 'medical practitioners'. Licences for massage parlours are obtained from a local magistrates court, and will be granted if the person making the application is judged to be suitable and if the police do not object. Any person can operate as a masseur or masseuse if he or she has not been convicted under sections 146–149 of the 1961 Crimes Act, or under legislation pertaining to the misuse of drugs. However, sections 147–149 of the 1961 Crimes Act deal specifically with 'brothel keeping' (section 147), 'living on the earnings of prostitution' (section 148) and 'procuring sexual intercourse' (section 149). Hence, while under the 1978 Massage Parlours Act application can be made for a licence to operate as a massage parlour, which is widely recognized as a location for sexual liaison, under section 147 of the Crimes Act, 1961, 'everyone is liable to imprisonment for a term not exceeding 5 years who keeps or manages, or acts or assists in the management of any brothel . . .'.

Part IV

Planning and community action

Introduction by Stephen Page

Within the literature on tourism, an ongoing debate has continued on the extent to which tourism planning exists as a discrete and integrated activity within the public and private sector (Page and Thorn, 1997, 1998). While a range of tourism texts now exist on the theme of tourism planning (Gunn, 1979; Inskeep, 1991, 1994; Gartner, 1996; Hall et al., 1997; Wilkinson, 1997), in only a few contexts (e.g. Languedoc-Roussillon) does tourism planning exist as a specialist and integrated activity (Getz, 1986). In many cases, tourism planning is an all-embracing term used to encompass a wide variety of activities, often including tourist development (see Pearce, 1989). This makes any definitive analysis of the field of study complex, and an almost impossible task to review in a coherent and meaningful manner. This is made even more complex when considering new paradigms that approach tourism planning from the planning literature perspective (Hall, 1999). In fact Hall's (1999) new and stimulating review attempts to avoid sterile, check list and pedantic reviews of tourism planning by placing people, politics and the irrational explanations of planning decisions as central to his thesis.

Probably the most notable development in the tourism planning field in the 1990s is the focus on sustainability (Hall and Lew, 1998). This is part of the evolution of tourism thought and practice described in detail by Hall (1991), where an economic–industry approach, boosterism, the land-use approach or community approach and sustainability have characterised tourism planning and development principles and practices. Many of the articles published in the *Journal of Sustainable Tourism* with a planning focus reflect the development of this new all-embracing paradigm for tourism, although one common criticism is the failure to provide operational perspectives on integrating sustainable tourism planning in practice. For small historic cities such as Venice and Canterbury, which have major problems of capacity and physical space, it immediately focuses attention on managerial perspectives in relation to tourism and sustainability (Page, 1995). In each case, the concern with sustainability requires appropriate baseline data and indicators of tourism that can be used to monitor and evaluate change. In urban areas, this becomes more complex than in natural, remote and urban fringe locations, since establishing the impacts caused directly or indirectly by tourism are often difficult to disaggregate from the impact of residents, recreationalists, workers and other city-users (e.g. the military). However, the sustainability paradigm is raising appropriate planning questions related to the value of mass versus more responsible tourism (Cooper and Ozdil, 1992; Alipour, 1996) in particular destinations. As a result a greater questioning of the value of mass tourism and the myriad of planning headaches and consequences it causes for the built and natural environment has certainly raised an applied tourism focus on the interface of tourism and landscape design. There is also a neglected area of study – namely, the use of tourism to facilitate urban conservation (Smith, 1988; Ashworth and Tunbridge, 1990).

Research by Smith (1991; 1992a; 1992b) and more recently by King (1997) has focused attention on the planning needs for fragile tourism environments, particularly coastal areas and small islands (Wilkinson, 1997). Indeed, Craig-Smith and Fagence (1994) and Fagence (1996) provide telling critiques of national tourism plans for the Pacific Islands and the inappropriate philosophy and unrealistic visitor forecasts developed by Western-trained planning consultants funded by aid projects. In fact, Stiles and See-Tho (1991) examine the issue of integrated resort development and the tourism planning and investment issues in the Asia Pacific region.

This raises one immediate and telling question – Who is responsible for tourism planning? In the public sector, the role of national tourism organisations (NTOs) are commonly charged with tasks such as tourism strategy formulation, marketing and, in some instances, national plan development. Choy (1991) was highly critical of the failure of NTOs to link tourism plans to market forces, being static documents unable to gauge the dynamism of tourism growth and change. Ironically, countries such as New Zealand have swung to the complete extreme, dispensing with tourism planning at the NTO level, preferring to leave the market to decide the distribution, location, timing and impact of tourism. As Page and Thorn (1997, 1998) observed, this poses major strains for the next tier of planning – the regional, district or city level. This is in stark contrast to the integrated tourism planning model of Languedoc-Roussillon (Klemm, 1992) set in the highly centralised and directed French planning model with tourism infrastructure developed in anticipation of tourism growth.

One feature frequently overlooked in the analysis of NTOs and tourism planning in particular localities is the role of policy (Meethan, 1998) and the manner in which planning is negotiated, derived and steered through public sector processes. The politics of planning and the manner in which private sector interests articulate, lobby and influence the planning process has been largely overlooked in tourism research. In a rural context, Jenkins (1997) reviewed the development of rural tourism policy in Australia and the influence of state and local politics on grant allocations to pump prime development in marginal constituencies. While the published literature on tourism in rural areas has expanded (e.g. Page and Getz, 1997; Sharpley and Sharpley, 1997; Butler et al., 1998), planning issues have not assumed a major focus in many of the studies with a few exceptions (e.g. Gilbert, 1989; Davies and Gilbert, 1992; Evans and Ilbery, 1992) although the identification of impacts using survey methods have highlighted areas of concern for planners (Getz, 1994) and wider issues for individual countries (Fleischer and Pizam, 1997). Among the most significant issues for rural areas are the physical infrastructure needs to accommodate visitors and their activities (e.g. Ritchie, 1998).

It is interesting to also observe the gradual evolution of a greater planning interest in the effects of tourism on host communities and the need to accommodate their needs in planning processes. The innovative and influential synthesis of tourism–community relationships by Murphy (1985) and more recently by Pearce et al. (1996) has refocused attention on the obligations of planners and planning to the local community and in a thorough review of the area. Research by Prentice (1993) highlighted the critical role of community interests in tourism development while among the diversity of social impacts literature which has emerged, Teo's (1994) study of Singapore provided an interesting insight into a managed environment and the effects of tourism on the host population. In contrast, Falade's (1990) examination of tourism planning in Nigeria highlighted community issues for a less developed country.

From the private sector's perspective, comparatively few tourism studies have evaluated the practical planning requirements for successful tourism operations at a local or regional level. Few studies have ventured into the realms of evaluating the effects of specific planning policies (excluding European Union grants – see Pearce, 1990) and the likely effect on business prosperity. Page et al.'s (1999) evaluation of one region in New Zealand developed the innovative work on entrepreneurship and small businesses in tourism by Thomas (1998) and Shaw and Williams (1995). This study identified the absence of planning mechanisms by tourism organisations to promote small business prosperity in the tourism and hospitality sector, which reiterates the criticisms of tourism plans developed by Choy (1991): that they are not dynamic enough to facilitate tourism growth. In an environment where regions and places compete for tourists, planning and place-marketing and promotional activities assume a major role. Yet all too often, the needs of the lifeblood of the tourism and hospitality sector – small businesses – are often overlooked.

With the wide remit of tourism planning, a range of influential studies have been included in this section. These articles are divided into two sections: planning and community-oriented planning studies.

Planning

Getz, D. (1994). Residents' attitudes towards tourism: A longitudinal study in Spey Valley, Scotland, *Tourism Management*, August, 15(4): 247–58.

Community – oriented tourism planning

Robson, J. and Robson, I. (1996). From shareholders to stakeholders: critical issues for tourism marketers, *Tourism Management*, November, 17(7): 533–40.

Haywood, K.M. (1988). Responsible and responsive tourism planning in the community, *Tourism Management*, June, 9(2): 105–18.

Ritchie, J.B. (1993). Crafting a destination vision: Putting the concept of resident-responsiveness into practice, *Tourism Management*, October, 14(5): 379–89.

Getz's innovative longitudinal study of resident attitudes to tourism in Speyside, Scotland is included as one of the few longitudinal papers published within the tourism literature which has an important methodological and planning link to tourism research. In their paper, Robson and Robson examine both the philosophical and practical problems of this approach and the role of public relations companies in shaping ethical attitudes. In the last paper in this section, Ritchie extends the interest in community issues by emphasising the importance of a vision for particular estimations. In this sense, Ritchie's paper operationalises Haywood's (1988) ideas using the example of Calgary. In summary, it is evident that the literature on tourism planning remains a highly specialised and technical area as reflected in planning-based tourism publications. What have expanded are the studies with an implicit planning consequence or which highlight planning dilemmas and debates, although the literature still contains only a limited number of texts and synthesis of tourism planning. The literature is still at a relatively undeveloped stage, with only a limited attention to the process and implementation of planning and the formative influences on policy.

References

Alipour, H. (1996). Tourism development within planning paradigms: The case of Turkey, *Tourism Management*, 17(5): 367–77.

Ashworth, G. and Tunbridge, J. (1990). *The Tourist-Historic City*. London: Belhaven.

Butler, R., Hall, C.M. and Jenkins, J. (eds) (1998). *Tourism and Recreation in Rural Areas*. Chichester: Wiley.

Choy, D. (1991). Tourism planning – the case of market failure, *Tourism Management*, 12(4): 313–30.

Cooper, C. and Ozdil, I. (1992). From mass to responsible tourism: The Turkish experience, *Tourism Management*, 13(4): 377–86.

Craig-Smith, S. and Fagence, M. (1994). A critique of tourism planning in the Pacific, in C. Cooper and A. Lockwood (eds), *Progress in Tourism, Recreation and Hospitality Management*, vol 6. Chichester: Wiley. pp. 92–110.

Davies, E. and Gilbert, D. (1992). A case study of the development of farm tourism in Wales, *Tourism Management*, 13(1): 56–63.

Evans, N. and Ilbery, B. (1992). Advertising and farm-based accommodation: A British case study, *Tourism Management*, 13(4): 415–22.

Fagence, M. (1996). Planning issues in Pacific tourism, in C.M. Hall and S.J. Page (eds), *Tourism in the Pacific: Issues and Cases*, London: International Thomson Business Publishing. pp. 81–90.

Falade, J. (1990). Tourism planning in Nigeria, *Tourism Management*, 11(3): 257–62.

Fleischer, A. and Pizam, A. (1997). Rural tourism in Israel, *Tourism Management*, 18(6): 367–72.

Gartner, W. (1996). *Tourism Development: Principles, Processes and Policies*. New York: Van Nostrand Reinhold.

Getz, D. (1986). Models in tourism planning: towards integration of theory and practise, *Tourism Management*, March, 21–32.

Getz, D. (1994). Resident attitudes towards tourism: A longitudinal study in Spey Valley, Scotland, *Tourism Management*, 15(4): 247–58.

Gilbert, D. (1989). Rural tourism and marketing: Synthesis and new ways of working, *Tourism Management*, 10(1): 51–62.

Gunn, C. (1979). *Tourism Planning*. New York: Crane Rusak.

Hall, C.M. (1991). *Introduction to Tourism in Australia*, 1st edn. Melbourne: Longman Cheshire.

Hall, C.M. (1999). *Tourism and Planning*, Harlow: Pearson Education.

Hall, C.M. and Lew, A. (eds) (1998). *Sustainable Tourism: A Geographical Perspective*. Harlow: Addison Wesley Longman.

Hall, C.M., Jenkins, J. and Kearsley, G. (eds) (1997) *Tourism Planning and Policy in Australia and New Zealand: Cases, Issues and Practice*. Sydney: Irwin.

Haywood, K. (1988). Responsible and responsive tourism planning in the community, *Tourism Management*, 9(2): 105–18.

Inskeep, E. (1991). *Tourism Planning: An Integrated and Sustainable Development Approach*. New York: Van Nostrand Reinhold.

Inskeep, E. (1994). *National and Regional Tourism Planning: Methodologies and Case Studies*. London: Routledge.

Jenkins, J. (1997). The role of the Commonwealth Government in rural tourism and regional development in Australia, in C.M. Hall, J. Jenkins and G. Kearsley (eds), *Tourism Planning and Policy in Australia and New Zealand*. Sydney: Irwin.

King (1997). *Creating Island Resorts*. London: Routledge.

Klemm, M. (1992). Sustainable tourism development: Languedoc-Roussillon thirty years on, *Tourism Management*, 13(2): 169–82.

Meethan, K. (1998). New policy for old? Policy developments in Cornwall and Devon, *Tourism Management*, 19(6): 583–94.

Murphy, P. (1985). *Tourism: A Community Approach*. London: Metheun.

Page, S.J. (1995). *Urban Tourism*. London: Routledge.

Page, S.J. and Getz, D. (eds) (1997). *The Business of Rural Tourism*. London: International Thompson Business Press.

Page, S.J. and Thorn, K. (1997). Towards sustainable tourism planning in New Zealand: Public sector planning responses, *Journal of Sustainable Tourism*, 5(1): 59–77.

Page, S.J. and Thorn, K. (1998). Sustainable tourism development and planning in New Zealand: Local government responses, in C.M. Hall and A. Lew (eds), *Sustainable Tourism: A Geographical Perspective*. Harlow: Addison Wesley Longman.

Page, S.J., Forer, P. and Lawton, G.R. (1999). Small business development and tourism *Terra incognita*, *Tourism Management*, 20(4): 435–60.

Pearce, D.G. (1989). *Tourism Development*. 2nd edn. Harlow: Longman.

Pearce, D.G. (1990). Tourism and regional development in the European Community, *Tourism Management*, 9(1): 11–22.

Pearce, P., Moscardo, G. and Ross, G. (1996) *Tourism Community Relationships*. Oxford: Pergamon.

Prentice, R. (1993). Community-driven tourism planning and residents' perceptions, *Tourism Management*, 14(3): 218–27.

Ritchie, B. (1998). Bicycle tourism in the South Island of New Zealand: Planning and management, *Tourism Management*, 19(6): 567–82.

Sharpley, R. and Sharpley, J. (1997). *Rural Tourism*. London: International Thomson Business Press.

Shaw, G. and Williams, A. (1995). *Critical Issues in Tourism: A Geographical Perspective*. Oxford: Blackwell.

Smith, R.A. (1988). The role of tourism in urban conservation – The case of Singapore. *Cities*, 5(3): 245–59.

Smith, R.A. (1991). Beach resorts: A model of development evolution, *Landscape and Urban Planning*, 21(3): 189–210.

Smith, R.A. (1992a). Coastal urbanisation: Tourism development in the Asia Pacific region, *Built Environment*, 18(1): 27–40.

Smith, R.A. (1992b). Review of integrated beach resort development in Southeast Asia, *Land Use Policy*, 9(3): 209–17.

Stiles, R.B. and Wilke See-Tho (1991). Integrated resort development in the Asia Pacific, *Travel and Tourism Analyst*, 3: 22–37.

Teo, P. (1994). Assessing socio-cultural impacts: The case of Singapore, *Tourism Management*, 15(2): 126–36.

Thomas, R. (ed.) (1998). *The Management of Small Tourism and Hospitality Firms*. London: Cassell.

Wilkinson, P. (1997). *Tourism Policy and Planning: Case Studies from the Commonwealth Caribbean*. New York: Cognizant.

9

Residents' attitudes towards tourism: a longitudinal study in Spey Valley, Scotland

Donald Getz

Department of Tourism and Hospitality Management, University of Calgary, 2500 University Drive NW, Calgary, Alberta, Canada, T2N 1N4

As part of a comprehensive longitudinal evaluation of the development and impacts of tourism in the Badenoch and Strathspey District (often called Spey Valley) of the Scottish Highlands, perceptions and attitudes of local residents were measured in 1978 and again in 1992. Based on the results, implications can be drawn for policy, planning and destination management. As well, methods and results are discussed in the context of theoretical approaches to explaining resident attitudes, and their relationship to the planning and impacts of tourism.

Although there has been a considerable volume of research published on the impacts of tourism, there has been a noticeable dearth of longitudinal studies.[1] This is particularly true in the measurement and evaluation of residents' perceptions and attitudes towards tourism, of which there have been many one-time efforts (for a review, see Ap[2]).

The purposes of longitudinal research are several. Pearce[1] suggested (p. 233) that the evaluation of resident attitudes could be an important component in identifying and measuring tourism impacts, and this is especially relevant over a long period of time during which social and cultural evolution will occur in response to tourism development. Equally important are the policy, planning and management implications: determining public support for tourism and specific types of development; evaluating perceptions of problems that should be solved or opportunities to be exploited. For example, local attitudes and resultant levels of hospitality towards visitors have been identified as a factor shaping the attractiveness of a destination,[3] and negative attitudes could constitute a key threshold in determining the capacity of an area to absorb tourism.[4] Longitudinal studies of perceptions and attitudes can also make substantial contributions to theory. Identification of causal mechanisms is a major theoretical challenge,[5] and residents can provide the local knowledge necessary to link developments with their consequences – particularly the distribution of costs and benefits.

Theoretical background

'Attitudes' have been defined as 'a state of mind of the individual toward a value'[6] and as 'an enduring predisposition towards a particular aspect of one's environment'.[7] They are reinforced by perceptions and beliefs of reality, but are closely related to deeply held values and even to personality – unlike opinions, they do not change quickly. Many researchers feel that attitudes are structured along three dimensions: the cognitive (perceptions and beliefs); the affective (likes and dislikes, based on evaluation); behavioural (actions or expressed intent).[7] However, while attitudes are generally thought to be good predictors of behaviour, the link is not deterministic; situational factors, and the importance people attach to objects of attitudes, intervene.

Ap[8] used the term 'perception' instead of 'attitude', defining perceptions as 'the meaning attributed to an object'. He argued that many residents might attribute meaning to the impacts of tourism without necessarily having knowledge or enduring predispositions. This difference is important, as many studies appear to use the term 'attitude' when, in fact, they have measured 'perceptions'. In the Spey Valley research, perceptions are measured on a satisfaction scale which asks for residents' levels of satisfaction with quality-of-life indicators, while attitudes are measured on a Likert scale. These scales are discussed in detail in an ensuing section.

According to Ap,[8] existing attitudinal research regarding tourism has been primarily exploratory and descriptive (p. 666). Studies have revealed major impacts of tourism and related variables, but theory is underdeveloped: 'Currently there is limited understanding of why residents respond to the impacts of tourism as they do, and under what conditions residents react to those impacts' (p. 666). Husbands concurred, saying that 'There is, so far, no theoretical justification of why some people are, or are not, favourably disposed to tourism'.[9]

Several models have been developed to help explain the impacts of tourism and their relationship with residents' attitudes. Doxey's well-known 'Irridex'[10] suggests that resident attitudes towards tourism evolve from initial 'euphoria', through 'apathy' and 'annoyance' to 'antagonism', as perceived costs outweigh the real or expected benefits. Research by Long et al.[11] provided support to this model by concluding that resident attitudes commenced favourably and later reached a threshold after which support for tourism would decline.

The sequential Irridex model should not be interpreted as being deterministic. Rothman[12] believed that communities with long experience of tourism are able to develop mechanisms to accommodate inconveniences, which suggests that resident attitudes might also change as time goes by. A more complex model has been suggested by Butler,[13] featuring the potential for a community simultaneously to hold positive and negative attitudes along with active and passive support or opposition. This model can help explain political reactions to tourism, including the influential role of small interest groups. As well, the direction of attitudes is shown to be flexible, in response to changing conditions and perceptions. Support for this model comes from Murphy,[14] who found distinct attitude differences among administrators, business persons and residents in English tourist centres. Also supporting a non-linear model is the hypothesis of Dogan[15] who believed that resident attitudinal and behavioural responses to tourism could include resistance, retreat, boundary maintenance, revitalization and adoption. He argued that the initial response to tourism development, especially in rural or Third World settings, might be uniform within the resident population. However, attitudes and behavioural responses would evolve as groups became differentiated by their relationship with, or perceptions of tourism.

Perhaps the most promising approach, as explained by Ap,[8] is 'social exchange theory'. Applying the theory to tourism, Ap suggested that residents evaluate the expected benefits and costs which are realized in exchange for resources and services. He formulated a number of propositions which can be used as hypotheses, the essence of which is that positive resident attitudes towards tourism occur when perceived rewards, as opposed to costs, are satisfactory and balanced. Principles of 'rationality' (reward seeking), 'satisficing' (satisfying minimal aspirations), 'reciprocity' (mutual gratification) and 'justice' (fairness or equity) must be met. Support for the tenets of social exchange theory can be found throughout much of the related literature, as demonstrated in the following review, although results are somewhat mixed on specific relationships and causes.

Perdue et al.[16] concluded from a review of research that most perception and attitude studies have looked at differences in perceived impacts of tourism among resident types. They summarized the research by saying that: it revealed little difference in perceived tourism impacts by socio-demographic characteristics; perceived impacts decrease as the distance between the respondent's home and the tourism sector of the community increases; overall favourability of tourism impact perceptions increases with the individual's economic dependency on tourism. Following social exchange theory, they concluded that the literature supports the contention that people who benefit from tourism perceive greater economic and fewer social and environmental impacts from tourism than those who do not benefit. When controlling for personal benefits in their Colorado research, Perdue et al. observed that 'perceived positive impacts of tourism are much more closely related to personal benefits than are the perceived negative impacts' (p. 593), and support for additional development was positively related to personal benefits and to perceived positive impacts. One implication of their research was that public relations campaigns could be used to increase local support for tourism if they improved tourism's image – particularly among people who do not benefit directly. It was also suggested by these researchers that support for tourism was higher in communities pessimistic about their economic future – they called this the 'doomsday phenomenon'.

Schroeder[17] also found that socio-economic variables were not good predictors of perceptions in his Flagstaff, Arizona sample. However, Husbands[9] reported that age and education were important variables in his Zambian study, and that social class must be considered. Other researchers have concluded that certain socio-demographic variables are important, including age and language.[18] Several writers[19] have mentioned proximity to tourism development or activity as a factor in explaining attitudes, but Sheldon and Var[20] found that residents in North Wales who lived in high-density tourist areas were not more negative in their attitudes towards tourists. Conversely, Haukeland[21] found that more negative attitudes toward continued growth existed in the most developed tourism areas he studied, so the available evidence is mixed.

The types and intensity of visitor–resident contacts have been suggested as variables important in shaping resident attitudes. Most significant of these, at least in terms of attention paid by researchers, is employment and economic dependency on tourism.[22] Dependency is generally felt to account for positive attitudes towards tourism, although Liu and Var[23] reported that residents of Hawaii were so uniformly aware of tourism and related issues that direct contact or dependency on tourism did not explain attitudinal differences. In the Hawaii research it was found that ethnicity and length of residence were the most important socio-demographic variables explaining attitudinal differences. Liu and Var note that other writers have suggested length of residence to be important,[23] but this factor could be based on varying levels of knowledge and perceptions, as well as motivations for moving to the area.

Several researchers have focused on specific costs and benefits of tourism in seeking to explain attitudes. For example, Murphy and Andresson[24] concluded that residents of different areas on Vancouver Island saw tourism as a means to preserve cultural heritage, justify public amenities or create jobs. Wilkinson and Murray,[25] in a study of the Town of Collingwood, Ontario, saw evidence of an insider versus outsider attitude (i.e., permanent versus seasonal residents), with the permanent residents seemingly welcoming tourism and recreation-related jobs but resenting changing lifestyles, traffic and higher taxes. Impacts on residents' leisure have also been explored frequently,[26] revealing both problems of resident–visitor competition for resources and appreciation of tourism-related opportunities. Many of these studies, however, have measured perceptions of costs and benefits rather than attitudes.

Murphy[27] suggested that the types of recreational or tourist development in a community will affect attitudes, as day-trip impacts are different from short- and long-stay effects. He also concluded that in major tourism centres residents' perceptions were similar, owing to high levels of information about impacts. One other factor identified as shaping resident attitudes is that of political control. Keller[28] said that a loss of financial control will change resident attitudes, while D'Amore[29] concluded that local investment and ownership is necessary for avoiding social carrying capacity problems.

Not all theoretical issues can be addressed in the Spey Valley analysis, but arising from this theoretical review several key research questions are addressed: (1) have there been changes in attitudes over a long period of time, and if so, what explains them?; (2) do results in this case study support social exchange theory for explaining resident attitudes towards tourism?; (3) what are the theoretical implications of perception and attitude measurement for a better understanding of the long-term impacts of tourism? In addition, very practical implications for tourism planning and policy in the case study area are evaluated.

The Spey Valley case study

The Badenoch and Strathspey District lies within the Highland Region of Scotland (a regional government unit) and within the jurisdiction of Highlands and Islands Enterprise (formerly Highlands and Islands Development Board). It includes part of the granite plateau of the Cairngorm mountains and contains some of the most attractive rural and natural resources in Scotland: a rich variety of valley and wild mountain scenery, Caledonian forests, unique wildlife, lochs and rivers. The limitation of physical resources in the Spey Valley, while impeding the development of primary and manufacturing sectors, has favoured the development of tourism and recreation.

Small-scale, traditional patterns gave way suddenly to large-scale tourism in the 1960s. Government and private investors combined to develop the Aviemore Centre – completed in 1966 – which resulted in Spey Valley becoming Great Britain's first truly four-season resort destination. The development was intended to provide all-weather leisure facilities to help expand the tourist season.

While the Aviemore Centre facility was featured prominently in marketing the Spey Valley through the 1970s and into the 1980s, by 1992 it was in a run-down condition and the Aviemore and Spey Valley Tourist Board did not include any photos of the Centre in its tourist guide. The physical decline can be attributed to a lack of re-investment in the facilities, and to decline in demand which was at least partially due to two recessions in the early 1980s and 1990s plus several poor skiing seasons. The original owners sold the Centre to a hotel company in 1986, and a year later the new owners shut down the Santa Claus Land family attraction and its related shops; the indoor swimming pool was closed permanently in 1991. In 1992 the Centre's facilities and undeveloped land were sold to a property development company, but ownership of three large hotels in the Centre and the nearby Coylumbridge Hotel was retained.

Badenoch and Strathspey District has grown slowly since the development of large-scale tourism. In 1961 there were 9093 residents; by 1981 the population was 9363, and in 1989 it had grown to 10 800.[30] The Regional Council's forecast was for growth to a population of 11 508 by 1993. But growth was concentrated in Aviemore (population approximately 2400) and the other main villages (Grantown: 3241; Kingussie: 1461; Newtonmore: 1172), while depopulation continued in the rural portions. The characteristics of the population also changed, becoming younger and less Scottish in terms of birthplace, as many individuals and families moved to the area for employment.[31]

This trend, in a region which had experienced heavy depopulation for many decades, is confirmation of the success of tourism as a job creator and growth generator. Although out-migration has continued, it has been compensated by in-migration for jobs and retirement. However, this growth peaked by the mid-1980s. Economic dependence on tourism was evident as early as the late 1970s, and tourism remains the dominant employer in the 1990s.

In 1978 detailed interviews within the local industry were carried out by the author and assistants, permitting a very accurate measure of direct employment. Data were collected for the accommodation sector (except bed and breakfast and self-catering establishments) plus sport/recreation facilities and attractions (but not restaurants or retailing). The total was estimated to be 1100 full-time, all-year positions (about 30% of all jobs in the district). Of these jobs 42% were for males. About 209 all-year, part-time jobs were measured (mostly for females) and there were also seasonal increases in jobs, both summer and winter.

Aviemore and the immediate area extending through Coylumbridge to Cairngorm (the ski facility) is the focus of tourism/hospitality employment in the district. In 1978 this central portion of Spey Valley accounted for 65% of the permanent jobs for males (it includes the ski facility) and 59% of those for females. In 1992 this concentrated pattern had not changed.

Methodology

To measure attitudes and obtain other detailed information concerning the impacts of tourism on residents, random household surveys were necessitated. In 1978 the research was completed during the height of tourism development and in-migration in Spey Valley. Aviemore Centre was 12 years old and tourism demand was growing. Residents had clear perceptions of tourism's impacts and strong opinions on related political and development issues, such as the controversy surrounding proposed expansion of skiing facilities on Cairngorm. By 1992, conditions had changed markedly. Two recessions and several poor skiing seasons had weakened the industry, resulting in well-publicised bankruptcies, hotel sales and the decline of Aviemore Centre. Dependence on tourism had not lessened, and residents were worried. The Cairngorm ski-expansion issue was still at the fore, despite refusals by the Secretary of State in both 1982 and 1992 to allow expansion.

The 1978 survey consisted of 132 households, randomly selected from district property valuation lists which were geographically stratified to ensure full coverage of the district – 4% of households from each village and rural sub-area, were selected. The researcher and several paid assistants made repeat visits, as necessary, and achieved a very high completion rate of 86%, thus ensuring a very representative sample. Comparison of the sample with census data revealed that only single-female households (usually older persons) were under-represented. Structured interviews were used; some questions pertained to household heads (self-defined), others to all household members. A combination of random and quota selection within households was used to obtain a gender and age-balanced subsample for the satisfaction and attitude scales.

Conducted under the auspices of the Scottish Tourist Board, the 1992 household survey consisted of a random postal survey with postage-free mailback, drawn from the list of voters. A 4% sample was taken from each village and rural sub-area, thereby closely replicating the 1978 sample frame. However, the postal method resulted in a 40% response rate ($n = 79$). While this reduced response rate might suggest that the 1992 sample is somewhat less representative than the earlier one, the samples are quite similar (see Table 1). Gender is roughly balanced, but there was a higher proportion of males in 1992. The age spread is similar, particularly when comparing the categories of 29 years and under, and 50 years and over. The portion of local-born respondents is lower in 1992, but length of residence is similar if one compares the percentages in the categories 5 years and less, and 16 years and over. In 1978, 41 of 130 households (31.5%) in the survey reported at least one member working in a tourism establishment. In 1992 the respondents were asked if they felt their job, if any, was part of the tourist industry: 28 responded yes (35.4%), 26 no and 25 were not applicable. Although the questions were not identical, the results suggest that a slightly higher proportion of tourism-dependent respondents was obtained in 1992. Overall, characteristics of the two samples suggest that they should not account for major differences in responses.

Table 1. Characteristics of household survey respondents.

	1978		1992	
	No	%	No	%
Male	61	46.9	43	54.4
Female	69	53.1	36	45.6
Total	130		79	
Age	1978 (%)		1992 (%)	
16–19	5.4		3.8	
20–29	12.3		13.9	
30–39	26.2		15.2	
40–49	15.4		20.3	
50–59	13.1		19.0	
60+	27.7		27.8	
Origin	1978 (%)		1992 (%)	
This District	29		13.9	
HIDB area[a]	17		21.5	
Elsewhere Scotland	35		40.5	
Other UK	16		21.5	
Europe	2		2.5	
Length of residence (years)	1978 (%)		1992 (%)	
1–5	20		19.2	
6–10	13		26.9	
11–15	12		7.6	
16–20	7		12.8	
Over 20	48		33.3	

[a] Highlands and Islands Development Board area.

Two other samples were covered by the 1978 research, to provide a comparison with the general population. The first consisted of 47 resident owners and one resident manager of businesses, selected specifically to represent a cross-section of the tourism sector. This sample is balanced geographically and includes: 13 guest houses; 23 small hotels; four self-catering; five sports establishments; one outdoor centre; one manager of another tourism establishment. Six industry respondents were Spey Valley natives, five others were born elsewhere in the Highlands and Islands, 17 came from other parts of Scotland, 15 from elsewhere in the UK, and four from abroad. Thirty-three had purchased their establishments in 1970 or more recently, so a majority were newcomers. The 'conservation' sample consisted of 23 members (out of the full 35 to whom a postal questionnaire was sent) of the local conservation club. Many of these respondents were newcomers to the district.

Satisfaction and attitude scales

To test the perceptual or cognitive dimension of attitudes a satisfaction scale has been used. This provides a relatively straightforward measure of how residents evaluate objects – in this case elements of quality of life in Spey Valley. To measure the affective dimension, emotive statements in a Likert scale were used, with the specific goal of differentiating subgroups of the population which hold different attitudes towards one or more domains. Some of the statements in the Likert scale also reflect perceptions of impacts, similar to the satisfaction scale; it is the pattern and direction of scores from all six statements in each domain that reveals underlying attitudes.

Ideally, a batch of statements is derived from thorough knowledge of the subjects being explored, then tested on a subsample of the population. Item analysis can be employed to produce a list of statements which best discriminate positive and negative attitudes; this increases internal consistency. Factor analysis can be used to identify and eliminate highly correlated items. To assess validity, measures from special-interest groups can be compared with those from a random sample.[7]

For the 1978 research, statements were grounded in local knowledge of the nature of the industry, its apparent impacts, and issues identified by local media and key informants. Item and factor analysis were not used, and while this resulted in a few statements that did not differentiate well (i.e., everyone answered the same way), this is not felt to be a problem because each domain contained multiple statements. Special-interest samples were employed as a validity check. The same items were used in 1992, but special-interest samples were not achievable.

Four 'domains' were selected as having strong relevance to the Spey Valley (see Table 2). The primary interest was with resident attitudes towards tourism. Other major issues in the area engendered three domains: 'conservation', 'newcomers' and 'growth and change'. These four domains proved to be somewhat overlapping, but each possessed statements that clearly differentiated attitude groups. Statements were placed in random order on the questionnaires, with half of the 24 worded so that agreement constituted a favourable attitude toward the domain, and half the opposite.

Analysis of Likert scales usually employs means, with the scale items ranging in value from 1 to 5; the higher the mean, the more positive the attitude towards the domain. However, even though such scales are often interpreted to be interval in nature, statistical analysis is restricted if this assumption is not made. For this reason, as well as the policy and planning orientation of the research, the Spey Valley attitudinal data have been analysed primarily by way of an index of consensus developed by the author. This index of consensus has the advantage of revealing the weight of public attitudes towards the issues being assessed (see Figures 1 and 2).

Complete consensus is indicated by a value of 1.0 (plus or minus), which can only be obtained if all respondents agree/strongly agree or disagree/strongly disagree, and none selects the 'uncertain' category. Consensus is therefore low on items gathering a large number of 'uncertains', and when there is a split between positive and negative responses. Calculation of the index is as follows: (1) addition of the number of respondents who selected agree/strongly agree, and the number who selected disagree/strongly disagree; (2) subtraction of the smaller sum from the larger; (3) division of the difference by the total number of respondents; (4) assignation of a positive or negative sign, according to the *a priori* determination of whether agreement with the statement represents a positive or negative attitude towards the domain. The scales cannot be interpreted without this determination, so in Table 2 each one is labelled 'favourable' (F) or 'not favourable' (NF).

Table 2. Changes in attitude, 1978–92.

Domains and statements	*	SA	A	U	D	SD	a.	i.
Tourism:								
5. Tourism can be thanked for bringing	1978	17	67	21	21	2	3.6	0.48
good facilities to this area. (Favourable [F])	1992	8	28	18	23	3	3.2	−0.13
6. The truly local people do not benefit much	1978	12	40	20	40	16	3.1	0.03
from the tourist industry. (Not favourable [NF])	1992	5	27	7	31	10	3.1	0.11
9. Tourism is this area's big advantage over	1978	12	70	22	21	3	3.5	0.45
other parts of the Highlands. (F)	1992	6	35	21	18	0	3.4	0.29
11. Tourists bring money and jobs and that is more	1978	16	65	13	29	5	3.5	0.37
important than the nuisance they cause. (F)	1992	7	31	11	21	10	3.1	0.09
15. The tourist industry has become an	1978	2	11	22	80	13	3.7	0.63
insult to the Scottish heritage. (NF)	1992	4	8	21	41	6	3.5	0.44
22. Tourists are responsible for more	1978	3	9	24	75	17	3.7	0.63
damage than they are worth. (NF)	1992	4	8	14	45	9	3.6	0.52
Growth and change:								
1. Now that the district has started to develop, more	1978	27	42	23	34	2	3.5	0.26
must be done to keep it growing. (F)	1992	12	34	6	14	13	3.2	0.24
7. We need more manufacturing	1978	32	42	17	27	10	3.5	0.29
industry in this area. (F)	1992	11	32	12	20	5	3.3	0.23
8. Much of what was the best of Spey Valley has	1978	7	10	33	69	9	3.5	0.48
already been ruined by needless growth. (NF)	1992	4	18	17	38	2	3.2	0.23
19. Not enough effort is being put into	1978	15	31	25	50	7	3.0	−0.09
modernizing the Highlands. (F)	1992	8	16	18	34	3	2.9	−0.16
20. The point has been reached when no more growth	1978	4	26	35	54	9	3.3	0.26
should be permitted in this area. (NF)	1992	8	17	12	32	10	3.2	0.22
23. Each new development just adds	1978	3	14	22	80	9	3.6	0.56
to our problems. (NF)	1992	4	18	10	41	6	3.3	0.32
Newcomers:								
3. If we get a lot of new people moving here	1978	9	27	31	52	9	3.2	0.20
it will spoil things for everyone. (NF)	1992	12	20	15	27	4	2.8	−0.01
13. I sometimes feel like a stranger in my own	1978	5	28	9	69	17	3.5	0.41
community because of all the newcomers. (NF)	1992	11	18	5	41	5	3.1	0.21
17. Newcomers have become a valuable part of	1978	15	65	36	12	0	3.7	0.53
this community. (F)	1992	8	43	13	11	5	3.5	0.44
18. A lot of trouble makers have moved into this	1978	6	20	20	68	14	3.5	0.44
area lately. (NF)	1992	6	13	9	40	10	3.4	0.40
21. It is good to see this district attract ambitious	1978	12	89	21	6	0	3.8	0.74
people to live here. (F)	1992	9	40	17	11	3	3.5	0.44
24. The Highlands need more new	1978	15	58	25	28	2	3.4	0.34
faces and new ideas. (F)	1992	10	34	18	12	6	3.4	0.33
Conservation:								
2. It would have been nicer living in the Spey Valley	1978	14	30	29	51	4	3.0	−0.08
twenty years ago. (F)	1992	15	23	21	17	4	3.4	0.21
4. Not nearly enough has been done to protect	1978	14	37	14	56	7	3.0	−0.09
our attractive countryside. (F)	1992	12	33	8	22	4	3.3	0.24
10. It is more important to get jobs for local people	1978	25	58	27	16	2	2.3	−0.51
than to preserve scenery for others. (NF)	1992	6	25	20	22	7	3.0	−0.03
12. We must protect wildlife even at the expense of	1978	37	69	11	10	1	4.0	0.74
some development. (F)	1992	23	40	9	5	3	3.9	0.69
14. More skiing facilities would not hurt the	1978	12	57	27	23	9	2.7	−0.29
Cairngorms too much. (NF)	1992	18	21	13	6	21	2.9	−0.15
16. Nature reserves are here for people to use and	1978	24	71	16	16	1	2.2	−0.61
more access should be provided to them. (NF)	1992	9	35	18	13	4	2.6	−0.34

Key: a. Average out of 5.00; i. Index value out of 1.00 (+ or −); numbers of responses: SD = strongly disagree; D = disagree; U = uncertain; A = agree; SA = strongly agree.

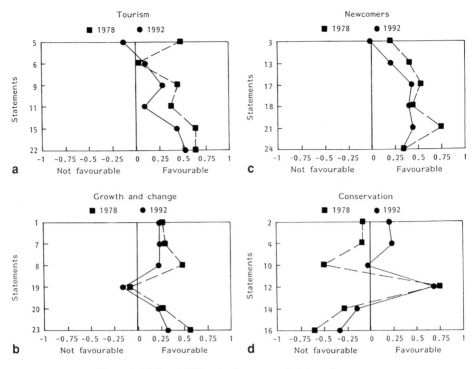

Figure 1. 1978 and 1992 attitudes compared: index of consensus.

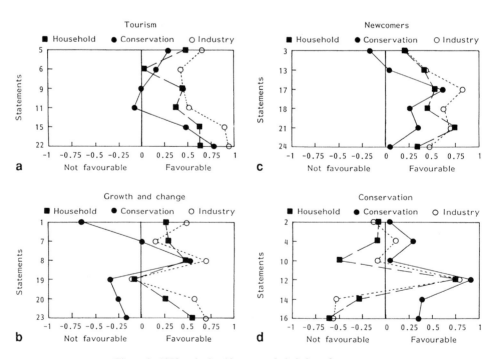

Figure 2. 1978 attitudes (three samples): index of consensus.

Analysis

Tourism

Table 2, column (a.) shows the mean scores, out of a maximum value of 5.0. 'Strongly agree' is scored 5 in 'favourable' statements, but for 'not favourable' statements the scoring is reversed. Mean scores for the six tourism statements had diminished from 1978 to 1992, signifying a somewhat more negative overall attitude towards tourism.

Index values shown in Table 2, column (i.), reveal that in both years attitudes towards tourism were mostly positive. Figure 1 graphically compares the index scores for 1978 and 1992, revealing an overall lower level of consensus in 1992. The index value of statement 5 ('Tourism can be thanked for bringing good facilities to this area') fell into the negative side in 1992, reflecting a major change in perceived impacts. Closure of the Santa Claus Land and swimming pool facilities in Aviemore Centre, as well as the resort's general decline, probably explains this increased negativism; in 1978 the facilities had been looked upon as major benefits of tourism.

Results of the other tourism-related statements strongly suggest that most residents do not believe tourism is an insult to the Scottish heritage, or that tourists cause more damage than they are worth. Spey Valley residents recognize that tourism gives an advantage over the rest of the region, but are not at all certain that native Highlanders benefit much from the industry.

Figure 2 compares the three 1978 samples, revealing (as expected) a highly positive attitude towards tourism on the part of owners/managers. The response pattern of the household sample was similar to the industry sample, but notably more negative (with no consensus) on statement six: many more residents felt that local people were not benefiting from tourism. Also as expected, the conservation sample was somewhat more negative towards tourism, yet their consensus scores were mostly on the favourable side.

Growth and change

The pattern of responses was remarkably consistent over the 14-year period, revealing continued, but slightly lesser support for growth and change; means and index scores were lower on all six statements. In both years one item ('Not enough effort is being put into modernizing the Highlands') generated a negative (i.e., anti-change) response, either reflecting a belief that the efforts were in fact adequate, or that too much modernization is not desirable. Other responses suggest that the latter interpretation is correct. The substantially lower index values for two statements (No 8 and No 23) in 1992 reveal an increased belief that problems and growth are related.

Comparing the three 1978 samples, it can be seen that the conservation sample was mostly negative, and the industry sample was the most positive. Nevertheless, a fairly high degree of consensus was evident in all three samples on statement No 8: few respondents believed that 'needless growth' had already ruined the area.

Newcomers

The overall positive attitude towards newcomers endured through 1992, although means and index values fell. The one negative index value in 1992 (No 3) reveals an increased concern about continued in-migration. There was also a major change regarding the statement: 'It is good to see this district attract ambitious people to live here'. The attitude remained positive in 1992, but with a much lower mean score and index value. Figure 2 shows that the three 1978 samples were all largely positive towards newcomers, although the conservation sample feared continued high levels of in-migration.

Conservation

The results suggest that a more positive attitude towards conservation had emerged in 1992, although there are both positive and negative responses to the statements. In both years there was near unanimity on the No 12 statement: 'We must protect wildlife even at the expense of some development'. Whatever the interpretation of the other responses, this shows that most residents share some degree of conservation ethic. Responses to items No 14 and No 16 reveal a belief (although somewhat diminished in 1992) that ski development and access to nature reserves can be increased, and while this is interpreted as being negative towards conservation (the responses of the conservation group in 1978 corroborate this interpretation), it may be that residents genuinely believe that development and conservation are not incompatible.

The 1978 samples, as expected, revealed the conservation group to hold the most positive attitude towards conservation. The fact that their consensus scores were not high on several of the items could be interpreted in two ways: that conservation club members recognized the need for some development, or that they believed some development would be compatible with conservation.

Satisfaction changes

Table 3 compares the 1978 and 1992 household sample on satisfaction levels. In 1978 the question allowed for 11 responses (from 0 to 10), but in 1992 the question allowed only 10 responses (from 1 to 10). To facilitate direct comparison the data were grouped into low, medium and high categories (scores of 0, 1, 2 and 3 = low; 4, 5, 6 = medium; 7, 8, 9, 10 = high). Percentages are used (excluding non-responses) in order to compare the changes over the 14-year period.

Because the scales are not of an interval nature, interpretation of changes in scores over time requires judgement. Most of the items reveal a change for the worse, which is revealed by fewer responses in the high and/or more in the low categories. Increased negativism is particularly clear with regard to 'the way in which the Spey Valley is changing' and 'the way in which local people have a say in important decisions made for this area'. As well, the decline in satisfaction with sport and recreational facilities is very pronounced, reflecting in part the closures in Aviemore Centre.

Table 3. Changes in satisfaction, 1978–92.

	1978			1992		
How satisfied are you with/that	Low (%)	Med (%)	High (%)	Low (%)	Med (%)	High (%)
1. your present job	1	14	85	4	21	75
2. the choice of jobs you could have in this district	58	26	16	52	31	16
3. the way in which the Spey Valley is changing	18	42	40	33	46	21
4. the choice of housing you could have in this district	43	24	32	39	32	29
5. the health services here, compared with the rest of Scotland	11	11	78	6	5	88
6. the public bus transportation service in this district	76	16	8	55	27	18
7. sport and recreational facilities in this district	17	19	64	44	22	35
8. the way in which local people have a say in important decisions made for this area	35	33	33	39	43	18
9. that crime and vandalism are being kept under control in this area	15	11	74	14	22	65
10. that your village (or nearest village) provides all the facilities and services you think are needed	19	30	52	32	37	32
11. that schools and education are as good here as in the rest of Scotland	6	9	85	5	16	78
12. that social and welfare problems are being well looked after in this area	6	22	72	15	23	63
13. that the Spey Valley is a good place in which to bring up children	2	9	90	5	6	88

It is doubtful that the general negativity of residents is an artefact of the sample, or an unthinking cynicism that might reflect general economic and social patterns. This conclusion is warranted by the increase in satisfaction with public transport and health services, which reflect tangible improvements made in this district. As well, the final item provides a kind of overall indicator of satisfaction with life in the Spey Valley. A large majority of residents in both 1978 and 1992 strongly believed 'that the Spey Valley is a good place in which to bring up children'.

The link between satisfaction and attitude scores is apparent. More negative satisfaction scores reveal perceptions that many aspects of life in the area have become worse, and this is reflected in the attitude scales which revealed generally lower levels of consensus in favour of tourism, growth and change. Because many of the perceived benefits of tourism development have not been realized, or have declined in recent years, residents seem to be more cautious about supporting tourism and growth.

Conclusions and implications

From a planning and policy perspective, the measurement of perceptions and attitudes in Spey Valley has important implications. Residents have been found to be largely supportive of tourism and the changes that development has brought. But while the general pattern of attitudes remained consistent from 1978 to 1992, an increasing negativism is apparent. This probably reflects the industry's poor performance in recent years (especially the decline in Aviemore Centre), a feeling that 'truly local people' are still not receiving sufficient benefits, and perhaps a stronger conservation ethic. The industry and planners can count on public support for resort revitalization and even some growth in tourism, but not necessarily for every project.

Turning to specific issues, the attitude and satisfaction scales reveal a major disappointment in the closing of facilities in Aviemore Centre. Providing resident-orientated leisure facilities should be a priority in future redevelopment. There is also a modest consensus for more skiing development and access to nature reserves, but it is also known that considerable organized opposition exists. Given the two-time failure to secure approval for Cairngorm skiing expansion, planners and industry leaders might better concentrate on restoring the Aviemore Centre's attractiveness and expanding nature-based services and packages. Providing more support to foster employment and business opportunities for Highlanders, such as local training opportunities recently introduced by the Moray, Badenoch and Strathspey Enterprise company, should help overcome much of the increased negativism.

Methodologically, the attitude scales worked well. They differentiated subgroups, as evidenced by the three 1978 samples, and demonstrated remarkable stability over the 14-year interval. These facts suggest that a high degree of validity was achieved, although item and factor analysis could have been employed to refine the scales. The satisfaction scale also worked well to reveal issues and perceptions of changing conditions.

Case study results cannot necessarily be generalized for wider application. Because the Spey Valley is a rural area with few development alternatives, residents are aware of their dependence on tourism. And because development and tourist demand peaked in the 1980s, this destination can be said to be in a mature state in which elements of growth, decline and planned rejuvenation coexist. Accordingly, the case study is not typical of destinations which continue to grow and expand, resulting in more and more negative impacts. Generalization to high-growth or to urban areas might therefore be inappropriate.

However, this study does contribute to theoretical understanding of tourism impact causation and resultant resident attitude formation. Specifically, the Spey Valley case study lends support to the social exchange theory of attitude formation. Although this research did not test specifically for a relationship between economic dependence and attitudes towards tourism, the 1978 samples clearly revealed that owners and managers of businesses were the most positive about tourism, growth and change. Also, the general state of economic dependence on tourism and knowledge about the industry in Spey Valley are very high. Accordingly, the overall positive attitude towards tourism and growth reflects the belief that the industry's benefits outweigh the costs to residents. However, increased negativism and dissatisfaction over the 14-year interval suggests that residents believe benefits have declined, or have not matched expectations.

The decline in favourable scores and satisfaction levels appears to support the Irridex model of increasing negative attitudes over time (in response to the negative impacts of tourism development), but the evidence does not totally support such a conclusion. Rather, it appears that the negativism witnessed in 1992 reflects specific economic problems related to recession, and decline in the Aviemore Centre. An economic rebound and improvements to the resort would probaby result in improved levels of satisfaction and more positive attitudes towards tourism. In other words, attitudes follow perceived costs and benefits, and these are not necessarily of an ever-worsening nature. Even if benefits do decline and costs or problems increase over time, recognition of the absence of viable economic alternatives could result in both lowered satisfaction and continued support for tourism. This reflects the conclusion of Perdue et al.[16] that positive attitudes increase during economic downturns.

These findings also have implications for the destination life-cycle concept and the issue of capacity.[32] Increasing negativism in Spey Valley residents' attitudes appears to signal displeasure over perceived costs and benefits, which is both a manageable problem and subject to cyclical evolution. The Spey Valley evidence shows that most residents are not increasingly hostile towards tourism and tourists, nor have they become very negative on growth and change. Capacity thresholds in Spey Valley relate more to the restrictions on skiing development and general concern about environmental impact than they do to resident attitudes.

Acknowledgements

The author is greateful to the Scottish Tourist Board for their participation in this research. Thanks go to Darren Joncas for his technical support, and to Tazim Jamal for valuable comments. All opinions, and any errors, are those of the author alone.

References

1. Pearce, D *Tourist Development* 2nd edn, Longman, Harlow (1989) 228 pp
2. Ap, J 'Residents' perceptions research on the social impacts of tourism' *Annals of Tourism Research* 1990 **17** (4) 610–616
3. Inskeep, E *Tourism Planning* Van Nostrand Reinhold, New York, (1991) 85
4. Butler, R 'The concept of a tourism area cycle of evolution: implications for management of resources' *The Canadian Geographer* 1980 **24** 5–12
5. Getz, D 'Models in tourism planning: towards integration of research and practice' *Tourism Management* 1986 **7** (1) 21–32
6. Allport, G 'Attitudes in the history of social psychology' in Warren, N and Jahoda, M (eds) *Attitudes* Penguin, Harmondsworth (1966) 24
7. McDougall, G and Munro, H 'Scaling and attitude measurement in tourism and travel research' in Ritchie, B and Goeldner, C (eds) *Travel, Tourism and Hospitality Research* Wiley, New York (1987), 87, 88
8. Ap, *op cit*, Ref 2, 671
9. Husbands, W 'Social status and perception of tourism in Zambia' *Annals of Tourism Research* 1989 **16** (2) 239
10. Doxey, G 'A causation theory of visitor–resident irritants: methodology and research inferences' in *The Impact of Tourism, Sixth Annual Conference Proceedings of the Travel Research Association* (1975) 195–198
11. Long, P, Perdue, R and Allen, L 'Rural resident tourism perceptions and attitudes by community level of tourism' *Journal of Travel Research* 1990 **28** (3) 3–9

12. Rothman, R 'Residents and transients: community reaction to seasonal visitors' *Journal of Travel Research* 1978 **6** (3) 8–13
13. Butler, R 'Tourism as an agent of social change' in *Tourism as a Factor in National and Regional Development* Occasional Paper 4, Department of Geography, Trent University, Peterborough (1975) 85–90
14. Murphy, P 'Perceptions and attitudes of decisionmaking groups in tourism centers' *Journal of Travel Research* 1983 **21** (3) 8–12
15. Dogan, H 'Forms of adjustment: sociocultural impacts of tourism' *Annals of Tourism Research* 1989 **16** (2) 216–236
16. Perdue, R, Long, P and Allen, L 'Resident support for tourism development' *Annals of Tourism Research* 1990 **17** (4) 586–599
17. Schroeder, T 'Host community perceptions of tourism's impacts: a cluster analysis' *Visions in Leisure and Business* 1992 **10** (4) 43–48
18. Brougham, J and Butler, R 'A segmentation analysis of resident attitudes to the social impact of tourism' *Annals of Tourism Research* 1981 **7** (4) 569–590
19. Belilse, F and Hoy, D 'The perceived impact of tourism by residents: a case study in Santa Marta, Columbia' *Annals of Tourism Research* 1980 **7** (1) 83–101
20. Sheldon, P and Var, T 'Resident attitudes to tourism in north Wales' *Tourism Management* 1984 **5** (1) 40–47
21. Haukeland, J, 'Sociocultural impacts of tourism in Scandinavia: studies of three host communities' *Tourism Management* 1984 **5** (3) 207–214
22. Milman, A and Pizam, A 'Social impacts of tourism on central Florida' *Annals of Tourism Research* 1988 **15** (2) 191–204
23. Liu, J and Var, T 'Resident attitudes toward tourism impacts in Hawaii' *Annals of Tourism Research* 1986 **13** (2) 193–214
24. Murphy, P and Andersson, B 'Tourism development on Vancouver Island: an assessment of the core–periphery model' *Professional Geographer* 1988 **40** (1) 32–42
25. Wilkinson, P and Murray, A 'Centre and periphery: the impacts of leisure and tourism on a small town' in Smale, B (ed) *Leisure Challenges: Bringing People, Resources, and Policy Into Play* Proc of Sixth Canadian Congress on Leisure Research, Unversity of Waterloo, Ontario Research Council on Leisure (1990) 237–278
26. McKercher, B 'Tourism as a conflicting land use' *Annals of Tourism Research* 1992 **19** (3) 467–481; and Snepenger, D and Johnson, H 'Potential self-identification and perceptions of tourism' *Annals of Tourism Research* 1991 **18** (3) 511–515
27. Murphy, P 'Community attitudes to tourism: a comparative analysis' *Tourism Management* 1981 **2** (3) 189–195
28. Keller, P 'Centre–periphery tourism development and control' in *Leisure, Tourism and Social Change* Congress Proc, Edinburgh, Tourism and Recreation Research Unit (1983)
29. D'Amore, L 'Guidelines to planning in harmony with the host community' in Murphy P (ed) *Tourism in Canada: Selected Issues and Options* Western Geographical Series Vol 21, University of Victoria (1983) 135–157
30. Highland Regional Council, *HRC Structure Plan* Inverness (1989)
31. Getz, D 'Tourism and population change: long-term impacts of tourism in the Badenoch and Strathspey District of the Scottish Highlands' *Scottish Geographical Magazine* 1986 **102** (2) 113–126
32. Getz, D 'A rationale and methodology for assessing capacity to absorb tourism' *Ontario Geography* 1982 **19** 92–102

10

From shareholders to stakeholders: critical issues for tourism marketers

Jane Robson

*University of Northumbria at Newcastle, Northumberland Road,
Newcastle upon Tyne, NE1 8ST, UK*

Ian Robson

*Centre for Marketing Practice, Dundee Business School, University of Abertay,
Dundee DD3 6HF, UK*

This article has two objectives. First, it explores the implications for tourism marketing decision makers of the current debate on the 'stakeholder society', the concept of which is being seen as an increasingly necessary corrective to free-market capitalism. Second, it identifies and examines the practical and philosophical problems of this approach and whether it offers a real solution to social inequality, exemplified in this case by the position of women. The potential role of public relations companies in shaping more ethical attitudes is also explored.

The reality behind the rhetoric

Tony Blair, Leader of the Labour Party in the United Kingdom, unveiled the concept of the stakeholder economy in a speech in Singapore on 7 January 1996. The idea of the stakeholder concept represented a criticism of the 'enterprise culture' which, New Labour argue, has not provided a just, market-led form of wealth distribution that was promised. Moreover, they claim that the glorification of wealth creation has contributed to crime and to the destruction of the environment. However, the perceived ambiguity of the stakeholder concept was seized upon by the newspaper columnists and Conservative ministers. They called it a 'Trojan horse', representing, according to its critics, an attempt to disguise New Labour's hidden agenda of state and union interference in business. Critics of the concept cite its inherent promotion of public accountability as a prescription for state regulation, therefore posing a threat to entrepreneurialism and profit.[1]

New Labour, however, sees it as a voice against the highly individualistic form of capitalism offered by Conservative social theory, for a return to the notion of a consensual contract between free and equal citizens.[2] Society in the socialist sense implies the *whole* community and signifies a set of beliefs linking democracy, property and ownership within a moral context. Paradoxically, the ideology of the free market claims moral superiority over systems of government allocation of resources owing to the notion of welfare creating a dependency and thus a loss of liberty.[3] In spite of this, it seems that New Labour are justified in attacking the morality of the free market in terms of social and economic performance where crime rates, homeless and jobless figures are appalling, and where the environment is constantly referred to as being under threat.

Stakeholder theory is a tool that facilitates the formulation of corporate strategy along ethical lines. A stakeholder is defined by Freeman[4] as any individual or identifiable group who is affected by or can affect the achievement of corporate objectives. Although Freeman[4] would argue that governments should provide the regulatory framework for business activities, many authors, such as Ekins,[5] point to the existence of the global poor and the injustice and inequality of the market-place as evidence of the failure of this mechanism to deliver environmentally and socially sustainable economic activity.

In terms of the perceived need to develop a more caring, sharing society, stakeholder theory must be taken seriously. For tourism businesses, this essentially means that stakeholders need to be drawn in to the decision-making process. Stakeholders need to be identified, and relationships nurtured to ensure that analysis of concerns, goals, values and responsibilities are understood and synthesized into the strategic framework of the business.[6] The ethical context of business is thus brought to the fore, with greater facilitation of choices relating to the things businesses ought to do for the good of themselves and society collectively. This process is examined further below using the example of the tourism industry.

Stakeholder management in the tourism industry

The application of stakeholder management to any industry presupposes that moral questions can indeed be answered by the business organizations concerned. While authors such as Ferrell and Fraedrich[7] assert that many business managers feel that moral decisions are extrinsic to the business context, it is a widely accepted doctrine among moral philosophers, such as Midgley,[8] that moral decisions are a fundamental part of everyday life. It is therefore an empirical fact that businesses do make decisions and choices which are directly related to moral issues.[9] The term itself implies that moral decisions can be overtly implanted within the decision-making system of a business. This stance would be a fundamental part of Blair's stakeholder society since the business organization is at the heart of the capitalist economy the current government has nurtured.

This part of the discussion turns to the example of the world's largest service industry, tourism, in seeking to establish a substantive role for stakeholder management. The subject has been discussed before, notably by Wheeler.[10] Other authors, e.g. Simmons,[11] have sought to develop models that involve community participation in tourism, but none has explored the conceptual and ideological issues which underpin the approach. This analysis, therefore, looks at the potential for stakeholder management to work in practical terms before outlining some of the key issues surrounding its conception and implementation.

Moral issues for business encompass many factors such as equal opportunities, human rights, animal rights, industrial democracy, honesty and fairness and the environment. The tourism industry itself has a major concern for environmental issues given that tourism products either largely or entirely consist of a physical location or place. In addition, tourism is held responsible for pollution as a result of increased visitor numbers and for a number of other negative impacts such as house price rises, cultural imperialism and pressure on local services such as water and refuse collection.[12] A key phrase coined in recent times in connection with these problems and the ways in which the tourism community can solve them is 'sustainable tourism'.

McKercher[13] defines sustainable tourism as follows:

When tourism is sustainable, the natural and cultural resources and the environmental, social and economic well-being of an area are maintained forever.

Sustainable tourism is therefore a utopian term which is widely used to describe the nature of future tourism development. This 'new tourism' has attracted a great deal of interest worldwide, although the method of its delivery has not been fully explored. Stakeholder management is one such methodology which has been cited by some[13] as the framework within which sustainable tourism development can be delivered.

The complexity of this approach becomes apparent when we consider the overlap of tourism activity and operation into the leisure, entertainment and sports industries. For the approach to be workable, the many thousands of small businesses involved in tourism service provision would clearly need to be drawn into the network.

The tourism industry, as March[14] points out, is complex, dynamic and contains vastly different cultural perspectives from service providers and consumers around the world. In addition to this, March indicates that tourism research and literature has a 'Eurocentric' flavour which is clearly not useful in gaining useful insights and developing models of wholesaler/retailer activity in the global market-place. Markets around the world are largely heterogeneous, with vastly different infrastructures and legislative frameworks regarding the environment, grant aid, employment contracts, government involvement and so on.

The general lack of understanding and education concerning the environment are a huge barrier to engendering a new ethos for sensitive tourism. Robinson and Towner[12] add that the environmental impact of tourism is difficult to assess and isolate from other economic and recreational activity. Therefore the tourism industry has been reluctant to shoulder the blame for such damage. The special problems of sustainability are outlined in the English Tourist Board's (ETB) publication *Tourism and the Environment – Maintaining the Balance*.[15] For the ETB the problems concern:

- overcrowding;
- traffic congestion;
- wear and tear, e.g. footpath and river bank erosion;
- inappropriate development, e.g. design, size, use;
- conflicts with local community.

The need for greater knowledge of visitors is identified by the ETB, but one of the key suggestions put forward was that of greater coordination among stakeholders. If we identify the private sector-based tour operator as an example of a key player in the

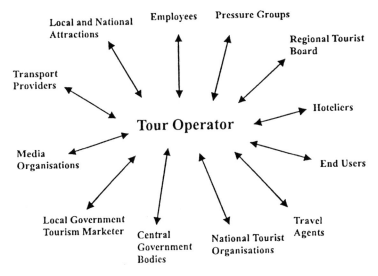

Figure 1. Stakeholder groups for the tour operator.

tourism market-place, we can begin to evaluate the methodology in terms of its applicability. The key principle of stakeholder theory is that a company, in this case the tour operator, is granted a licence to operate by virtue of its social contract with stakeholders. As long as society sees a benefit of company activity, it will allow the company to operate. Figure 1 illustrates the stakeholder groups for the tour operator.

Several issues arise immediately in relation to the stakeholder concept. First, it appears that each stakeholder, other than end-users, will have its own unique group of stakeholders. Figure 2 shows the array of stakeholders for the local government tourism marketer (adapted from Wheeler[10]).

The list of potential stakeholders for any one given player in the tourism industry is almost endless, to the point where it becomes virtually impossible to see how corporate objectives can be derived from such an analysis. Not only is the physical act of identifying stakeholders very complicated, but potentially so too is the process by which social contracts are drawn up, agreed and built in to a strategic planning framework.

Corporate governance and stakeholder orientation

The rationalization of corporate intentions regarding social responsibilities has been analysed by Spratlen.[16] Table 1 describes the five key theses for socially responsible action identified by Spratlen. The power thesis is an acceptance that power over stakeholders, as in the case of persuasive advertising, must go hand in hand with accepting social responsibility for such groups. Mutual benefits may concern sensitive design and choice of materials for new tourism development, or perhaps employee welfare considerations. Enlightened self-interest refers to the adoption of an ethical stance such as developing an environmental code of conduct for tourists (for example Thomson Holidays), with a view to gaining long-term competitive edge or, in the case

Figure 2. Stakeholder groups for the local government tourism marketer.

Table 1. Five key theses for social responsibility.

Thesis	Brief description
Power	Equates 'power off' with 'responsibilities for'
Mutual benefit	Mutual benefit accrues to the firm and the stakeholder group involved
Enlightened self-interest	Based on anticipation of societal needs with benefit to long-run objectives
Enterprise defence	To protect autonomy of the firm against possible interference
Ethical	Biblical, moral or social conscience

Source: Adapted from Spratlen.[16]

of defensive enterprise, protecting market share. Finally, the ethical thesis provides that companies may choose to act in a moral manner (for example as in the case of Traidcraft Ltd or Turkish Delights – tour operator) in the same way as individuals.

The European Societal Strategy Project[17] identified 10 possible responses (see Table 2) to the challenge of corporate responsibility. These responses are governed by the adopted role of the organization, which in turn governs its behaviour and attitudes. The first main category comprises firms which reject social responsibility for reasons of the overriding need to pursue profit and growth objectives. Many private sector visitor attractions operators would fall into this category. Firms in the second category look on social responsibility as a matter of common sense. Social investment through active involvement in a stakeholder network would be a natural activity for

Table 2. Responses to the challenge of corporate responsibility.

Firm type	Role	Economic	Behaviour and attitude		
			Social	Political	
Efficiency seeker	Profit maximizer	Profit dominates	Impediment to profit	Avoids political involvement	
	Profit satisficer	Growth dominates	Reacts against social	Avoids interaction	
	Defender of free enterprise	Business is business	Outside scope of firm	Lobbies for free enterprise	
	Lone wolf	Emphasis on profit	Voluntary unilateral acceptance of social role	Avoids involvement	
Social investor	Societally engaged	Emphasis on profit	Interactive engagement	Negotiation of rules of the game	
	Societally progressive	Emphasis on profit	Interactive engagement	Formulation of industrial policies	
	Global actor	Emphasis on profit	Interactive engagement	Assumes responsibilities for balance between national and international policies	
Progressive	Developer of society	Financial self-sufficiency	Improvement through innovation	Active in planned development of social infrastructure	
Social servant	Social servant	Second to social objectives	Provides essential non-economic goods and services	Formulation of national policies with social emphasis	
	Employment provider	Subsidized	Provides jobs	Subsidized with government support	

Source: Adapted from the European Societal Strategy Report.[17]

this type of organization. 'Progressives' would incorporate organizations such as the National Trust and the Rural Community Council, both of which are actively engaged in planning activities and contribute to the development of society, albeit in contrasting ways. The 'social servant' category covers a multitude of public sector organizations as well as English Nature, the Sports Council and the various Regional and National Tourist Boards. Clearly, the local government tourism marketer would probably fit into this category, although a gradual reduction in grant aid and public sector investment in tourism has been witnessed for several years.

The problems of a stakeholder approach

The notion that organizations within the tourism industry should have any interest at all in social responsibility and stakeholder management is normative in the sense that there exists a general agreement that these organizations ought to do so. Stakeholder management based on the concept of social responsibility has been found so far to have both the initial problem of identifying the stakeholders themselves, and the added problem outlined above of differing social roles stemming from different responses to, and rationalizations of, the challenge of social responsibility. This then begs the question of how success could be measured, since the various stakeholders have vastly different missions and value platforms. The determination of values for each stake is a question posed by Ambler and Wilson,[18] along with serious doubts concerning the representation of stakeholders and the treatment of competitors. Questions of who selects stakeholder groups and who is responsible for policing agreements have not been addressed in the literature so far.

The planning issue

Recent articles covering the broader topic area of tourism planning (e.g. Brownlie[19]) fail to consider the role of stakeholder management or that of environmental issues. Where environmental issues are mentioned, Baum[20] reports that they are set within the context of growth objectives and aggressive marketing. The achievement of a coordinated and well-informed tourism service provider network clearly depends on many factors, the most crucial of which must be a clear national framework for consultation and negotiation and nationally agreed environmental standards. Baum found that just over half of the respondents to his international tourism policy research acknowledged a concern for the effects of tourism on the environment. The actual functions of NTOs covered the activities listed in Table 3 in rank order of popularity.

It seems clear from Baum's research that many NTOs are concerned with environmental impacts, but do not necessarily engage in direct action to pursue the approaches of either sustainable tourism development or stakeholder management. Clearly more research needs to carried out into the detail of categories of NTO activity such as items 6, 7, 8 and 10 in Table 3 to deduce the exact role of NTOs in managing the problems of delivering sustainable development. Further light can be shed on the growing area of countryside tourism. The Countryside Commission[21] recognizes a strong trend towards increased visitor numbers and therefore land usage in the UK. They also acknowledge the role of increased marketing activity from a wide variety of service providers, which inevitably capitalizes on the appeal of the landscapes and

Table 3. Tourism planning concerns.

Function	Overall sample (%)
1 Tourist information	83
2 Statistics collection	81
3 Marketing – international and domestic	74
4 Policy development	74
5 Product grading	60
6 Product development – accommodation	52
7 Training	50
8 Product development – attractions	48
9 Marketing – international only	36
10 Other functions	12
11 Marketing – domestic only	7

Source: Adapted from Baum.[20]

physical beauty of the place products themselves. This attaches even greater importance to the need for a workable approach in dealing with increasing environmental
problems in this industry.

In marketing planning, we need to recognize that frameworks and approaches
are, in the main, theoretical constructs. The notion of reciprocity, as proposed by
Nooteboom,[22] for example, has strong philosophical and theoretical underpinnings in
terms of literary coverage of market justice, but we can find little empirical evidence to
suggest that this approach has been adopted. Where planning frameworks are concerned we find that conceptual frameworks, such as Robin and Reidenbach's[23]
or Simmons',[11] fail to consider details regarding implementation. As abstract or
philosophical contributions to the subject, they are valuable in themselves, but
academics and practitioners need to address the practical aspects of implementation.

Public relations from an ethical perspective

We can conclude at this stage of the debate that stakeholder management is an
idealistic method of handling ethical issues *per se*, even if we narrow things down to just
one ethical domain, namely the environment. In practical terms, it is argued here, we
are essentially reducing stakeholder management to a function which bears a close
resemblance to public relations, particularly as it was originally conceived in the earlier
part of the 20th century.

The potential for an ethical role for public relations within the maelstrom of codes of
practice, environmental legislation, aggressive public and private sector marketing
activity and active pressure groups is not fully appreciated by many academics and
practitioners. In the main, marketing is still regarded by many as a tool for achieving
primarily growth-related objectives for all types of organizations. Public relations is a
tool of the marketer which helps change attitudes and encourage support for business
organizations in a vast array of contexts and circumstances. The complexity of this PR
role has not escaped the attentions of contemporary critical thinkers in marketing
academe. Recent discourses, e.g. Brown,[24] suggest that the 'postmodern condition'
supports the view that relationship-driven marketing and business approaches have
more relevance to the chaotic characteristics of contemporary business. This criticism
of mass marketing approaches appears to open the door for the public relations
function to attain a more expansive role within the relationship ethos supported by a
strong philosophical basis which other marketing and business functions would envy.

Historically, however, we can see that the embryonic role of public relations was
almost entirely concerned with a moral imperative which had developed out of a need
to communicate honestly and openly with a newly formed and mobilized 'public
opinion'. The First World War had been a major catalyst in this process of delivering a
mass communication and media industry in response to the demand by the masses for
wartime news. National leaders had also played their part through the promotion of
public speeches and addresses to encourage, pacify and enthuse the masses. As a
defined function public relations was born in the 1920s where the roots of the consumer
society also lie. John W Hill[25] alludes to an awakening of public interest in world affairs
at this time, which necessitated the development of the public relations function for
governments and, importantly, industry.

The boom-and-bust years of the 1920s and 1930s delivered chaotic and turbulent economic and social conditions which resulted in civil unrest, particularly in relation to the actions of private sector industry. The return of control of the mining industry in the UK from the public to the private sector caused uproar in the wake of wage cuts and redundancies. The Prime Minister, Lloyd George, was forced to call out the army to deal with the unrest. It was at this time that businesses began to look to the media for help. This was the case on both sides of the Atlantic where links between public relations practitioners and journalists is very strong. The case of Du Pont in the 1920s illustrates the trend. The Du Pont news agency was set up to implement a policy of honesty and transparency with the public, following a series of factory explosions which had been misreported in the press, subsequently nurturing a negative public image for the company.

Darrow, Forrestal and Cookman[26] point out that, at this time, the prevailing view on the social role of a private company was that it should operate in the public interest – *pro bono publico*. They further add:

Public goodwill is a powerful asset but public opinion that is misinformed or uninformed can be hostile and damaging. Without corporate integrity, public relations cannot succeed. Corporate actions must be in the public interest since businesses in free markets operate on a franchise from the society it serves. This franchise can be damaged or even withdrawn if strongly negative public opinion develops.

A Japanese influence?

The notion of consumer sovereignty and the general ability and propensity of organizations to maintain this orientation has been severely criticized by authors such as Brownlie and Saren.[27] Nevertheless, while seemingly idealistic, Tony Blair is in effect placing the issue of customer orientation and public service high on the business agenda. To an extent, the motivation for doing so is seen to come from the example of our Japanese competitors. The Japanese, it is argued, are adept at succeeding in the global market-place, while asserting a social role for their businesses. Keegan[28] presents us with the view that Japanese business is deeply concerned with developing management philosophy, citing the case of Konosuke Matsushita.[29] As the founder of Matsushita Electric National and Panasonic brands he declares that, without a proper management philosophy, sound business development is not possible. Critically, Matsushita postulates that 'A management philosophy must be founded on a view of what is right for life, society and the world'. Kotabe and Okoroafo[30] argue that their research demonstrates a definite long-term customer satisfaction orientation which is significantly stronger than that of their European counterparts. A stakeholder society based at least in part on the emulation of Japanese culture directly relates to the moralistic industrial origins of public relations.

Current discourse on the implementation of the stakeholder society in the United Kingdom typically ignores the detail of how this would take place. In relation to the business community, it is also clear that stakeholder management is seen, perhaps mistakenly, as something completely different from public relations. The major conceptual differences concern the pivotal role of ethics and the social contract in stakeholder management. However, in practice, we may see that the complexity of impracticality of stakeholder management can reduce the approach to something resembling public relations, albeit in its earlier form. It seems from references included here to the historical development of public relations that the ethical and social context of its use has been overlooked of late and that manifestations have taken its place which perhaps reflect today's political economy.

The feminist perspective

The idea of the stakeholder economy should encompass not just the issues of ownership (stake), as described earlier, but also the social organization of production to allow people to identify and articulate the nature of their oppression. We have already seen that stakeholder management nurtures an extremely complex and largely unmanageable communication network which may hinder business planning rather than assist in making the approach more overtly ethical. It is hardly likely, therefore, that the concept of stakeholder management offers an antidote to inequality, since women do not own an obvious stake in the new economy (lower pay and part-time work characterize the role of women in today's economy).

The contractualism embedded within the stakeholder concept also has its problems, as Scanlon[31] points out: 'an act is wrong if its performance under the circumstances would be disallowed by any system of rules for the general regulation of behaviour which no one could reasonably reject on the basis of informed, unforced general agreement'. The central feature of this statement is that for an action to gain legitimacy, there must be a general consensus. Jagger[32] is sceptical of contractualist approaches, suggesting that general moral agreement can never be attained owing to inequalities in power and knowledge suffered particularly by women. Women cannot give fully informed and rational consent because of the impediments of the social world, and it cannot be assumed that hypothetical consensus symbolizes actual consent. Therefore, the stakeholder society is unlikely to include the moral consensus of women. If we relate this argument to Figures 1 and 2, we can see further evidence of this inequality. The stakeholder groups labelled in these diagrams are further proof that male domination in society would be transferred to the stakeholder management context.

A stakeholder society as suggested, while seeking to reform the economy in a moral sense, fails to present a challenge to the social oppression of women. This undermines their role as potential stakeholders. Implicit in the stakeholder concept is the notion of the attempt to build a 'just society and moral community that is congruent with private property'.[33] However, as women are largely invisible in the economy, the new attempts at corporate governance could represent the formation of an economic and social cartel, according to Vincent.[34] Moreover, the notions of equality in the workplace may merely serve to conceal the unequal relationship between men and women, making it more difficult for women to identify sources of their oppression.

Socialist feminists, according to Eisenstein,[35] present the vigorous argument that 'male supremacy and capitalism are defined as the core relations determining the oppression of women today'. Seidler[36] is in support of this and adds that the powerless and oppressed have been dispossessed by the capitalist society when in fact the imperative should have been to foster a greater level of responsibility for all individuals. However, the feminist critique suggests that capitalism, whether under the

Socialist or Conservative umbrella, relies on the entrenchment of women in domestic labour for the accumulation of profit. Thus the inherent exploitation of women renders them unequal in society and therefore not 'paid up' stakeholders.

Conclusion

The idea, then, that the recent support for a stakeholder society can fundamentally change the ethical performance of our businesses is highly dubious. Stakeholder management can go some way to nurturing a more favourable business culture, but is in some senses fraught with practical problems and, as discussed, is in other ways just as likely to reinforce gender inequality. When reduced to a practical level where businesses are concerned, we have seen that the result is something akin to public relations. This is perhaps a useful step forward, being similar to contemporary micro approaches exemplified by concepts such as relationship marketing and integrated marketing. However, we must take note that the selection of stakeholders is assumed to take place hierarchically, and from the perspective of the company. This is perhaps one of the most serious flaws within the concept itself, since we are placing the business organization at the head of the process. At the very least, within this limited sphere of coalition, companies and their customers would become closer to enable faster and more accurate marketing responses to dynamic social structures and systems. The ability of companies to observe patterns in the supplier chain and the end-user market in the short term becomes greatly enhanced, while the folly of long-term planning and the resource wastage associated with transactional marketing is avoided.

The question of the environment and the need for social and ecologically sensitive business development is, however, not fully answered by these modern approaches. Stakeholder management is arguably another form of business activity which is more relevant to the complex relationship management situation facing industry today. Whether this approach is fundamentally different from the concept of public relations as it was first conceived remains to be seen, but in essence the likely complexity of any given stakeholder system would seem to provide an insurmountable challenge to business. As Sisman[37] argues, the regulatory framework of the tourism industry provides a critical but not all-consuming framework for more overtly moral business practice to take place. Tourism providers *and* tourists must take some responsibility for their behaviour and attitudes. It is argued that the stakeholder society is a *utopian* concept. However, according to Bauman[38], *utopia* has two meanings, the dominant usage implying 'a place which does not exist'. Importantly, it was also associated with 'a place to be desired' or *eutopia*, thus the stakeholder concept implies the beginning of a new ethical paradigm, particularly for business. The stakeholder approach may comprise a praiseworthy endeavour for marketing managers in tourism to follow, in spite of its complexities and weaknesses.

References

1. Jamieson B 'The Casino Model for Stakeholder Blair' *Sunday Telegraph, City and Business* 1996 (14 January)

2. Heelas, P and Morris, P *The Value of the Enterprise Culture. The Moral Debate* Routledge, London (1992)
3. Friedman, M and Friedman, R *Free to Choose* Penguin, Harmondsworth (1980)
4. Freeman, R E 'Strategic management: a stakeholder approach' *Advances in Strategic Management* 1983
5. Ekins, P *Wealth Beyond Measure: An Atlas of New Economics* Gaia Books, London (1992)
6. Goodpaster, K 'Business ethics and stakeholder analysis' in Winkler, E and Coombs, J *Applied Ethics* Blackwell, Oxford (1993)
7. Ferrel and Fraedrich *Business Ethics* Houghton Mifflin (1994)
8. Midgley, M *Can't We Make Moral Judgements?* Bristol Press, Bristol (1991)
9. Ground, I *Business Ethics Workshops* Newcastle University Working Paper, Newcastle (1995)
10. Wheeler, M 'Applying ethics to the tourism industry' *Business Ethics, A European Review* 1992 **1** (4)
11. Simmons, D G 'Community participation in tourism planning' *Tourism Management* 1994 **15** (2) 98–108
12. Robinson, M and Towner, J *Beauty, Health and Permanence* University of Northumbria Working Paper (1993)
13. McKercher, B 'The unrecognised threat to tourism' *Tourism Management* 1993 **14** (April)
14. March, R 'Tourism marketing myopia' *Tourism Mangement* 1994 **15** (6) 411–415
15. English Tourist Board *Maintaining the Balance* ETB (1991)
16. Spratlen, T H 'Marketing: A social responsibility' *American Management Association* 1973 (34) 65–75
17. European Institute for Advanced Studies in Management *Facing Realities: The European Societal Strategy Report* EIASM (1981)
18. Ambler, T and Wilson, A 'Problems of stakeholder theory' *Business Ethics, A European Review* 1995 **4** (1) 30–35
19. Brownlie, D 'Market opportunity analysis: a DIY approach for small tourism enterprises' *Tourism Management* 1994 **15** (1) 37–45
20. Baum, T 'The development and implementation of national tourism policies' *Tourism Management* 1994 **15** (3) 185–192
21. Countryside Commission *Visitors to the Countryside* Countryside Commission, Cheltenham (1991)
22. Nooteboom, B 'Marketing reciprocity and ethics' *Business Ethics, A European Review* 1992 **1** (2)
23. Robin, D P and Reidenbach R E 'Social responsibility, ethics, and marketing strategy: closing the gap between concept and application' *Journal of Marketing* 1987 **51** 44–58
24. Brown, S *Postmodern Marketing* Routledge, London (1995)
25. Hill, J W *Corporate Public Relations* (1963) cited in Darrow, R W, Forrestal, D J and Cookman, A O *Public Relations Handbook* (1967)
26. Darrow, R W, Forrestal, D J and Cookman, A O *Public Relations Handbook* Dartnell Corporation, London (1967)
27. Brownlie, D and Saren 'The 4 P's of Marketing' *European Journal of Marketing* 1992
28. Keegan, W 'Strategic marketing planning: the Japanese approach' *International Marketing Digest* 1992
29. Matsushita, K 'Why have a management philosophy?' *PHP* 1979 (March) 78–83
30. Kotabe, M and Okaroafo, C O 'A comparative study of European and Japanese multinational firms' marketing strategies and performance in the United States' *Management International Review* 1990 **30** (4) 353–370
31. Scanlon, T M 'Contractualism and utilitarianism' in Sen, A and Williams, B (eds) *Utilitarianism and Beyond* Cambridge University Press, Cambridge (1981)
32. Jaggar, A 'Taking consent seriously: feminist practical ethics and actual moral dialogue' in Winkler, E and Coombs, J (eds) *Applied Ethics* Blackwell, Oxford (1993)
33. Hutton, W 'Raising the stakes' *Guardian Society* 1996 (17 January)
34. Vincent, A *Modern Political Ideologies* Blackwell, Oxford (1992)
35. Eisenstein, Z *Capitalist Patriarchy and the Case for Socialist Feminism* Monthly Review Press, New York (1979)
36. Seidler, V J *The Moral Limits of Modernity: Love, Inequality and Oppression* Macmillan, London (1991)
37. Sisman, D 'Sustainable tourism development – regulation or self-regulation?' *Tourism* 1995 (summer edn)
38. Bauman, Z *Socialism: The Act of Utopia* Allen & Unwin, London (1976)

11

Responsible and responsive tourism planning in the community

K Michael Haywood

Associate Professor, School of Hotel and Food Administration, University of Guelph, Ontario N1G 2W1, Canada

Healthy, thriving communities are the touchstone for a successful tourism industry. Unfortunately the substantial development, activity and income generated by tourism is not always compatible with a community's other social and economic objectives. In fact the purely economic rationale for tourism development has been challenged. Tourism planners are now being asked to be more responsive to a broader set of economic and social needs.[1] If this is to occur local governments should recognize that they will have to become more responsible to the local citizens whose lives and communities may be affected by tourism.[2]

While the complexity of the operating environment and the intensity of the rhetoric demanding change in the way tourism is planned at the community level, differs from one region to another, the underlying theme is a call to include a greater degree of public participation. The rationale is as follows – the positive and negative aspects of tourism (economic, social and ecological) have their most profound impact in and on host communities. Whenever tourism activity is concentrated in time and space, builds rapidly, dominates a local economy, disrupts community life, endangers the environment, and ignores community input, the seeds of discontent are sown. Whenever the residents' thresholds of tolerance for tourism and tourists are exceeded, host–tourist encounters sour, and the industry has a tendency to peak, fade and self-destruct.[3] Peter Murphy expresses the importance of viewing tourism as a community industry as follows:

The term 'community industry' acknowledges that tourism is an industry which must attract visitors and remain competitive if it is to succeed in the world market, but at the same time it extends decision-making beyond the business sector to consider the long-term interests of the host community on which the industry is so dependent. The host community is the destination in which individual, business and government goals become the tangible products and images of the industry. A destination community provides the community assets (landscape and heritage), public goods (parks, museums and institutions), and hospitality (government promotion and welcoming smiles) that are the backbone of the industry. To attract visitors with a viable product and to maintain a destination's amenities and support, tourism should be viewed as a resource industry, a resource industry in a corporate sense in that the industry gives back to the community while extracting a living from it, so that both the industry and the community base can benefit mutually from a long-term partnership.[4]

Recognition that tourism and tourists are consumers and users of community resources implies that the community is a commodity.[5] The naturalness of the community, its way of life, its institutions, and its culture are bought and sold. In fact, some communities are intentionally planned and constructed for consumption by tourists, e.g. Cancun, Mexico and Hilton Head, South Carolina. Since most communities are 'natural' arenas in which local citizens play out their lives and in which their needs are met, tourism can generate profound social concerns. For example, tourism creates employment opportunities (often low paying and seasonal) that necessitate intensive interaction with visitors. Local residents obviously become part of the tourist product attracting tourists through their culture and hospitality, and consequently the resident, as a community member, is affected by tourism in all its positive and negative manifestations.

Whenever communities become venues of and for consumption, 'social sensitivity' comes to the fore and a call goes out – often unheeded – to incorporate representative democracy into the planning process. The net effect can be an increased populist quality in planning, an extension of planning constituencies, and the increased influence of citizens in establishing planning agendas and directions.

The clarion call for greater community involvement in the tourism planning process, particularly from religious organizations and environmental groups, is becoming more widespread and deserves close scrutiny.[6] A framework for encouraging a more participatory approach to tourism planning needs to be developed. As a caveat, however, the abandonment of, or a diminishing need for, centralized government tourism planning is not suggested. But well developed and stronger tourism planning at the community level is vital if any region or country wishes to deliver exciting and novel tourist experiences in which there is an emphasis on quality and high value-added components at the destination points. As in any business, strategic planning is meaningless unless it is accepted and implemented at the operational level. There is a need for a partnership – the wholesale participation of, and gain sharing with, all people concerned with the tourism product.

Community level tourism planning

Community participation in tourism planning is a process of involving all relevant and interested parties (local government officials, local citizens, architects, developers, business people, and planners) in such a way that decision making is shared. This ideal, inherent in such a partnership, is likely to be quite elusive. There exists a wide variety of institutional and system obstacles to fuller representation in the planning process, e.g.:

- Extensive bureaucratic organizations across diverse tiers and levels exist in connection with tourism. Not only do national and regional levels of government have ministries or departments of tourism, but, the diverse nature of the tourism pheno-menon creates a situation whereby other ministries are involved by virtue of their mandates. Consequently, in many countries or regions, tourism planning suffers from fragmentation and overlapping interests, which in turn dilutes the integrity of the network of national, regional and local governmental units, and precludes cooperation and collaboration.

- In most communities comprehensive tourism planning is, at best, either non-existent or, *ad hoc*. For example, few cities or specific tourist destinations make mention of tourism in their official plans or industrial strategic plans. Many areas are content pursuing an 'unmanaged adaptation' policy toward tourism and/or may believe that the individual and collective planning (read 'marketing') activities of local hotels, attractions and visitor and convention bureaux are adequate.

- Public participation may be viewed as unnecessary, unwieldy, time consuming, and an idealistic dream. The costs are not merely financial but can be classified as 'executive burdens'. These burdens include the possible dilution of power, the lack of time to interact with citizens, the patience to educate others, the forbearance to be educated by 'outsiders', the determination to improve negotiating skills, the cour-age to risk some loss of control over matters previously internal to the industry, and, ultimately, the danger of failure and the pain of bad publicity. These costs are not small.

- Efforts to integrate and appraise the impinging economic/social/environmental factors into an existing urban or regional planning process are perceived as requiring the efforts of large planning departments, continuous task forces and a host of external consultants. Besides the scarcity of time and money resources, there is the concern of maintaining a tight reign on specialization and professional domination that can lead to more bureaucracy.

- Equally worrying is the impact at the managerial and operational levels of the industry. Efforts to generate a more comprehensive approach to tourism planning, one that incorporates social and environmental objectives, for example, may be thwarted if the recommendations are perceived as adding to the cost of doing business or as irrelevant to the earning of a profit.

- Finally, there is the problem of alienation from the centres of decision-making which concerns citizens and community groups. These people may need help in establish-ing a role for themselves in tourism planning vis-à-vis local authorities and industry representatives. Admittedly, though, this may be impossible in countries or areas where the officials are not interested in encouraging representational democracy.

These and other constraints to community tourism planning are not easily overcome. Every community must struggle to find its own way. A first-order task, if a community has the 'political will', is to assess the costs and benefits of community involvement. While some costs can be inferred from the previous statements, the benefits can be substantial. They include:

- an opportunity to improve the management of the community's tourism life cycle;
- an improved understanding of the relevant elements in the community having an impact on tourism;
- better anticipation of the internal and external challenges to tourism;

- a change to ameliorate detrimental impacts, such as congestion; and
- a superior opportunity to accommodate the full range of publics that may be affected by tourism.

As a democratic and egalitarian movement, and as a fundamental instrument of constructive social and political change, public participation has the potential for providing new 'social bargaining tables' that can turn conflicting views into a truly integrated awareness of the wider implications of debated issues. By orientating tourism planning towards the probable, the desirable and the achievable, not only can the quality of community life be enhanced, but tourism can be properly integrated into the community. But consultation and collaboration is a complex undertaking and the forging of partnerships through public participation can be fraught with difficulty.

Public participation

Community involvement in tourism can exist in a variety of formats. Arenstein's 'participation ladder' indicates there are three levels of involvement of authorities with citizens – non-participation, tokenism, and citizen power.[7] Once involved in the process of participation, however, the participation may proceed through various stages as shown in Table 1.

In deciding whether to proceed with public participation, and if so how far to move, an appraisal of the community's tourism environment may be necessary – What are the issues? Who are the concerned publics and what are their reactions to these issues? Once a reading has been undertaken (an important step in getting a hesitant tourism industry to cooperate in the venture at all) the design and terms of participation must be decided upon. Typically, logistical costs and administrative convenience tend to argue for a small group, while the need for adequate representation can necessitate a large one. Trade-offs also arise in the determination of what specific individuals or representative groups will serve as participants. While there is a desire to chose individuals who are, by industry standards, informed and reasonable, the community

Table 1. Participation ladder based on process of participation.

(1) information	introduction of existing tourism policy to citizens by the authority
(2) animation	stimulation of perception among citizens
(3) participation (stage 1)	opening of dialogue between citizens and authority
(4) participation (stage 2)	initiation of tourism planning on a basis of partnership
(5) participation (stage 3)	joint research – identification of strengths and weaknesses, opportunities and threats, etc.
(6) participation (stage 4)	determination of tourism objectives and strategies
(7) participation (stage 5)	joint decision making regarding resource allocation, development and management
(8) operationalization	implementation of tourism strategy by administrators
(9) participation (stages 6 and 1)	review of tourism policy and achievements

Source: Adapted from Richard Pine, 'Community development and voluntary associations: case studies in Finland, England and Ireland', *Leisure Studies*, Vol 3, 1984, p 119.

constituencies should be allowed to name their own representatives. To do otherwise is to run the risk that the public participants will be seen as a token body, and the participation as a hollow exercise. Public participation that is seen as being deferential, or as a way to develop sanction and overcome political resistance, will definitely not work.

Having accepted authoritative people as participants, there is an expectation that these representatives will 'deliver' their constituencies. But this is not a *quid pro quo* that can be met. Desirous of having an influential role, but wary of being co-opted in the process, participants may insist that their advice is not equivalent to their constituency's consent. While industry representatives may accept this arrangement as necessary, they may resent it as unfair. That is, industry representatives may see the public participants as taking authority to shape industry policies in private, while giving no assurances they will support these policies in public. This may strain relationships among participants, so the issue of commitment must be addressed at an early stage.

If the planning process is to succeed, the public participants must have good information, and, to be fully informed, the participants must have access to full information on the tourism industry. Industry members must be willing to invest time in briefing meetings and the like. Similarly, if the commitment of time is to be fruitful then everyone may have to learn new negotiating skills. As the participants increase in number and variety, so do the outlooks to be reconciled. 'A persistent condition underlying social conflict is the differing set of subjective assumptions and levels of awareness by which groups perceive the same objective set of circumstances.'[8] Clearly, participants need a range of tools on which to draw. These include conciliation, mediation, arbitration and the establishment of superordinate goals.

As a final point, if the participatory planning process is to succeed, then no single organization should be allowed to become convinced that its best interest lies in an action that subverts citizen or public involvement. Many factors can lead a government, trade association or a company to scuttle the joint enterprise. For example, it is rare to find a trade association that embraces all companies in an industry. Therefore, an association may not be able to control the actions of its non-members, let alone its own members. However, the biggest obstacle is the fact that public participation usually begins without a legacy of collegial interaction. Many of the participants who come together do so as strangers. In an undertaking calling for openness and agreement, a lack of prior dialogue is a considerable liability.

These obstacles to public participation are not insurmountable.[9] By working out a set of recommendations, the participation process can create a sensible set of policies, which, through accord, will guide the vetting of the tourism industry within the community for years to come.

Diversified approach to tourism planning

A practical challenge for tourism planners today is to match the planning approach to the needs of the community. If public participation is to become the norm then tourism planning as a central community activity may be judged wanting. Planning may be rational, but it must also be creative and intuitive. It may be bureaucratic, yet it must also be dynamic and involving. It may be political, but, at the same time, it must be concerned with important choices between human values.

Recent attempts to apply systems theory as a way of integrating our knowledge of tourism with a systematic planning approach is helpful but, from a practical point of view, burdensome.[10] Experience from the world of business indicates that the imposition of a comprehensive approach to the organization of planning activities is illusory.[11] Rather than seeking panaceas through planning models, emphasis should be placed on finding planning modes to fit different situations. For example, if a community faces an uncertain situation and many interest groups are involved, it may be advisable to use an incremental or organizational learning process to improve mutual understanding, to explore the problem, and possibly to evolve a consensus. If it is necessary to influence decisions in other organizations there may be a need for special arrangements to improve formal and informal contacts through joint committees or liaison officers. If there is a 'crisis of identity' within the community with regard to tourism it may be particularly important to re-examine the role of the industry. In circumstances where growth and further development are being pursued it may be important to organize for new projects.

The need for a situational approach is based on planning realities as well as the difficulties in getting a participatory community-based tourism planning process underway. In other words, planning, as currently practiced, cannot help but be *ad hoc*, informal, non-rational and concerned with values and power. In contrast planning theory is deliberate, rational, and sequential. The need for a flexible approach to community tourism planning does not advocate a rejection of rationality, a neglect of systems and procedures, and a return to 'muddling through'. On the contrary, by introducing a new set of evaluative criteria into the tourism planning process as well as an enlarged set of actors, urgently needed improvements in the decision-making process will be required.

Specifically, a more responsible and responsive approach to tourism planning is one that is multidisciplinary and continues to recognize the importance of formal planning. It is also an approach that should be designed to encourage innovative and creative thinking, attempt to improve the overall understanding of tourism, recognize the political aspects of planning, i.e. power inside and outside the industry, speculate on the future as an essential background for current planning, and consider broadly based qualitative considerations (instead of viewing all decision-making as resource allocation). Each of the following five perspectives that can enhance a diversified approach towards tourism planning will be discussed in more detail below:

- planning as a process for designing the future;
- planning as a process for innovation;
- planning as a process for learning;
- planning as a process for influencing; and
- planning as a process for managing.

As we shall see, each of these perspectives creates a basis for making tourism planning a legitimate process within a community.

Designing the future

Planning has been defined as the design of a desired future and of effective ways of bringing it about.[12] Not surprisingly, an important function of planning is to muse about the future. There are three variations to this musing. The most popularized aspect is the emphasis on vision, speculation, and the utopian. By focusing on perceptions of the future – the 'possible' or the 'can be' – participants in the planning process can learn to paint appropriate images of tourism for their communities. They can alert the community to new opportunities that they result from market and technological breakthroughs, and they can sensitize perceptions, and challenge assumptions.

This popularized, visionary side of planning for the future is counterbalanced by a more rational, analytically-driven approach. This domain of planning focuses on the evaluation of alternatives, the estimation of probabilities and the determination of the consequences or impacts of a particular tourism project or event. Such a focus forces tourism planners to flesh out the 'may be' and alert the community to opportunities or dangers that may be lurking.

The third dimension of the future deals with expressing preferences for particular futures as the precursor for guiding action. In contrast to the visionary and exploitative objectives of the previous two dimensions, the emphasis here is on the normative. In other words tourism planners can emphasize education, help people discover and choose preferences, win support for preferred alternatives or choices, and help bring about change. The focus is on what 'should or ought to be'.

It has been suggested that tourism planners in general have not only neglected the normative aspects of planning but have ignored, by and large, the whole area of long-term tourism futures research.[13] At first glance this is quite discouraging. If community tourism planning is to have any significant impact it must emphasize the importance of goals and values in planning, particularly as they apply to the critical economic, environmental and sociocultural issues that ultimately determine the long-term viability of the community.

Setting goals is, however, a complex social process. In fact the 'goal first, plan second' hypothesis is not always suitable or achievable, particularly as there may be many value systems competing for dominance. The challenge in community tourism planning, therefore, may not be the setting of explicit goals – goals that may be inappropriate in a turbulent environment – but in sensitizing others to the repercussions and value implications associated with various courses of action.

Innovation

Tourism life-cycle concepts and evolutionary models suggest that a community, whose maturing consists simply of acquiring more firmly established ways of doing things, is headed for the graveyard – even if it learns to do these things with greater and greater skill.[14] In the ever-renewing community what should mature is a system or framework within which continuous renewal and rebirth can occur.[15] One of the concerns of tourism planners, is how to foster this innovation.[16] In many communities there is a conflict of values between order and freedom.

Without order, planning, predictability, central control, accountancy, instruction to the underlining, obedience and discipline, nothing fruitful can happen because everything disintegrates. And yet without the magnanimity of disorder, the happy abandon, the entrepreneurship venturing into the unknown and incalculable, without the risk and the gamble, the creative imaginative rushing in where bureaucratic angels fear to tread – without this, life is a mockery and a disgrace.

The centre can easily look after order; it is not so easy to look after freedom and creativity. The centre has the power to establish order, but no amount of power evokes the creative contribution. How then can top management at the centre work for progress and innovation?[17]

This dilemma is particularly evident in communities troubled by economic sluggishness and strong negative thinking. Even in those communities that are contemplating public participation in planning, there is always the worry that 'anti-tourism interests' will forestall or control development and other innovative measures. While a coalition of citizens truly interested in managing, i.e. in controlling and innovating tourism, may exist within the community (particulary in chambers of commerce) problems occur when others wish to impose a broader focus on the issues of tourism development. However, the problem is not simply a matter of resolving a conflict between values. The problem is one of gaining or transferring power in order to exert influence so as to resolve the conflict. Only when an equitable decision-making base has been established, however, can the community identify the relationship between what 'can be' and 'what should be'. For example, there may be no difficulty in attracting new development but it is important for the community to be assured that the development is appropriate. In other words successful innovation only occurs if the community has a clear idea of its values:

The formation of an institution is marked by the making of value commitments, that is, choices which fix the assumptions of policy-makers as to the nature of the enterprise, its distinctive aims, methods and roles. These character defining choices are often not made verbally, they might not even be made consciously . . . the institutional leader is primarily an expert in the promotion and protection of values . . . leadership fails when it concentrates on sheer survival. Institutional survival, properly understood, is a matter of maintaining values and distinctive identity.[18]

Learning

The feeling of uncertainty produced by the pressures of change make it necessary to develop tourism planning as a learning process. For example, the social technologies for understanding and defining complex tourism systems are underdeveloped, we have almost no experience in effectively incorporating different stakeholder groups into the long-range planning process, and there are no ready-made, tested 'solutions' or even humane coping procedures for dealing with major tourism issues or tasks.

In these situations, tourism planning and public participation in planning is a process of trial and error. It is incremental, experimental, managed, shared and based on recent information.[19] By 'learning to plan and planning to learn' a community tourism planning process can be set up to involve public participation.[20] It should move at the group's pace, and deal with the issues they choose to consider. The discussions which take place can strengthen understanding between a variety of constituent groups and may help to evolve a concensus about what needs to be done. Finally, as the approach tends to be incremental and proceeds in steps, with the various groups participating at each stage, there is likely to be less anxiety than with the installation of a comprehensive planning system.

Influencing

The planning process is highly political. The various constituencies may have their own agenda or may form coalitions in which the balance of power is crucial. This makes it difficult to gain agreement to long-term commitments. The nominal leader will have to proceed through incremental steps, taking one issue at a time. Again, the idea of developing a comprehensive, rational, long-range plan may be unrealistic.

Since a wide coalition of interests may make the development of specific objectives and policies impossible, the only way to keep the coalition together may be through the use of well-phrased platitudes. However, penultimate measures, such as mediation and related practices, may have to be employed if disputes erupt. Gradually success in community tourism planning will come as a result of building informal contacts and networks throughout the community.[21] The argument for 'network building' is based on the observation that an organization's scope and influence tend to be defined in practice through establishing relationships, bargaining, and gradually developing policies.

As the community tourism planning process moves toward greater consultation and participation with a variety of constituency groups, there will have to be an appreciation that tourism planning must be concerned with identifying, appraising and modifying the values or belief systems in certain sectors of the industry or community. Similarly, there will have to be effort to ensure a better 'fit' between the dominant ideas or values within the tourism industry and the expectations of the community in which it exists.

Planning, of course, is about change. The capacity of institutions to resist change is legendary. They exhibit not merely 'inertia' – a tendency to move steadily along their present courses unless a contrary force is exerted upon them – but 'dynamic conservatism', i.e. they fight to remain the same.[22] Tourism planners must therefore take precaution to anticipate the social impact of change, and to facilitate its absorption by the community.

Managing

As tourism changes from a purely economic to a socioeconomic instrument of a community, tourism planners are confronted with the problem of reformulating a viable role for tourism within the community. In other words tourism may have to be legitimized, and shown to be a socially responsible industry. As a consequence, existing community and individual business tourism strategies may have to be altered to reflect the new *raison d'être* of tourism within the community. This means that planning as a

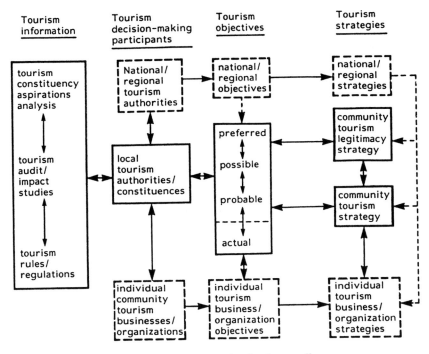

Figure 1. A sample community planning paradigm.

process for designing the future, for encouraging innovation, for learning, and for influencing must ultimately be integrated into a process for managing.

A schematic representation of tourism planning as a process of managing is depicted in Figure 1. This is not an attempt to explain how community planning should or could work, but is simply an attempt to recognize that tourism is a community affair, and that a variety of representatives from interested community, business and governmental constituencies should get together in order to determine an ideal approach to managing tourism within the community as a whole. In other words tourism legitimation, goal and objective determination, and strategy development should represent an ideal set of outcomes.

It is necessary to identify the various constituencies and determine their aspirations regarding tourism, e.g. owners of tourism enterprises may be most concerned about the short-term financial performance of their companies. Management on the other hand make trade-offs between corporate strategy and career strategy, and are likely to favour high returns on investment criteria. Visitors or tourists, of course, will be concerned with the delivery of customer satisfaction, while the political players will be desirous of tourism's ability to generate community prosperity. In other words, jobs lead to votes, and tourism expenditure increases taxes to help pay for government programmes and services. Society, in general, will want to ensure that tourism enhances the quality of community life, not only for today but for future generations.

Each of these constituencies may desire studies to be undertaken or commissioned in order to evaluate the economic/social/ecological impacts of tourism within the community. All of this information, together with data on the existing rules and regulations currently governing all aspects of tourism will then be submitted for review and scrutiny by the planning committee.

The tourism planning committee, consisting of representatives from local government, business and the community, then sorts out the information base, begins to evaluate existing objectives and strategies, if any, and gradually works toward the development of new objectives and strategies. (Of course, this systematic approach assumes that the obstacles obscuring the rational planning process can be dealt with.) While the actual timing and sequence of work by any committee will vary according to the particular circumstances in each community, the process of objective setting could begin with a determination of preferred objectives – objectives of social and environmental responsiveness, objectives of responsiveness to the needs of visitors (tourists), and objectives of performance and growth.[23] For practical purposes, however, it must be recognized that the respective sets of aspirations may be in conflict and cannot all be served equally. For example, there may be a conflict between profitability and employment maintenance or generation. Therefore, the tourism planning committee will have to recognize that the choice of objectives will have to be limited to those aspirations which it believes the industry can serve and which are most appropriate to serve.

While there exist a wide variety of tools, techniques and methods for clarifying objectives, a broadly based technique, described in the following section, is scenario writing. Its usefulness is in clarifying goals by providing planners with broad theories, concepts and information about the interaction of tourism and tourists in the contexts of their community. Ideally scenarios reduce commitments to *a priori* conceptions, theories or goals, and can help reduce the problem of stereotypes and stereotypical thinking. Once the planners have widened their sights in this way, they can specify the role of tourism in their community more carefully and clarify their goals more authentically.

One of the outcomes of these deliberations on objectives is what might be called a legitimacy strategy, i.e. a clear delineation of the role of tourism within a community, together with a set of guidelines outlining what needs to be done to make tourism more socially, ecologically and economically responsive and responsible.[24] For example, the Northwest Territories, Canada, has made a concerted attempt to legitimize community based tourism:

...Our final destination is a community based tourism industry in the NWT. It will be an industry which stimulates NWT purchases, and profits for NWT residents, across the NWT; which employs NWT residents in jobs compatible with both wage and traditional community lifestyles; which offers tourists a variety of quality offerings at a fair price; which is environmentally clean; and, does not compete with the activities of hunters and trappers for scarce renewable resources. Most important of all, it will be an industry which reflects the interests and aspirations of the communities in which it is located.[25]

Once the tourism planning committee can agree on a preferred *raison d'être*, the next step in the legitimizing process is the determination of what is possible and probable given existing resources and capabilities and the ability to access further resources. Obviously there will be gaps between the probable and the preferred. These gaps will have to be bridged as each constituency, whether represented or not on the planning committee, has its own set of objectives and priorities that must be reconciled.

Consequently, a series of bargaining strategies will have to be decided upon. Finally, an overall community tourism strategy focusing on future development projects, and marketing strategies, can be decided upon. Theoretically this is the ideal planning sequence, but, in reality, development projects and marketing campaigns form continuing processes, and thus may proceed the legitimizing and strategic development process.

The community tourism planning process, as described, recognizes the importance of external linkages and makes sure that these linkages are tied back or related to the internal arrangements within the community, e.g. the unique structural arrangement of, and objectives for, tourism. Therefore, the focus in community tourism planning is not merely on the formulation of strategy as a problem solving process, but on the problem of implementation and control. Analysis of the economic, ecological, technological and informational aspects of strategy making is similarly linked to an analysis of the social and political factors inside and outside the industry. Community tourism planning, therefore, is part and parcel of a tourism management process.

Scenarios to integrate tourism objectives

The goals of community tourism planning are three-fold:

- to identify the possibilities and choices about the future of tourism within the community;
- to examine each possibility carefully in terms of probable impacts; and
- to include in the planning process the real preferences of the people in the community whose lives and home environment are influenced by the decisions made.

While this delineation of goals necessitates a separation of thinking skills – conceptual, analytical and advocacy – an integrative approach to goal determination will be required if the community tourism planning process is to fulfil its purpose, i.e. to provide direction for the future development of tourism.

A variety of techniques have been used to help fulfil this integrative role – gaming simulations, the Delphi approach, and the nominal group technique.[26] Another promising approach is the use of scenarios. So far their use in tourism has more or less been restricted to 'projective' or 'prospective' looks into the future but it has been suggested that they could also be used to reflect preferences.[27] This is an exciting prospect because many communities currently face a 'mission or value crisis' with regard to tourism. It has been suggested that scenario development can lead to tentative goal clarification, to more precise goal formulation and finally to the determination of plans, strategies, tactics and actions.[28] In this case scenarios are not attempts to predict but are designed to:

- provide perspective;
- sensitize;
- stimulate intensive examination of the present and its possibilities;
- help structure uncertainty; and
- optimize the 'fit' between the community and the changing impacts of tourism.

But, to do justice to a concept that has been described as 'difficult' and 'hazardous' scenarios must be developed and written in such a way as to compel understanding and insight, to spark not only intellectual interest but, most important, to change behaviour.[29] For example, everyone has a mental model of the community or world in which he or she acts – this is based on experience and knowledge. Whenever a person must make a decision, he or she thinks of behaviour alternatives within this mental model. When a decision is good, others will say the person had good judgment. In other words, the person's mental map matches the fundamentals of the real world.

Similarly, there is a business view of the world. In any given community, therefore, each tourism business may act differently or assign different priorities to certain goals. Each will act rationally, given its world view. Therefore, a particular company's perception of its business environment is vitally important as its strategy comes from this perception.

The ultimate challenge facing tourism planners, therefore, is to ensure that the general objectives of each tourism business are synchronized with the community's objectives for tourism. If this cannot be accomplished, then the behaviour of individual decision-makers within each business may not correspond to the desired community view. For this reason a participatory approach to tourism planning at the community level is of utmost importance. Only by engaging the various decision-makers and stakeholders in conversation, and by getting everyone to listen to each other's deepest concerns, can scenarios be written so as to reflect the community's preferences, possibilities and probabilities.

Development and application

While no attempt is made to review and evaluate the scenario development process in this article, there is a rich literature on how scenario construction methodology can turn scenarios into disciplined explorations of the future.[30] But, as the Royal Dutch/ Shell Group has discovered, scenario development should not be viewed simply as a new formula in planning but more as a way of thinking.[31] It is in this regard that scenarios have significant implications for the community tourism planning process.

As the Royal Dutch/Shell Group has found it is not enough to give people (decision makers) a more comprehensive world view. To be meaningful, scenarios must be tied to the individual concerns of constituent groups. As such, scenarios have been found to be protective. They can be used to anticipate and understand the risks inherent in tourism. Scenarios help organize seemingly unrelated economic, social, environmental, technological, competitive and political information and translate it into a framework for judgment. Moreover, scenarios can illuminate the major forces driving tourism within the community, their interrelationships and critical uncertainties. By acknowledging uncertainty, scenarios aim to structure and understand uncertainty and help identify a few alternatives and internally consistent pathways into the future. Similarly, scenarios allow planners to evaluate existing or proposed alternative strategies and to assess the impact of each.

Scenarios deal with two worlds: the world of facts and the world of perceptions. They explore for facts but they aim at perceptions inside the heads of decision makers. Their purpose is to gather and transform information of strategic significance into fresh perceptions. This transformation process is not trivial – more often than not it does not happen. When it works, it is a creative experience that generates a heartfelt 'aha!' from your managers and leads to strategic insights beyond the mind's previous reach.[32]

Fundamental to the process of planning and the involvement of a variety of constituencies interested in ensuring a viable fit for tourism within a community, scenarios can provide learning experiences. They force people to see and understand other points of view and focus people's attention on the broader or community concerns. By allowing novel information outside the span of paritcipant expectations, scenarios help encourage creative and innovative thinking and expression. Scenarios, as pictures of the future, form the context or the perspective in which the desired profile and action path are conceived. In a sense the resulting strategies are planned responses to anticipated stimuli. The stimuli are the scenarios.

Summary

Tourism planning activity is increasingly being tested by the degree to which it enhances opportunity and reduces social, economic and environmental disparities. By accepting tourism as a community industry, by encouraging a participatory approach to tourism planning, and by introducing techniques such as scenarios in order to formulate community goals and strategies for tourism, it is hoped that the tourism planning agenda can be legitimized.

The path towards achieving and maintaining public participation, however, contains numerous obstacles. In addition to those previously discussed there is the difficulty in obtaining commitment over a long period of time. It is important, therefore, that continuity be ensured. This may require that leadership and management for tourism be vested in an individual or group of people who can sustain the necessary effort. It should go without saying, but the time, effort and commitment by all concerned must be rewarding and rewarded.

As a final comment, effective tourism planning at the community level must serve to enhance the operating effectiveness of tourism for all parties – visitors and concerned citizens, industry operators (including employees), prospective developers, the business community and various government agencies. If this can be accomplished community involvement in tourism planning has a bright future.

Notes and References

1. See e.g. Jost Krippendorf, 'Toward new tourism policies: the importance of environmental and sociocultural factors', *Tourism Management*, Vol 3, No 3, 1982, pp 135–148; and E. De Kadt, ed, *Tourism: Passport to Development?* Oxford University Press, Oxford, 1979.
2. The following articles provide some rationale for more sensitive planning: Cristos Spanoudis, 'Trends in tourism planning and development', *Tourism Management*, Vol 3, No 4, 1982, pp 314–318; Clare Gunn, 'Industry pragmatism vs tourism planning', *Leisure Sciences*, Vol 1, No 2, 1977, pp 84–94; Jacqueline R. Cheng, 'Tourism: how much is too much? Lessons for Canmore from Banff', *Canadian Geographer*, Vol 24, No 1, 1980, pp 72–80; and Donald Getz, 'Regional and local tourism planning in Ontario: review and critique', *Environments*, Vol 17, No 1, pp 67–70.

3. Alistair Mathieson and Geoffrey Wall, *Tourism: Economic, Physical and Social Impacts*, Longman, London, 1982 p 141; George Doxey, 'A causation theory of visitor–resident irritants: methodology and research inferences', *Proceedings of the Travel Research Association, 6th Annual Conference*, TRA, San Diego, California, 1975, pp 195–198; and R.W. Butler, 'The concept of a tourist area life cycle of evolution: implications for management of resources', *Canadian Geographic*, Vol 24, 1980, pp 187–201.
4. Peter E. Murphy, 'Tourim as a community industry: an ecological model of tourism development', *Tourism Management*, Vol 4, No 3, 1983, p 181.
5. Cristine Fry, 'The community as a commodity: the age graded case', *Human Organization*, Vol 36, No 2, Summer 1977, pp 115–122.
6. Ron O'Grady, *Third World Stopover: The Tourism Debate*, World Council of Churches, Geneva, 1981: and see the special topics issue 'Tourism and the physical environment', *Annals of Tourism Research*, Vol 14, 1987.
7. S.R. Arenstein, 'A ladder of citizen participation', *Journal of the American Institute of Planners*, Vol 35, 1969, 216–224.
8. Hazel Henderson, 'Toward managing social conflict', *Harvard Business Review*, Vol 49, May–June 1971, pp 86–87.
9. Mary Benwell, 'Public participation in planning – a research report', *Long Range Planning*, Vol 13, August 1980, pp 71–79.
10. Donald Getz, 'Models in tourism planning: towards integration of theory and process', *Tourism Management*, Vol 7, No 1, 1986, pp 21–32.
11. Yehezkel Dror, *Ventures in Policy Sciences*, Elsevier, New York, 1971, p 118.
12. R.L. Ackoff, *Redesigning the Future*, Wiley, New York, 1974.
13. Joseph W.M. Van Doorn, 'Can futures research contribute to tourism policy?' *Tourism Management*, Vol 3, No 3, September 1982, pp 149–166; and, 'Tourism forecasting and the policymaker: criteria of usefulness', *Tourism Management*, Vol 5, No 1, 1984, pp 24–39.
14. Butler, *op cit*, Ref 3.
15. K. Michael Haywood, 'Can the tourist-area life cycle model be made operational?' *Tourism Management*, Vol 7, No 3, 1986, pp 149–166.
16. K. Michael Haywood, 'The go system: generating opportunities for hospitality business', *International Journal of Hospitality Management*, Vol 4, No 1, 1985, pp 15–26.
17. E.F. Schumacher, *Small is Beautiful – A Study of Economics as If People Mattered*, Abacus, London, 1975, p 209.
18. Philip Selznick, *Leadership and Administration: A Sociological Interpretation*, Harper and Row, New York, 1975, p 28, as quoted in Thomas J. Peters and Robert H. Waterman Jr, *In Search of Excellence: Lessons from America's Best Run Companies*, Harper and Row, New York, 1982, p 281–282.
19. J. Friedmann, 'The future of comprehensive urban planning: a critique', *Public Administration Review*, 1971, Vol 31, No 3, p 325.
20. Donald N. Michael, *On Learning to Plan and Planning to Learn*, Jossey-Bass, San Francisco, 1973.
21. John K. Friend, J.M. Power and C.J.L. Yewlett, *Public Planning: The Inter-Corporate Dimension*, Tavistock, London, 1974.
22. Donald A. Schon, *Beyond the Stable State*, W.W. Norton, New York, 1971.
23. K. Michael Haywood, 'Criteria for evaluating, the social performance of tourism development projects', in *Tourism as a Factor in National and Regional Development*, Proceedings of the IGU Working Group on the Geography of Tourism and Recreation, Trent University, Peterborough, Ontario, 1975, pp 94–97.
24. Department of Economic Development and Tourism, Government of the Northwest Territories, *Summary Report – Community Based Tourism: A Strategy for the Northwest Territories Tourism Industry*, NWT, Yellowknife, 1983, pp 28–29.
25. Sadrudin A. Ahmed, 'Understanding resident's reaction to tourism marketing strategies', *Journal of Travel Research*, Vol 25, No 2, Fall 1986, pp 13–18.
26. Philippas J. Loukissas, 'Public participation in community tourism planning: a gaming simulation approach', *Journal of Travel Research*, Summer 1983, pp 18–23; H.A. Linstone and M. Turoff, eds, *The Delphi Method: Techniques and Applications*, Addison Wesley, Reading MA, 1975; and

J.R. Brent Ritchie, 'The nominal group technique: an approach to consensus policy formulation in tourism', *Tourism Management*, June 1985, pp 82–94.

27. Josef W.M. Van Doorn, 'Scenario writing: a method for long-term tourism forecasting', *Tourism Management*, March 1986, pp 33–49; Larry Hirschorn, 'Scenario writing: a developmental approach', *APA Journal*, April 1980, pp 172–183.

28. John M. Courtney, 'Developing alternative futures', *Journal of the Urban Planning and Development Division*, August, 1976, p 52.

29. H.A. DeWeerd, 'A contextual approach to scenario construction', *Simulation and Games*, April 5, 1974, pp 403–414.

30. General Electric Company, *Four Alternative World/US Scenarios, 1971–1980*, GEC, Fairfield, Connecticut, 1971; J. Gershuny, 'The choice of scenarios', *Futures*, December 1976, pp 496–508; Larry Hirschorn, 'Scenario writing: a developmental approach' *APA Journal*, April 1980, pp 172–183; R O'Connor, *Planning Under Uncertainty: Multiple Scenarios and Contingency Planning*, The Conference Board, New York, 1978; and Van Doorn, *op cit*, Ref 28.

31. Pierre Wack, 'Scenarios uncharted waters ahead', *Harvard Business Review*, September–October 1985, pp 73–89; and Pierre Wack 'Scenarios: shooting the rapids', *Harvard Business Review*, November–December 1985, pp 139–150.

32. *Ibid*, November–December 1985, p 140.

12

Crafting a destination vision: putting the concept of resident-responsive tourism into practice

J R Brent Ritchie*

Chairman, World Tourism Education and Research Centre, the University of Calgary, 2500 University Drive, NW, Calgary, Alberta T2N 1N4, Canada

One of the most compelling forces which has emerged in recent years is the desire of peoples all over the world to recapture control of the political processes which affect their daily lives. While the most dramatic examples of this movement have occurred in Central and Eastern Europe, equally important (although more subtle) manifestations of the same phenomenon are evident in other countries in Europe, in North America, and even in Asia. While the causes of this movement are many and varied, the end result is an increasing unwillingness on the part of educated and free peoples to bow to the unresponsive will of a few individuals for any extended period of time. One consequence of this movement has been a profound evolution of the socio-political ground rules which shape both policy formulation and decision-making at all levels of society. As a result, societies in all parts of the globe have had to radically rethink and reshape the organizations and the processes which have traditionally been used to develop national policies and to implement supporting programmes.

Tourism, as an important and integral part of the global social and economic fabric, has not escaped the pressures for change created by this metamorphosis of the democratic process. Increasingly, along with all important industry sectors, tourism is being critically assessed concerning its net contribution to the well-being of the community or region which it both serves and impacts on. As part of this process, the residents of communities and regions affected by tourism are demanding to be involved in the decisions affecting their development. This reality was emphatically highlighted as one of the major conclusions of the First International Tourism Policy

*The author served as Chairman of the Calgary Visitors and Convention Bureau during the period 1988–90 and subsequently chaired the 'Calgary: Host, Consultant and Educator to the World' Task Force activities on which the contents of this essay are based.

Forum held at George Washington University. To quote directly:

Resident responsive tourism is the watchword for tomorrow: community demands for active participation in the setting of the tourism agenda and its priorities for tourism development and management cannot be ignored.[1]

In effect, the above conclusion from the Forum and its associated recommendations stressed the need for consultation involving the local community in all forms of tourism development.[2]

It should be noted at this point that the idea of a community emphasis on tourism is not new.[3] A number of other authors have pointed out the desirability of providing broad-based citizen input into tourism-related policy and development decisions.[4] As well, a range of approaches for obtaining consensus, or at least unbiased input into the decision-making process, have been developed and tested.[5] However, none of these previous works has reflected the unanimous emphasis placed on meaningful citizen involvement by members of the Tourism Policy Forum. As such, it would appear that this strong desire for meaningful input into tourism development decisions is a fairly recent reality.

Level and nature of resident input

Great care must be taken in identifying the kinds of input from community residents that are desirable and useful. This concern has three dimensions. First, the inputs and impact of citizens must be real; tokenism has no place in the new democratic processes which the public is demanding. Second, from a practical perceptive, citizen input provided on a volunteer basis is a limited and valuable resource. As such, it can be obtained only in limited amounts and on a periodic basis. Finally, in terms of content, it is acknowledged that the views which residents furnish represent non-technical advice designed to provide direction concerning the nature and type of tourism development that the community wishes to support. Such input is not a version of professional or consulting advice pertaining to the implementation of strategies or plans on an ongoing basis. This role is the responsibility of professional managers.

Given this caveat, it becomes clear that the solicitation of resident input involves a process designed primarily to define the broad parameters within which tourism development should take place for a given destination or region. The intent of the process is to formulate a framework which provides the industry with broad guidelines as to the kinds of major facilities, events and programmes that residents find most consistent with their values and aspirations for the long-term development and well-being of the community. In traditional management terms, such a framework is often referred to as a 'long-term strategic plan'. More recently, the concept of 'visioning' or 'vision management' has emerged.

Strategic planning and visioning

While strategic planning and visioning are clearly related processes, there are some useful distinctions. Writings by Mintzberg and his colleagues in the field of strategic management provide some insights in this regard. As noted by Mintzberg,[6] the traditional approach to strategic planning (referred to as the 'Design School' model) can be described as 'prescriptive' in orientation. This terminology implies that strategy formation is viewed as a process of conceptual design, of formal planning and of analytical positioning. The essence of the Design School model is that it is by nature structured, logical and somewhat mechanical. It emphasizes that strategy formation should be a controlled, conscious process of thought for which ultimate responsibility lies with the chief executive officer of the entity involved in strategy development. The outcome of this process is a simple, unique and explicit 'best' strategy for a given situation.

At the other end of the spectrum is what Mintzberg defines as the 'crafting' of strategy. Under this conceptualization, a strategy is a dynamic, evolving process in which strategies take form as a result of learning over a period of time – as opposed to being formulated at a fixed point in time. He emphasizes that the crafting of strategy reflects an ongoing iterative process of thinking and acting – and then thinking some more. One idea leads to another until a new pattern forms. As such, strategies can form as well as be formulated. A strategy can emerge in response to an evolving situation, or it can be brought about deliberately, through a process of formulation followed by implementation. Crafting strategy requires dedication, experience, involvement with the material, the personal touch, mastery of detail, a sense of harmony and integration.[7]

The process of 'strategic visioning' – or simply 'visioning' – like the crafting of strategy, is seen as a dynamic, interactive phenomenon.[8] From a conceptual perspective, the process can be broken down into three distinct stages:

- the envisioning of an image of desired future organizational state, which,
- when effectively communicated to followers,
- serves to empower those followers so they can enact the vision.

Crafting a tourism vision

In traditional terms, the vision for an organization is provided by leaders, such as a Lee Iacocca, who 'developed an agenda . . . that included a bold *new vision* of what Chrysler could and should be'.[9] Whether or not this model of the single, charismatic leader remains appropriate in a world of flat organizations, shared expertise and networking is open to discussion. What is significant, however, is the importance of developing a vision for a given organization in relation to its particular mission. In the present context, the task is to establish a framework and a process by which to provide leadership to a community, a region or a country in its efforts to formulate a vision as to what it can or should seek to become as a tourism destination.

In undertaking to craft a vision for a destination it should be kept in mind that such a process is a new but important extension of the more common process of strategic planning in tourism.[10] In extending the concept of visioning to tourism, it is found that three characteristics of the process need to be kept in mind when compared with its application in organizations such as the Chrysler Corporation.

- The vision for a tourism destination must bring together the views of many organizations and individuals in the industry and the community. As such, the process is much more complex than that carried out within a single firm.

- Because of the number and diversity of the stakeholders involved in the crafting of a destination vision for tourism, the value system brought to the process can be greatly different, even to the point of being diametrically opposed. As such, the task of reaching consensus and obtaining endorsement of the destination vision is a challenging and often delicate task.
- Compared with a firm, the vision developed for a destination tends to define the nature of extremely long-term major developments, many of which are relatively irreversible. While the choice of the right vision is critical for any entity, it is absolutely critical for a tourism destination as it will set in motion the development of facilities, events and programmes which will do much to define the very essence of that destination for years to come.

Crafting a tourism vision for Calgary

To this point, the discussion has focused on the nature of vision formulation in a very abstract way. Because of the relative newness of the concept, particularly in a tourism context, it was felt useful to review its origins so as to provide some basic insights into its purpose and characteristics.

In the remainder of this article, attention turns to the application of the visioning process for a specific destination that has used the approach in an attempt to provide both direction and support for future tourism development. The destination in question is the city of Calgary, Canada – a city for which tourism is a major economic and social force. As previous studies have shown,[11] the destination is best known for three things, two of which are tourism oriented: the oil and gas industry, the annual Calgary Stampede and the hosting of the 1988 Winter Olympic Games.

Some background to the visioning process

Calgary is a rapidly developing city of some 750 000 residents. Its relatively isolated location just east of the Canadian Rocky Mountains in Western Canada has engendered a relatively strong feeling of the need for self-generated development initiatives. While clearly acknowledging that the quality of life enjoyed by its residents owes much to the oil and gas reserves with which the region is blessed, there is also a recognition of the need to plan for the future diversification of the economy. While this desire is driven primarily by economic motives, it also reflects a desire to develop a broader range of activities and interests for residents so as to make the city an even more vibrant and exciting place to live.

The success of the 1981 bid to host the XVth Winter Olympic Games represented the beginning of an important new phase in the city's history. From relative obscurity, Calgary achieved a level of international awareness that, at its height in 1988, made it nearly as well known as the three largest Canadian cities of Toronto, Montreal and Vancouver.[12] Perhaps more important, the preparation for, and actual hosting of this mega-event provided a unique opportunity for community development, both in economic and social terms.[13]

Recognizing that many of the benefits derived from the successful hosting of the Olympics would end as soon as the Games were over, community leaders sought to determine how best to capitalize on the reputation and the contacts generated by the event. Towards this end, just following the Games, community leaders called together over 100 residents of the city to address this issue. The community leaders directing this initiative included both the Mayor of Calgary and the President of the local Chamber of Commerce. This collaboration took place formally under the auspices of the Calgary Economic Development Authority (CEDA), a joint public–private sector entity reporting to both elected officials on City Council and to the Board of Directors of the city's main business organization. While undoubtedly imperfect, this approach to public–private collaboration sought to ensure that the interests of city residents at large were represented, while at the same time involving the business community which, in the end, would be expected to implement many of the programmes resulting from the strategic planning process.

The result of the initial meeting of residents from all segments of the community was the creation of a 'Core Group' of 12 volunteer citizens whose formal mission was 'to develop a strategic plan that will positively influence the development of Calgary in directions that will strengthen our city as we know it today'. Approximately one year later, after extensive deliberations, this group released its report which outlined a strategy for economic development for the city into the 21st century.[14] This report was circulated widely and discussed extensively by residents of the city. In this way, every attempt was made to ensure that members of the community were generally in agreement with the directions being proposed for the future development of the city. While it is indeed difficult to ascertain the extent to which the overall contents of the CEDA report were endorsed by all sectors of the community, local press coverage appeared to indicate general acceptance of the strategic directions proposed.

Perhaps the most significant immediate outcome of the 'Calgary . . . Into the 21st Century' report was the creation of 10 ongoing Task Forces whose mandate was to further explore the opportunities identified by the core group. The specific focus of each of these task forces is summarized in Table 1. From a tourism standpoint, the most critical task force was that charged with the responsibility of attempting to establish Calgary as 'Host, Consultant and Educator to the World'. While no doubt grandiose in its terminology, the mandate of this task force was to determine how the city could best build upon its fleeting international reputation from the Olympics, its

Table 1. Focus of the 10 task forces established to support the economic development of 'Calgary . . . Into the 21st century'.

No	Focus
1	Capitalize on free trade
2	Modernize, develop and expand Calgary's existing industries
3	Find new economic drivers – diversification
4	Develop and mobilize our human potential
5	Increase capital availability
6	Establish Calgary as 'Host, Consultant and Educator to the World'
7	Internationalize and respond to globalization
8	Establish Calgary as the world's first information port
9	Enhance and maintain Calgary's enviable quality of life
10	Align to the 21st century

legacy of sports facilities built for the Games, its proximity to the scenic Rocky Mountains, its world-class technical expertise in key sectors of the economy (notably oil and gas), and its situation as the most highly educated city in Canada, in order to develop itself as a major international travel destination.

Host to the World Task Force

Using this general mandate as a starting point, the task force developed a more detailed mission statement within its formal Terms of Reference (Table 2). As seen from this table, the critical initial component of the mandate of the task force was:

...to develop a vision concerning the kind of tourism destination it believes Calgary should become as we move into the 21st century...

It is this initial part of the task force mandate, the development of a destination vision, which is the primary focus of the present discussion. This said, the reader should keep in mind the importance of the subsequent activities related to the implementation of the vision which was developed. While these implementation details will be noted only briefly, they are clearly important. Although discussion is minimal here, they required a considerable amount of time and effort on the part of task force members.

Table 2. Terms of reference of Task Force No 6: 'Calgary...Host, Consultant and Educator to the World'.

The formal terms of reference defined the overall mandate of the task force as being:

...to develop a vision concerning the kind of tourism destination it believes Calgary should become as we move into the 21st century in order to truly establish the city as a major host, consultant and educator to the world. It should subsequently prioritize the major initiatives that will be essential to achieving this vision. Finally, it should recommend and initiate specific actions/implementation steps that will be required to translate the vision into reality.

In seeking to fulfil this mandate, the task force set itself seven specific tasks. These were:

1. To formulate, in a reasonable amount of detail, a *vision* describing the Calgary of the 21st century as a tourism destination. This vision will define the kind of destination we want Calgary to be, and the kind of people we are likely to attract if such a vision is realized.
2. To identify and prioritize the *major facilities* that it will be necessary to put in place over the next 20 years as Calgary moves to establish itself as the kind of host, consultant and educator to the world defined by the above noted vision statement.
3. To identify and prioritize the development and/or enhancement of *major events* that are consistent with the vision statement and which will be necessary to realize it as we move into the 21st century.
4. To identify critical aspects of the *support and educational/training infrastructure* that it will be necessary to develop/enhance as we move towards realizing the vision.
5. To provide concrete specifications of the *image of Calgary* that will be portrayed nationally and internationally so as to accurately, yet competitively, position Calgary in the markets it seeks to serve.
6. To provide useful *estimates of the amount of funding* likely to be required to implement initiatives related to the facilities, events, infrastructure and other programmes identified by the task force. As well, the issue of *possible sources of funding* should be addressed. It is felt necessary, the task force may authorize additional feasibility studies to be undertaken where financial support for such studies can be successfully solicited.
7. To identify *organizations/individuals* who can be encouraged to assume responsiblility and/or leadership in implementation and/or development of the various facilities, events, infrastructure and programmes deemed to be a priority by the task force.

Integrating task force efforts with those of existing tourism efforts

One obvious issue of significance which might be raised is the potential for conflict between a short-term community strategic planning group for tourism and those existing tourism-related organizations which have had, and continue to have, a very strong and ongoing involvement in the industry. In the present case, this issue was dealt with directly by asking the local Convention and Visitor Bureau to assume a leadership role within the task force. In practical terms, this involved inviting the Bureau to recommend a person to chair the task force and convening its first meeting at the offices of the Bureau. At the same time, the core group took steps to ensure that membership of the task force was not restricted to 'industry insiders' only. The end result was a larger task force (18 persons) than might have been required from a strictly functional standpoint but one which did provide for broader community representation than is often the case. In retrospect, it is felt (in the author's view) that an even broader range of individuals from the community at large could have been incorporated into the process. There are, however, practical limits to the size of a strategic planning group such as the present task force.

Integrating tourism with other sectors

Despite the importance which professionals in the field attach to their sector, it is essential to keep in mind that tourism is only one of several sources of income and employment, within most communities. As such, any effort which tends to focus exclusively on the development of tourism for a destinition must be concerned about the relationship of tourism to other sectors. This concern was addressed by Task Force No 6 before undertaking the detailed work related to its mandate through an examination of its relationship with the mandates of the other nine task forces. In particular, it noted it relationship with:

- The Task Force (No 7) on Internationalization and Globalization – particularly that tourism will play an important role in internationalizing Calgary businesses and other institutions.
- The Information Task Force (No 8) – specifically, that the consulting and educational aspects of the 'Host to the World' mandate will rely heavily on efforts of this task force.
- The Human Resource Task Force (No 4) – notably, the fact that the educational dimension of Task Force No 6 depends very heavily on human resource development. It was also noted that this same dependency on human resources applied across several task forces.

Principles underlying the vision

In the initial phases of its work, the 18 persons on the task force attempted to establish a framework within which to develop the vision for Calgary as a tourism destination. In particular, considerable attention was devoted to identifying principles on which to base development of the vision. These principles are summarized in Table 3.

Table 3. Principles underlying the vision of 'Calgary...Host, Consultant and Educator to the World'.

- Developments related to the vision must always seek to ensure that Calgary and region residents are net beneficiaries (i.e. positive impacts must clearly outweigh any potential negative consequences)
- The vision should focus on initiatives which reflect our natural strengths, lifestyles and heritage
- The vision should incorporate and build upon the high quality of the natural, visual and built environment enjoyed by Calgary and the surrounding regions
- The vision should focus on significant themes and initiatives which will help position and develop Calgary as a major international destination and knowledge/education centre [and]
- Although the concept of 'host, consultant and educator' is clearly applicable to all areas of excellence that Calgary enjoys, the vision proposes that we learn about the strategic combination of these areas through an initial focus on the oil and gas, agribusiness and tourism sectors. In brief, we will first strive for excellence as hosts, consultants and educators in these areas.

Elements of the vision

Once the mandate of the task force and the principles on which to base the process had been agreed to, attention then focused on the primary goal of attempting to define a common vision of what Calgary could and should look like as a tourism destination some 15 to 20 years from now.

As might be expected this process required several sessions and a considerable amount of iterative reflection, reaction and reformulation. As a result of this process, task force members agreed on a series of nine statements which, in their totality, provided a composite picture as to how they envisage the Calgary of the future from a tourism perspective. These nine vision statements are given in Table 4.

An examination of this set of vision statements reveals that they fall into two general categories. The first category contains those that reflect some general values as to how the city should develop – almost without reference to tourism. The first two in particular fall into this category. It is important to keep in mind, however, that task force members insisted that such elements as overall liveability of the city and environmental protection were indeed major tourism appeals. Furthermore, they insisted that if Calgary could not be maintained as a city which appealed to residents, it could not develop its attractiveness for others. The knowledgeable reader will immediately be able to provide examples as to exceptions regarding the generality of this assertion. Nevertheless, it was judged important by Calgary residents.

The second category of vision statements described more explicitly the key dimensions of the city's character on which tourism should build as Calgary enters the 21st century. It is believed that each of these vision statements fully respects the principle presented in Table 4.

Before leaving the vision statements, it should also be pointed out that the report of the task force contains a more extensive discussion concerning the manner in which members decribed and interpreted each statement. This information is available to those wishing for a more detailed understanding of the process and its results.[15]

Realizing the vision

The definition of the nine vision statements and the subsequent elaboration of their specific meaning was viewed as fulfilling the first of the seven tasks contained in the

Table 4. The vision of Calgary as 'Host, Consultant and Educator to the World'.

Calgary in the 21st century should be:

- A city which is safe, clean, attractive and efficient, and whose priority is maintaining and enhancing its liveability
- A city which values and preserves the high quality and beauty of the natural environment, waterways and setting with which it has been blessed
- A city which reflects its proud and dynamic western heritage and native cultures
- A city which values and supports knowledge and education, particularly in those spheres upon which it depends for its well-being and development
- A city which actively encourages and facilitates knowledge transfer between those who generate the knowledge and those who use it
- A city which genuinely welcomes visitors from all parts of the world in an environment that encourages the exchange of insight and understanding while striving to create new personal and professional friendships
- A city which values its cultural diversity and its artistic achievements
- A city that thrives in all seasons – and which is therefore attractive to visitors at all times
- A city which attracts attention and acclaim by providing first-class attractions and by hosting high-profile events which are of interest to its citizens.

overall mandate of Task Force No 6 (Table 1). As the next step in the total process outlined by the Terms of Reference, task force members subsequently focused their attention on efforts to both identify and prioritize the major facilities, events and programmes that it was felt would be necessary to put in place over the next 20 years if Calgary was indeed to establish itself as the kind of 'Host, Consultant and Educator to the World' defined by the composite vision statement.

With this goal in mind, the task force first generated a large number of possible initiatives and then selected a more limited set of higher priority items. The outcome of this process is shown visually in Figures 1, 2 and 3. These figures identify the specific Facilities (Figure 1), Events (Figure 2) and Programmes (Figure 3) which members felt would contribute to the realization of each of the nine elements of the vision. It should be noted that each of the figures contains facilities, events or programmes that reflect:

- projects that are already in place and which requires additional support to encourage evolution towards recognized international excellence;
- projects that have been proposed by others and that are currently under review; and
- suggested new projects that flow logically from the vision defined by the task force.

While the individual facilities, events and programmes in Figures 1, 2 and 3 are by nature very specific to the community in question, a number do have characteristics which could be generalized to other settings. The important point to be emphasized, however, is that each of the various facilities, events or programmes bears a direct relation to one or more of the vision statements developed by members of the community.

Developing an action plan

While space does not allow discussion here, the final steps in the process defined by the task force Terms of Reference was to develop a relatively detailed action plan which specified, as far as possible, the organization(s) most appropriately responsible for

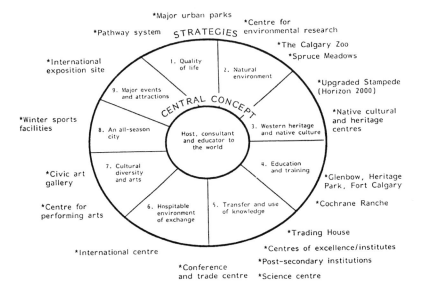

Figure 1. Facilities required to realize the vision.

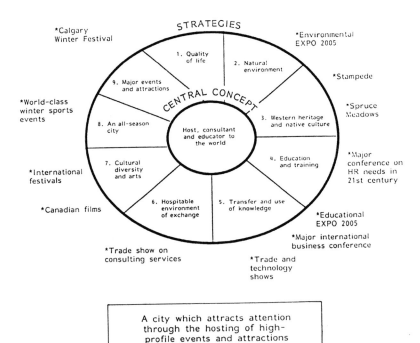

Figure 2. Events required to realize the vision.

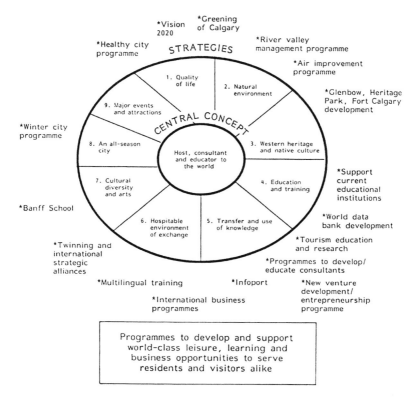

Figure 3. **Programmes required to realize the vision.**

undertaking each proposed initiative, the desired timing of various actions, and some preliminary estimate of the magnitude of the resources that would be likely to be required to develop a particular facility, event or programme. Again, readers having an interest in the details are referred to the original documentation.[16]

Some observations on the crafting of a tourism vision

While one must be cautious not to exaggerate the significance of the present effort to develop a process for the crafting of a vision for tourism destinations, it is felt that the work does break some new ground. In the process of doing so, it is acknowledged that other cities have undertaken similar economic renewal initiatives (for example, Pittsburgh, Pennsylvania). However, most have not emphasized the visioning process in tourism to the extent of the present example. As well, it is recognized that certain things could certainly be done better – and hopefully will be in the future. Towards this end, a number of observations concerning the process may be of interest.

- *Where's the beef?* In total, the Host to the World Task Force held 10 sessions over a period of 12 months. Readers may wish to note that, of these 10 meetings, the first four were devoted to the crafting of the actual vision statement – and that these sessions were by far the most challenging and the most stimulating. The remainder focused on identifying the details related to the specific initiatives and actions required to realize the vision. While these implementation sessions were acknowledged to be important, they did not generate the same level of energy – even electricity – that was associated with the crafting of the vision statements. The lesson to be retained is that making a vision operational requires a considerable amounts of staff work. To ensure that this work occurs, it is important to start involving industry professionals and to start transferring ownership of the vision to them. In order for this to take place, it is advisable to have a number of these professionals actively involved as members of vision crafting task forces. This said, care must be taken to ensure they do not dominate the process. Visioning is an exercise which must allow for genuine, broad-based resident input.

- *Visions of sugarplums, gifts of coal – combining intellect with experience*: The process of 'visioning' requires a carefully balanced combination of creative, intellectual insights carefully sprinkled with flakes of reality derived from practical experience. Visioning is by nature a process designed to tap the imagination. As such, it is obviously essential that organizers include in the process a number of individuals who are prepared to explore new avenues, who are willing to reveal their true values, and who are prepared to dare to dream. This said, it must also be recognized that, while vision should challenge a community, they must also bear some relation to the ability of the destination to realize the vision. The challenge, of course, is to strike the right balace.

- *Camelot or Caracas? Defining the appropriate unit of analysis*: The example described in this essay focused on a well-defined metropolitan destination of moderate size. To a certain degree, because of Calgary's isolation, its fairly homogeneous value system and its strong community focus, it might well qualify as one of the so-called emerging 'city states'. In this setting, the process of visioning was well received and appeared to work well. This said, it is fair to question whether or not the process is applicable to settings in which there is more diversity, greater land mass or less focused commitment. For example, a similar process of visioning is currently being carried out at the level of the entire Province of Alberta (in which Calgary is located). It remains to be seen whether or not this attempt to formulate a vision for a much larger area will be successful. Taken to yet another level, even more serious questions might be raised if one attempted to craft a vision for an entire country – particularly one as vast and diverse as Canada. The answers to these questions await further experience.

- *Maintaining perspective*: While the visioning process is extremely important for all those involved in the development of a tourism destination, it is essential to recognize that tourism is not always the most critical or most valued component of a city or region's overall economic development priorities. Thus, in addition to defining the vision, its advocates and supporters must also be prepared to deal with both apathy and resistance with respect to both the vision itself and the initiatives proposed for its realization. To the extent that the task force which crafts the vision reflects the general views of the community, this concern will be minimized.

- *Patience is indeed a virtue!* Visions are not realized overnight. As such, it is absolutely essential that, once the initial excitement has faded, there exists a true core of believers who are prepared to persist in efforts to transform wishes into reality. In this regard, it is usually a few key individuals who make the difference. At the same time, it must be recognized that an individual's circumstances change over time. As a consequence, if the vision is to be realized, it is also important to attempt to gain an ongoing commitment from those leading tourism organizations whose support is essential in the long term.

Concluding remarks

As stressed at the beginning of this article, peoples around the world are attempting to achieve greater control over the decisions that affect their daily lives. While reality dictates that many forces which determine their well-being are beyond such control, this in no way minimizes the importance of attempting to do whatever is reasonably possible to shape the future in ways that increase the possibility that desirable futures will be realized. This article has described one such attempt by residents of one very small corner of the world to define and influence how their tourism sector should develop over the next several decades. Whether or not the exercise will make any difference is still unclear. Whether or not the vision will be realized remains to be seen. At the very least, the process provided the residents of Calgary with some shared expectations concerning the kind of tourism development that seems appropriate for the place they call home.

Acknowledgement

The author wishes to express his appreciation to Lorn R. Sheehan for his assistance in support of the work on which this essay is based. As well, the invaluable contributions of the citizens of Calgary who participated in the work of the Task Force 'Calgary: Host, Consultant and Educator to the World' are gratefully acknowledged.

Notes and references

1. J.R. Brent Ritchie, 'Global tourism policy issues: an agenda for the 1990's', *World Travel and Tourism Review*, Vol 1, 1991, pp 149–158.
2. The full text of the section in the summary report discussing this conclusion is as follows:

'Resident responsive tourism is the watchword for tomorrow: community demands for active partici-pation in the setting of the tourism agenda and its priorities for tourism development and management cannot be ignored.

For too long, much of the concern related to tourism development has been focused on the needs of the consumer of the tourism service. While in a competitive world this concern will continue to be of sub-stantial importance, there is a strong and growing recognition that a greater balance needs to be struck in weighing the desires of visitors against the well-being of their hosts. There is a need to recognize that tourism must benefit the local community and that there must be broad-based participation in tourism development decisions at the community level. There is a realization that while tourism enhances com-munity life, it can also threaten the well-being of residents as well as the values they hold.

Several policy recommendations emerged.

1. In general, there is a need to recognize that tourism development must be in harmony with the socio-cultural, ecological, heritage, goals, values and aspirations of the host community.

2. Similarly, the economic benefits from tourism must be equitably accessible to all participants in the overall tourism process.

3. Creative approaches to foster host country participation in the equity and ownership of tourism facilities and services must be developed. There is genuine concern that if host communities do not benefit from tourism they will become alienated and reject tourism in all its forms. In this regard, there is particular concern with respect to Third World Countries and the need to optimize economic benefits from tourism – a recognition that this has not always been the case in the past.

In effect, these policy recommendations reflect a thematic need for consultation involving the local community in all forms of tourism development. In particular there is a sensitivity to the cultural disparities that may exist between the host region and the visitors to this region. This results in the need to avoid the potential for social alienation on the part of host communities.'

3. Peter Murphy, *Tourism: A Community Approach*, Methuen, New York, 1985; and K. Michael Haywood, 'Responsible and responsive tourism planning in the community', *Tourism Management*, Vol 9, No 2, 1988, pp 105–118.

4. Brian Keough, 'Public participation in community tourism planning', *Annals of Tourism Research*, Vol 17, 1990, pp 49–465.

5. J.R. Brent Ritchie, 'Tourism education and training in Canada', *Global Village: Journal of the Canadian Hospitality Institute*, Vol 13, No 4, 1985; J.R. Brent Ritchie, 'Alternative approaches to teaching tourism', paper presented to the Teaching Tourism into the 1990s conference, University of Surrey, 1988.

6. Henry Mintzberg, 'The Design School: reconsidering the basic premises of strategic management', *Strategic Management Journal*, Vol 11, 1990, pp 171–195.

7. Henry Mintzberg, 'Crafting strategy', *Harvard Business Review*, July–August 1987, pp 66–75.

8. Frances Westley and Henry Mintzberg, 'Visionary leadership and strategic management', *Strategic Management Journal*, Vol 10, 1989, pp 17–32.

9. John P. Kotter, *The Leadership Factor*, Free Press, New York, 1988, pp 18–24.

10. See, for example, David Gilbert, 'Strategic market planning for national tourism', *The Tourist Review*, No 1, 1990, pp 18–26; Clare A. Gunn, *Tourism Planning*, Taylor & Francis, New York, 1988; Charles Kaiser Jr and Larry E. Helber, *Tourism Planning and Development*, CBI Boston, 1978.

11. J.R. Brent Ritchie, Charlotte M. Echtner and Brian H. Smith, *A Survey of the Views of Canadian Residents Concerning Calgary's Image as a Tourist Destination*, World Tourism Education and Research Centre, University of Calgary, Calgary, Alberta, 1989.

12. J.R. Brent Ritchie and Brian H. Smith, 'The impact of a mega-event on host region awareness: a longitudinal study', *Journal of Travel Research*, Vol 30, No 1, 1991, pp 3–10.

13. J.R. Brent Ritchie, 'Promoting Calgary through the Olympics: the mega-event as a strategy for community development', in Seymour H. Fine, ed, *Social Marketing*, Allyn and Bacon, Boston, 1989, pp 258–274.

14. CEDA, *Calgary...Into the 21st Century*, Calgary Economic Development Authority, Calgary, Alberta, 1989.

15. CEDA, *Calgary: Host, Consultant & Educator to the World*, Calgary Economic Development Authority, Calgary, Alberta, 1991.

Part V

Urban tourism

Introduction by Stephen Page

The 1980s saw the emergence of new and popular research areas in tourism, and urban tourism was no exception to this. One indication of the growing interest in this area was the proliferation of journal articles and, during the 1990s, a range of mainstream texts and edited collections of books on urban tourism. In the seminal texts on tourism, such as Mathieson and Wall (1982), urban tourism received a balanced treatment while in the burgeoning interest in the geography of tourism, Pearce (1987, 1995) discussed urban tourism and highlighted its significance for cities.

Probably the most influential and widely cited study on urban tourism is the seminal and classic study by Ashworth (1989) which documented both the literature and interest in urban environments. Ashworth (1989) also observed an 'imbalance in attention' was explicitly reflected in that it is '. . . remarkable because most tourists originate from cities, many seek out cities as holiday destinations and the social and economic impacts of tourism are substantial in urban areas. The failure to consider tourism as a specifically urban activity imposes a serious constraint that cannot fail to impede the development of tourism as a subject of serious study'. This was further developed by Ashworth (1989: 33) where a 'double neglect has occurred. Those interested in the study of tourism have tended to neglect the urban context in which much of it is set, while those interested in urban studies, itself, a rapidly growing focus of academic interest, have been equally neglectful of the importance of the tourist function in cities'. Despite recent advances in research, Ashworth's (1989) comments still remain valid and poignant because the progress in research has been slow and bogged down by a large proliferation of descriptive case studies and analytically devoid assessments of tourism in individual city environments. These studies have often contributed little to the development of theory or new conceptual frameworks. A range of books on the subject area have provided recent syntheses of urban tourism as a serious area of research, arguing that it needs to be moved much higher up the research agenda. These books include Law (1993), Page (1995) and

Ashworth and Tunbridge (1992), as well as the influential Ashworth and Voogd (1990) and Law (1996).

Urban tourism research has also suffered from a range of seemingly novice tourism researchers attempting to write on the subject area, which appears simple, uncomplicated and well suited to descriptive case studies. One might argue that this problem has become sufficiently acute during the 1990s and that one has to question whether sufficient theoretical and conceptual development has taken place in the area to justify the delineation of urban tourism as a sub-field of tourism studies. In other words, has the published research been of the quality and significance that a discernible sub-area called urban tourism thrives. This is compounded by a major conceptual problem that has never been adequately addressed – the need to understand the complexity of the urban tourism system and sub-systems which exist and co-exist alongside other economic, social and environmental systems. Yet few consultancies or academic studies are sufficiently large to gain a comprehensive understanding of the relationships and operation of urban tourism in specific environments. This still remains a major challenge for decision-makers and researchers. To the contrary, tourism in cities remains a looser and more apt description of the research efforts with a common focus – the urban environment, lacking unity and direction around the theoretical and conceptual frameworks necessary to give the area direction and development. The problem is also compounded by the wide range of journal and publication outlets which researchers can now seek for a one-off urban tourism-related publication. However, a sign of the continued interest is reflected in the launch in 1999 of a new quarterly journal – *City Reports* – which to all intents and purposes is an urban tourism journal aimed at decision-makers, published by Travel and Tourism Intelligence.

The international literature on urban tourism can be reviewed under a number of headings: theory and conceptual developments; demand and supply issues; tourist behaviour; management, planning and policy; and modelling and forecasting. In terms of theoretical developments, the literature has not advanced significantly in the last decade from a theoretical perspective, as few studies have advanced the research frontiers and led to a reconceptualisation of urban tourism, However, developments in social theory have had some impact on the research approach adopted towards urban areas as places producing tourist experiences and as places which have been consumed for pleasure. A notable study which focuses on the globalisation of the postmodern metropolis is Hannigan's (1998) *Fantasy City*, with the city as an entertainment hub. Such studies have adopted earlier theoretical developments in social science such as postmodernity and the city. Similarly, the contribution made by other critical debates in social theory on the form, processes shaping urban economies and role of tourism as integral elements of the economic base are certainly leading a limited number of researchers to rethink their approach to tourism in cities. In the journal literature, many of the articles published in the 1980s and 1990s have been concerned with demand (e.g. Buckley and Witt, 1989) or supply, particularly in terms of development (e.g. Timothy and Wall, 1995; Hall and Hamon, 1996; Oppermann et al., 1996; Cockerell, 1997; Bramwell, 1998; Heung and Qu, 1998; Hughes, 1998; Pearce, 1998).

One of the least researched areas of urban tourism, in part linked to demand and supply, is tourist behaviour (Page, 1997). The literature which exists is largely situated within the social psychology paradigm, epitomised by the work by Jenkins and

Walmesley (1993) on perceptual mapping and images of the urban environment. While this type of research is grounded in urban studies research, the major contribution lies in the recognition of the ways tourists settle into and become familiar with the urban environment and developmental maps and images of places. The wider planning and marketing implications have, in the main, not been widely recognised by city planners and the private sector who still base location decisions for mega-attractions and flagship projects in unsuitable locations off the main tourist routeways. They fail to adequately signpost or make attractions accessible or pay attention to tourist behaviour in the planning and development of attractions. There are a wide range of examples in the literature (e.g., see Page, 1995 for the case of London Docklands) which explain the failure to understand tourist behaviour and learning processes to offer an environment conducive to visitation, spending and a positive experience. This remains an important area for further research, as Lawton and Page (1997) observe, in relation to understanding how tourist images of places and their activity patterns are shaped and affected by promotional literature.

Probably the most researched area within tourism in cities is the focus on what can be categorised as management, planning and policy. For example, the real growth area has been in the place-marketing literature (Ashworth and Voogd, 1990; Kotler et al., 1993; Gold and Ward, 1994; Gold and Gold, 1995; Limburg, 1998; Ward, 1998). While this is part of the wider interest in the postmodern city and the competition between places for tourists, it also focuses on the manner in which the place image is constructed and marketed as part of the commodification of places.

In terms of the modelling and forecasting for urban destinations, this has remained the domain of a small number of specialist economic forecasters, reviewed in Mazanec (1997), which is the most comprehensive review of the field to date. The complexity of disaggregating urban tourism systems and their inter-relationships from other economic activities still remains a major obstacle to the modelling and forecasting activities that would sit firmly in the practitioner contribution. But inadequate data sources and information still precludes detailed analysis for many destinations. In contrast, quality issues have assumed a growing significance for individual activities (see Murphy, 1997), which also emerges in Tyler et al. (1998) under the wider management theme although urban-wide approaches to quality initiatives remain largely industry sector specific (e.g. the hospitality sector) and comprehensive quality approaches to the urban tourist experience remain in the too hard basket for many destinations and tourism organisations. Clearly, the scope for research on urban tourism remains significant as many edited collections are still at the stage of assembling overviews of individual destinations (e.g. Law, 1996). Against this background, two papers have been selected for this section. These are

Jansen-Verbeke, M. (1991). Leisure shopping – a magic concept for the tourism industry?, *Tourism Management*, March, 12(1): 9–14.

Getz, D. (1993). Tourist shopping villages – development and planning strategies, *Tourism Management*, February, 14(1): 15–26.

Jansen-Verbeke's (1991) paper is probably one of the more influential studies published on urban tourism in *Tourism Management* over the last 20 years. Aside from highlighting a new concept, which has subsequently received substantial treatment in retailing literature and in the urban regeneration literature, it highlighted the essential role which tourist spending on shopping in urban environments makes to the economy of towns and cities. Although it is not as significant in conceptual terms as her study of the tourist use of the inner city (Jansen-Verbeke, 1986), it certainly builds on the conceptual inroads she has established, along with Ashworth (1989), in making urban tourism a serious area of research. It certainly kickstarted a research area which culminated in a range of consultancy and academic research studies designed to re-engineer the way in which tourism is sold to interest groups in cities, businesses and residents as a major element underpinning the range and nature of shops in each locality. It was also a forerunner of the subsequent development of the tourism and leisure component in the town centre management concept in the UK (Page and Hardyman, 1996), where retailers began to adopt more sophisticated approaches to their customers, their needs and contribution to the area.

Getz's (1993) analysis of tourist shopping villages further developed the concept of tourist shopping as a major activity of urban visitors, examining the development of tourist shopping villages, established as retailing areas to encourage and attract tourists near urban areas. In the UK, the concept of out-of town shopping centres and the subsequent concern for town centres (see Page and Hardyman, 1996) equally developed the theme of tourist shopping, based on these innovative studies. Getz's contribution provided a broad evaluation of the tourist shopping village concept, development strategies and highlighted the important role of entrepreneurs in recognising and developing the market for such facilities. In fact the role of the entrepreneur in tourism research has only come to the fore in recent years, as reflected in a number of specialist publications surveying the field.

In summary, it is perhaps fair to add that *Tourism Management* has not attracted a great deal of research on urban tourism over the last decade, despite the rise in publications on the area. One obvious explanation is that there has not been sufficient experimental work undertaken on this area to take the frontier forward. Those studies published in the journal have made a contribution, particularly the two discussed above, but there is a clear need for further research on the different facets of the tourist experience of cities, the activities which tourists attend (see also Part VI Theme Parks in this book) and the wider tourist system.

References

Ashworth, G. (1989). Urban tourism: An imbalance in attention in C. Cooper (ed.), *Progress in Tourism, Recreation and Hospitality Management*, vol. 1. London: Belhaven.

Ashworth, G. and Tunbridge, J. (1992). *The Tourist-Historic City*. London: Belhaven.

Ashworth, G. and Voogd, H. (1990). *Selling the City*. London: Belhaven.

Bramwell, B. (1998). User satisfaction and product development in urban tourism, *Tourism Management*, 19(1): 35–48.

Buckley, P. and Witt, S. (1989). Tourism in difficult areas II: Case studies of Calderdale, Leeds, Manchester and Scunthorpe, *Tourism Management*, 10(2): 138–52.

Cockerell, N. (1997). Urban tourism in Europe, *Travel and Tourism Analyst*, 6: 44–67.

Gold, J. and Gold, M. (1995). *Imagining Scotland: Tradition, Representation and Promotion in Scottish Tourism since 1750*. Aldershot: Scholar.

Gold, J. and Ward, S. (eds) (1994). *Place Promotion: The Use of Publicity and Marketing to Sell Towns and Regions*. Chichester: Wiley.

Hall, C. M. and Hamon, C. (1996). Casinos and urban redevelopment in Australia, *Journal of Travel Research*, 34(3): 30–6.

Hannigan, J. (1998). *Fantasy City*. London: Routledge.

Heung, V. and Qu, H. (1998). Tourism shopping and its contribution to Hong Kong, *Tourism Management*, 19(4): 383–6.

Hughes, H. (1998). Theatre in London and the inter-relationship with tourism, *Tourism Management*, 19(6): 445–52.

Jansen-Verbeke, M. (1986). Inner-city tourism: Resources, tourists and promoters, *Annals of Tourism Research*, 13(1): 79–100.

Jenkins, J. and Walmesley, D. (1993). Mental maps of tourists: A study of Coffs Harbour, New South Wales, *GeoJournal*, 29(3): 233–41.

Kotler, P., Haider, D. and Rein, I. (1993). *Marketing Places: Attracting Investment, Industry and Tourism to Cities, States and Nations*. New York: Free Press.

Law, C. (1993). *Urban Tourism: Attracting Visitors to Large Cities*. London: Cassell.

Law, C. (ed.) (1996). *Tourism in Major Cities*. London: International Thomson Business Press.

Lawton, G. and Page, S. J. (1997). Analysing the promotion, product and visitor expectations of urban tourism: Auckland, New Zealand as a case study, *Journal of Travel and Tourism Marketing*, 6(3/4): 123–42.

Limburg, B. (1998). City marketing: A multi attribute approach, *Tourism Management*, 16(5) 475–8.

Mathieson, A. and Wall, G. (1982). *Tourism, Economic, Physical and Social Impacts*. Harlow: Longman.

Mazanec, J. (ed.) (1997). *International City Tourism: Analysis and Strategy*. London: Pinter.

Murphy, P. (ed.) (1997). *Quality Management in Urban Tourism*. Chichester: Wiley.

Oppermann, M., Din, K. and Amri, S. (1996). Urban hotel location and evolution in a developing country, *Tourism Recreation Research*, 21(1): 55–63.

Page, S. J. (1995). *Urban Tourism*. London: Routledge.

Page, S. J. (1997). Urban tourism: Analysing and evaluating the tourist experience, in C. Ryan (ed.), *The Tourist Experience: A New Introduction*. Cassells: London. pp. 112–35.

Page, S. J. and Hardyman, R. (1996). Place marketing and town centre management: A new tool for urban reviatlisation, *Cities: The International Journal of Urban Policy and Planning*, 13(3): 153–164.

Pearce, D. (1987). *Tourism Today*. Harlow: Longman.

Pearce, D. (1995). *Tourism Today*. Harlow: Longman.

Pearce, D. (1998). Tourist districts in Paris: structure and functions, *Tourism Management*, 19(1): 49–66.

Timothy, D. and Wall, G. (1995). Tourist accommodation in an Asian historic city, *Journal of Tourism Studies*, 6(2): 63–73.

Tyler, D., Guerrier, Y. and Robertson, M. (eds) (1998). *Managing Tourism in Cities: Policy, Process and Practice*. Chichester: Wiley.

Ward, S. (1998). *Selling Places: The Marketing and Promotion of Towns and Cities 1850–2000*. London: E&F N Spon.

13

Leisure shopping: a magic concept for the tourism industry?

Myriam Jansen-Verbeke

Department of Urban and Regional Planning, The Catholic University of Nijmegen, Post bus 9044, 6500 K D Nijmegen, The Netherlands

These reflections about the relationship between tourism, leisure and shopping are based on a series of aspects and assumptions inspired by a literature study and to some extent supported by empirical findings.[1] How valid are the arguments to look upon shopping areas as a tourism resource? This central question is related to a set of factors which can explain why shopping areas are being developed as leisure settings and why shopping is seen as a leisure activity. The article includes some reflections on:

- leisure shopping as a tourism resource;
- the leisure environment as a tourist attraction;
- leisure shopping (the activities and the perception).

According to the results of recent surveys the discussion on shopping tourism is related to both the attractiveness of the environment and the actual activities and the perception of this environment. The characteristics mentioned in different survey and marketing studies all indicate a strong relationship between behaviour, perception and the environmental setting, without really disentangling the complexity of this interaction.[2] The preconditions to develop a shopping environment as a tourism product and an attractive leisure environment are to be questioned. So far there are no results known which could give a clue to the priority of the characteristics and conditions.

How, where and when can a shopping environment function as a tourist attraction? This question needs further research of the environmental conditions for shopping tourism and shopping as a leisure experience.[3] The actual differences between intentional shopping and intentional leisure-tourism activities may give a first indication. In this analysis a set of criteria is taken into consideration, introduced here by a number of keywords.

Motives of visitors

Intentional shopping or intentional leisure and tourism.

Behaviour pattern of visitors

- trip length – short, possibly longer;
- length of stay – limited or rather unplanned;
- time of stay – a few hours during the day, an evening, a full day;
- kinds of activity – window shopping, intentional buying or impulsive buying, drinking, eating, various leisure activities, cultural activities, sightseeing;
- expenditure – goods, possibly some souvenirs, drinks, meals, entrance fees to leisure facilities.

Functional characteristics of the environment

- wide range of retail shops, department stores, catering, leisure and other facilities, tourist attractions, spatial clustering of facilities;
- parking space and easy access;
- street retailing, pedestrian priority in open spaces.

Qualities of the environment

- image of the place, leisure setting, display of goods on the street, street musicians and artists;
- accessibility during leisure time, including weekends and evenings;
- aesthetic value, image of maintenance and safety;
- architectural design of buildings, streets, shops, windows, signboards, lighting;
- social affective value, liveliness of the open space;
- animation, entertainment, amusement and surprise.

Hospitableness of the environment

- social, visual, physical;
- orientation, information, symbolism, identification.

In many cases, however, a distinction between a predominant shopping function and an area with an additional attraction is hardly realistic as many intermediate behaviour patterns, combined motives and mixed environments will blur the model. The range of motives is complex, so is the behaviour pattern in terms of time–space and expenditure budgets. The pattern of shopping tourism and leisure shopping is not always the outcome of explicit motives – people do not come to visit, to eat or to shop, but to be there. People are coming for the delight.

Nevertheless, the leisure-shopping function as well as the tourist attraction can to a certain extent be predicted by the range of facilities, the proportion of retail and leisure facilities and the nature of tourist attractions in a particular place.

Tourist and leisure experience

The current interest in shopping tourism can be explained by an increasing demand for leisure activities in general and the search for new experiences in particular. A series of interconnected social, economic and cultural trends are creating new behaviour patterns and new demands. As a consequence many shopping areas are now being developed as a core element in many tourist products.

The importance of shopping tourism is widely recognized; it has become a magic concept for the tourism industry despite the fact that little is known about the actual behaviour and expectations of tourists.[4]

Expenditure patterns have occasionally been studied. Indicators such as personal characteristics, the company during the shopping visit, visitors' motives, kind of purchases, have proved to be useful in analysing shopping tourism. In addition, a large number of external conditions are assumed to play a role, such as the weather circumstances and the time of the year (e.g. Christmas shopping is different from bargain shopping in the sales period).

According to several surveys dealing with visitors' behaviour there is a relationship between the leisure dimension and the duration of the visit. The longer a visitor tends to loiter in the shopping area, the more the leisure aspect is becoming predominant – the visit then tends to include other activities such as having a drink or a meal, going to the cinema or any other kind of cultural activity. In addition, the longer tourists can be held in a place, the greater the chances that time and money will be spent on shopping.

Analysing the mix

Undeniably, the quality of the environment plays a vital role. However, little is known about the characteristics which particularly contribute to the tourist attraction and the leisure setting of a shopping area. The role of the environment can be understood by analysing the functional tourism–leisure–shopping mix in different settings with regard to their capacity to attract tourists.

Leisure shopping as a tourist activity has always existed, but the shopping element has recently become an important instrument in the promotion of tourist places, even the solution for marketing tourism in places with a rather weak tourism profile. Shopping trips still stand for an important segment of the tourism market, although the tourist product should include more than just an attractive shopping area.

The search for the unique shopping and leisure experience accounts for numerous trips, especially day trips to the so-called shopping paradises. Many places acquired this image thanks to their situation in a national border area, through favourable fiscal systems (tax-free shopping) or through a tradition of offering a wide range of specialized goods. Shopping tourism in border areas is a well known pattern all over the world, and the tourist flows are changing in intensity and direction according to the price fluctuations of neighbouring countries.[5]

Taking into account the global standardization in products, the downgrading in the quality of the souvenir products, the equalization in prices, these places need to add additional attractions to their image as shopping paradises. Their future attraction to the tourism market will largely depend on the capacity to develop leisure facilities, which can maintain the image of a unique shopping and leisure experience.

In addition, the *competition between the shopping paradises is becoming extremely fierce* to the extent that only those which can offer a complete tourist product will survive. This reality needs to be faced by many tourism promoters who tend to see shopping as a tourism resource.

It will be most interesting to follow the development of some well known European shopping paradises in the context of the new Common Market. They have so far benefited from the differences in prices, in tax regulations, in goods, in opening hours and have established the image of interesting shopping places, worth a trip. How will they survive after 1992? The hypothesis is that their future attraction will depend on the site, on their situation within the European tourist market and not in the least on the local tourism resources. The policy of integrating tourism attractions, historical buildings, interesting sightseeing objects and recreational facilities into the shopping environment is common nowadays.

West Edmonton Mall

Undeniably, North American experiments have been a source of inspiration and a model for several projects in Europe. West Edmonton Mall, Canada, is the most debated and reported experiment. This project for an indoor shopping leisure mall was unique at the time, offering more than 800 shops, parking space for 27 000 cars and a wide range of attractions. Leisure facilities account for about 10% of the total floor space. The leisure 'ambience' dominates the entire mall by the integration of catering facilities into the project and the theming of special shopping areas (European Street and Bourbon Street). In addition to this shopping-leisure complex there is the Fantasy-land Hotel, contributing to the 'Fantasia' theme of this mall. This large-scale project was the first experiment in creating a 'complete' leisure-shopping environment based on a new concept in terms of mixing retail shops, leisure facilities, food courts and services. Beyond the gaudiness, glitter, 'hype' and utter weirdness of this project lies a planning, a forecast of consumer behaviour and demands and an interesting financial story, which makes it a worthwhile lesson for researchers in the field of leisure shopping and shopping tourism, especially for project developers who feel tempted to imitate this success formula.[6]

The objective was to concentrate theme elements from Europe, Hawaii, Disneyland and many other places under one roof, so that people could have all these experiences in just one day. This city on its own, with a compact pedestrian area, where there is no winter (and this in the North of Canada) apparently meets a particular demand in the leisure and tourism market. Many researchers have tried to understand the factors of success. This successful mix of shopping and leisure has been copied since 1985, in different places in the USA, now even bigger in Minneapolis (Riverside) and recently also in Europe (e.g. Metrocentre in Gateshead).

Meanwhile, this five-year-old experiment already shows some signs of fizzling out. This can be concluded from the shift from high-quality goods and retail shops to mediocrity in general. Trying to find the right mix between shops and leisure facilities and promoting the place as a tourism destination will remain a continuous challenge. Furthermore the effect of *déjà vu* when it comes to spectacular attractions will soon affect the visitor rates, so there will be an increasing need for product renovation.[7]

Could the conclusion be that this kind of attraction can only have a short life span, because the product mix is based on intensive, expensive, trendy and superficial experiences?[8] Does this well-staged leisure setting hold enough incentives for people to return? Can the glitter and the blitz continue to satisfy the public?[9] The answer will have to wait until the results are known of the second generation of megamalls turning up all over the world, each of them trying to find the gaps in the tourism-leisure market.

Urban shopping tourism

Traditionally urban tourism centres offer all the possibilities of combining shopping, sightseeing and various leisure activities. To some extent they are still the focus of shopping tourism. As long as cities have existed, the pattern of 'going into town' has included a leisure experience, and visiting towns is an essential part of the tourist market. Why then is the concept of 'leisure shopping' now being introduced as a new phenomenon and referred to as a marketing instrument in the tourism industry?

Over the past few years new retailing schemes have been reported in many places, with one feature in common – leisure facilities are a must in the new retail environment. Is this combination of leisure facilities and a renewed retail environment a sufficiently strong basis to look upon the place as a tourism resource?

Usually shopping areas include catering facilities (pubs, restaurants, fast food outlets, take-aways). Apparently this set of facilities is no longer matching the customers' demands or, to put it differently, shopkeepers, urban planners and tourism promoters are looking for additional attractions. Leisure facilities and attractions are assumed to function as a magnet for the retail environment.[10] The vitality of the place and night-time traffic stimulate people to stay longer. Furthermore there is a strong tendency to see tourism as a vehicle to revitalize traditional shopping centres. The development of a tourism function improves the quality of the environment both in quality of design and in the range of facilities offered.

Not every urban shopping area has the same credentials to become a tourism destination or even an attractive leisure environment. Undeniably, the structure, symbolism and image of the town play an important role. Strong symbolic values of historic centres assure their significance as meeting places, places for shopping and eventually for fun and entertainment. Empirical research in different historic inner cities confirms the hypothesis that the combination of a historical setting and a shopping area holds potential as a tourism attraction.[11] Contrary to the American example mentioned, in most west European cities the concept of a tourism–leisure–shopping mix is usually implemented on a small scale.[12] The first step has been to create pedestrian precincts, find solutions to the parking demand and developing a theme, which should then be closely related to the traditional image or the strong points of the town. Cultural and historic theming offers plenty of opportunities in the current tourism market. Many new initiatives tried to improve the image and the design of the traditional urban shopping area, e.g. including indoor shopping galleries, refurbishing the façades, improving the design, the pavement, the street lighting, the signboards, introducing new decorations, adding benches, flowers, water fountains, music, promotion leaflets, tourist information material, etc.

One major consequence of this trend is the growing emphasis on a particular type of retailing. Tourism-oriented shopping areas are characterized by a growing predominance of speciality shops, gift shops, souvenir shops and not least catering facilities. A good example of this change is demonstrated in the well known tourist streets such as the Kalverstraat in Amsterdam, Ponte Vecchio in Florence, Carnaby Street in London, Place du Montmartre in Paris, or the small streets around the main market square in Brussels. These are examples of an unplanned development of shopping as a tourism resource.

In fact the current search for planning and marketing tourism development which could stop the process of deterioration in many older cities found a solid basis in the current changes towards a more leisure-oriented society in which urban tourism and recreation plays a vital role.[13] However, *many traditional urban shopping areas are in need of major refurbishment*.[14] Theme shopping is the new challenge.[15] Especially in the USA and the UK the development of festival marketplaces indicates the trend.[16] This kind of shopping area is energizing the heart of many cities and opens new perspectives to promote the place as a tourism destination. The introduction of the concept 'festival' is in some way misleading, for it refers to an event and not to a permanent setting. It seems that festival market centres are a success. The preconditions for this success are:

- The location of the festival market centre has to fit into the existing urban network and make use of the environmental resources, facilities and tourist attractions already there. It should reinforce the existing elements and be reinforced by them.
- Major public attractions should be in the neighbourhood, such as office complexes and schools, but also tourism attractions such as museums, cultural facilities and hotels. Spatial clustering and functional association is of vital importance.[17]
- The festival market centre should be easily accessible to the different groups of visitors.
- The uniqueness and identity of the place should be supported by a strong promotion campaign.

The capacity of these traditional shopping areas to compete with new tourism developments in out-of-town locations needs to be questioned.

Out-of-town shopping

The attraction of urban centres is threatened by an increasing trend towards decentralization in tourism attractions, retail supply and leisure facilities. In addition, the poor accessibility of towns, the perceived crowding, noise, pollution and inadequate safety precautions are yet other points of weakness in the competition with out-of-town tourism destinations and shopping areas. The growth of suburban shopping since the 1970s, their favourable location and the way these shopping areas are expanding their range of facilities, including hotels and recreational facilities, should also be taken into consideration.

In addition, the countryside as a whole is getting more and more involved. In most cases the tourism–leisure–shopping function is the best alternative for declining rural areas or industrial premises no longer in use. Many examples can be given of old warehouses, derelict harbour areas and old industrial buildings now being re-used for retail shops, hotels, restaurants, pubs and various entertainment facilities. Depending on the characteristics of the site and on the promotion activities, some of these experiments have become tourism attractions in their own right. The effect of this trend on the interest in urban tourism might become problematic. For this reason there are plenty of restrictions, in most countries, to the development in the countryside of large-scale tourism projects including major shopping facilities. Nevertheless they are appearing, in different forms and in different places.

Themepark shopping

Managers of large theme parks are fully aware of the opportunities of a combined leisure and shopping environment. The tourism attractions and leisure facilities they already have, the real threats of declining visitor numbers and the fierce competition are the incentives to look for a product enlargement. Again a US example (Disneyland) is taken and imitated in many different ways. The policy of catching other target groups by including a series of retail shops, initially related to the theme of the park, has now been expanded into a wider range of retail shops with all kinds of gadgets.

At the moment the main motive for visiting a theme park is not really shopping, so marketing techniques have to be developed to stimulate impulsive buying. This can include special theme markets, events, curiosity shops and aggressive selling techniques. The list of international capital investments in leisure theme parks in Europe, with an increasing accent on the 'shopping' element of their product, is astonishing but at the same time alarming. The old market principle of 'supply creates demand' becomes questionable, even if there is plenty of creative thinking about the leisure–shopping mix and highly efficient marketing in the tourism industry.

Future scenario

A 'total experience' seems to be the slogan for the future leisure–shopping scenario and a major challenge for the tourism industry. Taking part in the experience makes one part of modern society. Apparently the well-staged settings which are now offered by festival markets, theme parks, megamalls and shopping paradises are capable of attracting large numbers of visitors. It seems to be rather irrelevant whether the setting is newly built, a simulation of, or a genuine cultural setting. Being there (or having been there) is important and this experience is carefully staged.

The message for the tourism industry would then be to promote those places which allow for many different experiences and offer the possibility to do many different things, to the extent that the impulses for buying are unavoidable.[18]

This scenario seems vulnerable and questionable – not least because of the growing competition on the supply side but also the growing awareness of being fooled as a tourist in the search for a 'unique experience'.

This conclusion provides an incentive to look more closely and above all more critically at the myth of leisure shopping in order to reveal the actual preconditions for a synergetic relationship between shopping and tourism.

References

1. M. Jansen-Verbeke, 'Leisure + shopping = tourism product mix', in G. Ashworth and B. Goodall, eds, *Marketing Tourism Places*, Routledge, London, 1990, pp. 128–135.
2. A. Jansen, ' "Funshopping" as a geographical notion', *Tijdschrift voor Economische en Sociale Geografie*, No 80, 1989, pp. 171–183.
3. G. Boudreau, *Shopping for Recreation*, Canadian Parks, Recreation Association, 1983, pp. 13–14.
4. W. Kent, 'Shopping: Tourism's Unsung Hero(ine)', *Journal of Travel Research*, 1983, Spring, pp. 2–4.
5. K. Weigand, '*Drei Jahrzehnte Einkauftourismus ber die deutsch–dänische Grenze*', Geographische Rundschau, 1990, May, pp. 289–290.
6. *West Edmonton Mall*, Shopper Intercept Survey, Canada, 1985, 1986.
7. G. Blomeyer, 'Myths of malls and men,' *The Architects' Journal*, May 1988, Vol 187, No 20, pp. 38–47.
8. B. Gilmour, 'Mall, Fantasyland bring in millions of tourists–study', *Edmonton Journal*, October 1986.
9. R. Johnson and R. Mannell, 'User satisfaction with malls as shopping versus non-designated recreation areas', *Third Canadian Congress on Leisure Research*, University of Waterloo, 1981.
10. P. Brand, 'What are you doing here? asked Milligan, or the physics and metaphysics of town centers', *The Planner*, April 1987, pp. 23–26.
11. M. Jansen-Verbeke, 'Leisure, recreation and tourism in inner cities', *Netherlands Geographical Studies*, No 58, Amsterdam/Nijmegen, Netherlands, 1988.
12. J. Hadju, 'Pedestrian malls in West Germany: perception of their role and stages in their development', *Journal of the American Planning Association*, Vol 54, No 3, 1988, pp. 325–335.
13. M. Jansen-Verbeke, 'Future leisure scenario in the inner city', in S. Parker and A. Tomlinson, eds, *Work, Leisure and Life-styles, Part 2, Leisure Studies Association, Conference papers no 34*, LSA, London, 1989.
14. C. Owen, 'Tourism and urban regeneration', *Cities*, August 1990, pp. 194–201.
15. Jones Lang Wootton, *Speciality Shopping Centres*, JLW, London, 1986; and Jones Lang Wootton, *Retail, Leisure and Tourism*, JLW, London, 1989.
16. D. Sawicki, 'The festival marketplace as public policy', *Journal of the American Planning Association*, Summer 1989, pp. 347–361.
17. M. Jansen-Verbeke and G. Ashworth, 'Environmental integration of recreation and tourism', *Annals of Tourism Research*, Vol 17, No 4, 1990, pp. 618–622.
18. C. Keown, 'A model of tourists' propensity to buy: the case of Japanese visitors to Hawaii', *Journal of Travel Research*, Winter 1989, pp. 31–34.

14

Tourist shopping villages: development and planning strategies

Donald Getz

Associate Professor of Tourism and Hospitality Management, University of Calgary, 2500 University Drive NW, Calgary, Alberta, Canada T2N 1N4

Tourist shopping villages (TSVs) can be defined as small towns and villages that base their tourist appeal on retailing, often in a pleasant setting marked by historical or natural amenities. They are found along touring routes, in destination areas and near urban centres, but are markedly different from urban business and shopping districts in terms of their small scale, speciality retailing and distinct ambience. In this article the focus is on three TSVs situated close to large urban populations, with recognition of the likelihood that TSVs in touring and destination areas will display differences (Figure 1 also shows a fourth community identified later as a potential TSV).

Tourist shopping villages are part of the broader phenomenon of leisure shopping and are associated with heritage conservation and small-town development planning. Little attention has been paid, however, to the role of shopping as an attraction, and to pertinent questions on its planning and impacts on the host community. A major uncertainty is whether or not shopping, by itself, is a complement to the basic product or a viable alternative to other types of tourist attractions.

Analysis of case study TSVs, such as the three documented in this article, quickly reveals both similarities and differences, as well as numerous planning and marketing issues. Although a considerable amount of research is needed before a thorough understanding of the tourist shopping village phenomenon can be gained, the paper does conclude with three alternative strategies for developing and planning TSVs. Deriving planning strategies from a limited number of case studies is inherently risky, so recommendations are also made for expanding pertinent research.

Leisure and tourist shopping

At one time a daily routine far removed from leisure, shopping is now often a leisure pursuit. As noted by Howard,[1] 'People can more and more choose where they go

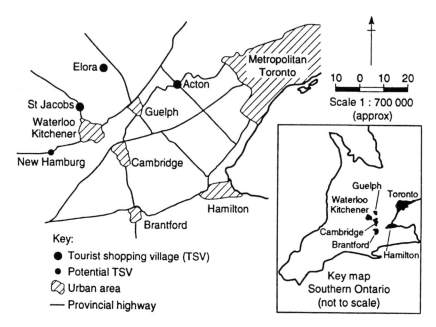

Figure 1. Location map of the three shopping villages.

shopping', making it possible to attract customers through provision of leisure opportunities and more pleasant settings. Martin and Mason[2] noted that non-essential shopping in particular is seen by consumers as being a leisure activity, and the retail sector has adapted in different ways to this trend. Johnson[3] has identified three leisure/ shopping models. The first is called 'ambient leisure', which involves the 'creation and underpinning of a pleasant environment for shopping'. The goals are to extend the duration of a shopping trip and to gain competitive advantage over less attractive shopping areas. This approach is manifested in shopping centre design and also in the proliferation of speciality shopping in historical or architecturally unique areas.

The second type is the 'new generation mall', such as the West Edmonton mega-mall, which lures shoppers by means of added recreational attractions, and also attracts purely recreational custom. In the case of West Edmonton Mall the developers sought to create a mixed shopping and leisure environment powerful enough to become a major tourist attraction.

A third type is 'heritage-destination leisure'. Exemplified by European cathedral cities, according to Johnson, this category attracts niche-position retailers and appeals both to shoppers and sightseers. The tourist shopping villages assessed in this article seem to fit this category, but are smaller and lack the grand focal point provided by a cathedral.

The aim of combining leisure with shopping, according to Johnson, is 'synergy', with specific benefits to the retailers and developers being: attraction of longer distance and longer staying shoppers; higher per capita spending; more targeted customers; competitive advantage; and a marketable image.

Research to date

Research on leisure shopping and the connection with tourism is not well developed, and has primarily been directed at urban settings. As a starting point, however, it has been shown that shopping is an important tourist activity. Kent et al.[4] reported on household interviews conducted to reveal preferences and behaviours of visitors to the Atlanta, Georgia, region. Shopping ranked as the most popular activity among all tourist-visitors interviewed, with expenditures on shopping accounting for 18% of the total. The researchers advocated more emphasis on shopping in tourism advertising. Bussey[5] reported that shopping is the number one activity of foreign visitors to the UK, accounting for 36% of total visitor spending. A study of tourist shopping in Australia determined that shopping accounts for approximately 20% of foreign tourist spending in that country.[6]

Gratton and Taylor[7] reported that two-thirds of day visitor spending and one-third of overnight visitors' spending in the historic English towns of Winchester and Salisbury was made on shopping. Most published visitor surveys will confirm that tourists spend a lot of time (often just browsing) and money on shopping, but such data shed little light on whether shopping is a trip motivator, or on how destination attributes might influence travel and shopping patterns.

Jansen-Verbeke[8] discussed the difficulties inherent in defining leisure shopping behaviour, as leisure is a state of mind. In addition, even though shopping is a common activity of tourists, it does not necessarily mean that shopping heightens an area's relative attractiveness. However, her research in The Netherlands suggested that shoppers with a leisure motive for a trip tend to stay longer in an area and take part in more activities, such as eating and drinking. Research in different historic inner cities also confirmed the hypothesis that historic settings and shopping together present an inviting leisure environment. But research has not proved the relative values of environmental attractiveness, visitor activities and perceptions of the environment in explaining tourist shopping behaviour.

Specific criteria for assessing leisure shopping environments were suggested by Jansen-Verbeke,[9] and these can be considered as tentative planning and design criteria for improving shopping area attractiveness:

- clustering of a wide variety of shops, catering, leisure and other activities and attractions;
- good accessibility and parking;
- pedestrian priority over vehicles;
- a positive image;
- attractive design (aesthetics);
- availability during leisure time (e.g. Sundays);
- hospitableness (visitor orientation, adequate information, symbolism, identification);
- social affective value;
- liveliness or animation, with surprises.

Similarly, Lichfield[10] suggested that leisure shopping areas must provide a sense of freedom, make shopping a pleasure, and facilitate social interaction. Roberts[11] referred to a number of studies which demonstrated how pedestrianization of streets in town centres was often a response to competition from suburban shopping centres. Most projects were undertaken in towns with little in the way of heritage attractions. Hence, environmental improvements followed competitive decline. The trend reinforced comparison and speciality shopping in the pedestrian precincts.

What remains unproven is the supposition that shopping in villages can attract tourists without some other form of attraction, notably natural or heritage resources. In the cases assessed later, the links to heritage resources in particular are highlighted.

Finally, researchers have not previously reported on the role of entrepreneurs in developing or fostering the tourist shopping village. Dahms[12] did, however, observe the entrepreneur's importance in an overview of trends affecting small towns in Ontario, Canada. Regarding the Lake Huron village of Bayfield, he noted that it was an example of how location, amenity and heritage factors were at work in revitalizing many small communities:

Not only is it inherently an extremely pleasant place in which to reside or to visit, but it has increased in attractiveness because of the initiatives of entrepreneurs who have renovated buildings and risked starting specialty shops.

Three case studies

The three cases were selected because of their convenient location and their reputation as day-trip shopping destinations. Elora and St Jacobs both promote themselves regionally as quaint or historic shopping villages, while the major private corporation in Acton advertises its shopping attractions widely. Accordingly, these cases cannot be said to represent an empirically determined class of town or village. Figure 1 shows their location relative to major population centres and highways in Southern Ontario, Canada. The other three figures illustrate the specific forms of natural and heritage attraction and types of shopping developments in the villages.

Research consisted of the following: reviews of local planning documents and published research; selected interviews with local entrepreneurs and officials; field observation, consisting of video-tape, photographic and written records of types and locations of retailing, services and possible attractions. The research was not quantitative, but was intended to identify planning issues and strategic development alternatives. Currently, more systematic analysis and case studies are being conducted in a quite different region to verify the concept of tourist shopping villages and the generalizability of the identified issues and suggested planning approaches.

Acton

Acton, population 7000, is approximately a 45-minute drive from several major cities in populous Southern Ontario. It has a commuter train service into Toronto – a metropolis of three million people. Acton is the largest and fastest growing of the three case study villages, with new suburban estates changing its character. Its downtown area, however, is a typical, resident-oriented main street, lacking outstanding architecture or heritage features and suffering from high volumes of automobile

Figure 2. Acton: renovated 1899 tannery is the centrepiece of The Olde Hide House retail developments.

through-traffic. The only unique feature of the town, relative to tourism, is the development of a 'Leathertown' theme by a dominant corporation. This company has converted an old tannery (built 1899) into a large shopping and dining complex, has built two related theme stores in the town, and in 1991 added a golf course.

The dominant company, called The Olde Hide House, has three of seven partners who are local residents and who wish to develop the village rather than reinvest elsewhere.[13] Their original investment was a leather-goods and furniture store (1980) and restaurant (1981) in a renovated tannery building (see Figure 2). It was conceived as a tourist attraction, and the intent has been to expand the general attractiveness of the town and its surrounding area. Hence, two new shops were subsequently opened by the company (both are themed leather-goods stores) and they were deliberately placed at the opposite end of the main street from the original store in order to spread visitor activity, and to encourage independent development initiatives. To a degree this has worked, with four or five other leather, furniture and tourist-oriented shops opening in the vicinity. Most recently (1991), The Olde Hide House has developed a championship golf course on the edge of Acton. Related to this project, executive estate housing and overnight accommodations are in the development phase, partly in the hope of attracting Japanese golf and shopping tour parties.

The company's philosophy is to be marketing driven and tourism based. In addition to promoting their own attractions, they have developed a 'Canada's Leathertown' logo and theme which is being increasingly used by other establishments in Acton, and they promote other town and regional attractions in their publications. An attractive information package has been developed, aimed at up-market tour groups. It features material on group dining, guest services, shopping, the golf course and other activities in the area. The primary market area is Southern Ontario, cultivated systematically through multi-media advertising. A very high recognition factor has been achieved for their slogan: 'It's worth the drive to Acton'. As well, television advertising in border states of the USA has been employed.

From an initial staff of 20 in 1980, the Olde Hide House company has grown to employ over 200, and attracts some 300 000 visitors annually (as of 1991) – not counting the new golf course. These visitors are actual shoppers or diners at Olde Hide House stores and include tour groups as well as car-based, independent travellers. The attractiveness of this operation is not explained by the town, which has yet to revitalize its main street or capitalize on its potential heritage assets, but by a unique shopping/dining product, compelling advertising and an emphasis on hospitality.

Much work will be needed to eliminate some of the town's negative features, notably a messy railway yard right next to the Olde Hide House, and the congestion that clogs its main street. With the added lure of the golf course, new market segments will probably be drawn to the town. Further expansion of the tourist shopping component can therefore be expected, along with important environmental changes.

St Jacobs

St Jacobs is the smallest of the three villages (population 1500), and the closest to a city. Situated just a mile from the Waterloo city limits, it is within easy daily shopping range of a large urban population (over 300 000), although weekend demand dominates. The village possesses a number of heritage buildings and a river, giving it an advantage over Acton, but it is not as visually attractive or historically unique as Elora. St Jacobs does have the added advantage of a close association with 'Mennonite Country', and that fact has shaped its evolution into a tourist shopping village. More so than the other two cases, a dominant corporation has steered the village's growth.

Milo Shantz, a local entrepreneur, developed a restaurant in 1975, then established the Mercedes Corporation for additional tourist-oriented development.[14] Part of the motivation of this individual, who is a Mennonite, was to avoid exploitation of that culture and to include an educational component in the tourist village. Hence, the 'Meetingplace' interpretive centre is a prominent part of the main street attractions. Since 1975 the corporation's achievements have included the development of a restaurant and inn, guest house, multiple shops in several restored or redesigned buildings – most notably an old feed mill (see Figure 3) – and a small maple syrup museum which acts as a lure in an old factory renovated into a shopping complex. Other, independent initiatives have followed this lead, but the corporation acts as a dominant mover and shaper of the village shopping environment, right down to storefront design and the theming of signs.

The local retail committee has estimated that the village attracts one million visitors a year who account for some C$13 000 000 in sales[15] (there have been no published studies indicating the proportion of day-trippers from nearby Kitchener-Waterloo, versus more distant origins, but given the absence of large-scale accommodation or other major trip motivators, it is clear that day-trips, leisure shopping and dining predominate). This committee fought hard for official designation from the regional municipality as a tourist area, thereby permitting Sunday shopping. Without it, considerable business opportunities were being missed, as weekends are the dominant

Figure 3. St Jacobs: renovated feed mill is the centrepiece of this community's shopping attractions.

visitation period. The village also attracts tourists during nearby special events (Kitchener-Waterloo Oktoberfest and the Elmira Maple Syrup Festival).

In 1991 the Mercedes Corporation launched a pre-Christmas television advertising campaign to encourage 'country' themed shopping trips from within the urban region. A village brochure produced by the retail committee features the historic buildings, shopping and visitor services of St Jacobs. This combination is also noted in a brochure for the restored inn and restaurant: 'Benjamins is nestled in the heart of St Jacobs, a village known for its historical richness and its artistic traditions'. The Inn itself was built in 1852 and restored in 1987 by the Mercedes Corporation with financial assistance from Ontario provincial tourism programmes. It is a self-admitted 're-creation' which approximates the original building: 'And even though everything inside is new, an old world theme invites guests to stay awhile and absorb an atmosphere of days gone by'.[16] Other buildings in the village have been adapted to retailing and visitor services while still retaining their original looks, but one major shopping building, called Riverworks, possesses merely the facade of authenticity – in reality it is a recycled factory of no architectural importance. To the visitor, however, this deception might not be noticeable, for the building inside is very much like a modern shopping centre.

One other element of the village's attractiveness, as noted in the previously cited brochure, is that of artisans. When the feed mill was first refitted for shopping, the concept was to feature local artisans who would manufacture and sell goods on the premises. This proved to be difficult to sustain, and most of the operations have been replaced by more mainstream specialty shops. Some artisans do remain in the village, however, and this adds to the country shopping theme.

The effectiveness of St Jacobs's heritage and shopping mix is apparent in its continued growth, although the confidence and marketing strength of the dominant corporation propels this expansion. A combination of authentic and inauthentic buildings and facades is apparently sufficient to satisfy most visitors, but this is a hypothesis requiring testing.

Elora

Elora is a village of 3000 persons, situated within a 30-minute drive of Kitchener-Waterloo and Guelph and an hour's drive west of Toronto. This village boasts an attractive river and limestone gorge, a popular conservation park, restored mill and many fine stone buildings. Particularly important is the Mill Street collection of buildings dating from the 1800s. Owing to its historic flavour and charming ambience, Elora and area has been the site of several Hollywood films. The village has long been a popular day-trip destination, so a tourist-oriented service industry has naturally evolved. This trend has been encouraged by the Chamber of Commerce, which recognizes shopping as an important attraction. Special events, including a music festival and antique sale and show, draw tourists to the village and generate publicity. There is also an annual historic homes tour for lovers of antiques and architecture.

Elora has not been influenced to the same degree as the other two cases by a dominant corporation or individual, but it does have a major business. The old mill was renovated into an up-market inn and restaurant that serves as the major attraction and anchor on the main tourist shopping street (see Figure 4). Without private investment in the adaptive reuse of this landmark there would certainly be the risk of structural decay. Tourism provided the means by which heritage conservation could be

Figure 4. Elora: the old mill is now a hotel and restaurant in a beautiful village setting.

economically justified. Similarly, tourism contributes to the renovation and economical use of many other Elora buildings, although not without controversy.

Because the built heritage had been so well preserved in Elora, any restoration project faces scrutiny on grounds of authenticity and design compatibility. Several out-of-character tourist-oriented structures have been developed among the original stone buildings, and other trappings of tourism – such as signage and outdoor cafes – are potential visual detractors. Furthermore, heavy peak traffic and parking problems can be attributed to the village's tourist attractiveness. Residents of the nearby village of New Hamburg, while desiring designation of their downtown area as a heritage conservation district, expressed fears that it might become another Elora![17]

The Elora Chamber of Commerce publishes a shopping and activity guide which, in 1991, carried the slogan: 'Elora: Come for the charm . . . stay for the value'. Shopping and heritage ambience are thereby explicitly linked and promoted, but the village's attractiveness is wider. Commercial accommodation is more important in Elora than in the other two cases, in terms of the total supply. There are two hotels, including the mill, and a number of bed-and-breakfast establishments in historic homes. The Grand River Conservation Authority maintains a large campsite in the adjacent park. It is also an event-oriented village, with its popular music festival and antique show and sale attracting significant numbers of day-trip and overnight visitors.

Sunday shopping has been legal in Elora for over a decade, making it a popular weekend destination. This had given the village a competitive advantage over places like St Jacobs which had not been designated a tourist area until quite recently.

A previous study of Elora by Mitchell and Wall[18] used Dunn and Bradstreet historical data to demonstrate how local businesses had evolved towards a tourist orientation. The historic trend had been one of decline in retailing and resident-oriented services, but with a surge in tourism there was considerable growth in antique shops, art galleries, and craft and gift stores. In 1986 47% of surveyed businesses said their main source of revenue was from non-locals.

Previous visitor surveys undertaken in Elora, as reported by Coppack et al.,[19] identified scenery, the country atmosphere, peace and quiet and the historical nature of the village, followed by shopping, to be the most important attractions among tourists in general (i.e. other than festival patrons). Of note, however, was the finding that shops were ranked first by only 13% of first-time visitors compared with 41% of return visitors – presumably people find Elora for a variety of reasons but are more likely to come back because of the shopping. The same visitor surveys found that unique crafts and gifts were cited as important shopping attractions, while high costs, crowding and too much commercialism were some of the complaints of Elora visitors. The findings suggest that tourist shopping development in historic places can lead to the spoiling of the original attractiveness if it is poorly planned or gets too commercial, at least in the perception of some visitors.

Planning issues for the TSV

From the literature and cases cited above, a number of specific issues become evident regarding the planning of tourist shopping villages.

Shopping, services and business evolution

Tourism, or leisure shopping in general, influences the types and evolution of retailing in a community. Speciality shops (sometimes dominated by souvenirs), catering and entertainment businesses evolve to meet the different demands expressed by the visitor and the leisure shopper. The development of these services can either displace traditional, resident-oriented businesses or expand the range of shopping and service opportunities. There might also occur a displacement of resident owners in favour of in-migrant investors or chain stores; there has been no research reported on this point.

In St Jacobs and Elora, tourism-oriented services are dominant, while in Acton they are still emerging. Elora's Mill Street and the main street shopping area of St Jacobs have largely been taken over by tourist-oriented businesses, and in Elora the transition to visitor-oriented services has spread along adjacent Metcalfe Street and is now threatening to displace the remaining resident-oriented section. Acton has a resident-oriented business district, but the deliberate spreading of investment by the dominant corporation is having the effect of stimulating spin-off, tourist-oriented shops. This is not necessarily a negative impact, as small towns and villages often have a difficult time sustaining viable businesses.

It is, however, difficult for a planning agency to control the process, as normal commercial land use designations do not differentiate between resident and tourist-oriented services. Possibly zoning laws can be used to discriminate on the basis of scale or type of development. Also, business opening hours can be regulated to affect orientation; certainly the issue of Sunday shopping was revealed to be critical in one of the case study villages.

Heritage

Adaptive reuse to retail and service functions has preserved many historic buildings in the three case study communities. As well, deliberate architectural and historic theming appears to be an entrepreneurial tool in developing tourist attractiveness, with the community as beneficiary. The risks of tourist shopping developments must also be noted, including inauthentic 're-creations' or inappropriate new designs, and conversion from traditional uses to visitor-oriented uses. A cost–benefit evaluation of the process would be difficult to undertake without a heavy emphasis on values. One problem certain to arise is the trade-off between commercial viability and maintenance of authentic designs and uses.

Stewart[20] warned of a related problem, noting that some communities fabricated a quaint or historic look, becoming 'theme' villages in the process. Dalibard[21] cautioned that mega-projects should be avoided, specifically in downtown revitalization schemes, as they are more likely to destroy attractiveness. He also advised against pedestrian malls, describing them as 'quick fixes' which can become a liability.

In North America there have been successful programmes launched to encourage the use of tourism and heritage conservation for main-street revitalization in small towns and cities.[22] The US National Trust for Historic Preservation and Heritage Canada have actively promoted this link through education and demonstration projects. Distinctiveness of place is encouraged through community-based action, with retailing and visitor services fitting in to the community's character, not changing it.

Investment

In light of the importance of individuals and dominant corporations revealed in the three case studies, planning for the tourist shopping village should highlight entrepreneurship and find ways to stimulate and assist local investments. Maintaining local control, albeit at the corporate level, will enhance economic impacts and should foster better community support for tourism initiatives in general. Once a major attraction or service infrastructure has been initiated, assistance to spin-off businesses would logically follow.

Investment in special events is a related strategy, as a small amount of capital can generate substantial economic impacts.[23] The events attract attention to the shopping areas, contribute to their pleasant ambience, and encourage longer stays and repeat visits. Many urban downtown business authorities develop programmes of special events for these reasons, and even small shopping villages can do the same.

Tourism planning and marketing

The absence of accommodation in small villages is often an obstacle to realizing local economic benefits, but small inns and bed-and-breakfast establishments are natural complements to the country shopping experience and can be developed without much visual or social impact. Financial assistance can be targeted to residents, to achieve maximum community benefits.

Joint marketing (both destination-wide and inter-business) is likely to be needed for most small villages, unless a dominant corporation emerges to meet the community's needs. Theming adds to the overall marketability of the TSV, as revealed in all three of the case studies, but obtaining agreement on, and use of the theme might be problematic. In particular, concern for preserving authenticity might clash with the desire to develop architectural uniformity, and a dominant developer might come into conflict with municipal officials or other businesses in its attempt to develop a design theme.

Environmental planning

Parking and traffic flow can become serious problems in tourist villages and can lead to negative resident attitudes, especially where visitor volume exceeds the physical capacity of small villages. Getting heavy through-traffic off the main shopping streets should be a priority. Where tour buses are attracted, special access and parking arrangements become critical. Developers can be required to incorporate parking in their expansion plans, but often the municipality will have to secure space outside the main shopping areas because old downtowns seldom left room for the automobile.

In addition to heritage attractions, natural and man-made amenities are important to the TSV. Businesses can contribute, but the appropriate public agencies will have to coordinate amenity planning. The long-term value of pedestrian malls is not known, but streetscaping and pedestrian comfort zones are clearly needed. Coordinated and themed signage is important.

Social capacity

Small villages have inherent physical limits to growth or redevelopment, as evidenced by the parking and traffic problems in the case studies. As well, social capacity must be considered, as villagers are likely to be more aware of, and concerned about change in general and tourism developments in particular. Several studies have shown how local control over the process is an important mitigating factor and how the measurement and consideration of resident attitudes must form an important part of local tourism planning.[24] Specific to the TSV, key issues are likely to be residents' fear of the loss of traditional shopping and its replacement by tourist-oriented services, higher costs in stores and general disruption of the quiet village or small-town life. A related question is that of economic dependency, particularly the possibility that tourist shopping might make the village overly dependent on one company or on a narrow range of products and services.

TSV development strategies

Results of this review and case study analysis suggest three distinct strategies for developing tourist shopping villages.

Natural evolution

In Elora it appears that tourist-oriented services evolved naturally in response to gradually increasing demand. No single business or individual dominated. The resulting tourism infrastructure has been substantial, so this mode of development has to be recognized as having considerable potential. Local planning and environmental controls are likely to be necessary to make it work without loss of heritage and natural amenities.

In general, targeted funding can be used to help the most capable entrepreneurs in increasing local investment. Fostering joint promotion would overcome the inherent problem of insufficient investment potential in those TSVs lacking dominant developers. Encouragement of a tourist development plan, integrated with normal community planning, would be likely to achieve better community support and avoid social capacity problems.

Entrepreneur-driven

In this mode, demonstrated clearly in St Jacobs and Acton, an individual or corporation takes initiatives which are followed by others. The first developments are a catalyst, which it is hoped will generate enough tourist demand to stimulate community-wide initiatives, and provide leadership in heritage and environmental conservation or adaptive reuse. The risks include over-dominance, and possible sell-out to non-residents. Those residents opposed to rapid or large-scale change might select the dominant entrepreneurs as targets for their opposition, or even initiate obstructionist political tactics.

From a planning perspective it is probably easier – though not necessarily better – to deal with, and obtain development results through a single, dominant entrepreneur. A modest level of support and facilitation might achieve major results in generating tourist demand. The marketing of TSVs through a single enterprise can also be highly cost-effective, if their scale of operations warrants widespread advertising. Financial and planning assistance tied to community residence, while discriminatory, could maximize local economic impact and community support. Enterpreneurs based in the community should have a better understanding of local sentiment and how to avoid negative effects.

Planned TSVs

Conceivably, TSVs can be created where none exists. A developer could be enticed to invest in the necessary attractions and infrastructure. A village with heritage or natural attractiveness could be targeted by tourism development agencies and provided with assistance to plan for growth. This strategy runs the risk of encountering a negative reaction, or of encouraging external control of the development process.

In keeping with principles of community-based planning[25] and sustainable tourism,[26] a preferred approach would be to:

- offer the community advice on preparing a tourism strategy;
- implement an adaptable planning and control process which fosters community-based planning;
- undertake a cost–benefit assessment, using long-term sustainability, rather than immediate profit, as the key criterion for measuring net benefits;
- gradually assist local investment and development efforts;
- balance the needs of residents and visitors, based on research into attitudes and behaviour;
- avoid large-scale and sudden changes;
- avoid inalterable changes;
- plan the service sector developments to respect the scale, nature and character of the place;
- anticipate and address traffic congestion and other negative impacts before they occur;
- ensure that heritage and environmental goals are not compromised when fostering entrepreneurial activity; this can be settled in a public forum where criteria are established.

Research needs

To validate the concept of the TSV and issues and strategies suggested in this article, a region-wide analysis of near-urban, rural and resort villages is being conducted in western Canada. Systematic analysis of this type is intended to ascertain the relative dependence of villages on tourism, and the importance of their retailing and service sectors. Local planning efforts are also being studied, to see if retailing and service functions are receiving any specific consideration in municipal and tourism plans. Ideally, longitudinal research is desirable to detect evolutionary patterns, such as shifts in types of products offered and impacts on the economic base.

Consumer surveys are needed to explore further the environmental base of leisure shopping in villages, and particularly its relationship with heritage resources. A working hypothesis, based on the three cases, is that heritage resources are in themselves the initial attraction, but tourist-oriented shopping and other services provide the draw for repeat visits. Retail surveys are also needed to test tourist preferences for types of goods and services, especially the assumption that arts and crafts, 'country' goods and souvenirs are preferred. Advertising themes and messages should be tested, as well as the semantics of tourist shopping environments (e.g., what type of design or signage signifies to tourists that they are welcomed and that suitable product lines or services are provided in a village or inside a building?).

Relative strengths and weaknesses, along with the costs and benefits of employing the three development strategies, should be scrutinized through evaluative research. As a starting point, more case studies of each mode would be beneficial, as tests for the above-mentioned hypotheses.

Finally, resident surveys are required to evaluate community participation, attitudes and preferences for tourism in general, and the shopping village strategy in particular. Planners must be especially sensitive to physical and social capacity in small towns and villages, with a number of issues being specific to shopping-based development strategies.

References

1. E. Howards, 'Trends', in Oxford Institute of Retail Management, *Leisure and Retailing*, Longman, 1990.
2. B. Martin and S. Mason, 'Current trends in leisure', *Leisure Studies*, Vol 6, No 1, 1987, pp 93–97.
3. S. Johnson, 'The leisure market: consumer choice and consumer activity', in Oxford Institute of Retail Management, *Leisure and Retailing*, Longman, 1990.
4. W. Kent, P. Schock and R. Snow, 'Shopping: tourism's unsung hero(ine)', *Journal of Travel Research*, Vol 21, No 4, 1983, pp 2–4.
5. K. Bussey, 'Leisure + shopping = ?', *Leisure Management*, Vol 7, No 9, 1987, pp 22–24.
6. Department of the Arts, Sport, The Environment, Tourism and Territories, Report of the Committee of Enquiry, *Tourism Shopping in Australia*, Canberra, 1988; report of the Tourism Shopping Implementation Committee, *Tourism Shopping in the Nineties*, Canberra, 1990.
7. C. Gratton and P. Taylor, 'Leisure and Shopping', *Leisure Management*, Vol 7, No 3, 1987, pp 29–30.
8. M. Jansen-Verbeke, 'Leisure + shopping = tourism product mix', in G. Ashworth and B. Goodall, eds, *Marketing Tourism Places*, Routledge, London, 1990, pp 128–135.
9. M. Jansen-Verbeke, 'Leisure shopping: a magic concept for the tourism industry?', *Tourism Management*, Vol 11, No 1, 1991, pp 9–14.
10. D. Lichfield, 'From combination to integration', in Oxford Institute of Retail Management, *Leisure and Retailing*, Longman, 1990.
11. J. Roberts, 'Buying Leisure', *Leisure Studies*, Vol 6, No 1, 1987, pp 87–91.
12. F. Dahms, 'Diversity, complexity and change: characteristics of southern Ontario towns and villages', *The Canadian Geographer*, Vol 30, No 2, 1986, pp 158–166.
13. S. Holloway, personal interview, 1991.

14. C. Mitchell, R. Nolan and F. Hohol, 'Tourism and community economic development: a case study of St Jacobs, Ontario', Department of Geography, University of Waterloo.

15. *Kitchener-Waterloo Record* (Kevin Crawley), 'Sunday shopping favoured for St Jacobs', p B5, 18 May 1991.

16. Brochure entitled 'Benjamin's Retaurant and Inn', no date.

17. *Kitchener-Waterloo Record* (staff), 'New Hamburg residents back heritage destination', 19 June 1991.

18. C. Mitchell and G. Wall, 'Impacts of festivals: A comparative analysis', a report submitted to the Ontario Ministry of Citizenship and Culture, University of Waterloo Department of Geography, 1986.

19. P. Coppack, K. Beesley and C. Mitchell, 'Rural attractions and rural development: Elora, Ontario case study', in F. Dykeman, ed, *Entrepreneurial and Sustainable Rural Communities*, Mount Allison University, 1990, pp 115–128.

20. J. Stewart, 'A strategy for main street', *Canadian Heritage*, Vol 40, 1983, pp 4–7.

21. J. Dalibard, 'Bringing them back to life', *Canadian Heritage*, Vol 40, 1983, pp 32–36, 44.

22. J. Weiler, 'Making places livable: a collaborative consensual approach', *Plan Canada*, January 1992, pp 30–36.

23. D. Getz, *Festivals, Special Events, and Tourism*, Van Nostrand Reinhold, New York, 1990.

24. See, for example, L. D'Amore, 'Guidelines to planning harmony with the host community', in P. Murphy, ed, *Tourism in Canada: Selected Issues and Options*, University of Victoria, Western Geographical Series 21, 1983, pp 135–159.

25. See, for example, P. Murphy, *Tourism: A Community Approach*, Methuen, New York, 1985.

26. See, for example, *Tourism and the Environment: Maintaining the Balance*, London, Department of Employment/English Tourist Board, 1991.

Part VI

Theme parks

Introduction by Stephen Page

Since the opening of Disneyland in Anaheim, California in 1955, the global growth of theme parks (also known as amusement parks) has emerged as a major element of leisure, recreational and tourist activity patterns in the developed world. Camp (1997) defines a theme park as being

- an outdoor attraction which combines rides, attractions and shows;
- designed around a central theme or group of themes; and
- charging a pay-one-price admission fee to visitors. (Camp, 1997: 4–5)

The global theme park industry has grown to a US$11 billion a year business, with an estimated 119 major theme parks spread across the world. These parks received in excess of 300 million visits in 1996, many attracting over 1 million visitors each a year. This is complemented by a large array of parks which attract less than a million visitors a year. The visits per capita to theme parks varies from 0.6 in the USA and Japan to 0.5 in Australia to 0.23 in Europe. These statistics illustrate the global impact of theme parks, which have attracted a great deal of debate among researchers on their wider significance to contemporary society.

Probably one of the most incisive and current syntheses of the debates associated with the rise of theme parks in modern society is Hannigan's (1998) *Fantasy City*. Hannigan's (1998) analysis considers theme parks as one facet of the development of Fantasy City, with its roots in tourism, sports, culture and entertainment. It also signifies the rise of the postmodern city, with its explicit focus on these centres for consumption compared with their original rationale of production. Hannigan (1998) identifies six fundamental characteristics of Fantasy City:

- A focus on themocentricity; namely, that it is based on a scripted theme.
- The city is aggressively branded, which is reflected in the place-marketing strategies and product range.

- Day and night operation is a common feature, unlike shopping malls which are largely day-time operations.
- Modularisation of products, where a diverse array of components are assembled to produce a wide range of experiences.
- Solipsisticity, where the city is economically, culturally and physically detached and isolated from surrounding neighbourhoods in a City of Illusion.
- Postmodernity, where the city is constructed around the technologies of simulation, virtual reality and the thrill of the spectacle. The city draws a major source of inspiration from the Disney model, which is widely imitated. The Disney model merges the concept of the motion picture and amusement park into a fantasy world using technologies which create conditions of hyperreality. Soja (1989) has termed such creations, postmodern agglomerations, with their antendant concerns for globalisation.

From the entertainment, leisure and tourism industry perspective, many powerful business interests have recognised these trends as part of the growth sector for the future. Yet, as early as the 1980s, critics of the recreation of historical events in the UK dubbed it the 'heritage industry' (Hewison, 1987), which was seen as a worrying trend pervading the tourism industry. Critics of the entertainment value of formerly dry and uninspiring museum exhibits being transformed into living heritage were seen as lacking authenticity, accuracy and integrity. Instead they were seen as part of the crass commercialisation of the Fantasy City concept. Goldberger (1996) criticised Fantasy City for its creation of new landscapes of leisure based on urbanoid environments, where cloning and reality were distorted by the eradication of the former living city in downtown areas.

City authorities have seized upon the urban regenerative effects of Fantasy City for inner cities which lost former productive functions, as conspicuous consumption creates a controlled, organised and measured urban experience. However, theme parks, which are part of the Fantasy City experience, have been criticised as the high technology playgrounds of the middle classes, of little benefit to local communities. What is clear is their role in the liminality of the tourist experience, where pleasure and thrill seeking in postmodern cities is a traded commodity.

An interesting perspective proffered by the French sociologist Bordieu (1984) interprets the patronage of theme parks as part of the acquisition of cultural capital: 'been there, done that', which confers status in the postmodern society. In fact, Christiansen and Brinkerhoff-Jacobs (1995) progress this argument a stage further, suggesting that the architects of Fantasy City are creating a new kind of experience for the consumer. In the context of theme parks, this consumer is requiring a constant and technologically dazzling level of amusement incorporated into their repertoire of cultural capital. Yet, Rojek (1993a) observes that an important element in the packaging of the fantasy experience is the provision of a safe, reassuring and predictable environment, termed the 'recurrence of reassurance'. This is part of what Ritzer (1993) has termed the *McDonaldization of Society*, based on the principles of efficiency, calculability, predictability and control epitomised in the theme park environment. A further element is the easy to decipher signs, the standardised behaviours and limited human interactive experiences. Although critics may be concerned that in the postmodern city we may be amusing ourselves to death (Postman, 1985), these developments are not confined to Europe (Jenner and Smith, 1996) and North America (Loverseed, 1994). The development of theme parks in the Asia Pacific region is emerging as a globalisation of the Fantasy City.

One of the key concerns in the spread of the concept to South East Asia is the diversity of ethnic groups (Hall and Page, 1999a) and the wider consequences for ethnic representation in view of the development of cultural theme parks. To reiterate McCannell's (1976) seminal study, these theme parks are basing their product on staged and reconstructed authenticity for the purposes of tourist gazing (Urry, 1990). The ramifications for wider inter-ethnic conflict are significant where ethnic divisions are not sensitively integrated into the theming of such entertainment complexes. There is also a wider equity concern where theme parks globally are becoming private spaces, with entry and participation controlled by tariffs and entry fees which can exercise social exclusivity policies to generate the appropriate target market.

Within the tourism literature, the research studies on theme parks and the wider issues of visitor attractions remains a neglected area, although a number of overview studies do exist (Oliver, 1989; Stevens, 1991; Jones, 1994) along with the more substantive study by Swarbrooke (1995) and a specialist study of heritage attractions by Leask and Yeoman (1999). One of the principal problems with theme park and attraction research is the relative paucity of data (see Hanna, 1998 for a UK-wide survey). Studies for entire countries such as the UK (Hanna, 1998) are comparatively rare, with much of the data deemed confidential and commercially sensitive by operators. Leiper (1997) provides an excellent example of one attraction which sought to make the transition from a roadside attraction to a theme park. Leiper (1997) highlighted one of the major requirements of a theme park – a substantive base market. In the Australian case, the roadside attraction traditionally relied on a large number of low-spenders as transit visitors on a major routeway. However, this was inadequate to meet the needs of a capital-intensive theme park, which required high-spending tourists visiting the region for more than a day. Similar findings emerged with the initial opening of Euro Disneyland near Paris. In what it is certainly an over-researched theme in the literature, (i.e. EuroDisney), Roisne (1997) highlighted the success of appropriate pricing and marketing strategies to attract the Workers Councils trade. In a similar vein, Vogel (1998) also examines the economic considerations associated with successful theme park development and operation.

Although Disney has attracted considerable interest, Rojek (1993b) provided an incisive and thoughtful analysis of their films and theme parks to conclude that they were part of a specific moral order. In one sense, Disney culture has parallels with the rational recreation era of the 19th and early 20th century (Hall and Page, 1999b) where organisation, control and rigid rules existed. D'Hauteserre (1997) adopted a different perspective in the analysis of Disney, highlighting the French government's utilisation of the theme park development process to create a growth pole within its new town strategy. In an exploratory study of the Tang Dynasty in Singapore, Kau (1994) examined pre-opening attitudes to the theme park while Thach and Axinn (1994) identified the main attributes sought by consumers: cleanliness, attractive scenery, an uncrowded family atmosphere, water rides and roller coasters. Kau provided an analysis of Singapore's tourism attraction system and the role of theme parks, while

Teo and Yeo (1997) examined Haw Paw Village to assess local images and tourist attitudes to the development. While a wide range of research has been published on theme parks in non-tourism journals, such as the German-language publication *Amusement Technology and Management*, many of the studies remain descriptive and lacking in analysis. In this respect, the studies published in *Tourism Management* over the last decade have added a significant dimension to the analysis of tourist patronage of theme parks. The papers selected for this section are

McClung, G.W. (1991). Theme park selection: Factors influencing attendance, *Tourism Management*, June, 12(2): 132–40.

Fodness, D.D. and Milner, L.M. (1992). A perceptual mapping approach to theme park visitor segmentation, *Tourism Management*, February, 13(1): 95–101.

Kau, A.K. (1993). Evaluating the effectiveness of a new theme park: A cross-cultural comparison, *Tourism Management*, June, 14(3): 202–10.

In McClung's (1991) paper, the continuously changing nature of market trends in the individual's choice and expectations of theme parks is considered. Using multi-segmentation strategies, marketers seek to address new market expectations from consumers and this paper examines a research study designed to achieve this objective. The study not only draws a substantive sample size, geographically dispersed across the Eastern seaboard of the USA, but uses factor analysis to derive attraction and theme park preferences for urban consumers. On the basis of this research, strategies to more effectively position theme parks are developed.

Fodness and Milner argue that theme park visitors constitute a widely described but poorly understood segment of the tourism industry. Using a perceptual mapping technique, the marketing implications of consumer choice in Florida are investigated. While traditional response variables were reported (e.g. consumer demographics, socio-economic characteristics, characteristics of the party size, trip and trip planning characteristics and expenditure patterns) novel and traditional analytical techniques were employed (e.g. visitor interchange analysis, multi-dimensional scaling, cluster analysis and market segmentation analysis). This provided a detailed analysis of theme park visitor choice behaviour which provides a basis for the discussion of market positioning of theme parks, theme park selection and promotional strategies.

Kau's (1993) discussion of Tang Dynasty Village theme park in Singapore set out to establish the perceptions of potential visitors to the newly created park. The study also examined perceptions of other tourist sites in Singapore, as well as tourist inclination to visit new attractions like the Tang Dynasty Village. The study adopted a cross-cultural method of analysing Asian and Caucasian visitor perceptions which displayed marked variations. The study emphasised the complexity of marketing attractions to different ethnic groups and visitors with different cultural backgrounds and expectations. The study also illustrated that European and North American theme park models cannot simply be replicated and applied to the Asia Pacific region without a major refocusing and development work to understand the needs, expectations and attitudes of the market.

These three articles certainly produce a wide range of research findings which need to be set against the social and cultural critiques of theme park development in the postmodern society. As Hannigan (1998: 198) concludes, the theme park city sanctions disengagement; that it is serendipitous, and casual encounters between visitors in theme parks are largely restricted to those who accompany you on the trip. Hannigan (1998: 198) cites the example of Disney World, where 'most of the rides are intentionally designed to disallow you seeing anyone, much less touching or talking to them: contact with fellow guests is "only minimally available and not at all desirable"' (Kuenz, 1993: 72). Whether such entertainment experiences and the social dimensions are problematic for society leaves a great deal of scope for research. What is certain, is that the theme park is an artificially created medium for meeting the needs of the mass tourism market, efficiently servicing their needs and expectations in a pleasure society.

References

Bordieu, P. (1984). *Distinction*. London: Routledge and Kegan Paul.

Camp, D. (1997). Theme parks in Europe, *Travel and Tourism Analyst*, 5: 4–21.

Christiansen, E. and Brinkerhoff-Jacobs, J. (1995). Gaming and entertainment: An imperfect union?, *Cornell Hotel and Restaurant Quarterly*, 36(2): 79–94.

d'Hauteserre, A. (1997). Disneyland Paris: A permanent economic growth pole in the Francilian Landscape, *Progress in Tourism and Hospitality Research*, 3(1): 17–33.

Goldberger, P. (1996). The rise of the private city, in J. Vitullo Martin (ed.), *Breaking Away: The Future of Cities*. New York: The Twentieth Century Fund.

Hall, C.M. and Page, S.J. (eds) (1999a). *Tourism in South and South East Asia: Critical Issues*. Oxford: Butterworth–Heinemann.

Hall, C.M. and Page, S.J. (1999b). *The Geography of Tourism and Recreation: Environment, Place and Space*. London: Routledge.

Hanna, M. (1998). *Visits to Tourist Attractions 1997*. London: British Tourist Authority/English Tourist Board.

Hannigan, J. (1998). *Fantasy City: Pleasure and Profit in the Postmodern Metropolis*. London: Routledge.

Hewison, R. (1987) *The Heritage Industry: Britain in a Climate of Decline*. London: Metheun.

Jenner, P. and Smith, C. (1996). Attendance trends at Europe's leisure attractions, *Travel and Tourism Analyst*, 4: 72–93.

Johnston, P. and Thomas, B. (1991). The comparative analysis of tourist attractions, in C. Cooper (ed.), *Progress in Tourism, Recreation and Hospitality Management*, vol. 3. London: Belhaven. pp. 114–29.

Jones, T. (1994). Theme parks in Japan, in C. Cooper and A. Lockwood (eds), *Progress in Tourism, Recreation and Hospitality Management*, vol. 6. London: Wiley. pp. 111–26.

Kau, A.K. (1994). Assessing the market receptivity of a new theme park in Singapore: An exploratory study, *Journal of Travel Research*, 32(3): 44–50.

Kuenz, J. (1993). It's a small world after all: Disney and the pleasures of identification, *The South Atlantic Quarterly*, 92(1): 63–88.

Leask, A. and Yeoman, I. (eds) (1999). *Heritage Visitor Attractions: An Operations Management Perspective*. London: Cassell.

Loverseed, H. (1994). Theme parks in North America, *Travel and Tourism Analyst*, 4: 51–63.

Leiper, N. (1997). Big success, big mistake, at big banana: Marketing strategies, roadside attractions and theme parks, *Journal of Travel and Tourism Marketing*, 6(3/4): 103–21.

McCannell, D. (1976). *The Tourist: A New Theory of the Leisure Class*. New York: Schocken.

Oliver, D. (1989). Leisure parks present and future, *Tourism Management*, 9(3/4): 233–4.

Postman, N. (1985). *Amusing Ourselves to Death*. New York: Viking.

Ritzer, G. (1993). *The McDonaldization of Society*. Thousand Oaks, CA: Pine Forge Press.

Roisne, S. (1997). Magic Kingdom in the realms of Works Councils: The Commercial Policy of Disneyland, Paris, *Cahiers Espaces*, 53: 38–41.

Rojek, C. (1993a). *Ways of Escape: Modern Transformations in Leisure and Travel*. Basingstoke: Macmillan.

Rojek, C. (1993b). Disney Culture, *Leisure Studies*, 12(2): 121–35.

Soja, E. (1989). *Postmodern Geographies*, New York: Verso.

Stevens, T. (1991). Visitor attractions: Their management and contribution to tourism, in C. Cooper (ed.), *Progress is Tourism, Recreation and Hospitality Management*, vol. 3. London: Belhaven. pp. 106–13.

Swarbrooke, J. (1995). *The Development and Management of Visitor Attractions*. Oxford: Butterworth – Heinemann.

Teo, P. and Yeo, B. (1997). Remaking local heritage for tourism, *Annals of Tourism Research*, 24(1): 192–213.

Thach, S.V. and Axinn, C.N. (1994). Patron assessment of amusement park attributes, *Journal of Travel Research*, 32(3): 51–60.

Urry, J. (1990). *The Tourist Gaze*. London: Sage.

Vogel, H. (1998). *Entertainment Industry Economics: A Guide for Financial Analysis*. Cambridge: Cambridge University Press.

15

Theme park selection: factors influencing attendance

Gordon W McClung

Assistant Professor of Marketing, West Virginia University, Morgantown, WV 26505-6025, USA

Inflation is eroding real income; uncertainty regarding oil supplies and fuel price increases are causing dramatic shifts in consumers' perception of the cost of travel; and consumers grouped by how far they are willing or able to travel are likely to differ in their responses to marketing strategies. Throughout the developed world employment conditions are creating a workforce with increasing leisure time. We can add theme parks to the traditional guardians of American culture – theatres, libraries and museums. In the past 25 years, parks have increasingly appropriated historic 'themes' as a medium for entertainment and communication with the travel markets.

A theme park offers a controlled, clean environment. Contrary to popular beliefs, the parks are not aimed at children. Only one visitor in four to Disneyland is a child. Market research has shown that if family members have to spend more than two hours in each other's company they tend to bicker. Theme parks are arranged with a sufficient variety of distractions to resolve this problem.

Theme parks are continually changing and adding dimensions. Disney World has become a resort in itself. The latest trend is to provide education as an integral component of theme parks. Recent technological developments are used to involve park visitors in learning games. Youngsters and adults can solve puzzles, play competitive games, make words and letters, create musical compositions, etc. Even the fast-food restaurant has an educational goal – to make healthy foods interesting and to make popular foods healthy. Waiting in line at the Food Factory provides an opportunity to watch dough and ice cream being prepared from scratch.[2]

Manufacturers are beginning to produce 'mental rides', where the audience is seated and the visual environment is manipulated to create the illusion of movement. 'We are seeking a teaching moment that can only happen when someone is entertained', says Larry Pontius, a Disney EPCOT executive.[3] People are becoming more physical today – they are going in for active pursuits, perhaps in reaction to the passivity of television and movies. The objectives are still the same – socializing with others and making them happy while they play.

Some theme parks have experienced difficulty in maintaining their customer base. Changing customer tastes can interfere with success if the park fails to anticipate the customers' needs. Beyond the basic threat to survival, miscalculating the public's taste may result in lost revenues. Some parks with 'hard' rides would need to bring in 'soft' rides. Other options are 'live' shows. A lunchtime performance relieves the pressure on a park's restaurants, while an evening extravaganza encourages visitors to stay for supper and the show. Frequently suggested methods to entice customers to visit theme parks are:

- offer new rides and attractions every year;
- introduce 'live' entertainment;
- institute special promotions.

The objective of this study is to identify factors that play a role in consumers' selection of theme parks. Market segmentation information is of considerable value in the development and operation of theme parks. Markets have been subdivided by desti-nation, trip demographics, media exposure, travel method, benefits received, social influences, personal demographics and involvement.[4] Tourism marketers are now faced with a situation that suggests the need for market segmentation. In fact, parks which feel the effects of reduced visitation and are eager to stimulate increased demand are already practising segmentation. Offerings tailored to specific segments will enhance the park's ability to compete. Effective decisions require considerable know-ledge of the prospects. In contrasting near-home with distant travellers, the manager might ask what kind of experiences they have and what types of benefits they perceive. Are their personal or family demographics different? What do they seek? Is one more accessible through a particular medium?[5] For any market segmentation strategy to work:

- the use of segmentation must be justified on the criteria of costs versus profits;
- the market segment must be accessible through existing distribution channels;
- the segment must be sufficiently large to be profitable.

Segmentation criteria include:

- demographics;
- geography;
- pertinent market behaviour;
- benefits;
- psychographics.

Although some authors mentioned trends in planning and development of theme parks, no recent major study has addressed the identification and segmentation of pertinent markets.[6] A recent study by Milman suggests that certain internal variables pertinent to the park, rather than external variables relating to travel behaviour or demographics, should be considered in the development of the park.[7] As to the factors influencing the decision to visit a park, the study found that about 46% of the respondents were influenced by the recommendations of friends/relatives and about 38% made the decision based on previous experience in the parks. Children influenced 20% of the respondents and traditional marketing activities (newspaper advertisements, billboards, television commercials etc) were influencing about 7–17% of respondents. The study has its limitations, however, in that from all 4222 adults who were asked to participate, 3007 were unqualified owing to local residency and 636 owing to language barriers. The usable sample was about 300 respondents drawn from the 579 qualified subjects.

In identifying segmentation factors for theme park selection, one must look at the 'purchase' and how the vacation/leisure decision is influenced. The service offered by the theme park must be unusual enough to differentiate the park. The major concerns are to increase the interest in and likelihood of visitation.

This study was conducted to:

- identify the influencing factors in the selection of a theme park;
- profile visitors and non-visitors;
- analyse what attractions are preferred;
- identify appropriate themes based on preferences.

Methodology

Data were collected from several sources. The West Virginia Department of Commerce provided background information. Individual theme parks were contacted by mail to obtain information about each park and the industry. The International Directory and Buyers Guide to Amusement Parks and Attractions, published by the International Association of Amusement Parks and Attractions (IAAPA), provided information on head counts, admission fees, owners, locations, size and attractions. Additionally, census data was obtained for every country in Kentucky, Maryland, North Carolina, Ohio, Pennsylvania, Tennessee and West Virginia.

Questionnaires were administered to heads of households from 10 metropolitan areas (Pittsburgh, Baltimore/Washington, Richmond, Roanoke/Lynchburg, Lexington, Columbus, Canton/Akron/Youngstown, Cleveland, Charlotte and Winston-Salem/Greensboro). Random telephone calls were made throughout each and every day for 30 days. The overall response rate was 53% with 3039 useful responses.

The questionnaire consisted of three main parts. The first section asked general travel behaviour questions dealing with frequency of travel and if respondents visited a theme park during the year before. In the second section respondents rated the importance of distance, expense, crowd, like/dislike of parks, climate, lodging and children's interest. The rating scale for importance was on a five-point scale ranging from very important (1) to very unimportant (5). The third section of the questionnaire asked respondents to identify the attractions that are important in choosing a theme park. The 13 different attractions to be examined on a similar five-point scale were the following – roller coasters, water rides, thrill rides, big name entertainment, movie-based rides, exhibits or attractions to promote learning, rides for small children, animals and their natural habitats, animal shows, gift/souvenir shops, cartoon characters.[8]

The fourth section of the questionnaire posed 14 different themes to be ranked on a five-point scale to determine which general themes held the greatest appeal. The suggested themes were the following – showcase of fantasy, technology, history, culture, natural preserve or botanical garden, flower displays, river trips, wilderness, exotic animals/natural setting, live entertainment/dinner theatre, educational exhibits, animal shows, water rides and nightclub type entertainment. The final section gathered general demographic data on respondents' age, marital status, number of children and income level.

Findings

Demographic profile

The basic profile of respondents shows a mix of men (43%) and women (57%) across all age and income categories (Table 1) – 52% of the respondents were between 25–44 years, and 43% reported household income of $25000 to $44900. The majority of those responding were married (66%). Over 58% of the households reported no children under 18 years of age living at home.

Demographic profile by visitation

An examination of the demographic profile of park visitors versus non-visitors revealed several key differences. Park visitors were identified as individuals reporting

Table 1. Demographic profile.

	Respondents	%
Sex	Male	43
	Female	57
Income ($000)	under $15	11.3
	$15 to 24.9	20.2
	$25 to 34.9	22.8
	$35 to 44.9	20.0
	$45+	25.7
Marital status	Married	65.5
	Single	21.6
	Divorced/widowed	12.9
Age	18 to 24	12
	25 to 34	27
	35 to 44	25
	45 to 54	14
	55 to 64	12
	65	9
Children under 18	No children under 18	58.5
	1 child	17.2
	2 children	16.6
	3+ children	7.7

visitation to a theme park during 1988. Park visitors tended to be somewhat younger with 59.2% in the age group 25–44 years whereas 46% of non-visitors were in this age category (Table 2). A larger number of visitors had children under 18 in the home compared to 67% of non-visitors having none (Table 3). Visitors seemed to earn more (45% of the visitors earn more than $35 000 compared to 41.4% of the non-visitors earning the same income) (Table 4). The demographic profile of park visitors (Table 5) parallels the profile of visitors from Simmons Market Research Bureau.

Attendance patterns

Over 45% of those responding stated they had attended a theme park during 1988. Of the park visits, 73% occurred during July (27.5%), August (24.7%) and June (20.8%). Attendance dropped off significantly to only 8% in September and 5.8% in May. Attendance for the remaining months was less than 3% per month. There was a heavy concentration of attendance during the three summer months and at weekends during this period.

Table 2. Age – park visitors versus non-visitors (%).

Age (years)	Did not visit	Visited	Total
18–24	4.86	6.78	11.64
	(8.83)[a]	(15.06)	
25–34	13.32	13.39	26.71
	(24.22)	(29.76)	
35–44	12.23	13.26	25.49
	(22.24)	(29.46)	
45–54	9.09	5.45	14.55
	(16.53)	(12.12)	
55–64	8.73	3.67	12.40
	(15.87)	(8.16)	
65+	6.77	2.45	9.22
	(12.32)	(5.44)	

Notes to Tables 2–4: [a]Figures in brackets refer to column percentages, i.e. percentages among visitors and non-visitors.

Table 3. Children under 18 in household – park visitors versus non-visitors (%).

No of children under 18	Did not visit	Visited	Total
0	37.40	21.12	58.52
	(67.92)	(46.99)	
1	7.78	9.46	17.23
	(14.12)	(21.04)	
2	6.75	9.82	16.57
	(12.27)	(21.85)	
3+	3.13	4.54	7.67
	(5.69)	(10.12)	

Table 4. Income – park visitors versus non-visitors (%).

Income	Did not visit	Visited	Total
under $15000	6.93	4.35	11.28
	(12.87)	(9.43)	
$15000 to $24999	11.32	8.92	20.24
	(21.00)	(19.35)	
$25000 to $34 999	12.78	9.97	22.75
	(23.71)	(21.63)	
$35000 to $44999	9.60	10.38	19.98
	(17.80)	(22.52)	
$45000+	13.27	12.48	25.75
	(24.62)	(27.07)	

Table 5. Demographic profile by visitation.

	Visitors	Non-visitors
Sex	–	–
Income	Higher income	–
Marital status	–	Divorced or widowed
Age	Under 44	–
Children	Children under 18 in home	–

Influencing factors

The climate was consistently rated as the most important influencing factor in the decision to attend or not to attend a theme park. It should be noted that the focus on east coast markets may bias the importance of climate. Though the question was directed at factors influencing park selection and visitation, climate may not be as significant in market areas with less seasonal variation in climatic conditions.

Children's desire to visit the park, and cost, were rated third and fourth in importance, while preference for this type of park was second (Table 6). Factors considered important by visitors paralleled the overall rating (with indexes such as climate 1.2; preference 1.09, children 1.07) (Tables 7 and 8). Non-visitors rated lodging (1.17) and crowds (1.04) higher in influence than visitors (0.79 and 0.97 respectively). Children's desire to visit the park was rated lower by non-visitors (0.89) than the overall rating (1.07). This discounting of children's influence may be reflective of the higher incidence of no children under 18 living at home with non-visitors (67.9%).

Attractions

Thirteen different attractions were examined to determine which attractions held the greatest appeal. Indexing attractions by the overall mean score, it becomes apparent that learning (as found in themes) is the highest rated attraction (1.91), followed by variety/quality restaurants (1.177) and animals in their natural habitat (1.140) (Table 9).

Table 6. Influencing factors' importance, ranked by city.

Factor	Distance	Cost	Crowds	Preference	Climate	Lodging	Children
Pittsburgh	5	4	6	2	1	7	3
Baltimore/Washington	4	6	5	2	1	7	3
Richmond	6	5	4	2	1	7	3
Roanoke/Lynchburg	7	4	5	2	1	6	3
Lexington	6	5	4	2	1	7	3
Columbus	6	5	3	4	1	7	2
Canton/Akron/Youngstown	4	6	5	3	1	7	2
Cleveland	6	5	4	2	1	7	3
Charlotte	6	2	5	4	1	7	3
Winston-Salem/Greensboro	6	3	5	2	1	7	4
Overall	#6	#4	#5	#2	#1	#7	#3

Table 7. Influencing factors – park visitors.

Rank	Variable	Index[a]
1	Climate	1.20
2	Preference for this type park	1.09
3	Children	1.07
4	Cost	0.99
5	Crowds	0.97
6	Distance	0.94
7	Lodging	0.79

Note: [a]Mean/grand mean.

Table 8. Influencing factors – non-visitors.

Rank	Variable	Index[a]
1	Lodging	1.17
2	Climate	1.04
3	Crowds	1.04
4	Preference for this type park	1.03
5	Cost	1.00
6	Children	0.89
7	Distance	0.82

Note: [a]Mean/grand mean.

Attempting to match attractions by examining their relative ranking is difficult at best. On closer examination, it would appear that several of the attractions are closely related. Analytically, factor analysis is a technique for examining these relationships. The objective of factor analysis is to simplify (reduce the complexity of) the interpretation of multiple items (e.g. 13 attractions) by putting multiple items into single factors without losing the original value of the information provided by respondents.

Table 9. Attractions.

Rank	Variable	Label	Index[a]
1	Attraction 8	Exhibits/attractions promoting learning	1.191
2	Attraction 5	Variety/quality of restaurants	1.177
3	Attraction 10	Animals in their natural habitat	1.140
4	Attraction 6	General shows and entertainment	1.106
5	Attraction 11	Animal shows	1.035
6	Attraction 2	Water rides	1.026
7	Attraction 3	Thrill rides	0.970
8	Attraction 4	Big name entertainment	0.965
9	Attraction 9	Rides for small children	0.947
10	Attraction 1	Roller coaster	0.929
11	Attraction 13	Cartoon characters	0.919
12	Attraction 7	Movie-based rides entertainment	0.818
13	Attraction 12	Gifts of souvenir shops	0.776

Note: [a]Mean/grand mean.

Table 10. Attractions – mean scores.

Attraction	Visited	Did not visit
Family[a]	3.45	3.37
Thrill[b]	3.58	2.85
Leisure	3.28	3.27

Note: [a]Significant difference at $p < 0.05$. [b]Significant difference at $p < 0.01$.

Using factor analysis to help simplify the multiple attractions to a set of related attractions, we see three major factors emerge which can be classified as family, thrill and leisure attractions. The first attracting factor, family, consists of attractions for learning, rides for small children, animals in their natural habitat, animal shows and cartoon characters. The second attraction factor, thrill, consists of roller coasters, water rides and several thrill rides. The third attraction factor, leisure, consists of big name entertainment, general entertainment, variety/quality of restaurants, and gifts or souvenir shops.

Comparing the difference in importance of these three attraction factors for visitors and non-visitors, we see no difference in the importance of leisure attractions (mean scores of 3.28 and 3.27 respectively) (Table 10). Family attractions were considered more important by visitors (3.45) than non-visitors (3.37). The greatest disparity in ratings exists for thrill attractions. Visitors rated thrill attractions as the most important aspect (3.58), while in sharp contrast, non-visitors rated thrill attractions as the least important factor (2.85).

Themes

Fourteen different themes were examined to determine which general themes held the greatest appeal. Indexing themes by the overall mean score facilitates the interpretation of the relative importance of each individual item. Overall, educational exhibits were the highest ranking theme (1.17), followed by exotic animals (1.09) and technology and botanical gardens (1.05) (Table 11).

Attempting to match themes by examining their relative ranking is difficult. Applying factor analysis to facilitate the interpretation of multiple themes, we find four factors. These four factors represent general themes of learning, wet and wild, night-owl and botanist. The first theme factor, learning, consists of fantasy, technology, history, culture and educational. The second theme factor, wet and wild, consists of river trips, wilderness, exotic animals, animal shows and water rides. The third theme factor, night-owl, consists of dinner theatre and nightclub entertainment. The fourth and final theme factor, botanist, consists of botanical gardens and floral displays.

Given these four theme categories, we can make comparisons between those who visited a park and those who did not (Table 12). Interestingly, learning was highly rated by both visitors and non-visitors (3.51 and 3.45 respectively). On the other two theme factors, visitors and non-visitors were in sharp contrast. Visitors rated wet and wild themes significantly higher (3.46) than non-visitors (3.32). In contrast, non-visitors rated the botanist theme significantly higher (3.43) than visitors (3.24).

Table 11. Themes.

Rank	Variable	Label	Index
1	Theme 11	Educational exhibits	1.170
2	Theme 9	Exotic animals	1.090
3	Theme 2	Technology	1.058
4	Theme 5	Botanical gardens	1.043
5	Theme 8	Wilderness	1.028
6	Theme 3	History	1.025
7	Theme 7	River trips	1.018
8	Theme 4	Foreign cultures	0.984
9	Theme 10	Live entertainment	0.969
10	Theme 13	Water rides	0.963
11	Theme 12	Animal shows	0.952
12	Theme 6	Flower displays	0.949
13	Theme 1	Fantasy	0.937
14	Theme 14	Nightclub	0.813

Table 12. Themes – mean scores.

Theme	Visited	Did not visit
Learning	3.51	3.45
Wet-wild[a]	3.46	3.32
Night-owl	3.00	2.98
Botanist[a]	3.24	3.43

Note: [a]Significant difference at $p < 0.01$.

Table 13. Themes and attractions – correlation coefficients.

	Attractions		
Themes	Leisure	Family	Thrill
Learning	0.40	0.53	0.07
Wet/wild	0.35	0.58	0.32
Night-owl	0.53	0.15	0.18
Botanist	0.43	0.38	−0.09

Themes and attractions

Examining the correlations between major themes and key attractions, we find a strong positive relationship between a learning theme and both family ($R = 0.53$, $p < 0.001$) and leisure ($R = 0.40$, $p < 0.001$) attraction factors (Table 13). There is also a strong positive relationship between a wet/wild theme and family attractions ($R = 0.53$, $p < 0.001$). The botanist theme has a strong positive relationship with leisure ($R = 0.43$, $p < 0.001$) and family ($R = 0.38$, $p < 0.001$) attractions.

Conclusions

Predicting theme park attendance and recognizing potential market segments is difficult. This study attempts to identify tourist preferences involving theme parks. The findings underscored the fact that several key demographic aspects differentiate park visitors from non-visitors, including age, children in household and income. The visitor/non-visitor distinction was based on attendance within a 12-month period. From a marketing perspective any non-visitor represents new market potential. Realistically, a portion of the non-visitors have a low expressed interest in theme parks as an entertainment alternative (13.4% in the present study). It may be prohibitively expensive and time consuming to convert this group to visitor status.

Park visitors were younger, with children under 18 living at home, and earning more than non-visitors. Of the households contacted 45% reported park attendance. The vast majority of park attendance occurs during the months of June, July and August.

Respondents indicated four important influencing factors in their consideration of whether or not to attend a theme park. The most important factors influencing park attendance are climate, preference for theme parks, chilren's desire to attend and cost.

Climate, which represents the single most important aspect, (visitors' index 1.2 and non-visitors' index 1.04) would appear to be operationally uncontrollable. Yet, it is possible to influence potential visitors' perception of climate in addition to providing a variety of activities which can be enjoyed irrespective of climatic conditions. The second and third influencing factors, preference for the type of park and children's desire to attend, are both reflective of the marketability of the theme park. Design, operation and communication are three essential elements for addressing these two factors. Visitors and non-visitors are influenced greatly by their underlying preference for theme parks (indexes 1.09 and 1.03, respectively). Further, for visitors, children's influence is important (index 1.07), whereas non-visitors indicated great concerns for lodging (index 1.17) and crowds (index 1.04).

Therefore, it is suggested that theme parks could direct their marketing activities to capitalize on childrens' influence as a primary factor for attracting more visitors. To target non-visitors, theme parks must take appropriate measures to position the park favourably on criteria such as quality and availability of lodging and limited crowds. The analysis of attraction factors reveals that visitors prefer family (learning exhibits, rides for children, animal shows, cartoon characters), thrill (roller coasters, water rides, thrill rides), and leisure (big name entertainment, general entertainment, variety/quality restaurants, gift/souvenir shops) with means of 3.45, 3.58 and 3.28 respectively. Non-visitors on the other hand prefer family and leisure (means of 3.37 and 3.27 respectively), but do not favour thrill attractions (mean of 2.85).

- In order to position the park to visitors, an emphasis should be placed on family, thrill and leisure attractions. Special attention should be paid to children's influence on making the decision to visit a theme park.
- To attract non-visitors, family and leisure attractions can be developed and promoted. However, considering that non-visitors seemed to be older and crowd averse, special attention should be given to educational exhibits and big name shows with good leisure activities that might also be appropriate for families with older children.

According to the preference for themes, visitors indicated learning, wet/wild and botanist as the most preferred themes (with means of 3.51, 3.46 and 3.24 respectively). As a comparison, non-visitors indicated learning (mean of 3.45) and botanist (mean of 3.43) as the preferred themes. The fact that non-visitors expressed a certain dislike for wet/wild themes might be explained by their concern for crowds and aversion to thrill attractions. These results suggest that parks with learning themes and botanist themes can be positioned to both visitors and non-visitors. However, non-visitors might stay away from parks that offer wet/wild themes exclusively or as the primary attractor. Wet/wild themes were highly preferred by visitors and they might complement family attractions but should not be used to target non-visitors.

Correlation of themes and attractions provided these results:

- Theme parks with learning themes could draw attendance from both visitors and non-visitors. This can be explained by the strong relationship between family and leisure attractions and learning themes. Floral displays and botanical gardens can be both educational and relaxational. Therefore, this type of theme park can attract both visitors and non-visitors. Consideration should, however, be given to children's influencing factor (age, preference);
- Given that the wet/wild themes correlate highly with family attractions, this type of theme can be used to attract younger people and families with children looking for thrills and excitement activities and good/variety restaurants.
- The night-owl theme goes well with leisure attractions. Therefore, this theme could be positioned to older segments, primarily adults seeking entertainment activities and good/variety restaurants.

Multisegmentation strategies

Overall, the study suggests some important marketing strategies. Combining themes with attractions, it is suggested that learning themes with family and leisure attractions, and botanist themes with leisure and family attractions, can increase the likelihood of attracting more non-visitors while maintaining the visitors' status. The requirement for this strategy is to create an environment where learning is enjoyable and is positioned not only to youngsters but also to adults. Learning themes such as fantasy, technology, history, and culture can provide the 'teaching moment'.[9] The challenge of creating a musical composition or the opportunities to learn how popular food is prepared are appropriate strategies to make theme parks appealing to an older crowd who are not traditionally attracted to theme parks. A theme park should provide sufficient distractions to meet the diverse needs of family members.

However, park management is important. Since crowds may be a deterrent to older segments, facilities should be properly managed. In addition, combinations of attraction/theme factors are essential for competitive attractiveness. For instance, with family attractions, themes like learning, wet/wild and botanist can be blended. However, factors such as children's influence or non-influence and personal preferences for a theme, also contribute to making a selection to attend or not attend. Looking at leisure attractions, themes like botanist would suit the older segment whereas wet/wild is preferred by thrill seekers who are normally young adults and older children. Therefore, a selection of certain themes and attractions is mandatory for the successful marketing of the park. Strategic targeting is needed to attract the most desirable and feasible segments:

- To attract both younger and older segments (visitors and non-visitors) emphasis should be on learning themes with family and leisure attractions and/or botanist themes combined with leisure and family attractions.
- Wet/wild themes attract younger thrill seekers but scare older adults (non-visitors). Possible target market is visitors with children. Parks could emphasize learning themes and combine them with family attractions.
- Night-owl themes attract older, leisure seeking adults. Combined with big name entertainment activities, shows, and family restaurants a park can be positioned to attract families and younger adults (visitors).

The recent trends in attendance patterns, the changing expectations of family members related to amusements and relaxation, and the market conditions underline a need for family activities that provide a learning environment with enjoyment. Also the more active lifestyle of our population calls for parks and facilities that challenge adults and provide a novelty experience. The benefits sought by attending a theme park have changed and, therefore, marketers would need to address the new expectations of these segments.

Theme parks are typically comprised of multiple themes to appeal to a wide range of potential visitors; however, the study suggests that combinations of the desired themes and attractions are essential for competitive attractiveness. The suggested strategies provide a starting point for the formulation of different combinations of the desired themes and attractions for competitive differentiation.

Acknowledgement

The author gratefully acknowledges the financial support provided for this research by the West Virginia Department of Commerce and the West Virginia University Center for Economic Research. The author gratefully acknowledges the assistance provided by Georgine Konyu-Fogel and Nikos George, both graduate students at West Virginia University.

References

1. *The Economist*, 'The American dream and the great escape', 11 January 1986, p 83.
2. S. Hanna, 'An amusement park that also educates', *Video Technology*, 1981, p 37.
3. A. Meredith, 'Revolution on the Midway – an exotic world unfolds', *Scientific Digest*, August 1979, pp 58–63.
4. C.D. Schewe, D.R. Scott and D.G. Frederick, 'A multi-brand/multi-attribute model of tourism state choices', *Journal of Travel Research*, Vol 17, No 1, Summer 1978, pp 23–29; J. Graham and G. Wall, 'American visitors to Canada, Study in market segmentation', *Journal of Travel Research*, Vol 16, Winter 1978, pp 21–24; W. Darden and W. Perreault Jr, 'A multi-variate analysis of media exposure and vacation behaviour with lifestyle covariates', *Journal of Consumer Research*, Vol 25, September 1975, pp 93–103; D.K. Hawes, 'Empirically profiling four recreational vehicle market segments', *Journal of Travel Research*, Vol 16, Spring 1978, pp 13–20; A.G. Woodside, E. Moore and M.J. Etzel, 'Vacation travel behavior and perceived benefits of home state residents', *Business and Economic Review*, University of South Carolina, Vol 26, April 1980, pp 28–35; J. Burnett and M. Etzel, 'Developing marketing strategy in the tourism and travel industry using market segmentation', in, J. Sumney and R. Taylor, eds, *Evolving Marketing Thought for 1980*. Proceedings of the Southern Marketing Association, New Orleans, LA, November 1980, pp 441–444; A.G. Woodside and R.E. Pitts, 'Effects of consumer styles, demographics and travel activities on foreign and domestic travel behavior', *Journal of Travel Research*, Vol 14, Winter 1976, pp 13–15; J. Gentry and M. Doering, 'Sex role orientation leisure', *Journal of Leisure Research*, Second Quarter, 1979, p 111; and D.R. Fesenmaier and B. Johnson, 'Involvement based segmentation', *Tourism Management*, Vol 13, No 1, December 1989, pp 293–300.
5. M.J. Etzel and A. Woodside, 'Segmenting vacation markets: the case of the distant and near-home travelers', *Journal of Travel Research*, Vol 20, Spring 1982, pp 10–14.
6. F.R. Lawson and M. Baud Bory, *Tourism and Recreational Development*, Architectural Press, London, UK, 1977; and C.Y. Gee, *Resort Development and Management*, MI Educational Institute of the American Hotel and Motel Association, East Lansing, MI, USA, 1979.
7. A. Milman, 'Market identification of a new theme park: an example from Central Florida', *Journal of Travel Research*, Vol 26, Spring 1988, pp 7–11.
8. *Ibid.*
9. *Op cit*, Ref 3.

16

A perceptual mapping approach to theme park visitor segmentation

Dale D Fodness and Laura M Milner

Department of Business Administration, School of Management,
University of Alaska Fairbanks, Fairbanks, Alaska 99775–1070, USA

Theme park consumers are a frequently described, though little understood, component of the hospitality market-place. While tourism marketers often utilize survey techniques to develop profiles of theme park visitors, the analysis of such data is typically restricted to questions of who is visiting and what they do. Alternative analyses of simple survey data, however, can also enable the marketer to find answers to more involved and, arguably, more interesting questions such as why individuals visit one theme park and not another, and what the determinants of theme park choice are.

If relatively homogeneous segments of theme park visitors could be identified based on their choice behaviour, this information could be used by theme park marketers to more effectively target marketing efforts. In order to understand what factors are important to consumers when they evaluate theme park alternatives, tourism research can focus on the behavioural aspects of consumer choice.

The present study used survey data and perceptual mapping techniques to investigate the marketing implications of consumer choice of theme parks. To accomplish this, consumer choice data were collected from recent theme park visitors. The data were then analysed by the techniques of consumer interchange, multidimensional scaling, cluster analysis, and market segmentation analysis.

Hypotheses

The primary objective of this study was to investigate the underlying dimensions of visitor choice of theme parks. Are there discernible patterns of visitor behaviour and/or characteristics that might enable a tourism marketer to explain, predict or possibly influence theme park choice? Accordingly, two hypotheses are tested.

Hypothesis 1

The substantive hypothesis is that differences in leisure travellers exist, so that homogeneous clusters can be formed based on their theme park visitation patterns. The null hypothesis is that no such differences in theme park visitation patterns exist. In order to test this hypothesis, leisure traveller theme park attendance data will be analysed via visitor interchange, multidimensional scaling and cluster analysis.

Hypothesis 2

The second hypothesis is concerned with whether or not the resulting theme park visitation clusters can be considered viable market segments. The substantive hypothesis is that there will be statistically significant differences between theme park visitation segments with respect to managerially relevant variables. The null hypothesis postulates no differences between theme park visitation segments with respect to the dependent variables. In order to test this hypothesis, cluster profiles of travellers derived from the test of the first hypothesis will be analysed using standard marketing segmentation techniques.

Methodology

Empirical setting: Florida tourist attractions

The empirical setting for this study was Florida and the sampling frame for this data collection effort consisted of car travellers who stopped at official Florida welcome centres and completed a short, self-administered questionnaire. The instrument used in this programme required travellers to return the card with their names and addresses in order to receive an incentive item. It was this list of names and addresses of recent visitors to Florida which formed the sampling frame for this study.

One thousand surveys were mailed to a random sample of the approximately 1800 visitors who returned cards from January to June 1990. Of the 716 surveys returned, 585 were usable for the purposes of this study.

The data collection instrument

The Florida Department of Commerce Division of Tourism conducts approximately 9000 person-to-person interviews annually with out of state visitors as they are completing their stay and leaving the state. Questionnaires are administered by field workers employed by private marketing research firms under contract to the state of Florida. In order to make it possible to compare the independent data collection effort of this study with the on going Florida exit survey programme data, the data collection instrument used in this study was based on the Florida questionnaire and was rewritten only as needed to facilitate its use as a self-administered mail questionnaire.

In general, the match between the two samples was quite good, indicating that the data used for this study are reasonably representative of the Florida tourism drive market.

The data

Response variables of interest to this study included traditional consumer demographic, socioeconomic and behavioural data. Included in the behavioural data were the subjects' reported attraction visits. On the survey form subjects could report up to six attractions they had visited. This study viewed the relevant product set as consisting of the top ten attractions reported. Table 1 lists these attractions, the percentages of respondents reporting visits to these attractions, and their rankings.

Synopsis of analytical techniques

Four alternative and complementary analytical techniques were used to address the hypotheses: visitor interchange, multidimensional scaling, cluster analysis and market segmentation. By using alternative techniques to develop a structural representation of the relationships between theme parks and visitor characteristics and behaviour, the researcher can identify relatively stable patterns emphasized by more than one method. The following section briefly describes each of these techniques and its relationships to the other techniques.

Visitor interchange. A visitor interchange matrix can be used by theme park marketers to understand what other theme parks their own visitors patronize as well as to identify the other theme parks from which they draw their customers. Data are collected by asking theme park visitors what attractions they have visited. A matrix of conditional probabilities of visiting any particular pair of theme parks in a given market is developed from the raw data. When a large probability exists between any two theme parks on the matrix, high customer interchange occurs between the theme parks. When the identified probabilities are low, little visitor interchange occurs between given theme parks.

Multidimensional scaling. Like visitor interchange, multidimensional scaling (MDS) may help the tourism researcher to determine which theme parks are most competitive with one another. MDS goes beyond simply identifying similarly perceived theme

Table 1. Top ten major attractions of visitors surveyed 1990 first and second quarter auto travellers.

Attractions	%	Rank
Disneyworld	32.7	1
Sea World	13.2	2
EPCOT Center	10.7	3
Spaceport USA	10.0	4
Parks and preserves	8.9	5
Everglades National Park	7.9	6
Busch Gardens	6.8	7
Disney-MGM Studios	6.5	8
Cypress Gardens	6.0	9
Silver Springs	3.2	10

parks, however; its focus on underlying relationships may suggest market segments based on consumer perceptions of theme parks. That is, MDS not only identifies the level of interchange among theme parks, it suggests underlying dimensions which may explain the nature of the interchange pattern.

Cluster analysis. While MDS is used to group similarly perceived theme parks, cluster analysis is used to identify theme park patrons with similar visitation patterns. If fairly homogeneous clusters of theme park visitors can be identified from their visitation patterns, this information can be used to target various types of marketing efforts.

Market segmentation. The well-established principle of market segmentation suggests that marketing strategies for theme parks should be designed for a restricted segment (or segments) of visitors whose needs and wants are best satisfied by the offering marketed. Utilizing cluster analysis to identify more homogeneous groups of theme park visitors, market segmentation provides guidelines for the selection of target market segments and for the mix of marketing resources to be applied to each.

Analyses and results

Visitor interchange

A customer interchange matrix was created from the raw data by tabulating the number of respondents who reported a visit to both attractions in all $n(n-1)/2 = 45$ pairs of the top ten attractions. Each row of the resulting 10×10 matrix (Table 2) was then transformed into conditional probabilities. A literal interpretation of Table 2 shows, for the sample previously described, that:

- Of the Disneyworld visitors (DW) 26% went only to DW; 2% also visited EPCOT Center; 11% visited Sea World; 3% visited Busch Gardens; 8% reported a visit to Spaceport USA; 2% visited Cypress Gardens; 2% visited Silver Springs; 5% visited

Table 2. Visitor interchange matrix.

	% of each attraction's customers also attending									
	BUS	CYP	EPC	EVE	MGM	PAR	SEA	SIL	SPC	DW
Busch Gardens (BUS)	20	13	23	•	10	•	10	•	5	13
Cypress Gardens (CYP)	14	9	29	3	6	3	14	3	6	9
EPCOT Center (EPC)	15	16	6	2	24	3	8	2	6	5
Everglades (EVE)	•	2	2	30	4	15	11	•	4	13
Disney-MGM Studios (MGM)	10	5	38	5	18	•	3	•	•	5
Parks and preserves (PAR)	•	2	4	13	•	31	8	•	•	17
Sea World (SEA)	5	6	6	6	1	5	5	5	8	27
Silver Springs (SIL)	•	5	5	•	•	•	21	32	5	16
Spaceport USA (SPC)	3	3	6	3	•	•	10	2	3	26
Disneyworld (DW)	3	2	2	3	1	5	11	2	8	26

parks/preserves; 3% visited the Everglades National Park; and 1% visited Disney-MGM Studios.
- When the conditional probability between attractions is large, high visitor interchange occurs between theme parks. For example, 24% of EPCOT's visitors also reported a visit to Disney-MGM and 38% of the Disney-MGM visitors also attended EPCOT. When the percentages are low, there is little visitor interchange between attractions. Only 1% of Sea World's visitors, for example, reported a visit to Disney-MGM, and only 3% of Disney-MGM visitors went to Sea World.
- While Spaceport USA attracted 26% of DW's visitors, DW attracted only 8% of Spaceport USA's visitors. Such inequalities have implications for strategic planning and promotion, which will be discussed in the final section of this article.

Multidimensional scaling

MDS analysis. The conditional probabilities generated for the visitor interchange matrix may also be regarded as measures of similarity suitable for multidimensional scaling analysis. The data used for the MDS analysis differ from the visitor interchange data only in that subjects who visited only one theme park were excluded.

The conditional probabilities/similarity data were submitted to the ALSCAL procedure to obtain a perceptual map in which the distances between theme parks reproduced as closely as possible the original similarities in input data. Thus, the closeness (or distance) between the theme parks on the perceptual map reflects the degree to which they tended to be visited by the same (or different) visitors. Kruskal and Wish discuss general techniques for deriving MDS solutions from similarities data.[1] ALSCAL was accessed via SPSSX in this research and the specific approach was equivalent to Young's asymmetric multidimentional scaling model.[2] To aid the interpretation, the model was directed to fit the data in two dimensions. The resulting perceptual map appears in Figure 1.

MDS goodness of fit. A reliable measure of fit when using ALSCAL is R^2.[3] The R^2 roughly approximates to its counterpart in regression analysis, and indicates the

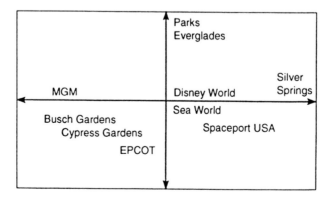

Figure 1. MDS perceptual space.

proportion of variance of disparities (optimally scaled data) that can be accounted for by the MDS procedure. The MDS solution generated a high R^2 (0.931), which indicates a good fit for the two-dimensional model.

MDS interpretation. An examination of the perceptual map (Figure 1) suggests that the two dimensions might represent underlying constructs related to the age of the visitor and the nature of the attraction. The horizontal dimension, for example, groups Disney-MGM Studios, Busch Gardens, Cypress Gardens, and EPCOT Center at one extreme and Disneyworld, Sea World, Spaceport USA and Silver Springs at the other. Familiarity with the data would support a tentative interpretation of theme parks which tend to appeal to an older visitor in the left cluster and theme parks which appeal to younger visitors on the right. The vertical dimension, with Everglades National Park and parks and preserves grouped at one extreme and all other theme parks grouped at the other, suggestes a natural versus man-made attraction distinction.

Results from the visitor interchange analysis tend to corroborate the perceptual maps developed from the multidimensional scaling. Disney-MGM Studios, Busch Gardens, Cypress Gardens and EPCOT fall closely together on the perceptual map and they have relatively high levels of visitor interchange. The other two groups display similar characteristics. In other words, the MDS groupings demonstrate high levels of customer interchange for theme parks within groups and lower levels of interchange between theme parks in different groups.

Cluster analysis

An agglomerative hierarchical cluster analysis procedure available via SPSSX was used in the present study to group theme park visitors according to their theme park visitation patterns. This method of cluster analysis begins with each observation (theme park visitor) as its own cluster, and successively merges observations and clusters of observations until all of those which show a common pattern are joined in a single cluster. Formation of clusters is defined by the researcher's choice of a similarity measure and an algorithm that provides the rule for joining observations.

The data in this study were binary, i.e. subjects either visited, or did not visit, each of the top ten attractions. It was therefore necessary to utilize the SPSSX procedure Proximities to compute a special similarity measure. Using the Kulczynski similarity measure 2, the binary data were transformed into values interpretable as conditional probabilities, that is, this measure gives the conditional probability that one theme park was visited given that the other theme park was visited. This measure was chosen based on its similarity to the analyses conducted via visitor interchange and MDS, which also utilized conditional probability data.

Cluster analysis goodness of fit. There is no single best solution to a clustering problem. Six alternative solutions were generated based on clustering method: average linkage between groups, average linkage within groups, single linkage, complete linkage, centroid clustering, median clustering, and Ward's method. When evaluated in the light of previous visitor interchange and MDS results, and with an emphasis on

Table 3. Cluster solution (%).

	Cluster 1, $n = 71$	Cluster 2, $n = 71$	Cluster 3, $n = 32$
Busch Gardens	21.1	18.3	3.1
Cypress Gardens	23.9	12.7	12.5
EPCOT Center	53.5	15.5	9.4
Everglades	9.9	7.0	40.6
Disney-MGM Studios	32.4	8.5	9.4
Parks and preserves	14.1	11.3	31.3
Sea World	35.2	52.1	28.1
Silver Springs	2.8	12.7	6.3
Spaceport USA	31.0	38.0	18.8
Disneyworld	70.4	78.9	75.0

interpretability, Ward's method appeared to offer the most reasonable three-cluster solution.

Cluster analysis interpretation. A three-cluster solution was suggested by the results of the MDS analysis. Table 3 presents the results of a three-cluster solution of theme park visitors which exactly replicates the three dimensions found in the MDS procedure which grouped theme parks.

Test of the first hypothesis

Based on the results of the visitor interchange matrix, the multidimensional scaling, and the cluster analysis, the first hypothesis, that no differences in theme park visitation patterns will exist which will enable leisure travellers to be clustered together on this basis, is rejected. Rather, all three analyses solidly support the notion of three distinct patterns of theme park visitation. One cluster of visitors is more likely to choose from among Disney-MGM Studios, Busch Gardens, Cypress Gardens, and EPCOT Center. A second cluster of visitors is more likely to restrict its choices to Disneyworld, Sea World, Spaceport USA, and Silver Springs. A third distinct cluster tends to visit Everglades National Park and other parks and nature preserves (bold figures identify in which cluster the majority of other theme park visitors fall).

Visitor segmentation

The second hypothesis is concerned with whether or not the resulting theme park visitation clusters can be considered viable market segments. The dependent variable framework used to develop and compare the profiles of the functional segments included demographic characteristics, travelling party characteristics, trip characteristics, trip planning characteristics, trip behaviour characteristics, and expenditure patterns. Descriptor variables were selected on the basis of managerial relevance, as suggested by the tourism literature. Descriptor variables were chosen which either would seem to contribute to a manager's understanding of his or her product or which conceivably could be influenced by the manipulation of the marketing mix.

For each of the following data tables, a brief discussion of each segment's characteristics relative to the variables presented in the table will be held. Discrete dependent variables were compared across segments using χ^2 distribution tables to determine if any statistical dependencies existed. Analysis of variance using Duncan multiple range tests on means was used to compare continuous dependent variables across segments. Those variables for which the null hypothesis of no differences could be rejected are indicated by asterisks which indicate the associated level of significance.

Demographic characteristics (Table 4). The members of cluster 1 were the most likely to be retired (38.0%), while cluster 2 members were the most likely to be a couple in the empty nest stage of the family lifecycle (16.9%). The third cluster contained the highest percentage of families with children, whether young children (21.9%), teenagers (12.5%) or grown children (12.5%).

Although not statiscally significant, the data suggest that cluster 1 members were the least educated, with only 28.2% reporting education beyond high school. Cluster 2 and 3 members both reported nearly 45% with higher education.

No statistically significant differences were found across the clusters in regard to income; however, the data indicate higher incomes in the third cluster and lower incomes in the first.

Travelling party characteristics (Table 5). While all three clusters were primarily composed of families, cluster 3 travelling parties were significantly the largest, with an average of four persons. Cluster 2 travelling parties were the smallest, with a mean number of 2.9 persons. No doubt the larger travelling party size for cluster 3 was due to the greater likelihood of there being children in the travelling party (50.0%).

Table 4. Comparison of demographic characteristics across multiple attraction visitor segments (%).

Demographic variables	Cluster 1, $n=71$	Cluster 2, $n=71$	Cluster, 3 $n=32$
Lifecycle ($\chi^2 = 14.8^a$)			
Single adult	11.3	15.4	3.1
Married without children	9.9	8.5	6.3
Family with young children	16.9	12.7	21.9
Family with teenagers	12.7	5.6	12.5
Family with grown children	7.0	8.5	12.5
Empty nest	4.2	16.9	6.3
Retired	38.0	32.4	37.5
Education ($\chi^2 = 8.0$)			
High school	71.8	54.9	56.35
College/Vocational or technical	16.9	33.8	21.9
Postgraduate	11.3	11.3	21.9
Income ($\chi^2 = 5.0$)			
< $29 999	35.2	28.1	15.6
$30 000–$49 000	50.7	59.2	71.9
> $50 000	14.1	12.7	12.5

Note: [a]Significant at alpha = 0.05.

Table 5. Comparison of travelling party characteristics across multiple attraction visitor segments.

Travelling party variables	Cluster, 1 $n = 71$	Cluster 2, $n = 71$	Cluster 3, $n = 32$
Travelling party composition ($\chi^2 = 0.8$)			
Family	73.2%	76.1%	81.3%
Size of travelling party (F $= 7.3^{b}$)			
Number of persons	3.1	2.9	4.0
Children in travelling party ($\chi^2 = 5.8^{a}$)			
Children present	28.1%	26.8%	50.0%

Notes: [a]Significant at alpha $= 0.05$; [b]Significant at alpha $= 0.001$.

Table 6. Comparison of trip characteristics across multiple attraction visitor segments (%).

Trip variables	Cluster 1, $n = 71$	Cluster 2, $n = 71$	Cluster 3, $n = 32$
Mode of travel ($\chi^2 = 5.2^{a}$)			
Car	63.4	76.1	62.5
Recreational vehicle	16.9	14.1	12.5
Truck or van	19.7	9.9	25.0
Time of trip ($\chi^2 = 1.7$)			
First quarter	59.2	49.3	59.4
Second quarter	40.8	50.7	40.6

Note: [a]Significant at alpha $= 0.05$.

Trip characteristics (Table 6). There was a greater percentage of cluster 2 visitors travelling by car (76.1%). Cluster 3 travelling parties, on the other hand, were the most likely to travel by truck or van. The timing of the trip, i.e. whether the respondents travelled in the first or second quarter, was fairly evenly disbursed among the two quarters for all three clusters.

Trip planning characteristics (Table 7). Statistically significant differences were found in trip planning variables across clusters. Planning times appeared to be the shortest for cluster 1 travellers and the longest for cluster 3 travellers.

Statistically significant differences were also found in information sources used to plan the trip. Cluster 1 members were the least likely to utilize the services of auto clubs (28.2%), but the most likely to rely on past experience (23.9%). Cluster 2 members were the least likely to depend on past experience (7.0%), but the most likely to use a state travel guide (22.5%). Cluster 3 members were unlikely to use a state travel guide (6.5%), but highly likely to use auto club services (54.8%).

Trip behaviour characteristics (Table 8). While clusters varied little in numbers of destinations and attractions visited, cluster 3 travellers tended to use more different types of lodging per trip (1.7) than the other clusters. Cluster 3 members were the most likely to stay with friends and relatives (26.9%).

Table 7. Comparison of trip planning characteristics across multiple attraction visitor segments (% except where indicated).

Trip planning variables	Cluster 1, $n = 71$	Cluster 2, $n = 71$	Cluster 3, $n = 32$
Planning time ($\chi^2 = 14.4$[a])			
< 2 weeks	9.9	9.9	3.1
2 weeks–1 month	9.9	4.2	3.1
1–3 months	23.9	38.0	38.0
3–6 months	23.9	12.7	31.3
6 months–1 year	26.8	33.8	21.9
> 1 year	5.6	1.4	3.1
Information sources used			
Automobile clubs[b,c]	28.2	53.5	54.8
Brochures[b]	31.0	28.2	25.8
Guide books[b]	23.9	19.7	9.7
Friends or relatives[b]	49.3	42.3	61.3
Welcome centres[b]	46.5	57.7	54.8
Local tourist offices[b]	12.7	18.3	19.4
Magazines[b]	19.7	21.1	25.8
Newspapers[b]	16.9	7.0	12.9
Past experience[b,d]	23.9	7.0	12.9
State travel guide[b,c]	12.7	22.5	6.5
Travel agency[b]	11.3	11.3	6.4
Mean number of sources used[e]	3.0	3.0	3.1

Notes: [a]Significant at alpha = 0.05; [b]χ^2 test of dependency; [c]Significant at alpha = 0.001; [d]Significant at alpha = 0.01; [e]ANOVA F test of differences.

Table 8. Comparison of trip behaviour characteristics across multiple attraction visitor segments.

Trip behaviour variables	Cluster 1, $n = 71$	Cluster 2, $n = 71$	Cluster 3, $n = 32$
Mobility (F = 0.9)			
Number of destinations visited	2.8	2.6	2.9
Attraction visitation (F = 1.7)			
Number of attractions visited	3.5	3.2	3.6
Lodging type (%)			
Hotel/motel[a]	45.7	52.4	36.0
Friends or relatives[a,b]	16.5	15.7	26.9
Campground/RV park[a]	20.6	15.5	18.1
Timeshare unit[a]	4.6	7.2	7.3
Condominium, apartment, home[a]	10.6	9.2	8.5
Other[a]	1.9	—	3.1
Number of lodging types[a,c]	1.5	1.4	1.7

Notes: [a]ANOVA F test of differences; [b]Significant at alpha = 0.05; [c]Significant at alpha = 0.01.

Expenditure patterns (Table 9). When calculated on a per person per day basis so as to negate the effects of travelling party size and length of stay, cluster 2 members had the highest total expenditures ($50.13). When looking at discrete expenditure categories, however, cluster 1 travellers spend the most on entertainment ($9.00), cluster 2

Table 9. Comparison of expenditure patterns across multiple attraction visitor segments.

Expenditure variables	Cluster 1, $n = 71$	Cluster 2, $n = 71$	Cluster 3, $n = 32$
Expenditure categories			
($ per person per day)			
Lodging[a]	14.16	15.63	12.46
Petrol[a,b]	4.48	6.00	3.76
Restaurant[a]	8.67	9.88	9.59
Entertainment[a,c]	9.00	8.95	6.47
Gifts[a,c]	2.16	4.08	2.90
Grocery[a,b]	2.16	3.51	2.81
Personal souvenirs[a]	1.80	2.76	2.25
Total expenses[a,b]	42.42	50.13	40.23

Notes: [a]ANOVA F test of differences; [b]Significant at alpha = 0.05; [c]Significant at alpha = 0.01.

travellers spent the most on petrol ($6.00), gifts ($4.08) and groceries ($3.51). In total, cluster 3 members tended to spend the least.

Profiles

Typical cluster member profiles are presented below.

Cluster 1. The members of this cluster tended to visit Disney-MGM Studios, Busch Gardens, Cypress Gardens and EPCOT Center. These travellers were the most likely to be retired, with the lowest educational levels and income. Their trip planning times were among the lowest, with nearly 20% of the members of this cluster planning their trips within one month of departure. The primary trip planning information source used was past experience. These travellers spent the most on entertainment on a per person per day basis.

Cluster 2. These travellers most often visited Disneyworld, Sea World, Spaceport USA and Silver Springs. Cluster 2 members were the most likely to be a married couple without children and in the empty nest stage of the family lifecycle. Accordingly, Cluster 2 travelling parties were among the smallest, with an average of nearly three persons. These travellers were the most likely to be travelling by car and they were heavy users of state tourism travel guides. They were among the least likely to depend on past experience to plan their trip. Cluster 2 travellers had the highest total expenditures, as well as the highest expenditures for petrol, gifts, and groceries.

Cluster 3. Members of cluster 3 were most likely to visit the Everglades National Park in conjunction with other Florida parks and nature preserves. This cluster contained the most families with children of all ages. Cluster members were highly educated and reported high incomes. The travelling parties in this cluster were the largest, averaging four persons, and they reported the longest trip planning lead times. These travellers were the most likely to travel by truck or van and they were highly likely to use auto club services. Cluster 3 travellers were also the most likely to stay with friends or relatives and they reported the lowest total expenditures.

Test of the second hypothesis

The second hypothesis was concerned with whether or not the theme park visitation clusters could be considered as viable market segments. The market segmentation analysis demonstrated that there were statistically significant differences between theme park visitation segments with respect to managerially relevant variables. Thus, the null hypothesis, that there would be no differences between theme park visitation segments with respect to the dependent variables is rejected.

Summary and implications

Summary

The combination of visitor interchange analysis, multidimensional scaling, cluster analysis and market segmentation analysis used in this study presents a detailed picture of theme park visitor choice behaviour. Hypothesis tests based on these results suggest that not only do theme park visitors display identifiable choice patterns, but that these patterns of visitation can be used as the basis for segmentation of the theme park visitor market. The fact that all four techniques revealed the same basic patterns allows for greater confidence in the overall results.

Limitations. Implications to be drawn from the present study are, of course, subject to limitations. First, it must be kept in mind that the sample of visitors studied here was composed only of auto travellers who stopped at official Florida welcome centres. Given the non-random nature of the sample, generalization of these results to the larger population of Florida visitors is impossible. The data collected for this study, however, are consistent with these collected of the same type by the Florida Department of Commerce.

   Although segmentation based on theme park visitation patterns were found to have merit, there is no way of telling whether or not it is an optimal segmentation base for theme park marketers.

Theme park marketing implications

The positioning of theme parks. The most relevant perspective on positioning for this study is one which focuses on the competitive structure of the theme park marketplace. Each cluster represents the competitive environment in which the theme parks operate. Busch Gardens, for example, completes more directly with EPCOT Center than with Sea World. Understanding the true nature of competition in the industry enables the marketer to more effectively formulate both offensive and defensive marketing strategies.

Theme park target market selection. The analytical procedure described in this study gives the marketer a clear understanding of his or her current customers. The marketer may then investigate whether or not current marketing efforts match consumer profiles. In addition, the procedure clearly identifies the profiles of other potential markets as well and provides clues as to how the marketing mix might be adjusted so as to attract those markets, if desired.

Promotional strategies for theme parks. The segmentation analysis based on the perceptual mapping procedures in this study provides the marketer with ample information on how to develop the promotional mix. Information on pre-trip planning periods, usage of information sources, and demographic/socioeconomic variables are all readily available to direct promotional efforts.

Given that the theme park visitor's resources of time and money are typically limited, an important promotional consideration of competitive theme parks should be whether they substitute for, or are a complement to, their competition. If they complement, and thus offer significantly different experiences, such as those of Sea World and Spaceport USA, joint promotional efforts might be of benefit to both. If, however, theme parks are direct competitors and visitors may substitute one for the other, it becomes even more important for the marketer of a given theme park to understand consumers' perceptions of the choices confronting them so as to be able to differentiate an attraction from the competition and demonstrate to potential visitors some sort of differential advantage in the product offering.

References

1. J.B. Kruskal and M. Wish, *Multidimensional Scaling*, Sage, Beverly Hills, 1978.
2. F.W. Young, 'An asymmetric Euclidean model for multiprocess asymmetric data', *Proceedings of the US–Japan Seminar on Multidimensional Scaling*, 1975.
3. Joseph F. Hair, Rolph E. Anderson and Ronald L. Tatham, *Multivariate Data Analysis*, Macmillan, New York, 1987.

17

Evaluating the attractiveness of a new theme park: a cross-cultural comparison

Kau Ah-Keng

Associate Professor, Department of Marketing, National University of Singapore, 10 Kent Ridge Crescent, Singapore 0511, Republic of Singapore

Tourist arrivals in Singapore reached 5.31 million in 1990, giving Singapore first rank in the Asia Pacific region in terms of per capita tourist arrivals. However, in absolute numbers, Singapore attracted fewer tourists compared with Malaysia (7.08 million) and Hong Kong (5.93 million) but was ahead of Thailand (5.30 million) and Japan (3.24 million). As shown in Table 1, the bulk of tourists arriving in Singapore were mainly from the five other ASEAN countries of Brunei, Indonesia, Malaysia, the Philippines and Thailand. These countries generated 27% of Singapore's total tourist arrivals. This was followed by Japan (18.3%), Europe (17.8%) and Australia and New Zealand (10.4%). On the whole, Asians accounted for slightly more than 64% of the total arrivals of which over 86% (55.2/64.3) of them were from the Asia Pacific region. The Caucasians, representing the Americans, Canadians, Europeans and Australians and New Zealanders, accounted for the remaining 36% of the total arrivals.

According to the *Survey of Overseas Visitors to Singapore* published by the Singapore Tourist Promotion Board, the tourist expenditure contributed S$4811 million[1] to the Singapore economy in 1989. As Singapore is moving fast into a service-oriented economy, it is therefore essential that the tourism sector should continue to play an important role in propelling the engine of economic growth for Singapore. As such, the Singapore government in 1986 announced a tourist product development programme to invest over S$1 billion over a five-year period to provide better and more infrastructure and facilities for the tourism industry. The government also hoped that the private sector would also invest a further S$2 billion to complement the efforts made by the government. Included for consideration were the enhancement of current tourist attractions as well as the development of new products such as theme parks and cultural villages. The development of man-made attractions in the case of Singapore is even more imperative as it lacks natural scenery. It possesses no competitive advantage in this respect when compared with the neighbouring countries such as Malaysia, Indonesia and Thailand.

Table 1. Visitor arrivals in Singapore by country of residence, 1990.

Country	%
Asia	
ASEAN	27.0
Japan	18.3
Taiwan	4.2
Hong Kong	3.7
Korea	2.0
Indian subcontinent	5.6
Middle East	0.6
Others	2.9
Subtotal	64.3
Americas	6.3
Europe	17.8
Oceania	10.7
Others	1.2
Total	100.0

Source: Yearbook of Statistics, Singapore, 1990.

The development of man-made tourist attractions was therefore high on the agenda. Inspired by the success of a historical and cultural theme park called the Sung Village in Hong Kong, the Economic Development Board of Singapore decided to invite the developer of that village to consider a similar project in Singapore. The project was named the Tang Dynasty Village with an investment estimated at S$50 million in the first instance.

The Tang dynasty (618–906 AD), from which the name of the theme park was derived, was praised as a glorious era in Chinese history, which saw the blossoming of Chinese diplomacy, commerce, architecture, literature and art. Its capital, Chang An, was regarded not only as the political but also as the cultural and trading centre of the 'world'. It received an influx of traders, merchants, scholars and diplomats mainly through the famous Silk Road as well as from Japan and Korea and this period was considered an apex of Chinese civilization. It was on this basis that the Tang dynasty was chosen as the theme of this park. The hope was that the theme park would be able to recreate the grandeur of this period of Chinese history in modern-day Singapore.

The Tang Dynasty Village is located on 12 ha of land on the west coast of Singapore island. Several tourist attractions, including the Chinese Garden, Japanese Garden, Bird Park and Crocodile Paradise, are found in its vicinity. The concept was to develop the village into a leisure and entertainment theme park, emphasizing ancient Chinese culture and history blending with the conveniences of modern and cosmopolitan Singapore. It aimed to provide foreign tourists and local visitors with superb entertainment within a leisure, entertainment, historical and dining complex. When fully completed, the village is expected to have an open city, an underground palace, a pagoda, a temple, three television and movie filming studios, a shopping arcade, and an exhibition and convention hall as well as several restaurants.

The prime objective of this paper is to determine whether there were differences between Caucasian and Asian tourists in: (1) their receptivity to this theme park; (2) how much each group would be willing to pay for admission; (3) their evaluations of the various attractions and activities to be staged within the theme park. If this information were available to the management of the park, they would be able to plan their marketing mix strategies much more appropriately. However, as this research is more of an exploratory nature, no formal hypotheses were to be tested.

Review of past work

Studies of tourist characteristics have been carried out extensively. Both demographic and psychographic variables have been developed to cluster tourists into different segments. Anderson and Langmeyer[2] studied the under-50 and over-50 travellers and found that, although both age-groups journeyed for relaxation and to visit relatives, the over-50 travellers were more inclined to visit historic sights while their younger counterparts were more likely to go for outdoor recreation and to visit man-made amusement facilities. Employing lifestyle variables, Mayo and Jarvis[3] noted that the peace-and-quiet travellers preferred the outdoor life and were family oriented while aggressive and active travellers were sociable and confident and wanted new experiences. Pitts and Woodside[4] examined the relationship between personal values and travel or leisure decisions. They found important value differences between visitors and non-visitors to 10 selected travel attractions.

Research studies have also been carried out to examine the characteristics of international travellers. Yavas[5] investigated the preferences of Saudi Arabian tourists. He discovered that some Saudis perceived a higher level of risk associated with foreign travel and preferred to visit Islamic countries. Bakkal[6] analysed West German demand for international tourism in six Mediterranean nations. He found that the demand was mostly income-elastic. Muller[7] used personal values to define market segments in international tourism. He found three segments with distinctive value profiles. Hakam et al.[8] discovered that tourists coming to Singapore could be profiled as three types: the budget travellers, the novelty seekers and the general-purpose travellers. Other studies (e.g. Fish and Gibbons[9]) also confirm that international tourists do differ in a variety of ways.

Although many studies have been conducted to study tourist (both domestic and international) profiles and segmentation, very few major research works have investigated the identification and segmentation of theme parks. Two of these are examined here. Milman[10] tried to identify potential markets and predicted the likelihood that tourists would visit a horse-oriented theme park in central Florida. He found that his model consisted of variables related to the features of the park rather than variables concerning the demographic and psychographic characteristics of the visitors. McClung[11] studied a sample of over 3000 heads of households from 10 metropolitan areas in the USA with regard to the factors influencing the choice of theme parks. The important factors were found to be climate, preference for a particular type of park, children, cost, crowds, distance and lodging availability. In addition, respondents were also given 14 different themes to rate. The greatest appeal was found to lie in educational exhibits, followed by exotic animals, technology and botanical gardens.

Research about theme park receptivity has not previously been conducted in Singapore. This exploratory study therefore represents a preliminary effort in this direction. It was hoped that the findings would reveal the different characteristics exhibited by tourists from different cultures. Such information would assist the theme park marketers in better matching the needs of such visitors and make them satisfied customers.

Method of study

This study was a result of a practical project planned as partial fulfilment of a course in marketing research taught by the author. To provide a real-life experience in marketing research to complement classroom teaching, students enrolled on this course were to complete a real-life project. The management of the Tang Dynasty Village (which was then still under construction) was contacted to sponsor a project which would provide practical market research experience to the students and would also give benefits to the sponsoring company. After some discussion, the company agreed to finance the project. The broad objective was to assess the perceptions of potential visitors to this newly created theme park. The management of the project provided a briefing to the students in August 1991 and the final project presentation by the students was made at the end of the year.

A structured research questionnaire was used for the survey. A total of 15 questions were incorporated. The first part of the questionnaire required the respondents to mention three tourist spots they had seen and enjoyed most in Singapore. This was followed by checking with them whether they had heard of the new theme park called the Tang Dynasty Village. As most of the respondents were not aware of the existence of the village, they were shown a copy of the coloured flyer with a description of the park. Although it would be better if a model of the village could have been shown to the respondents to facilitate the understanding of the concept, it was not possible to do so in practice. The respondents were then requested to rate their interest, using a five-point Likert scale, in the nine activities to be staged in the park. They were also asked to propose other activities or attractions which they thought would be interesting to visitors. Their propensity to visit the park was also assessed through a dichotomous yes–no answer. If they gave a negative answer, the interviewer would probe further for reasons.

As the inclination to visit the village would be affected by the level of price charged, two questions on pricing were included. One of them dealt with the admission charge. The other asked how much the respondent would be willing to pay if the admission charge were to include a light lunch and a guided tour, as well as transport from the visitor's hotel. This information would help the management of the theme park to price correctly their entrance fee, which is an important factor in influencing park attendance.

A set of nine psychographic statements was also incorporated to help determine the profile of tourists who would want to visit the park. Respondents were required to rate each statement using a five-point Likert scale ranging from 1 (disagree strongly) to 5 (agree strongly), Finally, a host of demographic questions was included for cross-classification purposes. The original questionnaire was first prepared in English but was also translated into Chinese and Japanese. Pilot testing of the questionnaire was also done to eliminate any ambiguity in wording or meaning.

The sampling process was completed on a combination of quota and convenience basis. It was decided to engage about 500 local residents and 1200 foreign visitors to participate in the survey. For the purpose of this paper, only the tourist sample was analysed. The tourists were approached primarily at points of departure such as airport terminal buildings and the railway station. Some of them were also selected at the tourist shopping areas. A certain quota for each nationality was set up to ensure that the important sources of visitors to Singapore would be covered. The final sample yielded about 1600 respondents, from which about 1000 questionnaires were analysed for the purpose of this paper.

Main findings

Profile of respondents

The tourists were divided into two groups: Caucasians and Asians. The 379 Caucasians included those from North America, Europe and Oceania. The 639 Asian tourists came mainly from ASEAN (345), followed by those from Hong Kong and Taiwan (181) and Japan (116). As detailed in Table 2, approximately 58% of these tourists

Table 2. Demographic profile of respondents.

	Caucasian (%)	Asian (%)
Gender[a]		
Male	57.8	58.6
Female	42.2	41.4
Age group[b]		
15–24	16.9	20.2
25–29	21.6	21.3
30–34	10.8	17.0
35–39	11.1	12.8
40–49	19.5	15.2
50 and above	20.1	13.5
Occupation[c]		
Admin/managerial	14.3	17.6
Professional	33.3	14.6
Technical and related	9.8	11.5
Homemaker	5.8	8.8
Clerical and related	4.8	6.6
Student	7.9	9.3
Sales and service	5.5	7.4
Production and transport	1.1	3.3
Retired	6.1	3.5
Others	11.4	17.4
Total (all categories)	100.0	100.0

[a]Chi-square value = 0.0685; level of sig. = 0.7935; [b]chi-square value = 17.44; level of sig. = 0.0037; [c]chi-square value = 60.72; level of sig. = 0.0000.

were male and there were no significant differences in gender make-up between the Caucasians and Asians. However, significant differences were observed in the age profiles of the two groups of tourists. Asian tourists were generally younger as compared with their Caucasian counterparts. For instance, while about 40% of the Caucasians were aged 40 and over, the comparative figure for Asians was only 29%.

In terms of occupational status, there were again significant differences between the two cultural groups, as shown by the chi-square value (Table 2). The professionals made up about one-third of the Caucasian tourists but only 15% of the Asian visitors. On the other hand, there were slightly more Asians belonging to the administrative and managerial category as compared with the Caucasians. The percentage differences between the two groups were less than two percentage points for most of the other occupational groups.

Purpose of visit

As shown in Table 3, about one half of these tourists came to Singapore for pleasure and vacation. However, about 30% of the Caucasians were on a stopover, as compared with 9% of the Asians. On the other hand, proportionately more Asians came to Singapore on business and to visit friends and relatives. In terms of type of tours taken, a higher percentage of the Asians came on package tours, as compared with the Caucasians who favoured non-package tours on their own. This finding has marketing implications for tour agents as well as marketers of tourist attractions: different channels for accessing the tourists must be planned.

Place of interest enjoyed most

The respondents were requested to name three places they visited and enjoyed most in Singapore. The percentage distribution of their choices is shown in Table 4. It is noted that the two groups of tourist were different in their choices, both in terms of the

Table 3. Purpose of visit and type of tour.

	Caucasian (%)	Asian (%)
Purpose of visit[a]		
Pleasure and vacation	50.4	49.4
Stopover	28.8	8.7
Business and pleasure	11.3	13.3
Business	5.5	12.5
Visit friends/relatives	3.2	9.3
Others	0.8	6.8
Type of tour by tourists[b]		
Package tour	20.6	30.0
Non-package tour	70.4	58.6
Not applicable	9.0	11.3
Totals (both categories)	100.0	100.0/99.9

[a]Chi-square value = 102.47; level of sig. = 0.0000; [b]chi-square value = 14.50; level of sig. = 0.0007.

Table 4. Place of interest enjoyed most.

Place of interest	Caucasian (%)	Asian (%)
Sentosa Island	41.9	63.6
Orchard Road	34.8	30.1
Chinatown	24.2	9.2
Zoological Garden	22.1	14.2
Botanical Garden	13.9	10.7
Jurong Bird Park	9.7	19.9
Haw Par Villa (Dragon World)	7.4	14.7
Elizabeth Walk/Merlion Statue	3.2	8.3
Chinese Garden	2.9	6.8
Science Centre	2.4	3.7

ranking or preferences and percentages expressing such preferences. For instance, Sentosa Island was picked by both groups as the most popular tourist attraction. However, while 42% of the Caucasians mentioned this as the place of interest enjoyed most, the figure was much higher for the Asians (64%). Similarly, while 22% of the Caucasians favoured the Singapore Zoological Garden, only 14% of the Asians expressed such a liking. Another big contrast was also observed in the case of China-town: 24% of the Caucasians favoured this tourist spot; however, only 9% of the Asians expressed such a sentiment. One of the possible explanations could be that a large proportion of the Asians could be Chinese, most of whom would have seen a Chinatown in their own countries, especially those from ASEAN, Hong Kong and Taiwan.

In general, it is observed that Asians liked to see more touristic places such as Sentosa Island, Jurong Bird Park, Haw Par Villa, Chinese Garden and the Merlion Statue close to Elizabeth Walk. The Caucasians, in addition, also enjoyed local culture more.

Awareness and likelihood of visiting theme park

When asked if they were aware of the Tang Dynasty Village (Table 5), only 13% of the Caucasian tourists answered in the affirmative. However, about one quarter of the Asian tourists knew of the existence of the theme park. It is obvious that more promo-tional work needs to be done to raise awareness to a significant level before and after the opening of this new attraction. When the concept of the theme park was made known to these tourists, almost all of them expressed a desire to visit the village. This could be an expression of a genuine desire to try the new tourist attraction. On the other hand, one must guard against the possibility that such responses could be a reflection of the respondents wanting to please the interviewers.

The respondents were further asked to pick one out of three descriptions of the park given to them; the majority (about 60%) felt that the village could be described as 'the largest historical and cultural theme park'. This was followed by describing it as 'an attraction for entertaining, shopping and food'. It is noted that almost 15% of the Asian tourists favoured it being called the 'Universal Studio of the East', as compared with 8% of the Caucasian tourists.

Table 5. Awareness, intention of visit and description of theme park (in percentage distribution).

	Caucasian	Asian
Awareness[a]		
Yes	13.2	25.3
No	86.8	74.7
Intention of visit[b]		
Yes	94.7	95.3
No	5.3	4.7
Best description[c]		
An attraction for entertainment, shopping and food	29.6	26.6
Universal Studio of the East	7.7	14.7
Largest historical and cultural theme park	62.7	58.7
Totals (all categories)	100.0	100.0

[a]Chi-square value $= 21.08$; level of sig. $= 0.000$; [b]chi-square value $= 0.1666$; level of sig. $= 0.6831$; [c]chi-square value $= 10.66$; level of sig. $= 0.0048$.

Table 6. Admission fee respondents willing to pay.

Category	Caucasian (S$)	Asian (S$)	p-value[a]
1 Admission only	18.14	17.92	0.866
2 Admission plus transport, guided tour and lunch	36.36	40.37	0.055

[a]Level of significance for t-test.

Admission fee

After gauging propensity to visit the theme park, the respondents were also asked to indicate the amount of admission they would be willing to pay. For direct admission only, there were no significant differences between the amount favoured by the Caucasians and Asians. The average admission charge was around S$18. However, for admission charge also to include transport, a guided tour and lunch, the Asian tourists were prepared to pay about S$4 more. The difference was significant at the 0.055 level as shown in Table 6.

Interest in the planned attractions and activities

A list of planned attractions and activities to be staged in the theme park was shown to the respondents and they were asked to evaluate each of these using a five-point Likert-scale ranging from 1 (not at all interested) to 5 (most interested). The results indicated that both groups enjoyed eating very much (Table 7). They gave a rating of about 4 (the highest for all activities listed) for tasting of Tang delicacies. The other attractions where no significant differences were found between the Caucasians and Asians were the display of terracotta soldiers and fortune telling.

Table 7. Interest in the planned attractions and activities.

Attraction/activity	Mean value[a] Caucasian	Asian	*p*-value[b]
Tang delicacies tasting	4.150	4.046	0.125
Chinese cultural show	4.058	3.551	0.000
Terracotta soldiers display	3.651	3.698	0.578
Calligraphy demonstration	3.444	3.209	0.006
Motion-picture making	3.356	3.845	0.000
Kung fu demonstration	3.103	3.401	0.001
Photo-taking in Tang costume	2.916	3.376	0.000
Horse/camel riding	2.825	3.390	0.000
Fortune telling	2.652	2.820	0.075

[a]Measured on a five-point scale ranging from 1 (not at all interested) to 5 (most interested). [b]Level of significance for *t*-test.

Table 8. Results of *t*-tests between Caucasians and Asians in each of the six age-groups.

Attraction/activity	15–24	25–29	30–34	35–39	40–49	50+	Total
Tang delicacies tasting	a	b	ns	ns	ns	ns	0.125
Chinese cultural show	a	a	b	b	a	ns	0.000
Terracotta soldiers display	ns	ns	ns	ns	b	ns	0.578
Calligraphy demonstration	b	a	ns	ns	c	ns	0.006
Motion-picture making	a	c	b	a	ns	a	0.000
Kung fu demonstration	ns	ns	b	ns	ns	a	0.001
Photo-taking in Tang costume	a	a	b	ns	ns	b	0.000
Horse/camel riding	b	a	c	ns	c	a	0.000
Fortune telling	ns	ns	ns	ns	ns	a	0.075

Note: a = significant at the 0.01 level; b = significant at the 0.05 level; c = significant at the 0.10 level; ns = not significant.

For all other activities to be staged, the levels of interest between the two groups were significantly different. The Asians appeared to favour motion-picture making, horse/camel riding, kung fu demonstrations and photo-taking in Tang costume. The Caucasians, on the other hand, preferred watching Chinese cultural shows and even a calligraphy demonstration. It is therefore obvious that the interests of the two groups differed and marketers must be prepared to consider such differences in the planning of theme park activities.

As the sample was made up of different age-groups and age was perceived to influence the types of activities taken or preferred,[12] *t*-tests were performed between Caucasians and Asians in each of the six age-groups to determine whether age was an important factor in influencing the choice of attractions/activities (Table 8). The results indicate that of those activities/attractions which were found to be significantly different between the two groups in the total sample, such differences were generally observed in at least three of the six age-groups. For example, in the case of 'Chinese cultural shows', the only age-group where no significant differences were observed between the two groups was those aged 50 and over. One exception did occur: in the case of the 'kung fu demonstration', only in two age-groups were significant differences found between Caucasians and Asians, and for those aged 30–34 and 50 and over respectively.

Psychographic profiles of respondents

To better understand the psychographic make-up of the tourists, eight statements were provided for each of the respondents to rate their agreement or disagreement. The Caucasian tourists liked to know more about a country's culture and history, enjoyed local cuisine, and wanted to understand Chinese culture and history. The Asian travellers enjoyed being near to nature and liked to know more about a country's culture and history, as well as trying local cuisine.

There were significant psychographic differences observed between the Caucasians and Asians (Table 9). For instance, the Caucasians were more interested to know about a country's culture and history when they travelled, when compared with their Asian counterparts. They liked exotic places and wanted to know more about Chinese culture and history. The Asians preferred to be near the beach and sun, as compared with the Caucasians in this sample. However, little difference was found between the two groups in terms of enjoying local food, shopping, being close to nature and going to museums.

The *t*-tests were also similarly performed to examine whether the age of respondents affected their responses to the various psychographic statements presented. The general conclusion was that if significant differences were noted between the two groups in the total sample, at least three of the age-groups would also report similar differences. On the other hand, when no such differences were found, it would be possible to find one or two age-groups reporting differences between the two cultural groups. Details are given in Table 10. The above findings concerning the responses of the respondents to the various psychographic statements could be used to plan communication strategies more appropriately.

Table 9. Psychographic profiles of respondents.

Statement[a]	Mean value Caucasian	Asian	*p*-value[b]
1 When I travel, I like to know more about a country's culture and history	4.512	4.274	0.000
2 I enjoy local cuisine when I travel	4.356	4.259	0.106
3 I like to know about Chinese culture and history	4.323	4.035	0.000
4 I enjoy being near to nature	4.291	4.317	0.653
5 I like to explore exotic places like Tibet and the Silk Road	4.189	3.816	0.000
6 I often shop when I go to another country	4.021	3.936	0.221
7 I like to go to museums	3.618	3.680	0.401
8 When I travel, I prefer to be near to the beach and the sun	3.220	3.614	0.000

[a]Statements were measured on a five-point scale ranging from 1 (for strongly disagree) to 5 (strongly agree). [b]Level of significance for *t*-test.

Table 10. *T*-test of psychographic statements between Caucasians and Asians in each of the six age-groups.

Statement	15–24	25–29	30–34	35–39	40–49	50+	Total
1 When I travel, I like to know more about a country's culture and history	ns	a	ns	b	a	ns	0.000
2 I enjoy local cuisine when I travel	ns	a	ns	ns	ns	ns	0.106
3 I like to know about Chinese culture and history	ns	a	b	c	a	ns	0.000
4 I enjoy being near to nature	ns	ns	ns	ns	ns	ns	0.653
5 I like to explore exotic places like Tibet and the Silk Road	b	b	c	ns	b	a	0.000
6 I often shop when I go to another country	ns	ns	ns	a	ns	a	0.221
7 I like to go to museums	ns	b	ns	ns	ns	ns	0.401
8 When I travel, I prefer to be near to the beach and the sun	ns	c	ns	ns	b	a	0.000

Note: Notations used (a, b, c, ns) as in Table 7.

Table 11. A theme park should have exciting rides and hi-tech amusement.

	Caucasian (%)	Asian (%)
Disagree strongly	10.6	8.8
Disagree	22.5	11.4
Neither	32.0	19.8
Agree	21.4	27.3
Agree strongly	13.5	32.6
Totals	100.0	100.0

Chi-square value = 70.84; level of sig. = 0.000.

Rides and hi-technology amusement in theme park

It is generally perceived that a theme park should have rides and other high-technology amusement. As such, it was found appropriate to gauge how visitors to Singapore would react to such a suggestion. The responses to this statement differed significantly between the Caucasians and Asians (Table 11). More of the Asian respondents either agreed strongly or agreed with statement. About 60% expressed such an attitude, as compared with only 34% of their Caucasian counterparts. This finding indicates that the marketers of this theme park must be able to dispel this misconception and to impress upon their visitors that a theme park can have a lot to offer other than just rides and high-technology amusement.

Summary and conclusions

The research findings have so far indicated that international tourists with different cultural backgrounds exhibit distinct patterns of preference when they travel. Even when age is considered, such differences often still exist. Caucasian visitors enjoyed various tourist attractions in Singapore to a different extent than their Asian counterparts. For instance, about 42% picked Sentosa Island as the favourite tourist spot. This percentage was much lower than the 64% indicated by the Asian tourists in the sample. Similarly, while almost one in four (or 24%) enjoyed visiting Chinatown, the corresponding figure for the Asians was only 9%. In addition, there were also significant differences observed between the Caucasians and Asians in their psychographic profiles. The former liked to know more about a country's culture and history when they travelled. They were also more inclined to want to know more about Chinese culture and history and to visit exotic places.

With regard to the new theme park, both groups exhibited an intention to visit and were prepared to pay around S$18 as an admission charge. However, the two groups rated the attractions and activities to be staged in the theme park differently. The Caucasians liked Chinese cultural shows and calligraphy demonstrations more than the Asians. the latter group favoured seeing motion-picture making, kung fu demonstrations and horse/camel riding more than the Caucasians. The Asians also wanted to see more rides and high-tech amusement facilities in a theme park than did the Caucasians.

With these differences between the two visitor groups clearly observed, it is evident that the marketers of this theme park must attempt to plan their communication strategy accordingly. For the Caucasian visitors, the accent of the theme park must be on the culture and events of this period in Chinese history. For the Asians, the action-oriented activities of theme park, such as kung fu demonstrations and motion-picture making, must be duly emphasized. This strategy is no different from the marketing of consumer goods when varying aspects of products must be communicated to the different market segments in an appropriate way. Only with such strategies will the theme park in this particular study be able to meet the expectations of the different cultural groups and make all of them satisfied customers.

Acknowledgement

I would like to acknowledge the assistance given by Mr David Leong, former Director of Finance and Marketing, Tang Dynasty Village private limited company, for providing information and sponsoring this research project. Thanks also go to my students who took the Marketing Research course in the academic year 1990–91 for their efforts in conducting fieldwork and data entry.

References

1. Singapore Tourist Promotion Board, *Survey of Overseas Visitors to Singapore*, STPB, Singapore, 1990.
2. B.B. Anderson and L. Langmeyer, 'The under-50 and over-50 travellers: a profile of similarities and differences', *Journal of Travel Research*, Vol 20, 1982, pp 20–24.
3. E. Mayo and L.P. Jarvis, *The Psychology of Leisure Travel*, CBI Publishing, Boston, MA, 1981.
4. R.E. Pitts and A. Woodside, 'Personal values and travel decisions', *Journal of Travel Research*, Summer, 1986, pp 20–25.
5. U. Yavas, 'Foreign travel behaviour in a growing vacation market: implications for tourism marketers', *European Journal of Marketing*, Vol 21, No 5, 1987, pp 57–69.

6. I. Bakkal, 'Characteristics of West German demand for international tourism in the Northern Mediterranean region', *Applied Economics*, Vol 23, No 2, 1991, pp 295–304.

7. T.E. Muller, 'Using personal values to define segments in an international tourism market', *International Marketing Review*, Vol 8, No 1, 1991, pp 57–70.

8. A.N. Hakam, Chow Hou Wee and C. Yang, 'Lifestyle segmentation of the international tourists: the case of Singapore', in K.D. Bahn, ed, *Developments in Marketing Science*, Vol XI, 1988, Academy of Marketing Science, Blacksburg, VA, pp 142–146.

9. M. Fish and J.D. Gibbons, 'Target market for the US international tourism industry', *Mid-Atlantic Journal of Business*, Vol 24, No 1, Winter 1985/86, pp 15–30.

10. A. Milman, 'Market identification of a new theme park: an example from Central Florida', *Journal of Travel Research*, Spring, 1988, pp 7–11.

11. G.W. McClung, 'Theme park selection: factors influencing attendance', *Tourism Management*, Vol 12, No 2, 1991, pp 132–140.

12. *Op cit*, Ref 2.

Part VII

Tourism and the natural environment: marine and ecotourism

Introduction by Stephen Page

It is widely accepted within the tourism and environmental science literature that tourism activities are dependent upon the concept of attractivity: without this element in a given context, it is unlikely that tourist visitation will occur. Although the concept of attractivity has not been studied in its own right to understand the motivation, behaviour and response of tourists from different cultural backgrounds, most visitors have rated natural environments highly in simple surveys of what they like about particular places. Although a substantial literature exists on the complexity of developing scales, adjectives and measures to assess landscape attractiveness for tourists (see Hall and Page, 1999, for a review), the natural environment has emerged as a particular focus for tourism research. Although Hall and Page (1999) point to the artificial division of the use of natural environments into tourist and recreationalist activities, in practice, use of the same resource base often blurs the distinction between these groups with different motives, behavioural traits and the demand they place on the resource. To understand the natural environment as a tourist resource, one needs to recognise the continuum of the resource base from the urban, man-made environment through to the urban-fringe, rural areas to wilderness areas. In addition, one should also not overlook the significance of specific tourism attributes which can run through the continnum of resources, such as rivers and waterways, marine and coastal areas that also comprise district environments. While specific models of the resource-base for tourism and recreation have been used since the 1950s and 1960s (see Pigram, 1983; Hall and Page, 1999, for a review), the paradigm guiding research on the natural environment has undergone profound changes over the last decade. It has moved from a primary focus on the resource-base, use and problems of monitoring and evaluating impacts to a new conceptualisation of different tourist typologies and their differential impact on the environment. In particular, new philosophical stances have developed to show how tourist use of the natural environment may be beneficial for wildlife conservation and preservation, rather than simply condemning tourism for its negative environmental impacts.

These changes have emerged as a response to new research agendas in environmental research and a growing concern for the fragility of many resources when subjected to tourist use. In this respect, tourism research has been informed by wider developments in environmental awareness and concern such as sustainability and limits of acceptable change replacing 1970s concerns such as 'Limits to Growth'. Probably the greatest impact has been the reaction to the mass tourist phenomenon during the 1980s, as new resources were discovered (e.g. the Turkish coastline) and the rapidity with which development took place. The systematic destruction of natural environments in pursuit of tourist numbers, expenditure and market share raised a wide range of environmental, ethical and moral questions. The last decade has also seen the integration of new concepts and modes of analysis into tourism to study the effects of such activities on the natural (and built environment). If one accepts the analogy that tourism suffers from the 'snowball effect' (i.e. as it proceeds on its journey downhill it gathers momentum, gets bigger and is virtually unstoppable due to its increasing size), then it is not surprising to find new modes of analysis to seek to displace the mass tourism idiom. A wide range of analytical standpoints have emerged since the 1970s, ranging from soft measures such as environmental impact assessment and environmental auditing (Hunter and Green, 1995) to more radical reconceptualisations of tourism – such as ecotourism, alternative tourism, nature tourism (Whelan, 1997) and radical critiques advocating limits to tourism (Krippendorf, 1987). These perspectives combine to provide a wide-ranging continuum of analytical approaches to tourism and the natural environment with a variety of conflicting and complementary standpoints.

These new critiques of tourism and its relationship to the natural environment are far more complex in philosophical and operational terms than can be easily reviewed here. Indeed, among the plethora of books that have emerged to fuel the debate on tourism and its use, impact and degradation of natural environments, there has been little universal agreement over the definition of concepts, meanings and a common acceptance of basic principles. Perhaps the most apt description of the literature, approaches and research agendas is one of complete intellectual bewilderment. The same comments may also apply to the term 'sustainability' which has also entered into the debate on the natural environment. Therefore, any attempt here to provide a meaningful synthesis of the literature is going to be fraught with problems of clarity, definition and precision. For this reason, the discussion does not seek to debate the tautological proposition – What is ecotourism? – since an entire encyclopaedia is currently being developed around this theme by David Weaver, Griffith University, Australia. Instead, readers are directed towards some of the recent studies of two themes which this section examines – marine tourism and ecotourism.

In many respects, marine tourism is a comparatively straightforward area to review; the recent publication of *Marine Tourism*, which is an excellent synthesis of this field by Orams (1999), provides the most accessible, concise and comprehensive review of an emerging field of research. What Orams (1999) achieves is a synthesis of the growing body of literature from marine scientists, with an overarching interest in tourism, with the contributions made by geographers (Fabbri, 1990), planners and environmental scientists in the analysis of the coastal littoral and marine environment stretching from the beach through to deep sea environments. The impact of cruise ships, recreational yachting, scuba diving and other marine activities such as dolphin-watching and whale-watching are also evaluated. There is little doubt that the marine environment is an emerging interest among researchers and it is developing a momentum which is largely driven outside the framework of tourism studies. The ecotourism literature is the complete antithesis of the marine tourism literature in terms of attempting to gain an overview of its development, research agendas and direction. In fact, to the uninitiated, it is a sprawling mass which has its own momentum: ironically, it is like the mass tourism phenomenon it frequently criticises as destructive. For that reason, this review highlights a number of key texts and some of the more recent publications in the field which are juxtaposed with the papers on this theme selected for this section.

According to Weaver (1998: 1) 'terms such as sustainable tourism, alternative tourism and ecotourism, which were not even in the lexicon 20 years ago, are not the objects of intense scrutiny, debate and controversy. At present, there is no consensus at all surrounding the use of the term ecotourism', a feature poignantly emphasised by Orams (1995). Not surprisingly, the question of semantics now appears to be occupying a significant portion of the research agenda as researchers seek to debate its meaning and value. 'Further confusion results from the use of related terms, such as sustainable tourism and alternative tourism, to name only two of the more prominent ecotourism affiliates' (Weaver, 1998: 1). Ecotourism has been recognised as a subset of alternative tourism (i.e. an alternative to mass or large-scale tourism), where the major motivation for travel is to use, see and experience the natural environment (Cater and Lowman, 1994). The seminal study of this area is widely acknowledged as Boo's (1990) *Ecotourism: The Potential and Pitfalls*, which widely popularised the area where passive and active forms of activity patterns among tourists have been observed (Woods and Moscardo, 1998).

Jaakson (1997) explores the epistemology of ecotourism, a feature expanded and developed by Malloy and Fennell (1998) in relation to ethical issues. Among the most accessible and comprehensive overviews of this growth area for research are the excellent syntheses by Weaver (1998), Fennell (1999) and Neil and Wearing (1999). Each text contains a detailed bibliography and a wide-ranging discussion of the area. From an economic perspective, Choongki et al. (1998) provide a much needed economic appraisal of ecotourism resources in South Korea while Mananyi (1998) examines mechanisms for the economic management of ecotourism. In a similar vein, McKercher (1998a) and McKercher and Robbins (1998) examine the development issues facing nature-based tourism operators in Australia. A more specialist study by Burton (1998) examines quality issues among ecotourism operators. At a strategic level, Fagence (1997) reviews the nature of ecotourism on a variety of Pacific Islands and the first generation of ecotourism strategies. McKercher (1998b) examines the explicit politics of tourism and conservation organisations among the Victorian National Parks Association since 1952.

From the ecotourist's perspective, Luzar et al. (1998) develop a profile of the nature-based tourist while Hvenegaard and Dearden (1998) examine the conflict between tourist and ecotourist in a Thai National park. In a marine context, Mason and Moore (1998) examine the potential effects of ecotourism in two Australian marine environments and Holland et al. (1998) examine the role of angling as an ecotourism activity, while Douglas and Taylor (1998) consider river-based ecotourism. In contrast, Chirgwin and Hughes (1997) discuss the perceptions of ecotourists participating in ecotourism activities from an economic standpoint. In a country-based study, Loverseed (1997) provides an overview of the adventure tourism industry in North America, highlighting trends, market segmentation, nature tourism, cycling, birdwatching and canoeing which fall within the wide remit of ecotourism. Probably one of the most wide-ranging sources to consult in the recent literature on ecotourism is the *Earthscan Reader in Sustainable Tourism* (France, 1997), which republishes many of the key studies published in journals and books. This offers a useful synthesis of the field and many of the classic studies are reprinted in this volume.

What is clear from this brief overview of key studies and recent publications in the journal literature is both the diversity, range of disciplinary perspectives adopted towards ecotourism and the development of new domains for tourism research. Therefore, in selecting the studies published in *Tourism Management* over the last decade, there were a wide range of potential contributions which could have been included (including Orams, 1997). In the marine tourism area, one notable study published offers a range of interesting perspectives. This is

Davis, D., Banks, S., Birtles, A., Valentine, P. and Cuthill, M. (1997). Whale sharks in Ningaloo Marine Park: managing tourism in an Australian marine protected area, *Tourism Management*, August, 18(5): 259–71.

In Davis et al.'s chapter, a survey of consumer's expectations and experiences among 464 divers in a marine park highlights the highly educated nature of the visitors. A high-income level highlighted the niche nature of this nature-tourism activity, with the most favourable experiences resulting from interaction with sharks. The study yielded important findings in relation to closeness of contact, and satisfaction levels, with implications for regulations for minimum distance between swimmers and sharks. It also raised issues related to the number of vessels which should be licensed to operate and the most appropriate economic rent to derive from the use of a natural resource that is a public good. The second set of papers on this theme are

Owen, R.E., Witt, S.F., and Gammon, S. (1993). Sustainable tourism in Wales: From theory to practice, *Tourism Management*, December, 14(6): 463–74.

Orams, M.B. (1995). Towards a more desirable form of ecotourism, *Tourism Management*, February, 16(1): 3–8.

Laarman, J.G., and Gregersen, H.M. (1996). Pricing policy in nature-based tourism, *Tourism Management*, June, 17(4): 247–54.

Wight, P.A. (1997). Eco-tourism accommodation spectrum: does supply match the demand? *Tourism Management*, June, 18(4): 209–20.

Boyd, S.W., and Butler, R.W. (1996). Managing ecotourism: an opportunity spectrum approach, *Tourism Management*, December, 17(8): 557–66.

Owen et al. examine the concept of sustainable development and tourism in Wales. Although this paper does not explicitly deal with ecotourism, it does consider the significance of policies and partnerships established by the Wales Tourist Board as crucial to the application of sustainable development with a nature-tourism component. In Orams's short 'Current issues' article on ecotourism, the difficulty of defining the term is addressed, with ecotourism presented as a continuum and model for discussion. It highlights the role of management strategies, which can shift the ecotourist experience from simple enjoyment and satisfaction through stages of greater understanding. A model is presented which offers a number of indicators to measure this transition. Laarman and Gregersen examine visitors to public resources (national parks and wildlife reserves) and a pricing policy for nature-based tourism. This is suggested as a fairer and powerful tool for achieving sustainable management goals.

In Wight's discussion of an ecotourism accommodation spectrum, surveys of accommodation provision in Canada are used to confirm the existence of a spectrum ranging from 'soft' tourists at one end through to experienced ecotourists at the harder end. It also illustrates strange paradoxes in provision and gaps in supply in the smaller, rustic, adventure-type segment of the market. Using a similar conceptual framework – a spectrum approach – Boyd and Butler propose a model to manage the many different types of ecotourism experience. Using the widely cited Recreational Opportunity Spectrum (ROS) and Tourism Opportunity Spectrum (TOS), a modification is proposed to derive an Ecotourism Opportunity Spectrum (ECOS). Eight components are proposed: accessibility, relationship between ecotourism and other resource uses, attractions in a region, level of social interaction, degree of acceptance of impacts and control over level of use and type of management which are needed to ensure the long-term viability of areas.

What the selection of papers infers is that ecotourism has now become central to the analysis and conceptualisation of tourism–environment relationships and the effect on the natural ecosystems. An enormous research effort has developed in the 1990s and *Tourism Management* has published both an eclectic and yet cutting-edge series of papers with an emphasis on both philosophical and management implications.

References

Boo, E. (1990). *Ecotourism: The Potential and Pitfalls.* (2 vols). Washington, DC: World Wildlife Fund.

Burton, R. (1998). Maintaining the quality of ecotourism. Ecotour operators' responses to tourism growth, *Journal of Sustainable Tourism*, 6(2): 117–42.

Cater, E. and Lowman, A. (eds) (1994). *Ecotourism: A Sustainable Option?* Chichester: Wiley.

Chirgwin, S. and Hughes, K. (1997). Ecotourism: The participants perceptions, *Journal of Tourism Studies*, 8(2): 2–7.

Choongki, L., Juhee, L. and Sangyoel, H. (1998). Measuring the economic value of ecotourism resources: The case of South Korea, *Journal of Travel Research*, 36(4): 40–6.

Douglas, A. and Taylor, J. (1998). Riverine based ecotourism: Trinity River non-market benefit estimates, *International Journal of Sustainable Development and World Ecology*, 5(2): 136–48.

Fabbri, P. (ed.) (1990). *Recreational Uses of Coastal Areas: A Research Project of the Commission on the Coastal Environment*, Dordrecht: Kluwer.

Fagence, M. (1997). Ecotourism and Pacific Island countries: The first generation of strategies, *Journal of Tourism Studies*, 8(2): 26–38.

Fennell, D. (1999). *Ecotourism.* London: Routledge.

France, L. (ed.) (1997). *The Earthscan Reader in Sustainable Tourism*. London: Earthscan Publications Ltd.

Hall, C.M. and Page, S.J. (1999). *The Geography of Tourism and Recreation: Environment, Place and Space.* London: Routledge.

Holland, S.M., Ditton, R. and Graefe, A. (1998). An ecotourism perspective on billfish fisheries, *Journal of Sustainable Tourism*, 6(2): 979–1116.

Hunter, C. and Green, H. (1995). *Tourism and the Environment: A Sustainable Relationship?* London: Routledge.

Hvenegaard, G. and Dearden, P. (1998). Ecotourism versus tourism in a Thai National Park, *Annals of Tourism Research*, 25(3): 700–20.

Jaakson, R. (1997). Exploring the epistemology of ecotourism, *Journal of Applied Recreation Research*, 22(1): 33–47.

Krippendorf, J. (1987). *The Holidaymakers.* Oxford: Butterworth-Heinemann.

Loverseed, H. (1997). The adventure travel industry in North America, *Travel and Tourism Analyst*, 6: 87–104.

Luzar, E., Diagne, A., Gan, C. and Henning, B. (1998). Profiling the nature – tourist: A multinational logit approach, *Journal of Travel Research*, 37(1): 48–55.

McKercher, B. (1998a). *The Business of Nature-Based Tourism.* Melbourne: Hospitality Press.

McKercher, B. (1998b). The politics of tourism and conservation organisations: The case of the Victorian National Parks Association 1952–1996, *Progress in Tourism and Hospitality Research*, 4(2): 141–57.

McKercher, B. and Robbins, B. (1998). Business development issues affecting nature-based tourism operators in Australia, *Journal of Sustainable Tourism*, 6(2): 173–88.

Malloy, D. and Fennell, D. (1998). Ecotourism and ethics: Moral development and organisational cultures, *Journal of Travel Research*, 36(4): 47–56.

Mananyi, A. (1998). Optimal management of ecotourism, *Tourism Economics*, 4(2): 147–69.

Mason, D. and Moore, S. (1998). Using the Sorensen Network to assess the potential effects of ecotourism on two Australian marine environments, *Journal of Sustainable Tourism*, 6(2): 143–54.

Neil, J. and Wearing, S. (1999). *Ecotourism*, Oxford: Butterworth-Heinemann.

Orams, M. (1995). Towards a more desirable form of ecotourism, *Tourism Management*, 16(1): 3–8.

Orams, M. (1997). Historical accounts of human–dolphin interaction and recent developments in wild-dolphin based tourism in Australasia, *Tourism Management*, 18(5): 317–26.

Orams, M. (1999). *Marine Tourism.* London: Routledge.

Pigram, J. (1983). *Outdoor Recreation Management.* London: Croom Helm.

Weaver, D. (1998). *Ecotourism in the Less Developed World.* Wallingford: CAB International.

Whelan, T. (1997). *Nature Tourism.* London: Earthscan Publications Ltd.

Woods, B. and Moscardo, G. (1998). Understanding Australian, Japanese and Taiwanese ecotourists in the Pacific Rim region, *Pacific Tourism Review*, 1(4): 329–39.

18

Whale sharks in Ningaloo Marine Park: managing tourism in an Australian marine protected area

Derrin Davis and Simon Banks

Centre for Coastal Management, Southern Cross University, PO Box 157, Lismore, NSW 2480, Australia

Alastair Birtles, Peter Valentine and Michael Cuthill

Reef Cooperative Research Centre, James Cook University, Townsville, QLD 4810, Australia

Introduction

A large number of opportunities exist around the world for people to interact with wildlife. These range from mountain gorillas in Rwanda, to fairy penguins at Phillip Island in Southern Australia. Orams[1,2] noted that the demand for opportunities to experience wildlife in their natural environment is growing rapidly, particularly in the case of marine animals such as dolphins and whales. A new marine based human–animal interaction opportunity developed recently off the coast of Western Australia. This experience is that of diving or swimming with whale sharks, the largest fish in the ocean.

The whale shark is a docile animal with which snorkellers and divers can interact when the opportunity arises. Since 1993, Ningaloo Marine Park, on the coast of Western Australia, has become well known internationally among recreational scuba divers and naturalists as the only readily accessible place where whale sharks congregate in significant numbers. This congregation occurs for only about seven weeks from March to May each year. The reasons for such a congregation are unknown, although Taylor[3] suggested that it might relate to the mass coral spawning that occurs in the same period on Ningaloo Reef. Karniewicz[4] noted, however, that scientists consider the species to be highly migratory and 'it is more likely that their occurrence on Ningaloo Reef is one part of an annual migratory pattern' (p. 15). A tourism industry, based on the 'whale shark experience', where divers may swim (usually on snorkel rather than scuba) with the sharks, has developed since 1993. The management of this industry is evolving as tourism operators and the park managers gain experience in managing tourists, the park, and the animal. An important characteristic of the industry presently is that it is confined to the marine park because that is where the animals are known to gather, and also where they are most accessible.

Ningaloo Marine Park encompasses more than $4572\,km^2$, some $1200\,km$ north of Perth, the capital of Western Australia (Figure 1). The park features the world's longest fringing reef, stretching along $260\,km$ of coastline. It was declared a marine park in 1987 with a principal aim 'to provide for conservation of the marine environment with recreational use [allowed] to the extent that it is compatible with conservation of its natural environment' (Department of Conservation and Land Management, p. 1).[5] The park is managed by the state of Western Australia's Department of Conservation and Land Management (CALM). The principal attraction of Ningaloo Marine Park was, until 1993, recreational fishing, while the fringing reef also constituted a popular scuba diving destination. Since then, however, the area has become well known, at least among the scuba diving fraternity and naturalists, as a place where whale sharks congregate for a few weeks each year.

The whale shark is the largest fish in the ocean, most commonly being 4–$12\,m$ in length, and thought to grow to a length of $18\,m$.[4] The largest accurately measured animal was $12.18\,m$ in length, and weighed 11 tonnes. While a true shark, the whale shark is a plankton feeder which, consequently, spends lengthy periods of time close to the surface of the water. The shark is a filter feeder with no teeth, and feeds by filtering large quantities of water through gill slits behind its head. It is also a docile animal and one with which divers and snorkellers can interact at close quarters, sometimes for quite long periods of time.

Very little scientific information is available on whale sharks. For example, there is almost no information on their migratory patterns and breeding behaviour.[3] However, since the early 1980s, whale sharks have been known to congregate in the waters of Ningaloo Marine Park although, as noted above, the reasons for such a gathering are unknown. Lent[6] noted that Ningaloo Marine Park is the only readily accessible place known where whale sharks can be counted on to appear annually in large numbers. It is thought that between 200 and 400 whale sharks, mostly juvenile males, spend time in the park, principally from mid-March to mid-June. Again, the reasons for the predominance of young male sharks are not known.

Nothing is known about the likely impacts of humans on whale sharks over the longer term. Consequently, some attention has been paid to the biological aspects of the management of whale sharks in Ningaloo Marine Park. For example, shark sighting data and information on contacts with sharks have been collected by CALM officers and various individual researchers. Following one such study,[7] it was observed:

Although estimates of the proportion of fish in contact provide a guide for managers, difficulties in determining appropriate licence numbers remain until there is clear understanding of a) the levels of harassment associated with different fish contact rates, b) the occurrence of peak and shoulder periods, and c) the relationship between vessel numbers and fish contact rates during both peak and shoulder periods. (p. 2)

While these are valid points, in a recent report recommending a representative marine reserve system for Western Australia,[8] it was stated that marine protected areas are intended to contribute not only to the maintenance of biological diversity (and other conservation values) but also to a sustainable and enjoyable environment. That is, recreational values are considered as being important, although they should

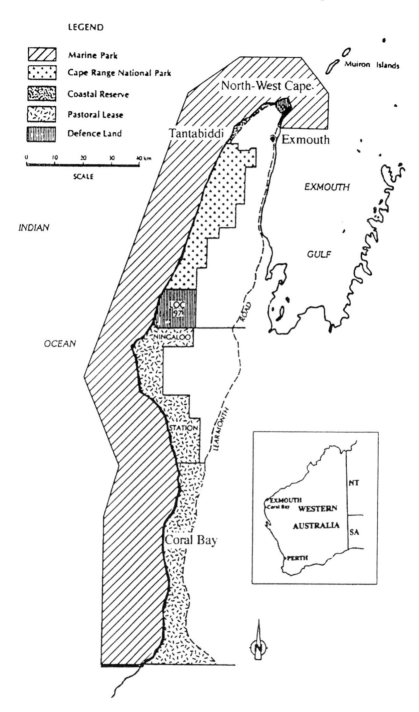

Figure 1. Ningaloo Marine Part – location map.

be compatible with the ongoing protection of natural values. The International Union for the Conservation of Nature (IUCN), now renamed the World Conservation Union, provides a listing of eight classifications of marine park and protected areas, ranging from strict nature reserves to multiple use management areas.[9] Ningaloo Marine Park is a multiple use area with conservation, recreation, commercial, educational and research values. Consequently, management considerations need to take account of human values as well as the biological values emphasised by Osborne and Williams.[7] This, of course, presents a potential dilemma to management agencies such as CALM as they seek to balance conservation and human use of an environmental resource in a multiple use management area. But it does drive home the point that these other values need to be considered when questions like limiting the number of licences in activities such as whale shark viewing are being considered. While the mandate for management clearly signals that conservation values have priority over recreational use, Davis and Tisdell[10] found that, in many cases, it will be human and recreational values which impose a greater constraint on the use of marine resources than will biological considerations. For example, loss of amenity through crowding or visual impacts might reduce demand for the attraction before biological impacts become severe and result in the need to limit use. Devlin[11] also reviewed the likely conflicts between recreation and environmental management, and concluded that priority should be given to maintaining the highest possible environmental quality, thereby also ensuring a future for recreation that is based on accessing the natural resource in question.

In summary, biological data are critical to decisions about the management of the whale shark industry, but so too are data and information on the recreational aspects of the industry, particularly the expectations and experiences of users and their willingness to pay for a quality experience. Furthermore, the ability of the operators to provide that experience within the confines of the present management system, infra-structure, and financial constraints, must also be considered in decisions about management of the resource. At present, however, these types of information are not generally available to either charter boat operators or CALM. It was for this reason that the research reported in this paper was undertaken.

Human–animal interactions in the marine environment

As previously noted, the demand for tourism activities based on interacting with wildlife has increased rapidly in recent years. Orams[2] summarised the spectrum of tourist–wildlife interaction opportunities, noting that these range from viewing captive animals in facilities such as zoos, aquaria and aviaries, through accessing semi-captive animals such as in safari parks where animals are fenced in or marine enclosures where, in some cases, tourists may swim with marine animals, to animals in natural or 'wild' environments. Orams,[2] along with Willman de Donlea,[12] explained that interactions between humans and 'wild' animals commonly occur within national or marine parks, and usually centre on breeding sites, along migratory routes or at feeding and drinking sites. For example, Limpus[13,14] explained the nesting behaviour and locations of marine turtles in locations such as Mon Repos and Lady Musgrave Island in the southern Great Barrier Reef area in Eastern Australia, with Mon Repos a particularly popular tourist attraction during the breeding season.

Willman de Donlea[12] noted that more than 600 000 people participate in whale and dolphin watching activities in Australia each year, based on the migration of humpback and southern right whales from Antarctica to breeding grounds in warmer waters along the southern, eastern and western coastlines of Australia. Dalton and Isaacs[15] prepared a guide to whale and dolphin watching in Australia, while Tucker[16] provided information about the species of whales likely to be seen, along with regulatory guidelines for interacting with whales. Species such as humpback whales are viewed in many parts of the world, while killer whales are a popular attraction in areas such as Canada's Pacific coast, where a combination of resident populations (making use of food resources provided by migrating Pacific Salmon) and migrating populations are accessed by tourism operators.[17]

Examples of the use of feeding sites for interacting with marine wildlife include interactions with dolphins at locations such as Tangalooma, Queensland, Australia,[1] and at Monkey Mia on Australia's west coast.[18] Frohoff and Packard,[19] in a review of human–dolphin interactions, noted the popular demand for human encounters with dolphins, with such demand resulting in organised encounters at many sites around the world. Encounters such as those at Tangalooma and Monkey Mia are based on feeding dolphins. Around 100 000 visitors interact with dolphins at Monkey Mia each year,[18] while more than 200 kg of fish are fed to the Tangalooma dolphins each week.[1] The use of feeding to facilitate interactions with marine life occurs also in cases such as the Cod Hole, located in the northern Great Barrier Reef, where the feeding of giant potato cod and moray eels by divers became popular after the site was discovered by recreational scuba divers in 1972.[20,21] In some cases marine animals have been fed, in defiance of codes of conduct, so as to maximise the chance that visitors will see an animal. Shackley[22] reported that this happens with manatees in Florida, a species considered to be under considerable threat but for which there is a thriving consumer demand for interactive experiences. Shackley concluded that

Anyone who wants to ensure the survival of the species would be well advised to avoid visiting them (p. 316)

The brief review of human–marine animal interactions provided above, while not intended to be at all exhaustive and while largely Australian in focus, nonetheless serves to emphasise the popularity of such tourism activities. The popularity of human–animal interactions seems set to continue and is likely to increase. Hall and Weiler[23] explained the increasing interest among tourists for more active vacations, particularly in natural settings, and interactions with 'wild' animals – whether terrestrial or marine – provides one opportunity for such active pursuits. Orams suggested that

Opportunities for interaction [with 'wild' animals] typically involve greater effort on the part of the tourist to view the animal in its natural setting (p. 41)

Interacting with whale sharks in Ningaloo Marine Park, Western Australia, represents one such tourist activity, one that has developed quite recently, and one that involves considerable active effort on the part of tourists who choose to swim with a highly mobile wild animal.

Commercial activity in the industry

While occasional voyages to interact with whale sharks had been run by an Exmouth dive charter operator in the early 1990s, the whale shark tourism industry only began in earnest in 1993. During that season approximately 1000 charter boat passengers interacted with the sharks, with up to 14 charter boats and five spotter planes catering for those visitors.[24] The number of divers increased to nearly 1800 in 1994, and exceeded 2000 in 1995, while the number of charter operators remained stable.

Prior to 1995, licences were issued for only one year, with all applicants being granted a licence to operate whale shark charters. Beginning in 1995 licences were issued for a three year period to 13 operators and a one-year period for two operators on a trial basis at Coral Bay, towards the southern end of the marine park (Figure 1). Licence holders are required to pay a deposit of $750 each year, while a charge of $15 per adult and $7.50 per child (under 16) came into force in 1995. The fee is designed to allow CALM to meet the costs of bringing their own vessel, crewed by Wildlife Officers, to Ningaloo Marine Park to monitor the industry. The $750 deposit is deducted from the total user fees payable in a season, and represents the minimum annual charge payable by operators. That is, the daily charges constitute a management levy on the operators, a levy that is on top of their ticket price to consumers. However, it is made obvious to consumers that a levy is being charged, and that that charge is being passed on to them, via the provision to all participants of a souvenir quality validation pass for swimming with whale sharks. The question of how many operators should be allowed into the industry remains to be resolved.

Whale sharks are fully protected under Western Australia's Wildlife Conservation Act with additional specific regulation under the state's Fisheries Act. The CALM Act of Western Australia addresses licensing and conditions for commercial operations. A code of practice, developed in conjunction with the industry, was incorporated into both the Western Australian Wildlife Conservation (Closed Season for Whale Sharks) Notice 1995 (which carried provision for fines up to $10 000 for proposely touching or otherwise interfering with whale sharks) and the License Conditions set by the state. These regulate the operation of vessels in the vicinity of whale sharks, limit the number of swimmers in the water with a whale shark to a maximum of 10 at any one time, and prohibit touching, or attempts to touch the animals. In 1995 swimmers were required to maintain a minimum distance of at least 1 m from the head or body of a shark and 4 m from its tail. They were not allowed to block a shark from its chosen direction of movement, use flash photography, or employ any form of motorised propulsion aid. The human–shark separation distances are particularly notable and contrast to interactions such as whale watching where swimmers must stay a minimum of 30 m from animals.[15,16] The potential for interference by swimmers with whale sharks and, therefore, for negative impacts upon the animals, are likely greater because consumers are allowed to get so close to the animal.

The majority of commercial vessels operate through Tantabiddi Passage at the northern end of Ningaloo Reef (Figure 1). Spotter planes are used to locate a whale shark and the mother ship is guided towards it by radio until the skipper is in visual contact. Most of the animals at Ningaloo are observed cruising along the reef front, at or near the surface. The interactions between whale sharks and visitors are, therefore, subject to Indian Ocean swells and, although the reef slope is occasionally visible to swimmers, encounters are often in deeper water. Snorkellers enter the water in front of the animal (license regulations stipulate a minimum of 30 m) either directly from the mother ship or from its inflatable tender. They then wait for the shark to come to them or, more commonly, are directed into the path of the animal by the skipper or a deck hand. Once they sight the shark snorkellers swim with it until they tire or the whale shark dives and disappears. If the shark is moving relatively slowly and staying at or near the surface, tired swimmers are usually picked up by an inflatable tender and, if they wish, are again dropped into the path of the shark. Only one vessel may be 'in contact' with a shark, with any other vessels standing off a minimum distance of 250 m. The vessel 'in contact' may stay in contact for a maximum of 90 minutes. Other vessels may, however, queue and take over contact with an animal beyond the 90-minute time limit. This is an important point in terms of the management of the industry. While most regulations – including those described below – relate to environmental management, the regulations on vessels-in-contact appear to constitute a sharing mechanism amongst operators, rather than a means of reducing stress on the animals. All activity on the water is monitored by Wildlife Officers from CALM, with surveillance conducted from CALM's own vessel.

The season is very short, with the first charter voyages in 1995 commencing on 26 March and the last occurring on 24 May (although occasional 'one-off' charters occurred outside these dates). While the peak of activity occurs during April, the season is effectively only about seven weeks in duration. Coupled with a maximum of 15 operating licences and strict controls over the number of divers allowed in the water at any one time, this means that the experience is available only to limited numbers of consumers. It is also an expensive experience because of the isolation of the area and the costs of travelling to it, and because of the high costs of servicing demand (e.g. spotter planes are used by charter operators to find sharks). This results in the daily charter cost of the experience being around $300 for most of the season.

The seasonality of whale shark tourism means that industry operators tend to make few specific investments – other than in promotion – in the industry. Rather, as with the game fishing tournaments that are held each year in the region, and potential interest in new attractions such as whale watching and diving with manta rays (Myers, pers. comm.), whale shark charters allow operators to make greater use of existing investments in vessels and other equipment. Most local operators also run fishing charters and other dive charters, while some are also involved in professional fishing for much of the year. Furthermore, a number of the whale shark industry operators are from outside the North-West Cape area. These operators undertake specific voyages to Ningaloo Marine Park for some or all of the whale shark season and, again, are generally seeking to make additional use of existing vessels.

Research objectives

As previously noted, data and information relating to the recreational aspects of the whale shark industry, including data on the expectations and experiences of consumers, along with their ability and willingness to pay for the experience, are virtually non-existent. Important questions regarding matters such as how many snorkellers should be in the water at any one time so as not to interfere with each other or with the whale sharks, relate to such matters as the desirable separation distance between swimmers and sharks. Information on the experiences realised by participants, along with financial and other data, is likely to be useful to both the management agency and to individual operators in the industry as they attempt to ensure a quality experience but also minimise impacts on the sharks.

Consequently, the principal objectives were:

(1) to gather information on the demographic characteristics of the participants in the whale shark experience;
(2) to gather data on the incomes of respondents, along with information on the amounts they expended both on interacting with whale sharks and on other attractions in the local area; and
(3) to elicit information on the quality of the experience realised by consumers of the whale shark experience.

Methods

A pilot survey of consumers of the whale shark experience was undertaken in 1994. The focus in the pilot survey was the collection of demographic and economic data, including expenditure on visiting Exmouth and the incomes of survey respondents. Experience gained during the pilot survey was, subsequently, used in developing the approach to the main survey and, in 1995, a survey of visitors participating in the whale shark experience was undertaken. Questionnaires were delivered to each of the charter operators who, in turn, were asked to distribute them to their customers following each day's charter. Respondents were also provided with a reply-paid envelope to facilitate the return of completed questionnaires.

Japanese visitors were identified in 1994 as comprising a large proportion of the visitors. To cater for these divers, 400 Japanese language questionnaires were distributed, along with 1500 in English. The approach adopted was to distribute survey questionnaires and envelopes (along with a large supply of pens) to the whale shark tour operators who were asked, in turn, to hand them to each of their customers after they had completed their day's swimming with the whale sharks. Questionnaires were completed either on the boat during the return journey from the whale shark trip, on the bus journey from Tantabiddi back to Exmouth, or at the dive shop. Such an approach was required because of the experiential questions being asked. Respondents were requested to complete sections on demographic characteristics, their expenditure on the whale shark trip, and on several experiential aspects of swimming with whale sharks. Japanese language questionnaires were translated to English by a Japanese speaking research assistant.

A total of 464 completed surveys were eventually returned. The breakdown of responses by nationality or region of residence is shown in Table 1. The completed surveys included 188 Japanese language questionnaires which were translated to English by a Japanese speaking research assistant. Log book returns indicate that

Table 1. Place of residence of survey respondents (*n* = 444).

Country	Responses
Japan	188
Australia	155
Germany	25
England	23
Switzerland	14
USA	10
Other	29

around 2000 visitors participated in whale shark cruises in 1995 (CALM, pers. comm.). The overall response rate was, therefore, approximately 23%. Using age as the key variable, and based on a standard approach to calculating a significant sample,[25] the sample was representative of the population from which it was drawn (at the 95% confidence level). The response rate was, however, less than hoped for, and resulted because there was heavy reliance on support from the various charter operators. Some of the operators were extremely supportive, while many apparently disregarded the survey and made no effort to distribute the questionnaire to their customers.

Results and discussion

Socio-economic data

Japanese and Australian visitors made up the bulk (74%) of all visitors, with European visitors also comprising a significant group (Table 1). Notably, the largest operator of whale shark charters has specifically targeted the Japanese market which is a growing and lucrative dive market.

The breakdown of the sample was 218 males (47.3%) and 243 females (52.7%) (*n* = 461). More than half the survey respondents were in the age bracket between 20 and 30 years of age, although the mean age was 33 years.

A significant number of respondents were found to be employed in professional (25%), managerial (7%) and para-professional occupations (12%) (e.g. nurses, fire officers and ambulance personnel). These three categories accounted for 181 (44%) of the total of 413 people who responded to the question on occupation. More than half of the respondents were employed in occupations requiring some level of post-high school education. Just over 20% of the sample consisted of either full-time students, or people who were unemployed or stated 'no occupation'.

As shown in Table 2, respondents were generally well educated, with 262 (72.6%) of 361 respondents having a university degree, either at Bachelors or postgraduate level. A further 90 were found to have trade or technical qualifications. Unfortunately, 103 respondents did not answer this question. By taking the most conservative approach, that these 103 people had no formal qualifications, then 56% of the total sample (*n* = 464) are educated to degree or higher levels (compared, for example, to 27.3% of

Table 2. Education levels (*n* = 361).

Education level/qualification	Number	Percent (%)
No response	103	28.5
Year 12 school	9	2.5
Trade/technical qualification	90	24.9
Undergraduate degree	191	52.9
Postgraduate degree	71	19.7

Table 3. Incomes of survey respondents ($).

Income Category	Mean	SD	Min.	Max.	*n*	Median
Personal annual income (single)	51 888	75 252	3800	1 000 000	268	38 000
Family annual income	127 088	137 242	7000	1 000 000	122	90 000
Australian mean single income*	28 288	na	na	na	na	12 000–16 000
Australian mean family income*	na	na	na	na	na	25 000–30 000

*Australian Bureau of Statistics figures, February, 1995.

all Australians between the ages of 15 and 65). Similar high levels of formal education have been found amongst samples of divers in other surveys.[26,27]

The incomes of the respondents are reported in Table 3, where it is shown that the mean single income was almost $52 000 per annum, while the mean of the combined incomes reported exceeded $127 000 annually. The existence of a small number of very high or low figures can, however, bias means upwards or downwards. The range and standard deviations of the incomes reported are shown in Table 3 and, with individual and combined incomes of up to $1 000 000 being stated, it is almost certain that the mean income will be biased in an upward direction. Consequently, median incomes are reported and, as shown, these are also well above Australian average levels.

Visitor experiences

Pearce[28] emphasised the importance of considering the 'tourist's own perspective' (p. 8) in tourism research. Pearce, along with Strongman,[29] Crandall,[30] and a number of other authors, was interested also in the motivations of leisure seekers. Strongman noted that recent interest has been particularly strong in terms of the distinction between extrinsic and intrinsic motivation for participation in leisure activities. According to Strongman, extrinsic motivation leads to activities with an external reward such as money or status, while intrinsic motivation leads to activities that appear to be engaged in for their own sake – the rewards are internal. The nature-based whale shark experience is likely to be typified most by intrinsic motivations, although extrinsic, status-type motivations might also be important to many participants who, after the experience, can 'brag' about swimming with the largest fish in the ocean. Furthermore, Harper[31] argued that, in addition to consideration of motivational forces, it is important to study the experience of leisure via reflective description.

Information on visitors' personal experiences with whale sharks was, therefore, gathered during the 1995 survey using questions that encouraged Harper's reflective description. Many of the responses and statements clearly reflect the profound nature of visitor's reactions (their intrinsic responses) to an encounter with 'the biggest fish in the world'. Visitors were asked to use a scale of 1–5 to rate how important each of 12 variables was in contributing to their enjoyment of the whale shark trip/s (Table 4). As shown in Table 4, the most highly ranked variables related to 'naturalness' and the marine life, particularly large animals.

In an open-ended question. visitors were asked to list their three best experiences while participating in a whale shark charter. A total of 1374 responses were obtained from 464 respondents. Two major themes emerged when these responses were coded: 'Whale Sharks' and 'Other Activities or Experiences'. These themes included many sub-themes, however, providing rich detail on visitors' best experiences.

As expected, visitors indicated that their best experiences involved some type of interaction with whale sharks. Under the first theme 'Whale Sharks', visitors indicated that, overall, the most positive experience came simply through having the chance to see the whale sharks with comments such as: 'seeing these wonderful animals', 'watching it swim past' and 'I could observe a whale shark'. Similarly, visitors indicated that they enjoyed swimming with the animals, commenting on 'actually being able to swim with them' and 'being in the water with them'. Being close to whale sharks emerged as the next most important sub-theme: 'getting so close to such a large animal' and 'the excitement of being close to huge fish'. Further comments related to the size or the numbers of animals: 'seeing the biggest fish in the world'; and to the animals behaviour: 'watching them feed'.

Other responses related to the amount of time spent swimming with whale sharks or the importance of the first sighting. Many people offered emotional descriptions of the experience including 'the calmness of it', 'feeling the peaceful character of the whale shark', and 'the grace and beauty of whale sharks'.

Under the second theme group 'Other Activities or Experiences', visitors again reinforced the importance of the natural components of their trip with the sub-theme 'other animals, reefs or nature' recording the most responses. These included

Table 4. Factors contributing to the enjoyment of the experience ($n = 450$).

Ranking/variable	Mean response
1. Being close to nature	4.58
2. Seeing large animals	4.42
3. Many different types of marine life	4.24
4. Feeling of excitement	4.12
5. Learning about the marine environment	4.11
6. Feeling of adventure	4.10
7. Underwater scenery	3.94
8. Diving somewhere new	3.75
9. Feeling of freedom	3.71
10. Relaxation	3.54
11. Being with friends	3.32
12. Element of risk	2.72

comments such as 'swimming with a large manta ray', 'just being in the ocean with wild animals', and 'seeing the corals and many fishes'. There were many favourable comments about the staff, food, boats and the way the operations were run. Many visitors indicated that they were happy just to be in the water scuba diving or snorkelling: 'simply snorkelling the reef' and 'scuba diving was very good'. Social interactions and good weather conditions were also mentioned by small numbers of people as contributing to visitors' best experiences.

The overall quality of the whale shark experience was rated very highly by visitors. The mean score was 4.56 on a 5-point scale ($n = 459$) from 'poor' (1), through to 'excellent' (5). This very positive result was to be expected given the responses about 'best experiences'.

Closeness of swimmers to the whale sharks was a key element mentioned in both the open-ended question on best experiences and in the 12 variables which contributed to enjoyment (Table 4). Given that this is also a central issue of concern to managers, this factor was further explored by dividing the respondents into three fairly equal groups according to how close they said they came to a whale shark. These three groups are shown in Table 5. As shown in the table the quality of the whale shark experience (scored on a 5-point scale) did not alter significantly between the three groups (ANOVA, $\alpha = 0.05$). Therefore, although closeness of visitors to the whale shark emerged as an important component of the best experiences, it was found not to affect overall satisfaction.

Despite the potential of an A$10 000 fine, 34 visitors indicated they had physical contact with a whale shark (Table 6). It is noted that some participants might not be aware of the potential for such a fine, although all are briefed that they should not touch the sharks. This question provided a total of 50 responses as to why swimmers touched the whale sharks, as some visitors indicated more than one reason (e.g. 'an *accidental touch* as the whale shark *moved towards me*').

Table 5. Quality of interaction with whale sharks by group.

Group	Mean response
Group 1 (1 m; $n = 159$)	4.5975
Group 2 (between 1 and 3 m; $n = 139$)	4.5755
Group 3 (3 m or more; $n = 124$)	4.5484

Table 6. Reasons for touching whale sharks ($n = 34$).

Reason for touching	No. of responses
Because the whale shark deliberately moved towards you	24
An entirely accidental touch	15
Your curiosity about the texture of its skin	5
Your desire to be close to the animal	3
Interference from another snorkeller	2
The excitement of touching such a larger animal	1

The findings on closeness, satisfaction and physical contact have immediate management implications with respect to the minimum distance between swimmers and whale sharks. If the quality of the experience does not alter, then there is every reason to regulate for a minimum distance of at least 3 m from the whale sharks. The 1995 season minimum distance of 1 m (from the head of the animal) undoubtedly resulted in the relatively high levels of physical contact (whether accidental or deliberate) found in this study. Being only 1 m from the head of a large animal that is swimming at about one knot gives very little time for evasive action if the animal banks even slightly.

When asked about worst experiences, crowding emerged as a major area of concern among visitors, closely followed by specific problems with other snorkellers. These two sub-themes together accounted for 25% of all negative experiences. The first category included responses such as: 'too many people in the water at one time'; 'too many people crowding the shark'; and 'less people would be better'. The second sub-theme included a litany of collisions, obscured vision and interrupted photography, e.g. 'people's flippers knocking me in the head'; 'too many people swimming close to each other and consequently being kicked by each others fins'; 'when we swam with a whale shark I couldn't see him/her well, because of lots of bubbles from other snorkellers fins'; and 'several [photographic] shots ruined by people swimming in front of me'. The lack of snorkelling experience of a number of visitors may have contributed to these collisions between swimmers.

Snorkelling with whale sharks presents a situation where crowding may impact upon the animal, and may also detract from the experience of the human participants. Consequently, survey respondents were asked how many people they thought should be in the water with a whale shark at one time (current regulations allow a maximum of 10 people in the water at one time). Of 434 respondents, 308 (71%), thought that six or less divers should be in the water at one time, while less than 13% suggested that 10 or more participants was acceptable (Table 7).

Some operators avoided crowding by rotating groups of about four people in the water at any one time with a strictly enforced time limit for each. Other operators were reluctant to reduce their group size below 10 and the maximum remained at this level in 1996 (CALM, pers. comm.). However, the proposal to move people further away from the whale sharks will have the additional advantage of helping to address many of the crowding problems without reducing the group size. If the minimum distance between

Table 7. **Preferences for numbers of divers in the water ($n = 434$).**

Number of divers in the water	Responses (No.)	Percent (%)
< 4	20	4.6
4	72	16.6
5	101	23.3
6	27	6.2
8	38	8.8
9	6	1.4
10	46	10.6
> 10	9	2.1

the shark and surrounding swimmers is increased, the perimeter of the area (from which swimmers are excluded) grows and there should be a corresponding decrease in the frequency of contact with other snorkellers, along with an improvement in the view for all those in the water at the time. The quality of the experience might also be improved, while there should also be less interference with the sharks.

Economic aspects of the whale shark industry

In considering the economic impact of an industry such as that based on swimming with whale sharks the expenditure by visitors on the activity is important. Additionally, however, expenditure by visitors attracted by the whale shark icon, but who then participate in other activities, is also important. The breakdown of visitor expenditure is shown in Table 8. Importantly, two averages are shown – the mean and the median – because of the wide range of expenditures and the consequent high standard deviations (e.g. one respondent reported expenditure of $10 000 on restaurants, meals and drink). It is suggested that both averages are worth considering here but that, in most cases, the median will be the best measure of the level of expenditure because a few very high data points will serve to inflate the mean.

One item that makes the data in the table more difficult to interpret is that of 'package costs'. Some visitors, particularly those from overseas, were on package holidays which included transport, accommodation and diving. These components of those divers' costs, therefore, do not show up in the averages in the preceding parts of the table. Conversely, expenditure on items such as restaurants and gifts will be separate to package costs and are picked up in the earlier items in the table.

Reference to Table 8 shows that significant amounts of money are spent on 'the whale shark experience'. It should be noted, however, that not all of the costs shown relate totally to diving with whale sharks in Ningaloo Marine Park. More than 90% of visitors who are attracted to the area by the opportunity to swim with whale sharks also undertake other activities such as recreational diving at a range of locations, along with visits to nearby national parks and four wheel drive outings. Furthermore. 87% of overseas tourists stated an intention to visit other places in Australia, particularly in

Table 8. Expenditure by survey respondents ($).

Item	Mean	SD	Min.	Max.	Sum	*n*	Median
Restaurants, meals and drink	442	876	5	10 000	129 178	292	200
Accommodation	558	942	10	6500	156 197	280	268
Snorkel – Whale Sharks	512	601	81	8000	165 283	323	300
Other diving in Coral Coast	280	414	10	3000	47 368	169	125
Other recreation	398	572	10	3500	60 157	151	200
International travel costs	2322	2631	95	15 000	348 268	150	1500
Gifts/souvenirs	182	254	3	2000	35 361	194	100
Travel costs in Australia	817	972	20	8000	217 310	266	500
Other costs	779	1137	40	5000	35 074	45	300
Package costs	3325	4442	250	21 000	242 724	73	1800

Note: All figures are rounded to the nearest dollar.

Western Australia. Therefore, assuming that the prime motivation of most overseas participants is to interact with whale sharks, the benefits arising from the existence of the whale shark industry flow on to other regions. In subsequent analyses the proportion of expenditure devoted to whale shark viewing will be separated out and a more accurate *picture* of the economic importance of the industry will be available. Reference to Table 8 shows, however, that the existence of the whale shark industry means that a considerable amount of money is injected into a small local economy in a short period of time. Considering only expenditure in Exmouth and Coral Bay (that is, excluding all travel costs and package holiday costs, and also excluding the 'Other costs' category which is difficult to interpret), the mean expenditure was of the order of $2370 per diver. Based on 2000 divers who visited to see whale sharks, this translates to a primary injection of funds to the local economy of around $4.7 million annually. Clearly, the whale shark industry, though highly seasonal, is important to local and regional economic activity and development, as well as allowing greater use of a range of infrastructure than might otherwise occur.

Additionally, a review of the information in Table 8 shows that the benefits from the whale shark industry are spread through many parts of the local economy. These are benefits that would not be realised without this industry, given that the survey respondents are mostly people who are attracted to Exmouth because of whale sharks. The local accommodation, restaurant and food services sector, other recreational providers (outback tours and so on), gift retailers and, of course, airlines, all benefit from the presence of whale sharks in Ningaloo Marine Park.

Managing the industry

As previously noted, the management of the whale shark industry is the responsibility of the Western Australian Department of Conservation and Land Management (CALM). Whale sharks are fully protected under the state of Western Australia's Wildlife Conservation Act with additional specific regulation under the State's Fisheries Act. Additionally, the CALM Act of Western Australia addresses licensing and conditions for commercial operations.

The system for, and approach to licensing has evolved since the industry began to expand in 1993. In 1993 licensing was under the Western Australian Wildlife Conservation Act, requiring an 'Animal Interaction License'. Licensing was of vessels rather than individual operators, and no fees, other than a small application fee, were payable. These licences were for one year only and were granted to any and all applicants with the capability to run commercial charters.

In 1994, licenses were issued under the Conservation and Land Management Act, with licensing again being of vessels and, again, being for only one year's duration. In early 1994, CALM announced the imposition of an A$15 per diver per day cost, with that fee payable by tour operators in the industry. The fee was designed to allow CALM to meet the costs of bringing their own vessel, crewed by Wildlife Officers, to Ningaloo Marine Park to monitor the industry. This was an important point in the evolving relationship between CALM and the operators. The operators argued two points. First, the announcement of such a fee only two months from the beginning of the season imposed an extra and unexpected cost burden on commercial operations because their promotion had been completed and many tours pre-sold. Second, they argued that the operators themselves had a vested interest in the sustainable development of the industry and, therefore, that self-monitoring was both possible and desirable. The resulting negotiations led to the imposition of a $7 per diver per day fee in 1994, a cost that was absorbed by the operators. This also provided the impetus for the operators to develop an industry steering committee to represent their interests when management proposals were to be discussed.

A question which also came under greater scrutiny in 1994 was that of one-year licensing, with operators arguing that this limited tenure did not allow for adequate planning of promotional and other activities, nor did it encourage investment in the industry. Subsequently, beginning in 1995 licences were issued for a three year period to 13 operators operating through Tantabiddi Passage in the north, and for a one year period for two operators on a trial basis at Coral Bay, towards the southern end of the marine park (Figure 1). As previously explained, licence holders were required to pay a deposit of $750 each year, while a charge of $15 per adult and $7.50 per child (under 16) came into force in 1995. Importantly, while the $15 (or $7.50) represents a charge on operators, it is made clear to consumers through the provision to them of a souvenir quality 'validation pass' for swimming with whale sharks. Consequently, the charge, which operators pass on to users, is made transparent to those users. Furthermore, it is made clear that money collected via the charge is spent directly in the industry, being committed to management, research and consumer education.

There are at least four management considerations that are of importance in terms of managing the whale shark industry within the context of sustainable tourism. First, the question of the impacts on the sharks themselves is of concern to the management agency and the wider community. The question of human impacts on marine animals, and of likely changes in animal behaviour is a prime concern in most interaction-based experiences, with Frohoff and Packhard,[19] Shackley,[22] Capaldo,[32] Carter[33] and Sweeney[34] being amongst researchers who have considered the impacts of interactive activities on animals such as dolphins and manatees. Furthermore, Department of Conservation and Land Management[18] has expressed concern that human–animal interactions should not impact adversely upon the animals in question. In the case of Ningaloo's whale sharks, human impacts on the animals are unclear but are the subject of monitoring by CALM. Only with the experience of a number of years will such impacts become evident if, indeed, they are important. Examples of possible indicators of impact include decline in whale shark numbers over a period of a decade or more, health problems in the population, or if the behaviour of the animals begins to change– they become more aggressive (as reported in other situations)[20] or dive as soon as swimmers enter the contact zone. It is implicit within the meaning of sustainable tourism that there should be no significant negative impacts on the whale sharks.

Second, there are management strategies which relate to the experiential aspects of whale shark tourism. Management needs to balance the continued high quality experiences which visitors enjoy against potential impacts. The discussion presented in this paper on crowding issues, on the distance between swimmers and whale sharks and the effects on visitor experiences strongly supports the CALM proposal (based on a recommendation of the authors of this article) to increase the minimum shark-to-swimmer distance to 3 m during the 1996 season (this change was, sub-sequently, introduced for the 1996 season). This is a good example of how research can be used constructively to improve regulatory guidelines and maintain the quality of visitor experiences. It is essential that the effects of these changes on both sharks and people be monitored.

Third, there are questions that relate to the management of the operations of the industry. These include considerations of how many vessels should be allowed to operate, what the licensing arrangements should be, and who should appropriate the economic rent from the use of a natural resource which is a public good. This last issue relates closely to questions about who should pay and who should benefit from the availability of the natural resource in question, and has been the subject of consi-derable discussion in the environmental economics literature.[35–37] However, many of the generalised problems associated with managing open access goods which may occur at, for example, popular scuba diving sites, might not be experienced in the case of Ningaloo's whale sharks. The figures reported in earlier sections of the discussion indicate that the whale shark experience constitutes a niche market, that the season is very short, and that the isolation of Exmouth drives costs up and keeps visitor numbers down. Furthermore, interaction with whale sharks requires visitors to go to sea (in often fairly rough sea conditions), and to participate in snorkelling in deep water. Because the sharks are generally on the move it is also a very active pursuit, one that requires a good level of fitness and capability in the water. The industry and the sharks, therefore, might have a degree of 'protection' from the large visitor numbers experienced at sites such as Monkey Mia, further to the south, where the dolphin interaction occurs at the water's edge, relies on feeding the animals, is a year round activity, and requires little or no active effort on the part of human visitors.

Fourth, the economic data reported indicate a high level of ability and willingness to pay for the whale shark experience. Costs such as the $15 fee per visitor day payable by the charter operators but passed on to the participants – a fee which is made transparent through the issuing to divers of a souvenir quality validation pass – are unlikely to affect demand at their present level. Furthermore, the fact that the industry is totally centred in a marine protected area means that open access and boundary problems,[38] typical in many natural environments, may be reduced to some degree (although not completely removed). For example, even though private vessels are not prevented from placing divers in the water near whale sharks, they must still adhere to the rules for standing off when another vessel is in contact, and to regulations govern-ing such matters as contact, and to regulations governing such matters as contact time with individual sharks. Conversely, even though CALM closely monitors activities from their own vessel, because much of the interaction occurs underwater it is difficult to enforce regulations such as those on separation distances and touching – the co-operation of the industry operators and their divemasters is critical to the effective implementation of such regulations.

Is reliance entirely on regulation the best strategy for managing this particular resource? The argument is advanced here that it is not, and that a judicious blend of the use of institutional regulation, self-regulation and economic instruments (such as user-pays and transferable licences) is a more efficient and effective management strategy. It also provides an opportunity for direct contributions by users to the management and protection of the natural environment they enjoy, a requirement of sustainable tourism. In this context at least two further issues arise. First, the aims of management need to be clearly formulated and transparent to all stakeholders. Usually, they will be couched in broad terms relating to the desire to manage the use of natural resources in an ecologically sustainable manner. Specific objectives which form part of the strategy to achieve stated aims might include restricting numbers of users at a site (thereby minimising congestion and possible environmental damage), or the development of guidelines or other information about appropriate use. Objectives may also relate to the appropriation of some or all of the economic rent from the use of a public good.

Second, such objectives raise the further question of how they might be achieved. The nature of the industry in Ningaloo Marine Park opens up the possibility of imaginative approaches to management. Regulation will always be required because of the public good nature of the resource, while increased self-regulation and management by the industry – actions which are already being pursued by industry participants – is desirable and necessary to ensure that the industry is sustainable. One feature of the operators at Ningaloo is a very strong willingness to provide their knowledge and experience to the development of a high quality management environment. Continuing recognition of this by CALM will help achieve compliance with the regulations, testing of their validity and the development of further innovative approaches to management. The best example of the need for self-regulation relates to the regulations on human–shark separation distances and the associated prohibition on touching the animals.

Licensing arrangements could also be reviewed in the near future. Licensing of operators has moved from one year to three year licenses, with the present three year licenses due to expire at the end of the 1997 season. The question of allocating still greater property rights to operators through, for example, selling licenses with no time restriction, might usefully be appraised at that time. Such a system would require that the licenses be transferable, but include provisions that prevent speculative buying of licenses by, for example, forfeiture of unused licenses (a condition that currently applies to licensing), along with provisions preventing monopoly holdings of licenses. Such a move would be an extension of the property rights presently afforded to licensees in the whale shark industry. Before such arrangements were implemented, however, there would need to be careful consideration of the legal implications and likely difficulties of revoking the licence of an unethical operator, if such an operator were to enter the industry.

Finally, the importance of education as a management strategy cannot be overstated. Orams,[2] Clark, Dwyer and Forsyth.[38] Crabtree and Gibson,[39] and Forestell[40] are amongst the many authors to have emphasised the importance of education as a management strategy in nature-based tourism. Clark, Dwyer and Forsyth noted that management strategies such as price and quantitative instruments are ways of controlling visitor numbers, 'but they will have no influence on the way visitors behave once they are inside the sensitive area' (p. 279). Furthermore, they emphasised that both the tourism operators and the consumers of environmental tourism attractions need to be educated, thereby influencing 'behaviour through specific environmental education' (p. 279). The whale shark tourism experience is one where education and associatcd codes of conduct will be important to the overall approach to the management of both industry operators and visitors.

In conclusion, the research reported here not only describes ecological, experiential and economic elements of whale shark tourism in Ningaloo Marine Park, but also demonstrates how management can significantly improve both protection and experience through the application of this knowledge. Conversely, small human–animal separation distances, coupled with the fact that vessels may queue and a shark be passed from one vessel to the next, means that there is potential for negative impacts on sharks, and this potential requires ongoing monitoring of the behaviour of both the sharks and of consumers of the experience. There is significant potential to further improve both management of the whale shark industry and the experiences provided by industry operators. As a new industry, located in an isolated but protected area, both the management agency (CALM) and the operators have the opportunity to develop innovative approaches to the management of this exciting industry and, thereby, to also provide lessons about more effective marine tourism management for other agencies and areas.

Acknowledgements

Support received from industry operators and the Western Australian Department of CALM for the research reported in this paper is gratefully acknowledged. Funding support was provided by Southern Cross University, the Reef Cooperative Research Centre and The University of Queensland. The useful comments of two referees and the editor are gratefully acknowledged.

References

1. Orams, M. B., Tourism and marine wildlife: the wild dolphins of Tangalooma, Australia: a case report. *ANTHROZOOS* 1994, **VII**(3), 195–201.
2. Orams, M. B., A conceptual model of tourist–wildlife interaction: the case for education as a management strategy. *Australian Geographer* 1996, **27**(1), 39–51.
3. Taylor, G., The whale shark. *Australian Natural History* 1990, **23**(4), 282–283.
4. Karniewicz, R., *The Whale Sharks of Ningaloo Reef* (interpretive booklet). Department of Conservation and Land Management, Perth, Western Australia, 1995.
5. Department of Conservation and Land Management, *Ningaloo Marine Park: Management Plan 1989–1999*. Department of Conservation and Land Management, Perth, Western Australia, 1989.
6. Lent, L., A whale of a time on Ningaloo Reef. In *Ranger*, Western Australian Department of Conservation and Land Management, Perth, Autumn, 1995, pp. 9–10.
7. Osborne, S. and Williams, M., Monitoring of whale shark tourism in Ningaloo Marine Park by aerial survey. Report, Western Australian Department of Conservation and Land Management, Perth, 1995.
8. Marine Parks and Reserves Selection Working Group, *A Representative Marine Reserve System for Western Australia*. Department of Conservation and Land Management, Perth, 1994.
9. IUCN, *Review of the Protected Areas System in Oceania*. IUCN Commission on National Parks and Protected Areas, Gland, Switzerland, 1986.
10. Davis, D. C. and Tisdell, C. A., Recreational scuba diving and carrying capacity in marine protected areas. *Ocean and Coastal Management* 1995, **26**(1), 19–40.

11. Devlin, P. J., Outdoor recreation and environment. In *Leisure, Recreation and Tourism*, eds H. C. Perkins and G. Cushman. Longman Paul, Auckland, 1993, pp. 84–93.

12. Willman de Donlea, E., Whale and dolphin watching in Australia. Paper presented at the 1996 World Congress on Coastal and Marine Tourism, Honolulu, Hawaii, 19–22 June, 1996.

13. Limpus, C. J., The Marine Turtles in Australia 1988 Review. In *International Symposium on Sea Turtles in 1988*. Hiwasa Chelonia Museum, Japan, 1988.

14. Limpus, C. J., *Mon Repos Turtle Rookery Volunteer Kit—Breeding Data and Information for Australian Sea Turtles* (manual). Department of Environment, Brisbane, Queensland, Australia, 1993.

15. Dalton, T. and Issacs, R., *The Australian Guide to Whale Watching*. Weldon Publishing, Sydney, 1992.

16. Tucker, M., *Whales and Whale Watching in Australia*. Australian National Parks and Wildlife Service, Canberra, 1989.

17. Duffus, D. A. and Deardon, P., Recreational use, valuation, and management of killer whales (*Orcinus orca*) on Canada's Pacific Coast. *Environmental Conservation* 1993, **20**(2), 149–156.

18. Department for Conservation and Land Management, *Monkey Mia Reserve: Draft Management Plan 1993*. Department of Conservation and Land Management, Perth, Western Australia, 1993.

19. Frohoff, T. G. and Packard, J. M., Human interactions with free-ranging and captive bottlenose dophins. *ANTHROZOOS* 1995, **VIII**(1), 44–53.

20. Adler, J. and Haste, M., The cod hole: a case study in adaptive management. In *Recent Advances in Marine Science and Technology*, eds O. Bellwood, H. Choat and N. Saxena. James Cook University, Townsville, Australia, 1995, pp. 427–436.

21. Mellor, B., Loving the reef to death. *Time* 1990, **45**, (November 5), 48–55.

22. Shackley, M., Manatees and tourism in Southern Florida: opportunity or threat? In *Proceedings of the 1990 Congress on Coastal and Marine Tourism*, Vol II, eds M. Miller and J. Auyong. National Coastal Resources Research and Development Institute, Newport, OR, US, 1990, pp. 311–316.

23. Hall, C. M. and Weiler, B., Introduction: what's special about special interest tourism? In *Special Interest Tourism*, eds B. Weiler and C. M. Hall. Belhaven Press, UK, 1992, pp. 1–14.

24. Jones, L. W., *North West Cape Tourism Development Study*. Perth, Western Australia, 1993.

25. Mason, R. A., Lind, D. A. and Marchal, W. G., *Statistics: An Introduction*, 3rd edn. Harcourt Brace Jovanovich, New York, 1991.

26. Skin Diver, Skin Diver Subscriber Survey 1992. *Skin Diver magazine*, United States, 1993.

27. Davis, D. C., Banks, S. A. and Davey, G., Aspects of recreational scuba diving in Australia. In *Tourism and Hospitality Research: Australian and International Perspectives*, ed. G. Prosser. Australian Tourism and Hospitality Research Conference, Coffs Harbour, February 1996, published by the Bureau of Tourism Research, Canberra, 1996, pp. 455–466.

28. Pearce, P. L., *The Social Psychology of Tourist Behaviour*. Permagon Press, Oxford, 1982.

29. Strongman, K. T., The psychology of leisure. In *Leisure, Recreation and Tourism*, eds H. C. Perkins and G. Cushman. Longman Paul, Auckland, 1993, pp. 143–156.

30. Crandall, R., Motivations for leisure. *Journal of Leisure Research* 1980, **12**, 45–54.

31. Harper, W., The experience of leisure. *Leisure Sciences* 1981, **4**(2), 113–126.

32. Capaldo, T., Animal welfare tests the water of a human–dolphin bond project. *Psychologists for the Ethical Treatment of Animals Bulletin* 1989, **8**(2), 7–8.

33. Carter, N., Effects of psycho-physiological stress on captive dophins. *International Journal for the Study of Animal Problems* 1982, **3**(3), 193–198.

34. Sweeney, J. C., Marine mammal behavioural diagnostics. In *Handbook of Marine Mammal Medicine: Health, Disease and Rehabilitation*, ed. L. A. Dierauf. CRC Press, Boston, 1990.

35. Turner, R. K., Pearce, D. and Bateman, I., *Environmental Economics: An Elementary Introduction*. Harvester Wheatsheaf, Brighton, 1991.

36. Tisdell, C. A., *Economics of Environmental Conservation: Economics for Environmental and Ecological Management*, Developments in Environmental Economics, Vol. I. Elsevier, Amsterdam, 1991.

37. James, D., *Using Economic Instruments for Meeting Environmental Objectives: Australia's Experience*. Environmental Economics Research Paper No. 1, Department of the Environment, Sport and Territories, Canberra, Australia, 1993.

38. Clarke, H., Dwyer, L. and Forsyth, P., Problems in use of economic instruments to reduce adverse environmental impacts of tourism. *Tourism Economics* 1995, **1**(3), 265–282.

39. Crabtree, A. E. and Gibson, A., A case-history of symbiosis between reef tourism, education and research. In *Ecotourism: incorporating the Global Classroom*, 1991 International Conference Papers. Bureau of Tourism Research, Canberra, Australia, 1991.

40. Forestell, P. H., Marine education and ocean tourism: replacing parasitism with symbiosis. In *Proceedings of the 1990 Congress on Coastal and Marine Tourism*, Vol, I, eds M. Miller and J. Auyong. National Coastal Resources Research and Development Institute, Newport, OR, US, 1990, pp. 35–39.

19

Sustainable tourism development in Wales: from theory to practice

R Elwyn Owen*

Director of Research and Corporate Planning, Wales Tourist Board, Brunel House, 2 Fitzalan Road, Cardiff CF2 1UY, UK

Stephen F Witt

Lewis Professor of Tourism Studies, European Business Management School, University of Wales, Swansea SA2 8PP, UK

Susan Gammon

Research Assistant in Tourism, European Business Management School

The purpose of this paper is to show how the principles of sustainable development may be interpreted within a tourism context. The policies and partnerships of the Wales Tourist Board are used for illustrative purposes, and three case studies which demonstrate the successful practical application of sustainable tourism development are then presented: the first is an example of rural tourism development; the second focuses upon a World Heritage Site; and the third is garden festival event. Whilst the projects chosen all share the common goal of sustainable tourism development, they strive to achieve this aim in a variety of ways.

Sustainable development

The World Commission on Environment and Development defines sustainable development as: 'development that meets the needs of the present without compromising the ability of future generations to meet their own needs'.[1] The notion of sustainable development recognizes that the earth's resources are finite and subject to a number of unprecedented threats which are global in scale. These include population growth, global warming, destruction of the ozone layer, degradation of the environment, the loss of biological species and habitats, and pollution in all its forms.

*In compiling this paper Mr Owen has drawn heavily from his experience gained within the Wales Tourist Board. The views expressed are his own, which may not necessarily be those of the Board.

Such problems derive to a greater or lesser extent from the fact that the pursuit of economic growth in order to improve the material quality of life has been achieved only at the cost of resource exploitation and environmental asset stripping. It follows, therefore, that the solution lies in more careful management of the earth's resources in order that they can be safeguarded and replenished. Good husbandry and careful stewardship are central to sustainable development. Each generation has a duty to maintain the earth's assets so that they can be passed on intact rather than squandered.

The concept of sustainable development need not be in conflict with the notion of economic growth. Proponents of sustainable development accept that economic vitality is essential in order to combat poverty, improve the quality of life and drive the process of environmental protection. However, balances have to be struck in order to ensure that growth does not make excessive demands on natural resources. Furthermore, proponents of sustainable development do not claim that this is a prescription for doing nothing or for standing in the way of change. Rather, acceptance of the need for sustainable development throws down a challenge to use resources creatively in a way which will ensure their long-term survival. This means managing the process of change in such a manner that it occurs in as benign a way as possible rather than by accident.

Gradually, the concept of sustainable development is infiltrating the policy framework of many government organizations and agencies. The challenges that face policy makers should, however, not be underestimated, and certain conditions need to be met for effective policies to be realized:

- *Compromise* – striking a balance between growth and conservation. This requires the present generation to make sacrifices in favour of a generation that is not yet born.
- *Commitment* – recognizing that sustainability requires deeds as well as fine words. Politicians who have traditionally founded their campaigns on the promise of greater short-term material wealth face the challenge of selling to the electorate the less tangible and less immediate benefits of lower but sustainable rates of growth.
- *Control* – putting in place a framework of planning and other policies to regulate the pattern and scale of development. These policies need to be imaginative, well thought out and practical, rather than simply restrictive. They must be implemented fairly, consistently and with vigour.
- *Cooperation* – recognizing that the search for sustainable development has an international dimension. The richer and the poorer countries of the world need to work together to secure a more equitable use of resources.

Sustainable tourism development

The notion of sustainable *tourism* development follows naturally from the above discussion. It embraces several key principles:[2]

- Tourism is a potent economic activity which brings tangible benefits to the host community as well as to the visitor; however, tourism is not a panacea and must form part of a balanced economy.

- The physical and cultural environments have intrinsic values which outweigh their values as tourism assets; their enjoyment by future generations and long-term survival should not be prejudiced by short-term considerations.
- The scale and the pace of tourism development should respect the character of the area. Value for money and a high-quality tourist experience should be provided.
- The goal of optimum long-term economic benefit to the community as a whole should be pursued, rather than short-term speculative gain for only a few.
- Tourism development should be sensitive to the needs and aspirations of the host population. It should provide for local participation in decision-making and the employment of local people.

Considerable criticism has, however, been directed towards the sustainable tourism development concept. In particular, Wheeler expresses grave doubts regarding its relevance, given the overriding problems of ever-increasing tourist numbers and tourist movements mass tourism moving towards 'megamass' tourism).[3] However, he does acknowledge the potential importance of the notion of sustainable tourism development at the individual project level: 'what we have at best are small-scale, isolated examples of "success" – micro solutions to what...remains a macro problem'.[4] A clear distinction therefore needs to be made between micro-level tourism (e.g. an individual tourism project) and macro-level tourism (i.e. tourism *per se*):

Tourism on a micro-level can perhaps be sensitively planned for but at the macro-level, because of the enormity and complexity of the task, it becomes cumbersome, uncontrollable and 'unplannable'.[5]

Jones, on the other hand, argues that micro-level sustainable tourism development might yield 'clues and solutions ... [which] can be used to inform and advise policy and practice in the development and management of mass tourism'.[6]

This paper concentrates on micro-level tourism development. In order for sustainable tourism development to occur, strong partnerships need to be forged and appropriate practices need to be implemented. Concerning the former, effective partnerships are generally characterized as being dynamic and long term in nature. Within the tourism industry, the public sector is often a major player in the early stages of a project's development, allocating, in some cases, substantial funding and marketing resources. This is turn can stimulate investment from the private sector. Community involvement is also encouraged both prior to and during the development stages of a project, in order to foster commitment and ensure that the needs of the host community are recognized.

Regarding appropriate practices, certain mechanisms have evolved to prevent and redress some of the environmental and socio-cultural problems associated with various forms of development – including tourism. Examples are:

- design and control of development;
- transport planning and management;
- provision and management of access;
- soft technology;
- resource management and maintenance;

- consultation; and
- information services.

It may be helpful to clarify what is meant by the term 'soft technology'. Soft technologies are those of a planning and process nature, and include institutional structures and planning systems related to the initial stages of development, management decision-making strategies integral to the ongoing operation of tourism facilities and services, and public participation and conflict resolution methodologies.[7] Of course, education and training are also significant components of soft technology.

It is likely that all of the mechanisms cited above will be required to a greater or lesser degree either to rectify, where possible, inappropriate tourism developments, or to face the challenge of establishing new development projects which are sustainable in nature.

Sustainable tourism development in Wales

Background

Wales offers a remarkable scenic diversity within a small area. Approximately one-fifth of the land lies within the three National Parks of Brecon Beacons, Pembrokeshire Coast and Snowdonia. In addition, there are five areas of Outstanding Natural Beauty and 40% of the coastline is designated as Heritage Coast. Two environmentally sensitive areas have been established, namely, the Cambrian Mountains and the Lleyn Peninsula, and there are 45 National Nature Reserves and 730 Sites of Special Scientific Interest – intended to conserve flora, fauna and geological formations.[8] Wales has been, and continues to be, proactive in the conservation and enhancement of the environment.

However, in some parts of Wales a major obstacle has had to be overcome – the legacy of derelict, contaminated land resulting from the rapid industrialization which occurred in the South Wales Valleys (and to a lesser extent in Mid- and North Wales). In the 18th century, the copper and iron industries flourished in South Wales, followed by the growth of the coal industry. The latter dominated the way of life in the Valleys, and along with the other major industries of copper and iron contributed substantially to Britain's industrial revolution. In the latter half of the 20th century, the decline of these traditional industries has led to urban deprivation and high unemployment in the South Wales Valleys and has incurred environmental degradation in the form of industrial dereliction (such as slag heaps and water pollution). Consequently, negative images have been associated with this particular area of Wales.

Indications are that this region is determined to reverse (where possible) damage to the environment and to diversify and strengthen its economy. Tourism has made, and continues to make, a substantial contribution in these areas.

Wales Tourist Board

The Wales Tourist Board (WTB) is the statutory body for tourism in Wales and receives the bulk of its resources from government (through the Welsh Office).

This section focuses upon the WTB in order to illustrate the possible policies and potential partnerships associated with sustainable tourism development.

The policy framework of the WTB is set out in two principal documents. In 1988 the Board published a major report, *Tourism in Wales – Developing the Potential*, which set out a tourism strategy for a five-year period.[9] That document was produced following extensive consultation with other official bodies and the tourism industry. It included a strong commitment to conservation and improvement of the environment, and the preservation of the Welsh language and culture. (The WTB is currently preparing its new strategy in consultation with private and public sector partners.)

The WTB also submits an annual corporate planning statement to the government in order to support its case for financial resources. This sets out detailed programmes and targets for the ensuing year, and is intended to complement and add detail to the five-year development strategy. The corporate planning framework has as its cornerstone a brief mission statement, which describes the key aims of WTB policies:

In accordance with the Development of Tourism Act 1969, the Wales Tourist Board seeks to develop and market tourism in ways which will yield the optimum economic and social benefit to the people of Wales. Implicit within this objective is the need to sustain and promote the culture and the language of Wales, and to safeguard the natural and the built environment.[10]

The words in this statement have been chosen with care. The term 'optimum' rather than 'maximum' makes it clear that the Board is more concerned with long-term advantages than short-term gain. Similarly, the expression 'people of Wales' is introduced in order to emphasize that the benefits from tourism should accrue to the community as a whole rather than simply to certain individuals.

Although the WTB is the lead agency for tourism in Wales, other bodies have an indirect interest in tourism or responsibility for allied recreational matters, and the WTB seeks to work closely with these other organizations in order to ensure that resources are used wisely and in an integrated manner. The bodies include:

- other UK Tourist Boards;
- other statutory bodies with an interest in economic development, recreation, conservation and the environment;
- non-statutory organizations with an interest in conservation, the environment and heritage; and
- local authorities and national park authorities.

One of these partnerships is now briefly described. Responsibility for national parks and countryside recreation matters rests with the Countryside Council for Wales, and the WTB has established a productive working relationship with it and its predecessor the Countryside Commission. As early as 1978, the Board and the Commission entered into a formal policy agreement regarding tourism in national parks. This recognized that tourism is a major component in the economy of national parks and that the economic and social well-being of the residents is an essential consideration in achieving national park objectives. However, it also recognized that recreation and tourist use should not be such as to impair the natural beauty and amenity balance of the parks. Where irreconcilable conflicts occur between conservation and public enjoyment objectives, then priority should be given to the former.

The Board has supported this principle by launching a number of practical initiatives which provide advice and information to the tourism industry. For example, a guide to good practice by tourist operators in national parks has recently been issued. In essence, its purpose is to identify ways in which operators can make use of their special location in order to benefit their business, whilst at the same time helping to support the objectives of national parks.[11]

Rural tourism development

The natural environment is the most important tourism asset of Wales, and one which lends itself to rural tourism development. Whilst 'it is difficult to find an adequate all-embracing definition of rural tourism',[12] its major aim is 'the planned use of resources for a countryside area which will lead to an increase in the general welfare of the environment, the community and the visitor'.[13] According to Lane two forms are emerging: the first is large-scale rural tourism (as exemplified by Center Parcs), and the second is alternative rural tourism (as illustrated by the Mid-Wales Festival of the Countryside).[14]

He goes on to point out that attractions such as Center Parcs provide recreation for a large number of tourists in a controlled rural setting, as well as considerable employment opportunities, but that major criticisms can nevertheless be levelled against this form of rural tourism development; for example, the ventures and activities are not directly rooted in rural life and tradition, and such large enterprises are often owned by outside interests whose policy-making is more likely to be carried out for the benefit of the owners rather than the community.

Alternative rural tourism is characterized as being small scale and locally controlled, and offering indigenous tourism products or programmes, often with a strong natural resource and conservation component.[15] One of the major criticisms against this form of rural tourism is the difficulty in gaining cooperation and agreement among numerous small businesses, which is essential for determining marketing strategies and campaigns, standards and limits on growth.[16]

Case Study 1: Mid-Wales Festival of the Countryside. Established in 1985, the Mid-Wales Festival of the Countryside is a summer-long, region-wide programme of events and activities in rural Wales 'which combines tourism with environmental education and rural development'.[17] The programme attracts about 250 000 visitors and includes approximately 600 rural events and activities clustered under five major themes:

- *Nature and Wildlife* – nature reserve visits, bird and mammal watching, natural history courses;
- *Working Landscape* – visits to farms, forests, reservoirs, markets and water mills;
- *Rural Rides* – narrow-gauge railway trips, white-water rafting, pony trekking, mountain biking;
- *Arts and Crafts* – art, sculpture, and photographic exhibitions, visits to craft workshops; and
- *History and Tradition* – tours of castles, iron age hill forts, historical exhibitions, re-enactments.

The idea of a 'festival of the countryside' was put forward in 1984 by the Development Board for Rural Wales (DBRW). It became a reality through a joint venture between the DBRW, CYNEFIN[18] and the then Countryside Commission Office for Wales. These three organizations, along with the Nature Conservancy Council and the Royal Society for the Protection of Birds, comprised the original steering group. However, as the festival gained momentum, the number of organizations involved increased to include the WTB, the Mid Wales Tourism Council, and the Heart of Wales Tourism Association, as well as many community groups.

The festival is seen as a major initiative intended to promote conservation, stimulate the economy and manage/satisfy the increasing demand for holidays and recreational activities in the countryside. The festival has several specific objectives, such as:

- improving access to the countryside whilst protecting the most sensitive and fragile areas of Mid-Wales;
- providing environmental education through interpretive walks, lectures, exhibitions, leaflets and other means;
- increasing public awareness of natural history, rural issues, historical and cultural dimensions of Mid-Wales;
- encouraging participation in environmentally acceptable sports;
- stimulating the purchase and use of rural foods and crafts; and
- involving a wide range of organizations, groups and individuals in the development, planning, delivery and review of the programme.

Initially, the DBRW provided significant funds (£60 000 per annum), primarily for marketing purposes, recognizing that time would be required to establish a strong identity.[19] Operating costs are now provided by the eight local authorities in Mid-Wales, the private sector, the Countryside Council for Wales and the DBRW. Direct funding for some of the festival's programme, particularly the more innovative events, has been provided by the DBRW social development grants and social promotion support, the Countryside Council, CYNEFIN and private sector sponsorship. The WTB has very much welcomed the Festival of the Countryside, which provides a potent marketing tool to complement the Board's own initiatives.

The economic impact of the festival includes the creation of approximately 20 full-time job equivalents and the generation of £5 million annual turnover in the rural economy of Mid-Wales. The jobs and income which result from the Mid-Wales Festival of the Countryside help to sustain the rural communities in Mid-Wales. In addition, the Festival offers 'an opportunity for low capital entry to encourage a local entrepreneurial culture thus reducing the dependence upon inward investment (and the inevitable high level of input jobs and profit leakages)'.[20]

The large number of relatively small-scale events and activities are dispersed throughout the region, thus helping to spread tourism growth spatially, and thereby fostering environmental conservation. In addition, holding the events and activities over the whole summer reduces the concentration of tourists in the peak holiday weeks, thus helping to spread tourism growth temporally also. Furthermore, an appraisal of existing attractions and visitor facilities is conducted with a view to assessing which attractions can sustain continued long-term use (i.e. where visitor numbers are low). The appraisal is based on dialogue between the DBRW, the Countryside Council for

Wales, 'green' agencies, and those individuals operating the attractions. For areas that are sensitive nature reserves, a decision regarding one of the following courses of action must be taken:

- not to market those areas;
- develop lower key presentations; or
- monitor the situation as an early warning process.

As Denman points out, 'The dependence of tourism on the quality of the environment places it in a very special position in the whole debate about sustainable tourism'.[21]

It is clear that the Mid-Wales Festival of the Countryside is a good example of a successful sustainable development project.

Heritage tourism

Case Study 2: Project Conwy. Conwy is a small town situated on the northern coast of Wales, at the estuary of the river which bears the same name. It lies on the fringe of the Snowdonia National Park and is within close proximity to Wale's main holiday resort of Llandudno. Conwy's historic significance has been recognized by the designation of its 13th century castle and town walls as a World Heritage Site by UNESCO. The town has a long-established tourism industry which remains the mainstay of the economy.

Conwy's character and location have traditionally been an asset and a constraint. North Wales's principal industrial and tourism access route has hitherto been routed straight through the town, whose narrow streets are ill-equipped to deal with modern-day traffic. The result has been frequent traffic congestion, with its associated noise, loss of amenity and pollution. This has marred the enjoyment of existing visitors to the town and deterred others from going there. Conservation, interpretation and visitor management have all been hindered; the quality of urban fabric has diminished and both the quality of tourism and the quality of life generally have suffered.

A major road programme has been under way for some years, which has culminated in the bypassing of the town of Conwy by means of an estuarine tunnel (completed in October 1991). This has been built at substantial cost in order to protect the fabric of the town and to safeguard its amenity value.

Shortly before construction of the tunnel commenced, a group of official agencies in Wales got together in order to develop a long-term strategy for the town. The steering committee was led by the WTB; it comprised also the official agencies responsible for economic development and for historic monuments in Wales, the three local authorities with an interest in the town and the foremost non-statutory conservation body in Britain. Consultants were appointed to develop a cohesive package of measures to conserve and interpret the historic elements of the town, in order to enhance its appeal to the visitor and to bring economic benefit. The brief given to them emphasized the need for an integrated approach, which took careful account of the views of the host community.

On completion of the study, the consultants produced a combined strategy and action plan.[22] It began by setting out a vision of Conwy for the 1990s – as a town where the local community takes a real pride in its heritage and is equally proud to share it with visitors. The report detailed recommendations as to how the above-mentioned vision might be implemented. It emphasized that much of the initial investment would need to come from public sector agencies, rather than from the private sector. Such investment would be directed towards providing a sound infrastructure and conserving and interpreting the historic fabric of the town. In so doing a firm platform would be created upon which to base a sustainable and sympathetic tourism economy. Confidence would be engendered, in due course drawing in investment by the private sector in the form of improved accommodation, catering and retail services. A key recommendation was that a new body be established in order to help implement the agreed strategy in an integrated way. This body would receive core funding from existing public sector bodies; it would not remove executive functions from them but would exercise an enabling and coordinating role.

The major recommendations of the consultants' report are being implemented. In the first instance, an agency as been set up to market Conwy as an entity and to bring cohesion to the process of implementing the development and conservation strategy. Entitled 'Project Conwy', the agency has located its office in the main shopping street of the town as a visible symbol that the strategy is being implemented, and it is readily accessible to members of the community. Progress-to-date on five other major recommendations which incorporate the notion of sustainable tourism development is summarized in Table 1.

Major efforts and investment have taken place in Conwy in order to transform the town from what was once a down-market beach resort holiday destination for the 'candy-floss brigade' to an up-market, walled heritage town. Financial support has been received from all the official agencies and local authorities with the WTB providing up to £1 million over a three-year period. Improved infrastructure and accessibility, visitor management techniques, and conservation and enhancement of many historic buildings and structures all contribute to a quality visitor experience and the quality of life for local people.

One of the aims of Project Conwy is to spread the flow of tourists throughout the year in order to relieve congestion during the peak summer months (thus reducing pressure on the environment) and also to ensure that those working in tourism have permanent employment. However, it is too early as yet to determine the outcome of this particular marketing strategy.

Certain steps have been taken, and could be taken, to prevent and/or minimize the negative impacts of this tourism project. The re-routing of traffic via the estuarine tunnel and the creation of predominantly pedestrianized areas within the walled town have been undertaken to protect and preserve the historic fabric of buildings and structures for future generations, as well as to enhance the visitor experience. Sensitive to the potentially harmful impacts of tourism, Conwy is participating in the 'Walled Towns of Europe Survey', the aim of which is to examine the environmental impacts of tourism in walled towns and to determine ways in which the potential disadvantages may be minimized and the advantages from tourism maximized.

One component of sustainable tourism development is that it should provide for local participation in decision making. When Project Conwy opened its office several years ago, there was some resistance from the community towards the small organization for fear it would dictate what actions were to be taken. However,

Table 1. Project Conwy – progress to date.

Recommendations	Action
1. Conservation, maintenance and enhancement of the historic fabric of buildings and structures	*Major Schemes* (public sector investment): • Complete restoration of Seion Chapel as a new home for the Royal Cambrian Academy of Art • Repair and repainting of the Carmel Chapel to complement the restoration of the nearby Seion Chapel • Restoration and better interpretation of historic house, Plas Mawr, recently released into the care of *Cadw* (Welsh Historic Monuments) • *Cadw* is restoring the wall walk surrounding the town (a rolling programme) which will provide more opportunities for viewing the town
2. Creation of a predominantly traffic-free environment	• Car parks within walled town to be designated short-term parking • Large car park outside the walled town to be expanded and landscaped • Creation of 'flexible' pedestrianization, whereby pavements are widened and roads narrowed (and the latter are closed during peak summer months) • Approval pending for development of a park and ride scheme at Llandudno Junction
3. Creation of pedestrianized areas and environmental improvements which harmonize with historic buildings	• Resurfacing scheme for streets and pavements using stone and clay paving stones (partly completed) • A new system of pedestrian signposting using cast-iron posts and fingers with a Jackdaw design for the post tops incorporating the wording *Conwy* • Grants of 50% available for business and residential properties to improve the appearance of buildings • Replacement of chrome and glass telephone boxes with old style red boxes by British Telecom • A four-year plan for improved street lighting, lighting of key buildings and decorative lighting awaiting approval
4. Imaginative, coordinated interpretation of key aspects of Conwy's history	• Information boards which provide a brief history of Conwy, a map and comprehensive visitor information are located at car parks • A series of interpretive plaques have been placed on buildings and sites of interest, linked to a 'Town Trail' leaflet • An exhibition, 'Chapels in Castles', opened in the Chapel Tower at Conwy Castle (*Cadw*) • Aberconwy House, the oldest residential property in Conwy, is being refurbished with each room in the house depicting a different period in the house's history (National Trust)

Table 1. (Continued)

Recommendations	Action
5. Investment in new, appropriate development in sympathy with the town's history and environment, which adds to the resources for tourism	• Construction of the first phase of Conwy marina is complete, including 250 fully serviced berths and with potential to expand up to 450 to 500 berths (private sector developer) • A small, privately owned, attraction has opened – a Teapot Museum exhibiting novelty teapots and teapots from the 1700s to the present • A new Youth Hostel is planned, with the possibility of a nearby field studies facility being linked to the hostel • The Council is seeking a private developer to establish a quality, professionally catered caravan park – three developers have expressed interest • As space is confined in Conwy, development of small attractions is being encouraged. One year ago there were 22 empty commercial properties on the market, but only eight are presently still available. Small businesses (e.g. speciality clothing shops, Victorian tea rooms, gift shop) are being established

information was disseminated via talks with community groups and a quarterly newsletter, and views and ideas were solicited from local people. Furthermore, 'following the incorporation of Project Conwy as a company limited by guarantee, nine local people have been elected as Directors' including four business representatives, four Conwy community representatives and one representative for Llandudno Junction/Deganwy.[23]

The key principles necessary for the achievement of sustainable tourism development are clearly satisfied by Project Conwy.

Garden Festival Event

Case Study 3: Garden Festival Wales in Ebbw Vale. The 1992 Garden Festival Wales in Ebbw Vale was the last of five garden festival events to be held in the UK since 1984. Sponsored by Blaenau Gwent Borough Council and Gwent County Council, with contributions from the Welsh Development Agency (WDA), the WTB, the Welsh Arts Council and the Welsh Sculpture Trust, the garden festival was the only one established in a rural setting as opposed to an urban one.

In broad terms, garden festivals are intended to stimulate economic renewal and environmental rejuvenation. Their purpose is threefold: to encourage inward investment, to undertake land reclamation and to create a positive image for the area. The latter point is especially important. A key purpose of Garden Festival Wales was to change people's perceptions of the area – both to encourage local people's pride in the transformation which has occurred in the South Wales Valleys and to change the outside world's perceptions of the area so that it is viewed as a desirable area in which to invest. Located in South Wales, Ebbw Vale was at one time the country's most polluted area due to the fumes of steel mills and the slag and shale from adjacent collieries.

The site of the Garden Festival covered nearly 200 acres, 96 of which will remain permanently landscaped. The WDA has been responsible for reprofiling industrial debris into a site which ranged from 730 feet above sea level to 1250 feet at its highest point. The variety of plateaux enabled the visitor to view the entire site – a feature not possible with previous garden festivals. Three hundred thousand trees, 450 000 shrubs, 750 000 bedding plants and 300 000 bulbs were newly planted.

Although the horticultural exhibits formed the essential element of the festival, there were three major theme areas. The first area, entitled 'Land of Our Fathers' consisted of displays and exhibits depicting Welsh heritage, traditions and culture. Also included was a modern Welsh castle, a boulevard and a 'Festival Emporium' of retail units, restaurants, child care facilities and so on. The second area was the 'heart' of the festival and comprised not only the horticultural exhibits but also displays, exhibitions, special events and staged performances. Designated as 'Wales Celebrates', this area had a special theme each week throughout the duration of the festival. The third area, 'Journey into the Future', was dedicated to the preservation and conservation of the environment. New technologies (such as solar and wind power) were on display along with exhibits of space travel, satellites and robotics. A traditional Welsh farm was also incorporated:

... demonstrating that old skills have an essential role to play in the balance of seasons ... [indicating] man's place in nature and ... [highlighting] the need to care and protect rather than to simply exploit.[24]

Although the festival was in operation for only five months (May to October 1992), it achieved two of its three objectives in the short term. First, a derelict, industrial site was reclaimed and transformed with quality landscaping, and in addition the surrounding area was significantly improved. Second, some people's perceptions and image of Wales have changed for the better. The results of a Garden Festival exit poll conducted over the period May to August 1992 indicate that 27% of all visitors from outside Wales found that the festival had altered their image of Wales, and the main reasons for the change of image were the beauty of the landscape and the apparent improvements that had taken place. Nearly two-thirds of these visitors stated that the festival had made them want to revisit Wales, in particular the South Wales Valleys.[25]

In addition, Garden Festival Wales created employment opportunities for approximately 2500 people; 1000 involved in design, construction and preparation and a further 1500 people required for the operation and management of the entire event. Some of the local people received formal training which included nationally recognized certificates, thereby upgrading skills at the same time as gaining work experience.

The Garden Festival has had a positive impact on the community in terms of increased morale, and there is a desire to build on the momentum of the festival and the confidence it has brought to local residents.

The Blaenau Gwent Borough Council, Gwent County Council and the Welsh Development Agency (WDA) have formed a joint venture to manage the implementation of an End-Use Scheme for the Garden Festival site. A target has been set for development of the site by the end of the century. *Short-term* plans include:

- retaining 63 acres of the site for a Festival Park;
- conversion of two festival office buildings into office space; and
- availability of two other buildings constructed for the festival which are suitable for light industry assembly or business uses.

As part of the *long-term* development plans for the area, a residential/business plan for a self-contained village is being finalized. This is expected to be the centre-piece of the development and will incorporate light industry, commerce, housing, amenity areas and leisure facilities. Already, various commitments have been given to build housing. Furthermore, the WDA has agreed to rent/buy business units but, whilst interest has been expressed, no commitments from firms in business or technology have yet been received.

The Garden Festival has achieved two of its three goals – it has resulted in the reclamation of derelict land and created a positive image for the area – but the third one, that of encouraging inward investment, is likely to take longer to realize. Business development will depend on the economic situation. Furthermore, the outcome of the End-Use Scheme for the Garden Festival site will only be determined in the long run. However, the joint venture appears committed to providing commercial opportunities in tandem with improving the quality of life for the local community within a realistic time-frame.

The Garden Festival event differs from the other two tourism projects considered in that it was by its very nature temporary. Hence, the long-term considerations relate to what remains now that the festival is over, and are thus not necessarily tourism related. In the short term, various sustainable tourism development principles were satisfied: local participation in decision-making, the employment of local people, provision of a high-quality tourist experience, considerable improvement in the physical environment, emphasis on the importance of local culture, and so on. In the long term, the benefits to the physical environment will still remain. Furthermore, long-term economic and social benefits should accrue to the community from the End-Use Scheme for the Garden Festival site, and from the newly perceived positive image for the area which should encourage inward investment.

Conclusion

The concept of sustainable tourism development has been discussed, along with an illustration of effective policies and partnerships through the Wales Tourist Board. The practical application of sustainable tourism development has been demonstrated via three case studies.

The case studies presented in this paper are recent tourism projects which have all been undertaken with a view to regenerating the economy over the long term, improving and protecting the environment, enhancing the quality of life for the host population, offering the visitor and resident a quality experience of Welsh heritage and culture, and providing for local participation in decision-making and the employment of local people. They demonstrate that by adopting the principles of sustainable development within a sustainable policy framework and by implementing these through effective partnerships and practices, success in achieving sustainable tourism development can be realized.

Acknowledgement

The authors wish to thank Arwel Jones for information pertaining to the Mid-Wales Festival of the Countryside and for valuable comments on an earlier draft of this paper.

Notes and references

1. World Commission on Environment and Development, *Our Common Future*, Oxford University Press, Oxford, 1987, p 43.
2. For further discussion of these principles see English Tourist Board/Employment Department Group, *Tourism and the Environment: Maintaining the Balance*, ETB/Employment Department Group, London, 1991; Countryside Council for Wales/Wales Tourist Board, *Principles for Tourism in the National Parks of Wales*, CCW/WTB, Bangor and Cardiff, 1991; Countryside Commission/ Countryside Council for Wales/English Tourist Board/Rural Development Commission/Wales Tourist Board, *Tourism in National Parks: A Guide to Good Practice*, CC/CCW/ETB/RDC/WTB, Cheltenham, Bangor, London, Salisbury and Cardiff, 1991; and M. Lillywhite and L. Lillywhite, 'Low impact tourism', *World Travel and Tourism Review*, Vol 1, CAB International, Oxford, 1991, pp 162–169.
3. B. Wheeler, 'Is progressive tourism appropriate?', *Tourism Management*, Vol 13, No 1, 1992, pp 104–105.
4. *Ibid*, p 105.
5. See p 95 of B. Wheeler, 'Tourism's troubled times: responsible tourism is not the answer', *Tourism Management*, Vol 12, No 2, 1991, pp 91–96.
6. See p 103 of A. Jones, 'Introduction to alternative tourism', *Tourism Management*, Vol 13, No 1, 1992, pp 102–103.
7. Centre for Tourism Policy and Research, *Tourism, Technology and the Environment*, Simon Fraser University, Vancouver, 1991, p 2.
8. See White Paper, *This Common Inheritance: Britain's Environmental Strategy*, HMSO, London, 1990.
9. Wales Tourist Board, *Tourism in Wales – Developing the Potential*, WTB, Cardiff, 1988.
10. Wales Tourist Board, *Tourism in Wales: Developing the Potential, A Wales Tourist Board Strategy*, WTB, Cardiff, 1988.
11. Countryside Commission/Countryside Council for Wales/English Tourist Board/Rural Development Commission/Wales Tourist Board, *op cit*, Ref 2.
12. See p D5-3 of B. Lane, 'The future for rural tourism', *Insights*, English Tourist Board, London, 1989, pp D5-1–D5-5.
13. See p 40 of D. Gilbert, 'Rural tourism and marketing: synthesis and new ways of working', *Tourism Management*, Vol 10, No 1, 1989, pp 39–50.
14. See B. Lane, *op cit*, Ref 12.
15. See R. Denman, *Tourism and the Environment: Consultative Paper No. 2*, Wales Tourist Board, Cardiff, 1992, p 3.
16. See B. Lane, *op cit*, Ref 12.
17. A. Jones, *op cit*, Ref 6, p 103.

18. CYNEFIN is a voluntary body which is in the process of becoming a registered charity, limited by guarantee. It is Wales's contribution to the World Conservation Strategy sponsored by international agencies concerned with the environment.

19. M. Stone, *The Festival of the Countryside* (Initiative A385), The Planning Exchange, Glasgow, 1989.

20. See T. Stevens, *Tourism and the Community: Consultative Paper No. 3*, Wales Tourist Board, Cardiff, 1992, p 30.

21. See p 3 of R. Denman, *op cit*, Ref 15.

22. Land Use Consultants, *Conwy – A Strategy for the Future*, Aberconwy Borough Council/Cadw/ Conwy Town Council/Gwynedd County Council/National Trust/Wales Tourist Board/Welsh Development Agency [no location], 1988.

23. See p 2 of *Newyddion Project Conwy News*, Issue 3, Project Conwy, Conwy, 1992.

24. Garden Festival Wales, *Garden Festival Wales: Ebbw Vale 1992*, Garden Festival Wales, Gwent [undated], p 12.

25. Golley Slater Group, *Garden Festival Wales Exit Poll: Research Report*, Wales Tourist Board, Cardiff, 1992.

20

Towards a more desirable form of ecotourism

Mark B Orams

*Department of Geographical Sciences and Planning, University of Queensland,
St Lucia, Queensland 4007, Australia*

The term ecotourism has received much attention in recent years. There is considerable
debate over what the term means, and what it should mean. Professional associations
have been formed and codes of ecotourism ethics and standards produced.[1,2] This
paper reviews some of these definitions and discussions and builds on this debate. It
takes a subjective standpoint and argues that tourism operations, which are based on
the natural environment and which claim the positive connotations associated with
the prefix 'eco', should strive to be more than just that. It is suggested that ecotourism
operations should use education-based management strategies to prompt their customers to adopt more environmentally sensitive attitudes and, more importantly, change
to more environmentally sound behaviour. A conceptual framework, which outlines
the transition that ecotourism should strive to make, is outlined and indicators which
can be used to measure progress towards that more desirable state are offered.

Origins of the term ecotourism

The argument for the integration of tourism with conservation was first made
widespread by Budowski[3] in 1976 in an article entitled 'Tourism and conservation:
conflict, coexistence or symbiosis'. However, the use of the term 'ecotourism' can be
traced only as far back as the late 1980s.[4,5] Its invention is, in part, the result of the
increased recognition of, and reaction to, the negative impacts being caused by mass
tourism to natural areas:

Originating in a worldwide reaction against mass tourism, the idea of nature-based tourism,
which was protective of nature as well as enjoying it, has come to fruition in the last five years.[6]

The concept of ecotourism is probably equally due to the widespread and growing
interest in the natural environment and a corresponding recognition of the importance

of conserving natural environmental quality. The idea of visiting and experiencing high-quality natural environments and also protecting them from harmful impacts is now an acceptable and marketable one. As a result, a suitable term which evokes the positive images associated with the term 'eco', for example, in ecology, ecosystem, ecosphere and eco-sensitive, with the activity of tourism has been combined to create a name that expresses a concept which has become popular.

Defining the term ecotourism

Visiting areas for the purpose of observing and experiencing elements of natural environment is not new. Safaris to wild places in Africa to view wildlife were popular amongst explorers and adventurers from Western Europe during the last century. Recreational activities such as hiking, climbing, cross-country skiing, fishing, canoeing and boating are all based on natural environmental features and were popular long before the term ecotourism ever existed. The activities which fall under the category of ecotourism, therefore, are not new. Rather, it is a new term which has arrived because nature-based recreation and tourism has become increasingly frequent and, to a lesser degree, as a reaction against more traditional forms of mass tourism.[6,7]

There are a wide variety of names which refer to tourism which has, as its primary purpose, an interaction with nature, and which has, as an integral part of that inter-action, a desire to minimize or eliminate negative impacts.[6] Because of this wide variety of terms and the increasingly widespread adoption of ecotourism as the generic label to describe this kind of tourism, there is a need to define the term more accurately. However, when one reviews the various definitions that have been given to the term ecotourism, it becomes apparent that there are a wide variety of meanings attributed to this label.

Miller and Kaae[8] views this diverse number of definitions and connotations associated with the term ecotourism as a continuum (see Figure 1). This continuum of ecotourism paradigms is bounded by polar extremes. At one pole is the view that all tourism (including ecotourism) has negative impacts/influences on the natural world. Ecotourism is, in this view, impossible because any kind of tourism will have a negative effect. At the other extreme, humans are viewed as living organisms whose behaviour is natural and who have no obligation or responsibilities to consider other living things. As a result of this paradigm, people are literally unable to behave unnaturally

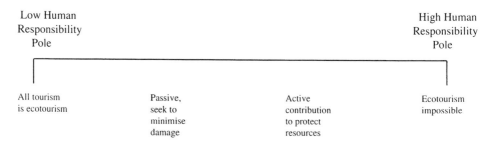

Figure 1. The continuum of ecotourism paradigms.
Note: derived from Miller and Kaae.[8]

or 'un-ecotouristically'. There is, therefore, no difference between the 'natural environment' and the 'human made environment' and all tourism is ecotourism.

These two positions represent extreme and unrealistic views. In reality, definitions of ecotourism can be considered as lying in a position somewhere within a range that lies inside these polar extremes (see Figure 1). Ecotourism definitions can, however, be classified according to their tendency to be consistent with a high – or a low – level of human responsibility. For example, definitions that promote the idea that ecotourism should be active and contribute to the improvement of the natural environment lie toward the high level of human responsibility pole on the continuum. Toward the low level of responsibility are more passive approaches. These are definitions that argue that ecotourists must simply be unobtrusive and seek to minimize their damage to the natural environment.

Examples of definitions of ecotourism can be considered in terms of a position along this continuum. Ceballos-Lascurain,[9] who was probably the first person explicitly to use the term ecotourism,[4] defines ecotourism as:

... travelling to relatively undisturbed or uncontaminated areas with the specific objective of studying, admiring, and enjoying the scenery and its wild plants and animals, as well as any existing cultural manifestations (both past and present) found in these areas ...

This definition lies toward the low responsibility pole and can be classified as a passive position. Additional definitions which also take a passive position in terms of the continuum include those by Zell,[10] who views ecotourism as tourism which is 'ecologically responsible', Muloin,[11] who sees ecotourism as 'tourism which is environmentally sensitive' and Figgis,[12] who states that ecotourism should avoid 'damage or deterioration of the environment'.

Definitions such as those by Valentine,[6] Richardson,[5] The Canadian Environmental Advisory Council[13] and Ziffer[14] fall into the 'active' category and can be located toward the high responsibility pole on the continuum (refer to Figure 1). Valentine[6] proposes the ecotourism is, or should be,

restricted to that kind of tourism which is:
(a) based upon relatively undisturbed natural areas,
(b) non-damaging, non-degrading
(c) a direct contributor to the continued protection and management of the protected areas used,
(d) subject to an adequate and appropriate management regime.

It is, therefore, a definition which, under part (c), requires that ecotourists take an active and responsibility role and contribute to the quality of the natural environment. Ziffer[14] takes a similar 'active' position:

The ecotourist practices a non-consumptive use of wildlife and natural resources and contributes to the visited area through labour or financial means aimed at directly benefiting the conservation of the site ...

A number of ecotourism definitions are general in nature and fall closer to a central or passive position on the continuum. For example, the United States Ecotourism Society's[15] definition states that ecotourism is:

... responsible travel that conserves the environment and sustains the well-being of local people.

Further examples of these types of definitions include those by Young[16] and the Ecotourism Association of Australia.[17]

This plethora of definitions does little to clarify what is meant by the use of the term ecotourism; however, this problem is probably best summarized by Miller and Kaae[8] who state:

> Of course, the merits or deficiencies of ecotourism (or any of its surrogates) are not to be found in any label *per se*, but in the quality and intensity of specific environmental and social impacts of human activity in an ecological system.

In summary, this review of the variety of ecotourism definitions shows that, at a minimum, ecotourism is tourism which is based on the natural environment and seeks to minimize its negative impact on that environment. However, many definitions argue that ecotourists should attempt to do more than simply minimize impacts. They should also contribute to the health and quality of the natural attractions which they visit. It may be that one of the challenges for the ecotourism industry is to assist in moving ecotourists from a minimal 'passive' position to a more 'active' contribution to the sustainability of 'eco-attractions'.

Problems associated with ecotourism

> Ecotourism is big business. It can provide foreign exchange and economic reward for the preservation of natural systems and wildlife. But ecotourism also threatens to destroy the resources on which it depends. Tour boats dump garbage in the waters off Antarctica, shutterbugs harass wildlife in National Parks, hordes of us trample fragile areas. This frenzied activity threatens the viability of natural systems. At times we seem to be loving nature to death.[18]

This statement typifies the concerns of many regarding the increasing number of tourists who are visiting natural areas and who are having a detrimental impact on those areas. Others, such as Wight[13] caution that the ecotourism label is being utilized to take advantage of a 'greening' of the economic marketplace and to 'eco-sell' tourism and travel. In some cases ecotourism may well be nothing more than a new marketing gimmick which dresses up existing tourism attractions in an attempt to increase market share.

> There is no question that 'green' sells. Almost any terms prefixed with the term 'eco' will increase interest and sales. Thus, in the last few years there has been a proliferation of advertisements in the travel field with references such as ecotour, ecotravel, ecovacation, ecologically sensitive adventures, eco(ad)ventures, ecocruise, ecosafari, ecoexpedition and, of course, ecotourism.[13]

Despite many countries and agencies looking towards ecotourism as an answer to both economic and conservation objectives[19] many remain unconvinced that such ventures are a panacea that both protects the environment and supports economic activity. Considerable debate exists over whether eco-tourism can be sustainable and what management regimes/strategies can be employed to minimize the negative impacts which are associated with anthropogenic influences on natural ecosystems.

The objectives of ecotourism management strategies

At a basic level, the overall goal of management strategies designed to control interaction between tourists and the natural environment is twofold: first, to protect the environment from detrimental impacts and, second, to provide for and promote enjoyable tourist experiences. However, it was suggested earlier that an objective of ecotourism experiences should be to attempt to move the visitor experience beyond mere enjoyment to incorporate learning and to facilitate attitude and behaviour change. Additionally, it is argued that ecotourism management regimes should attempt to move ecotourists from a passive role, where their recreation is simply based on the natural environment, to a more active role where their activities actually contribute to the health and viability of those environments. The success of a management regime can, therefore, be measured in terms of its effectiveness in moving the ecotourist experience towards these desired objectives (see Figure 2).

It is recognized that this view is somewhat idealistic. However, the relative youth of the ecotourism industry (or at least the relatively recent recognition of its existence and importance) and the apparent struggle to agree on a definition for it, suggests that a framework which allows ecotourism operations to be measured is needed. This kind of model can help clarify the place of various ecotourism operations within the wider ecotourism field.

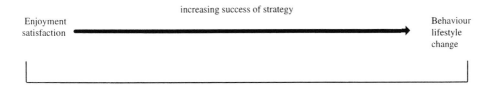

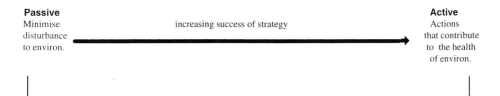

Figure 2. Objectives of ecotourism management strategies.

Using indicators to measure progress toward objectives

In order to measure the success of management strategies in achieving a shift towards the aforementioned objectives a number of indicators need to be selected. These outcome indicators are shown in Figure 3.

At the most fundamental level the success of any management regime can be measured in terms of its impact on tourist satisfaction and enjoyment. A good management regime will rank highly on this indicator. However, more complex educational and behavioural objectives may be achieved if the management strategies are particularly effective. The intermediate steps which assist in this transition from enjoyment to behaviour change are, initially, the facilitation of education and learning and, subsequently, the changing of attitudes and beliefs to those that are more environmentally and ecologically sound. These four indicators, satisfaction–enjoyment, education–learning, attitude–belief change and behaviour–lifestyle change, can be used to measure the effectiveness of a management strategy in achieving the transition illustrated in Figure 2.

It is also important to assess both the direct and indirect, short- and long-term effects of tourist use on the natural environment (the second objective). These impacts can occur in many ways and differ widely depending on the environment on which the ecotourism is based. Nevertheless, the second set of indicators shown in Figure 3 are

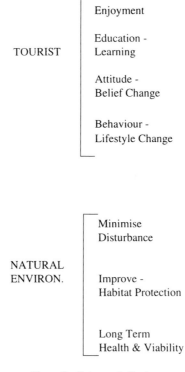

Figure 3. Outcome indicators.

suitably broad categories under which progress towards desirable ecotourism can be measured. More specifically, these indicators can assist in measuring the transition from a passive position, where the ecotourist seeks to minimize detrimental impacts on the natural environment, to an active position where the ecotourism actually contributes to the health and viability of the environment. These three indicators, to minimize disturbance, to improve habitat protection and to contribute comprehensively to the long-term health and viability of the natural environment represent suitable measures of the desired transition outlined in Figure 2.

Collecting data to test hypotheses from each outcome indicators for tourists is not difficult. Accepted social science information-gathering techniques such as questionnaires and intercept interviews can be used to gather data on tourist enjoyment and satisfaction. Similarly, the level of learning, the degree of attitude change and tourists' intention to change behaviour can be questioned. These data can be collected using a before-and-after type research strategy where the data collected before the ecotourism experience are compared with the data collected after to allow assessment of the effect of the ecotourism experience. Alternatively, a control–experiment situation can be tested where similar groups are exposed to different management strategies or experiences. The results are then compared and differences in indicators analysed.

In order to test for behaviour change a follow-up interview or questionnaire needs to be conducted. It is well recognized that intentions to change behaviour do not necessarily result in actual behaviour change.[20] The follow-up should attempt to gather information on whether the desired behaviour change actually occurred.

Collecting data which allow the testing of hypotheses pertaining to tourist impact on the natural environment is far more difficult. Each environment on which the ecotourism is based will be different and, therefore, indicators selected to monitor progress toward the desired state will need to be chosen carefully. However, for each setting, decisions should be made on what types and levels of change in the natural ecosystem are acceptable. Second, what critical indicators should be used to monitor this change should be determined and, third, what human actions are appropriate and inappropriate for that setting need to be decided. Various techniques can be used to make these decisions. For example, if adequate scientific knowledge is available for the resource, the most important indicators may already be known. In reality, however, this is seldom the case. Processes such as those developed for environmental and strategic planning (including public participation) can be used or an 'expert' panel can be employed to arrive at a consensus on the indicators. In this way hypotheses can be developed which allow testing of the level of disturbance to the natural environment.

Assessing whether tourists' actions improve habitat quality/protection is less difficult. If tourists provide financial support and/or labour which directly assists in the maintenance, protection or improvement of the natural resource they are visiting they are meeting this objective. The more desirable state occurs when a comprehensive and ongoing programme exists where tourists can not only contribute during their visit but are able to continue to support and contribute finance, labour, expertise to the resources on a long-term basis. Measurement of these indicators involves assessing the management regimes in place for specific ecotourism programmes to establish whether they facilitate this kind of tourist involvement.

Conclusion

This paper argues that ecotourism should strive to achieve objectives which result in better ecotourists and a better natural environment. It is recognized that what is seen as 'better', or a more desirable form of ecotourism, is very subjective and possibly contentious. Nevertheless, the wide variety of definitions of the term 'ecotourism' implies that the debate over what ecotourism is, and what it should be, continues. An analysis and presentation of these diverse definitions as a continuum allows the development of an argument that ecotourists should be encouraged, through the management strategy of the ecotourism operation, to become active contributors to the health and viability of the natural environment. This argument is not a new one; however, the means by which one can measure the desirability of an ecotourism operation in achieving this more desirable state will assist in the comparison of one ecotourism operation against another. Additionally it can provide a basis whereby the success of a new management strategy can be tested.

Acknowledgements

I wish to thank Associate Professor Greg Hill of the Department of Geographical Sciences and Planning, The University of Queensland for his assistance and advice in preparing this paper. I also wish to thank the referee for his/her helpful comments in the review of this paper. Financial support was provided by a University of Queensland postgraduate research scholarship.

References

1. Ecotourism Association of Australia 'Guidelines for ecotourists' in Richardson, T *Ecotourism and Nature Based Travel* Ecotourism Association of Australia (1993) 39–40
2. Ecotourism Society *The Ecotourism Society Document* Ecotourism Society, USA (1992)
3. Budowski, G 'Tourism and conservation: conflict, coexistence or symbiosis' *Environmental Conservation* 1976 **3** 27–31.
4. Commonwealth Department of Tourism *National Ecotourism Strategy* Australian Government Publishing Service, Canberra (1994)
5. Richardson, J *Ecotourism and Nature Based Holidays* Simon and Schuster, Australia (1993)
6. Valentine, P S 'Ecotourism and nature conservation: a definition with some recent developments in Micronesia' in *Ecotourism Incorporating the Global Classroom. International Conference Papers* (1992) 4–9
7. Moore, S and Carter, R W 'Ecotourism in the 21st century' in *Ecotourism Incorporating the Global Classroom. International Conference Papers* (1992) 140–146
8. Miller, M L and Kaae, B C 'Coastal and marine ecotourism: a formula for sustainable development?' *Trends* 1993 **30** 35–41
9. Ceballos-Lascurain, H 'Estudio de prefactibilidad socioeconomica del turismo ecologico y anteproyecto arquitectonico y ubranistico del centro de turismo ecologico de sian ka'an, quintana roo', study for SEDUE, Mexico (1988)
10. Zell, L 'Ecotourism of the future – the vicarious experience' in *Ecotourism Incorporating the Global Classroom. International Conference Papers* (1992) 30–35
11. Muloin, S 'Wilderness access for persons with disability: a discussion' in *Ecotourism Incorporating the Global Classroom. International Conference Papers* (1992) 20–25

12. Figgis, P 'Eco-tourism: special interest or major direction?' *Habitat Australia* 1993 (February) 8–11
13. Wight, P 'Ecotourism: ethics or eco-sell?' *Journal of Travel Research* 1993 **31** (3) 3–9
14. Ziffer, K *Ecotourism, an Uneasy Alliance* Working Paper No 1, Conservation International, Washington, DC (1989)
15. Blangy, S and Wood, M E 'Developing and implementing ecotourism guidelines for wildlands and neighbouring communities' *The Ecotourism Society Document* USA (1992)
16. Young, M 'Ecotourism – profitable conservation?' in *Proceedings of Ecotourism Business in the Pacific Conference*, University of Auckland, Auckland (1992)
17. Ecotourism Association of Australia 'Ecotourism associations' in Richardson, J *Ecotourism and Nature Based Travel* Ecotourism Association of Australia (1993) 49
18. Berle, P A A 'Two faces of ecotourism' *Audubon* 1990 **92** 6
19. Boo, E *Ecotourism: The Potentials and Pitfalls* World Wildlife Fund, Washington DC (1990)
20. Gudgion, T J and Thomas, M P 'Changing environmentally relevant behaviour' *Environmental Education and Information* 1991 **10** 101–112

21

Pricing policy in nature-based tourism

Jan G Laarman

Department of Forestry, Box 8008, North Carolina State University, Raleigh, NC 27695, USA

Hans M Gregersen

Department of Forest Resources, 115 Green Hall, 1530 N. Cleveland Ave, University of Minnesota, St Paul, MN 55108, USA

A small but rapidly growing segment of the world's tourism industry is nature-based tourism (NBT). This refers to travel motivated totally or in part by interests in the natural history of a place, where visits combine education, recreation and often adventure. It is certain that NBT provides substantial flows of hard currencies to several economies of the developing world.[1-3] It is also certain that only a small share of the money spent by visitors in NBT goes towards protecting the attractions they go to see.

A main attraction for NBT is publicly owned national parks, wildlife reserves and other protected areas.[4,5] Yet entrance fees and other charges for access to such areas frequently are below amounts visitors are willing and able to pay, and below amounts required to finance park operating budgets. The perverse result is that relatively poor countries subsidize visits of persons from relatively wealthy countries, who comprise a large proportion of all NBT participants. Moreover, the generation of only small revenue flows from parks and reserves provides governments with little political or fiscal rationale to augment funding for them in strategies of national development. The vicious circle is one of low fees, inadequate revenue and deficient public investment – followed by continued low fees, revenue and investment.

Although these principles are readily grasped in the abstract, only a few analyses examine them empirically.[6-7] Pricing and revenue allocation in NBT are seriously neglected in public policy, especially for the many governments around the world struggling with fiscal problems. Our paper has three objectives:

- to review briefly the economist's concept of willingness to pay as a basis for NBT pricing;
- to examine administrative criteria in NBT pricing from the perspective of a government agency; and
- to discuss the elements of success in NBT pricing at policy and project levels.

What price to access nature? Willingness to pay

Demand for NBT as willingness to pay

National parks, biological reserves and other natural attractions for NBT are valued for their existence and their use. Existence values explain the demand for preserving sites; use values reflect the demand for visiting them.

The choice to visit or not visit a particular site for NBT is determined by an individual's willingness to pay (WTP) for it in relation to the competing uses of his or her income. Demand studies indicate that WTP varies with income, education, occupation, demographic aspects and psychographic profiles.[8]

Additionally, WTP is higher or lower in relation to a site's attributes, or 'qualities'. These attributes comprise attraction factors and infrastructure factors. The special amenities of the Galapagos Islands, Serengeti Plain and other 'jewels of nature' explain high WTP. These sites have high scarcity value. Few persons will pay as much for access to 'ordinary' sites, i.e. those for which several alternatives provide roughly similar experiences. The WTP also reflects the presence and quality of ground transportation, accommodations, guide service and cooperative governments. The attraction factors and infrastructure factors jointly determine the amount of satisfaction provided by the tourism visit, and thus the WTP for it.

Determining WTP: travel costs and contingent valuation

Willingness to pay (WTP) is different in concept from ability to pay. Both can be different from the amount an individual actually pays (i.e. for access and use of NBT sites). The focus of demand studies is the WTP. Most studies of WTP rely on one of two analytical methods: travel costs and contingent valuation.

Decades ago, the economist Harold Hotelling inferred that the use value of a recreation site is given by the transportation, food, lodging and other costs to travel to and experience the site. Clawson and Knetch[9] built on this idea to relate travel expenditures to the numbers of persons visiting different recreation sites from different origins. The inverse relationship between travel costs and visitation rates is a demand curve. An individual's willingness to pay a fee for access or use (or both) can be derived from this relationship. In practice, however, the travel-cost approach is employed more often to value and defend NBT as a land use than to guide pricing, e.g. for the Monteverde Cloud Forest in Costa Rica.[10]

While the travel-cost method is grounded in observed market behavior, the contingent valuation method poses hypothetical 'what if' questions about how individuals would respond to specified fee types or amounts. Representative applications include contingent valuation studies at Nairobi National Park.[11] Tikal National Park[12] and several parks in Costa Rica.[13-14]

The answers on WTP are contingent upon the situations described by the interviewer. The choices – or contingencies – have to be realistic, well described and clearly understood by respondents. Through years of experience and hundreds of surveys, the limitations of contingent valuation are by now familiar.[15] However, they are no less a constraint in applied work.

The administrative framework: perspectives of the public agency

The economist's answer on WTP is only a starting point for the administrator of the public agency (e.g. for national parks and wildlife), who has numerous interests to serve and criteria to weigh. The matter of setting fees of NBT is complex because of multiple pricing objectives, visitor categories, NBT activities and fee instruments. Importantly, the context of charging fees is often surrounded by philosophical and legislative debates. In countries where access to nature has been considered 'every person's right', the discussion of new or higher fees is bound to stir controversy.

Pricing objectives

The agency's perspective on a new or elevated fee begins with reasons to impose it. Here we identify 10 pricing objectives, realizing that our list may be incomplete:

(1) The revenue goal is an obvious one for private NBT suppliers, and for public suppliers whose budgets are constrained. Even where fee collections must be turned over to a national treasury, budget allocations often reflect the amount of revenue generated.

(2) The collection of revenue from NBT indicates that natural areas have financial value. Demonstrating through user fees that visitors pay their way wholly or in part is important in political discussions of land use.

(3) If revenues from fees can be made to increase, this may enable public agencies to gain increasing independence from outside influences. In the example of Peru, an estimated 90% of financial input for the country's protected areas is from external sources.[16] The acceptance of external funds can be inseparable from external influence on policy making. Conversely, greater financial autonomy may lead to greater policy autonomy.

(4) Fees can be designed to reduce subsidization of groups perceived to receive unfair advantages, e.g. non-residents who pay no taxes for financing the NBT sites they visit. Conversely, fee policy may deliberately subsidize target groups or activities, especially if natural history is considered a merit good. In each context, defining what is just and meritorious is subjective, resting on political and administrative judgments.

(5) If fees are made high enough, they will discourage low-income visitors (except as they are granted access through other policies). This can be a deliberate step to restrain total visitation, and to ration it to a selected socioeconomic element (e.g. the relatively high-spending tourists).

(6) Fees can be a management tool to relieve crowding if fees are elevated during peak times and for congested sites. However, evidence on off-peak pricing to shift use patterns is inconclusive, possibly because even 'high' fees have been modest in most cases to date.

(7) Fee policy for publicly owned NBT sites can be designed to stimulate private business and regional economic development. Low fees contribute to high visitation. This increases the total number of persons who spend for hotels, guide and transport services, and other goods and services. However, the visitors may

include many who travel on low budgets, e.g. backpackers, students and nearby residents. Also, low fees at public sites make it difficult for private businesses to compete in direct production of similar NBT activities.

(8) Among recreation managers, a frequent assumption is that NBT visitors are more respectful of their surroundings if they have to pay for them. Those arguing this position assert that vandalism, littering and other negative behaviors decrease when visitors pay for use. This proposition merits more study than it has received to date, especially in a cross-cultural international context.

(9) The levy of one or more fees helps the public agency to educate its visitors. At the time of fee collection, information can be presented verbally or in writing to explain why fees are being collected. This gives the agency an opportunity to win visitor support for programs and special needs. Supplementary information may address natural history, risks and liability and other topics to enhance visitors' enjoyment and safety. Even though such information can be presented separately, its combination with fee payments is efficient for the agency, and helps visitors understand what they receive in exchange for their money.

(10) As a corollary of the preceding point, policy discussions of new or increased fees help to educate public agencies about their visitors. Proposals to increase fees require forecasts of acceptability, cost recovery and consequences for visitation patterns. Moreover, implementation of a new fee is wisely accompanied by monitoring and evaluation to determine actual impacts. The information collected for feasibility and later for evaluation provides profiles on visitor numbers, composition and likes and dislikes.

Hence pricing objectives are many, competing and varying from one area to another. Administrators are challenged to articulate their pricing objectives, and to make them feasible to attain. Table 1 offers guiding principles.

Pricing strategies

The strategy of how to set fees emerges from pricing objectives in combination with information about visitors' WTP. The strategy should change through time as visitor demand increases, and as administrators acquire experience with different types of fees. Table 2 shows an evolution that begins with small charges, and moves towards increasingly higher ones.

'Token charges' are below supply costs, do not deter use and do not raise significant revenues. However, the approach establishes a pricing policy (i.e. access is not completely free), and many improve data collection and analysis (e.g. on visitor numbers, periods of peak use, etc).

'Going-rate charges' reflect that pricing of a given NBT attraction should be equivalent to charges at comparable attractions after adjusting for differences in site quality, travel costs, visitors' incomes and other demand factors. This is a market-oriented strategy. However, implementation is made difficult by the uniqueness of certain NBT attractions. Also, because marketed-oriented pricing has not been widely practiced in the public sector, going-rate fees typically depart from frameworks of visitor supply and demand. Even fees at private nature reserves, which generally

Table 1. Guiding principles for fee policy in NBT.

Principle	Rationale
Fees supplement but do not replace general sources of revenue	Even for heavily visited sites, fee revenue rarely covers total costs, especially capital costs. Heavy dependence on fee revenue reduces visitor diversity and the scope of attractions that can be offered. Yearly fluctuations in fee revenue make fees an unstable income source
At least a portion of fee revenues should be set aside ('earmarked') for sites that generate them	Earmarking increases management's incentives to set and collect fees efficiently. Visitors may be more willing to pay fees if they know that fees are used on site
Fee should be set on a site-specific basis	National guidelines specify fee objectives and policies, yet management goals and visitor patterns vary across NBT sites, requiring local flexibility in assessing the type and amount of fee
Fee collection is not justified at all sites	Fees are not cost-effective at places with low visitation demand and high collection costs
Fee systems work best when supported by reliable accounting and management	Administrative decisions about fees require acceptable data on costs and revenues of providing NBT for different sites and activities

Source: Adapted from Lindberg and Huber[19] (pp. 103–104).

Table 2. An approximate evolution of pricing strategies in NBT.

Objectives	Experience
Introduction of token charges	Nominal fees become accepted as a way to impute value to visitation
Fees for revenue	'Reasonable' fees become accepted as a necessary budget supplement
Fees to offset costs	Fees are set to recover some or all of operating costs
Fees as management tools	There are many discussions but few test cases of using differential pricing to affect use patterns (e.g. fees varying by season, day of the week, and site)
Fees for profit	Profit can be appropriate even in public agencies, e.g. to build capital reserves and replace facilities. Yet there is little evidence to date of profit-making behavior in most parks agencies

Source: Adapted from LaPage, W F 'Financing the wilderness with user taxes' in Martin, B H (ed) *Fees for Outdoor Recreation on Lands Open to the Public: Conference Proceedings* Appalachian Mountain Club, Gorham, NH (1984) 95.

charge more than public reserves, are often subsidized by grants and other external financial support.[17]

'Cost-based charges' are self-explanatory. The approach is straightforward to explain and defend in concept. Usually, cost-based approaches imply fees that are higher than token charges and going-rate charges. Various manuals guide the collection and analysis of cost data, but a complete cost accounting is challenging. In most practice to date, the costs of ecological impacts and congestion are omitted as too difficult to quantify. Even costs of operation and maintenance can be difficult to completely define and estimate. In application, then, many cost-based charges are underestimates.

Fees, taxes and contributions

Various types of fees and charges are assessed in exchange for access to and use of NBT sites (Table 3). In a public agency, the choices are determined by cultural and legal norms, administrative costs and human imagination. Criteria governing the form and method of payment include the following:

- The system of fees and charges should be clear about which persons will pay what amounts; there should be no room for ambiguity.
- Fair fees reflect (1) ability to pay, and (2) payment in proportion to the benefits received. Efficient fees reflect payment in proportion to the costs of management and administration.
- Fee instruments should not distort economic efficiency, e.g. approaches should avoid large taxes in sectors such as transportation, hotels etc.
- The choices among alternative fee instruments should weigh expected revenues against expected costs of fee collection and administration.

Where ability to pay is an issue, approaches which combine different kinds of fees and charges can be attractive. For example, fees for general entry to a nature park can be kept low so that few persons are excluded at the gate. Inside the gate, individual services and facilities are priced at their cost of provision. This has obvious political appeal, but faces the drawback that collection of different fees at the same site can be costly for management and irritating for visitors.

Taxes levied on equipment (fishing gear, camping equipment, boats, diving equipment, cameras, etc) can generate substantial revenues in industrialized countries.[18] Yet this approach is less feasible in most developing countries, where foreign visitors typically enter the destination countries carrying equipment from their home countries.

Table 3. Categories of fees and charges in NBT.

Fee type	Observation
General entrance fee	'Gate fees' allow either free or priced access to facilities beyond the entry point
Fees for use	Examples: fees for visitor centers, parking, camp sites, guide services, boat use, trail shelters, emergency rescue, etc
Concession fees	Charges (or revenue shares) are assessed on individuals and business which sell food, accommodations, transportation, guide services, souvenirs and other goods and services to NBT visitors
Royalties and profit shares	Can be charged on sales of guidebooks, postcards, tee-shirts, souvenirs, books, films, photos, etc
Licenses and permits	For tour operators, guides, researchers, wildlife collectors, mountain climbers, river rafters, etc. The concept can be extended to individual campers, bikers, etc
Taxes	Examples: room taxes, airport taxes, vehicle taxes, excise taxes on sports and outdoor equipment, etc
Voluntary donations	Include cash and in-kind gifts, often through 'friends of the park' organizations

Source: Adapted from Sherman and Dixon[7] (pp. 109–112).

Taxes collected at airports, hotels and other facilities may be able to generate substantial revenues for allocation to national parks and other NBT sites. However, the funding of NBT sites from such broad-based taxes is less fair than collecting payments from NBT users.

Licenses and permits for mountain climbing, river rafting, safari opportunities, reef diving, etc, can be sold to high bidders through auctions. The successful bidders are expected to comply with agreements which specify conditions of access, liability and permit revocation. The auction approach is most viable where (1) administrative structures are efficient and honest, (2) access to NBT sites can be controlled, (3) numbers of allowed entries are restricted, and (4) revenue condiderations rank high among pricing objectives. Clearly, only a few NBT attractions meet all of these conditions. Furthermore, auctioning is often opposed by small tour operators, who fear that their larger competitors will apply political influence and bribes to capture all the permits.

Particularly in recent years, voluntary contributions of cash, land and labor have been increasingly important resources for NBT. From the criterion of meeting varying ability to pay, voluntary contributions are superior to mandatory fees. Tapping voluntary contributions is politically correct in 'green societies', and can be remunerative. As reported by Lindberg and Huber,[19] The Nature Conservancy solicited US$150 thousand for the Charles Darwin Research Station in the Galapagos Islands by mailing an appeal for contributions to visitors who signed the station's guest book. In Costa Rica, several private organizations have raised susbstantial funding for that country's protected areas through external grants and gifts.

More generally, the international conservation organizations direct what must be a large financial transfer from industrialized to developing countries for wildlife, national parks and other resources valuable for NBT. It is highly appropriate for these organizations to pay for existence value, which is widely enjoyed by citizens of all countries. It is less appropriate for them directly or indirectly to subsidize on-site visitation, which is a private rather than public good. Even more importantly, the recipient country may be expected to accept that 'he who has the gold makes the rules'. The philanthropy of cross-country nature protection is little explored. Nor is much known about possible neocolonial influences in 'nature sectors' where foreign contributions are significant.

Multi-tiered pricing

Multi-tiered pricing occurs when fees vary by category of visitor. Fees are often reduced for children, students, handicapped and retired persons – particularly for residents.

When WTP is lower for residents than non-residents, two-tiered pricing yields more revenue than either a high or low fee alone.[6] More generally, a public agency which aims to make as much revenue as possible charges different fees to different visitors in relation to their varying WTP. This promotes not only revenue objectives, but possibly also social equity.

However, multi-tiered pricing is not free of dilemmas. When carrying capacity is limited so that some visitors have to be excluded, the public agency makes more revenue by selling access to non-residents over residents. The trade-off between revenue versus local use has no answer except in a political framework.

Explanations for multi-tiered fees sometimes confuse social merit, fairness and ability to pay. Reduced fees for students may reflect an assumption that students have low incomes, even though some are from wealthy families. Ecuador's fee to visit the Galapagos Islands is many times higher for non-residents (foreigners) than residents (nationals), even though some Ecuadorians are wealthy and many foreigners are not.

In summary, multi-tiered pricing is highly imperfect as a policy instrument. It attempts to discriminate among individuals on the basis of broad but mythical averages, i.e. foreigners are rich, students and retirees are poor, etc. Furthermore, criteria for differential pricing are not solely fiscal, but also legal, political and cultural. For these reasons, the performance of multi-tiered pricing may depart from the economist's expectation of high revenue generation.

Public attitudes about fees

The charging of fees to access nature touches fundamental questions regarding which among a country's resources should be provided 'free' or at only nominal prices. In many settings, access to public wildlands has been everyone's right, particularly for dispersed uses of lands not privately claimed. If the use of public lands is everyone's right, then is it justifiable for a government to deny access to individuals who cannot or will not pay a fee?

It can be politically popular to favor free access. Some environmental organizations maintain that access to nature promotes self-reliance, independence and even democracy.[20] Moreover, nature-based activity fits the philosophies of 'green societies'. That NBT is perceived to be compatible with environmental protection provides an argument for subsidizing it. To the preceding premises can be added the concern for equity, i.e. that low-income people should not be excluded from nature appreciation, particularly in light of the alleged virtues it bestows.

This is a formidable list of cultural and psychological obstacles in the way of elevating fees for NBT. Even when governments are under pressure to adopt enterprise-like behavior, political leaders have been reluctant to increase fees in fear of public protest. Moreover, the natural resources agencies have been notably timid on this matter. Discussions to increase fees correlate well with periods of falling budget appropriations, but do not leads to long-term and sustained policy efforts.

Indeed, the models of NBT pricing in western societies may be poor examples for developing countries. To date, wealthy societies have seemed quite willing to subsidize NBT, despite mild undercurrents to the contrary. For example, fee revenues collected by the USA's National Park Service are equivalent to only 5–6% of the agency's expenditures.

This contrasts with the starker reality of low-income countries. Chronic shortages of public revenues imply that NBT visitors should pay, especially when they are (rich) foreigners. It is no surprise that fees for NBT are most differentiated and market-oriented in Costa Rica, Ecuador, East Africa and elsewhere in the developing world.

In the presence of public resistance to fees, administrators have several strategies to counteract it:[21]

- Visitors are less reluctant to pay fees when they know how and why their fees are used. Some evidence suggests that visitors are happier to pay when informed that their fees contribute to onsite management. Conversely, visitors should be informed of services that will be discontinued if fees are not collected.
- Support for fees increases when they are for 'quality' improvements. Visitors are sensitive to the quality of toilets, trails, maps, signs and other infrastructure.
- Visitors are less opposed to fees which offset costs than fees which control entry or ration use. Hence the way that fees are described can shape attitudes.
- Fee increases are more palatable in regular small increments than in large jumps, even when fees are comparatively low.
- Support for increased fees is only partly related to an individual's income and past amounts of use.
- More important is the past level of the fee for a particular type of activity in a particular place, i.e. a conditioned expectation.

The preceding observations from North America may be less relevant elsewhere, particularly in cross-cultural settings. For example, a study at Tikal (Guatemala) indicated no relationship between WTP higher fees and information that fees would be returned for park management.[12] More generally, the subject of public support for higher fees traverses difficult ground in psychology and communications. Comparatively little is known about this, especially when pricing is linked with emotional subjects such a nature protection and customary rights.

As indicated, one avenue to win support for fees is to open the issue for public education. The premise is that people will act rationally when presented with justifiable reasons for paying higher fees. Opposite to this strategy is hiding fees, particularly when they are high, so that visitors are unaware of them. For instance, high fees to view mountain gorillas in Central Africa have been included in the prices of tour packages.

Other indirect revenues include taxes for overnight lodging, transportation services etc. The fees and taxes are attached to expenditures such as hotel bills and airline tickets, where they are less conspicuous and less avoidable than if levied separately. Moreover, indirect methods transfer a part of the costs of fee collection from public agencies to private businesses. To be weighed against these apparent advantages, cooperation is unlikely where businesses are obliged to collect fees and taxes, but derive no benefit from them. Finally, indirect fees and taxes – where they are large – can distort prices in ways that hurt the larger economy.

Revenue sharing with local communities

There is no shortage of advice on the 'how to' aspects of cultivating local support for NBT in communities near protected areas.[22–24] One of many strategies is to encourage governments to share entrance and user fees with the communities. The revenues at any particular NBT site are insignificant for a national treasury, but can be important locally. Where it can be made to function, revenue sharing is a focal point for cooperation between parks administrators and local residents.

Yet revenue sharing is not widely practiced. In studies of 28 protected areas in Africa, Asia, and Latin America, Wells and Brandon[25] reported only three examples of it for Kenya, Nepal and Mexico. Revenue sharing is simple in concept, but governments have been reluctant to pursue it. In the first place, revenue sharing has to be supported by top-level authorities for revenue collection. Understandably, they can be highly unsympathetic to proposals which reduce inflows to the treasury. Second, revenue sharing works best when officials in parks and wildlife agencies invite community leaders to discuss NBT pricing and revenue disposition. Not every parks administrator is open to this, and the process can be long and difficult. For example, revenue sharing at Ranomafana National Park (Madagascar) extends to 160 villages, demanding an enormous effort in organization and dialogue.[26]

Perhaps most importantly, successful revenue sharing requires mutual trust between the government and local residents. Trust is often in short supply, particularly in respect of collecting and handling money. Typically, each side regards the other as incompetent and corrupt.

None of these obstacles is insurmountable. If revenue sharing spreads more widely in the future, local communities are likely to play a larger role in decisions about NBT pricing. Communities will want NBT to generate high and continuing yields of revenue. They can be expected to attempt to influence fee policy in ways that come close to market-oriented pricing.

Success in NBT pricing: final suggestions

In this review paper, we assert that pricing is a potentially powerful tool to move towards greater efficiency, fairness and environmentally sustainable NBT. To date, this tool is underutilized. We conclude with a few suggestions to advance pricing practice for administrators who take the issue seriously.

Money-making behavior is not part of the usual administrative culture for public authorities in charge of parks and wildlife. Most professional rewards are tied to program development, not entrance receipts. Perhaps the majority of sites for NBT cannot become self-financing, even under the most intelligent of pricing strategies. It is easy to understand why too much pressure to generate revenues would be an unfortunate distraction. Nor do visitors expect public nature reserves to be managed as businesses.

While we accept these qualifications, they do not stop us from arguing the importance of pricing. The proposition that contact with nature bestows social benefits cannot be accepted at face value. Even where the premise is valid, it does not warrant free or nearly free access to publicly owned natural attractions. These attractions are not costless to provide, and the concept of 'user pays' is perfectly appropriate for NBT as a private good (even when it is supplied through a public agency). For socially meritorious individuals (students, local residents, etc), the public agency can make exceptions to a pricing rule. There is ample precedent for this.

Regarding the amount of revenue to be collected, a politically defensible position is cost recovery. The provision of services at their cost (marginal-cost pricing) is a standard pillar of public finance. The costs to be recovered through user fees are an agency's expenditures to provide for NBT, not its total outlay for park protection and maintenance. The total outlay contributes existence value for the world, but visitors should not be charged for it. Rather, visitors should pay for their direct use, e.g. capital and operating costs of trails, interpretive centers, guide services and the like. Because many costs are indivisible, the accounting to separate user costs from all other costs is not easy. However, practice should be subordinated to principle, not the other way around.

In some cases, the agency's direct costs to support visitation may be high in relation to small numbers of visitors. Then, the agency has over-built its infrastructure in relation to user demand. Costs cannot be recovered through any reasonable level of fees. This indicates inefficient public spending, and obligates the agency to re-think how it should allocate its budget.

The elements of successful fee setting contain few surprises. The agency must be clear about its pricing objectives. It must be particularly mindful of how its fees affect businesses in the tourism sector. It must have reliable information about visitors' WTP. It must realize that visitors and tourism businesses are more accepting of small but regular fee increases than of large jumps. It must actively discuss its fee policy with revenue authorities, tour and hotel operators and local communities.

These guidelines are easily written but less easily followed, as illustrated by recent events in Costa Rica. In late 1994, the country's natural resources agency announced that daily park entrance fees for non-residents would rise from US$1.25 to US$15.00. The new fee is well above the middle range of WTP indicated by previous studies.[13] The steep increase provoked immediate protests, especially by tour operators. Newspapers interviewed angry tourists who claimed they were being exploited. In the town of Cahuita, where livelihoods depend on visitors to the adjacent national park, local people protested the fee increase by taking control of the park entrance. In just one year, non-resident visitation to Costa Rica's national parks fell by 47%. Critics attribute this to the new entrance fee, although that cannot be proved. More certain is that the fee increase has been exceptionally controversial, and that few people in the tourism sector were prepared for it.[27]

The preceding example takes us to our final issue, collaboration. One definition of success in NBT pricing is shared agreement (or not too much disagreement) that the types and amounts of fees contribute to national objectives for tourism and nature conservation. The focus on fees is an excellent means to promote a dialogue about these objectives. Various parties are invited to the table: park managers, revenue authorities, tour and hotel operators, managers of private NBT reserves and leaders of communities near NBT sites. The government's aim is to create a climate of good will by giving each party a voice in the deliberations. Just as importantly, the authorities hear all arguments for and against different fee proposals. In the end, the choices among alternatives are no less difficult, but they are informed.

Acknowledgements

The background research for this paper was funded by the Environmental Policy and Training (EPAT) project, funded by the United States Agency for International Development (USAID), and administered by the Midwestern University Consortium for International Assistance (MUCIA), USA.

References

1. Boo, E *Ecotourism: The Potentials and the Pitfalls* World Wildlife Fund, Washington, DC (1990)
2. Whelan T (ed) *Nature Tourism: Managing for the Environment* Island Press, Washington, DC (1991)
3. International Resources Group, Inc 'Ecotourism: a viable alternative for sustainable management of natural resources in Africa' US Agency for International Development, Bureau for Africa, Washington, DC (1992)
4. McNeely, J A *Economics and Biological Diversity* International Union for the Conservation of Nature and Natural Resources, Gland, Switzerland (1988)
5. Dixon, J A and Sherman, P B *Economics of Protected Areas* Island Press, Washington, DC (1990)
6. Lindberg, K 'Policies for maximizing nature tourism's ecological and economic benefits' World Resources Institutes, Washington, DC (1991)
7. Sherman, P B and Dixon, J A 'The economics of nature tourism: determining if it pays' in Whelan T (ed) *Nature Tourism: Managing for the Environment* Island Press, Washington, DC (1991) 89–131
8. Ryel, R and Grasse, T 'Marketing ecotourism: attracting the elusive ecotourist' in Whelan T (ed) *Nature Tourism: Managing for the Environment* Island Press, Washington, DC (1991) 164–186
9. Clawson, M and Knetch, J L *Economics of Outdoor Recreation* Johns Hopkins University Press, Baltimore, MD (1965)
10. Tobias, D and Mendelsohn, R 'Valuing ecotourism in a tropical rainforest reserve' *Ambio* 1992 **20** (2) 91–93
11. Abala, D O 'A theoretical and empirical investigation of the willingness to pay for recreational services: a case study of Nairobi National Park' *Eastern Africa Economic Review* 1987 **3** (2) 111–119
12. Barry, C C 'Nature tourism and its development in Guatemala: assessing current trends and future potential' MS thesis, University of North Carolina, Chapel Hill, NC (1992)
13. Baldares, M J and Laarman, J G 'User fees at protected areas in Costa Rica' in Vincent, J R (ed) *Valuing Environmental Benefits in Developing Economies* Michigan State University, East Lansing, MI (1991) 87–108
14. Hanrahan, M, Solorzano, R and Echeverria, J 'Valuation of non-priced amenities provided by the biological resources within the Monteverde Cloud Forest Reserve' Tropical Science Center, San Jose, Costa Rica (1992)
15. Mitchell, R C and Carson, R T *Using Surveys to Value Public Goods: The Contingent Valuation Method* Resources for the Future, Washington, DC (1989)
16. Barzetti, V (ed) *Parks and Progress: Protected Areas and Economic Development in Latin America and the Caribbean* International Union for the Conservation of Nature and Natural Resources and Inter-American Development Bank, Washington, DC (1993)
17. Alderman, C L 'A study of the role of privately owned lands used for nature tourism, education, and conservation' Conservation International, Washington, DC (1990)
18. Prosser, N S 'A successful excise tax: the Dingell-Johnson Program' in Martin, B H (ed) *Fees for Outdoor Recreation on Lands Open to the Public: Conference Proceedings* Appalachian Mountain Club, Gorham, NH (1984) 115–118
19. Lindberg, K and Huber, R M Jr 'Economics issues in ecotourism mangagement' in Lindberg, K and Hawkins, D E (eds) *Ecotourism: A Guide for Planners and Managers* Ecotourism Society, North Bennington, VT (1993) 82–115
20. Gould, E M Jr 'Culture and guides to action' in Martin, B H (ed) *Fees for Outdoor Recreation on Lands Open to the Public: Conference Proceedings* Appalachian Mountain Club, Gorham, NH (1984) 10–14
21. Driver, B L 'Public responses to user fees at public recreation areas' in Martin, B H (ed) *Fees for Outdoor Recreation on Lands Open to the Public: Conference Proceedings* Appalachian Mountain Club, Gorham, NH (1984) 45–48
22. Drake, S P 'Local participation in ecotourism projects' in Whelan T (ed) *Nature Tourism: Managing for the Environment* Island Press, Washington, DC (1991) 132–163
23. West, P C and Brechlin, S R (eds) *Resident Peoples and National Parks* University of Arizona Press, Tucson, AZ (1991)

24. Brandon, K 'Basic steps toward encouraging local participation in nature tourism projects' in Lindberg, K and Hawkins, D E (eds) *Ecotourism: A Guide for Planners and Managers* Ecotourism Society, North Bennington, VT (1993) 134–151

25. Wells, M and Brandon, K *People and Parks: Linking Protected Area Management with Local Communities* World Bank, World Wildlife Fund, and US Agency for International Development, Washington, DC (1992)

26. Peters, W J Jr 'Attempting to integrate conservation and development among resident peoples at Ranomafana National Park, Madagascar' PhD thesis, North Carolina State University, Raleigh, NC (1994)

27. Chase, L 'National park entrance fees in Costa Rica' Dept of Agricultural, Resource, and Managerial Economics, Cornell University, Ithaca, NY (1995)

22

Managing ecotourism: an opportunity spectrum approach

Stephen W Boyd

Geography Division, Staffordshire University, Stoke on Trent ST4 2DF, UK

Richard W Butler

Department of Geography, University of Western Ontario, London, Ontario, Canada N6A 5C2

Within the overall context of tourism, ecotourism has experienced rapid growth over the past decade. Although ecotourism has come to imply a form of tourism which fosters environmentally responsible principles, it appears that the economic benefits that can accrue from this activity have been the primary motivation for some nations to deliberately promote ecotourism within their borders. In other cases nations appear to have been willing to accept the development of ecotourism as a result of exogenous market pressures. The magnitude of the ecotourism industry is well illustrated by the fact that over US$25 billion are transferred from the northern to the southern hemisphere annually.[1] Established ecotourism destination areas are located predominantly in the developing nations[2–5] but recent growth in ecotourism has included new destination areas in Australasia,[6] and the remote landscapes of the polar regions.[7] Expansion has also resulted in opportunities being sought in the less exotic temperate landscapes of the developed world, such as Northern Ontario, Canada.[8] This last trend has emerged in response to the potential that ecotourism may offer the economies of marginal areas, and also the realization that there may be a declining number of new exotic and rare environments available that can be marketed as ecotourism destination areas in the more established regions. Early ecotourism destinations such as Kenya,[9] the Galapagos Islands[10] and Thailand[11] have already suffered extensive impacts as a result of increased numbers of tourists.

In light of the above, it is imperative that only those areas which are suitable for ecotourism be developed and that ecotourism criteria are matched with the resource base characteristics of the region. Once begun, ecotourism, like any other form of tourism, requires management. The impression is often given that a form of tourism which fosters environmental principles will have limited impact in the areas in which it is promoted. Unfortunately, just like other forms of tourism, ecotourism generates impacts that require management. As tourism has developed beyond an undifferentiated phenomenon, it can be segmented into numerous forms, and management frameworks are needed that focus on specific types of tourism, rather than tourism in general.

This paper proposes a framework to manage the ecotourism experience which will cover both the hard and soft range of the experience being sought. The overall concept proposed is not new but is one which is based on existing approaches used in the field of resource management. It incorporates ideas from the Recreational Opportunity Spectrum (ROS)[12] and the Tourism Opportunity Spectrum (TOS).[13] The framework proposed here modifies the ideas presented in TOS to specifically address ecotourism, and is termed the Ecotourism Opportunity Spectrum (ECOS).

There is a large and ever growing literature on ecotourism that has addressed a plethora of issues including how it can be defined,[2,14] the dimensions involved,[15-17] and the linkages with other types of tourism and environmental management concepts.[18-20] In light of this, the authors have purposefully used a broad definition of ecotourism namely, a form of tourism which fosters environmental principles, with an emphasis on visiting and observing natural areas. The emphasis on tourism, as much as this can be separated from recreation is deliberate. It is acknowledged that, in reality there is often very little difference in many respects between such day recreation activities as birdwatching and month-long ecotourism trips to observe birds, except the location where these activities take place, the length of time and the amount of expenditure involved. By definition, however, ecotourism in this paper does not include most of the short-term visits to natural and semi-natural areas, especially those in developed countries where the emphasis is on participation in an activity rather than experiencing nature. Thus a weekend or day visit to a national park in the United Kingdom or even in the United States is not the focus of this paper. Rather, it is on that form of tourism labelled and probably marketed as ecotourism. Implicit in the above definition are the concepts of sustainability and appropriateness to ensure the maintenance of the resource base of the destination area, which may also provide the livelihood for local inhabitants of the area. The emphasis in the model is on the relationship of ecotourism to the physical environment more than to social/cultural environment. The focus and purpose of the paper is to outline a framework for the management of ecotourism in destination areas. The model and framework suggested here may have applicability in other situations also, albeit after some modification. In developing this framework, the authors drew from the existing literature to determine what should be its various elements, beginning with a review of concepts and definitions.

Key concepts and related terms

It should be readily apparent from an examination of ecotourism that the relationship between that activity and the environment in which it takes place is of critical importance. Ecotourism, more than any other form of tourism, is dependent upon the quality of the environment, and extra care needs to be taken by managers and developers of ecotourism destinations to ensure that the impacts from the activity are controlled and minimized. It is important to appreciate that ecotourism, however benign it may be, will still have some impacts on the environment, and therefore requires management and control just as any other form of tourism or other resource activity. As well, the amount of use is a critical parameter for ecotourism, as for any form of tourism.

Two key issues interrelate here. One is the problem of maintaining the quality and ecological integrity of the resource base in which ecotourism is being undertaken, to ensure the maintenance of the resource for its own sake and to ensure that it remains attractive to tourists and to ensure that it remains attractive to tourists and to other users also (including, of course, local residents). The second is the problem of maintaining the quality of recreation experience of the ecotourists themselves, which is based not only on the quality of the natural environment but also on the levels and nature of the interaction between groups of users. Research over the last three decades, beginning with Lucas,[21] has shown clearly that key factors which affect the quality of the experience for the user include the number and type of other users encountered, as well as the expectations and experience of the users themselves.

Initially the solution to these problems was sought in the concept of 'carrying capacity', that is, placing a limit on the number of users who would be allowed access to a resource, at or below the level at which they would create irreparable damage to the resource. It became accepted quickly, however, that the concept of carrying capacity in recreational and tourist contexts was not as simple as initially thought, and that the mix of users was as important as, or more so, the actual numbers of users in some situations.[22] Stemming from this came the logical conclusion that the way in which the resource was managed was of at least equal significance to the above factors. Thus by the mid-1980s the concept of carrying capacity had moved from one of finding optimal numbers of users to one involving the management of resources, user expectations and preferences, and physical parameters of the resource.[23]

Some key elements can be identified from the carrying capacity literature. First, that limits on numbers of users are of little value unless they are placed in the context of management objectives. Second, that it is generally accepted that there are a number of measures of user satisfaction for any area, rather than only one and, related to this, that user dissatisfaction may not be simply a mirror image of satisfaction. Third, that compatibility or tolerance of different user groups to one another varies with the nature of the resource and other elements, including frequency, place, type and time of encounters. Fourth, that ecological effects of use in an area vary widely, and indicators of change may be numerous.[24]

Irrespective of the numbers and varieties of capacity, the fact remains that the concept still has applicability to tourism and recreation areas, particularly so in the context of ecotourism. Central to all of the issues is agreement over management of the resource and the user, and general acceptance that in the absence of such control (on levels, type and time of use in particular) overuse, misuse and abuse of the resource are likely to occur over time. If such problems continue, then the resource is likely to suffer irreparable damage to the point at which ecological integrity will be threatened.

'Control', therefore, becomes a key issue. In the context of parks and declared reserves, this remains an issue with regard to level of intervention, planning procedures, monitoring and enforcement, but the idea of control is normally accepted and established. In the case of many tourist resources and destinations, control is a major problem as there may be no specific agency which has control of the resources in question, or has a mandate for activities such as ecotourism. If numbers of tourists become excessive at a destination and the tourist experience declines, visitor numbers may decline because of the unattractive nature of the setting, but by this time it may be too late to restore the area to an attractive state.

Management procedures and frameworks

Over the last two decades a number of management procedures have been developed with particular reference to wilderness and natural areas to resolve the problems identified above. In general these frameworks have placed a focus upon recreation opportunities rather than identifying specific capacity limitations, although the issue of numbers of users, quality of experience and quality of environment underlie all of them. One of the first, and the most widely adopted framework was the Recreation Opportunity Spectrum (ROS)[12] which attempts to incorporate relationships between setting, activities, user expectations and the role of management. This framework takes a behavioural approach, defining the recreational setting as the combination of physical, biological, social and managerial attributes. It establishes a spectrum of recreational settings which vary from pristine wilderness to high-density urban recreation. It utilizes six specific attributes to define the nature of the opportunities for recreation which are deemed possible within each setting: access, management, social interaction with other users, non-recreational resource uses, acceptability of impacts from visitor use, and acceptable levels of control of users.

The ROS has proved attractive to managers of recreational resources because it has a high degree of flexibility in ways in which recreational opportunities can be supplied by integrating the setting with visitor priorities and preferences. By incorporating the spectrum concept into management plans, specific sensitive areas can be identified and protected, and other settings more capable of withstanding heavier levels of use can be earmarked for more intensive forms of recreation.

A variation of the ROS concept, the Tourism Opportunity Spectrum (TOS) was developed by Butler and Waldbrook.[13] This was created to adapt the ROS approach to a tourism context (tourism in the Canadian Arctic), and to provide a background and setting against which tourism development and change could occur. The purpose of the TOS and similar concepts is to provide a context and framework within which information and data can be examined prior to decision-making in respect of the activities which should be allowed or prohibited, and the kind of facilities which should be developed. The availability of accurate and up-to-date data is of crucial importance to the successful application of such concepts and frameworks.

In the above spectrums, the emphasis is upon opportunities for recreation and tourism. It is also important to consider the effects of visitor use on the resources base, and approaches to managing both the resource base and the visitor. One attempt to solve some of the problems of identifying maximum use levels was the Limits of Acceptable Change (LAC) approach, proposed by Stankey et al.[25] This concept accepted that, as the solutions to the issues of carrying capacity were likely to have to be found and instituted by resource managers, a process to assist them to identify acceptable use levels was required. The LAC concept places an emphasis on positive planning and management pre-empting in-appropriate or over-use, thus avoiding the need for remedial or after-the-fact management actions. However, it places a considerable responsibility on managers, with no guarantee that managerial values and decision will be in line with user preferences, particularly as both of these elements are dynamic.[26]

Two other management concepts which have some relevance to ecotourism areas are the Visitor Activity Management Process (VAMP)[27] and the Visitor Impact Management Process (VIMP).[28] The VAMP process was developed by the Canadian Parks Service (CPS) for use in National Parks, and is incorporated into the CPS Natural Resources Management Planning Process. It is aimed at producing management decisions which are based on both ecological data and social information, and is, in reality, a generic planning model, incorporating objectives, terms of reference, analysis of data, options, recommendations and implementation.

Its counterpart, VIMP, was developed for use within the US National Parks, with the aim of reducing or controlling negative effects of use of parks areas. It focuses on identifying problems and unsuitable conditions, on identifying likely causal factors resulting in undesired impacts, and on identification of management strategies for mitigating or preventing unacceptable effects of use. It has proved reasonably effective as a management strategy where a system of control, data collection and analysis and management is in place.

Development of the Ecotourism Opportunity Spectrum (ECOS)

The ECOS model was developed to provide a conceptual management approach for ecotourism destinations, but it is acknowledged that the approach is evolutionary rather than revolutionary, that is, it builds on models already present within the literature. Figure 1 illustrates eight factors viewed as important to ecotourism: (1) accessibility, (2) relationship between ecotourism and other resource uses, (3) attractions in a region, (4) presence of existing tourism infrastructure, (5) level of user skill and knowledge required, (6) level of social interaction, (7) degree of acceptance of impacts and control over level of use, and (8) type of management needed to ensure the viability of areas on a long-term basis. The first seven factors are set against a spectrum of ecotourism opportunities which ranges from eco-specialists to eco-generalists. The spectrum suggested by Fernie[29] which has been adopted for the ECOS framework is very similar to other classifications of ecotourism[30] including the 'hard' and 'soft' categorization by Wilson and Laarman,[15] Laarman and Perdue[31] and Fennell and Eagles,[5] which was based on the interests of the tourist and the physical rigour of the experience itself. The eighth factor links decision makers and stakeholder groups that may be involved in managing a region for ecotourism.

According to Fernie[29] (p. 4), 'eco-specialists' may be perceived as those ecotourists who participate as individuals or in small groups, immersing themselves in the local natural and cultural environment, requiring minimal infrastructure and generally having minimal environmental impact. They may, however, desire and obtain close and lengthy contact with local inhabitants, and individually have considerable social and cultural impacts on such populations by entering the 'backstage' of the cultures

Ecotourism Spectrum

--Eco-specialist-------------Intermediate------------Eco-generalist

ACCESS

(i) Difficulty
arduous & hard..............
.....difficult & vigorous...
moderate & easy..

(ii) Access System
Transportation
waterways, trails........................
......aircraft (float planes)...................................
.................roads (loose surface)..................
................roads (logging)..........................
....roads (paved).......................

Marketplace
personal experience..............................
friends
local tourism......................
operators (camps & outposts)
travel companies.............

Information Channels
Channels
word of mouth..
advertisements (local tourism brochures).
..............travel company tours.....

(iii) Means of Conveyance
Transportation
foot, canoes, horses.................................
motorised vehicles................................

OTHER RESOURCE-RELATED ACTIVITIES

(i) Relationship
incompatible...........
......depends on nature and extent.....
..........compatible on a larger scale

ATTRACTIONS OFFERED
more oriented to natural environment.......
focus on cultural & urban aspects...

EXISTING INFRASTRUCTURE

(i) Extent
no development
development only in......
isolated areas
moderate development......

(ii) Visibility
none.............
....primarily natural....................
....obvious changes.........

EXISTING INFRASTRUCTURE (continued)

(iii) Complexity
not complex.............
level of complexity increasing...................

(iv) Facilities
none.............
search & rescue...............
rustic accommodation
(camps & outposts)
some comforts...........
(lodges)
....many comforts
(hotels & cottages)

SOCIAL INTERACTION

(i) Other ecotourists
avoid or little contact...........
some contact..................
(travel in small groups)
frequent contact.........
(travel in large groups)

(ii) Hosts (local population)
little contact.......................
some interpretation............
& use of basic services
frequent contact..............
services & source for
handicrafts

LEVEL OF SKILL & KNOWLEDGE
professional.........
and extensive
extensive to limited.......
minimal to.........
no knowledge

ACCEPTANCE OF VISITOR IMPACTS

(i) Degree of Impact
none..............
......low to moderate..........
.........high degree............

(ii) Prevalence of Impact
minimal or uncommon........
prevalent in small areas...
prevalent...........

(iii) Level of Control
no control.........
minimum control........
moderate to strict control.

Figure 1. Components of the Ecotourism Opportunity Spectrum (ECOS).

visited. They often have specialized knowledge and obtain a high skill level to participate in activities. In comparison, 'eco-generalists' are usually involved in larger
groups, often organized in ecotourism tour packages, prefer a certain level of comfort
which requires a tourism infrastructure and, as a result, tend to make greater demands
on the host culture and environment. The intermediate forms of ecotourism are similar
to the 'mainstream nature' type suggested by Ziffer[16] in her typology of ecotourism,
which ranged from 'hard-core' to 'casual-nature' types of experience. This intermediate form of ecotourism is seen developing as visitor patterns are established,
numbers increase, expectations change, and awareness of the destination area and the
attractions it offers develops.[29,31,32] Intermediate ecotourists generally travel in small
groups rather than individually, use basic forms or transportation and local
infrastructure and services, and rely on prearranged facilities and touring services.

Access

Access within the ECOS framework includes the level of difficulty in travelling to an
area, the nature of the access system in place in the area, the type of transportation
used to travel to and within areas, and the channels of information available to
promote ecotourism within the region. In terms of difficulty, this may range across the
ecotourism spectrum from left to right, with access classed as being arduous and hard
for eco-specialists, difficult and vigourous for the intermediate type and moderate and
easy for eco-generalists. It is expected that most ecotourists would use some form of
mechanized transportation (e.g. car, train, float plane) to reach an access point to the
ecotourism region. Some specialists may prefer to use non-motorized means to reach
access points, travelling along waterways or trails from communities located close to
access and egress points. Within an ecotourism area, it would be expected that the
specialist would prefer to use natural routeways, such as rivers or pathways created by
wildlife. Generalists, on the other hand, may be viewed as preferring an access system
comprising both paved and gravel roads. The intermediate type, while accepting the
existing road network, would be more willing to use trails created for other purposes
such as resource-related activities which may be present in an area.

The market-place would differentiate ecotourists.[33] The eco-specialist is perceived
as preferring to travel alone, often gaining knowledge about the opportunities an area
affords for ecotourism based on personal experience of travelling through an area
previously or based on information obtained from contacts who have visited the
region. In contrast, the eco-generalist prefers to travel as part of an organized tour, set
up by companies that specialize in catering to ecotourism. This market is therefore
diverse but not as general as that perceived for mass tourism. The intermediate form of
ecotourist may be identified and catered for by local tourism operators who own camps
and outposts within an ecotourism area and provide guides who accompany tours.
The information channel used may include word of mouth of previous users, or advertisements that describe the facilities and operations available within the ecotourism
destination area.

The last aspect of access involves the means of conveyance used. It is expected
that the ecospecialist would select non-mechanized forms of transportation to limit the
impact on the environment. Motorized forms of transportation would be more

acceptable for the other types of ecotourism, with the use of motorized forms of transportation being reduced as one moves closer to the left of the ecotourism spectrum.

Other resource-related activities

Butler[19] (p. 224) stated that in the context of the integration of resource uses, complementarity was the highest goal, implying that 'each use or activity is not only not in conflict or competition with the others, but by their presence and interaction add something to each other'. A position of compromise may be viewed as where compatibility exists between users in terms of neither use nor activity detracting from or harming the other. The problem of ensuring compatibility between uses is compounded by the fact that 'the relationships between different uses may be extremely dynamic and subject to sudden and significant change' ([19] p. 226). At the opposite end of a spectrum of integration is the condition of competitiveness, where incompatibility exists (the situation in which two or more uses or activities cannot exist in the same area at the same time using the same resource).[19]

The degree to which ecotourism should be compatible with other resources users and other tourism users is an important part of the definition for ecotourism within any area. The presence of other resource users and their relationship with ecotourism is treated as an important factor within the ECOS framework, and it is unlikely that a position of complementarity can be reached in many cases where there is a range of uses. Often, compatibility is a possible goal but one which would be dependent on the nature and extent of ecotourism promoted within a region and the nature of the other uses. The level of compatibility would be less for eco-specialists as they are perceived to avoid and to be less accepting of other activities in an area, particularly when those activities may detract from the experience they are seeking. The presence of logging, trapping or mining activities, for example, would impact negatively on an eco-specialist's experience, and would be avoided. The eco-generalist's perception of ecotourism may be such that the level of compatibility between uses is higher, but there may still be conflicts between specific resource-related uses and ecotourism activities and experiences within areas. Where a cultural experience is an anticipated part of the ecotourism experience in a particular area, for example trekking in the Himalayas, all participants may view landscape elements, such as those created by traditional agricultural practices, as enhancing rather than detracting from their overall experience.

Attractions offered

This element represents the first departure from the factors developed in the ROS[12] and TOS[13] frameworks. Attractions are taken to mean the types of experience an area may offer given the characteristics of the setting. The inclusion of attractions within the ECOS framework was considered to be important as it is the nature of the experiences which characterizes this form of tourism.

Ferine[29] explored how the type of previous ecotourism experiences influenced the perception of ecotourism. She concluded that an ecotourist more orientated to the natural environment may not perceive cultural-urban settings as being important or appropriate for ecotourism, and that the type of past ecotourism experiences may also influence perceptions of specific settings as acceptable destinations for ecotourism.[29] In terms of the ecotourism spectrum, the eco-specialist can be perceived to be most orientated to the natural environment, focusing more on exploring, viewing and admiring vegetation and diversity of wildlife, paying less attention to the cultural aspects found within the region.

In contrast, the eco-generalist is more likely to enjoy attractions of the cultural environment equally with those of the natural environment. It should be noted, however, that the attraction of viewing elements of the natural environment is still of major importance to eco-generalists, and a major part of the experience may often be the chance to view wildlife seldom seen elsewhere.

Existing infrastructure

This refers to what is labelled 'tourism plant' in TOS. Within the context of ecotourism, the infrastructure differs markedly from that found in other tourism areas, which often includes the provision of shopping and entertainment facilities. Existing infrastructure is used in place of tourism plant as the emphasis is primarily on provision of suitable accommodation for ecotourists along with minor modification of existing infrastructure to conform to meet other essential needs of the ecotourists themselves. Modifications of existing infrastructure for elements such as water, power and sewage will vary in terms of extent, scale, visibility , complexity and the number as well as the type of facilities involved, but for eco-specialists would be minimal and not irreversible.

Eco-generalists may accept more extensive development that suits their wider preferences, while those in an intermediate position may accept limited developments in isolated areas. As for visibility, a range from none to obvious changes would result as one moves from left to right across the ecotourism spectrum. The aspect of complexity anticipates eco-specialists preferring simple development with the level of complexity increasing for both the intermediate type and eco-generalists, With respect to the last factor, facilities, eco-specialists do not desire formal facilities, while the intermediate type may accept rustic accommodation (e.g. camp cabins, outpost huts) along with services such as search and rescue operations and the modification and creation of new trails. In contrast, eco-generalist may desire a minimum level of comfort and convenience, such as a hotel or cottage with modern conveniences.

Social interaction

Over the past few decades a substantial amount of research has focused on tourist interaction, including that with the host (local population) and with other guests (other tourists).[34] The extent to which such interaction occurs has important implications for the opportunities an area may offer as it brings into play the variable of experiential or social carrying capacity and how this influences the level of satisfaction of tourists. In recent years the level of satisfaction (which may represent a measure of the acceptable level of interaction), has been expressed in terms of norms. Social interaction beyond norms or expected encounter levels may result in changes in the experience obtained within a region, and, in turn, impact on the opportunities that a region may present to tourists.

Much of the research undertaken on norms has been focused either on water-based recreation or on recreational activities undertaken within backcountry wilderness-type settings.[35–37] While recreation rather than tourism has been the focus of such research, the types of activities which have been considered are common to ecotourism destinations, and the use of norms may be an appropriate approach to indicate the level of social interaction acceptable.

In terms of interacting with other ecotourists, the level of contact would increase as one moves from left to right across the ecotourism spectrum. Eco-specialists would tend to avoid contact with other tourists, focusing on their desire to explore the natural environment and view wildlife present in a state of relative isolation. In contrast, the intermediate type of ecotourist would be in contact with others as they would be travelling in a group which may include the use of a guide. The size of such groups would normally be small as too many people would detract from the level of satisfaction desired from the trip. In contrast, eco-generalists would normally traverse a region as part of a larger organized party using a guide, and accept the presence of other tourists and even other organized groups. Their overall ecotourist experience, even though it often may represent only a small part of their overall vacation, might still be negatively affected if they visited locations at which the level of use was impacting visibly on the natural environment and reducing the quality of the experience.

The extent to which ecotourists use the services and facilities present in a region influences how much interaction occurs between guest and host. The type of experience itself, whether the interest is solely in the natural environment or includes the cultural heritage of the area, also influences the extent to which such interaction will occur and the level which will be acceptable. Eco-specialists, because their greater knowledge of an area and skill of coping within a setting may negate the need for local people as guides, may have little direct contact with residents, and use the local community only as a base from which their trip originates, unless it had significant cultural appeal. In contrast, eco-generalists, because of the services used by providers of the trip, will tend to find themselves in greater, if less personal, contact with locals, especially if local communities are used for accommodation.

Level of skill and knowledge

Ecotourists' levels of skill and their prior knowledge have implications for the opportunities that an area may offer and the type of experiences that may be obtained. Eco-specialists' skill and knowledge level may be viewed as extensive, reflected in the fact that they may engage in trips of considerable duration. These skills and knowledge allow them to survive with a low level of interaction and limited contact with others. The knowledge and skill level of the intermediate group will range from limited to extensive, and their trip duration and prior knowledge about the region may determine whether or not they will use a guide. Eco-generalists will probably have minimal skills and knowledge about an area and its ecology or culture, the visit will generally be of a short duration (weekend to day trips), in an organized party, following a specific itinerary, with accommodation provided and a guide present to offer interpretation.

Acceptance of visitor impacts

This factor involves the degree and prevalence of impact and the need for control to be exercised over impacts that occur. As numbers of users increase across the ecotourism spectrum from left to right, the range and severity of impact they cause will also increase. It should be noted that eco-specialists may have greater impacts than is often suggested, as they frequently enter less accessible areas which may be highly sensitive to human intrusion. In terms of prevalence, impacts by eco-specialists may be minimal or uncommon. In contrast, the incremental impacts of larger numbers of eco-generalists will probably be confined to specific trails and viewing areas that are heavily used, but not be evident away from these areas, as the majority of this group will keep to trails and pathways.

When level of control over use is considered, for the most part, the eco-specialist normally leaves only a limited impact on the environment and little direct control may be needed. Such users often find unacceptable the impacts generated by other users, and seek out new experiences and opportunities in areas not yet considered ecotourism destinations. Eco-generalists may be aware of the impacts occurring from ecotourism in a region, and be willing to accept moderate to strict control over the number of groups permitted, their size and the types of activities they are permitted to undertake. However, impacts may still be considerable and prevalent.

Acceptance of a management regime

In developing the TOS framework, Butler and Waldbrook[13] alluded to the problems of attempting to control tourism development and identifying responsibility for this control, problems which apply equally in the case of ecotourism. Successful or sustainable ecotourism development may be regarded as where the product (opportunity and experience) can be maintained over the long term ensuring the viability of the resource base on which it is based. It is equally important that ecotourism in an area be compatible with established local activities. To attempt to introduce or impose ecotourism into an area or a community with which it is incompatible or in which it is unwanted should clearly be unacceptable. Part or all of the purpose of establishing ecotourism in an area is normally to improve the economic and social viability of the local communities. If ecotourism is not appropriate to or compatible with established local activities and cultural beliefs, then it will not achieve goals established for it, will not be accepted locally or be sustainable, and may even be actively opposed or undermined.

Many of the factors within the ECOS framework need to controlled through management. Figure 2 shows the components of a management regime in which it is recognized that decision making is ultimately a political process. However, as the model shows, the decisions on how ecotourism should be managed in a region, especially where other resource-based uses exist, have to involve all of the various stakeholders present in the area. This will include the tourism industry, resource-based industries, local communities and other public and private agencies. It has to be recognized that in most communities there is rarely complete agreement on any

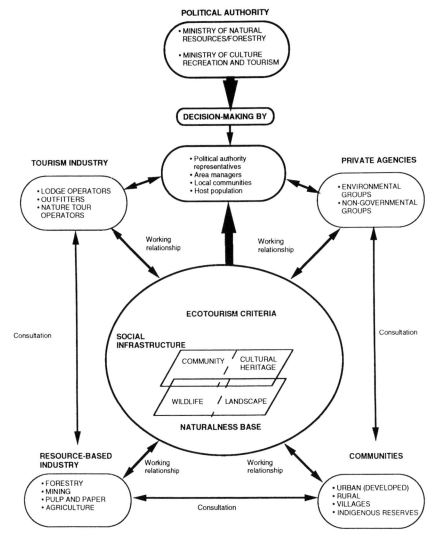

Figure 2. Stakeholders and decision-making framework.

issue, and that within the groups noted above there also will almost certainly be divergence of opinion about development.

Conclusion

This paper has proposed a framework by which opportunities for ecotourism may be identified and located. An obvious next step is the application of the framework within a destination area seeking to promote ecotourism. Of the eight elements that comprise the ECOS framework, the first four can be determined from on-site study.

The remaining factors, excluding the last one concerning an appropriate management regime, require input from ecotourists themselves, preferably from those visitors who have experience in the region under consideration. The eighth element requires dialogue with all the groups and interests involved, both on an individual basis and collectively in order to reach areas of consensus over how ecotourism could be promoted and who should be responsible for overseeing the management of ecotourism within the region. To assist with these tasks, a number of conceptual frameworks have appeared in the ecotourism literature in the past few years[5,32] which have the potential to be applied to the development of ecotourism. They have addressed non-consumptive wildlife-orientated recreation as well as the function of the resource tour (group led by a competent guide), and its relationship with and impact on the visitors and the service industry.

Other researchers have commented on how tourism within an area may change over time, noting possible stages in the process of tourism development.[38] Understanding that the type of ecotourist, and hence ecotourism itself, may shift in the early stages of an area's development away from catering for eco-specialists to serving an eco-generalist population has a bearing on the type of opportunities for ecotourism which an area may create.[39] As a result, marketing may come to play a more significant role in shaping ecotourism opportunities in regions. If marketing is successful in attracting and maintaining the desired and appropriate type of ecotourist to a destination, then it could reduce the pressure on the area which a set of undifferentiated users would exert.[33] The need for strict management and control over the types of ecotourism activities that could be undertaken could therefore be reduced. If ecotourism regions are to be developed, then the specific developments should be based on guidelines which evaluate the relative priority of ecotourism activities and opportunities compared with other resource uses and community needs, and assess the significance of their environmental and social impacts, and marketing efforts should be in line with such guidelines.

It is important, however, to be able to apply a management framework and management principles to the development of ecotourism destinations. Ecotourism development is often different from many other forms of tourism development in that it is frequently small scale, environmentally responsible and selectively marketed, at least in its early stages. It also occurs mostly in remoter areas. The potential for public sector intervention, control and management is much higher than in the case of a multinational large-scale mass tourism development in an established urban area, for example. Unlike many forms of tourism which take place in urban or developed areas on private land with no public sector management role possible, much of the ecotourism development occurs on public lands and the potential for the establishment of a management regime normally exists. As noted earlier in the paper, ecotourism is often 'sold' as beneficial and harmless to destination areas[40] for a variety of motives ranging from ignorance to uncaring exploitation. It is up to decision makers in these areas to ensure an appropriate management framework is in place before development occurs. The framework proposed in this paper is a model, and it is recognized that any model, by nature, includes a considerable degree of generality. Divergent views can be expected to change over time in many directions, just as the type of tourism will also change. Reality is always more complex than any model can portray. That, however, should not prevent the introduction of management controls, particularly where vulnerable physical and social communities may be placed at risk. The fact that ecotourism development tends to occur in the more remote and marginal areas of the world, often in fragile and endangered ecological and human communities, makes the need for such appropriate management all the more critical.

References

1. Whelan, T (ed) *Nature Tourism: Managing for the Environment* Island Press, Washington, DC (1991)
2. Boo, E *Ecotourism: The Potentials and Pitfalls* Vols 1 and 2, World Wildlife Fund, Washington, DC (1990)
3. Dearden, P 'Tourism in developing societies: some observations on trekking in the highlands of North Thailand' *World Leisure and Recreation* 1989 **31** (4) 40–47
4. de Groot, R S 'Tourism and conservation in the Galapagos Islands' *Biological Conservation* 1983 **26** 291–300
5. Fennell, D A and Eagles, P F J 'Ecotourism in Costa Rica: a conceptual framework' *Journal of Park and Recreation Administration* 1990 **8** (1) 23–24
6. Valentine, P S 'Review: nature-based tourism' in Weiler, B and Hall, C M *Special Interest Tourism* Belhaven Press, London, UK (1992) 105–127
7. Marsh, J 'Tourism in Antarctica and its implications for conservation' paper presented at the IVth Congress on National Parks and Protected Areas, Caracas, Venezuela (1992)
8. Boyd, S W, Buttler, R W, Haider, W and Perera, A 'Identifying areas for ecotourism in Northern Ontario: application of a Geographic Information Systems Methodology' *Journal of Applied Recreation Research* 1994 **19** (1) 41–66
9. Olinda, P 'The old man of nature tourism: Kenya' in Whelan, T *Nature Tourism – Managing for the Environment*, Island Press, Washington, DC (1991) 23–28
10. Kenchington, R A 'Tourism in the Galapagos Islands: the dilemma of conservation' *Environmental Conservation* 1989 **16** (3) 227–232
11. Dearden, P and Harron, S 'Tourism and the hilltribes of Thailand' in Weiler, B and Hall, C M *Special Interest Tourism* Belhaven Press, London, UK (1992) 96–104
12. Clark, R N and Stankey, G H *The Recreation Opportunity Spectrum: A Framework for Planning, Management, and Research* US Department of Agriculture Forest Service, Pacific Northwest Forest and Range Experiment Station, General Technical Report PNW-98 (1979)
13. Butler, R W and Waldbrook, L A 'A new planning tool: the Tourism Opportunity Spectrum' *Journal of Tourism Studies* 1991 **2** (1) 1–14
14. Wood, M E, Gatz, F and Lindberg, K 'The ecotourism society: an action agenda' in *Ecotourism and Resource Conservation: A collection of papers* Vols I and II, Ecotourism and Resource Conservation Project, compiled by J A Kusler (1991) 75–79
15. Wilson, M A and Laarman, L G 'Nature tourism and enterprise development in Ecuador' *World Leisure and Recreation* 1988 **29/30** (1) 22–27
16. Ziffer, K *Ecotourism: The Uneasy Alliance* Conservation International and Ernst and Young, Washington, DC (1989)
17. Scace, R C, Grifone, E and Usher, R (SENTAR Consultants Ltd) *Ecotourism in Canada* Report produced for the Canadian Environmental Advisory Council, Ottawa (1992)
18. Lane, B 'Sustainable tourism: a new concept for the interpreter' *Interpretation* 1991 **49** 2
19. Butler, R W 'Integrating tourism and resource management: problems of complementarity' in Johnston, M E and Haider, W *Communities, Resources, and Tourism in the North* Lakehead University, Centre for Northern Studies (1993) 221–236
20. Cater, E 'Ecotourism in the Third World: problems for sustainable tourism development' *Tourism Management* 1993 **14** (2) 85–90
21. Lucas, R C 'Wilderness perception and use: the example of the Boundary Waters Canoe Area' *Natural Resources* 1964 **3** (3) 394–411

22. Butler, R W, Fennell, D and Boyd, S *Canadian Heritage Rivers Recreational Carrying Capacity Study* Heritage Rivers Board, Environment Canada, Ottawa (1992)
23. Stankey, G H and McCool, S F 'Carrying capacity in recreational settings: evolution, appraisal and application' *Leisure Sciences* 1986 **6** (4) 453–473
24. Shelby, B and Herberlein, T A 'A conceptual framework for carrying capacity determination' *Leisure Sciences* 1986 **6** (4) 433–451
25. Stankey, G H, Cole, D N, Lucas, R C, Peterson, M E and Frissell, S S *The Limits of Acceptable Change (LAC) System for Wilderness Planning* USDA Forest Service General Technical Report INT–176, Intermountain Forest and Range Experiment Station, Odgen, Utah (1985)
26. McCool, S F and Stankey, G H 'Managing for the sustainable use of protected wildlands: the limits of acceptable change framework' paper presented at the IVth World Congress on Parks and Protected Areas, Caracas, Venezuela (1992)
27. Graham, R, Nilsen, P and Payne, R J 'Visitor management in Canadian National Parks' *Tourism Management* 1988 **9** (1) 44–62
28. Loomis, L and Graefe, A R 'Overview of NPCA's *visitor impact management process*' paper presented at the IVth World Congress on Parks and Protected Areas, Caracas, Venezuela (1992)
29. Fernie, K J '*Ecotourism: a conceptual framework from the ecotourist perspective*' unpublished MSc thesis, Department of Forestry, University of Toronto, Toronto (1993)
30. Twynam, D G and Robinson, D W *A Market Segmentation Analysis of Desired Ecotourism* Northern Ontario Development Agreement Project 4052, Final Report, Thunder Bay, Ontario, Lakehead University (1996)
31. Laarman, J G and Perdue, R R 'Science tourism in Costa Rica' *Annals of Tourism Research* 1989 **16** 205–215
32. Duffus, D A and Dearden, P 'Nonconsumptive wildlife-oriented recreation: a conceptual framework' *Biological Conservation* 1990 **53** 213–231
33. Eagles, P F J, Ballantine, J L and Fennell, D A 'Marketing to the ecotourist: case studies from Kenya and Costa Rica' paper presented at the IVth World Congress on National Parks and Protected Areas, Caracas, Venezuela (1992)
34. Smith, V *Hosts and Guests* University of Pennsylvania Press, Philadelphia (1987)
35. Manning, R 'Crowding norms in backcountry settings: a review and synthesis' *Journal of Leisure Research* 1985 **17** (2) 75–89
36. Vaske, J J, Grafe, A R, Shelby, B and Heberlein, T A 'Back-country encounter norms: theory, method and empirical evidence' *Journal of Leisure Research* 1986 **18** (3) 137–153
37. Vaske, J J, Donnelly, M P and Shelby, J 'Establishing management standards: selected examples of the normative approach' unpublished manuscript supplied by the principal author (1992)
38. Butler, R W 'The concept of a tourist area cycle of evolution and implications for management of resources' *Canadian Geographer* 1980 **XXIV** (1) 5–12
39. Dixon, J A, Scura, L F and Hof, T van't 'Meeting ecological and economic goals: marine parks in the Caribbean' *Ambio* 1993 **XXII** (2–3) 117–125
40. Wheeller, B 'Sustaining the ego' *Journal of Sustainable Tourism* 1993 **1** (2) 121–129

23

Ecotourism accommodation spectrum: does supply match the demand?

Pamela A Wight

Tourism Consultant, 14715-82 Avenue, Edmonton, AB, Canada, T5R 3R7

Market demand

Ecotourism is a growing tourism market. Further, ecotourists are now influencing general travellers' preferences. Until recently, there has been little market information on ecotourists' characteristics, preferences and motivations, and one gap in information has been their accommodation preferences. This paper presents demand information related to accommodation, and identifies a gap in the supply side.

Types of accommodation preferred by ecotourism markets

Recently, Alberta Economic Development and Tourism, the Government of British Columbia and two Canadian federal departments commissioned an Ecotourism Market Demand Assessment.[1] General consumers, experienced ecotourists, and the ecotourism travel trade were surveyed. General consumers were those North American travellers who had taken (77%) or wished to take (23%) a vacation involving nature, adventure, or cultural experiences in the countryside or wilderness. They should be considered as consumers who enjoy more general interest ecotourism, and they were surveyed by telephone. Experienced ecotourists were surveyed by mail, from a travel trade lists of clients. Markets were asked what kind of accommodation they preferred. Figure 1 shows the range of preferences.

General consumers chose hotels/motels most often (56%), but they also selected a range of other camping and fixed roof options. By comparison, hotels/motels were only selected by 41% of experienced ecotourists (12% of responses). They were far more likely to select from a range of intimate, adventure-type accommodation, such as cabins lodges/inns, camping, bed and breakfasts (B and Bs), or ranches. One might suggest that the degree to which hotels/motels are mentioned by general consumers has a bearing not only on the demand, but on the accommodation *supply* and their degree of familiarity with that supply. In addition, general consumers may have tended to

Accommodation Type	Experienced Ecotourist %	General Consumer %
Cabin/cottage	66	14
Lodge/Inn	60	14
Tent Camping	58	17
Bed & breakfast	55	10
Hotel/motel	41	56
Ranch	40	1
Cruise ship	20	4
Sail boat	3	1
RV	2	5
Private home/friends	1	6
Hostel/dorm/university residence	1	1
Condo, house, apartment	0.4	3
Other	1	1
Total Number of Respondents	422	1377
Av. No. of Choices	3.5	1.3

N.B.   Percentages do not total 100% due to multiple responses
(*Source*:   HLA/ARA Consulting, 1994[1])

Figure 1. Accommodation preferences of North American ecotourism markets.
(*Note*: RV = recreational vehicle.)

give only a first choice of accommodation due to the mode of survey (telephone vs mail).

Of possibly greater significance that the desire for smaller, adventure-type accommodation by ecotourists, is the *number of responses* made by each respondent; general consumers made 1.3 selections each, while experienced ecotourists provided an average of 3.5 responses each. This higher incidence of multiple responses may, in part, be attributable to the fact the experienced ecotourist survey was by mail; however, it also relates to their experiences and desires. They make a broad range of choices in the area of smaller, more intimate accommodation. Focused interviews with the travel trade and other evidence[2] supports the conclusion that the overall vacation experience seems to determine the accommodation; the accommodation is not the critical determinant. For example, European travel trade customers generally want comfortable accommodation which has character. However, they are prepared to 'rough it' if this is part of the experience.[3]

Surveys of the ecotourism travel trade (120 firms) indicated camping was the commonest accommodation type, followed by hotels and variety of other types.[1] The prominence of camping may reflect the types of preferred activities (the top 6 were: hiking, rafting, canoeing, cycling, kayaking and rafting), or the type of accommodation offered, or the actual supply of accommodation available.

Accommodation demand ranges along a spectrum

Accommodation is a key component of the tourism industry – tourists need a place to stay. It could be a campsite or some fixed roof accommodation (e.g. cabin, hut, lodge,

ECOTOURISM ACCOMMODATION SPECTRUM

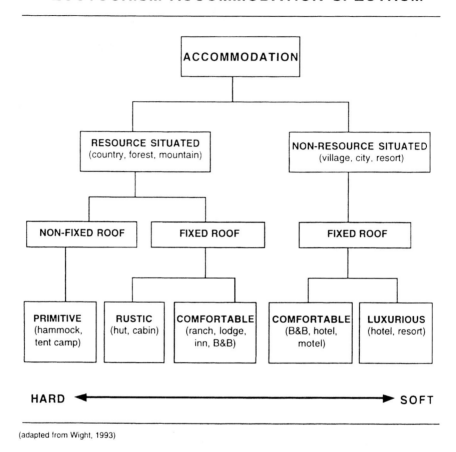

(adapted from Wight, 1993)

Figure 2. Ecotourism accommodation spectrum.

B and B, farm, ranch, motel, hotel or resort. Apart from campsites, accommodation is some form of fixed roof facility. A range or spectrum of land-based accommodation types can be appropriate for ecotourism (Figure 2), and may range from hard to soft.[4] Accommodation may be situated in the resource in which ecotourism activities and experiences take place, or outside the resource, in nearby towns or other centres. When accommodation is located outside the resource, the centres in which they are located act as base-camps to ecotourism activities.

The Alberta/British Columbia market demand assessment study confirmed that ecotourism accommodation demand does, indeed, range along this type of spectrum. The actual demand is illustrated on Figure 3, as a series of pie charts. Each chart represents stated demand for each accommodation type, and these are presented according to the accommodation spectrum, ranging from hard to soft. In most other preference categories, general consumers are tending to move toward the preferences of the experienced ecotourists;[5,6] we may therefore expect that demand for more

DEMAND FOR ECOTOURISM ACCOMMODATION

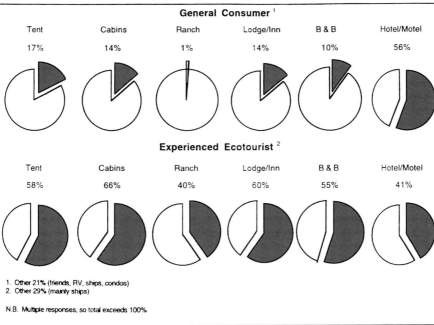

General Consumer [1]

Tent	Cabins	Ranch	Lodge/Inn	B & B	Hotel/Motel
17%	14%	1%	14%	10%	56%

Experienced Ecotourist [2]

Tent	Cabins	Ranch	Lodge/Inn	B & B	Hotel/Motel
58%	66%	40%	60%	55%	41%

1. Other 21% (friends, RV, ships, condos)
2. Other 29% (mainly ships)

N.B. Multiple responses, so total exceeds 100%

HARD   SOFT

Figure 3. Demand for ecotourism accommodation.

intimate, 'resource-situated' accommodation types will be increasing relative to the demand for more urban-based hotels and motels. Although Andersen has suggested that a typical ecotourism facility is of limited size, precluding the participation of major hospitality corporations, he acknowledged that 'there is increasing interest in eco-tourism by major hoteliers, where the economics of resort operations seem to be directing the ecotourist marketplace towards larger facilities'.[7] This could be unwise from a number of perspectives, including market preferences.

Level of luxury preferred

A 1991 survey of US tourists interested in outdoor adventure vacations found that 47% wanted mid-range accommodation, 34% wanted basic accommodation, and 15% desired first class or better.[8] Subsequent surveys and travel trade focused inter-views confirmed that most market segments do not prefer luxury.[1] All groups prefer middle range levels of luxury (consumers 60%, ecotourists 56%) followed by basic/budget (Figure 4). Only 9% of consumers and 6% of ecotourists want luxury. Representative consumer comments include 'something in middle – not too classy,' or 'want small affordable place, not looking for much comfort, as would be out hiking and enjoying evening.'[1] These surveys show that the desire for luxury has decreased somewhat in the last few years. For specific types of accommodation, there is evidence

Accommodation	General Consumer %			Experienced Ecotourist %		
Type	Luxury	Mid	Budget	Luxury	Mid	Budget
Hotel/motel	10	66	23	9	59	32
Lodge/inn	9	67	24	8	64	53
Cabin/cottage	4	60	36	4	57	39
Tent	3	41	56	5	42	53
Bed & breakfast	8	66	25	8	60	32
Ranch	19	69	13	6	59	36
Other	9	58	30	8	67	25
Total (number)	9(117)	60(799)	31(406)	6(24)	56(236)	38(160)

NB: 1. Values may not total due to multiple responses, or rounding.
        2. Totals may not equal total sample size since not all respondents answer all questions.
        (Source: HLA Consultants, 1996[6])

Figure 4. Accommodation preference by level of luxury preferred.

that the experienced ecotourist has a lower desire for luxury than does the general consumer. Figure 4 presents the levels of luxury desired.

Figure 4 also presents the level of luxury cross-tabulated against the accommodation preference. It reads: for the general consumers who prefer hotel/motels, 10% prefer luxury (vs 9% for the total sample), 66% prefer mid range (vs 60%), and 23% prefer basic budget (vs 31%). It shows that those general consumers who prefer ranches prefer more luxury and mid range accommodation than the average (19% vs 9%); and those who prefer cabins or tents want more basic budget accommodation (36% vs 31% and 56% vs 31%). For experienced ecotourists, campers prefer more basic budget than average (53% vs 38%) and those who prefer lodge/inns want more mid range (64% vs 56%) and basic budget (53% vs 38%).

In focused group discussions with the ecotourism travel trade, it was also found that it is the activity which determines the experience, not the accommodation.[1] Japanese operators indicated that until about 10 years ago, accommodation preferences were major hotels. Recently, markets have wanted chalets and guest ranches, although they want a higher level of amenities. Adventure resorts are in demand, but few Japanese want rustic accommodation. They do not want deluxe, just good, and they prefer to stay in mountainous areas, but not in the wilderness. European travel trade customers want comfortable accommodation with character. The British want a mix of accommodation and enjoy something rustic, but not for the whole trip – the trip should end with a more upscale experience, Germans prefer remote, or fly-in accommodation, preferring very small fixed roof with running water. There is a general tendency for most markets to want a higher degree of comfort at the end of their trip. For example, after a week of hiking, hikers want amenities like a bed and a tub or shower, while those with rustic accommodations may want comfort or luxury.[1,9]

Accommodation influencers: activity preferences and
other market and trip characteristics

There has been an ongoing debate in government, non-governmental organization, and other circles, whether or not ecotourists who do not wish to camp would be happy to stay in towns and other centres, and 'visit' the resource by day. In order to examine this question, the relationships between activities and accommodation preferences of general consumers were examined (Figure 5).[6] It was found that those who preferred activities considered to be more ecotourism in nature (hiking, boating, camping, or fishing, and experienced in relative wilderness settings, were more likely to select accommodation likelier to be found in those settings (tent, cabin/cottage) than average; the opposite was found for activities less associated with ecotourism. For example, on average 56% of consumers preferred hotels/motels, but only 50% of hikers indicated hotels/motels, while 64% of those interested in touring indicated hotels. Similarly, while on average 14% of consumers responded cabin/cottage, 19% of hikers and 24% of those who wanted to fish indicated cabin/cottage; conversely, only 8% of those who preferred touring, and 7% of those interested in local culture, wanted cabins/cottages.

There were similar findings for the experienced ecotourist sample, although these are not presented as cross-tabulations, due to the smaller overall sample, thus small cell sizes (418 respondents). It should be noted that experienced ecotourists had a considerable preference for ranch accommodation (40%). Those who preferred fishing, riding horses, walking and enjoying mountain scenery were likelier to select ranch accommodation than others in the sample. Experienced ecotourists also selected backpacking with a relatively high frequency. Those who selected backpacking preferred tents more than the sample average (79% vs 58%), but they preferred hotel/motel and lodge/inn accommodation less (28% vs 41% and 47% vs 68%).

General consumers and experienced ecotourists also rated select activities and attributes on a 5-point scale, with '1' being most important. Those considered to be

Preferred Activities	Hotel/Motel %	Lodge/Inn %	Cabin/Cottage %	Tent %	Total Number
Hiking	50	14	19	27	528
Touring	64	11	8	8	278
Camping	40	14	22	39	261
Boating	48	14	15	27	234
Walking	65	11	6	7	231
Fishing	51	15	24	21	212
Other scenery	55	19	19	13	184
Swimming	61	3	10	16	164
Local Cultures	68	17	7	12	115
Cycling	57	11	11	15	114
Skiing	60	25	14	15	96
Wildlife Viewing	56	22	16	16	93
Horse Riding	55	16	13	30	84
Mountain scenery	53	15	16	10	61
Total	**56%**	**14%**	**14%**	**17%**	**1368**

(*Source*: HLA Consultants, 1996[6])

Figure 5. Activities and accommodation preferences.

most strongly oriented toward ecotourism were: wilderness setting, mountain climbing, hiking/trekking, and wildlife viewing. The relationships between accommodation and activity/attribute preferences were examined. General consumers who assigned a '1' importance value to the strongest ecotourism activities had a greater preference for accommodation that is likely to be found in remote settings; that is, in the resource where these activities are provided (tent, cabin/cottage).[6] Those who preferred hotels/motels were more likely to give these strong ecotourism activities a '5' (least important) rating. Their preferred activities were more likely to be 'softer' ecotourism activities.

The preference for certain types of accommodation also had a relationship with general consumer demographics (household composition and age).[1] For example: lodge/inns were preferred by the 45–64 age groups; tents by younger ages (ages 18–24, 30% and ages 25–34, 21%, vs 17% overall); and cabins by younger to middle ages (ages 18–44).

Accommodation preference may also be influenced by other factors such as the travel party. For example, consumers (who traveled with children more than ecotourists) made comments such as: 'with buddies, a backpack and tent; with wife, a trailer park; with kids, a motel'. Destination may also have an influence; relevant consumer destination comments include 'in Yosemite, want a cabin; in Hong Kong, want hotel/motel.' Trip purpose may also have an influence. Comments about trip purpose include 'if nature trip, want cabin; if sight-seeing, want hotel.'[1]

Other elements desired in accommodation

There are a number of relevant considerations related to providing ecotourism accommodation.[4,10] These include:

- Accommodation type (is it more rustic, intimate and adventure-type, representative of its setting?)
- Environmental sensitivity (does it demonstrate credibility and sensitivity to its environment, regarding location, building and 'green' or conservation practices?)
- Cultural sensitivity (does it fit in with cultural or local community preferences?)
- Programming (does it feature a package or environmentally-based interpretive experiences?)

Accommodation is part of the infrastructure necessary for the ecotourist to be able to stay overnight in the area. But the add-ons (type, programs, guides, activities, interpretation, sense of place, and environmental sensitivity) will determine whether or not the accommodation is looked upon as just 'another bed in the wilderness', or regarded as an extension of the ecotourism experience, worthy of a recommendation, extended stay, or return visit. Marketing ecotourism accommodation involves selling a destination and an experience, not a stop-over place to stay. The add-on elements enable the operator to promote and encourage extended stays. For example, at Coconut Beach Rainforest Resort in Australia, after introducing a comprehensive list of nature tours and activities, the guest length of stay increased by 30% (Kerr 1992).[11]

There has also been increasing concern that ecotourism properties demonstrate credibility in their concern for environmental conservation, regarding the built facility, site and operations. Some properties demonstrate this;[12,13] others have less genuine concern. Yet even the average tourist share an interest in this. Australia has a guide which is designed for the general traveller. In it, Australian outdoor opportunities and experiences are described: parks, heritage areas, wilderness, outdoor activities, cultural heritage, and so on.[14] In addition, a range of operators and attractions are featured in the guide. What is interesting, however, is the *manner* in which the accommodation operation is described. Each is featured on a matrix, along with whether or not they have a number of elements detailed in the matrix. These are summarised in Figure 6.

Some categories are examined in great detail, and one may wonder if, in fact, the general visiting public is equipped to understand and evaluate the information as presented (e.g. is it environmentally 'better practice' to dispose of solid waste by burying it on the property, composting, burning, or shipping to the mainland). Nevertheless, the matrix *does* present many of the detailed practices at a property, highlighting their environmental protection perspectives. This guide serves to respond to increasing market desire for environmentally responsible travel and accommodation products, to make visitors more aware of environmentally sensitive practices, and to demonstrate that the overall Australian destination, as well as individual properties, is environmentally sensitive.

AUSTRALIA'S NATURAL HOLIDAY GUIDE
Accommodation Information Matrix Elements

ENVIRONMENT
Description of Accommodation
Camping
Wilderness lodge
Resort complex
Hotel
Caravan
Cottage
Farmhouse
Cabins
Motel
Landscaped
Native plants
Exotic plants
Gardens and Lawns
Pesticides
Herbicides
Fertilizers
Wildlife
Do you have a program to encourage native wildlife?
Do you practice elimination of feral animals?
Do you have wildlife?
Do you have a wildlife breeding program?
Do you have plant or wildlife sanctuary areas?
Do you plant bird attracting plants?
Do you have accessible nature areas in excess of 20 hectares within walking distance from the complex?

SEWERAGE TREATMENT
Primary
Secondary
Tertiary

CHEMICALS
Do you use phosphate-based detergent?
Do you offer dry-cleaning?
Do you use chlorine bleaches or cleaners?

WATER CONSERVATION
Program to minimize water use?
Guests to conserve water (e.g. for showering)?
Dual-flush toilets?
Low-flow shower heads?

RECYCLING:
Use of Non-Recycled Products
Polystyrene cups
Paper plates
Plastic plates
Plastic utensils
Recycled paper in promotional materials?
Unbleached paper for domestic use?

SOLID WASTE DISPOSAL SYSTEM
Shipped back to the mainland
Buried on property
Municipal garbage system
Minicipal recycle garbage system
Removed from the site
Burnt
Composting

ENERGY
Solar Power System
Hot water
Lighting
Heating
Heated swimming pool
Electricity
Energy key program

WASTE MINIMIZATION
Sewerage Disposal System
Septic
Composting
Free disposal
Town
Pit
Removed from site
Other

(*Source:* derived from Australian Tourism Commission, 1994[14])

Figure 6. Environmental categories in Australian accommodation.

Whatever the specific type of accommodation markets prefer, there is market interest in environmentally sensitive accommodation, as evidenced by:

- Results of traveller surveys: (87% of US travellers are likely to very likely to patronise travel companies which protect the environment,[15] and over 50% of UK adults said that when arranging holidays or business trips it would be important for them to deal with a company that took into account environmental issues[16])
- Willingness to pay: (US travellers are willing to pay, on average, 8.5% more for environmentally sensitive accommodation;[15] 30% of UK adults are willing to pay extra to ensure environmentally friendly accommodation, for an average of US $13[16])
- Results of ecotourist surveys: (64% of US travellers who are likely to patronize companies which support the environmental are likely to take an ecotourism trip[15]
- Environmental (green) ratings of accommodation[17] (e.g. Denmark, Thailand, Switzerland, Auckland, Toronto)
- Green conference destinations (green meetings handbooks[18] and green conference literature, e.g. Vancouver,[19] Toronto, Auckland, and Finland's Tampere Hall)
- Green events: (books on how to green events,[20] and the Sydney Olympics promoting the greening of the games[21])
- Travel businesses seeking environmentally responsible partners: (e.g. the National Tour Association and American Bus Association[22]).

A recent ecolodge sourcebook has a strong focus on resort accommodation and luxury lodges.[13] Some of the cases provide an appropriate range of examples, from tent campgrounds, to mountain cabins, to seashore lodges, and facilities within existing villages. However, a number of examples are luxury resorts; a nature-based holiday village in the Amazon with pool and conference centre; wilderness resorts; a 50-room ecotourism hotel in the Caribbean run by an international hotel chain lodge which is part of the world's largest hotel franchising system; or a luxury ecotourist retreat in Northern Australia with 5 star resort and bar. The concept of an ecoresort is being equated with the concept of ecotourism increasingly frequently, generally due to their conservation measures: Shundich describes ecotourism as being 'where ecotourists visit ecoresorts'.[23] While the term 'ecoresort' has yet to be more fully defined, it seems to include a range of luxury accommodation, from international hotels in the heart of an African national park, to a hotel, cabana and bungalows in the heart of an ancient Mayan trade route, to a Maldives resort with private gardens, sumptuous views, and large sybaritic bathrooms.[23]

The concern that ecotourism may lead the way to the devastation of natural areas may yet be realised if the trend to building larger, internationally funded and managed facilities in the heart of the resource continues – 'as ecotourism grows, so does the demand for new resorts in faraway, pristine lands'.[23] A partner in Mountain Travel Sobek voices concern that ecotourism might be 'a crass marketing tool used by the travel industry to legitimize the hedonism of wilderness travel'.[24] As he says, 'resort tourists too often see what cannot naturally occur, an idyllic insulated retreat with all the amenities of a Beverly Hills hotel,' whereas 'ecotourists seek out locally owned inns and eateries'. Resorts (or ecoresorts) certainly have a place in the ecotourism accommodation spectrum, but *outside* the resource, where they should act as base camps for ecotourists, rather than be located in the heart of pristine areas. Environmentally sensitive construction and operational technologies, and unobtrusive architecture may otherwise be used as a justification for an inappropriate location.

It is probable that as the 'next wave' of concern, ecotourism accommodation (and other tourism operations) will expand from a sensitivity to environmental aspects to encompass social and cultural aspects. In fact, the more proactive tourist accommodations have been involved with communities already.

Accommodation supply

Desire for alternative accommodation types

Some locations have a good supply of small, fixed roof accommodation. In Britain, the B and B system has been widespread for years. In addition, visitors to national parks enjoy some alternative types of accommodation. These may be camping barns, which provide very simple accommodation in converted buildings, for low cost; or bunkhouse barns, which are more elaborate than camping barns, with separate rooms; or converted country houses. Demand has increased steadily, with demand for bunkhouse barns, for example, increasing 20% over 2 years in the Peak District National Park.[25] Use of these structures may also contribute to the conservation of heritage buildings and regions.

The literature, too, indicates that a range of accommodation is desired and supplied, with considerable emphasis given to smaller scale, rural and adventure-type accommodation, representing the middle range on the spectrum. One piece of market research divided Americans into five psychographic motivational groups. Naturebased travel, including ecotourism, was associated with a group called 'Get Away Active'. Among other traits, the accommodations for this group tend toward the more rustic than the lavish.[5] Similarly, for Indonesia, 'appropriate accommodations for the (nature tourism) sites should be motels, cottages, and other small lodging types, instead of five-star hotels'.[26] This echoes a similar comment for Australia that 'there is usually more truly Australian character in half-star developments than those of 5-stars'.[27] These examples are in the middle range of the spectrum.

While some indicate that South-East US nature-based travellers stay in hotels or motels,[28] others found that there are a range of accommodation preferences from 'condos to campgrounds'.[29] Other studies have found that there was relatively high use of rural and village-level accommodations by nature-oriented tour operations to underdeveloped countries: 40% rural/village; 27% camping; 21% luxury hotels; and 33% other hotels.[30]

In a Caribbean destination which offers a tent/cottage site and also two resort sites, guests' preferences have been monitored for 19 years. Those who had experienced the resorts subsequent to the tent cottages, missed the close-to-nature experience of tent cottages. 'It was quite amazing to me that my customers preferred a $7000 Maho tent cottage to an $80 000 Harmony luxury unit'.[31]

In the US there has been recent interest in a range of ranch accommodation which may not involve luxury ranch resorts or even the ranch house. Ranches in many areas are looking to share lifestyle experiences with visitors as one of many agricultural diversification activities. The intent is to provide visitor satisfaction, while maintaining ranch lifestyles in the face of increasing economic pressures.[32] Some of the new, naturalist-type ranches offer a range of accommodation, from wood-frame tents to log cabins. These may be near or apart from the ranch house, and range from A frame cabins, to hand notched and refurbished hand-built cabins.[33]

An advantage of smaller, more intimate fixed roof accommodation is that it may also reflect, or be more easily built in the vernacular style of the destination (e.g. ranches in the North American Midwest, thatched huts in the tropics, hammocks with shelters in the Amazon, or barns in Great Britain). Tourist developments, especially hotels and motels, are often not distinctive. Many were built to some presupposed international appeal. However, ecotourists come to a destination to experience it, not to see an echo of their own cities.

Accommodation supply: Canadian examples

It has been said that 'very few ecolodges exist in North America as the markets appear to favour independent camping, and/or comfortable recreational lodges'.[34] However, the results of recent market research[1] do not indicate that this is due to market preference: markets actually *demand* a range of accommodation types, and experienced ecotourists, in particular, are expressing a preference for intimate, adventure-type accommodation. If there is considerable demand for such alternative accommodation, the pertinent question may then become: What is the range of accommodation types *supplied* by any destination area? In many cases, the supply is an abundance of the conventional hotels and motels, together with considerable opportunity for camping. The gap in many destinations appears to lie in the middle range of the spectrum, in the area of adventure-type, more rustic, small scale, fixed roof accommodation.

In Canada, the accommodation industry has been surveyed in order to provide industry benchmarks and indicators. All sizes and types of properties were surveyed, in all provinces and territories, including hotels, motels and 'others'.[35] The 'other' category included tourist courts and cabins, guest houses and tourist homes, lodging houses, camping grounds, travel trailer parks, hunting and fishing camps and other recreation and RV camps; most are located in rural areas. These are the types of properties that ecotourists are likely to patronise. Indeed, when customer base was examined (Figure 7), it was found that while hotels and motels are of least importance to foreign and leisure visitors, the other/alternative accommodation appeals to 88% of such travellers. However, collectively this other/alternative accommodation only represents around 12% of the accommodation surveyed.

In Alberta, studies have found a demand for small, fixed roof accommodation, which exceeds actual supply. There is a demand for lakeside and wilderness cabins (both road accessible and inaccessible) which far exceeds supply,[36] and a strong, but unsatisfied demand for small fixed roof accommodation, such as front and back country lodges and cabins, and hut to hut facilities.[37]

In a Canadian survey of *adventure* operators, the most common form of accommodation used was cabins/cottages (41%) followed by tents (40%); and 44% of operators, when asked about the services they provided, indicated very basic utilities

Customer Base	Hotels & Motor Hotels % (1,349)	Motels % (385)			Other* % (231)
		Small	Medium	Large	
Foreign	16	6	10	7	28
Leisure	35	52	55	57	60
Business	38	34	29	28	11
Government	11	8	6	8	1

* Includes cabins, guest houses, camping & travel trailer parks, outfitting camps, & other recreation & vacation camps
(*Source*: CTC[35])

Figure 7. Customer base of Canada's accommodation supply.

(e.g. running water, electricity, showers, or washrooms).[38] It is fortunate that for some areas of Canada, such as the North, accommodation supply is more responsive to demand. However, in other areas, there seems to be greater current emphasis on the *ends* of the spectrum (camping, or high end fixed roof, such as hotels).

The *demand* for accommodation may be known (see Figure 1). However, it is difficult to measure the *supply* of accommodation precisely: the number of properties is one potential measure of supply; the number of beds is another. But while the *exact* numbers of each category of accommodation supplied is not precisely known, the availability of each category is usually known at an order of magnitude level. This can be plotted on a Supply-Demand Matrix. This matrix will vary for different destinations and different markets (Figure 8). In Alberta, there has been a tendency for fixed roof accommodation to be conventional hotels and motels, which are located in urban centres, while only camping is allowed in wilderness and natural areas. In general, there are legislative and other problems with attempting to construct any form of fixed roof accommodation in wildlands areas or crown lands, regardless of whether or not potential environmental issues will be addressed, or alternative and low impact technologies proposed for construction and operation. Alberta has some alternative forms of accommodation, such as cabins, ranches and lodges. However, this supply is limited, and even the newer inns and lodges are tending to be built in urban areas, and many are really redesigned hotels/motels with different names.

Ecotourism accommodation demand will vary, depending on the markets attracted to a destination's range of experience opportunities. It should be noted, however, that the interest of ecotourists is tending to be mainstreamed in more general markets. Thus, destinations would be well advised to examine their supply side for the degree to which they are able to respond to current and future demand.

This is not to suggest that fixed roof accommodation should be allowed in any location simply because demand exists. It is important that the suitability of the location and site for a fixed roof facility should be examined, and the acceptability of such accommodation to the local community should be examined. However, this should be done within the context of the planning, design, construction and operational technologies and techniques which are proposed, and the relationship with the local community. As has been asked 'why is it that camping is acceptable but a low-key lodge is unacceptable?'[39]

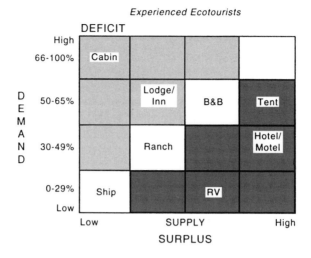

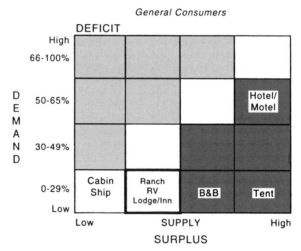

Figure 8. Ecotourist accommodation: demand vs supply.

Relationship of accommodation to ecotourist motivation

Ecotourists seek a range of products, and it is clear that the setting is critical to an ecotourism experience. However, this desire for settings is not unique to ecotourists. Elements which distinguish between ecotourists and other travellers have been determined.[40,41] While mass tourists are more interested in nightlife, attractions, dining, and shopping, those experiences ranked as most important to ecotourists are:

- uncrowded
- remote, wilderness
- learning about wildlife, nature

- learning about natives, cultures
- community benefits
- viewing plants and animals
- physical challenge.

As discussed earlier, it is the *experience* which determines the accommodation, not vice versa. The lodgings chosen are an enabler for tourists to experience a place; they are not the primary motivator. Tourists choose the environment (whether it be natural, cultural or urban) which they want to experience, *then* they choose the accommodation. When the motivations which most differentiate ecotourists from mass tourists (uncrowded, remote/wilderness, learning about nature/culture) are considered, it is clear that the conventional type of large, urban-based property will not provide the experience sought. Such experiences currently may be more easily be found at the more rustic end of the accommodation spectrum. From the discriminant characteristics, one can see that 'on-site' accommodation, in the resource setting, would logically be most attractive to many ecotourists. Accommodation would generally fall on the hard to middle range of the spectrum of accommodation. There will, of course, continue to be a demand for accommodation along the middle to soft end of the spectrum.

There is considerable evidence that there is a shift of interest by travellers interested in nature, adventure and culture. It has been described as a 'mainstreaming' of ecotourists' preferences, and reflects the interest 'pioneered' by ecotourists.[42] The place of accommodation and related amenities and elements relative to this shift is illustrated on Figure 9.

When it is considered that the more general interest ecotourism traveller tends to 'follow' the preferences of experienced ecotourists, it is clear the the *demand* for intimate accommodation is there. However, the supply is not. As has been pointed out, decisions on what type of accommodation to provide should be based on a combination of supply and demand factors related to environmental, social, and economic goals.[4]

Conclusions

It has been shown that a range of accommodation may be appropriate for ecotourism and that demand ranges along this spectrum. However, specific preferences may vary with specific ecotourism markets: general consumers interested in ecotourism as part of their vacation may exhibit a preference which is at the softer end of the spectrum, while experienced ecotourists may prefer the middle or harder end of the spectrum. However, there is a tendency for mainstream tourism markets and perhaps other tourism niche markets, to be shifting their preferences in the direction of ecotourists.

Destination areas and operators need to understand this range of accommodation desired, and to match their accommodation supply to the current and shifting market preferences, taking into account the local community preferences and environmental constraints. For those areas which tend to have a seasonal constraint, fixed roof accommodation, rather than camping, could also enable extension of the season of operation. Resource managers should be aware that there are now a range of

Tourism Component	Traditional Tourism	Current and Future Tourism & Ecotourism Market Trends
Facilities/ Accommodation	• Accommodation as bed • Accommodation provides luxury and pampering • Accommodation on "island" enclave • Upscale design & operation	• Accommodation as part/facilitator of the experience • Accommodation as extension of the conservation ethic • Accommodation integrated with surrounding environment • Environmentally sensitive planning, design & operation
Service	• Functional requirements of the guests	• Total experience of the guests: understanding their activity, Intellectual, spiritual & other needs
Luxury	• Structures to service guests • Mid range to luxury • Fun • Service	• Environments available to guests • Basic budget to mid range • Education, satisfaction, appreciation • Style
Marketing	• Mass markets • Enjoyment • Sell image • Green image (eco image)	• Speciality market niches–nature/adventure/culture/education • Wilderness ethic, environmental stewardship, enlightenment • Describe benefits plus responsibilities • Green reality (eco ethic)
Programming	• On-site activities • Contact during vacation, possible education • Observing & relaxing • Activities specific & specialised, few to no guides	• On-site experiences, plus off-site nature-based activities & experiences • Contact and education: pre, during and post-vacation • Experiencing & being active • Activities and experiences interlinked, often guided
Motivation	• Nightlife, attractions, dining, shopping	• Uncrowded, remote, learning about nature/culture, wildlife viewing & physical challenge
Benefits	• Operator ($) • Customer benefits during vacation	• Resource, community, operator (varied benefits) • Benefits last longer than actual vacation
Measures of Success	• Volume-based • Number of visitors • $$ spent	% of repeat visits and word of mouth • Customer enlightenment & commitment • Community & operator quality of life, cultural renewal & pride • Spreading out visitation period • Positive economic impact & viable business • Resource conservation

(*Source:* derived from Wight[10,42])

Figure 9. Shift from traditional tourism.

alternative technologies and practices which may enable smaller scale environmentally sensitive accommodation to be built in areas previously limited to camping. They should also be aware that market preferences are moving in this direction. Conversely, it may be that the most luxurious accommodation, which often tend to reflect a consumptive, rather than conservation-oriented lifestyle, may be inappropriate, when located within the resource. Operators should be aware that it is not the accommodation, itself, which is the attraction, but the overall experience. It is that experience which will determine the accommodation selected.

References

1. HLA Consultants and the ARA Consulting Group, *Ecotourism – Nature/Adventure/Culture: Alberta and British Columbia Market Demand Assessment*. Canadian Heritage, Industry Canada, British

Columbia Ministry of Small Business, Tourism and Culture, Alberta Economic Development and Tourism, and the Outdoor Recreation Council of British Columbia, 1994.

2. HLA Consultants, *Tour Operator Market for Alberta Ecotourism Experiences*. Alberta Economic Development and Tourism, Edmonton, Alberta, 1994.

3. ARA Consulting Group, Eureka Tourism and Hospitality Management Consultants, and the Tourism Research Group, *Yukon Wilderness Adventure Travel Market Awareness Study*. Yukon Department of Tourism, Whitehorse, Yukon, 1991.

4. Wight, P. A., Sustainable ecotourism: balancing economic, environmental and social goals within an ethical framework. *Journal of Tourism Studies* 1993, **4** (2), 54–66.

5. Reingold, L., Identifying the elusive ecotourist. In *Going Green*, a supplement to *Tour and Travel News*, 1993. (October 25), 36–39.

6. HLA Consultants, *Ecotourism Accommodation: an Alberta Profile*. Alberta Economic Development and Tourism, Edmonton, Alberta, 1996.

7. Andersen, D. L., A window to the natural world: the design of ecotourism facilities. In *Ecotourism: A Guide for Planners and Managers*, eds K. Lindberg and D. E. Hawkins. Ecotourism Society, North Bennington, Vermont, 1993, pp. 116–133.

8. Campbell Goodell Consultants, *United States Market Match Survey – Outdoor Adventure Vacations*. BC Ministry of Development, Trade and Tourism and Industry Science and Technology Canada, Victoria, 1991.

9. Sorensen, L,. The special-interest travel market. *The Cornell H.R.A. Quarterly*, 1993, June, 24–30.

10. Wight, P. A., Ecotourist preferences: what markets want from their nature and culture-based vacations. Keynote address to *Opportunities in Ecotourism Conference* hosted by the Forest Diversity/Community Survival Project, the Ottawa Valley Tourist Association, and the Ontario Parks Association, Renfrew, Ontario, April 26, 1996.

11. Kerr, J., Making dollars and sense out of ecotourism/nature tourism. In *Ecotourism: Incorporating the Global Classroom 1991 Conference Papers*, ed. B. Weiler. University of Queensland, Bureau of Tourism Research, Canberra, Australia, 1992, pp. 248–252.

12. Development Services Branch, *Environmentally Sensitive Facilities: Remote Tourism Case Studies*. Alberta Economic Development and Tourism, Edmonton, Alberta, 1994.

13. Hawkins, D. E., Epler Wood, M. and Bittman, S., *The Ecolodge Sourcebook*. The Ecotourism Society, North Bennington, Vermont, 1995.

14. Australian Tourist Commission, *The Natural Holiday Guide*. Sydney, Australia, 1994.

15. Cook, S. D., Stewart, E. and Repass K., US Travel Data Center *Discover America: Tourism and the Environment*. Travel Industry Association of America, Washington, DC, 1992.

16. Mori and Green Globe, New bulletin updates international environmental initiatives. *Green Hotelier*, 1996, **1** (3), 29.

17. Wight, P. A., Greening tourism operations and blackening the bottom line. Presentation to the *Opportunities in Ecotourism Conference* hosted by the Forest Diversity/Community Survival Project, the Ottawa Valley Tourist Association, and the Ontario Parks Association, Renfrew, Ontario, April 26, 1996.

18. Sims, S., *How to Plan Meetings that Don't Cost the Earth: An Environmental Handbook for Meeting, Incentive and Convention Professionals*. Eco Logic, Hawaii, 1993.

19. Greater Vancouver Regional District, *Green Conference Planning Guide*, Burnaby, BC, 1994.

20. Chernushenko, D., *Greening Our Games: Running Sports Events And Facilities That Won't Cost The Earth*. Centurion Publishing, Ottawa, 1994.

21. Sydney Organising Committee for the Olympic Games, *Environmental Guidelines and Greening Up for the Games*. Sydney, 1995.

22. National Tour Association and American Bus Association, *Group Travel and the Environment: Users Kit*, 1995.

23. Shundich, S., Ecoresorts: dollars, sense and the environment. *Hotels* 1996, **30** (3), 34–40.

24. Bangs, R., Clean, green and meant to be seen: the ethos of eco-tourism. In *Proceedings of the 1993 World Congress on Adventure Travel and Eco-Tourism Manaus, Brazil*. The Adventure Travel Society Inc., Englewood, Colorado, September 20–23, 1993, pp. 97–101.

25. Denman, R. (ed), *Tourism In National Parks: A Guide To Good Practice*. Countryside Commission, Countryside Council for Wales, English Tourist Board, Rural Development Commission and Wales Tourist Board, Glasgow and Associates.

26. Nababan, A. and Aliadi, A., 'Nature tourism profile: Indonesia'. In *Nature Tourism and Asia: Opportunities and Constraints for Conservation and Economic Development*, eds J. Nenon and P. B. Durst. USDA, Forest Service, USAID, USDA, Office of International Cooperation and Development, Washington, DC, 1993, pp. 43–54.

27. Amdal, D., Marketing by adding value. In *Ecotourism: Incorporating the Global Classroom 1991 Conference Papers*, ed. B. Weiler. University of Queensland, Bureau of Tourism Research, Canberra, Australia, 1992, pp. 253–254.

28. Backman, K. F. and Potts, T. D., *Profiling Nature-Based Travelers: Southeastern Market Segments*. Strom Thurmond Institute, South Carolina, 1993.

29. Silverberg, K. E., Backman, S. J. and Backman, K. F., A preliminary investigation into the psychographics of nature-based travelers to the southeastern United States. In *Proceedings of the 25th Anniversary Conference*, Travel and Tourism Research Association, Bal Harbour, Florida June 18–22, 1994, pp. 36–40.

30. Ingram, C. D. and Durst, P. B., Nature-oriented tour operators: travel to developing countries. *Journal of Travel Research* 1989, **28** (2), 11–15.

31. Selengut, A., 1995 'Foreword'. In *The Ecolodge Source Book*, ed. D. Hawkins, M. Epler Wood and S. Bittman. The Ecotourism Society, North Bennington, Vermont, 1993, v, vi.

32. Wight, P. A., Ranch ecotourism: principles, issues and options. Paper prepared for the *5th Stockmen's Range Management Course*, Maycroft, Alberta June 12–14, 1996.

33. Kramer, J., 'Dude ranches . . . with a difference'. *Snow Country*, 1996, Summer, 36–39.

34. ARA Consulting Group, *Ecolodge Survey*. A Supporting Technical Paper for the Government of Trinidad and Tobago Tourism Master Plan, 1994.

35. Canadian Tourism Commission, *A Window on Canada's Accommodation Industry* Ottawa, February, 1996.

36. Nichols Applied Management, *Cabin Development Potential in Alberta*. Alberta Tourism, Edmonton, Alberta, 1991.

37. Ernst and Young, *Kananaskis Country Small, Fixed Roofed Accommodation Study*. Prepared for Alberta Economic Development and Tourism, Edmonton, 1995.

38. Tourism Canada, *Adventure Travel in Canada: An Overview of Product, Market and Business Potential*. Industry Canada, Ottawa, 1995.

39. Hackett, M., Solving the ecotourism dilemma. In *Ecotourism: Incorporating the Global Classroom 1991 Conference Papers*, ed. B. Weiler. University of Queensland, Bureau of Tourism Research, Canberra, Australia, 1992, pp. 208–211.

40. Crossley, J. and Lee, B., Ecotourists and mass tourists: a difference in 'benefits sought'. In *Proceedings of the 25th Anniversary Conference*, Travel and Tourism Research Association, Bal Harbour, Florida June 18–22, 1994, pp. 22–29.

41. Wight, P. A., Tapping into market potential for ecotourism. Keynote address to workshop *Ecotourism in Ontario – New Business Opportunities*, Sir Sandford Fleming College, Haliburton Campus, Ecotourism Management Program, 24–25 November, 1995.

42. Wight, P. A., Planning for success in sustainable tourism. Paper presented to *Plan for Success*, Canadian Institute of Planners National Conference, Saskatoon, Saskatchewan, June 2–5, 1996.

Part VIII

Marketing and service quality – wider perspectives

Introduction by Chris Ryan

Tourism as a 'service' product

It is a truism to state that, within the marketing literature, tourism is regarded as a service. It thus possesses the attributes of being intangible, non-storable, hetero-geneous in consumer–supplier interactions, and where client satisfaction is heavily dependent upon the nature of those interactions with the supplier's representative. However, within this conventional model of what constitutes a 'service', it is immediately obvious that tourism possesses some specific differences. Ryan (1999) concludes that, unlike many service encounters described in the retail services literature, the holiday has:

- important emotional involvement for the tourist;
- a strong motivation for successful and satisfactory outcomes on the part of the client;
- a significantly long period of interaction between the tourist on the one hand and, on the other, the place and people in the holiday destination – a period wherein the tourist can manipulate his or her surroundings to achieve the desired outcomes;
- manipulative processes that are themselves part of the holiday experience and a source of satisfaction and need not require confrontation that may not be acceptable to some;
- a number of holiday services, so that the tourist can select among alternatives – also while a distribution chain may be said to exist between these services, in terms of satisfaction creation, the direction of the chain may not be causal;
- has a structure whereby the tourist can play several different roles – each role may have separate determinants of satisfaction and each role may have unequal con-tributions to total holiday satisfaction;

- a temporal significance not found in many service situations – it resides in the memory as a preparation for the future and is a resource for ego-sustainment during non-holiday periods.

For these reasons he argues that the tourist 'product' differs significantly from those normally considered in the services marketing literature. A further reason has also commonly been pointed out, and that is the issue of who is the customer? Generally, a customer is one who pays for a product and consumes it. As a 'product' though, tourism is often 'paid for' by residents in a location through taxes and tax incentives (i.e. income forgone), and in addition they 'consume' the impacts of tourism through the benefits of jobs, business opportunities, added costs of water and sewage treatment, infrastructure support and crowding that might occur. In short, if not a 'consumer' in the conventional sense, residents are important stakeholders who must also be satisfied by the process of tourism. Hence, the marketing of tourism is thought to involve not only the creation of satisfaction for clients and businesses but also has to recognise the need to satisfy other stakeholders (for discussion of this see, for example, Haywood, 1990; Ryan, 1991; Wheeller, 1991; Allen et al., 1988; Getz and Jamal, 1994; Gill and Williams, 1993; Jamal and Getz, 1995; Ritchie, 1993; Robson and Robson, 1996).

Discussions of tourism as a service and its marketing might therefore be said to fall into two broad categories. First, there are those that draw upon the services marketing literature based upon, for example, the gaps analysis models associated with authors like Parasuraman et al. (1994) and the much cited SERVQUAL model. Examples of this would include Ryan and Cliff (1996, 1997), who applied the conventional SERVQUAL scale to travel agencies, or the work of Tribe and Snaith (1998), who adapted the concept to develop their own specific scale, HOLSAT, to measure tourist satisfaction in Varadero, Cuba. These studies are characterised as psychometric in approach, and may include technical discussions of measurement issues and scale construction. The second type of discussion may be more general, may or may not be empirical, but draws upon a wider range of contexts. Additionally, it will tend to see marketing within a strategic sense of developing forms of tourism that generate, where possible, optimal solutions for as many stakeholders as is possible. One such example of this approach is that of Bramwell (1998). He discusses place-marketing, images of places and what attributes constitute the urban location (in this case, Sheffield in the UK) as a locus of touristic and recreational activities available for both visitors and residents. Both types of discussion can be commented upon.

Technical measurement and interactive relationships in service quality

Fisk et al. (1993) identify three stages in the literature of services marketing. Prior to 1980 the debate was primarily about the way in which services marketing required an approach which differed from that of product marketing, which had hitherto been dominated by the fast-moving consumer goods sector. They argue that from about 1980 to 1985, the debate turned to issues of service quality and critical encounters which, in turn, gave birth to models like that of SERVQUAL and its various gaps. Foremost among these gaps was the consumer confirmation/disconfirmation paradigm created by a difference between expected and perceived service. Contemporary concerns have sought to distinguish more clearly between service quality, customer satisfaction and the nature of the relationship between the two and the measurement of that relationship. Much of this latter debate was initiated by the inability of some researchers to duplicate the five dimensions of 'tangibility', 'reliability', 'responsiveness', 'empathy' and 'reassurance' that Parasuraman et al. had structured into their SERVQUAL instrument. Additionally, it was commented that much of the variance in consumer gaps was 'explained' by the perceptions rather than the expectations scale, thereby rendering the need for a gap as being surplus to requirements. Also, over time, the concept of 'consumer gaps' between expectations and perceptions was replaced by a concept of 'zones of tolerance' (for example, see Carman, 1990; Bakabus and Boller, 1992; Brown et al., 1992; Peterson and Wilson, 1992; Mansfeld, 1995; Danaher and Haddrell, 1996; Ryan and Cliff, 1997; Suh et al., 1997). Parasuraman et al. (1994) were sensitive to these and similar comments and developed a new version of their SERVQUAL instrument that sought to incorporate zones of tolerance and respond to criticisms by, for example, introducing a nine-point scale to permit more discrimination among responses. Generally speaking, the tourism literature has been conversant with these debates, but to the mind of this author, it has only just begun to catch up with the interactive modelling that has characterised market research in the final years before the millennium. Essentially, this new approach has questioned the assumption of a linear relationship between expectation, perception, quality and satisfaction, and has argued that the gap between perception and expectation should be seen not simply as an outcome but as a contributory factor to expectations and perceptions. Hence, mathematically, the relationship becomes one of higher orders and is reiterative in process.

It is thus argued that tourist satisfaction is not simply an outcome but an input variable into decisions to repurchase an activity, revisit a destination or repeat a specific type of holiday. So consumers make a purchase decision based upon expected quality, perceived quality, the perceived quality as against criteria of that which is thought to be ideal or tolerable, and past satisfaction with the service. From this perspective the gap between expectation and perception is not only an outcome which is a *measure* of service quality, but is itself a *determinant* of future purchase decisions. Equally, satisfaction is not solely determined by the recent experience of purchase, but an appraisal of that satisfaction within an assessment of past satisfactions. A linear representation of a service satisfaction model might be said to be

$$\text{Purchase} = a + b \text{ Expected Quality} + c \text{ Perceived Quality} + d \text{ Gap} + e \text{ Satisfaction Intention}$$

where a = intercept term and b, c, d and e are coefficients to be empirically determined.

However, if customer satisfaction and service attributes are determinants of both service quality and customer behaviour; the relationship can be rewritten as

$$\text{Purchase} + b \text{ Perceived Quality} = a + c \text{ Expected Quality} + d \text{ Gap} + e \text{ Satisfaction Intention}$$

Statistically, this formulation presents problems of interdependence of variables, i.e. multicollinearity (e.g. see Sincich, 1992). It has also been noted that the relationships of expectation, perception and resultant satisfaction are not necessarily linear; that is, any model may be of the form

$$Y = a + b_1X + b_2X^2 + e$$

Such a model refers to a single curvilinear independent variable and hence is insufficient on the premise that it lacks additional variables, and more importantly ignores the reiterative nature of the argument. To overcome these objections Aiken and West (1991) suggested that marketers should consider the use of hierarchical multiple regressions analysis (HMRA) using unstandardised regression coefficients. They noted that it is the *shape* rather than just the *slope* of the curve that is important and that, 'The simple slope of the regression of Y on X is the first (partial) derivative of the overall regression equation with respect to the variable X' (Aiken and West, 1991: 75). This means that the slope of the derived regression equation at alternative levels of a moderating independent variable (e.g. satisfaction) can be determined on the basis of the first derivative of the obtained regression equations. Taylor (1997) used this approach when questioning 937 respondents as to their purchase intentions, level of satisfaction, perception of quality, and disconfirmation measures by comparing products to expectations and competitors. He found clear evidence of higher-order and interactive effects. Thus 'the slope of the quality/satisfaction iteration appears to consistently decrease as satisfaction judgements increase' (Taylor, 1997: 149). Following Taylor (1997), the purchase intention towards a given holiday can be derived whereby the relationship between quality and intention, and between satisfaction and intention are both of a higher order and are fully interactive. Such a quadratic relationship would take the form:

$$Y = a + b_1X + b_2Z + b_3X^2 + b_4Z^2 + b_5XZ + b_6XZ^2 + b_7X^2Z + \cdots + b_nX^2Z^2 + e$$

where Y = purchase intention, X = quality perception, Z = satisfaction judgement, a = intercept and $b_1 \ldots b_n$ are coefficients to be established empirically. The confirmation/disconfirmation paradigm is included by the satisfaction judgement being assessed by questions such as, 'I would generally characterise this holiday as being . . . than expected' with the value being selected from a Likert-type scale.

However, a debate exists as to whether such global as against transaction-specific forms of quality perceptions and satisfaction judgements is valid. It may be that $X = \Sigma x_1, x_2, x_3 \ldots x_n$ and likewise with Z. Iacobucci et al. (1994) argued that consumers do not make this type of distinction when assessing a consumer experience, while Ryan and Glendon (1998) report that tourists had little difficulty in undertaking a global assessment of their holiday experience when assessing levels of satisfaction. They note that

The relationship between motivation, performance and resultant satisfaction invites consideration of a number of variables. From a psycho-sociological perspective, following concepts of involvement (Laurent and Kapferer, 1985; Dimanche, Havitz and Howard, 1991), the perceived importance of an activity in terms of self-development, self-enhancement, ego, role fulfilment, and responding to perceived requirements of significant others, can be argued to be important variables determining motivation, behaviour and derived satisfaction. (Ryan and Glendon, 1998: 170–1).

Service quality with reference to holidaying becomes not a simple matter of expectation/evaluation but also of the nature and degree of involvement and issues of status, ego enhancement and the presence or absence of significant others. Unless this is explicitly incorporated into the research design, as is done by Suh et al. (1997), a simple confirmation/disconfirmation model does not take these considerations into account. The nature of the issue may be shown by briefly assessing a not uncommon holiday experience and that is the search for sex. Any analysis of sex and tourism, and the satisfaction derived from 'holiday sex' needs to take into account a myriad of issues including sexual need, satisfaction, ego enhancement, self-identity, sexual identity, self-exploration, exploitation, the marginal and liminal natures of commercial sex and those who provide those services, issues of responsibility over sexually transmitted diseases, assessment of guilt – in short, a whole series of emotions and social issues. Obviously, gap models are not designed to tackle these sorts of issues. Additionally, gap models have traditionally been orientated towards the satisfaction of the individual holidaymaker, whereas the wider view of service quality and marketing has been to place the tourist–supplier relationship within a wider context of place and the other stakeholders in that place.

Service quality, marketing and stakeholder interests

If the literature derived from services marketing has become more technical in terms of specific measurement, the wider literature of what Ryan (1991) termed the symbiotic relationship between tourism and marketing, and more explicitly, societal marketing, has increasingly been better informed by conceptual considerations. Notable here has been the contributions by Ap (1992) who utilised exchange theory to analyse the nature of hosts' responses to tourism, although it should be noted that he was not explicitly concerned with societal marketing. Similarly, Lindberg and Johnson (1997) utilised structural equation modelling to develop a model of determinants of resident attitudes towards tourism impacts which highlighted issues within product design that affect residents' consumption of tourism and the levels of satisfaction they derive from it. They note the importance of traffic congestion, and also how the theories of cognitive consistency and social judgement might help to explain resident perceptions.

From a microanalytical viewpoint it might be said that residents' intention to reside in a tourist location could be defined in a manner similar to that of tourists' intention to visit, i.e.

$$R = a + b_1Q + b_2S + b_3Q^2 + b_4S^2 + b_5QS + b_6QS^2 + b_7Q^2S + \cdots + b_nQ^2S^2 + e$$

where R = residence intention, Q = quality perception, S = satisfaction judgement, a = intercept and $b_1 \ldots b_n$ are coefficients to be established empirically. The societal marketing issue becomes one of seeking to maximise Y and R. The constraints under which maximisation can occur would relate to existing structures of place for which the objective measures might be traffic flow figures, police records, sales revenues, water quality and other environmental indices and employment records.

If this debate seems removed from the normally considered concerns of marketing then the response would be that marketing is about not only promotion and pricing but also product design. In tourism, the product is an experience of place, and the interactions between tourist, place and the other actors in that place, i.e. businesses, residents and other tourists. Marketing thus becomes an inherent component of planning, as is discussed with reference to urban issues by Page elsewhere in this book.

Various viewpoints

The articles selected from past issues of *Tourism Management* all reflect facets of this discussion. The articles are

> Haywood, K.M. (1990). Revising and implementing the marketing concept as it applies to tourism, *Tourism Management*, September, 11(3): 195–205.
>
> Witt, C.A. and Muhlemann, A.P. (1994). The implementation of total quality management in tourism: some guidelines, *Tourism Management*, December, 15(6): 416–24.
>
> Otto, J.E. and Ritchie, J.R.B. (1996). The service experience in tourism, *Tourism Management*, May, 17(3): 165–74.

Haywood's paper commences with Krippendorf's (1987: 138) call that 'all suppliers of tourist services acknowledge their responsibility towards travellers, the host population and the tourist environment', and to do so in terms of concrete policy statements and in the enacting of those plans. Haywood characterises marketing as being conventionally customer and profit focussed with the business organisation structured to achieve its ends of greater profit. It is noted that tourism allocates little of its resources to research, and what little it does rarely builds on corporate and community strengths. For Haywood, marketing activities that engage in the development of an 'organisational/community capability' provide the way forward as it is in this manner that value is constantly added to the product whereby the needs of both visitor and resident are met. His paper represents a common theme in the literature of the 1990s: namely, that sensible marketing is orientated towards longer-term horizons and issues of sustainability. Yet, he admits, while it is easy to make such clarion calls, the problem is how to enact them in practice.

In the May 1996 issue of *Tourism Management* the articles by Otto and Ritchie (1996) and Oppermann (1996) represented two pieces of empirical research that reported attempts to achieve these ends. The former paper, replicated here, argued that while the terms 'visitor satisfaction' and 'service quality' are often used, no practical measures can take place until specific criteria are identified. Management needs measurable performance indicators that are 'real' in the sense that they measure those things that are important. Otto and Ritchie argued that service quality in tourism services revolves around the satisfaction of four dimensions – 'hedonics', 'peace of mind', 'involvement' and 'recognition'. To that end they constructed a scale and applied it to samples using hotels, airlines and tours and attractions. From this research they argued that 'service experience factors are not 'soft', elusive abstracts, but rather are specific dimensions that can readily be measured to better understand satisfaction' (Otto and Ritchie, 1996: 172). They noted the importance of various marketing messages – for example, that for airlines a primary need is to reassure clients that they are 'safe'. For his part, Oppermann concentrated on the fast-growing convention market and used not gap analysis but the related importance-evaluation approach. He illustrated this with specific reference to the destinations of San Diego, Honolulu and Quebec City, showing how each city has a different profile.

The final article is that of Witt and Muhlemann (1994), which was selected as carrying the debate about issues of quality in tourism into the wider literature about total quality management. They too discuss the ways in which tourism differs from other products but seek to specify issues that management should seek to define in three key areas. These are

1 elements of the product/service package;
2 human aspects of the delivery service; and
3 measurement issues in service quality.

As such, their paper establishes a management context which shows how service quality is not simply a marketing issue, but a strategic one which requires co-ordination between product design, personnel selection, training and empowerment, and the clarification of performance indicators. Read together the three papers illustrate how service quality infiltrates strategic thinking, product design and delivery, satisfaction measurement, and the need to think holistically as well as at the concrete level. The papers reinforce how tourism experiences may be the outcome of a complex process of interaction between tourist and place, and where both these latter variables are not immune to management planning.

References

Aiken, L.S. and West, S.G. (1991). *Multiple Regression: Testing and Interpreting Interaction Effects.* Newbury Park, CA: Sage.

Allen, R.L., Long, P.T., Perdue, R.R. and Kieselbach, S. (1988). The impact of tourism development on residents' perceptions of community life, *Journal of Travel Research*, Summer, 16–21.

Ap, J. (1992). Residents' perceptions of tourism impact, *Annals of Tourism Research*, 19(4): 665–90.

Bakabus, E. and Boller, G.W. (1992). An empirical assessment of the SERVQUAL scale, *Journal of Business Research*, 24: 253–68.

Bramwell, B. (1998). User satisfaction and product development in urban tourism, *Tourism Management*, 19(1): 35–48.

Brown, T.J., Churchill Jr, G.A. and Peter, J.P. (1992). Improving the measurement of service quality, *Journal of Retailing*, Spring, 69(1): 127–39.

Carman, J.M. (1990). Consumer perceptions of service quality: an assessment of the SERVQUAL dimensions, *Journal of Retailing*, 66: 33–55.

Danaher, P.J. and Hadrell, V. (1996). Spring, A comparison of question scales used for measuring customer satisfaction, *International Journal of Service Industry Management*, 7(4): 4–26.

Fisk, R.P., Brown, S.W. and Bitner, M.J. (1993). Tracking the evolution of the services marketing literature, *Journal of Retailing*, 69(1): 61–103.

Getz, D. and Jamal, T.B. (1994). The environment–community symbiosis: A case for collaborative tourism planning, *Journal of Sustainable Tourism*, 2(3): 152–73.

Gill, A. and Williams, P. (1993). Tourism growth management in mountain communities. Paper presented at the 24th Annual TTRA International Conference, Whistler, BC, Canada, 14 June 1993.

Haywood, K.M. (1990). Revising and implementing the market concept as it applies to tourism, *Tourism Management*, 11(3): 195–205.

Iacobucci, D., Grayson K.A. and Ostrom, A. (1994). The calculus of service quality and customer satisfaction: theoretical and empirical differentiation and integration, in T.A. Swartz, D.E. Bowenand, S.W. Brown (eds), *Advances in Services Marketing and Management*, vol. 3. Greenwich, CT: JAI Press. pp. 1–67.

Jamal, T.B. and Getz, D. (1995). Collaboration theory and community tourism planning, *Annals of Tourism Research*, 22(1): 186–204.

Krippendorf, J. (1987). *The Holiday Makers*. Oxford: Heinemann.

Lindberg, K. and Johnson, R.L. (1997). Modelling resident attitudes towards tourism, *Annals of Tourism Research*, 24(2): 402–24.

Mansfeld, Y. (1995). The 'value stretch' model and its implementation in detecting tourists' class-differentiated destination choice, *Journal of Travel and Tourism Marketing*, 4(3): 71–92.

Oppermann, M. (1996). Convention destination images: analysis of association meeting planners' perceptions, *Tourism Management*, May, 17(3): 175–82.

Otto, J.E. and Ritchie, J.R.B. (1996). The service experience in tourism, *Tourism Management*, 17(3): 165–74.

Parasuraman, A., Zeithaml, V.A. and Berry, L.L. (1994). Alternative scales for measuring service quality: a comparative assessment based on psychometric and diagnostic criteria, *Journal of Retailing*, 70(3): 201–30.

Peterson, R.A. and Wilson, W.R. (1992). Measuring customer satisfaction: fact or artifact, *Journal of the Academy of Marketing Science*, 20(1): 61–71.

Ritchie, J.R.B. (1993). Crafting a destination vision: putting the concept of resident-responsive tourism into practice, *Tourism Management*, 14(5): 379–89.

Robson, J. and Robson, I. (1996). From shareholders to stakeholders: critical issues for tourism marketers, *Tourism Management*, 17(7): 533–40.

Ryan, C. (1991). Tourism and marketing – a symbiotic relationship, *Tourism Management*, 12(2): 101–11.

Ryan, C. (1999). From the psychometrics of SERVQUAL to sex—measurements of tourist satisfaction, in A. Pizam and Y. Mansfeld (eds), *Consumer Behavior in Travel and Tourism*. Binghamtom, NY: Haworth Press, pp. 267–86.

Ryan, C. and Cliff, A. (1996). Users and non-users on the expectation items of the ServQual Scale, *Annals of Tourism Research*, 23(4): 931–4.

Ryan, C. and Cliff, A. (1997). Do travel agencies measure up to customer expectation? An empirical investigation of travel agencies' service quality as measured by SERVQUAL, *Journal of Travel and Tourism Marketing*, 6(2): 1–32.

Ryan, C. and Glendon, I. (1998). Application of leisure motivation scale to tourism, *Annals of Tourism Research*, 25(1): 169–84.

Sincich, T. (1992). *Business Statistics by Example*. New York: Macmillan.

Suh, S.H., Lee, Y.-H., Park, Y. and Shin, G.C. (1997). The impact of consumer involvement on the consumers' perception of service quality – focusing on the Korean hotel industry, *Journal of Travel and Tourism Marketing*, 6(2): 33–52.

Taylor, S.A. (1997). Assessing regression-based importance weights for quality perceptions and satisfaction judgements in the presence of higher order and/or interaction effects, *Journal of Retailing*, 73(1): 135–59.

Tribe, J. and Snaith, T. (1998). From SERVQUAL to HOLSAT: holiday satisfaction in Varadero, Cuba, *Tourism Management*, 19(1): 25–34.

Wheeller, B. (1991). Tourism's troubled times: responsible tourism is not the answer, *Tourism Management*, 12(2): 91–6.

Witt, C.A. and Muhlemann, A.P. (1994). The implementation of total quality management in tourism: some guidelines, *Tourism Management*, 15(6): 416–24.

24

Revising and implementing the marketing concept as it applies to tourism

K Michael Haywood

*Associate Professor, School of Hotel and Food Administration,
University of Guelph, Guelph, Ontario, Canada N1G 2W1*

'I want to call on all suppliers of tourist services to acknowledge their responsibility towards travellers, the host population and the tourist environment, to state clearly what contribution they are prepared to make to a more human tourism and what regulations they are willing to observe. I propose that they should formulate and make public a code of practice and the principles of their internal and external business conduct. Not in a few beautifully worded and vague sentences but in concrete and practicable policy statements, to which they would be answerable.'[1]

In the context of needed development in tourism marketing, it is vital that we examine the premises and presumptions that underlie marketing activity. This examination is necessary because many marketers are neglecting issues central to the outcome of touristic activities, namely satisfaction and harmonious relationships. For example, we constantly hear about tourists who complain about being duped, misinformed, or mistreated by travel, transport and hospitality firms as well as by individuals in tourist-receiving regions.[2] Then there is the intensifying social and environmental backlash being voiced about the more negative impacts of tourism development and tourist activity in and on tourism regions.[3] Despite the numerous benefits provided by tourism there is sufficient empirical evidence to suggest that there have been major failures to deliver value to customers and to communities. From philosophical as well as operational perspectives these failures are problematic. They suggest that tourism organizations and the destinations themselves are failing to meet their obligations.

Since the marketing concept represents the foundation of the theory of tourism marketing and the base on which organizational strategy and structure is based, perhaps it is the marketing concept itself which is at fault. In exploring this issue it is worth emphasizing that no differentiation is made between different types of tourism activity or the location of tourism activity. However, it is recognized that debate with regard to the appropriateness of the marketing concept is most relevant in those communities in which tourism dominates or is becoming a major economic force. As such, this paper will be divided into four sections:

- an explanation of the marketing concept;
- an identification of issues revolving around the implementation of the marketing concept;
- a clarification of the marketing concept as it applies to tourism; and
- prescriptions to facilitate the implementation of revised marketing concept.

Marketing concept

Since the 1950s the prevailing philosophy of business, as stated in word, though not always in deed, has revolved around the preeminence of the customer. Peter Drucker put it best when he said:

There is only one valid definition of business purpose: to create a satisfied customer. It is the customer who determines what the business is.[4]

With the unfolding of the marketing revolution, the doctrine of consumer sovereignty became an accepted philosophy of business. It was John McKitterick of General Electric who made the doctrine legitimate, put it into a marketing framework, called it the marketing concept, and suggested it as a guide to corporate strategy.

So the principal task of the marketing function in a management concept is not so much to be skillful in making the customer do what suits the interests of the business as to be skillful in conceiving and then making the business do what suits the interests of the customer.[5]

By emphasizing that marketing should become a general management responsibility, McKitterick and subsequent proponents of the marketing concept identified three normative prescriptions:

- develop a customer orientation;
- integrate this orientation into all functional areas of the firm; and
- use the customer orientation as a means of earning profits.

Prevailing marketing concept

(1) *Customer orientation.* Management thought and action should have an external focus rather than merely an internal focus. Production and sales orientations are poor guides to management action because neither are focused on the needs of the marketplace. Instead management should develop a customer orientation. This means that management action should be based on a thorough knowledge of customers, their needs, wants, expectations and behaviour patterns. The implication is that products and services should be designed, developed and sold in such a way that consumer problems will be solved, and their needs satisfied.

(2) *Integrated effort.* It has been recognized that successful development of a customer orientation could not be accomplished without company-wide acceptance and

support. In other words, people in all functional areas of a firm have to be committed to a customer orientation. This requires a willingness to work cooperatively so that all obstacles in the way of achieving a customer orientation can be removed.

(3) *Profitability focus.* While a customer orientation has the appeal of being altruistic, this objective is rarely manifest. Organizations exist to achieve their own purposes. A customer orientation is pursued, therefore, because it provides greater opportunity to achieve an enviable long-term competitive position. Through the application of appropriate marketing techniques, management expects that a customer focus will result in greater profits.

Issues in implementing the marketing concept

Tourism organizations and industry trade associations have come to accept the intuitive logic of the marketing concept. Indeed many of them pay homage to a customer orientation in their mission statements as well as their advertisements. Even the 1980 Manila Declaration of the World Tourism Organization with its reference to 'total fulfillment of the human being' is sympathetic to the marketing concept.

For numerous reasons, however, many organizations have encountered considerable difficulties in putting the marketing concept into operation.[6] As a result it has been suggested that an attempt be made to distinguish between the concept's philosophy and its implementation.[7] In this section, therefore, we examine reasons why implementation of the marketing concept is complex and fraught with difficulty.

Characteristics of tourism services. Tourism businesses and organizations are providers of services, but the generic attributes of services pose vexing problems for managers. For example, the core offerings of tourism companies are performances not objects. Performances require interaction between tourists and service providers, and, as such, are difficult to standardize and control. Courtesy, competence and responsiveness, for example, reflect the behaviour of personnel who may or may not be properly trained, motivated, or committed to the task of serving others. Therefore, there is potential for high variability in the performance of services. Because tourists participate in the service performance they too can affect the transaction. Therefore, tourist input and actions must be managed and monitored. Obviously quality control is difficult because it is hard to know if the service is being delivered in a manner consistent with what was originally planned and promoted.

Certain aspects of quality control can be achieved through the process of standardization. Despite the intangibility of services, attempts to standardize are possible.[8] But some critics argue that this process of 'industrializing services' across the globe has resulted in a homogenization of culture designed to obliterate any distinctive features of place or community. As a consequence, standardization has not always been successful and may indeed backfire. Many tourists are looking for customization and personalization of service.[9] Indeed much of the satisfaction derived from foreign travel and unique tourist experiences is based not on standardization but on complexity, novelty and diversity.

Another characteristic of services is an inability to adapt. Tourist facilities such as hotels, airlines and restaurants have a non-fluctuating number of spaces available. More spaces cannot suddenly be created during peak times. During slow times the spaces are still there and often empty. This puts tremendous pressure on the selling function. As such, a lot of time and effort is put into matching supply and demand.[10] Production and sales orientations must play a prominent role in shaping the thoughts and actions of industry managers.

Unprecedented change. Within the past few years the tourism industry has experienced rapid and unanticipated upheaval. The deregulation of airlines, the increasing level of competition and supply of facilities in excess of demand, new information technologies, and a vast array of social changes giving rise to new patterns of demand, have made the marketing concept difficult to put into operation. For example, when change leads to cutting costs, staff must be laid off, certain levels of service have to be eliminated, and tourists may have to be encouraged to perform some services themselves.

The current manpower shortage, coupled with low wage rates and poor working conditions, is creating unnecessary stress on those who remain to serve. In many firms the working environment is deteriorating to the point where the desire to be customer-oriented is dissipating.

Some tourists may revise their expectations but generally they are not interested in the problems facing a business or whether a business is trying harder. They want their expectations met or exceeded. It is no longer good enough just to give good service – tourists must perceive that they are getting good service. Unfortunately few tourist organizations really understand service as seen and experienced from the tourist's perspective.[11] This problem can be attributed partially to a lack of, or to poorly designed, market research.[12]

Product/market interface. Every tourism organization attempts to match its unique set of products and services with particular customers or market segments. However, no single organization provides or has control over the entire tourism product. Indeed the tourism product is difficult to identify because it differs for every single traveller and varies with the purpose of travel and the objectives to be achieved. The product itself is an amalgam of information, goods and services. It encompasses both a sojourn and a stay, and it involves a set of experiences involving not only interactions with people (other travellers, ordinary citizens and employees of business) but also interactions with natural and man-made settings and different cultures.[13]

Satisfaction with the tourism product and the resulting experiences is virtually dependent on the abilities and expertise of individual businesses and their employees who are expected to deliver services in such a way as to meet or exceed expectations. Independently each business may be successful. But over the period of a visit or a trip, there are bound to be 'moments of truth' in which the resulting experience is unsatisfactory. Not only are nasty experiences upsetting, but they may jeopardize the goodwill built up over a series of more satisfactory encounters or experiences.

Identifying and matching markets to tourist products or destinations is not easy and is often left to chance. First of all tourist markets may be widely dispersed and difficult to segment. Second, many tourism organizations lack the time, money and capability to research markets.

Another problem is that tourists represent a frequently maligned market. *En masse* tourists may be undifferentiated and viewed as demanding and ignorant – unworthy of any attempt to form long-standing allegiances. Some tourists are not even considered desirable, e.g. in the 1970s drifters converging on Amsterdam aroused anger among residents. In addition, some tourists are viewed as 'easy marks'. Understandably tourists may feel victimized and wary of falling into 'tourist traps'.[14]

These feelings are exacerbated when tourists encounter a lack of commitment to service, mediocrity, unfriendly systems, and rude and uncooperative employees, though blame can often be attributed to careless management.[15] Unless tourist organizations see themselves as existing to serve the needs of the people who are serving the customer, service disintegrates and dissatisfaction reigns.

Strategic considerations. The marketing concept is based on a long-term commitment to the satisfaction of tourists' needs. Typically, however, the strategic focus within many firms is short-term. This is partially due to a preoccupation with survival from season to season. As such, research and forecasting tend to be short-run exercises. Even executive compensation schemes are tied to short-run performance.

This short-term emphasis usually results in the application of 'market-pull strategies' to make minor product/service changes. However, this strategy has come under severe criticism for offering little guidance in assessing potential demand for offering either discontinuous innovations or existing products/services under radically different environmental conditions. What is missing according to the critics is acceptance and use of a technology-push strategy.[16] Indeed the shortening of tourist area life cycles demands various and creative strategies to ensure long-term survivability.[17]

The attack on the marketing concept and use of a market-pull strategy is based on the belief that customers are often unable to articulate new ideas that will result in product/service breakthroughs. Perceptiveness is limited by personal experience and education. Technology-push advocates argue, therefore, that tourist wants should be determined through means beyond those confined to consumer research. This would require a greater commitment to research and development and a strengthening of products and services built on a base of corporate and community strengths.

Unfortunately industry-by-industry comparisons of research and development activity reveal that tourism organizations commit little money to this effort. The research that is done tends to focus on improving short-term efficiency.[18] Even national and multinational firms that are more likely to pursue competitive, long-range investments, have learned to be extremely cautious. Tourist markets can be quite volatile and certain destinations can be politically unstable. As a result many of these firms have a tendency to stick with the tried-and-true. In all fairness, however, there is a need to capitalize on existing economies of scale and to standardize operations effectively. Not only is it necessary to copy what has been successful elsewhere but it is costly to make fundamental changes across the board. This conservatism may account for the so-called homogenization of tourist facilities and services, but it is incorrect to suggest that it is just the result of a misguided application of the marketing concept.

While critics of the marketing concept claim that ardent followers of the concept ignore the inherent capabilities of firms to create new products and services, there is little evidence to suggest that tourism organizations would pursue such a rigid and highly dubious policy.[19] Since many tourism organizations can be criticized for being focused internally, the more likely scenario is fixation with a particular corporate strength or a strategic focus. In other words, if there is a lack of originality or innovativeness it may be due more to decisions to 'stick to the knitting', to remain true to a particular market segment, or to uphold traditional levels of service when such decisions are 'out-of-synch' with the marketplace.

A significant but often disregarded obstacle in making a long-term commitment to the satisfaction of tourist needs is ignoring the fact that tourism is a community industry.[20] A successful tourism industry is built not only on the strengths of individual tourism organizations but also on the strengths of the community in which these organizations may be located. To a large extent it is the community that represents or provides the tourism product. But, tourism development has a reputation of being insensitive to the community, the quality of life of the people who reside there, and to the cultural and environmental milieu.

The uniqueness of tourism suggests that a philosophy that concentrates solely on the needs of the market is not the best orientation, even for the market itself. Tourism supply is oriented toward the resources of a community. To become totally marketing oriented, all aspects of the community would have to be oriented toward satisfying the needs and wants of the tourist. The risk for the community as well as for the tourist ultimately is that by orienting strictly and totally for the tourists' needs, the needs and integrity of the community may be abused . . . Destination areas that have attempted to adapt their resources to satisfy tourist needs may have lost the very thing that has made them attractive and unique in the first place.[21]

Imposition of product- or community-related goals on customers may seem antithetical to the marketing concept, but there are situations when it is common, expected and frequently successful. For example, it occurs among artists and craftsmen, who have established product/service standards that they do not want to compromise. It occurs among marketers who may be unable to redesign existing products or services.[22] But firms cannot afford to be lulled from a dedicated customer orientation.[23] A strict product or production orientation, or a sales orientation that emphasizes a quest for market dominance, can be captivating and take the focus of attention away from providing quality and value and satisfying the needs and wants of customers.

Marketing concept revisited

It is quite evident that managers of tourism organizations encounter numerous externally and internally driven reasons that make it difficult to implement to marketing concept. While these reasons have less to do with a literal and short-sighted interpretation of the marketing concept as it was originally formulated, further clarification of the concept is required. In order to relate the concept to tourism, a broader and more balanced view is warranted.

Orientation

Balancing customer and community needs. Tourism organizations exist in order to consummate exchange transactions with tourists. The traditional assumptions of the marketing concept suggest that this is best accomplished when organizations gain knowledge of tourists' needs and then create products and services to fulfill those needs. In this regard the marketing concept represents a useful and powerful guidance system.[24] However, as previously indicated, not every organization is able or even wants to bring forth products and services according to this precept.

For a moment reconsider the argument that tourism activity not only takes place in communities but that communities provide many attractions for tourists – culture, landscape, museums, parks, hospitality. We should be able to agree that these attractions are part of tourism product. Yet few, if any, of these attractions are ever designed explicitly for tourist use or consumption.

We should also recognize that the needs and wants of tourists are not merely economic in nature. Tourists expect a destination to be safe and clean, and they want to feel welcome and at ease. But clean, safe and friendly communities exist only if the local citizens care about them. And local citizens only care about their communities if the community demonstrates care for its citizens.

Citizens of a community are direct and indirect recipients of the economic and social costs and benefits derived from tourism. If tourism is seen as contributing to the economic and social well-being of their community it will be accepted. However, if tourism, through the actions of developers, politicians and tourists, shows a callous disregard for the culture, way of life, or the values and beliefs of citizens, it is unlikely to be tolerated. In other words, if the long-term success of tourism and the development of tourist facilities and services occurs with only the tourist in mind it may be short-lived.

Just as the long-term satisfaction of customer needs and wants in any single company hinges on how well the organization can continue to satisfy its own goals and objectives, the same is true in a community. Since no single tourism organization can determine, or has control over, a tourist's overall experience, tourist satisfaction is tied ultimately to how well tourists are received within the community. If there is community dissatisfaction with tourism, then tourists may not be welcomed and served in a hospitable manner. Tourist dissatisfaction ultimately leads to negative word-of-mouth reports and a quick demise for the industry.

From the perspective of tourism, then, a consumer orientation needs to be balanced with a community, or product-based orientation. This can be achieved or implemented through what could be called a 'community-push strategy'. At first glance this suggestion may appear preposterous, but tourism development is already subjected to community scrutiny through urban or regional planning processes and political debate. By taking an implicit strategy, and making it legitimate and more explicit, a community could articulate a vision as to how tourism should fit into, and contribute to, community life.[25]

Like every institution, a community is marked by the making of value commitments. A community orientation would incorporate primary values that lay the foundation to community life. Included could be statements related to heritage, uniqueness of the community, future aspirations, commitments to citizens, and integrity. Integrity, as it refers to tourism, for example, could make reference to a priority to serving the tourist with an assurance and devotion to quality. This care and concern would not only reflect an interest in tourists but also in the relationship of tourists with tourists, tourists with citizens, tourists with tourist organizations, and tourists with the environment. Since integrity is honesty and the consistent, responsible pursuit of a stated course of action, everyone who is part of a community should be able to feel more secure from the resulting imperative of trust, and feel that there really is a focus on long-term objectives that serve their best interests.

In turn this community orientation would then be communicated to individual entrepreneurs who would be encouraged to fashion the orientation into appropriate projects, facilities, products and services that could capitalize on a community's strengths and other unique tourism assets. By encouraging tourism organizations to take a long-term and broad view of tourism, tourists and their needs should be served better.

Implementation of a customer orientation would flow from a community orientation, and a customer orientation would form the basis for the development of a tourist organization's service strategy. Since each tourism organization needs to position itself in the marketplace this service strategy would represent a distinctive formula for the delivery of a service. The strategy would be adapted to the needs and unique attributes of the community along with a well-chosen benefit package that would be determined as valuable to targeted tourist markets. In other words, the chosen strategy would be based on:

- a thorough assessment of community strengths, weaknesses and desires;
- an evaluation of tourist expectations;
- an analysis of competitive strengths and weaknesses; and
- an alignment of tourist expectations with service capabilities.

Integrated effort

Tourism organizations are easily distracted from the task of achieving customer satisfaction. Emphasis on putting out fires, reacting to external threats, and achieving short-term objectives may mean that tourists get treated as if they were the enemy.

Integrated effort is a difficult and continuing managerial assignment. It should begin with a clear and well-defined service strategy that is articulated to everyone within the organization.[26] The strategy would then be integrated with the service systems that must be put in place to ensure that the 'right' things are done correctly. Service system development, however, does require rigorous analysis and control.[27] Standards for quality and productivity must be set and monitored constantly. Since service is derived from the interaction of tourists with contact personnel in a wide variety of service settings and situations, then different functional departments – operations, marketing and personnel – would out of necessity have to become better integrated.

Integration is not easy to carry out. Independence tends to be the operative word. As a result a balance must be struck between different orientations (cost versus revenue), different time horizons (short versus long), different motivations (technology-driven versus customer-driven) and different attitudes toward change (traditional versus innovative).

Satisfaction – customer, corporation and community

Profit may be the most basic condition necessary for a firm's survival, but the purpose of a tourism organization is to deliver satisfying products/services to tourists rather than to create a profit. Profit is merely a test of the validity of how successful an organization is in this regard. Emphasis on earning a profit can be a major distraction in achieving a customer or even a community orientation. Attempts to wring more profit out of sales are frequently made at the expense of the environment and customer service and quality. Obviously this is false economy in the long run. Recent research emphasizes that quality drives successful companies:

The 1980s have shown that one factor above all others – quality – drives market share and when superior quality and large market share are both present, profitability is virtually guaranteed. But relative perceived quality is not identical to the traditional concept of 'conformance' quality. It demands an entirely new perspective – one that calls for viewing quality externally, from the customer's perspective, rather than internally, from a quality-assurance point of view.[28]

In the light of the positive relationship between quality and profitability it seems that more effort should be made to identify units of measure that identify the extent to which tourists are satisfied with the quality of their experiences and the extent to which tourism adds to or detracts from the quality of life in the community. To accomplish this, goal evaluation studies need to incorporate the nature of the fit between expectations and experiences.[29] A methodology for achieving this objective has been proposed.[30]

Implementing a revised marketing concept

Loss of sales and market share due to competition, costs of poor quality, and threats to communities, collectively add up to a crisis in tourism. This crisis is beginning to stimulate some communities and tourism organizations to re-examine their approach to the tourism business and the achievement of tourist satisfaction. To get rid of these deficiencies, communities and tourist organizations need to recognize the synergy between community and customer orientations. Out of necessity communities and tourism organizations are partners in the tourism enterprise, therefore, some form of collaboration is in order.

Community-level prescriptions

Prescriptions for collaboration and for implementing a revised marketing concept at the community level include the following:

Getting started. Since most communities have a tourist office and/or persons responsible for tourism and tourism marketing activities, they could assume responsibility for establishing a committee to coordinate an approach to tourism within their communities. This committee should include representatives of departments of economic development, parks and recreation, planning, chambers of commerce, individual tourism organizations, and *other* concerned or interested citizens. While forming such a committee and getting public participation may be difficult, pariculary if citizens hold diametrically opposed views as to the merits of tourism, or if there exist distinct communities within a city or region, the role of the committee would be to coordinate the establishment of *policies* and goals for tourism.

Tourism policies. Policy as used here is a guide to managerial action whether at the community or individual company level. The committee would publish policy statements based on a good deal of deliberation followed by an approval process at a high level (e.g. a city council). Without exception, all published tourism policies should declare the intentions to meet the needs of the community at large and in specific locales, as well as the needs of tourists. The wording would include identification of specific needs to be met. Published tourism policy should also make reference to three other ongoing activities:

- a formal process for quality improvement;
- methods by which the abilities of organizations and individuals serving tourists might be enhanced; and
- how tourism policies might be enforced perhaps through a process of independent review.

Tourism goals. A goal is not achieved without effort. The committee should set community-wide goals for tourism and establish a system for deployment, i.e. subdividing the goals and allocating sub-goals to tourism organizations or other groups and individuals. The community committee is a logical place for receiving nominations for potential tourism goals. Use could be made of the concept of sponsors or 'champions' for specific goals or projects.

Planning to meet goals. The deployment of goals is itself a part of the planning process. It starts off with the needs of the community and tourism organizations. It translates those needs into sub-goals and projects that can be accomplished by tourism organizations. It identifies resources required to meet the goals. It optimizes the relationship between the value of the goals to the effort required to reach them.

By its very nature, the bulk of tourism planning must be done by tourism organizations. For example, the committee may give specific tourism organizations a mandate to evaluate the competitive quality of the community's tourism product. However, the methods for doing this may have to be left to the tourism organizations.

Evaluating performance. Evaluation requires units of measure. Since profit is, by itself, an imprecise and inadequate measure of tourism performance, particularly at the community level, new measures have to be devised. For every goal an associated means of evaluation is required, along with the basic data to serve as inputs for evaluation. Day-to-day operations provide extensive data on occupancy rates, expenditure patterns, etc. What is missing is the processing of those data into summaries, ratios, and indexes which then become part of the evaluation system used at the community level.

Special provision must be made to create new data sources. For example, measures may be required of tourism product salability, performance on quality improvement, competitive performance, tourist satisfaction, and specific environmental problems. It may also be necessary to carry out specialized audits – or independent reviews of tourism performance. These could be conducted by members of the committee. Such participation signals the high priority placed on tourism and how well tourism organizations are serving both the needs of tourists and the community.

Providing motivation. In some tourism organizations a collaborative effort involving the community will encounter some resistance on the grounds of 'community inter- ference'. This interference can involve goal setting, planning and evaluating. Sug- gestions for overcoming resistance or introducing change which have been evolved by behavioural scientists include:

- Allow for participation both in planning and executing change.
- Provide enough time for everyone first to evaluate the merits of change in relation to the threat of habits, status, beliefs, and second to find an accommodation with the advocates of change. This means 'no surprises' 'starting small', and 'choosing the right time'.
- Keep the proposals free of excess baggage. Do not clutter the proposals with extraneous matters not closely concerned with getting the results.
- Work with the recognized leadership.
- Treat everyone in a dignified manner.
- Look for alternatives, e.g. consider changing proposals to meet specific objectives. Offer something for something. Try a programme of persuasion, or forget a pro- posal if it might not succeed.

Individual tourism enterprise prescriptions

Individual tourism organizations should take much of their lead from this collabora- tive effort. Suggestions for implementing the revised marketing concept from their point of view, however, is equally demanding.[31]

Develop a guiding premise. Specialize, create niches and differentiate your tourism products/services in such a way that they capitalize on inherent community and corporate strengths.

Add value constantly:

- provide top quality as perceived by both tourists and local citizens;
- emphasize superior service in the tourist's terms;
- pay particular attention to the intangible qualities of the tourism product;
- work with the community, competitors, and customers in order to respond quickly to changing community and tourist requirements;

- constantly seek out new markets that are appropriate to the organization as well as the community;
- develop tourism products that seem to display symbolic and synergistic qualities vis-à-vis the organization, and the community's other tourism facilities and assets; and
- achieve uniqueness in the tourist's mind.

Build organizational/community capability:

- listen and become acutely sensitive to tourists' and local citizenry/community needs;
- engage in more innovative research and development activity;
- make service delivery systems and operations the prime marketing tool by paying attention to details and by fostering effective tourist – employee interactions;
- invest more in people, their education and training; and
- empower people by supporting them and removing obstacles that inhibit their effective performance.

In revising the marketing concept as a guiding philosophy, fundamental changes will have to be made in how we think and act about tourism. Laying down prescriptions for change is the cosy part. The challenge of achieving a more balanced community and customer orientation is more daunting – it requires a management revolution. If tourism is to become a truly successful community industry and be received enthusiastically by tourists and the citizenry, a revised marketing concept needs to be implemented now.

References

1. Jost Krippendorf, *The Holiday Makers*, Heinemann, Oxford, 1987, pp 138–139.
2. John A. Hannigan, 'Reservations cancelled consumer complaints in the tourist industry', *Annals of Tourism Research*, Vol 7, No 3, 1980, pp 366–384; John Moynahan, *The Tourist Trap*, Pan Books, London, UK, 1985; and Brian Moores, *Are They Being Served? Quality Consciousness in Service Industries*, Philip Alan Publishers, Oxford, 1986.
3. George Young, *Tourism, Blessing or Blight*, Penguin, Harmondsworth, 1973; and Alister Mathieson and Geoffrey Wall, *Tourism: Economic, Physical and Social Impacts*, Longman, Harlow, 1982.
4. Peter Drucker, *The Practice of Management*, Harper and Row, New York, 1954.
5. John B. McKitterick, 'What is the marketing management concept?', *Frontiers of Marketing Thought and Action*, American Marketing Association, Chicago, 1957, pp 71–82.
6. Hiram C. Barksdale and Bill Darden, 'Marketers' attitudes toward the marketing concept, *Journal of Marketing*, October 1971, pp 37–42.
7. M. L. Bell and C. W. Emory, 'The faltering marketing concept', *Journal of Marketing*, October 1971, pp 37–42.
8. Theodore Levitt, 'Production-line approach to services', *Harvard Business Review*, Vol 54, September–October 1972, pp 42–52; and Theodore Levitt, 'The industrialization of service', *Harvard Business Review*, Vol 50, September–October 1976, pp 63–74.
9. Carol F. Surprenant and Michael R. Soloman, 'Predictability and personalization in the service encounter', *Journal of Marketing*, Vol 51, No 2, 1987, pp 86–96.
10. Bernard H. Berry, A. Parasuraman and Valerie A. Zeithaml, 'Synchronizing demand and supply in service businesses', *Business Horizons*, Vol 34, October–December 1984, pp 35–37.

11. Michael Nightingale, 'Defining quality for a quality assurance program – a study of perceptions', in R. Lewis et al., eds, *The Practice of Hospitality Management II*, AVI Publishing, Darien, CT, 1986, pp 37–53.

12. Karl Albrecht and Ron Zemke, *Serivice America: Doing Business in the New Economy*, Dow-Jones Irwin, Homewood, IL, USA, 1985.

13. S. Medlik and V.T.C. Middleton, 'Products Formulation in Tourism', *Tourism and Marketing*, Vol 13, AIEST, Berne, 1973.

14. John Moynahan, *op cit*, Ref 2.

15. *Op cit*, Ref 12.

16. Roger C. Bennett and Robert G. Cooper, 'The misuse of marketing: an American tragedy', *Business Horizons*, 1981, pp 50–61; Joe Kent Kirby, 'The marketing concept: suitable guide to product strategy?', *The Business Quarterly*, Summer 1972, pp 31–35; and Robert Hayes and William T. Abernathy, 'Managing our way to economic decline', *Harvard Business Review*, Vol 58, July–August 1980, pp 67–77.

17. K. Michael Haywood, 'Can the tourist-area life cycle be made operational?', *Tourism Management*, Vol 7, No 3, 1986, pp 154–167; and K. Michael Haywood, 'Managing strategic change', *FIU Hospitality Review*, Vol 6, No 2, 1988, pp 1–7.

18. Pauline J. Sheldon, Juanita C. Liu and Chuck Y. Gee, 'The status of research in the lodging industry', *International Journal of Hospitality Management*, Vol 6, No 2, 1987, pp 89–96.

19. Andrew G. Kaldor, 'Imbricative marketing', *Journal of Marketing*, Vol 35, April 1971, pp 19–25; Roger C. Cooper and Robert G. Cooper, 'Beyond the marketing concept', *Business Horizons*, June 1979, pp 76–83; and Roger C. Cooper and Robert G. Cooper, 'The misuse of marketing, an American tragedy', *Business Horizons*, December 1981, pp 50–61.

20. Peter E. Murphy, *Tourism: A Community Approach*, Methuen, New York, 1985.

21. Robert Christie Mill and Alastair M. Morrison, *The Tourism System: An Introductory Text*, Prentice-Hall, Englewood Cliffs, NJ, 1985, p 360

22. Franklin S. Houston, 'The marketing concept: what it is and what it is not', *Journal of Marketing*, Vol 50, April 1986, pp 81–87.

23. Frederick E. Webster Jr, 'The rediscovery of the marketing concept', *Business Horizons*, May–June, 1988, pp 29–39.

24. A. Parasuraman, 'Hang on to the marketing concept', *Business Horizons*, September–October, 1981, pp 38–40.

25. The community push strategy is explained in K. Michael Haywood, 'Responsible and responsive tourism planning in the community', *Tourism Management*, Vol 9, No 2, 1988, pp 105–118.

26. K. Michael Haywood, 'Service management concepts: implications for hospitality management', *FIU Hospitality Review*, Vol 5, No 2, 1987, pp 43–60.

27. Lynn Shostak, 'Designing services that deliver', *Harvard Business Review*, January–February 1984, pp 33–39.

28. R. O. Buzzell and B. Gale, *The PIMS Principles: Linking Strategy to Performance*, The Free Press, New York, 1987.

29. P. L. Pearce and G. Moscardo, 'Visitor evaluation – an appraisal of goals and techniques', *Evaluation Review*, Vol 9, No 3, 1985, pp 281–306.

30. K. Michael Haywood and Thomas Muller, 'The urban tourist experience: measuring satisfaction', *Hospitality Research and Education Journal*, Vol 12, No 2, 1988, pp 453–459.

31. The following outline is an adaptation of ideas in Tom Peters, *Thriving on Chaos: Handbook for a Management Revolution*, Alfred A. Knopf, New York, 1987.

25

The implementation of total quality management in tourism: some guidelines

C A Witt and A P Muhlemann

The Management Centre, University of Bradford, Emm Lane, Bradford BD9 4JL, UK

This paper examines the potential of total quality management (TQM) to improve the competitiveness of the tourism industry. The various approaches to the TQM process are presented, and the experiences in manufacturing reviewed briefly to identify the lessons for the service industries. The key differences between manufacturing and services are presented in order to determine the influence of these on the successful adoption of TQM. This is used as the basis for developing three sets of guidelines for the successful implementation of TQM in the tourism sector.

Total quality management: an overview

Total quality management (TQM) emerged as a philosophy in the UK in the late 1970s and early 1980s. However, the term and this attitude towards quality is sometimes accredited to Feigenbaum[1] for his work in what he called total quality control (TQC). This required the involvement of *all* functions in the quality process, not just manufacturing.[2]

It was born out of a much earlier quest for quality which can be traced back to the pioneering work of Juran, Deming and others with Japanese industry in the 1950s. They had been largely unsuccessful in introducing the well-established statistical and other techniques to US manufacturers in the era of the postwar boom in production. The Japanese were looking to 'rebuild' their industry, and to change their reputation for 'shoddy' goods. It was natural that they would look for support from wherever possible.

The success of the Japanese in improving their quality standards became a major concern for the remaining manufacturers in the rest of the world. Attempts were made to identify, catalogue and copy what were seen as the key features of this success. Generally, the focus was initially on the manufacturing function within enterprises.

Statistical techniques (largely statistical process control – SPC) were used to establish what processes were capable of achieving and to monitor and detect changes. These ideas were not new and had been in the public domain since the 1930s (for example, Shewhart[3]). The base broadened with the attempt to involve the workforce more directly in the quality achievement process. In Japan this had been implemented successfully in part using quality circles, teams of workers, meeting voluntarily outside normal work hours to identify, discuss, examine and try to solve work place problems. Frequently these groups had a leader whose responsibilities included training the group in the analytic tools of quality control. Ishikawa is possibly the best known of the pioneers of the quality circle movement in Japan[2] and an interesting discussion of the development of this movement appears in Ishikawa.[4] At one point these were seen as a major contributory factor to the Japanese quality success story. However, as many attempts at setting up circles outside Japan failed to deliver the expected benefits it became apparent that the issues were more complex than originally perceived, and that quality was an important issue throughout the organization. The need for TQM was beginning to be recognized in the West.

TQM has been defined by Oakland[5] as:

>. . . a way of managing the whole business process to ensure complete 'customer' satisfaction at every stage, internally and externally. (p. ix)

Kanji[6] shows the following development of the concept of TQM: *quality*: to satisfy customers' requirements continuously; *total quality*: to achieve quality at a low cost; *total quality management*: to obtain total quality by involving everyone's daily commitment.

Implicit and crucial to both of these (and other) 'definitions' is that all organizations have chains of customers and suppliers. The idea of the supplier of materials to an organization or the customer for the organization's product or service is totally familiar; normally these are external to the organization. What is normally less evident and more important is the proposal that *everyone* within an organization has customers and suppliers and that many of these are internal to the organization. Thus the cook in the restaurant supplies the waiter with the meal for the diner, while the washer-up supplies the cook with clean plates. This recognition of these chains is a key building block in introducing TQM.

A number of quality gurus have appeared over the years and each appears to have his own unique view of how TQM should be developed within the organization. Some have supported their perspectives with texts: typical examples are: Deming, Juran, Ishikawa, Corsby.[4,7–9] Most have gone on and developed these themes in subsequent works. The practitioner, seeking help and assistance, is faced with a variety of 'messages' from these. What follows in this section draws in part on the analysis presented in Bendall.[2]

Feigenbaum[1] originally introduced the idea of *total* quality control to emphasize that the *entire* organization was involved, not just manufacturing (or operations). Much of his philosophy is biased towards the manufacturing company, although a number of his messages relate to all types of organization.

Deming[7] was responsible for a systematic approach to problem solving which he originally introduced to the Japanese: the Plan–Do–Check–Action cycle. This is extended in Oakland and Mortiboys[10] to the 'Helix of Never-Ending Improvement' based around 'Evaluate–Plan–Do–Check–Amend'. It is claimed that his famous '14 points' became the basis of the transformation of American industry and were 'a signal that management intend to stay in business, and aim to protect investors and jobs' (p. 23). These points cover a variety of both strategic and operational issues and, while some would have universal support, others are more controversial.

According to Bendall,[2] in order to fully exploit the potential of the 14 points, there is a tendency – indeed possibly a need – to use the tools developed by other gurus. However, Deming does stress the importance of management coming to terms with what he calls his 'Deadly diseases and obstacles' (to TQM).

In his earlier work Juran[8] adopts a somewhat analytically based approach to quality. However, in his later texts[11] he moves on and looks in more detail at 'softer' issues. Like many of the other writers he supports the idea of internal and external customers, and claims that the majority of quality problems are due to poor management rather than faulty workmanship.

Crosby[9] is probably the most flamboyant of the quality gurus, and well known for his views on 'zero-defects' or ZD. His 'Quality crusade' includes the 'Four absolutes of quality' and a 14-step approach to quality improvement.

Ishikawa[4] is most usually associated with the quality circle movement and the diagram which has his name. He is also linked to organization-wide quality initiatives in Japan which started in the 1950s (TQM). He claims that quality means not only the quality of the product (or service) but the after-sales service, quality of management, the company itself and the individuals within it.

The TQM model of Oakland[5] pulls together and develops further a number of the aspects and perspectives of some of the earlier writers. The idea of managing processes that relate to 'chains of customers and suppliers' is central to the model. This is surrounded by what he refers to as the 'soft' aspects of TQM: communication, culture and commitment, supported by 'harder management necessities' of systems, tools and teams.

The philosophy of TQM was developed and implemented originally largely within manufacturing environments. However it is increasingly being taken up within the so-called service sector. Dotchin and Oakland[12] report some statistics on this, indicating the rate of growth in reported applications. Indeed, if the basic frameworks, ideas and concepts of some of the key writers are examined they are largely presented in an environment-neutral context. The central concept of a 'process' in Oakland's model applies throughout an organization. It need not be a manufacturing process which produces a finished product for an external customer. It could be an internal process by which, for example, the work schedule for a tour company's representatives is prepared or the process followed to establish an organization's staff training needs. However, according to Dotchin and Oakland:[12]

Deming gives many examples of what might be studied with statistics in service operations, but does not include the less tangible processes which according to Morris and Johnson[13] are key differences between services and manufacture. (p. 139)

This will be developed in the next section.

Dale[14] carried out a survey of delegates at a recent TQM conference. Almost 42% of respondents claimed to use the teaching of one or more of the 'quality gurus' in their organization. It is interesting to note that over a quarter of these used more than one source, this in spite of suggestions that the approaches/methods of the gurus are in part mutually exclusive.

This can be contrasted with the comparison of the similarities between the various authors in Dotchin and Oakland[12] along a variety of dimensions:

Different authors place their individual emphases, and it might be inferred that substantially different philosophies are being represented. A more careful analysis, however, reveals surprisingly similar content. (p. 133)

Kanji[6] reports an application of TQM in ICI where the guidelines from Crosby, Juran and Deming were all considered and used selectively. It was commented that certain aspects of Crosby's approach has more relevance to the UK situation than others. Hence not all were used.

Dale[14] includes an assessment of the reasons for difficulties in starting and sustaining TQM. From his survey, all the inhibitors identified could apply equally to service and manufacturing environments. The top five inhibitors to introducing TQM are reported as: (1) lack of top management commitment and vision; (2) company culture and management style; (3) 'flavour of the month' type attitude; (4) departmental-based thinking and actions; and (5) poor appreciation of the concept and principles of TQM. The top five inhibitors to sustaining TQM include, in addition to (1), (3) and (4) above, (a) time pressure, work load and resources; (b) organizational restructuring.

Kanji[6] presents a set of principles and actions which will support an organization developing the TQM process. These key pairs are:

- approach – management led;
- scope – company wide;
- scale – everyone is responsible for quality;
- philosophy – prevention not detection;
- standard – right first time;
- control – cost of quality;
- theme – continuous improvement.

This is complemented by a four-stage process for the implementation of TQM:

- identification and preparation;
- management understanding and commitment;
- scheme for improvement;
- new initiative, new targets and critical examination.

This section has reviewed the philosophies of some of the major writers in TQM. In the majority of cases the broad frameworks are applicable in any type of environment. It is clear that some lessons can be learnt from the application of TQM in manufacturing organizations. Some of the key issues to recognize include: (1) ensure continued top management support; (2) manage the culture change; (3) set realistic expectations (potential improvement timescales); (4) provide continued support and training. These are equally important to service organizations planning to implement TQM.

It has been observed[14] that there are some fundamental differences between manufacturing and services which are not addressed fully by many of the various quality frameworks. The next section describes these differences in more detail, in order to evaluate the situation more fully.

Manufacturing and services: the differences

Lockyer[15] argues that basically no differences exist between manufacturing and services.

The proposal is made that the distinction between service and manufacturing industries should disappear, since effectively they carry out the same task ... (p. 5)

Operations managers are in both cases concerned with the transformation process of inputs into outputs. The nature of the inputs and outputs may be quite different – clearly the inputs for the manufacture of steel are not the same as those required when making furniture; the transformation process also differs. Lockyer argues that the differences between providing, for instance, a meal and making steel are no more significant than between any two examples.

Other authors[16–18] would not disagree with the argument that there is a common basic situation facing production and operations managers, i.e. that of transforming inputs into outputs. However, many talk of a continuum with outputs which are tangible (goods) at one end and intangible output (services) at the other. For example, a car would be at the tangible (goods) end of this continuum, with a small element of the intangible – the prestige of a Rolls Royce, the trendy element of a Peugeot 205, the raunchy image of a Ferrari. At the other end of the spectrum, the customer does not buy a bit of hotel room when purchasing a night's stay – only the use of the accommodation; nothing is bought which they can take away with them (except perhaps the unused shampoo or disposable shower cap!) This leads on naturally to the idea of providing a 'bundle of goods and services'[16–18] or 'service package'[19] which typically includes (1) supporting facility, (2) facilitating goods, (3) explicit and (4) implicit services.

Yet others would differentiate services from manufacturing using the degree of customer contact.[16–18,20] The purchaser of a car does not have to be present when a car is made. Not only that, but the production process is buffered from the customer by marketing and dealers/agents. By contrast, the purchaser of a hotel room for the night has to be physically present or the whole point of the operation is lost. Thus, when an operation involves either a high level of customer contact or has a product which is intangible in nature, it may be described as a service operation. As a consequence of these two attributes, services can clearly be seen to have characteristics which differ from those of an operation located at the tangible and low-contact end of the scale. The most comprehensive list of characteristics of which the authors are aware is presented by Murdick et al.[16] and reproduced here in Table 1.

The presence of these characteristics has implications for management. On the whole this fact seems to have been largely overlooked, or at least not explicitly addressed by the exponents of TQM. Relatively little work relating to TQM in services specifically has been reported and when TQM has been discussed in a service context, it is the tangible aspects which have been addressed or used as examples.[5,21] The majority of the work has related to manufacturing situations. If only the tangible

Table 1. Service characteristics.

1. Services produce intangible output
2. Services produce variable, non-standard output
3. A service is perishable; i.e. it cannot be carried in inventory, but is consumed in production
4. There is high customer contact throughout the service process
5. The customer participates in the process of providing a service
6. Skills are sold directly to the customer
7. Services cannot be mass-produced
8. High personal judgement is employed by individuals performing the service
9. Service firms are labor-intensive
10. Decentralized facilities are located near the customers
11. Measures of effectiveness are subjective
12. Quality control is primarily limited to process control
13. Pricing options are more elaborate

Source: Murdick, R G, Render, B and Russell, R S *Service Operations Management* Allyn and Bacon, Boston (1990) p 26.

deliverables of a service organization are considered, the various aspects of TQM can be accepted without too much concern.

In the next section, some of the more significant impacts that the differences have on the implementation of TQM are examined.

Services: the quality problems

Customer focus is central to all the models; for example Oakland[5] states: 'The ability to meet the customer requirements is vital' (p. 3). This is the underlying ethos of TQM and it is here that the problems start for services. First of all, how are these requirements identified and incorporated into a specification? The 'product' is intangible (characteristic 1). For example: airlines provide a means of getting from A to B; tour operators package together an experience. What is an experience? How may it be defined? What are the underlying attributes which may be incorporated in the design specification? Much of the work in this area derives from marketing. Dhir and Chandrasekar[22] found that potential customers are not themselves aware of how they make their decision to purchase when deciding between restaurants. Embacher and Buttle[23] point out:

The image of a location has been shown to have a significant impact upon its selection as a vacation destination. Measuring and managing this image therefore becomes a major priority for marketing and communications staff in hotels, resorts, national tourist offices and elsewhere. (p. 3)

They then used repertory grid analysis to identify the constructs along which 25 people judged holiday destinations. The constructs included built up, manmade environment/ beautiful countryside, boring destination/interesting destination, artificial 'tourist' culture/genuine culture etc.

Gartner[24] is also concerned with image, but he used multidimensional scaling to try and identify underlying factors. It appeared that in his study cultural based/natural resource based and in group social/out group social were the two underlying dimensions along which tourists viewed destinations.

A few studies[25-27] have sought to confirm the service-quality dimensions identified by Parasuraman et al.[28] The problem with all of these studies, however, is that the information gained is vague, making preparation of detailed design specifications difficult.

Additionally service produce variable, non-standard output (characteristic 2). The main reason for variable, non-standard output in services is people. Each customer who enters the door of a travel agency is different. Even the same person entering the same travel agency on different occasions will not have the same requirements every time. Not only that, but one person visiting three travel agents on the same day may well have a different attitude in each place – in between the visits they may have had a harrowing experience such that their patience has worn thin, or the accompanying child has had enough and decides to 'play' with the brochures on display.

In addition to the vagaries of the client, the contact-employee is also an individual who will have good days and bad days. Every interaction between employee and customer will be different.

These characteristics clearly make not only product design and specification difficult, but also make process design far more complex.

As a consequence of characteristics 1 and 2, measurement of performance is subjective. If there is no clear design specification there is no benchmark against which performance can be measured. It is easy to measure such things as miles per gallon and maximum speed of a car, but not so easy to measure a 'romantic atmosphere'. How does a manager 'check' that the customer requirements have been met? Parasuraman et al.[28] developed the SERVQUAL questionnaire to measure quality based on the presumption that service quality occurs when customers perceive received performance to equate with prior expectations. This has provoked much discussion.[26,29-31] Crompton and Mackay[29] write:

Assessing perceived service quality is not equivalent to assessing satisfaction. Satisfaction is a psychological outcome emerging from an experience, whereas service quality is concerned with the attributes of the service itself. (p. 368)

However, attempts to measure service quality usually involve the use of questionnaires.[25,29] In some cases the questions have been compiled as a result of focus group interviews[28,31] or from a literature search;[35] others do not describe how the questions were selected. Various techniques have been used to analyse the results of the questionnaires including factor analysis[26,28] principal components analysis,[35] multiple regression[22,26,31,32,34] and multidimensional scaling.[24] Some researchers[22,29,36] used constant sum scales rather than Likert-type scales in an attempt to overcome some of the problems associated with the latter (see Crompton and Mackay[29] for further discussion). Other analytical techniques used include repertory grid analysis[23] and conjoint analysis.[37]

However quality is measured and feedback obtained problems still remain. Dhir and Chandrasekar[22] show that relative importance of attributes changes between time of selection and time of consumption. Factors which draw new customers will differ from those of repeat purchasers.[36] Additionally Horovitz[38] points out that identifying 'defective service' is difficult because studies indicate that only 4% dissatisfied customers will actually complain, and while a dissatisfied customer will tell 11 potential customers of the experience, a satisfied customer talks to only four. The *underlying* problems, however, are subjectivity of assessment and heterogeneity of customers, making measurement of effectiveness and quality extremely difficult.

TQM demands study and development of processes and systems in order to ensure that customer requirements are met but, as already mentioned, as the customers are not homogeneous, a high level of variability can result. In addition the design of the process has to allow for non-employees in the system, with not only differing requirements, but also unpredictability of behaviour: the passenger who smokes on a non-smoking flight, the diner who drinks too much and becomes abusive to other customers, the child who is travel sick on the coach. These factors are not under the direct control of the service provider, but need to be considered when designing the process.

Culture change and commitment of employees are two other facets of TQM. Training is central to ensure success in both these dimensions. Two difficulties arise in services. First, the customer frequently participates in the process of providing a service (characteristic 5), whether it is helping to create the right atmosphere or serving themselves at the breakfast buffet. Thus 'training' needs to extend to the customer. Second, while much of the training in a manufacturing setting is largely restricted to the use of the TQM 'tools' (e.g. use of process control charts etc) and technical skills, in services, when skill is sold directly to a customer (characteristic 6), the possession of that skill is not enough. For example, on tours to Egypt the attendant historian requires interpersonal skills in addition to academic knowledge about the Pharaohs. Similarly, high personal judgement is frequently required by individuals performing the service (characteristic 8). This particularly applies to travel agents. In many cases customers are not necessarily aware of exactly what they do require. The agent needs to analyse the needs of the client and advise accordingly. Too much information will confuse the potential holiday-maker. Skill is needed to draw out the relevant information from the customer. Another example is the ski instructor who has to judge how hard to push his/her group – does this group want to win all the races at the end of the week or break the record for the highest number of schnapps stops in a week? Training in interpersonal skills and in the use of judgement is much more difficult. This is often aggravated by high labour turnover. The tourism industry in particular is susceptible to large fluctuations in demand, in part due to seasonality, which leads to the hiring of non-permanent staff. This high labour turnover also makes training costly and the development of a culture far more difficult to achieve.

Total quality management in tourism: applications

There are very few reports of organizations within the tourism industry adopting TQM. Van Borrendam[39] describes how KLM started to move towards a TQM system about 22 years ago. However, quality clearly appears on the agenda, even if not labelled TQM, of many firms in the tourism industry.

Airlines predominate in the literature. KLM believe a bottom-up approach is possible. 'Management quality targets' are used, with zero defects as the ultimate goal. These targets are set in consultation with (1) the department which needs to meet the targets, (2) the marketing department and (3) the costing department. KLM recognizes the difficulties involved in measuring service. They attempt to overcome this in part by using passenger questionnaires. Where the customer is not involved, standard checklists have been developed. KLM Quality Control then audit the systems. If problems are discovered on audit, quality assurance forms are distributed three months after the audit to identify how the matter has been solved. Thus systems are in place to ensure continual improvement[39].

SAS, under the influence of Jan Carlsen, has been credited with leading the realization that the individual employee has an important role to play in achieving customer satisfaction and of the need for a quality culture with empowerment of the individual employees.[40] Leirvaag[41] discusses the cultural changes which were made to facilitate this empowerment. Lilja[42] describes some of the operational systems that have been introduced but notes:

Although there is a long way to go towards TQM, the first steps have demonstrated to SAS how valuable the Quality Road is. (p. 176)

British Airways implemented a fairly well publicized 'Putting the Customer First' programme in the mid-1980s. Bruce[43] describes how a staff training programme was implemented which developed staff awareness of customer needs. A change of management style from bureaucratic to one which fostered flexibility was adopted, allowing staff to respond as necessary. More recently, blueprinting and benchmarking have been used to improve customer delivery service,[44] with effort being directed towards identifying problems with the process which lead to situations where customer expectations are not met, that is, fail points.

Alaska Airlines recognizes the need for customer focus, employee training and support, together with good communications:

We . . . take pride in serving our customers. To do it effectively, you've got to give your employees the training, tools, support and freedom to succeed. You also must maintain open communications so you can quickly identify and correct shortcomings. (R J Vecci, CEO Alaska Airlines, quoted in Miller,[45] p. 153)

Marriott Hotels have long realized the importance of training at all levels. The comprehensiveness of courses for all staff was reported by Hostage.[46]

Hilton International believe their improved service quality has given them a competitive edge. To gain this strengthened position in the market they studied both customer and employee attitudes and expectations of service, changed their culture, empowering their employees to set their own customer-orientated standards, and set up what they believe are objective measures of guest satisfaction.[47]

Saunders and Graham[48] report the results of a study which they undertook at the Sheraton Brisbane Hotel. They suggested that the main problem with TQM in services lies in the difficulty of measurement. This measurement may be external, that is, of the customer's perception of quality, or internal, which relates to measurements of performance from a control perspective. In the study, they develop internal 'measures' across four dimensions: timeliness, integrity (how complete the service is), predictability and satisfaction.

The measurement step is the second vital component of TQM, without which the supporting philosophies lack coherence. Once measurement methods have been developed and results derived the process being studied can be placed in this measured context and decisions made accordingly. The remaining aspects of TQM present no greater difficulties than in a manufacturing organization. (p. 248)

Thus, they argue that once appropriate measures of performance are identified, process control is possible.

Avant Hotel at Oldham was the first hotel in the UK to obtain BS 5750. Callan[49] describes the process of obtaining the accreditation. Unfortunately, however, the hotel later experienced trading difficulties and was sold. One of the problems with BS 5750 is that although it should ensure consistency of output, it does not necessarily have a customer focus.

Lane, Mansfield, Miller and Stratton[40,50-52] all discuss the approach to service quality taken by Disneyland/Disneyworld. The emphasis is on training and sound operations management techniques. Attention to detail ensures that the tangibles are working right first time. Every piece of equipment is on a preventive maintenance programme. Refurbishment of all attractions is scheduled. Design of new attractions takes account of maintenance and operational issues. Techniques such as value engineering are used to improve the design of seat belts, for example.[52] But the most important facet is the training of the staff:

At Disneyland the roadsweepers have a 5-day training course – 10 minutes on how to use a sweeper and the remainder on how to give information to guests ... (Lane,[40] p. 53)

and

For example, our sweepers are not just cleaning Main Street, they are helping to create an atmosphere of happiness ... (Holst as quoted in Miller,[51] p. 192)

Total quality management in tourism: guidelines

A number of authors have made suggestions as to how some of the problems of implementing TQM in services generally may be handled.[21,38,53-62] The guidelines proposed here for the successful implemenatation of TQM in services, developed in part from these suggestions, are presented below, grouped into three classes based on:

(1) elements of the product/service package;
(2) the human aspects of the delivery system;
(3) measurement issues in service quality.

While this classification may not be unique, it relates to some of the key differences identified earlier in Table 1, and facilitates presentation of the following guidelines.

Elements of the product/service package

- The organization should have a clear *strategy* in terms of the key features of the service, both *tangible* and *intangible* (quantified) and the specific markets served. This should be widely communicated within and without the organization so all expectations (internal and external) are clear. The concept of *focus* can help.

- The *design* of the service package should be approached in a structured and systematic manner so that quality can be designed into the provision.
- The service package should be decomposed into *processes* and each studied to develop the best approach; this should be completely documented and quantified where possible.
- The key *skills and competences* required for each process should be clearly identified.
- In designing delivery systems and examining processes, the key problem areas should be identified and *contingency* plans *developed.*
- Delivery systems should be *robust* and *under-utilization* of resources accepted as a consequence of fast response.
- The process should be *standardized* wherever possible to ensure *consistency* of delivery but not to the extent of losing competitive advantage, or in conflict with the organization's strategy.

Human aspects of the delivery system

- There should be *clear communication* of the organization's expectations given to staff.
- All staff should be fully *trained* in the skills and competences determined as relevant to their current and likely future role.
- Training in *interpersonal skills* is crucial for staff with direct customer contact.
- Training in *technical skills* should be provided for all staff involved in these areas, and they should be provided with appropriate equipment.
- Training should be used to develop *multiskilling, problem-solving* skills, and to promote *job enrichment.*
- *Recruitment* policies should take full account of skills and competences in the role to be filled.
- *Team working* should be used wherever possible, especially in the context of problem solving (quality action teams).
- Individuals should take over *ownership* of the processes which they work within and be responsible for satisfactory delivery.
- Staff should be *empowered* to make decisions to respond to requests to customize the service and handle local difficulties.
- Provision of *facilities for staff* should reflect their importance to the organization.
- Top management should demonstrate continuously *total commitment* to quality and this should be used in part to *motivate* the rest of staff.
- Management should instil a culture of *continuous improvement*, and be *role models.*
- Management should be *involved* and be *competent* to carry out the processes provided by those who respond to them.
- *Outdated values* should be eliminated.
- The *customer's roles* within the delivery system should be specified explicitly and communicated clearly.

Measurement issues in service quality

- In designing the service both tangible and intangible aspects should be *quantified*.
- The excuse should not be accepted that intangible aspects cannot be quantified – *focus-group questionnaires* can be used to establish expectations and set standards in these areas.
- Clear *standards* need to be set and communicated to both customer and provider.
- *Benchmarking* should be used to compare performance with the competition.
- Staff should be responsible for *feedback* on service performance: quantify factors – use of questionnaires, comment cards.
- Feedback should be seen as an *opportunity* not a *threat*.
- All negative feedback should be followed up and appropriate action taken.
- *Team work* can be used to evaluate and support resolution of problems identified through feedback.
- *All difficulties* which have arisen should be *recorded* and *analysed* and appropriate corrective action established. If necessary procedures *must* be modified/changed.
- Systems should be in place (questionnaires/follow-up interviews) to *monitor customer expectations*: changes in these may require modification to delivery systems, processes and so on.

Summary and conclusions

This paper has reviewed the various approaches to the TQM process, with specific reference to their impact on the key differences between manufacturing and services. This has facilitated the identification of three sets of factors which should contribute significantly to the successful introduction of TQM to the various sectors of the tourism industry. There is a need for further in-depth studies and documented implementations of TQM in tourism in order that the industry can learn through this process. This should focus on the generic issues rather than anecdotal evidence.

References

1. Feigenbaum, A V *Total Quality Control: Principles, Practices and Administration* McGraw-Hill, New York (1951)
2. Bendall, T *The Quality Gurus* Department of Trade and Industry, London (1989)
3. Shewhart, W A *Economic Control of Quality of Manufactured Products* Van Nostrand, New York (1931)
4. Ishikawa, K *What is TQC?* Prentice Hall, New York (1985)
5. Oakland, J S *Total Quality Management* 2nd edn, Heinemann, Oxford (1993)
6. Kanji, G 'Total quality management: the second industrial revolution' *Total Quality Management* 1990 **1** (1) 3–12
7. Deming, W E *Quality, Productivity and Competitive Position* MIT Press, Cambridge MA (1982)
8. Juran, J M *Out of the Crisis: Quality, Planning and Analysis* McGraw-Hill, New York (1970)
9. Crosby, P B *Quality is Free* McGraw-Hill, New York (1979)
10. Oakland, J S and Mortiboys, R *Total Quality Management and Effective Leadership* London, Department of Trade and Industry (1991)

11. Juran, J M *Juran on Planning for Quality* Free Press, New York (1988)
12. Dotchin, J A and Oakland, J S 'Theories and concepts in total quality management' *Total Quality Management* 1992 **3** (2) 133–145
13. Morris, B and Johnston, R 'Dealing with inherent variability: the difference between service and manufacturing explained' *International Journal of Operations and production Management* 1987 **7** (4) 13–22
14. Dale, B G 'Starting on the road to success' *Total Quality Management Magazine* 1991 **3** (2) 125–128
15. Lockyer, K 'Service – a polemic and a proposal' *International Journal of Operations and Production Management* 1986 **6** (3) 5–9
16. Murdick, R G, Render, B and Russell, R S *Service Operations Management* Allyn and Bocon, Boston (1990)
17. Sasser, E W, Olsen, R P and Wyckoff, D D *Management of Service Operations* Allyn and Bacon, Boston (1978)
18. Shostack, G L 'Breaking free from product marketing' *J of Marketing* 1987 (April) 133–139
19. Fitzsimmons, J A and Sullivan, R S *Service Operations Management* McGraw-Hill, New York (1982)
20. Chase, R B and Aquilano, N J *Production and Operations Management* 4th edn. Irwin, Homewood, IL (1985)
21. Clark, G 'Managing the intangibles of service quality' *Total Quality Management Magazine* 1989 **1** (2) 89–92
22. Dhir, K S and Chandrasekar, V 'Consumer subjectivity in selection and assessment of restaurants' in Lewis, R C, Beggs, T J, Shaw, M and Croffoot, S A (eds) *The Practice of Hospitality Management II* AVI (1986)
23. Embacher, J and Buttle, F 'A repertory grid analysis of Austria's image as a summer vacation destination' *Journal of Travel Research* 1989 **XXVII** (3) 3–7
24. Gartner, W C 'Tourism image: attribute measurement of state tourism products using multidimensional scaling techniques' *Journal of Travel Research* 1989 **XXVIII** (2) 16–20
25. Fick, G R and Ritchie, J R B 'Measuring service quality in the travel and tourism industry' *Journal of Travel Research* 1991 **XXX** (2) 2–9
26. LeBlanc, G 'Factors affecting customer evaluation of service quality in travel agencies: an investigation of customer perceptions' *Journal of Travel Research* 1992 **XXX** (4) 10–16
27. Saleh, F and Ryan, C 'Analysing service quality in the hospitality industry using the SERVQUAL model' *Service Industries Journal* 1991 **11** (3) 324–343
28. Parasuraman, A, Zeithaml, V A and Berry, L L 'SERVQUAL: a multiple-item scale for measuring consumer perceptions of service quality' *Journal of Retailing* 1988 **64** (1) 12–40
29. Crompton, J L and MacKay, K L 'Users' perceptions of the relative importance of service quality dimensions in selected public recreation programs' *Leisure Sciences* 1989 **11** (4) 367–375
30. Moores, B 'Management of service quality' in Jones, P (ed) *Management in Service Industries* Pitman, London (1989)
31. Oberoi, U and Hales, C 'Assessing the quality of the conference hotel service product: towards an empirically based model' *Service Industries Journal* 1990 **10** (4) 700–721
32. Geva, A and Goldman, A 'Satisfaction measurement in guided tours' *Annals of Tourism Research* 1991 **18** (2) 177–185
33. Kloppenborg T J and Gourdin, K N 'Up in the air about quality' *Quality Progress* 1992 **XXV** (2) 31–35
34. Lewis, R C 'Predicting hotel choice, the factors underlying perception' *Cornell Hotel and Restaurant Administration Quarterly* 1985 **25** (4) 82–96
35. Saleh, F and Ryan, C 'Client perceptions of hotels' *Tourism Management* 1992 **13** (2) 163–168
36. Whipple, T W and Thach, S V 'Group tour management: does good service produce satisfied customers?' *Journal of Travel Research* 1988 **XXVII** (2) 16–21
37. June, L P and Smith, S L J 'Service attributes and situational effects on customer preferences for restaurant dining' *Journal of Travel Research* 1987 **XXVI** (2) 20–27
38. Horovitz J 'How to check the quality of customer service and raise the standard' *International Management* 1987 **42** (February) 34–35
39. Van Borrendam, A 'KLM strives for customer satisfaction' *TQM Magazine* 1989 **1** (2) 105–109

40. Lane, C 'Putting people first – a company-wide approach to good service' in Moores, B (ed) *Are They Being Served* Philip Allan, Oxford (1986) 50–53
41. Leirvaag, S O 'The human factor or how do we organise SAS in the future?' Oslo (March 1988)
42. Lilja, O 'The SAS approach to quality' *TQM Magazine* 1989 **1** (3) 173–176
43. Bruce, L 'British Airways jolts staff with a cultural revolution' *Int Management* 1987 (March) 36–38
44. Davies, R J 'Mapping out improvement' *TQM Magazine* 1992 **4** (3) 181–183
45. Miller, B W 'High flyer' *Managing Service Quality* 1992 **2** (3) 153–156
46. Hostage, G M 'Quality control in a service business' *Harvard Business Review* 1975 **53** (4) 98–106
47. Hirst, M 'Newer and better ways' *Managing Service Quality* 1991 **1** (5) 247–251
48. Saunders, I W and Graham, M A 'Total quality management in the hospitality industry' *Journal of Total Quality Management* 1992 **3** (3) 243–255
49. Callan, R J 'Quality control at Avant hotels – the debut of BS 5750' *Service Industries Journal* 1992 **12** (1) 17–33
50. Mansfield, S 'Key in to visitor satisfaction' *Leisure Manager* 1987 **6** (3) 8–9
51. Miller, B W 'It's a kind of magic' *Managing Service Quality* 1992 **2** (4) 191–193
52. Stratton, B 'How Disneyland works' *Quality Progress* 1991 **XXIV** (7) 17–30
53. Asher, J 'Quantifying quality in service industries' *Total Quality Management* 1990 **1** (1) 89–94
54. Brockman, J 'Total quality management: the USA and UK compared' *Public Money and Management* 1992 **12** (4) 6–9
55. Gummesson, E 'Nine lessons on service quality' *Total Quality Management Magazine* 1989 **1** (2) 83–89
56. Hildebrandt, S, Kristensen, K, Kanji, G and Dahlgaard, J 'Quality culture and TQM' *Total Quality Management* 1991 **2** (1) 1–15
57. Horovitz, J and Cudennec-Poon, C 'Putting service quality into gear' *Quality Progress* 1991 (January) 54–58
58. Johnston, R 'A framework for developing a quality strategy in a customer processing operation' *International Journal of Quality and Reliability Management* 1987 **4** (4) 37–46
59. King, C 'A framework for a service quality assurance system' *Quality Progress* 1987 (September) 27–32
60. Kogure, M 'Some basic problems of quality assurance in service industries' *Total Quality Management* 1992 **3** (1) 9–17
61. Schvaneveldt, S and Enkawa, T 'Variability and quality loss in services: concepts and counter measures' *Total Quality Management* 1992 **3** (3) 233–241
62. Teboul, J 'De-industrialise service for quality' *International Journal of Operations and Production Management* 1988 **8** (3) 39–45

26

The service experience in tourism

Julie E Otto and J R Brent Ritchie

Faculty of Management, University of Calgary, 2500 University Dr NW, Calgary, Alberta T2N 1N4, Canada

The real challenge for the tourism industry is to create the right psychological environment, not to worry just about technical things. (John Crompton, addressing 'Quality Management in Urban Tourism' delegates, Victoria, BC, Canada, 1994)

Tourism is essentially a service industry or, perhaps more accurately, an amalgam of service industries. Consequently, its management practices are typically concerned with such issues as quality[1] and productivity[2] as they fall within the aegis of services marketing. While these concerns are critical, they encompass what Crompton refers to above as 'technical things', and may only be telling part of the management story.

The other side of the story is the 'psychological environment'; that is, the subjective personal reactions and feelings experienced by consumers when they consume a service. This phenomenon has been termed the service experience and has recently been found to be an important part of consumer evaluation of and satisfaction with services.[3] In tourism, understanding experiential phenomena is particularly important, as emotional reactions – and decisions – often prevail amongst consumers.[4]

To date, a model which captures the essence of the service experience across tourism industries has not been conceptualized. Further, most research into this and related constructs has employed qualitative and phenomenological methods, while a generalizable quantitative measure has yet to be developed. It must be noted that the intention here is not to downgrade the approaches typically used to study experiential phenomena; indeed, their richness and insightfulness can scarcely be matched by quantitative methods. Rather, given the ever-expanding range of products and markets in the tourism industry, the need to develop an instrument which is both managerially relevant and applicable in a broader context is evident. To this end, a quantitative approach, which could complement qualitative research, was deemed necessary.

The purpose of this research is to enhance our understanding of the service experience and, in so doing, to design a means for its measurement. Thus, the paper begins with a review of the literature concerning the leisure and tourism experience. Subsequently, we turn to the services marketing field for insights into the design and delivery of this experience. From an empirical perspective, the development of a scale was considered the most reliable and valid means to further accomplish the objective stated earlier. Accordingly, survey research was used to capture consumers' impressions of the experience of three tourism service sectors: hotels, airlines and tours and attractions. The dimensionality of scale items was then explored using factor analysis. The resulting factors are presented in the following pages, as are differences in the service experience across the three tourism sectors. Managerial implications and future research directions are then discussed. The authors conclude that the service experience scale can be applied to enhance our theoretical and managerial understanding of services marketing in the tourism industry.

Experiential perspectives in tourism

The 'experience' of leisure and tourism can be described as the subjective mental state felt by participants. This facet of consumption has received some attention from researchers in the field, mainly those concerned with its sociological, anthropological and psychological significance. The following sections review the importance of the experience to the meaning of leisure and tourism, as well as its relevance to motivation and satisfaction.

The meaning of leisure and tourism

In one context, the experience has been used as a vehicle to describe the *meaning* of various leisure and tourism activities and events, also called definitional research.[5] Such research refers to the phenomenology, dimensionality and characteristics of leisure pursuits,[6] the risk represented by various activities,[7] and the symbolic or cognitive representation of travel.[8]

Gunter[9] asks the rhetorical question, 'what is leisure?' Is it 'a kind of time, a state of mind, or a certain kind of pre-defined activities'?[9] He and others have since addressed this issue by assembling descriptive dimensions which typically comprise participants' experiences. Importantly, rather than describing actual leisure activities (such as scuba diving) and their tangible components (such as wetsuits, boat rides and oxygen tanks), this stream of literature describes how and where the activity sits in the psychological space of participants. For example, Celsi et al. found that the act of skydiving could be characterized by such things as feelings of communitas, or 'a sense of camaraderie that occurs when individuals from various walks of life share a common bond of experience' (p. 12)[10] and the existence of phatic communication, 'a special language... little understood by non-members... [comprising] verbal and nonverbal cues (p. 13).[10] Kleiber et al.[6] found that adolescent leisure activities were either relaxed (providing pleasure without physical demands) or developmental (necessitating effort and demand). The latter are seen as means by which youth could make the transition from the relative freedom of adolescence to the demands and constraints of adulthood. Gunter[9] found leisure in general to be characterized by a sense of separation from the everyday world, feelings of intense pleasure, freedom of choice, spontaneity, timelessness, fantasy, adventure and self-realization. No restrictions were placed on the means by, or time frame during which, one could achieve these desired states. Similarly, Unger and Kernan[11] provided empirical evidence that leisure activities are representing in varying degrees by the six conditions of intrinsic satisfaction, perceived freedom, involvement, arousal, mastery and spontaneity. Finally, in a related vein of research, Cheron and Ritchie[7] found that leisure-related activities could be characterized by the degree to which they represented two forms of risk: functional and psychosocial.

Tourism researchers have also sought to define and depict the act of travel in a psychological sense. Dunn Ross and Iso-Ahola assert that 'although such sociological factors as income and socioeconomic status affect tourism behavior, they are not significant determinants of the quality of the experiences. What matters is the individual's cognitions and feelings about the experience being undertaken.'[12] Building on the notion of sacred (non-ordinary) and profane (everyday) experiences, Graburn views tourism as one of many 'institutions that humans use to embellish and add meaning to their lives'.[13] Nash and Smith further extend this theme to describe tourism as a transitional rite of passage, comprising the three stages of separation from the community, liminality or transition, and reintegration.[8]

Hamilton-Smith[14] categorizes tourism on the two dimensions of existential reality and structural reality. The former represents the extent to which one feels 'high levels of satisfaction, freedom, and involvement, and [intrinsic] reward' (p. 334) while the latter entails the extent to which the activity is task-orientated and wherein completion is externally enforced. Clearly, overlap is evident between this categorization scheme and that of Kleiber et al., mentioned earlier. Combining low and high levels of each dimension, yields four spaces, such as 'Tourism-as-Quest' (both high existential and high structural), an example of which might be an African safari, wherein consumers can discover in themselves a new spirit of adventure while adhering to strict rules and procedural guidelines.

Motivation and satisfaction in leisure and tourism

As noted by Mannell and Iso-Ahola, the definitions cited above can help researchers and managers alike to understand the range of needs which people seek to satisfy through touristic behaviour. Indeed, meaning and motivation are arguably similar enough constructs to be discussed together; however, because the two are typically handled separately in the literature, they will be treated so here.

Motivational research is specifically concerned with the benefits one seeks and obtains from engaging in leisure and tourism activities. As noted by Celsi et al., these benefits are often nebulous, ambiguous or even paradoxical in nature:

Why would an individual purposefully seek physical and psychic risk? A paradox seems to exist when individuals who, for example, wear seat belts, obtain the best personal and property insurances, use condoms, and seek safety and security in the workplace spend their free time risking it all climbing granitic escarpments, hang gliding, or falling earthward at 150 miles per hour in free-fall. (p. 1)[10]

The study of motivation in risky or dangerous leisure and tourism pursuits does not seem conducive to traditional objective, utilitarian and functional frameworks.

Instead, Celsi et al. cite normative (sociological) and hedonic (psychological) incentives as prerequisites to initially undertake such activities. Notably, however, in skydiving, the motivation to *continue* comprises a different set of benefits: 'efficacy motives, the creation of a new self-identity, group camaraderie, and heightened experience' (p. 10). In other words, benefits move along a continuum from extrinsic to intrinsic as participants gain experience. Further, as participants became more skilled (in itself a motive), other motivations are more readily realized, thus highlighting the interdependence and potentially cumulative character of all facets of the psychological experience. However, the interplay of these dimensions represents a delicate equilibrium, in that individuals must feel challenged but not overwhelmed, and must manage the tension without giving into anxiety.

The question of satisfaction is really the other side of motivational research,[5] and it is further apparent that sources of satisfaction are conceptually similar, if not identical, to the constructs used to define the meaning of leisure and tourism. For example, Block and Bruce[15] found that a favoured form of leisure for highly product-centred individuals was product-centred activity, such as cleaning, displaying and discussing possessions. The resulting satisfactions fell into the categories of attention-seeking, power, recreation/escape, confidence/self-worth, self-importance and affiliation. The dual themes of seeking and escaping therefore appear to be universal in leisure and tourism consumption psychology. Again, however, it is the balance of the two which must be optimally managed.

Tourism as a service

Once recognizing the critical, yet delicate, interplay between the experience of, and satisfaction with, leisure and tourism activities, industry personnel are well advised to pay attention to the former dimension. Unfortunately, the socioanthropological perspectives discussed in the previous section, while critical to our understanding of the concept, are not necessarily readily transferable into managerial action. Viewing leisure and tourism as a service industry has permitted a framework in which actually to manage the experience while respecting and maintaining its integrity.

Service quality in tourism

Perhaps the most straightforward manner by which to apply a services marketing perspective is to borrow general marketing measurement instruments directly from the field and apply them to tourism. Indeed, most research of this nature has focused on the evaluation of service quality and on the more functional and technical aspects of service delivery, and in fact, traditional measures of service quality have been shown to apply in evaluation of services in the leisure and tourism industries. For example, the dimensions that LeBlanc[16] found travellers to use in evaluating service quality in travel agencies were not materially different from those captured by the SERVQUAL instrument (e.g. timeliness, competence, physical evidence, etc), nor were those used to evaluate service quality in organized tours, as noted by Luk et al.[17] Similarly, Fick and Ritchie[18] showed SERVQUAL to be adequate for monitoring and comparative purposes in service industries such as ski resorts. However, Fick and Ritchie also advocated the use of supplementary qualitative measures to capture key dimensions, noting that a strictly quantitative scale does not adequately address those affective and holistic factors 'which contribute to the overall quality of the "service experience" ' (p. 9). It is the application of this latter construct in leisure and tourism research to which we now turn our attention.

The service experience in tourism

Focusing only on the objective, technical aspects of tourism services leaves untapped a crucial resource; that is, the ability to understand and manage the true nature of consumer satisfaction as it occurs in the context of service delivery. In fact, research has shown that affective or emotion-based reports, which we argue form the basis of the quality of the service experience, contribute a significant, but often ignored, portion of explained variance in satisfaction evaluations.[19] We can conclude, then, that a measure of the quality of the service experience might be a useful complement – if not an alternative – to traditional quality of service measures.

Figure 1 is intended to depict, from a measurement standpoint, the difference between the 'quality of service' and the 'quality of experience'.[3]

Perhaps more than any other service industry, tourism holds the potential to elicit strong emotional and experiential reactions by consumers. Accordingly, at least two other researchers in the field have noted that utilitarian and rational information processing schemes which focus on functional or purely attribute-based elements are incommensurate with leisure and tourism. Dimanche and Samdahl[20] refer to tourism as unique owing to its symbolic expressive dimension, while Arnould and Price[21] focus on the extraordinary experience offered by extended leisure pursuits (in their case,

FRAMEWORK	QOS	QOE
Measurement	Objective	Subjective
Evaluative Model	Attribute-based	Holistic/Gestalt
Focus of Evaluation	Company/Service Provider/ Service Environment (External)	Self (Internal)
Scope	Specific	General
Nature of Benefits	Functional/Utilitarian	Experiential/Hedonic/ Symbolic
Psychological Representation	Cognitive/Attitudinal	Affective

Source: Otto and Ritchie 1995

Figure 1. Comparison of QOS and QOE frameworks.

white-water rafting trips), both of which render the experience incompatible with traditional evaluative paradigms. As an alternative, these authors advocate a focus on the self to truly understand satisfaction with such phenomena.

We further argue here that even when tourism sectors have a clear functional component to them, as do accommodation and transportation services, experiential benefits will remain a critical part of the process evaluation. The intimate, hands-on nature of the service encounter itself affords many opportunities for affective responses. Elements of the physical environment (what Bitner calls the 'servicescape'[22]) also have strong potential to elicit emotional and subjective reactions.[4] For example, the tranquil beauty of a mountain resort's setting affords psychological benefits that clearly transcend the physical need to 'sleep somewhere'. In addition, it has long been acknowledged that human interaction itself is an emotionally charged process. The extended interaction with a tour guide or other service provider can then also lead to experiential reactions.[21] In other cases, as in purely recreational activities, the experiential benefits will be ends in themselves.[23]

Given the importance of experiential benefits to satisfaction with all facets of the tourism industry, further understanding of this construct is necessary. To address this need, an empirical study was designed, the results of which will be presented in the remainder of this article.

Research method

Objective

The purpose of this research is to measure the nature of satisfaction with the service experience across tourism industries. While arguably the 'best' measurement of the quality of the service experience will employ both quantitative and qualitative components, we focused on the former, where it is felt that attention in both lacking and warranted at present. Thus, the empirical study presented herein is intended to develop a reliable and valid set of scales which can be used to assess the nature and quality of the affective component of the service experience. In the course of developing this instrument, a secondary objective was also addressed; that is, differences in the service experience across industries were examined. In summary, then, this research sought to answer two key questions:

- What is the overall structure of the service experience in selected tourism industries?
- How, if at all, does this structure vary across service sectors in the tourism industry?

Scale development procedure

The following sections present the methodology used in developing a set of scales to measure the quality of the service experience (also referred to as the affective component of the service experience), which was conducted according to the procedure developed by Churchill.[24] As an added confirmation of the research method, the authors consulted directly with researchers well seasoned in this measurement procedure, and used guidelines and protocols as they appear in other published materials referred to below.

Resource constraints limited the current study to completion of only the preliminary steps in Churchill's process. That is, this research addressed issues of content validity, dimensionality and internal reliability of the service experience scales, up to and including a factor analysis. Further tests as to validity and reliability of the scale itself will be undertaken in future empirical applications of the completed instrument.

Specifying the construct domain

The affective component of the service experience has been shown to comprise the subjective, emotional and highly personal responses to various aspects of service delivery which lead to satisfaction with the service overall.[3] Accordingly, this definition is specified as the domain of the construct for this scale development.

The next step was to generate an item pool that captured the domain of the quality of service experience as specified. To optimize the content validity of such a list, this research combined the results of exploratory research with a review of the literature in consumer behaviour, services marketing and leisure and tourism. The exploratory research comprised open-ended depth interviews with consumers of five different services.[3] A content analysis was performed on the results and an expert panel was used to sort the responses into dimensions. Figure 2 gives a summary of these content-analysed items and the dimensions which they appear to comprise. An underlying purpose of this research was to provide preliminary and statistically significant confirmation as to the existence of these six dimensions, and/or their respective elements, in the service experience.

Referring to the literature, the *hedonic, novelty* and *stimulation* dimensions which emerged from exploratory empirical research are consistent with experiential benefits described by Havlena and Holbrook,[25] Holbrook and Hirschman[23] and Bello and Etzel,[26] among others. *Safety* forms the basis of the Maslovian need hierarchy while *comfort* has been documented as a fundamental benefit of the service encounter.[27]

Dimension	Examples
Hedonic	• Excitement • Enjoyment • Memorability
Interactive	• Meeting People • Being Part of the Process • Having Choice
Novelty	• Escape • Doing Something New
Comfort	• Physical Comfort • Relaxation
Safety	• Personal Safety • Security of Belongings
Stimulation	• Educational and Informative • Challenging

Source: *Otto and Ritchie 1995*

Figure 2. Construct domain: the service experience.

Finally, the existence of *interactive* benefits in services consumption has been empirically corroborated and described by Hui and Bateson[28] and Arnould and Price.[21]

Based on elements derived from the aforementioned research studies, a list of items emerged which could be used to describe each dimension. To increase the reliability of the measure, the number of items used to measure each element should be greater than one. In this case, two items per element were deemed sufficient to enhance reliability while minimizing respondent wear-out during survey completion. This entire process yielded 56 items in total.

Tourism service sectors

The tourism study contained herein was part of a larger multi-industry study looking at the service experience in general. Complete generalizability across services, while desirable in the ideal, is unattainable given the reality of resource constraints. Thus, the current research was limited to the examination of three service sectors in the tourism industry: airlines, hotels and tours and attractions. These services were chosen based on the nature and degree of differences between them in the evaluation of the service experience which emerged in previous exploratory research.[21] Further, they differ in terms of such aspects as necessity, interpersonal contact, cost, accessibility and so forth. Finally, for the sake of convenience, these services were most likely to have higher usage incidence amongst the population at hand.

Research design and administration

The first part of the questionnaire used in this study consisted of 56 items each followed by a six-point Likert scale. For each service, respondents were asked the single-stem question. 'To be most satisfied with the experience of [service], I want to feel . . .' followed by the items. The second part of the study contained questions to help classify respondents on the basis of usage and demographics.

The surveys were handed out during late July and early August 1994, at the Tourism Vancouver Info-Centre in Vancouver, BC. Questionnaires were handed out at random to English-speaking respondents 18 years and older, and were distributed in alternating order for each particular service. This order was predetermined; that is, the survey administrator had no knowledge or control over who received a survey on which industry. Respondents were asked to complete the 15-minute survey on the spot or, if desired, to complete it at a later time and return it by mail in a pre-addressed and stamped envelope. As an added incentive, four prizes of C$100 were given out, the winners of which were drawn at random from the pool of returned surveys.

The scale was tested on 339 individuals, with a roughly equal distribution by sector (see Figure 3). This number was chosen to ensure that the number of cases for each service would be approximately two times greater than the total number of scale items for each of the three services to be tested. Demographic breakdowns are given in Table 1.

This sample was obtained in accordance with the procedures outlined by McDougall an Munro,[29] who assert that issues of randomness and generalizability are not critical in the initial stages of scale development. Consequently, convenience samples can be (and often are) used for this process, as was the case in this survey.

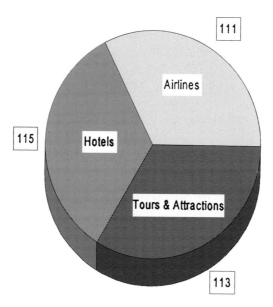

Figure 3. Sample by sector (*N* = 339).

Table 1. Sample demographics.

Factor	%
Gender	
Male	54.9
Female	45.1
Age	
19–29 years	37.8
30–39 years	27.4
40–49 years	13.9
50–59 years	9.7
60 years and over	11.2
Residence	
Canada	37.8
USA	12.1
UK	15.6
Australia/New Zealand	3.5
Asia	2.4
Other	19.8
No answer	8.8

Analysis

Once the data were transformed to correct a negative skew and adjusted for missing items, the dimensionality of the items were explored using factor analysis on SPSS PC. Specifically, principal axis factoring using a Varimax (orthogonal) rotation was used to indicate the number of underlying factors (or dimensions) in the data and to identify the set of items loading on each of these factors. To account for the greatest variance in each dimension, Echtner and Ritchie[30] advocate the elimination of factor loadings lower than 0.4. Because the objective was to develop a measure of the service experience that is generalizable across industries, this stage of the factor analysis was conducted on the pooled data set (i.e. data from all three sectors).

Next, Cronbach's alpha was calculated to measure the internal reliability for each of the significant factors identified in the exploratory analysis. In general, a value of 0.8 for Cronbach's alpha is the minimally acceptable point for scales.[31] If unsatisfactory alpha scores are obtained, item-to-total correlations are examined to determine which scale items should be dropped. In general, item-to-total values below 0.5 are deemed unacceptable.[32] An iterative sequence of deleting items with low item-to-total scores, recomputing alphas and item-to-total correlations, and so forth, was carried out until the maximum alpha was obtained.

Results

Three iterations of the above sequence were necessary until the final solution was realized. The results will be discussed with direct reference to the two research questions posed earlier.

What is the structure of the service experience?

In all, four factors with eigenvalues greater than or equal to one emerged from the data set, as given in Table 2. These four factors (comprising 23 items in total) explained 61.3% of the overall variance. Scale reliability was calculated at 0.899 (see Table 3).

From Table 2 it can be seen that *hedonics* account for not only the greatest individual variance (33.3%) but for more variance than the other three factors combined. Respondents confirmed the need to be doing what they loved or liked, to have their imaginations stirred and to be thrilled by the service activities. Further, they wanted to be able to have memories to keep to themselves and to share with others later on. The second most significant factor was *peace of mind*, accounting for 17% of the explained variance, in which consumers cited the need for both physical and psychological safety and comfort. The third factor, named *involvement*, seemed to have more to do with the process of service delivery than with outcome. Here, respondents indicated their willingness to be active participants in certain service systems, as indicated by the desire to have choice and control in the service offering. On the other hand, they also demanded that they be educated, informed and imbued with a sense of mutual cooperation. Finally, these consumers wanted to derive a sense of personal *recognition* from their service encounters, such that they could feel important and confident that they were being taken seriously.

How, if at all, does this structure vary across services?

In order to analyse how the structure of the service experience in tourism varies across sectors, means were computed to enable a ranking of each item by industry (Table 4) and to compare scores for each factor (Table 5).

Table 2. Factor loading matrix.

Dimensions/items	Fac 1	Fac 2	Fac 3	Fac 4	% Var.	EV
Factor one: Hedonics					33.3	7.65
Doing something I really like to do	0.471					
Doing something memorable	0.625					
Doing something thrilling	0.811					
Having a 'once in a lifetime' experience	0.777					
Share my experience with others later on	0.575					
A feeling of escape	0.579					
Being challenged in some way	0.678					
My imagination is being stirred	0.599		0.409			
On an adventure	0.842					
Having fun	0.695					
Doing something new and different	0.805					
Factor two: Peace of mind					17.0	3.9
Physically comfortable		0.765				
My property is safe		0.697				
Relaxed		0.637				
Personal security		0.737				
Privacy is assured		0.676				
Factor three: Involvement					6.6	1.53
Involved in the process			0.599			
Element of choice in the process			0.569			
Have control over the outcome			0.653			
Being educated and informed			0.43			
Cooperation			0.516			
Factor four: Recognition					4.4	1.0
Taken seriously				0.452		
Important				0.725		

Table 3. Scale reliability.

Factor	Cronbach's alpha
Scale (23 items)	0.899
Factor 1: Hedonics (11 items)	0.919
Factor 2: Peace of mind (5 items)	0.838
Factor 3: Involvement (5 items)	0.759
Factor 4: Recognition (2 items)	0.756

Looking at the data presented in Table 4, it can be seen that airlines and hotels appear to be generally similar in terms of the desired experience, while tours and attractions occupy a different space altogether. For airlines, the items making up peace of mind were the five most important overall. This pattern was reflected in hotels, with the exception of the fifth most important items, 'doing something I really like to do', instead of the 'assurance of privacy' which was fifth most important for airlines. For tours and attractions, on the other hand, hedonic elements such as 'doing something I really like to do', 'doing something new and different', 'having fun' and 'doing

Table 4. Rank importance of dimensions and items.

Dimensions	Total	Air	Hotel	Tour
Factor one: Hedonics				
That I am doing something I really like to do	4	6	5	1
As though I am doing something memorable	8	10	8	5
That I am doing something thrilling	19	19	19	13
That I am having a 'once in a lifetime' experience	20	20	22	12
That I can share my experience with others later on	12	14	13	11
A feeling of escape	13	11	11	14
That I am being challenged in some way	22	23	20	15
That my imagination is being stirred	15	17	16	7
Like I am on an adventure	16	18	14	10
Like I am having fun	6	7	6	3
That I am doing something new and different	10	15	15	2
Factor two: Peace of mind				
Physically comfortable	5	5	4	16
That my property is safe	1	1	1	6
Relaxed	2	4	2	9
A sense of personal security	3	2	3	4
That my privacy is assured	7	3	10	19
Factor three: Involvement				
That I am involved in the process	23	22	23	21
That there is an element of choice in the process	9	9	9	8
That I have some control over the outcome	14	12	17	17
That I am being educated and informed	17	21	18	4
A sense of cooperation	21	16	21	22
Factor four: Recognition				
That I am being taken seriously	11	8	7	20
That I am important	18	13	12	23

Table 5. Factor means.

Element	Factor 1 (Hedonics)	Factor 2 (Peace of mind)	Factor 3 (Involvement)	Factor 4 (Recognition)
Comparison within sectors				
Total	4.351	5.047	4.117	4.251
Airlines	4.081	5.473	3.936	4.435
Hotels	4.207	5.093	3.937	4.347
Tours	4.768	4.566	4.478	3.969
Comparison across sectors				
Total	4.351	5.047	4.117	4.251
Airlines	4.081	5.473	3.936	4.435
Hotels	4.207	5.093	3.937	4.347
Tours	4.768	4.566	4.478	3.969

something memorable' were the most important, although this was followed closely by the need for personal security.

At the other end of the continuum, four of the least important items for both airlines and hotels were to be 'doing something thrilling', to have a 'once in a lifetime experience', to be 'challenged in some way' and to be 'involved in the process'. For airlines, being 'educated and informed' was relatively unimportant, while for hotels, feeling a 'sense of cooperation' was also less important. With tours and attractions, respondents seemed least concerned with recognition factors, with being involved and feeling as though they are being cooperated with, and with having their privacy assured.

Examining differences in mean scores for factors also yields interesting insights (Table 5). Comparing means within sectors, peace of mind is the most important factor, while the involvement dimension is least important, for both airlines and hotels. Looking at tours and attractions, differences between factors are much less noticeable, indicating that its experience is much wider-ranging and multi-dimensional overall. It can be stated that hedonics is, directionally, the most important evaluative component for this sector, while recognition is evidently the least.

Comparing factor means across sectors, hedonics is most salient in tours and attractions, peace of mind is most important to airlines (wherein, recalling that this was a six-point scale, it is obviously critical), involvement is more important in tours and attractions, and recognition is slightly more important to airlines.

Managerial implications

Several managerial implications can be drawn from both the theory and the data presented in the foregoing analysis.

From a theoretical standpoint, it appears critical that both researchers and practitioners in the tourism industry not lose sight of the true nature of consumer benefits, motivations and subjective responses. The research presented here has shown that service experience factors are not 'soft', elusive abstracts, but rather are specific dimensions that can readily be measured to better understand satisfaction. Indeed, if industry managers use only service quality or attribute-based measures in their satisfaction evaluations, they may be forcing people to evaluate tourism services on more functional and utilitarian dimensions than is appropriate or even relevant.

From the perspective of marketing strategy, advertising 'experiential' benefits is not new to either product or services marketing. A clearer understanding of the customer-specific experience as it relates to your service and your company can contribute to a more effective positioning, promotional and communications strategy, a point which has been supported in previous research. Vogt et al.[33] found that travellers demonstrated the need for aesthetic information as well as for functional information. In other words, consumers will, consciously or otherwise, seek out information on what type of experience to expect at both the destination and, by extension, the company level. In practical terms, this means that the need for information on such aspects as pricing and operating hours may be supplemented (if not supplanted) by the need to promote psychological factors. While this may be obvious and commonplace in advertising for tours and attractions, incorporating experiential dimensions into more functional services may offer a unique competitive edge. As noted by Arnould and Price, 'although it may seem a stretch to promise a renewed sense of self from stopping at McDonald's for breakfast, several award-winning advertisements do just that.'[21] Effectively accomplishing this objective is tied into the type of medium used to convey product information. While glossy brochures are an advantage over newspaper, the current trend toward video-based advertising in tourism will provide even more opportunity to convey the richness of the customer experience in service encounters.

The multi-faceted nature of the service experience also implies that it could be a useful means by which to classify services. This data set has given evidence that both the nature and degree of the service experience differ significantly across service sectors. Clearly, the primary message emerging for tours and attractions is 'entertain me', while that for airlines and hotels is 'keep me feeling safe'. Of secondary importance to both airlines and hotels is the need for recognition as a customer, while for tours and attractions both involvement and peace of mind follow. Looking closely at these differences indicates a means by which one can categorize services based on their respective experiences. That is, certain services will offer experiential benefits as they relate to the way the business is run (that is, they are process variables), while others will offer experiential benefits as they relate to the overall purpose of your business (that is, they are outcome variables). An example of the former would be airlines, whose primary purpose is functional in nature (transporting passengers from A to B), while the delivery of the service can be enhanced by the incorporation of experiential benefits. An example of the latter would be a theme park, whose purpose is experiential in nature, but whose service environment would be enhanced by the incorporation of service quality or functional variables. In other words, then, the functional and the experiential are two ends of a continuum along which both service processes and outcomes might be evaluated and classified.

Of course, the challenge will lie in translating the service experience into service encounter, service delivery and service environment specifics. As noted above, the coexistence of these ostensibly opposing dimensions (thrills vs safety, functional vs experiential) underscores the need for service providers in tourism to understand their customers fully so that they can provide an environment which offers that critical balance. From a measurement standpoint, a related difficulty arises in the need to get more involved in measuring and understanding one's customers and their feelings rather than simply focusing on the more readily assessed and more easily controllable internal measures such as waiting time and uniform style. In the short term, implementation of service experience standards will potentially increase marketing costs, as the adminis-tration of customer surveys is naturally more expensive than internal audits and reviews. According to Ozment and Morash,[34] however, the payoff from an investment in this kind of consumer understanding is high. They further argue that it is in fact more efficient and economical to design all service standards based on the proper consumer understanding in the first place, rather than having to retrace one's steps and redesign systems that were built according to inaccurate, or even insufficient, information.

Limitations and future directions

Several limitations of the foregoing analysis are to be noted. First, this was a quantitative study with generalizability and reliability as its core objectives. Such investigations, especially those made into essentially phenomenological topic areas, are bound to sacrifice depth in favour of breadth. We recommend that both applied and theoretical survey research into the service experience be complemented with qualitative research to uncover the nuances and idiosyncracies related to each service sector and service company.

Similarly, research into the service experience should be as real and as recent as possible; that is, interviews should be done as close to consumption of an actual (as opposed to theoretical or scenario-based) service as possible, so that the evaluation remains fresh in consumers' minds and so that experiential benefits are not 'forgotten' or replaced with more cognitively accessible functional benefits. Finally, while this research has enhanced our understanding of the structure of the service experience, it is static in nature and does not lend insights into the dynamics of the service encounter. For example, the research does not indicate how consumers might trade off or weight their evaluations of different aspects of the service experience in arriving at overall satisfaction.

These limitations lead to suggestions for future research into the area. From an implementation perspective, one of the most critical areas requiring further explora-tion is that of causality. That is, to what extent are service experience elements influenced by attributes in the service encounter and perceptions of service quality? Similarly, how does the service experience impact on satisfaction, and how might this vary across services? Understanding questions such as these (which relate to the notion raised earlier about process vs outcome) can help in designing the service delivery process and the service environment itself. Finally, indications of how the service experience impacts upon company-favourable behaviours, such as positive word of mouth, repeat purchase and even price sensitivity, could further highlight the importance of this construct to managers in the tourism industry.

Acknowledgements

The authors would like to thank the staff of Tourism Vancouver for kindly and generously giving us access to their InfoCentre during our data collection period. The authors would also like to thank Dr Wilfred Zerbe for his assistance in the analysis.

References

1. McCutcheon, D M, Stuart, F I and Tax, S S 'Service quality planning in urban tourism: tradeoffs and resource deployment' in Murphy, P (ed) *Quality Management in Urban Tourism Proceedings* University of Victoria, Victoria, BC (1994) 56–66
2. Kirker, W, Crouch, G I 'Competing urban destinations: is productivity a relevant concept?' in Murphy, P (ed) *Quality Management in Urban Tourism Proceedings* University of Victoria, Victoria, BC (1994) 446–476
3. Otto, J E and Ritchie, J R B 'Exploring the quality of the service experience: a theoretical and empirical analysis' in Bowen, D, Swartz, T and Brown, S (eds) *Advances in Services Marketing and Management: Research and Practice* Vol IV, JAI Press, CT (1995)
4. Wakefield, K L and Blodgett, J G 'The importance of servicescapes in leisure service settings' *Journal of Services Marketing* 1994 **8** (2) 66–76
5. Mannell, R and Iso-Ahola, S 'Psychological nature of the leisure and tourism experience' *Annals of Tourism Research* 1987 **14** (3) 314–331

6. Kleiber, D, Larson, R and Csikszentmihalyi, M 'The experience of leisure in adolescence' *Journal of Leisure Research* 1986 **18** (3) 169–176

7. Cheron, J and Brent Ritchie, J R 'Leisure activities and perceived risk' *Journal of Leisure Research* 1982 **14** (2) 139–154

8. Nash, D and Smith, V L 'Anthropology and tourism' *Annals of Tourism Research* 1991 **18** 12–25

9. Gunter, B G 'The leisure experience: selected properties' *Journal of Leisure Research* 1987 **19** (2) 115–130

10. Celsi, R L, Rose, R L and Leigh, T W 'An exploration of high-risk leisure consumption through skydiving' *Journal of Consumer Research* 1993 **20** (June) 1–23

11. Unger, L S and Kernan, J B 'On the meaning of leisure: an investigation of some determinants of the subjective experience' *Journal of Consumer Research* 1983 **9** (March) 381–392

12. Dunn Ross, E L and Iso-Ahola, S E 'Sightseeing tourists' motivation and satisfaction' *Annals of Tourism Research* 1991 **18** (2) 226–237

13. Graburn, N H 'The anthropology of tourism' *Annals of Tourism Research* 1983 **10** (1) 9–33

14. Hamilton-Smith, E, 'Four kinds of tourism?' *Annals of Tourism Research* 1987 **14** (3) 332–344

15. Bloch, P H and Bruce, G D 'The leisure experience and consumer products: an investigation of underlying satisfactions' *Journal of Leisure Research* 1984 **16** (1) 74–88

16. LeBlanc, G 'Factors affecting customer evaluation of service quality in travel agencies: an investigation of customer perceptions' *Journal of Travel Research* 1993 (Spring) 10–16

17. Luk, S T K, de Leon, C T, Leong, F-W and Li, E L Y 'Value segmentation of tourists' expectations of service quality' *Journal of Travel and Tourism Marketing* 1993 **2** (4) 23–38

18. Fick, G R and Brent Ritchie, J R 'Measuring service quality in the travel and tourism industry' *Journal of Travel Research* 1991 (Fall) 2–9

19. Oliver, R L 'Cognitive, affective and attribute bases of the satisfaction response' *Journal of Consumer Research* 1993 **20** (December) 1–13

20. Dimanche, F and Samdahl, D 'Leisure as symbolic consumption: a conceptualization and prospectus for future research' *Leisure Sciences* 1994 **16** (2) 119–129

21. Arnould, E J and Price, L L 'River magic: extraordinary experience and the extended service encounter' *Journal of Consumer Research* 1993 **20** (June) 24–45

22. Bitner, M J 'Servicescapes: the impact of physical surroundings on customers and employees' *Journal of Marketing* 1992 **56** (April) 57–71

23. Holbrook, M B and Hirschman, E 'The experiential aspects of consumption: consumer fantasies, feelings and fun' *Journal of Consumer Research* 1982 **9** (September) 132–140

24. Churchill, G A 'A paradigm for developing better measures of marketing constructs' *Journal of Marketing Research* 1979 **16** (February) 64–73

25. Havlena, W and Holbrook, M 'The varieties of consumption experience: comparing two typologies of emotion in consumer behaviour' *Journal of Consumer Research* 1986 **13** (December) 394–404

26. Bello, D C and Etzel, M J 'The role of novelty in the pleasure travel experience' *Journal of Travel Research* 1985 (Summer) 20–26

27. Parasuraman, A, Zeithaml, V A and Berry, L L 'A conceptual model of service quality and its implications for future research' *Journal of Marketing* 1985 **49** (Fall) 41–50

28. Hui, M K and Bateson, J E 'Perceived control and the effects of crowding and consumer choice on the service experience' *Journal of Consumer Research* 1991 **18** (September) 174–184

29. McDougall, G H G and Munro, H 'Scaling and attitude measurement in travel and tourism research' in Ritchie, J R B and Goeldner, C (eds) *Travel, Tourism and Hospitality Research: A Handbook for Managers and Researchers* Wiley, New York (1994)

30. Echtner, C M and Brent Ritchie, J R 'The measurement of destination image: an empirical assessment' *Journal of Travel Research*, 1993 **31** (Spring) 3–13

31. Carmines, E G and Zeller, R A *Reliability and Validity Assessement* Sage University Paper Series on Quantitative Applications in the Social Sciences, 07–017, Sage, Beverly Hills, CA (1979)

32. Lankford, S V and Howard, D R 'Developing a tourism attitude scale' *Annals of Tourism Research* 1994 **21** (1) 121–139

33. Vogt, C A, Fesenmeier, D R and MacKay, K 'Functional and aesthetic information needs underlying the pleasure travel experience' *Journal of Travel and Tourism Marketing* 1993 **2** (2/3) 133–146

34. Ozment, J and Morash, E A 'The augmented service offering for perceived and actual service quality' *Journal of the Academy of Marketing Science* 1994 **22** (4) 352–363

Part IX

Indigenous peoples and tourism

Introduction by Chris Ryan

Introduction

The issue of indigenous peoples and tourism is not new as a topic, but what is beginning to emerge is more quantitative data. For a long time research into issues of tourism and its relationships with the cultures of the Aboriginal peoples of Australia, Maori of New Zealand, North American Indian peoples and the Inuit of Canada has been dominated by those approaching the topic from an anthropological perspective. Possibly the first major book on this subject was that Valene Smith's *Hosts and Guests: The Anthropology of Tourism*, an edited work that was first published in 1977. Other notable work has since been published, including in terms of analysis of imagery, the much cited works of Albers and James (1983, 1988), Cohen (1993) and Edwards (1996). Alternatively, some of the work has been concerned with various aspects of protection of sacred sites (e.g. Arsenault, 1997). Much of the work on the relationship between tourism and indigenous people's culture has been published as individual articles in the academic tourism journals, and has been, until recently, relatively infrequent in its appearance. However, in recent years there has been a significant increase in scholarly work, and it has also been increasingly accessible to students of tourism. Recent examples of edited books that have considered various aspects of 'indigenous tourism' include those of Butler and Hinch (1996), Price and Smith (1996), Lew and Van Otten (1998) and Robinson and Boniface (1999). That there is generally a greater awareness of the culture of tribal peoples was symbolised in the 1990s by the United Nations declaration of the International Decade of the World's Indigenous People (under General Assembly resolution 48/163, dated 21 December, 1993).

Definitions

Definitions of indigenous peoples are found in Convention 169, the Convention Concerning Indigenous and Tribal Populations in independent Countries, adopted by the International Labour Organisation (ILO) in June 1989; this convention has been important in the thinking surrounding the United Nations Declaration on the Rights of Indigenous Peoples. The ILO Convention defines indigenous peoples as follows:

tribal peoples in independent countries whose social, cultural and economic conditions distinguish them from other sections of the national community, and whose status is regulated wholly or partially by their own customs or traditions or by special laws or regulations;
peoples in independent countries who are regarded as indigenous on account of their descent from the populations which inhabited the country, or a geographical region to which the country belongs, at the time of conquest or colonisation or the establishment of present state boundaries and who, irrespective of their legal status, retain some or all of their own social, economic, cultural and political institutions. (ILO, 1991, Article 1)

The United Nations draft Declaration deals with this issue in Article 8, which states that

indigenous peoples have the collective and individual right to maintain and develop their distinct identities and characteristics, including the right to identify themselves as indigenous and to be identified as such.

More contentiously, Article 3 of the draft Declaration states:

indigenous peoples have the right of self-determination. By virtue of that right they freely determine their political status and freely pursue their economic, social and cultural development.

In international law the right of self-determination is associated with post-war de-colonisation. It is an accepted rule of customary international law, appears in the United Nations Charter, and was further recognised in the International Covenant on Economic, Social and Cultural Rights and Civil and Political Rights (1966). For a further discussion of these issues see Schulte-Tenckhoff and Ansbach (1995) and Martinez (1995). It is therefore of interest to peruse the contents of the books by Butler and Hinch (1996) and Robinson and Boniface (1999), for they cover cultural groups much wider than 'tribal peoples'. Cukier (1996), for example, describes the results of 60 interviews with vendors in Bali and notes that 'the majority of male vendors surveyed in both Kuta and Sanur were non-Balinese, while the majority of female vendors surveyed were Balinese' (Cukier, 1996: 69). No numbers of each respective group are provided. Again, Gurung et al. (1996) write of Nepali guides in Nepal. The purpose of these observations is not to criticise these authors, but rather to make the point that in spite of a growing interest in indigenous tourism, it is still nonetheless difficult for editors of books to find empirically based research which relates to tribal peoples living on lands once their own and on which they have a history of colonisation and now constitute a minority population.

A lack of information?

The absence of such research compared to the level of tourism promotion of the culture of Aboriginal peoples is significant. In Australia, Canada and New Zealand images of Aboriginal, Indian, Inuit and Maori peoples are used extensively in tourism promotional literature as national tourism boards seek to establish an identity unique to each of these countries. Governmental bodies have sought to promote tourism as a means of generating employment and income for such indigenous people. Tau Henare, Minister for Maori Affairs in New Zealand, in 1999, spoke of his belief that marae could be used to offer accommodation to tourists. In Australia the government has also, from time to time, exhorted Aboriginal people to consider tourism as a suitable form of enterprise initiative. However, the Aboriginal and Torres Straits Islander Commission (ATSIC, 1997) noted in its tourism strategy that

In the absence of good information, it is difficult to plan ahead. Indigenous people, government agencies and the mainstream tourism industry are handicapped in their support for increased indigenous participation in tourism by a lack of information of what is possible. This is particularly critical in the area of market research, where it is important to establish what tourists want from indigenous tourism, but where reliable data is lacking. (ATSIC, 1997: 44)

Thus, it appears from a tourism research perspective, that while opportunities for development have been identified, and indeed significant research has been undertaken in some directions (for example, in the case of New Zealand, see Urlich Cloher, 1998; Page et al., 1999), yet overall there still exists a lack of research into what visitors require. This is not to say that there is no research. For example, in Australia work has been reported by Pearce et al. (1997), Ryan and Huyton (1999), Pearce and Moscardo (1999), and Pitcher (1999) to cite but four examples which have all reported data drawn from survey work. In North America the developments of casinos on North American Indian reservations have attracted the attention of many researchers, including Lew (1996), Carmichael and Peppard Jr (1998) and Carmichael (2000) among others.

What is indigenous-based tourism?

Casino developments and luxury hotel developments by indigenous peoples are not unique to the Unites States. Hall (1996) notes how Maori interests sought a share in what has become the Sky City Casino development in New Zealand. Tanui, a Maori tribe in the Waikato region of New Zealand, have used part of their land settlement funds to help finance hotel development in Hamilton in partnership with Novotel. Such developments add a new dimension to what might be considered tourism products based on the culture of indigenous peoples. Traditionally, it might be argued, indigenous peoples have been viewed as primarily an exotic backdrop based on native arts and crafts. With significant land settlements being pursued in Canada and New Zealand, and with the wealth being generated by gaming in the United States, indigenous peoples have begun to develop enterprises in many areas of tourism. In addition to which, as increasing numbers begin to take advantage of more open educational and financial systems, indigenous people begin to start the same types of businesses in tourism that have been previously the preserve of majority populations. Barnett (1997, 2000), for example, points out that almost a quarter of Maori tourism business enterprises are actually in the accommodation sector, of which the most common form is motel ownership.

Ryan (1999) has developed a model that shows the range of tourism enterprises in which Maori are involved, and this might be extended to the indigenous people of most countries. He identified three dimensions:

- the ownership and size of the enterprise;
- the degree of indigenous culture portrayed in the enterprise; and
- the duration and intensity of the visitor experience.

He represents this in a diagram as shown in Figure 1. The three columns represent different types of experiences, and the three Ryan (1999: 242) selects are

A   Motel/hotel ownership   High in ownership by indigenous people
      (owned by Maori)   Low in cultural involvement
                                    Low in duration/intensity of visitor
                                        experience of cultural difference

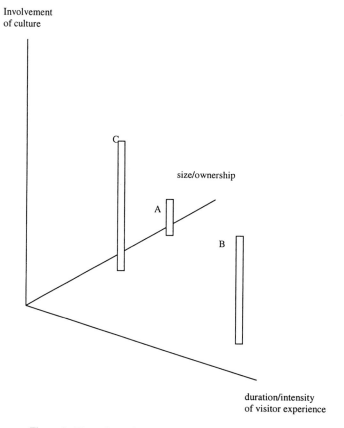

Figure 1. Dimensions of indigenous people's tourism product.

B   Stay in indigenous community   High ownership by indigenous people
                                                    High involvement of cultural presentation
                                                    High intensity by visitors of cultural
                                                       difference
C   Performing arts presentation   High ownership by indigenous people
                                                    High involvement of indigenous culture
                                                    Low to moderate intensity of experience
                                                       by visitors

This model is, however, simplistic in many senses. First, it is based upon many assumptions: for example, that the performing arts presentation is authentic in the sense that the dancers performing are indeed members of the portrayed peoples, and that those people have been involved in the organization of the event. Secondly, it also fails to take into account the situation within which the performing arts are being undertaken. For example, it does not assume that the performing arts presentation is a pseudo-event in Boorstin's (1961) terms: that is, it is solely undertaken for touristic purposes. On the other hand, research into the community events of North America that have involved indigenous peoples by Arnold (1997, 1999) and work currently being undertaken by Richards (1999) into the Aotearoa Traditional Maori Arts Performing Festival have both shown that quite high levels of intensity can be experienced by visitors. Indeed the Aotearoa Traditional Maori Arts Performing Festival has shown how indigenous people can create their own major tourism events, with 22 000 visiting the 1998 festival which was held in Wellington. Overseas visitors also attend this festival, some as contestants. Such events fulfill the need of reinforcing identities, which is referred to by commentators like Getz (1997). In short, the increasingly complex picture of tourism involving indigenous peoples must also take cognizance of the fact that the native peoples are tourists and entrepreneurs in mainstream as well as niche products.

Like much of tourism therefore, the certainties that informed research a decade ago – that the issues were primarily those of how tourism was seen to (negatively) impact on the culture of indigenous peoples, and how it commodified that culture into 30-minute packages of performance needs to be reappraised. Even the packages are changing. Nathan (pers. comm., 1999) in his role as being both a Maori and Chief Executive Officer of Tourism Rotorua, has noted how the hotel-based 'concert parties' are changing in order to involve audiences much more and thereby intensify the nature of the visitor experience. Commodification, once seen as a negative, is a means by which distinctions are made by indigenous peoples to distinguish between those events that have touristic value, and those that have value in other directions. The use of the term 'touristic value' is deliberately chosen as it represents the fact that tourism presentations of the values of indigenous cultures are normative statements of importance as indigenous peoples make new advances in the early years of the 21st century. Increasingly, indigenous people are able to use their control to leverage both profit and new understanding from both international and domestic visitors out of the tourist attractions that they increasingly control.

Two important caveats exist that limit this optimistic statement. First, the level of control exercised by indigenous peoples over the presentation of their culture is still uneven. Davis and Otterstrom (1998) provide examples of how, in the United States, Native American Indian people who wish to develop gaming are still facing actual and potential external constraints and internal tensions. Internally, elders still question the wisdom of gaming as an activity, and externally Indian initiatives may still be subject to State and Federal law or proposed law changes. Strang (1996) and Altman (1996) both describe how Aboriginal communities in Cape York, North Queensland, seek to negotiate tourism products from marginalised positions, and in doing so run the risk of a romantic stereotyping of 'alternative culture'. Aboriginal people in Australia seem to face the highest level of problems when seeking to undertake entrepreneurial activity – Altman et al. (1997: 6) described the position thus:

The historical experience of indigenous Australians in enterprise development is very chequered, partly due to a number of structural, locational, cultural, financial and human capital constraints in enterprise operation, and the labour force generally.

Secondly, it must not be thought that visitors are 'lay anthropologists'. It would seem that while tourists do want contact with indigenous people (Pearce et al., 1997), they may perceive such contacts within the wider framework of what constitutes their images of place. Ryan and Huyton (2000) have argued that many of the visitors to the Northern Territory wanted an experience of Aboriginal culture, but only within the tourists' perception of what forms an 'outback' experience; thus, visitors also wanted contact with nature, and scored highly on wanting to learn about flora and fauna and visiting national parks and taking outback tours. Pearce and Moscardo (1999) also found similar tendencies among visitors to the Tjapukai Dance Theatre. Furthermore, Ryan and Huyton claim that only 33 percent of their visitors had an interest in Aboriginal culture. The socio-demographics of this group were primarily young, female and non-Australian. This is reinforced by other research, both in terms of statistics derived from visitor monitoring (e.g. Blamey and Hatch, 1998) and from direct questioning at locations based on indigenous peoples culture (e.g. Pearce and Moscardo, 1986, 1999; Pitcher, 1999). Pitcher (1999) reported statements by a sample of 694 visitors to an Aboriginal community in the Northern Territory and commented that visitor perceptions were based in part upon easily accessible, popular literature, which is not always distinguished by high degrees of accuracy. Indeed, her study illustrates how visitors in search of authenticity often failed to perceive the authenticity that was around them in the sense of what was determining visitor–host interactions. For example, complaints made by some about eating arrangements revealed a possible lack of sensitivity to ritualistic taboos that may have been in force at certain times of the year. Additionally, she confirmed Strang's (1996) analysis of the romanticism of alternative cultures.

   Thus, the issue of authenticity which has been much discussed by tourism academics, yet again raises its head. It is not the purpose of this commentary to discuss this complex issue, other than to make a series of short points. First, in a sense the debate is circular in that initially much of the tourism research was about cultural impacts and cultural representations based upon observation and anthropological perspectives. Writers like Smith (1977) described how indigenous peoples changed their practices. More recently, writers have indicated that assumptions of passivity on the part of indigenous peoples are generally incorrect, particularly in some locations (see Strang, 1996; Ryan and

Crotts, 1997). Recent research drawn from a different research tradition based on psychometric testing of attitudes as well as qualitative research has shown that visitors create their own myths even while seeking what they perceive to be a 'reality' (e.g. Strang, 1996; Pitcher, 1999). In consequence, researchers turn back to the question of authenticity, asking whose authenticity? Hence, Hollinshead (1996) lists a number of research questions relating to processes of identification and disidentification that are implicit in contemporary tourism. He also warns us of treating 'culture-as-object' – for him this is a political act and one incomplete in its understanding as it ignores the social relations of production and consumption of cultural processes. To this complexity two more comments can be added. First, indigenous people are increasingly entering the mainstream of tourism, and as they do so, the nature of the indigenous experience and its representation thus changes – thereby creating new authenticities for both supplier and consumer. Secondly, such acts means that indigenous people occupy different worlds. This has been described thus:

Maori too have their 'gaze', but their 'gaze' is from at least three worlds, the world of their own culture which provides a traditional sense of identity, the post modern world of western dominated business practice and consumerism, and a world of interaction between these two cultures. To begin to understand Maori involvement in tourism is to require an understanding of concepts and applications of liminality and differences of culture. (Ryan, 1997: 259)

Tourism Management has published very few papers on indigenous tourism in the context discussed here whereby the concept is primarily applied to tribal peoples who have been subject to colonisation and who have become minorities in the countries in which they live. Yet, as seen from the dates of the cited works, there has been a new interest in this form of tourism, and even as this is written, two new papers are waiting to be published in later issues of *Tourism Management* (Carmichael, 2000; Barnett, 2000). From the past issues the following have been selected:

Lew, A.A. (1996). Tourism management on American Indian lands in the USA, *Tourism Management*, August, 17(5): 355–65.

Barnett, S. (1997). Maori tourism, *Tourism Management*, November, 18(7): 471–3.

The first, by Lew, is of importance because it considers the management and resource characteristics of tribal owned land in the United States. As such it sets a benchmark against which subsequent research can be compared as it describes the attitudes of tribal officers towards tourism development. In his sample Lew found that just over a third had many tourists, while about 14 percent had no plans for tourism development. He noted the irony that while for many tourists their concepts of native American Indians were based upon the plains Indian peoples of the west, it was the tribes in the eastern USA who displayed most sophistication and participation in tourism, in part explained by the nearness of large population centres. He also noted how Native Americans are also moving into niche markets not immediately associated with cultural issues, like river running and other adventure activities.

Barnett's paper is a short one, but is informed as being written by a Maori academic teaching in the subject of tourism. In her short paper Barnett identified the spheres within which Maori-based or -owned tourism operations exist, raised the question of what constitutes Maori tourism and located the issue within the realms of the relationship between Maori and New Zealanders of non-Maori background as governed by the 1840 Treaty of Waitangi.

As such, both of these papers represent a different stance to those adopted in research common at the commencement of the decade. Their overt concerns are not solely those of the impacts of tourism upon the culture of indigenous peoples, and both are based upon quantitative collections of data. Yet both in their way conclude that the process of development is culturally bound and, furthermore, exists within the framework of the history of past relationships between indigenous peoples and the majority population.

References

Albers, P. and James, W. (1983). Tourism and the changing photographic image of the Great Lakes Indians, *Annals of Tourism Research*, 10(1): 123–48.

Albers, P. and James, W. (1988). Travel photography: a methodological approach, *Annals of Tourism Research*, 15: 134–58.

Altman, J.C. (1996). Coping with locational advantage: tourism and economic development at Seisa Community, Cape York Peninsular, *Journal of Tourism Studies*, 7(1): 58–71.

Altman, J.C., Roach, L.M. and Liddle, L.E. (1997). *Utilisation of Native Wildlife by Indigenous Australians: Commercial Considerations*. Canberra: Australian National University, Centre for Aboriginal Economic Policy Research.

Arnold, N. (1997). Interviews with indigenous artists and cultural tourism specialists, ATIATI Inc., The National Service for Native American Arts, Soil of the Flame Festival., South Burnett, Four Winds Foundation, Queensland Arts Corporation, The California Arts Council for Indigenous Arts., The Cultural Arts Directors, Indigenous World Games. Queensland University of Technology.

Arnold, N. (1999). Marketing and development models for regional communities – a Queensland experience. *Part One, Proceedings of the 1999 Ninth Australian Tourism and Hospitality Research Conference*. Canberra: Bureau of Tourism Research. pp. 152–68.

Arsenault, D. (1997). L'impact du tourisme sur les sites sacrés en Amérindiens et Inuits du Bouchier Canadien I. Morrisset, L.K., (ed.), Turisme et religion, *Téroros, Revue de Recherche en Tourisme* 16(2): 21–5. Quebec: LELAT, Université Laval.

ATSIC (1997). *Tourism Industry Strategy*. Canberra: Aboriginal and Torres Straits Islander Commission.

Barnett, S. (1997). Maori tourism, *Tourism Management*, November, 18(7): 471–3.

Barnett, S. (2000). Maori accommodation – examples of Maori based tourism? *Tourism Management*, in press.

Blamey, R. and Hatch, D. (1998). *Profiles and Motivations of Nature-based Tourists Visiting Australia*. Canberra: Bureau of Tourism Research, Commonwealth of Australia.

Boorstin, D.J. (1961). *The Image – a Guide to Pseudo-events in America*. New York: Harper and Row.

Butler, R. and Hinch, T. (1996). *Tourism and Indigenous Peoples*. London: International Thomson Business Press.

Carmichael, B. (2000). A matrix model for resident attitudes and behaviours in a rapidly changing tourist area, *Tourism Management*, in press.

Carmichael, B.A. and Peppard, Jr. D. (1998). The impacts of Foxwoods Resort Casino on its dual host community: Southeastern Connecticut and the Mashantucket Pequot Tribe, in A. Lew and G.A. Van Otten, (eds), *Tourism and Gaming on American Indian Lands*. New York: Cognizant Communication Corporation.

Cohen, E. (1993). The study of touristic images of native people – mitigating the stereotype of a stereotype, in D.G. Pearce and R.W. Butler (eds), *Tourism Research – Critiques and Challenges*. London: Routledge. pp. 36–69.

Cukier, J. (1996). Tourism employment in Bali: trends and implications, in R. Butler and T. Hinch (eds), *Tourism and Indigenous Peoples*. London: International Thomson Business Press.

Davis, J.A. and Otterstrom, S.M. (1998). Constraints to the growth of Native American gaming, *Bottomline*, 13(1): 21–4, Provo, Utah: Brigham Young University.

Edwards, E. (1996). Postcards, greetings from another world, in T. Selwyn (ed.), *The Tourist Image: Myths and Myth Making in Tourism*. Chichester: Wiley.

Getz, D. (1997). *Event Management and Event Tourism*. New York: Cognizant Communication Corporation.

Gurung, G., Simmons, D. and Devlin, P. (1996). The evolving role of tourist guides: the Nepali experience, in R. Butler and T. Hinch (eds), *Tourism and Indigenous Peoples*. London: International Thomson Business Press, pp. 107–28.

Hall, C.M. (1996). Tourism and the Maori of Aotearoa, New Zealand, in R. Butler and T. Hinch (eds), *Tourism and Indigenous Peoples*. London: International Thomson Business Press. pp. 155–75.

Hollinshead, K. (1996). Marketing and metaphysical realism: the disidentification of Aboriginal life and traditions through tourism, in R. Butler and T. Hinch (eds), *Tourism and Indigenous Peoples*. London: International Thomson Business Press, pp. 303–48.

Lew, A.A. (1996). Tourism management on American Indian lands in the USA. *Tourism Management*, August, 17(5): 355–65.

Lew, A. and Van Otten, G.A. (1998). *Tourism and Gaming on American Indian Lands*. New York: Cognizant Communication Corporation.

Martinez, M.A. (1995). *Discrimination Against Indigenous Peoples*. Commission on Human Rights, Sub-Commission on Prevention of Discrimination and Protection of Minorities, United Nations Economic and Social Council, document E/CN.4/Sub.2/1995/27.

Page, S.J., Forer, P. and Lawton, G. (1999). Small business development and tourism: terra incognito. *Tourism Management*, 20(4): 435–61.

Pearce, P.L. and Moscardo, G.M. (1986). The concept of authenticity in tourist experiences, *Australian and New Zealand Journal of Sociology*, 22(1): 121–32.

Pearce, P.L. and Moscardo, G. (1999). Understanding ethnic tourists, *Annals of Tourism Research*, 26(2): 416–34.

Pearce, P.L., Moscardo, G., Green, D., Greenwood, T., Clark, A. and Tati, M. (1997). *Visitor Satisfaction at Tjapukai, First Report, An Analysis of Satisfaction Considering the Geographical Origin of Visitors*. Department of Tourism, James Cook University.

Pitcher, M. (1999). Visitors to Manyallaluk, an Aboriginal community. Unpublished PhD thesis, Northern Territory University, Darwin.

Price, M.F. and Smith, V.L. (1996). *People and Tourism in Fragile Communities*. Chichester: Wiley.

Richards, P. (1999). The Aotearoa Maori Performing Arts Festival. Paper given at *Tourism, Policy and Planning* – Oamaru, Otago, New Zealand, 30 August to 2 September 1999 – Regional meeting of the International Geographic Union's Study Group on the Geography of Sustainable Tourism, and The Centre for Tourism, University of Otago.

Robinson, M. and Boniface, P. (1999). *Tourism and Cultural Conflicts*. Wallingford: CABI Publishing.

Ryan, C. (1999). Some dimensions of Maori involvement in Tourism, in M. Robinson and P. Boniface, (eds), *Tourism and Cultural Conflict*. Wallingford, CABI Publishing.

Ryan, C. (1997). Maori and tourism: A relationship of history, constitutions and rites. *Journal of Sustainable Tourism*, 5(4): 257–78.

Ryan, C. and Crotts, J. (1997). Carving and tourism – a Maori perspective, *Annals of Tourism Research*, 24(4): 898–918.

Ryan, C. and Huyton, J. (2000). Aboriginal tourism – a linear structural relations analysis of domestic and international tourist demand, *International Journal of Tourism Research*, 2(1): 1–15.

Schulte-Tenckhoff, I. and Ansbach, T. (1995). Les minorites en droit international, in A. Fenet (ed.), *Le Droit et les Minorites*. Brussels: Brulant.

Smith, V. (1977). *Hosts and Guests: The Anthropology of Tourism*. University of Pennsylvania Press.

Strang, V. (1996). Sustaining tourism in Far North Queensland, in M.F. Price and V.L. Smith (eds), *People and Tourism in Fragile Communities*. Chichester: Wiley.

Urlich Cloher, D. (1998). *Sustainable Maori Tourism in Tai Tokerau – the South Hokianga and Kaikohe Regions*. The James Henare Maori Research Centre, The University of Auckland.

27

Tourism management on American Indian lands in the USA

Alan A Lew

Department of Geography and Public Planning, Northern Arizona University, Box 15016, Flagstaff, AZ 86011–5016, USA

Tourism has long been recognized as playing a significant role in more traditional societies.[1] Many authors have attempted to address the mechanisms and processes involved in this impact, but only a few have focused specifically on Native American reservations in the United States.[2–5] Smaller still is the number who have specifically examined the management of tourism on Native American reservations.

There are 318 federally recognized tribes in the continental USA, ranging in size from one or two members (as in several California bands) to over 200 000 on the Navajo Reservation.[6,7] Their distribution is shown in Figure 1. There are some 120 additional tribes that are currently seeking recognition by the federal government, including 12 that are recognized by state governments, but not yet by the federal government. Some tribes are combined with others on a single reservation, while other tribes are split among several reservations. Depending on the definition used, there are approximately 300 federally recognized reservations and 12 state recognized reservations. These range in size from under one acre (2.47 ha) to over 17 million acres (289 million ha), and total some 55 million acres (136 million ha). Approximately 20% of the federal reservation lands are privately owned; the remainder are held in trust by the federal government and reserved for Indian use only. Tribes also purchase land from non-reservation owners that can then be placed in trust and added to the reservation. The situation varies considerably from state to state depending on historical antecedents. For example, Oklahoma has 40 federally recognized tribes and 33 recognized tribal governments, but only one federally recognized reservation. Federally recognized reservations fall under the legal jurisdiction of the federal government and function largely independent of state law, although many areas of cooperation between reservations and local communities exist.

According to the 1990 US Census, there were 437 431 Indians living on reservations, which is 23% of all Indians in the country. About the same number live in close proximity to a reservation. On some reservations almost all of the residents are tribal

Figure 1. Number of Native American tribal governments per state in the USA.

members, while on others, such as the Flat-head Reservation in Montana, fewer than one in four are Indians. Although it varies from one tribe to the next, most will consider an individual to be a tribal member if they can prove that their blood line is between one-quarter and one-half from a given tribe. Exceptions to these proportions are numerous and problems of individuals with many different blood lines and those who cannot prove their blood line are common. Economic and social conditions on most reservations are alarming.[6] Average unemployment and poverty levels are both estimated at 45%, but they can be as high as 90%. A large, informal economy makes economic analysis on most reservations difficult. Only 52% of reservation Indians finish secondary school and only 4% have college degrees. Even though alcoholic beverages are illegal on most reservations, fetal alcohol syndrome is 33 times higher there than off the reservation and alcohol-related deaths are 10 times higher. Teenage suicide attempts are four times higher on reservations and rates of tuberculosis and diabetes are both approximately seven times greater.

The difficulties of life and livelihood on reservations in the USA has long been recognized and efforts to address these issues have been in place since most of the reservations were first established in the mid-1800s. Successive efforts at forced assimilation and acculturation were never successful, and many reservations ended up with a mixture of secular leaders who were recognized by the federal government and traditional leaders with religious and moral authority. These two groups were often at odds with one another over how best to meet the needs of their people.

The situation of tourism development on American Indian reservations parallels that of reservation administration overall. Government administration on many reservations has been characterized as complicated and requiring great expenditures of time, money and effort.[8,9] Less than effective management and development efforts have been attributed to a lack of skilled labour and managerial experience, bureaucratic and cultural resistance to change and complicated internal politics.[10-12] Further complicating tourism on reservations are the cultural differences that exist between Native Americans and the dominant American society. Indeed, administrative models developed for non-reservation communities have seldom been effective on reservations.[13]

Despite these difficulties, Browne and Nolan reported that tourism was a major component in the economies of the 49 of the 161 reservations in the western USA that responded to their tourism survey.[14] While their survey focused more on the perceptions and opinions of tribal officials toward tourism development and impacts, several management-related issues were also ascertained. For example, since it is difficult for non-tribal members to own private lands on most reservations, it is not surprising that over half (55%) of the tourism facilities on the responding reservations were operated by tribal members. In addition, the tribe itself is often the proprietor of major tourism facilities, and Browne and Nolan found that over two-thirds (68%) of the reservations responding to the survey used tourism revenues for tribal services and programs. Some indicated that tourism was their sole source of outside income. In order of frequency, decision making over tourism policy was the primary responsibility of:

- a tribal board of directors;
- an elected group of tribal members;
- a tribal office related to resource management;
- an economic development committee or office.

Questions related to managing and controlling the behaviour of visitors on reservation lands were included in the Browne and Nolan survey, with most (65%) stating that tourists are, or should be, restricted from some events, especially private religious activities, sacred dances, feasts, rites, pilgrimages to shrines, puberty rituals and funerals. However, only about half (48%) of the responding tribes had designated areas of the reservation that were off-limits to outside visitors for reasons of religion or traditional livelihood, suggesting a difference between the respondents' views and actual legal requirements. Some required the use of Indian guides to visit archeological sites, and one reservation was completely closed to visitors. A third (33%) of the respondents were concerned over existing or potential conflicts between tourists and their reservation's natural resources, including litter, damage to plants and disturbance of animals.

Overall, Browne and Nolan's findings suggest considerable diversity in tourism practices on reservations, with a general sense that major issues existed but were not being adequately addressed on most reservations that have some form of tourism. In the decade since their study (which was done in 1985), considerable changes have taken place on Indian reservations throughout the United States. These changes include:

- the establishment of high-stakes casino gaming on many reservation lands;
- a decline in federal aid to reservations and increasing pressure on self-reliance and economic development;
- an increase in the popularity of Indian reservations as tourist attractions in the 1990s.

Reservations today have better access to education, technology and transportation. Nearby transportation routes, in particular, bring large quantities of goods and people both to and from the reservation, thereby increasing the pressure on tribes to adopt the management techniques and economic and social values of the dominant American society. This is particularly true in the tourism services sector of the reservation economy. Though less overt than in the past, the process of externally induced cultural change on reservations is as great as ever – and the need to manage these changes effectively to protect the tradition and character of Reservation Lands is needed now more than ever.

Management

In spring 1994 a survey was sent to 337 Native American tribal governments in the USA. Included were those with various types of federal and state reservations and other tribal held lands, such as the non-reservation tribes of Oklahoma (see Figure 1).* The purpose of the survey was to determine the basic management and resource characteristics of tourism on tribal-owned land in the US. This report focuses on the management characteristics from the survey; it does not include the resource-related questions. A total of 118 surveys were returned, resulting in a response rate of 35% (Table 1). The response rate, however, varied from a high of 69% of tribes in the Rocky Mountain states to a low of 12.5% of tribes in the Northeastern USA.

Prior to the survey being sent, an initial inquiry was made of each reservation for information that might be of potential interest and value to a visitor. The information received was used to validate the mailing list and target, where possible, specific agencies within the tribes. The survey was then sent to either the agency responsible for tourism or to the tribal headquarters where no such department was found to exist. The survey form was kept brief (two sides of one page) to encourage completion, and comprised entirely closed-ended questions. Respondents were asked to provide open-ended comments on a separate page, but very few did.

Overall, the respondents to the survey represented tribes that either have a major stake in tourism or foresee some potential for tourism development in the future. Only 4.2% did not fall into either of these categories (Table 2). A review of tribes that did not respond to the survey indicated that most were tribal entities that were unlikely to be interested in tourism development in a significant way. Therefore, it is safe to assume that the respondents represented the bulk of tribes interested in tourism, and that about 35% of all tribes in the USA have such an interest.

For about two-thirds of the respondents, the tribe is a significant player in tourism development on tribal lands. This proves the findings of Browne and Nolan, who found about the same percentage of tribes that used tourism revenues for general reservation services and programs. Table 2 also includes a 'tourism intensity value' for

*The initial source for the survey address list was the Council of Energy Resources Tribes (Denver, Colorado), which publishes *Discover Indian Reservations USA: A Visitors Welcome Guide* (edited by Veronica E Tiller, 1992). This publication includes the addresses of all Indian tribes and other groups in the USA, whether recognized or not, that have a 'land base' or 'recognized community'. Even this list, however, was found to be incomplete and contained inaccuracies.

Table 1. Geographic distribution of survey respondents.

Region	No of tribes surveyed	% of tribes that responded	Tourism intensity value*
Rocky Mountains			
CO, WY, MT, ID	16	62.5	5.30
Midwest			
MN, WI, IA, MI, MO	33	57.6	6.00
South			
AL, FL, LA, MS, NC, SC, VA	13	38.5	4.89**
Desert West			
AZ, NM, NV, UT	67	35.8	5.08
Great Plains			
OK, SD, KS, ND, NE, TX	54	33.3	4.33
West Coast			
CA, OR, WA	130	29.2	4.17
Northeast			
CT, MA, ME, NJ, NY, RI	24	16.7	4.89**
Total	337	35.0	4.96 (national mean)

Notes:
*Tourism intensity value is based on a scale of 1 = little tourism and 7 = much tourism. See Table 2 for additional information on the definition of tourism intensity value.
**Due to the low number of respondents from the Northeast and South, these two regions were combined for a single, shared tourism intensity value.

Table 2. Perceived tourism intensity.

Intensity value	We receive on our reservation and tribal lands	And there is/are	%
1	No tourists	No plans to promote tourism in the future	4.2
2	No tourists	Plans to promote tourism in the future	10.0
3	Some tourists	No tribal or private attractions or tourism businesses	18.3
4	Some tourists	Private tourism businesses, with no tribal govt involvement	7.5
5	Some tourists	Tribal government is directly involved in tourism	23.3
6	Many tourists	No direct tribal government involvement in tourism	4.2
7	Many tourists	Considerable direct tribal involvement in tourism	32.5

each combination of visitor levels and tribal involvement. These values were self-identified by survey respondents and reflect the perceived level of visitation, as opposed to actual numbers, which are generally not available and, in any event, would vary as widely as the size and populations of different reservations.

An assumption was made that the person who responded to the survey was likely to be in a position of influence over, or at least considerable knowledge of, a tribe's tourism development. In addition, the department or office in which the respondent worked was assumed to have a major role in tourism administration and/or decision making for the responding tribe. For those individuals who gave their status and department affiliation, these assumptions held true.

Most of the tribes that responded have simple administrative structures, which partly accounts for the fact that so many respondents (44.5%) worked in the tribal chair's office (Table 3). This is also the office that is most likely to respond to tourist inquiries for information (Table 4). For a few of the very small tribal groups in California, the tribal chairperson was the one who completed the survey instrument. While this may be a suitable arrangement for smaller reservations, it is also more likely to make the administration of tourism, along with decision making on tourism-related

Table 3. Types of respondents to survey questionnaire.

No	%	Respondent type
53	44.5	Tribal Administrative Office
21	17.6	Planning and Community Development Departments including Natural Resources Departments
14	11.7	Economic Development Offices/Business Councils
6	5.0	Tourism Offices/Departments
6	5.0	Public Affairs/Community Relations
6	5.0	Commercial Enterprises: Casino or Gaming Corporation, Tribal Enterprise, Tribal Corporation, Tribal Hotel
5	4.2	Cultural Entities: Cultural Centre, Tribal Museum, Tribal Cultural Program, Tribal Historical Society, Cultural Preservation Office
8	6.7	Other: Library, Office of Grants and Contracts, Dept of Trust Responsibilities, Tribal Chamber of Commerce, Tribal Education Dept

Table 4. Responding to tourist inquiries.

Responses to question: Who typically responds to tourist/ visitor-related inquiries sent to your tribal government?	%*
We typically do not respond in any way to visitor inquiries	9.2
Tribal Government related:	
The Office of the Tribal Chairman/Governor/Principal Chief (or similar)	44.2
Tribal Economic Development or Business Council/Committee (or similar)	40.0
Tribal owned Hotel, Motel, Resort or Bingo/Casino enterprise	25.0
Tribal owned Museum, Cultural centre or Visitors centre	25.0
Tribal Public Relations Office/Department	22.5
Tribal Tourism Office	17.7
Other tribal office**	13.3
Non-tribal Government related:	
Off-reservation Chamber of Commerce	20.0
Regional or Multi-tribe organization	7.5
Reservation-based Chamber of Commerce	5.0
Other non-tribal entity***	10.8

Notes:
*Multiple responses were allowed.
**Other tribal offices included: information specialist, planning department, natural resources dept., pow-wow committee, tribal public library, marketing department, tour company, land office, cultural preservation office.
***Other non-tribal entities included: local school, local historian, regional economic development organisation, local museum, state's dept of transportation, National Park Service, county tourism and recreation association, county historical society, state Indian tourism association, state's dept of development.

issues, subject to the whims of each new political office holder. For many tribes, economic development offices and community development or natural resource departments are the principal agencies responsible for tourism management. As with the tribal chair's office, these agencies are more likely to view tourism as a secondary concern within their larger mission.

It is only in the tribes that already have motels, resorts, casinos, museums or cultural/visitors' centres that tourism is given more of an independent role within the tribal administration. For example, many tribes with these facilities use them to respond to tourist inquiries (see Table 4). Considering that the respondents to this survey were generally those tribes that are most interested in tourism development, surprisingly very few (17.7%) have offices dedicated exclusively to tourism, and in even fewer were tourism office administrators given the responsibility for completing the survey instrument (5%). This latter point might be due to the potential political implications that many tribal administrators see in anything related to tourism or economic development. Another possibility is that the tribe's tourism office may be temporarily unstaffed – a not uncommon situation on reservations.

Interestingly, some 20% of tribes also have a good working relationship with off-reservation Chambers of Commerce. This was especially true in Oklahoma where reservations are largely non-existent and Native peoples and their lands are closely integrated into the local population.

Characteristics

Table 5 shows the major characteristics of the eight respondent types identified in Table 3. All eight shared good highway access and good support for tourism among tribal leaders. These shared characteristics should not be underestimated. As mentioned above, the geographic isolation of most reservations has decreased in recent decades with better roads and more reliable transportation. Those with the best access to large population centres and the traveling public have a clear advantage in developing tourism. Leadership support for tourism is also crucial, but also it is the most susceptible to changes in political orientation, which can be a significant factor in the volatile arena of tribal politics.

Reservations that have existing commercial tourism enterprises (type 1 in Table 5) had the highest average tourism intensity values. Most of these reservations receive many tourists and have considerable tribal involvement in tourism development and promotion. Such reservations typically have a great diversity of attractions, easy highway access, and strong support for tourism both among tribal leaders and in the community overall. Many of these tribes have a tribal motel or gaming establishment, and a tribal public relations office. They are also more likely to be associated with regional tribal and non-tribal tourism associations.

Tribes that rely on public affairs-type offices to handle tourism (type 2) and those that have established tourism offices (type 3) also had relatively high tourism intensities. For some tribes, the public affairs office functions in the same manner as a tourism office. Both categories share a broad range of characteristics that are generally favorable for tourism development. Tribal public affairs offices also work closely with

Table 5. Characteristics of respondent types.

Respondent type*	Tourism intensity	Major distinguishing characteristics
(1) Commercial enterprises	7.0	Much attraction diversity; excellent highway access; strong community support for tourism; strong tribal leadership support; tribal-owned enterprises; very likely to be associated with a public relations office and/or a motel or bingo establishment; more likely to be associated with regional tribal and non-tribal tourism organizations
(2) Public affairs/ community relations	6.7	No major distinguishing characteristics; overall characteristics are favourable to tourism; most likely to be associated with a motel/bingo enterprise and/or a cultural centre
(3) Tourism offices/ departments	6.5	Much attraction diversity; excellent highway access; good support for tourism; good tribal leadership support; good planning
(4) Cultural entities	5.6	Few attractions; difficult access/remote location; good planning; tribal-run enterprises; some association with Economic Development Offices; good association with off-reservation Chambers of Commerce
(5) Planning and community development	5.3	No distinguishing characteristics; somewhat more likely to have privately owned tourism enterprises; some association with Economic Development Offices and off-reservation Chambers of Commerce
(6) Economic development offices	4.6	Excellent highway access; good financing available; some association with motel/bingo establishments and off-reservation Chambers of Commerce
(7) Tribal administrative office	4.1	No major distinguishing characteristics; somewhat less likely to have strong community support for tourism; least likely to respond to inquiries from potential visitors
(8) Other (see Table 2 for details)	5.1	Good highway access; financing most difficult to obtain; most likely to be associated with tribal administrative office in tourism development and with regional tourism organizations
Average intensity and most common characteristics	4.8	Good highway access; good tribal leadership support

Note: *See Table 2 for the definition of respondent types. Distinguishing characteristics are based on comparisons with the mean characteristics of the survey respondents, not in comparison with Indian reservations in general in the USA.

motel and gaming establishments on the one hand, and cultural centres and museums on the other.

The five remaining respondent categories had markedly lower intensity values. All of them represented respondents in agencies where tourism was only part of, or peripheral to, their broader mandate. These included planning departments, economic development offices and tribal administrative offices, among others. Tribal administrative office respondents (type 7) represented reservations with the overall lowest tourism intensity. These reservations were also the least likely to respond to inquiries from potential visitors. The fact that tourism is not part of a department other than the chairman's office suggests that while some tourism may be present, it is not important enough to generate separate administrative attention. The most distinguishing characteristic of these tribes is a lower level of support for tourism from tribal leaders. Given that this is the situation for the largest percentage of tribes in this survey, it would appear that a positive relationship exists between the support for tourism of tribal leaders and the intensity of tourism development on a reservation. The question of which of these two factors begat the other was not addressed by this survey.

Regional variation

Considerable diversity in cultures and lifestyles existed across the North American continent in pre-Columbian times.[15] In part, this reflected variations in physical conditions and resource opportunities. However, within the same place, such as in the American Southwest, very diverse Indian cultures were known to have existed side by side. This situation, combined with variations in the historical pattern of European conquest and settlement across the USA, has resulted in considerable regional differences in tourism on tribal lands today. For example, most of the tribes in the eastern USA have smaller reservations and share a longer history of European domination than those in the western USA. Table 6 shows variations that exist among the regions introduced in Table 1 and Figure 1. A few major patterns can be discerned from these data:

- Community support for tourism on reservations decreases as one moves from east to west.
- Tourism development is more likely to be sponsored by the tribe as one moves from east to west.
- Most western reservations are likely to use the tribal chairman's office or an economic development office to manage tourism, while those further to the east use tribal tourism offices, museum/visitors centres or tribal enterprises.
- Gaming is more likely on reservations in the east, while the natural environment and accompanying outdoor activities are more likely in western reservations.[†]

In general, tribes in the eastern USA appear to be more sophisticated and more assertive in tourism development, while those in the west are more cautious. The dividing region is the Great Plains, where the natural resources for tourism are more like those in the east, while the cautionary propensity toward tourism is more like that of the west. The Great Plains also has many large reservations, a characteristic more similar to the western USA than the eastern part of the country. This may explain, in part, the differences between the eastern and western USA. Larger reservations enable a greater sense of autonomy and sovereignty than do smaller reservations. This may make the residents of larger reservations slower to adapt to the dominant culture than those on a smaller reservation.

Another difference between the eastern and western USA is the history of European settlement. The west, including the Great Plains, was initially a dumping ground for

---

[†]The gaming situation on reservations in the USA is changing rapidly and gaming in the western USA is not properly reflected in this 1994 survey. Compare this with the National Indian Gaming Association (NIGA), *Fact Sheet* Washington, NIGA (1995).

Indians moved out of the east. It was only about a century ago that much of the Indian land in the west was confiscated for non-Indian settlers. This gives the Indian in the west a closer connection to the settlement period, and perhaps a more bitter resentment of the dominant society. It is ironic that the west is the American region which people most associate with Native Americans, and where both domestic and international

Table 6. **Major regional characteristics and tourism administration.**

Region*	Administration and characteristics	%
Rocky Mountain:		
Most likely administration	Economic Development Office	60
Least likely administration	Tourism Office	10
Major attractions	Natural environment, museums, dances/festivals	
Least likely to have	Leadership support for tourism	
Midwest:		
Most likely administration	Motel or resort	68
Least likely administration	Tribal Chairman's Office	26
Most likely to use	Off-reservation Chamber of Commerce	37
	Regional or multi-tribal organization	21
Major attractions	Gaming, restaurants/services, pow-wows	
Most likely to have	Available financing	
Highest	Mean tourism intensity = 6.0 (on a scale of 1 to 7)	
Desert West:		
Most likely administration	Tribal Chairman's Office	42
	Economic Development Office	33
Least likely administration	Public Relations Office	8
Major attractions	Natural environment, arts and crafts	
Great Plains:		
Most likely administration	Tribal Chairman's Office	50
	Economic Development Office	44
Least likely to use	Off-reservation Chamber of Commerce	6
Major attractions	Gaming, pow-wows, dances/festivals	
Least likely to have	Available financing	
West Coast:		
Most likely administration	Tribal Chairman's Office	45
	Economic Development Office	39
Least likely to	Respond to visitor inquiries	87
Major attractions	Natural environment	
Weakest	Community support for tourism	
Lowest	Tourism intensity = 4.17 (on a scale of 1 to 7)	
East (South and Northeast):		
Most likely administration	Museum or cultural/visitors centre	58
	Tribal Tourism Office	50
Least likely administration	Economic Development Office	11
Most likely	To respond to inquiries	100
Major attractions	Museums/visitors centres, arts and crafts, gaming	
Highest levels of	Community and leadership support for tourism	

Note: *For definition of the regions, see Table 1. Regions are listed in order from highest to lowest response rates. East is a combination of the Northeast and South regions in Table 1, with an overall response rate of 24.3%. For all of the regional tourism intensity values see Table 1.

tourists are most likely to go to see Indian culture. This, too, perhaps contributes to the different attitudes toward tourism on reservations in the western states. Whatever the reasons may be, the survey results show that Indian reservation tourism clearly varies in different parts of the country.

Examples

Tourism-related policies are formulated through a variety of administrative mechanisms on reservations, Some of these include:

- establishment and management of gaming;
- hunting and fishing regulations;
- establishment and management of a cultural or visitors' centre;
- regulations governing organized tours on a reservation;
- regulations governing visitors to a reservation;
- regulations governing the production and sale of arts and crafts;
- business codes and regulations;
- comprehensive plan goals and policies.

For larger reservations, each of these functions is likely to be managed by a different department or office. This is complicated when some of these departments are only minimally aware of the tourism aspects of their mission, and their relationship to other tourism-oriented sectors of tribal government. A comparison of several tribes from different parts of the country and with different tourism resources shows the diversity and regional differentiation among reservations.

The Eastern Cherokee reservation is in the Smoky Mountains of North Carolina and has the largest land area of any reservation in the east. Situated on the edge of the Great Smoky Mountain National Park, and close to the tourism and amusement centre of Gatlinburg, Tennessee, the Eastern Cherokee are in a prime location for tourism development. The tribe has taken advantage of this, having developed a major tourism centre with several motels, recreation and amusement attractions and shopping opportunities. While the tribe and tribal members own and operate many of these facilities, some also have non-Indian proprietors. Tourism development on the Cherokee reservation is primarily the responsibility of the Cherokee Tribal Public Relations and Travel Promotion Office (also known as Cherokee Travel and Promotion Services). The staff of this office is governed by an appointed board of directors and an advertising committee. This office is officially responsible for:

- advancing and promoting the tourism industry of the Cherokee Reservation;
- the promotion of the Cherokee Indian Reservation as a desirable destination vacation site;
- advancing information about the historic, scenic and cultural assets to be found on the reservation;
- promotions to increase the length of the stay at Cherokee by tourists, especially in the spring, fall and winter months.

The bylaws of the office go on to state:

The importance of the tourist industry to the Cherokee economy is recognized, and it is further recognized that a significant increase in this area will have a profound beneficial effect on the well-being of the Cherokee people by providing additional employment, more year-around employment and increasing the tribal tax base which will allow the Tribal Government more opportunities to provide services to tribal members.

For many smaller tribes where gaming has recently become prominent, tribal tourism management and development is synonymous with tribal gaming administration. This is evident in many tribes in Midwest and Northeastern USA, such as the Mashantucket Pequot Tribe (population 262) in Connecticut and the Shakopee Mdewakanton Dakota Community (population 153) in Minnesota. These two tribes operate the most successful (the Pequot's Foxwood Casino) and second most successful (the Dakota's Mystic Lakes Casino) reservation gaming establishments in the USA.[16] For these reservations, tourist inquiries are referred to the gaming enterprise or to an associated accommodations facility. These either function directly as a tourism office, or house such an office. The overall orientation is similar to that of the Eastern Cherokee, but, reflecting the reservations smaller populations and land areas, the administrative structure is much simpler.

In a very different mode, tourism on the Hopi reservation (population 7061) in the southwestern state of Arizona focuses more on visitor control than development. Regulations and proper protocol for visitors are posted throughout the Hopi Reservation, which also has a tribally owned cultural centre, consisting of a museum, motel and restaurant. Although each of the Hopi villages has its own set of posted regulations, they commonly include requirements to register with a village if spending a lengthy period there, and prohibitions against:

- possession or use of alcohol or drugs on the reservation;
- visitations to archeological sites and ruins;
- removal of artifacts;
- photography, sketching, and tape recording of villages and ceremonies.

Organized groups of visitors are also required to register with the tribe, and commercial tour companies are required to pay an annual fee, although neither of these regulations has been strictly enforced over the years. Tour registration was originally housed in the tribe's Public Relations office, which also responds to visitor inquiries. More recently, however, this function has been moved to the Cultural Preservation Office, further accentuating the tribe's visitor-control orientation. The importance of maintaining their religious and social traditions is utmost among the Hopis, who were never conquered militarily by European or American powers and are considered to have one of the most traditional cultures in the USA. Hopi villages are occasionally closed to outsiders during dances and other ceremonies, and on rare occasions a village will completely close itself to visitors for several weeks or months. This typically follows a series of perceived transgressions by tourists. However, such closures are never permanent due to the many village residents who earn good incomes selling arts and crafts to tourists. Even the lure of high profits from casino gaming is not enough to change the desire of most Hopis to keep a tight control over tourism. In May 1995, the Hopis voted against the establishment of a potentially successful gaming facility on land they owned near the city of Winslow, a one-hour drive away from the nearest Hopi community.

A final example of tourism management, again from the Southwest, is that of the White Mountain Apache Tribe (population 9825) in Arizona. Their large reservation is known as the Fort Apache Reservation and is situated in a pine-forested region high in the mountains, where fishing, hunting, hiking and camping are popular visitor activities. Three major forms of tourism are found here, each of which is managed by a different branch of tribal government. The Game and Fish Department establishes regulations and permit fees governing boating, camping, fishing and other outdoor recreation activities. The tribe operates a major ski area with year-round resort facilities, which is operated as a separate tribal business. Recently, the tribe opened a casino to serve the nearby mountain recreation communities, which also operates as a tribally owned enterprise. The Fort Apache Reservation is typical of the reservations in the Rocky Mountains and Desert West, from New Mexico to Montana and Nevada. Most of these are large reservations with pristine forests and other natural wonders. They are known for hunting and fishing opportunities that are superior to mountain areas outside the reservation, because they have not been logged or otherwise exploited to the same degree. Many of these reservations charge high fees to outdoor enthusiasts for fishing and hunting privileges, which typically includes an Indian guide. Staff in Game and Fish Departments, such as that of the White Mountain Apache, are educated and trained like those working for federal and state governments, and are generally very effective in management practices.

Summary and conclusions

These survey data provide a good representative cross-section of American Indian tribes interested in tourism development. Tribes that have no tourism and no interest in tourism represented only a few of the respondents to this survey, although they comprise most of the tribes that did not respond to this survey. Based on these findings, it is safe to state that at least a third, and probably not much more, of all recognized tribes in the USA have some involvement or interest in tourism. Tourism tribes, however, vary considerably in their resources and the way they manage tourism and make tourism development decisions. This is also affected by the perceived importance of tourism and its relationship to other tribal activities.

Regional variation exists in the development of tourism on American Indian lands. Eastern tribes are often more business oriented and have stronger tribal and community support for tourism. Tourism intensities are lower in many areas of the western USA, though they are the most associated with Native American culture. There is a greater sense of ambivalence toward tourism in the west, especially the West Coast.

The survey results presented here largely reconfirm the earlier findings of Browne and Nolan, although the great diversity in the way tribes manage tourism, both in the resources that they have and distinct regional variations, is made more evident. Overall, tourism development is not as prominent or successful as it might be. This is because of historical and cultural challenges, as well as by choice. For most tribes, the tribal chairman's office is the principal administrative and decision-making agency for tourism. However, a variety of other models also exist for tribes as they move from a more simple form of government administration to a more sophisticated one. Depending on their tourism resources and development goals. one or another of the models described in Table 5 would be an appropriate form of tourism administration.

In fact, the diversity of tribal experiences with tourism is enormous, from small and remote farming rancherias in California, to the large and diverse reservations of the Navajo in Arizona and the Eastern Cherokee in North Carolina. Every tribe is going to be different because natural and tribal resources vary from one place to the next. This diversity of resources has major implications for the marketing of tourism on Indian lands.[17] The primary market for gaming reservations has been, and will continue to be short-haul, domestic recreationists. Hunting and fishing are also largely domestically oriented, although the international big game hunting market offers lucrative opportunities for reservations that offer that type of activity. River running and other outdoor soft and hard adventure activities draw upon a mix of both domestic and international visitors. Partly in response to the recent popularity of Indian movies, cultural tourism has been the fastest growing international market in recent years for many tribes, but especially those in the Southwest and upper Great Plains. For some of the more traditional tribes, the visitor has as strong an interest in assuring the preservation of Indian culture as does the tribe itself. To capitalize on these trends, tribes need to become more aware of their resources and position in the international tourism economy.

Local cultural values and traditions also vary considerably and are possibly more important in determining how a tribe develops and manages its tourism resources than the nature of the resources themselves. Management practices need to reflect the physical and cultural environment of a particular reservation. It is best to choose from reasonable options carefully, and it is most important to be creative in looking toward the future.

References

1. Smith, V L (ed) *Hosts and Guests: The Anthropology of Tourism* 2nd edn, Philadelphia, University of Pennsylvania Press (1989)
2. Dietch, L I 'The impact of tourism on the arts and crafts of the Indians of the southwestern United States' in Smith, V L (ed) *Hosts and Guests: The Anthropology of Tourism*, 2nd edn, Philadelphia, University of Pennsylvania Press (1989) 223–236
3. Jett, S C 'Culture and tourism in the Navajo country' *Journal of Cultural Geography* 1992 **13** (1) 85–107
4. Luhan, C C 'A sociological view of tourism in an American Indian community: maintaining cultural integrity at Taos Pueblo' *American Indian Culture and Research* 1993 **17** (3) 101–120
5. MacCannell, D 'Tradition's next step', in Norris, S (ed) *Discovered Country: Tourism and Survival in the West* Albuquerque, Stone Ladder Press (1994) 161–179
6. Russell, G *The American Indian Digest* Phoenix, Thunderbird Enterprises (1993)
7. Hirschfelder, A and Kriepe de Montano, M *The Native American Almanac: A Portrait of Native America Today* New York, Prentice Hall (1993)
8. Kirst, L 'American Indian economic development policies' *Journal of Planning Literature* 1987 **2** (1) 101–110

9. Talbot, S 'Economic plunder of American Indians' *Today's Political Affairs* 1981 **60** (10) 29–37
10. Herzberg, H W 'Reaganomics on the reservation' *New Republic* 1982 **187** (20) 15–18
11. United Indian Planners Association (UIPA) *National Indian Planning Assessment* US Department of Housing and Urban Development and the Economic Development Administration, US Government Printing Office, Washington (1977)
12. United States General Accounting Office (USGAO) 'More Federal efforts needed to improve Indians' standard of living through business development' in *Report of the Comptroller* 15 February 1987, General Accounting Office Washington, DC, CED-78-50
13. Van Otten, G A 'A geographer's perception of land use planning in Arizona's Native American reservations' *Papers and Proceedings of the Applied Geography Conferences* 1985 **8** 303–307
14. Browne, R-J and Nolan, M L 'Western Indian reservation tourism development' *Annals of Tourism Research* 1989 **16** 360–376
15. Waldman, C *Atlas of the North American Indian* Facts on File, New York (1985)
16. Davis, J 'Spatial diffusion of Indian gaming in the United States' paper presented at the annual meeting of the Association of Pacific Coast Geographers, Northridge, CA, 15–19 June 1994
17. Lew, A A 'American Indian reservation tourism in Arizona', in Merrill, H (ed) *American Indian Relationships in a Modern Arizona Economy* University of Arizona, Tucson (1995)

28

Maori tourism

Shirley Barnett

Department of Management Systems, Massey University, Private Bag 11-222, Palmerston North 5301, New Zealand

Maori Tourism – What is it? This question has been debated and discussed since tourism to Aotearoa New Zealand began, which was almost as soon as the first colonizers arrived. A new country was there to be explored, complete with 'noble savages' and 'beautiful, entertaining women'. Many of the early tourists were from the whaling vessels that plied their trade in the cold Antarctic waters.

Tourism soon became more formalized and Aotearoa New Zealand was promoted to overseas countries as a holiday destination. Te Awekotuku (1991), writes that at Rotomahana, passengers were being ferried to the Pink and White Terraces as early as 1860.

In the 1870's with the formalisation of tourism in Aotearoa, Maori were romanticised as historical noble savages, replete in their barbaric and primitive culture, and as wild and 'tameable' as the new land. Early film, photography, travelogues and ethnographies concentrates attention on images or erotic/exotic game-playing Maori, while at the same time validating images of paternal, pioneering, civilising Pakeha.[1]

A Ngati Whakaue* elder is quoted as saying:

The Rotorua area, with its thermal wonders and lakes, was attracting visitors from overseas – the Pink and White Terraces were irresistible. The Government of the day – 1880 – realising the district had valuable assets to be exploited, decided that a town should be founded on a site central to those assets.[2]

Initially, tourists accommodation needs and guiding requirements were adequately met by Maori businesses – the first hotels and guiding operations in the district were either wholly or partly owned and operated by Maori. Gradually they were displaced by the Pakeha,[†] and Maori land alienation in the area began to accelerate.[2]

---

*A sub tribe of Te Arawa – main tribe in the Rotorua region.
†A person of predominantly European descent.

Prior to their destruction in 1886, Aotearoa New Zealand's Pink and White Terraces were, by all accounts, without equal. Tourists flocked here from all corners to view this 'eighth wonder of the world'[3] and the local Maori community benefited from tourism by some 4000 pounds per year. Despite the loss of the Terraces, travellers still came to New Zealand, but it was during the twentieth century that Maori began to be used by the tourism industry. Their image was used as a marketing tool to promote tourism and Maori were stereotyped into guides, carvers and entertainers. This was done without consultation and with very little commercial benefit to Maori.[4,5]

During the first half of the twentieth century Maori financial involvement in tourism development was almost non-existent and Pakeha were not slow to continue exploiting the Maori people in promotion and advertising for tourists. There was still a time (in the mid-twentieth century), when some overseas visitors believed that Maori still wore flax skirts and cooked in steaming pools (personal knowledge from being asked questions by visitors to the Tokaanu Thermal Reserve).

There is a paucity of information about the development of Maori tourism from the late 1870s until the 1980s. During this time Maori remained peripheral to tourism in Aotearoa New Zealand, only providing background colour and uniqueness to the national tourism product.

However, in 1989, at the New Zealand Tourism 2000 conference it was recognized '...that success in tourism means playing to our strengths which have enduring appeal to our customers. Those strengths are:

- the grandeur of our scenery
- the cleanness and greenness of our countryside
- our bicultural uniqueness...' (p. 9).

As Aotearoa New Zealand moves closer to the year 2000 it is being increasingly recognized that our bicultural uniqueness is becoming one of the biggest drawcards for international tourists. This bicultural uniqueness refers to the Maori culture which is indigenous and unique to Aotearoa New Zealand.

The last major trend in world tourism is the growing demand for different cultural experiences. The strong culture of the Maori – unique to New Zealand – is a major aspect of our national heritage which enhances New Zealand's appeal to the world's travellers.[7]

In 1993, the New Zealand Tourism Board wrote that world tourism trends favour New Zealand. These trends included, a growing demand for different cultural experiences. Marsh supports this when he said:

...what made New Zealand unique was its society and the different dimension given by the Maori culture.[8]

Marsh was referring to his original belief that international tourists visited Aotearoa New Zealand to see the scenery. After travelling to Yellowstone National Park he realised that the geysers in Rotorua are not what makes it a unique destination – it is the Maori culture.

In the latest International Visitors Survey compiled by the New Zealand Tourism Board for the period April 1995 to March 1996, it was reported that *ca.* 518 000 of all international visitors went to a Maori cultural performance and 259 000 experienced some other type of Maori tourism. There is no category for Maori historic sites, although *ca.* 518 000 people visited an historic site.[9]

We are now seeing that a resurgence of Maori culture over the last two decades has led to demand for Maori control over Maori tourism development, and control over the use of cultural artefacts and images in promotion. Therefore, as we enter the new millennium Maori people face substantial issues in terms of their involvement with the tourism industry.

One of the main issues being faced by Maori people in Aotearoa New Zealand is that many Maori cultural experiences and products are being presented to tourists in an inauthentic manner. Many cultural products are being provided or managed by non-Maori people and products and services have been commoditized for tourists. Most of our international visitors are now expressing a desire to see and experience Maori culture and history in a setting that is as authentic as possible. Work in this area is being undertaken by the Aotearoa Maori Tourism Federation who have prepared a preliminary report entitled 'A Mark of Authenticity for Maori Tourism Product'.[10]

There are many ways in which Maori are involved in tourism and this involvement is not restricted to the delivery of Maori tourism products, although many Maori are involved in this area. To help identify and cluster Maori tourism products the Aotearoa Maori Tourism Federation identified four categories. These four categories represent different ways in which Maori culture can be 'interpreted' for the visitor.

1 *Entertainment*: includes concerts performed in hotels, restaurants, on marae and in museums.
2 *Arts and crafts*: items produced for tourists that are generally sold in souvenir shops.
3 *History and display of artefacts* (*Taonga*): generally referring to treasures held in museums and art galleries.
4 *Guided tours*: many activities are included in this category ranging from a guided bush walk, to a half-day mini van tour, to a guided tour of a marae.

In 1996, 153 tourism operations in Aotearoa New Zealand were identified as being owned or operated by Maori or providing a Maori product.[12] These include operations in the categories as defined above:

- Entertainment: 6
- Arts and crafts: 21
- History/display of artefacts (taonga):   5
- Guided tours: 74

There were, however, a number of Maori tourism operations that did not fit into these categories, these were defined as accommodation and ranged from marae stays to Maori owned camping grounds, motels and hotels. There were 47 operations identified that were in the accommodation category.

However, Maori involvement in tourism is not restricted to the delivery of Maori tourism product. They are also involved at three different levels:

- *Individuals or small partnerships*: primarily small operations and many of the authentic Maori art and craft products that reach the market are produced in these businesses.

- *Hapu* and Marae†*: these businesses usually involve a larger number of people and tend to be in business for collective purposes (i.e. marae maintenance), rather than for individual wages. This does not affect the professionalism of these businesses and they are often able to provide a very authentic, often informal Maori cultural product, for example, a discussion with a kaumatua† about the area.
- *Iwi ¶*: Maori can become involved in tourism through land trusts, in corporations and joint ventures.[10]

So to return to the original question: what is Maori tourism? Does a Maori person taking a holiday constitute Maori tourism? Bennett defines Maori tourism as '...any contact that the visitor has with Maori culture' (p. 1).[10] This definition is based on the view point of the visitor and includes product that may not be seen by Maori or other New Zealanders as 'Maori'.

Bennett's definition is all encompassing and could include tourism operations providing Maori cultural products, as well as operations owned or operated by Maori. 'Contact with Maori culture' could be the specific Maori product that is provided for tourists or it could be a conversation with the Maori owner of a camping ground about the Maori history of the area.

There are strong views held by Maori regarding Maori tourism, many Maori espouse similar views to those expressed by Mahuta and Bennett. Mahuta writes that:

...tribes must act to retain their position as the controllers and regulators in any...venture and this must be written clearly into all contacts. They must always been seen as the kaitiaki§ of their resource be it cultural, spiritual or physical (p. 4).[12]

Only we can decide what is and is not for public consumption.

Our culture is our last frontier. Commercial exploitation of it, by others, for themselves, must not be part of our future (p. 8).[12]

Bennett sees the future of Maori tourism as lying in the development by iwi¶ of unique products in their different regions.[13] But it must be noted that:

Many Maori not only feel that they require control of the pattern and type of tourism development but that tourism is intimately related with the overall restoration of rights under the Treaty of Waitangi [Keelan (1993) cited in Hall[14] (p. 172)].

The issue of control is what lies at the heart of Maori tourism development in New Zealand and is the biggest concern of many Maori.

References

1. McGregor, H. and McMath, M., Leisure: a Maori and a Mangaian perspective. In *Leisure, Recreation and Tourism*, eds H. C. Perkins and G. Cushman. Longman Paul, Auckland, 1993.

---

*Section of a large tribe – an extended family group.
†Enclosed space in front of a house, meeting area, common village area.
‡Elder.
¶Tribe, nation, people.
§Custodian guardian, keeper.

2. Te Awekotuku, N., *Mana wahine Maori*. New Women's Press, Auckland, 1991, p. 154.
3. Stafford, D., *The Romantic Past of Rotorua*. A. H. Wellington and A. W. Reed, Wellington, 1977.
4. Hall, C. M., Mitchell, I. and Keelan, N., The implications of Maori perspectives for the management and promotion of heritage tourism in New Zealand. *GeoJournal*, 1993, **29**, 315–22.
5. Ormsby, O. J., Cultural tourism research development for Maori educational units in tourism. *Hikoi*, 1996, **2** (2).
6. *Tourism 2000 New Zealand Grow for it*. (1989, May). Conference Proceedings, Wellington, New Zealand.
7. New Zealand Tourism Board, *New Zealand Tourism in the 90's*. NZTB, Wellington, 1994, 195.
8. Smith, P., Tourism group says haramai to kia ora. *National Business Review*, 1992, April 24, 47.
9. New Zealand Tourism Board, *New Zealand International Visitors Survey*. NZTB, Wellington, 1995/96.
10. Bennett, R., Presentation to the rural tourism conference held in Methven, 12 March 1997.
11. Barnett, S.J., *Authenticity and Commoditisation of Culture: A Tourism Perspective*. 26.499 Research Report. Department of Management Systems, Massey University, 1996.
12. Mahuta, R. T., *Tourism and Culture: The Maaori Case*. Centre for Maaori Studies and Research, University of Waikato, Hamilton, 1987.
13. Community Employment Group, *From Mt Eden to Maungawhau*. Department of Labour, Wellington, 1996, p. 12.
14. Hall, C. M., Tourism and the Maori of Aotearoa, New Zealand. In *Tourism and Indigenous People*, eds R. Butler and T. Hinch, pp. 155–175, International Thomson Business Press, London, 1995.

Author Index

Subject Index